International Perspectives in Schizophrenia

Biological, Social and Epidemiological Findings

This book is dedicated to sufferers and their relatives.
Royalties will be applied to research.

International Perspectives in Schizophrenia

Biological, Social and Epidemiological Findings

Edited by
Malcolm Weller

John Libbey
LONDON · PARIS

British Library Cataloguing in Publication Data
International Perspectives in Schizophrenia
1. Man. Schizophrenia
I. Weller, M. II. Series
616.89'82

ISBN 0-861961-45-5

Published by John Libbey & Co Ltd
13 Smiths Yard, Summerley St, London SW18 4HR, UK. (01) 947 2777
John Libbey Eurotext Ltd
6 rue Blanche, 92120 Montrouge, France (1) 47 358552

Typeset by Activity Ltd, Salisbury, Wiltshire.
Printed by Dotesios, Trowbridge, Wiltshire.

Contents

Preface

There have been some exciting developments in the conceptualization and treatment of schizophrenia which are inaccessible without sifting a large and growing number of journals. Under the auspices of the National Schizophrenia Fellowship two conferences were organized recently in London which formed the basis of the chapters in this book. The audience was mixed, consisting of relatives of sufferers, the sufferers themselves and representatives of the medical and allied profession. Both conferences were warmly received by the audience and stimulated some interest in the National Press. The eminent contributors agreed to present their talks here and some additional chapters were added to provide a comprehensive overview of areas of significant advance.

A tension is sometimes felt between the proponents of biological and social models, at least of exacerbation if not of aetiology. It is hoped that a balance has been achieved by covering some demographic and social areas. What is apparent is that the resources which are devoted to the care and treatment are outstripped by the magnitude of the problem and our modern understanding of optimal resources.

Schizophrenia remains a widespread and devastating disease and I hope that the advances in our knowledge and the possibilities of new lines of treatment that are discussed here will soon be translated into more effective treatments.

London
1989

Malcolm Weller

I

BIOLOGY OF SCHIZOPHRENIA

Chapter 1

Clear consciousness and the diagnosis of schizophrenia An irreconcilable problem

Malcolm P. I. Weller

Friern Hospital, Friern Barnet Road, London N11 3BP, UK

Summary

Most diagnostic schemes take pains to differentiate schizophrenia, a 'functional' illness, from toxic confusional psychosis, and in general to exclude organic conditions by stipulating that the hallucinations, delusions and thought disorder of schizophrenia must occur in clear consciousness. In the light of the diverse organic findings discussed in this book it seems inappropriate to exclude such cases and it is inherently unlikely that there is a clear phenomenological distinction between 'functional' and organic psychoses.

The situation has been obscured by the fact that there are many examples of such clouding in schizophrenia, which precisely fit the criteria for clouding of consciousness specified by Engel & Romano (1959), Slater & Roth (1969) and Lipowsky (1980, see Appendix), which can be readily found in allegedly schizophrenic populations — this despite the diagnostic requirement that clouded consciousness is incompatable with a diagnosis of schizophrenia.

The organic and functional dichotomy

In order to distinguish schizophrenic phenomena from delirium, twilight states and intoxication, Schneider (1957) asserts that if a first rank symptom occurs '*in a non-organic psychosis* then we call that psychosis schizophrenia' (my italics). He lists a number of somatic factors which lead to clouded consciousness, such as an acute response to intoxication, GPI and other infections and internal disorders (p. 2). The Registrar General's (1968) *Glossary of Mental Disorders* specifies the need for clear consciousness in the assessment of those symptoms which form the basis for a diagnosis of schizophrenia. One of the intentions for invoking the term 'clear consciousness' is to distinguish schizophrenia from delirium, toxic psychosis and abnormal states of consciousness, such as hypnagogic and hypnapompic experiences, but it begs important questions. Aetiological theories of schizophrenia include: auto-intoxication, biochemical abnormalities, synaptic receptor abnormalities, traumatic brain damage, epilepsy, epileptic kindling and viral infections. If an organic explanation, such as one of the above, is vindicated, at least for some patients, is it likely that consciousness is indeed clear? Is it not equally plasusible that the psychotic experiences are manifestations of disordered brain mechanisms, postulated by Kraepelin (1920) as the source of the disorder, and that some disturbance of consciousness is an inevitable and central component of the experiences?

Roth & McClelland (1979), in accord with Ferraro (1943), consider schizophrenia to be a phenomenological rather than a neurological entity, and repudiate Schneider's view that 'the presence of a coarse brain disease excludes all other kinds of diagnosis'; they take the contrary view that, 'As its (schizophrenia's) aetiological basis, the hereditary factors apart, is not understood, it is illogical and circular to exclude cases with associated organic lesions from the outset'.

The problem may be more deeply ingrained than appears at first sight. Roth & McClelland imply that there is a substantial group of schizophrenic patients who are excluded from their discussion because they display organic phenomena. It is the burden of this chapter to stress that organic psychological phenomena are common in schizophrenic patients, an observation that is reinforced by evidence of brain lesions or malfunction, but that either this knowledge is suppressed to accommodate the requirement that consciousness should be clear in the definition of the disorder, or the clinical examination is insufficiently searching to reveal the clouding which is identified in the research literature.

The situation is inconsistent and relaxation of the exclusion of clouded consciousness is explicitly countenanced in the case of acute schizophrenic episodes, which are described in the 9th edition of the *International classification of diseases* as often being characterized by a dream-like state with slight clouding'. (There is a further problem in the implicit assumption that we can prospectively differentiate between acute and chronic conditions on the basis of the phenomenology.)

The problems of detection of clouded consciousness

The vigour with which we pursue investigations depends on our preconceptions. Leff (1977) has pointed out that in documenting a psychiatric interview, the importance attached to the phenomena is largely determined by the psychiatrist's theoretical frame of reference. When we are alert to the presence of a physical illness, as in a fever, it is not difficult to detect clouding of consciousness and natural to attribute the clouding to the illness. On the other hand, in the case of an occult physical illness accompanied by slight clouding, we may fail to detect the clouding for want of repeated, careful observations; and if detected, the cause of the clouding may remain obscure. 'In investigating the possible cause of the delirious state, it must be remembered that when associated with an acute infection such as pneumonia, the condition may not start until the convalescent stage, perhaps one or two weeks after the febrile illness has subsided. Careful history-taking is therefore essential if some specific cause is not over-looked'. (Slater & Roth, 1969, p. 602).

Is such a cause being overlooked when Kraepelin (1920) asserts (p. 19), 'Delirious states may appear under extremely varied conditions, not only as a result of toxic substances or infection, as in fever of brain injury, but also in epilepsy, general paresis, manic depressive insanity, dementia praecox,...'? This association between delirium and psychosis is implied in the description of acute schizophrenic episodes in the 9th edition of the *International classification of diseases*, already discussed, as often being characterized by 'a dream-like state with slight clouding of consciousness and perplexity'.

The organic – functional dichotomy

Slater & Roth (1969) stress the need for careful history taking, and careful observation is essential too since slight degrees of clouding may be difficult to detect (Russell, 1934). For example in testing for memory disturbance following head injury the problem of detection is surprisingly subtle; 'Such islands of memory are not uncommon and may be followed by further amnesia for a day or two: it is, therefore, the beginning of continuous memory loss which we prefer as our assessment. The second, though less common, error is to assume because a patient is aware of what is happening around him that he will be able to recall this later. This may lead to underestimation of the duration of post-traumatic amnesia in a patient who is under observation in the acute stage of his symptoms. It is, therefore, necessary in cases of this type to check the duration of the amnesia some time after the recovery of full consciousness ... ' (Symonds & Russell, 1943) (see also Whitty & Zangwill, 1966).

Similarities between delirium and the cognitive impairments of schizophrenia

Two statements describing clouded consciousness taken from Slater & Roth (1969) demonstrate the close similarily between this state and schizophrenia.

> 'Conceptual thinking (in clouded consciousness) breaks down and becomes cluttered with incoherent and fragmentary matter, often visualised and taking on an hallucinatory or delusional quality where even the self and the environment are incompletely differentiated'.
>
> 'An increase in suspiciousness, and the occurrence of delusional ideas is a feature of importance. These experiences may occur with suddenness and conviction, *in a form indistinguishable from the primary delusional experience* (my italics), in states of clouding so mild as to be unrecognisable as such'.

Kraepelin (1919) stated that, '(dementia praecox) patients complain frequently of passing dullness of consciousness which should probably be regarded as a condition of very slight stupor' (p. 17). Romano & Engel (1944) considered the corollary, 'essentially, delirium is a psychotic syndrome in which the basic psychologic symptom is a disturbance in the level of consciousness ... '. As Lipowski (1980) points out in his monograph on delirium, it may be doubtful whether a patient is suffering from delirium 'rather than from one of the functional psychoses. ... Acute schizophrenia, schizophreniform, or atypical psychosis is particularly likely to give rise to diagnostic difficulties' (p. 210).

In Table 1, defining characteristics of clouding of consciousness, as described by Slater & Roth (1969), are contrasted with statements in the literature on schizophrenia to illustrate how commonly clouding occurs, despite the fact that clouding of consciousness is an exclusion criterion for diagnosis (Registrar General's *Glossary of mental disorders*, 1968).

Nocturnal deterioration

In addition to these features, and in accord with Lipowski (1980), Slater & Roth mention fluctuations in the intensity of clouding of consciousness, with a tendency for it to become much more prominent at night. In order to differentiate 'true' schizophrenic phenomena from hypnagogic and hypnopompic experiences little regard is paid to experiences which occur in bed at night. Nevertheless, patients frequently report such experiences, particularly haptic ones of being touched or given electric shocks, and others describe an intensification of daytime auditory hallucinations. These features are so commonly

Table 1. *Characteristics of clouding of consciousness.*

States of clouding consciousness	*Quotations from the literature on schizophrenia*
'The patient has difficulty in maintaining attention.'	'It is our contention that many of the behavioural deficits seen in the schizophrenic can be accounted for by a primary attentional disorder.' (Kornetsky & Orzack, 1978)
'He tends to be easily distracted.'	'Thinking becomes distracted by external events. It also becomes distracted by irrelevant personal thoughts and emotions which may even become mixed up with the problem.' (Payne *et al.*, 1964)
'He cannot dismiss from his mind the irrelevant sensory experience or the irrelevant idea.'	'Schizophrenics have difficulty in maintaining a perceptual set and in concentrating on part of the perceptual field to the exclusion of other parts ... these patients are less capable of shutting off information which is irrelevant to the task in hand.' (Weckowicz & Witney, 1960)
'Perception is affected so that sense data are misjudged' (see Whitehead, 1939 Appendix I)	'In early phases of their illness, schizophrenic patients, together with difficulty in thinking, such as an inability to concentrate and to control their thoughts, may experience perceptual difficulty and may even complain of an impairment of vision.' (Weckowicz, 1960)
	'... distance constancy is poorer in schizophrenics than in non-schizophrenics and also ... related to the poorer size constancy found in these patients ... The lack of depth and 'flatness' of the visual world of schizophrenics has theoretical implications for the phenomenology of schizophrenia. Together with impaired form constancy it can change, foreshorten and distort the appearance of the perceived objects. Perhaps this change in depth perception would account for the complaint of some schizophrenics that things look different, unfamiliar and strange ... ' (Weckowicz, Sommer & Hall, 1958)
'Illusions, especially visual illusions ... are very much more likely to arise than in the normal state ...'	'Schizophrenics are more susceptible to the Muller-Lyer illusion than non-schizophrenics.' (Weckowicz & Witney, 1960)

'There are corresponding difficulties in comprehension shown at first only at the highest and most abstract level.'	'Some investigators (Cameron, (1939), Vigotsky (1934), Kasanin et al (1944)) have, on the basis of cognitive testing, concluded that the schizophrenic is unable to form the abstractions necessary for normal thinking in much the same manner in which the patient with organic brain defect is unable to deal with abstractions.' (Freeman, Cameron & McGhie, 1958)
'Called on to respond to a complex situation, the patient is likely to be slow'	'Although complete diagnostic specificity is lacking, there seems to be a remarkable correlation between ... reaction time phenomena and those behaviours that lead diagnosticians at many different times and places to a diagnosis of schizophrenia.' (Zahn, 1977)
'... and to show some perseveration in thought and speech'	'The tendency toward stereotyping, combined with a lack of purposeful goal in their thinking, leads on the one hand to "Klebendenken" (adhesive, sticky type of thinking), to a kind of *perserveration*, and on the other hand to a general impoverishment of thought.' (Bleuler, 1911, p. 27)
	'We frequently observe written verbrigeration in random repetition of words and sentences, and particularly of single letter and punctuation marks, either in a characteristic pattern or mixed with crosses, circles, triangles and other figures. For many years a hebephrenic always wrote the same row of numbers whose zeros were always continued to the end of each line.' (Bleuler, 1911, p. 159)
'Judgements, also will be less balanced and less adequate'	'... the weakening of judgement ... would have to be reckoned among the fundamental disorders of dementia praecox.' (Kraepelin, 1919, p. 248)
'Gestalts are not sharply circumscribed and finely differentiated; figure-background differentiation is blurred, and is much less open to goal directed action.'	'Selective perception becomes impossible so that instead of dealing with the essence of the problem irrelevant aspects are perceived and thought about ... ' (Payne, 1964)
'The difficulties in attention, comprehension etc., can be described as difficulties in raising the figure from the background, in maintaining it against disturbing forces arising from the background and in manipulating it.'	'these irrelevant associations to which the normal is also subject but to a much lesser degree would appear to arise from three sources: chance distractors from the environment; irrelevancies from the stimulus situation; and irrelevancies from past experience ... the mere presence of these irrelevant factors ... seems to lead the schizophrenic to give them focal rather than ground significance, signal rather than noise import' (Shakow, 1962).

encountered in clinical practice that it is difficult to find them specifically mentioned in contemporary accounts, but in the words of one early author describing a schizophrenic patient, 'he continued, however, to suffer much from noise in his ears, hearing voices, etc, especially at night' (Rorie, 1862–3). The abnormal night time experiences occurring without any such day time experiences probably represent an incipient phase when psychotic phenomena, like epileptic and delirious phenomena, are highlighted.

Memory

Memory disturbance is stressed by Slater & Roth (1969) as an indication of clouded consciousness. Subcortical neurones in the hippocampus and caudate nucleus compare stimuli and respond to novelty, and are therefore part of the mechanism of memory (see Luria 1973 and Buchwald & Humphrey 1973 for reviews, including the important Russian literature), and structural abnormalities have been found in the hippocampi and caudate nuclei of schizophrenic patients (Davison & Bagley, 1969; Roberts *et al.*, 1983; Roberts, this volume, p. 52).

Memory disturbances are common in schizophrenia, including delusional memories. The imagined events are often intensely significant and the false memory may become the basis of paranoid misinterpretation.

Dodge (1924), in an interesting article entitled 'Problems of human variability', wrote: 'Variations are not artifacts to be statistically lumped and treated as though they were errors of measurement, but they represent features which might well be quite as significant as the conscious aim of measurement in which they occurred'. The variability of the schizophrenic's performance on test procedures is notorious and any group of schizophrenics seemingly inevitably vary more than non-psychiatric controls. One would expect just such variability in a brain damaged group. In the World Health Organization's international pilot study of schizophrenia, the test-retest reliability had a mean intra-class correlation coefficient of only 0.49 (Hays, 1967). Since the patients were describing the same illness episode to trained observers, who used structured interview with which the inter-observer reliability averaged 0.83, the memory and reporting of the illness episode must have varied over the few days between the two interviews. This well authenticated example of recent memory disturbance cannot be easily disregarded.

There is no evidence of a temporal gradient to memories in schizophrenia, such as occurs in non-psychiatric patients, whereby the more recent memories are stronger than the more distant, and unmedicated as well as medicated schizophrenics rapidly forget verbal material (Calev *et al.*, 1987; Calev, this volume, p. 33).

A defect of cumulative memory in schizophrenia has been demonstrated experimentally (Kugler & Weller, 1983). In this study a chain of digits, exceeding the subject's memory capacity, was repeated seven times alternately with two novel chains. Control subjects, matched for initial digit span, improved their performance steadily and significantly on the repeated chain, while schizophrenic patients did not (Figure). This pattern of results is consonant with left hippocampal damage (Corsi, 1967), the deficits being proportional to the extent of the hippocampal damage.

Orientation

Memory defects may account for some of the temporal disorientation in schizophrenia. Stevens *et al.*, (1978), supplementing the work of Crow & Mitchell (1975), found that 25% of 357 patients with a consistent case note diagnosis of schizophrenia

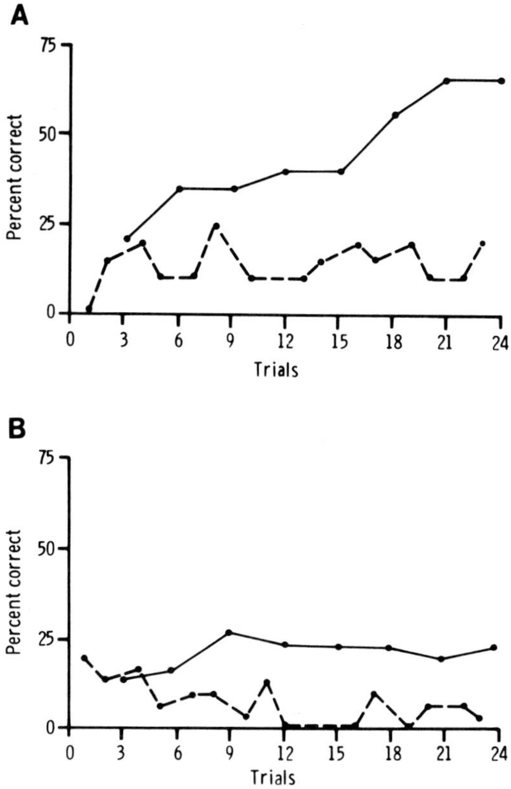

Fig. 1. *Performance on the Hebb recurring-digits test.* (A) Normal group; (B) schizophrenic group. (—) Recurring digit strings; (---) non-recurring digit strings. Figure reprinted from *Aspects of consciousness*, vol. 4. Clinical issues. Chapter 5, pp. 117–165 (1984) by permission of Academic Press, Inc.

underestimated their age by more than 5 years; 11% underestimated their age by a mean of 28.9 years. The phenomenon was associated with early onset and a poor prognosis. Six further studies were reviewed with similar findings; Crow & Stevens (1978) went on to demonstrate what they believed was a 'continuum of increasing temporal disorientation' which was associated with age disorientation.

The phenomenon of 'double orientation', admittedly of person rather than of place, is considered characteristic of schizophrenia and actually facilitated by clear consciousness (Slater & Roth, 1970, p. 276). However, these same authors (p. 602) also stated that a 'co-existence of two or more totally incompatible orientations' is a feature of clouding of consciousness. One patient treated by the author thought it was afternoon although he agreed that the clock told the right time (11 a.m.) and that he had not yet had his lunch (he has subsequently remained unwell for six years).

Perception

Many perceptual abnormalities have been described in schizophrenic patients, including phoneme recognition (Caudrey & Kirk, 1979), auditory acuity with normal otology and tympanography (Burtt & Weller, 1984), stereognosis under bimanual conditions (Beaumont & Dimond 1973; Green 1978) and unimanually (Weller & Kugler, 1979) and size and distance constancy (Weckowicz, 1957; Weckowicz, 1958).

Schizophrenic symptoms as a product of brain malfunction and the probability of altered consciousness

We must be sensitive to even slight indications of perceptual and cognitive impairment such as disorientation, since gross insults to the brain may result in only subtle changes, requiring careful testing and evaluation. Indubitable and substantial changes occur in cerebral function in advanced hydrocephalus, sub-total hemispherectomy and callosectomy yet such conditions betray nothing more than subtle changes in perception and cognition, advanced hydrocephalus being compatible with high intelligence (Lewin, 1981), and do not produce any obvious changes in consciousness. From the examples just cited, one may conclude that gross changes in cerebral functioning will not necessarily lead to obvious changes in the level of consciousness, and if there *is* evidence of clouding of consciousness it therefore probably implies marked alterations in brain functioning.

Subcortical abnormalities

Malfunctions of subcortical structures, particularly the basal ganglia and mid-brain, are particularly prone to cause disturbances of consciousness (Reichardt, 1929; Jefferson, 1944; Penfield & Jasper 1947; Cairns, 1952) and there is a concept of subcortical dementia (Foster, 1986). So-called schizophreniform psychoses have been associated with many different disease processes affecting the basal ganglia (Davison & Bagley, 1969), including post-encephalitic psychosis (Fairweather, 1947), hepatolenticular degeneration (Beard, 1959), Huntington's Chorea (Heathfield, 1967) and calcification of the basal ganglia (Kasanin & Crank, 1935; see Cummings *et al.*, 1983), which may include the striopallidodentate system (Lowenthal & Bruyn, 1968) and the cerebellum (Kalamboukis & Molling, 1962).

Cerebellar dysfunction (disorders of equilibrium, staggering, adiadochokinesia, and tremor) had been noted in schizophrenic patients before the introduction of phenothiazines (Dufour cited Kraepelin, 1919, p. 79) and tapping speed is slow in schizophrenia with a markedly different performance between the preferred and non-preferred hands (Weller *et al.*, 1988). The anterior cerebellar vermis has been found to be atrophic in some schizophrenic patients on CAT scans (Weinberger *et al.*, 1979, 1981; Reider *et al.*, 1981). The frequency is variable but reached 40% (34 out of 85 patients) in one study (Heath, Franklin & Shraberg, 1979). Recent animal experiments have shown that this structure is essential for long-term habituation (Leaton & Supple, 1986) and motor memories are probably stored (see Thompson, 1987). Although these recent findings were unknown to the anatomical workers, in accord with the general theme adopted here Heath *et al.* were clearly impressed by the brain pathology in a population allegedly suffering from a functional psychiatric disorder, and entitled their paper, 'Gross pathology of the cerebellum in patients diagnosed and treated as functional psychiatric disorders'.

Corpus callosal degeneration with demyelination and subsequent cavitation, and destruction of central axis cyclinders in the Marchiafava-Bignami syndrome, is associated with psychosis (Marchiafava 1932–3; Ironside *et al.*, 1961; Victor & Adams, 1961). The syndrome usually occurs in alcoholics, but can occur with accompanying psychosis without alcohol consumption (Nielsen, 1958). Anatomical evidence of abnormalities of the corpus callosum have been alleged in some schizophrenic patients (Bigelow *et al.*, 1983), and defects of stereognosis have been shown, suggestive of defects of corpus callosal function (Beaumont & Dimond, 1973; Green *et al.*, 1979, Weller & Kugler, 1979).

Evidence for structural abnormalities of subcortical structures in schizophrenia

Abnormalities of limbic neurones have been found in young schizophrenic patients whose brains were examined at necropsy (Averback, 1981 *a* & *b*). The youth of the patients made it unlikely that these abnormalities represented senile degenerative changes. More recently an abnormal cellular architecture has been found in the alpha and pre-beta layers of the parahippocampal/entorhinal cortex (Roberts, this volume, p. 53).

Neurotransmitter and neuromodular differences have been found in limbic structures of schizophrenic brains examined at necropsy. An abnormal asymmetry of dopamine has been found in the amygdalae of schizophrenic brains (Reynolds, 1983) (although this may also occur in depression; see Weller 1986*b*), and peptide abnormalities have been found in the hippocampus and amygdala (Roberts *et al.*, 1983).

The abnormalities of oculo-motor control (Holzman *et al.*, 1973; Latham *et al.*, 1981) are further examples of subcortical malfunction.

Electrophysiological abnormalities

Consonant with the pathological findings several neurophysiological abnormalities have been found in schizophrenic subjects which are interpreted as indicative of limbic malfunction. These include orientating response abnormalities (Gruzelier & Venables, 1972; Gruzelier *et al.*, 1981), which are particularly evident in those patients who respond poorly to treatment (Frith *et al.*, 1978; Zahn *et al.*, 1981) and illustrate a fundamental defect in the attentive mechanisms.

Abnormal discharges have been recorded from indwelling electrodes in the septal nuclei in schizophrenic patients, and the onset and offset of these correlated with psychotic experiences and behaviour (Heath, 1966). Such discharges could also be induced by low frequency stimulation of the hippocampus at 3–6 Hz, the same frequencies that showed excessive synchronous activity from temporal EEG derivations (Weller & Montagu, 1979). When the recording abnormality appeared, the patients showed what Heath (1966) described as 'classical psychotic symptoms', and in an interesting aside, he remarks, 'after recovering from the effects of stimulation, (the patients) described the experience as dream-like',

Electroencephalographic findings

Lipowski (1980, p. 41, see Appendix), influenced by the findings of Engel & Romano (1959), points out that in delirium slow waves are more prominent in the electroencephalogram. Statistical analysis of the EEG recordings from schizophrenic subjects have shown an excess of slow wave activity (Coger *et al.*, 1979; Weller & Montagu, 1979; Fenton *et al.*, 1980) and an increase in the degree of synchrony between certain brain regions (Flor-Henry & Yeudall, 1979; Weller & Montagu, 1979). Bilateral spikes and waves and paroxysmal slow wave activity have been described in non-epileptic schizophrenic patients (Hill & Parr, 1963). Non-specific abnormalities are detected in many psychiatric conditions, but, since they occur in a proportion of non-psychiatric patients, they do not have diagnostic implications. Nevertheless, the frequency of such abnormalities is greater among abnormal personalities (Schwade & Geiger, 1956; Hill, 1963) and borderline psychotic conditions are probably more frequent in this group (Hoch & Polatin, 1949).

Cerebral insufficiency

Engel & Romano (1959) consider that delirium is 'a syndrome of cerebral insufficiency', which takes its origin from changes in the functional metabolism of cerebral neurones. 'As with the more familiar concepts of organ insufficiency, this refers to what evolves when the function of the organ as a whole is interfered with, for whatever reason'. The metabolic rate and blood flow are lower in the frontal area in schizophrenia in all but one study, when there was a generalized reduction in metabolic activity (Buchsbaum & Ingvar, 1982, for experiments and review; DeLisi *et al.*, 1985; Weinberger *et al.*, 1986).

Conclusion

Differences between psychotic states and clouded consciousness are clearly difficult to demonstrate. This conclusion corresponds to Kraepelin's (1920, p. 19) position: 'There is a strong argument for classifying delirium as one of those forms of psychiatric disorder which are based on primarily mental reactions. It takes the place of orderly, clear, conscious thought, as soon as consciousness becomes clouded under the influence of any morbid process. It is not surprising that the particular form which delirium takes may be partly determined by the nature of the morbid process in question, as well as by the patient's own previous history.'

From the many examples that have been cited it is difficult to escape the conclusion that subtle examples of clouded consciousness can be detected in many schizophrenic patients. This would accord with organic explanations for at least a subgroup of patients, and reinforces the arguments of Ferraro (1934, 1943) and Roth & McClelland (1979), who challenge Schneider's (1957) view that 'the presence of coarse brain disease excludes all other kind of diagnosis'. There is no unequivocal diagnostic test of schizophrenia analogous to diagnostic tests in physical medicine. In the end one is reliant on the presenting phenomena, the previous history and clinical judgement. The desirability of excluding cases where there is a presumed organic aetiology inevitably results in an idiopathic group, in which the hope of finding a specific locus, or loci, of lesions causing the symptoms is diminished. It also creates a further group for whom there is no suitable diagnostic category. In any event organic features are so readily demonstrated in so many patients diagnosed as schizophrenic that attempts to exclude organic cases, and to sieve out a 'functional' disorder, are doomed to failure from the outset. The conviction of Kraepelin that organic explanations for dementia praecox would ultimately be shown is vindicated by the phenomenological features of clouded consciousness which are apparent in so many patients allegedly suffering from schizophrenia — despite the fact that none of them is schizophrenic if the diagnostic requirement of clear consciousness is rigorously enforced.

Acknowledgements—I thank the Wellcome Trust, the North East Thames Regional Health Authority, and the National Schizophrenia Fellowship for grants for the experimental work discussed in this paper, Dr K. Davison for helpful comments, and Friern Hospital and the Royal Society of Medicine for library assistance. An earlier formulation of the problem was first expressed in 'Some problems in the diagnosis of schizophrenia and the problems of clear consciousness' in *Aspects of consciousness*, vol. 4, ed. R. Stevens, Academic Press 1984.

Appendix

Lipowski (1980, p. 41) gives a comprehensive list of what he terms essential characteristics of delirium: 'an organic brain syndrome of acute onset and transient duration, characterized by global impairment, and due to widespread disturbance of cerebral metabolism. The term encompasses 'acute confusional states' and 'simple confusion' of other authors, provided that they use these terms to designate organic mental disorders' (pp. 38–39).

1. Impaired awareness of self and surroundings and their relationships.
2. Impairment of memory.
3. Disturbance of attention.
4. Impairment of directed thinking.
5. Diminished perceptual discrimination with a tendency to illusions and hallucinations.
6. Impairment of spatiotemporal orientation.
7. Increased or decreased alertness.
8. Sleep disturbance, usually drowsiness during the day, or insomnia at night, or both.
9. Relatively rapid fluctuations in awareness and severity of symptoms (2) through (7) during daytime and tendency to their exacerbation at night or in the dark.
10. Acute onset and relatively short duration.
11. Laboratory evidence of cerebral dysfunction, especially diffuse changes of background activity in the electroencephalogram.

Definitions

Definitions of consciousness are slightly different from one another. Some definitions are appended and clouded consciousness is discussed in relation to specified features.

Pillsbury (1911): By consciousness we mean a man's awareness of his own acts and their antecedents.

Whitehead (1933): That portion of experience irradiated by consciousness is only a selection. Thus consciousness is a mode of attention. It provides the extreme of selective emphasis.

Whitehead (1934): Without doubt the sort of observations most prominent in our conscious experience are the sense-perceptions.

Jefferson (1944): A state in which man (or animals for that matter) respond to the environment in a manner which shows insight.

Cobb (1948): An awareness of environment and self.

Hebb (1949): Mind can only be regarded, for scientific purposes, as the activity of the brain.

Sperry (1966): A functional property of the brain in action.

Concise Oxford Dictionary (1970): Awareness; totality of a person's thoughts and feelings; perception.

Van Till (1976): A result of brain activity, implying as a minimum level inner awareness; perception.

References

Averback, P. (1981*a*): Lesions of the nucleus ansae peduncularis in neuropsychiatric disease. *Arch. Neurol.* **38**, 230–235.

Averback, P. (1981*b*): Structural lesions of the brain in young schizophrenics. *Can. J. Neurol. Sci.* **8**, 73–76.

Beard, A.E. (1959): The association of hepato-lenticular degeneration with schizophrenia. *Acta Psychiatr. Neurol. Scand.* **34**, 411–428.

Beaumont, J.G. & Dimond, S.J. (1973): Brain disconnection and schizophrenia. *Br. J. Psychiatry.* **123**, 661–662.

Bigelow, L.B., Nasrallah, H.M.A. & Rauscher, P.R. (1983): Corpus callosum thickness in chronic schizophrenia. *Br. J. Psychiatry.* **142**, 284–287.

Bleuler, E. (1911): *Dementia praecox or The Group of Schizophrenias*, Translated 1950, J. Zinkin & N.C.D. Lewis. New York: International Universities Press.

Buchsbaum, M.S. & Ingvar, D.H. (1982): New visions in the schizophrenic brain: Regional differences in electrophysiology, blood flow and cerebral glucose use. In *Schizophrenia as a brain disease*, eds F.A. Henn & H.A. Nasrallah. New York and Oxford: Oxford University Press.

Buchwald, J.S. & Humphrey, G.L. (1973): An analysis of habituation in the specific sensory systems. In *Progress in physiological psychology*, vol 5, eds E. Stellar & J.M. Sprague, pp. 1–76. New York and London: Academic Press.

Burtt, C. & Weller, M.P.I. (1984): Diminished auditory acuity in schizophrenia. *J. Physiol. (Lond)*, **351**, 20P.

Cairns, H. (1952): Disturbances of consciousness with lesions of the brain-stem and diencephalon. Victor Horsley Memorial Lecture December 8, 1949. *Brain* **75**, 8–146.

Calev, A., Berlin, H. Lere, B. (1987): Remote and recent memory in long-hospitalized chronic schizophrenics. *Biol. Psychiatry,* **22**, 79–85.

Calev, A., Nigal, D., Edelist, S., Chazan, S., Kugelmass, S., Weller M.P.I. & Lerer, B. (1988): Amnesia in schizophrenia: Rapid forgetting of verbal material affected by emotion. Submitted for publication.

Caudrey, D.J. & Kirk, K. (1979): The perception of speech in schizophrenia and affective disorder. In *Hemisphere asymmetries of function and psychopathology*, eds J. Gruzelier & P. Flor-Henry, pp. 581–601. Amsterdam: Elsevier North Holland.

Cobb, S. (1948): *Foundations of neuropsychiatry*, p. 89 et seq. Baltimore: Williams and Wilkins.

Coger, R.W., Dymond, A.M. & Serafetinides, E.A. (1979): Electroencephalographic similarities between chronic alcoholics and chronic, non paranoid schizophenics. *Arch. Gen. Psychiatry,* **36**, 91–94.

Corsi, P.M. (1967): Unpublished M.A. Thesis, McGill University, Montreal; Reported in Milner B. (1971): Interhemispheric differences in localisation of psychological processes in man. *Br. Med. Bull.,* **27**, 272–277.

Crow, T.J. & Mitchell, W.S. (1975): Subjective age in chronic schizophrenia: Evidence for a sub-group of patients with defective learning capacity. *Br. J. Psychiatry,* **126**, 360–363.

Crow, T.J. & Stevens, M. (1978): Age distortion in chronic schizophrenia: The nature of the cognitive defect. *Br. J. Psychiatry,* **133**, 137–142.

Cummings, J.L., Gosenfeld, L.F., Houlihan, J.P. & McCaffrey, T. (1983): Neuropsychiatric disturbances associated with idiopathic calcification of the basal ganglia. *Biol. Psychiatry,* **18**, 591–601.

Davison, K. & Bagley, C. (1969): Schizophrenia-like psychoses associated with organic disorders of the C.N.S.: A review of the literature. In *Current problems in neuropsychiatry*. British Journal of Psychiatry Special Publication No. 4, p. 113. Ashford, Kent: Headley.

DeLisi, L.E., Buchsbaum, M.S., Holcomb, H.H., Dowling-Zimmerman, S., Pickar, D. et al. (1985): Clinical correlates of decreased anteroposterior metabolic gradients in positron emission tomography (PET) of schizophrenic patients. *Am. J. Psychiatry,* **142**, 78–81.

Dodge, R. (1924): Human variability. *Science* **59**, 263.

Engel, G.L. & Romano, J. (1944): Delirium II reversibility of the electroencephalogram with experimental procedures. *Arch Neurol. Psychiatry,* **51**, 378–392.

Engel, G.L. & Romano, J. (1959): Delirium, a syndrome of cerebral insufficiency. *J. Chron. Dis.* **9**, 260–277.
Fairweather, D.S. (1947): Psychiatric aspects of the post encephalitis syndrome. *J. Mental. Sci.* **93**, 201–254.
Fenton, G.W., Fenwick, P.B.C., Dollimore, J., Dunn, T.L. & Hirsch, S.R. (1980): EEG spectral analysis in schizophrenia. *Br. J. Psychiatry,* **136**, 445–455.
Ferraro, A. (1934): Histopathological findings in two cases clinically diagnosed dementia praecox. *Am. J. Phychiatry,* **90**, 883–903.
Ferraro, A. (1943): Pathological changes in the brain of a case clinically diagnosed dementia praecox. *J. Neuropathol. Exp. Neurol.,* **2**, 84–94.
Flor-Henry, P. & Yeudall, L.T. (1979): Neuropsychological investigation of schizophrenia and manic-depressive psychoses. In *Hemisphere asymmetries of function in psychopathology*, eds J. Gruzelier and P. Flor-Henry, pp. 341–362. Amsterdam: Elsevier, North Holland.
Foster, J.B. (1986): Subcortical dementia (leading article). *Br. Med. J.* **292**, 1035–6.
Freeman, T., Cameron, J.L. & McGhie, A. (1958): *Chronic schizophrenia.* London: Tavistock Publications.
Frith, C.D., Stevens, M., Johnstone, E.C. & Crow, T.J. (1978): Skin conductance responsivity during acute episodes of schizophrenia as a predictor of symptomatic improvement. *Psychol. Med.* **9**, 101–106.
Green, P. (1978): Interhemispheric transfer in schizophrenia: Recent developments. *Behav. Psychother.* **6**, 105–110.
Green, P., Glass, A. & O'Callaghan, M.A.J. (1979): Some implications of abnormal hemisphere interaction in schizophrenia. In *Hemisphere asymmetries of function and psychopathology*, eds. J.H. Gruzelier & P. Flor-Henry, pp. 431–448. Amsterdam: Elsevier/North Holland Biochemical Press.
Gruzelier, J.H. & Venables, P.H. (1972): Skin conductance orienting activity in a heterogeneous sample of schizophrenics: Possible evidence of limbic dysfunction. *J. Nerv. Ment. Dis.* **155**, 277–287.
Gruzelier, J.H., Connolly, J., Eves, F., Hirsch, S.R., Weller, M.P.I. & Yorkston, M. (1981): Effects of propranolol and phenothiazines on electrodermal orienting and habituation in schizophrenia. *Psychol. Med.* **11**, 93–188.
Hays, W.L. (1967): *Statistics for psychologists.* New York: Brooks-Cole.
Heath, R.G. (1966): Schizophrenia: Biochemical and physiologic aberrations. *Int. J. Neuropsychiatry,* **2**, 597–610.
Heath, R.G., Franklin, D.E. & Shraberg, D. (1979): Gross pathology of the cerebellum in patients diagnosed and treated as functional psychiatric disorders. *J. Nerv. Men. Dis.* **167**, 585–592.
Heathfield, K.W.G. (1967): Huntington's Chorea. Investigations into the prevalence of this disease in the area covered by the North East Metropolitan Regional Hospital Board. *Brain* **90**, 203–232.
Hebb, D.O. (1949): *The organisation of behaviour. A neuropsychological theory.* New York: John Wiley.
Hill, D. (1963) The EEG in psychiatry. In *Electroencephalography*, ed. D. Hill & G. Parr p. 368. London: Macdonald.
Hill, D. & Parr, G. (1963): *Electroencephalography. A symposium of various aspects*, 2nd ed. London: Macdonald.
Hoch, P. & Polatin, P. (1949): Pseudoneurotic forms of schizophrenia. *Psychiatr. Q.* **23**, 248–276.
Holzman, P.S., Proctor, L.R. & Hughes, D.W. (1973): Eye tracking patterns in schizophrenia. *Science* **181**, 179–181.
Ironside, R., Bosanquet, G.D. & McMenemy, W.H. (1961): Central demyelination of the corpus callosum (Marchiafava-Bignami disease). *Brain* **84**, 212–230.
Jefferson, G. (1944): The nature of concussion. *Br. Med. J.* **i**, 1–5.
Kalamboukis, Z. & Molling, P. (1962): Symmetrical calcification of the brain in the predominance in the basal ganglia and cerebellum. *J. Neuropathol. Exp. Neurol.* **21**, 364–371.
Kasanin, J. & Crank, R.P. (1935): A case of extensive calcification of the brain. *Arch. Neurol. Psychiatry* **34**, 164–178.
Kendell, R.E. (1974): The stability of psychiatric diagnoses. *Br. J. Psychiatry,* **124**, 352–356.

Kendell, R.E. & Brockington, I.F. (1980): The identification of disease entities and their relationship between schizophrenia and affective psychosis. *Br. J. Psychiatry* **137**, 324–331.
Kendell, R.E. Brockington, I.F. & Leff, J.P. (1979): Prognostic implications of six alternative definitions of schizophrenia. *Arch. Gen. Psychiatry* **36**, 25–31.
Kornetsky, C. & Orzack, M.H. (1978): Physiological and behavioural correlates of attention dysfunction in schizophrenic patients. *J. Psychiatr. Res.* **14**, 69–79.
Kraepelin, E. (1919): *Dementia praecox*, trans. M. Barclay, ed. G.M. Robertson. Edinburgh: Churchill Livingstone.
Kraepelin, E. (1920): Patterns of mental disorder. In *Themes and variations in European psychiatry*, eds M. Shepherd & S Hirsch. Bristol: Wright and Sons.
Kugler, B.T. & Weller, M.P.I. (1983): Memory impairment in schizophrenia: Hebbs's recurring digits. In *Laterality and psychopathology*, ed. P. Flor-Henry & J. Gruzelier, pp. 493–495. Amsterdam: Elsevier, North Holland.
Latham, C., Holtzman, P.S., Manschreck, T.C. & Tole, J. (1981): Optokinetic nystagmus and pursuit eye movements in schizophrenia. *Arch Gen. Psychiatry* **38**, 997–1003.
Leaton, R.N. & Supple, W.F. (1986): Cerebellar vermis: essential for long-term habituation of the acoustic startle response. *Science* **232**, 513–515.
Leff, J. (1977): International variations in the diagnostic of psychiatric illness. *Br. J. Psychiatry* **131**, 329–338.
Lewin, R. (1981): Is your brain really necessary? *Science* **210**, 1232–1234.
Lipowski, Z.J. (1980): *Delirium: Acute brain failure in man.* Illinois: Charles C. Thomas.
Lowenthal, A. & Bruyn, G.W. (1968): Calcification of the striopallido-dentate system. In *Handbook of clinical neurology, diseases of the basal ganglia* 6, ed. P.J. Vinken & G.W. Bruyn pp. 703–725. Amsterdam: Elsevier.
Luria, A.R. (1973): *The working brain: An introduction to neuropsychology*, Translated by B. Haigh. Harmondsworth, Middlesex: Penguin.
Marchiafava, E. (1932–3): The degeneration of the brain in chronic alcoholism. *Proc. R. Soc. Med.* **26**, 1151–1158.
Nielson, J.M. (1958) *Cerebral localization and the psychoses*, (research publication). Baltimore: Association for Research in Nervous and Mental Disease. **36**, 467–477.
Payne, R.W., Caird, W.K. & Laverty, S.G. (1964): Overinclusive thinking and delusions in schizophrenic patients. *J. Abnorm. Soc. Psychol.* **68**, 562–566.
Penfield, W. & Jasper, H.H. (1947): *Highest level seizures.* Association for Research in Nervous and Mental Disease, Proceedings **24**, 252–271. Baltimore: Williams and Wilkins.
Pillsbury, W.B. (1911): *Essentials of psychology.* London: Macmillan (cited by R.S. Woodworth (1931) in *Contemporary schools of psychology*, 3rd ed. London: Methuen).
Registrar General (1968): *A glossary of mental disorders.* London: HMSO.
Reichardt, M. (1929): Brain and psyche. Translated by F.I. Wertham. *J. Nerv. Ment. Dis.* **70**, 390–396.
Reider, R.O., Mann, L.S., Weinberger, D.R., van Kammen, D.P. & Post, R.M. (1981): CAT-scans in patients with schizophrenia, schizo-affective disorder and affective disorder. Presented at APA Annual Meeting New Orleans, cited by Weinberger D.R. & Wyatt R.J., Chapter 8, In *Schizophrenia as a brain disease*, eds F.A. Henn & H.A. Nasrallah. New York and Oxford: Oxford University Press, 1982.
Reynolds, G.P. (1983): Lateral asymmetrics in neurochemical measurements in human brains. Paper read at Schizophrenia Group Meeting 20th. April, Wellcome Trust, London. *Nature* (in press).
Roberts, G.W., Ferrier, I.N., Lee, Y., Crow, T.J., Johnstone, E.C., Owens, D.G.C., Bacarese-Hamilton, A.J., McGregor, G., O'Shaughnessey, D., Polak, J.M. & Bloom, S.R. (1984): Peptides, the limbic lobe and schizophrenia. *Brain Res.* **288**, 199–211.
Romano, J. & Engel, G.L. (1944): Physiologic and psychologic considerations of delirium. *Med. Clin N. Am.* **28**, 629–638.
Rorie, J. (1862–1863): The treatment of hallucinations by electrization. *J. Ment. Sci.* **8**, 363–365.
Roth, M. & McClelland, H. (1979): The relationship of 'nuclear' and atypical' psychoses. *Psychiatr. Clin.* **12**, 23–54.
Russell, W. (1934): The after-effects of head injury. *Med. J.* **41**, 129–141. [Extracts in *The traumatic amnesias.* London, Glasgow, New York: Oxford University Press, 1971.]

Schneider, K. (1957): Primary and secondary symptoms in schizophrenia. In *Themes and variations in European psychiatry*, ed. M. Shepherd. Bristol: Wright.

Schwade, E.D. & Geiger, S.G. (1956): Abnormal electroencephalographic findings in severe behaviour disorders. *Dis. Nerv. System* **17**, 307–317.

Shakow, D. (1962): Segmental set: a theory of the formal psychological deficit in schizophrenia. *Arch. Gen. Psychiatry* **6**, 1–1.

Slater, E. & Roth, M. (1969): *Clinical psychiatry*, 3rd edn. London: Bailliere Tindall and Cassell.

Sperry, R. (1966): Brain bisection and mechanisms of consciousness. *Pontificae Academiae Scientiarum Scriptavaria* **25**, 1–16.

Stevens, J.R. (1982): Neurology and neuropathology of schizophrenia. In *Schizophrenia as a brain disease*, eds F.A. Henn & H.A. Nasrallah, Chap. 7, pp. 112–147. New York and Oxford: Oxford University Press.

Stevens, M., Crow, T.J., Bowman, M. & Coles, E.C. (1978): Age disorientation in chronic schizophrenia: a constant prevalence of 25% in a mental hospital population? *Br. J. Psychiatry* **133**, 130–136.

Symonds, C.P. & Russell, W.R. (1943): Accidental head injuries: Prognosis in severe patients. *Lancet* **i**, 7–10.

Thompson, R.F. (1987): The cerebellum and memory storage. *Science* **238**, 1729–1730.

Van Till, M.A.H. (1976): Legal aspects of the definition and diagnosis of death. In *Handbook of clinical neurology*, eds P.J. Vinken, G.W. Bruyn & R. Braakman, vol 24 part 2 (Injuries of the brain and skull), pp. 787–828. Amsterdam, Oxford: North Holland.

Victor, M. & Adams, R.D. (1961): On the etiology of the alcoholic neurologic diseases with special reference to the role of nutrition. *Am. J. Clin. Nutr.* **9**, 379–397.

Weckowicz, T.E. (1957): Size constancy in schizophrenic patients. *J. Ment. Sci.* **103**, 432–486.

Weckowicz, T.E. (1960): Perception of hidden figures by schizophrenic patients. *Arch. Gen. Psychiatry* **2**, 521–527.

Weckowicz, T.E. & Witney, G. (1960): The Muller-Lyer illusion in schizophrenic patients. *J. Ment. Sci.* **106**, 1002–1009.

Weckowicz, T.E., Sommer, R. & Hall, R. (1958): Distance constancy in schizophrenic patients. *J. Ment. Sci.* **104**, 1174–1182.

Weinberger, D.R., Torrey, E.F. & Wyatt, R.J. (1979): Cerebellar atrophy in chronic schizophrenia. *Lancet* **i**, 718–719.

Weinberger, D.R., DeLisi, L.E., Neophytides, A.N. & Wyatt, R.J. (1981): Familial aspects of CT abnormalities in chronic schizophrenic patients. *Psychiatr. Res.* **4**, 65–71.

Weinberger, D.R., Berman, K.F. & Zec, R.F. (1986): Physiologic dysfunction of dorsolateral prefrontal cortex in schizophrenia. *Arch of Gen. Psychiatry* **43**, 114–124.

Weller, M.P.I. (1986*a*): Cognitive and sensory defects in schizophrenia. In *The long-term management of patients suffering from schizophrenia*, eds R.R.R. Tilleard-Cole & M. Lader. London and Geneva: Franklyn Scientific.

Weller, M.P.I. (1986*b*): Report of the 3rd Biannual International Workshop on Schizophrenia 1985, Schladmig. *Bull. R. Coll. Psychiatr.* **10**, 277.

Weller, M.P.I. & Kugler, B.T. (1979): Tactile discrimination in schizophrenic and affective psychoses. In *Hemisphere asymmetries of function in psychopathology* eds J. Gruzelier & P. Flor-Henry, pp. 463–474. Amsterdam: Elsevier, North Holland.

Weller, M.P.I. & Montagu, J.D. (1979): Electroencephalographic coherence in schizophrenia; A preliminary study. pp. 285–292 In *Hemisphere asymmetries of function in psychopathology*, ed. J. Gruzelier & P. Flor-Henry. Amsterdam: Elsevier, North Holland.

Weller, M.P.I., Kidd, J., Calev. A., Chazen, S., Nigal, D. & Lerer B. (1988): Laterality in schizophrenia measured by tapping speed. Presented at Biannual Workshop on Schizophrenia, Badgastein, Jan. *Int. J. Schizophrenia* abstract, in press.

Whitehead, A.N. (1933): *Adventures of ideas*, p. 269. New York: Mentor Book, The New American Library.

Whitehead, A.N. (1934): *Nature and life*. Chicago: University of Chicago Press. Abridged version in *The age of analysis: 20th century philosophers*, ed. M. White. New York: Mentor Book, The New American Library, 1961.

Whitty, C.W.M. & Zangwill, O.L. (1966): Traumatic amnesia. In *Amnesia*, eds C.W.M. Whitty & O.L. Zangwill. pp. 92–108. London: Butterworths.
Zahn, T.P. (1977): Comments on reaction time and attention in schizophrenia. *Schizophrenia Bull.* **3**, 452–456.
Zahn, T.P. *et al.* (1981): cited by Zahn, T.P., Rapoport, J.L. & Thompson, C.L. (1981): Autonomic efforts of dextroamphetamine in normal men: Implications for hyperactivity and schizophrenia. *Psychiatr. Res.* **4**, 39–47.

Chapter 2

Organic schizophrenia-like psychoses

Kenneth Davison

University of Newcastle and Newcastle General Hospital, Newcastle-upon-Tyne NE4 6BE, UK

Summary

Scrutiny of series of patients with a clinical diagnosis of schizophrenia reveals that 5–10% have a concurrent organic disorder directly or indirectly affecting brain function. From a review of the literature and study of a personal series of 50 patients with organic brain disorder and a psychosis resembling schizophrenia the following conclusions are reached: (1) Psychoses resembling schizophrenia occur in association with organic disorders affecting the brain more frequently than chance expectation; (2) They are not readily distinguishable from ordinary schizophrenia on clinical grounds; (3) They occur in patients without genetic loading for schizophrenia; and (4) In patients with brain lesions the location of the lesion may play an important role in the genesis of the psychosis.

Introduction

Careful examination of series of patients with a clinical diagnosis of schizophrenia, made according to phenomenological criteria, usually reveals a small proportion of patients with some form of organic disorder with the potential to affect brain function. One such report is by Johnstone *et al.* (1987), from Northwick Park Hospital. In a sample of 268 cases of 'first-episode schizophrenia' diagnosed on Present State Examination (PSE) criteria (Wing *et al.*, 1974), they found 15 (5.6%) with organic disorders which appeared relevant to their mental state (Table 1). As these patients had been screened for the

Table 1. *Organic disorders discovered in 268 patients with a first episode of schizophrenia, using PSE criteria (Johnstone* et al.*, 1987).*

Diagnosis	*Number of patients*
Alcohol abuse	3
Syphilis	3
Drug abuse	2
Sarcoidosis	2
Auto-immune disease	1
Bronchial carcinoma	1
Cerebral cysticercosis	1
Hypothyroidism, overtreated	1
Head injury/hemiparesis	1

Table 2. *Clinically undiagnosed organic brain disease revealed by CT scan in 136 patients with chronic schizophrenia (Owens* et al.*, 1980).*

Diagnosis	*Number of patients*
Cerebral infarction	7
Porencephalic cyst	1
Meningioma	1
Subdural haematoma	2
Pineal cyst	1

presence of organic disorder by the referring clinicians and this was an exclusion criterion for entry into the research sample, the true prevalence may have been much greater. A further consequence of the selection procedure was that the organic conditions eventually uncovered lay towards the more obscure end of the spectrum.

Examination of chronic schizophrenics, eg by CT scan, yields similar findings. For example, one CT scan study of 136 patients revealed 12 cases with abnormalities, which in 10 (7.4%) were regarded as of possible aetiological relevance (Owens *et al.*, 1980). The diagnoses in this study are listed in Table 2.

In a survey of 318 consecutive admissions to a large Newcastle Psychiatric Hospital with a clinical diagnosis of schizophrenia, 25 patients (7.9%) were found with an antecedent organic cerebral disorder (McClelland *et al.*, 1966), and one autopsy study of 200 schizophrenic patients yielded 22 (11%) with structural brain disease thought to be causally related (Khaime, 1967).

It seems reasonable, therefore, to conclude that between 5 and 10% of patients with a clinical diagnosis of schizophrenia will have an associated organic disorder of possible aetiological significance.

Does the association between the psychosis and concomitant organic disorder exceed chance expectation?

Some years ago, whilst working at the National Hospital, Queen Square (NHQS), a London Neuropsychiatric Hospital, I collected 50 such cases from former in-patients over a 10-year period. This was before the establishment of accepted diagnostic criteria, but the psychoses would fulfil Research Diagnostic Criteria (RDC) (Spitzer *et al.*, 1975) for schizophrenia. The organic diagnoses (Table 3) illustrate well that the type of disorder found depends upon the provenance of the case material.

Of the 50 patients, 29 had developed their psychosis after their first admission to the NHQS. During the same decade the admissions to the NHQS with diagnoses indicating cerebral disorder other than epilepsy (since patients with uncomplicated epilepsy had been excluded from my series) numbered 8029. On the unlikely assumption that all these patients were at the age of maximum risk for developing schizophrenia and had survived for the 10-year period, the expected number of cases of schizophrenia was 13. The observed number was 29 and there was no guarantee that every former patient who became psychotic was identified. Patients with organic brain disease, therefore, developed a schizophrenia-like psychosis at least twice as often, and very probably a good deal more, than expected on a chance association hypothesis (Davison, 1966).

An association greater than chance has been demonstrated in a number of specific brain disorders. Slater *et al.* (1963) confirmed this for epileptic schizophrenia-like psychoses and, in an up-to-date review, McKenna *et al.* (1985) concluded that the risk of developing

Table 3. *Diagnosis and origin of 50 patients with brain lesions and schizophrenia-like psychoses.*

Diagnosis	*Number of cases* *Queen Square*	*Other hospitals*	*Total*
Multiple sclerosis	7	2	9
Parkinsonism			6
Paralysis agitans	3	1	
Post-encephalitic	2	—	
Congenital lesions			6
Cerebral atrophy	2	—	
Cerebral diplegia	1	—	
Extra-pyramidal syndrome	1	—	
Hydrocephalus	1	—	
Sturge-Weber syndrome	—	1	
Cerebral tumour	5	—	5
Brain-stem thrombosis	3	—	3
Huntington's chorea	3	—	3
Post-traumatic	2	1	3
Narcolepsy	3	—	3
Torsion spasm	1	1	2
Cerebellar degeneration	2	—	2
Motor neurone disease	2	—	2
Post-meningitis/encephalitis	2	—	2
Post-cerebral abscess	1	—	1
Friedreich's ataxia	1	—	1
Wilson's disease	1	—	1
Kleine-Levin syndrome	1	—	1
	44	6	50

a psychosis of this type is increased by a factor of 6 to 12 in epileptic patients. A relevant example is Huntington's chorea.

Huntington's chorea

Psychoses diagnosed as schizophrenia and paranoid-hallucinatory psychoses resembling paranoid schizophrenia occur quite often in patients with Huntington's chorea. Prevalence rates in various series are listed in Table 4 (Davison, 1983) and considerably exceed chance expectation. (*Prevalence* is the number of cases per unit of population present at some specific point in time [point prevalence] or over some period of time [period prevalence], often 1 year or a lifetime. It reflects not only incidence but also duration. The point prevalence of schizophrenia in various parts of the world lies between 0.1% and 0.6% although an unusually high prevalence of over 1% is reported from parts of Sweden and Ireland [Torrey, 1987]). Three of these reports are population surveys and therefore unselected for psychiatric disorder (Bolt, 1970; Heathfield, 1967; Oliver, 1970). Some authors do not distinguish between diagnoses of schizophrenia and paranoid psychosis.

Schizophrenia is a common initial diagnosis in Huntington's chorea and is said to be the most frequent persisting misdiagnosis. A recent Norwegian review (Saugstad & Ødegard, 1986) comments: 'In several cases this diagnosis (of schizophrenia) was preserved during as many as 3 or 4 readmissions. The disease (HC) should be considered in the differential diagnosis of schizophrenia.'

Table 4. *Prevalence of schizophrenia and paranoid psychosis in Huntington's chorea (Davison, 1983).*

Number of cases of Huntington's chorea	*Schizophrenia (% ± SE)*		*Paranoid psychosis (% ± SE)*
461	5.0 ± 1.0		-------------
1200	1.7 ± 0.4		4.0 ± 0.6
102	6.9 ± 2.5		-------------
199	----------------	19.6 ± 2.8	----------------
71	14.1 ± 4.1		15.5 ± 4.3
43	2.3 ± 2.3		7.0 ± 3.9
334*	2.4 ± 0.8		15.0 ± 1.9
100*	12.0 ± 3.2		----------------
81*	11.0 ± 3.5		----------------

*population survey

Organic brain disease is of particular significance at the extremes of age. Childhood schizophrenia is often associated with a history of perinatal injury or anoxia or concurrent organic disease. Thus one series of 100 children with a diagnosis of schizophrenia contained 12 with epilepsy, one with congenital hemiplegia, two with cerebral lipoidosis (unsuspected in life) and two with other forms of brain damage (17% in all) (Creak, 1963). A series of 63 patients with 'infantile psychosis' included 18 (28%) with definite and 16 (25%) with possible brain damage (Rutter & Lockyer, 1967). Likewise groups of patients with paraphrenia, often regarded as late-onset schizophrenia (after age 60 years) yield prevalence rates for organic brain disorder of 5–17% initially, with an additional 8–18% appearing later (Davison, 1983). A recent 10-year follow-up of 42 cases of non-affective paranoid-hallucinatory psychosis occurring after age 60, diagnosed as late paraphrenia, found that five (11.9%) were symptomatic of organic disease on first referral and a further 13 (31%) became demented within 3 years. The organic group showed an excess of visual hallucinations but was otherwise clinically indistinguishable from the other cases at presentation (Holden, 1987).

Genetic disorders

In an important review of the literature on the association of genetic disorders with schizophrenia, Propping (1983) has listed those genetic disorders in which an increased risk of developing a schizophrenia-like psychosis is established or very probable, or possible (Table 5).

It will be seen that many of these conditions are associated with brain dysfunction, either primarily or secondary to metabolic defects. An example is Klinefelter's syndrome in which the sex chromosome constitution is XXY. A review of 48 studies involving 411 cases found 179 (43.5%) with a psychiatric disorder, including 26 (6.3%) with schizophrenia and 29 (7.1%) with 'psychoses of uncertain type with paranoid delusions' (Nielsen, 1969).

Without going into any further detail there would appear to be ample evidence that the association of a schizophrenia-like psychosis and organic disorder exceeds chance expectation. Association does not, however, necessarily indicate causation.

Table 5. *Genetic disorders with an increased risk of developing a schizophrenia-like psychosis (Propping, 1983).*

Established or very probable	*Possible*
Klinefelter karyotype (XXY)	Turner (45,XO) or Noonan syndrome
XXX karyotype	XYY karyotype
18q or r(18) constitution	Erythropoietic protoporphyria
Huntington's chorea	Niemann-Pick's disease, late type
Acute intermittent porphyria	Gaucher's disease, late type
Porphyria variegata	Fabry disease
Metachromatic leukodystrophy, adult type	Amaurotic idiocy, late type
Familial basal ganglia calcification	Congenital adrenal hyperplasia
	Homocystinuria
	Wilson's disease
	Haemochromatosis
	Ichthyosis vulgaris
	Laurence-Moon-Biedl syndrome
	Glucose-6-phosphate dehydrogenase deficiency
	Phenylketonuria
	Albinism
	Kartagener's syndrome
	Ataxia, dominant type
	Hyperasparaginaemia

How does the family loading for schizophrenia in the organic cases compare with that of ordinary schizophrenics?

Whether a single gene or multifactorial model is adopted, an absence of family loading for schizophrenia would argue strongly in favour of an aetiological relationship between organic disorder and psychosis. A family loading for schizophrenia greater than that of the general population would suggest either a non-specific stress precipitation effect or a non-aetiological connection.

Genetic studies from published reports are shown in Table 6. The appropriate comparison is the lifetime morbidity risk which for schizophrenia in the general

Table 6. *Morbidity risk for schizophrenia in the families of patients with a schizophrenia-like psychosis and CNS disease compared with ordinary schizophrenics and the general population (Davison & Bagley, 1969).*

CNS disorders accompanying psychosis	*Number of probands*	*Morbidity risk for schizophrenia (mean ± SE)*			*Author (Cited in Davison & Bagley, 1969)*
		Parents	*Siblings*	*Children*	
Epilepsy	69	———	0.7 ± 0.24%	———	Slater *et al.*, 1963
Cerebral trauma	240	0.4 ± 0.4%	1.3 ± 0.6%	0.7 ± 0.7%	Zerbin-Rüdin, 1966
	55	—	2.9 ± 1.3%	—	Schulz, 1932
Cerebral tumour	10	5.1 ± 4.9%	9.3 ± 6.1%	—	Wanner, 1950
Multiple sclerosis	9	———	1.0 ± 0.59%	———	Riegel, 1940
Schizophrenia		5.07%	8.53%	12.31%	Shields & Slater, 1967
General population		———	0.86%	———	

Table 7. *Incidence of psychosis in first degree relatives of 50 probands with 'organic schizophrenia' (Davison, 1966).*

Age group	*Parents*	*Relationship* *Siblings*	*Half-siblings*	*Total*
0–39yrs (0)	—	16	—	16
15–39 (½)	10	41	4	55
40+ (1)	85	95	4	184
No information	5	—	—	—
Total	100	152	8	260
Diagnoses:				
Schizophrenia	1	2	1	4
Depressive illness	3	3	—	6

Incidence of schizophrenia $= \dfrac{4}{½(55) + 1(184)}$

$= 1.9 \pm 0.95\%$ (1.5% without half-siblings)

Incidence of depressive illness $= 3.4 \pm 1.4\%$

population is 0.8% from birth to age 40 and 1% to age 55 (Registrar General, 1964), with the maximum risk between the ages of 15 and 40. A genetic study of my own 50 cases is shown in Table 7, which also demonstrates the Weinberg shorter method of calculating the family loading (Weinberg, 1925). Relatives below age 15 are not counted, those aged from 15 to 39 count as half-persons, and those aged from 40 onwards count as whole persons for calculating the denominator of the percentage incidence calculation. The morbidity risk for schizophrenia in the first degree relatives does not exceed that of the general population to a statistically significant extent (less than twice the standard error) and thus an aetiological role for the organic disorder is supported.

Is any particular brain locus preferentially involved?

Tables 8 and 9 show the pathology and locations of a large series of cases of cerebral tumour and 'schizophrenia', culled from the literature (Davison & Bagley, 1969),

Table 8. *Distribution of types of cerebral tumour in 70 psychotic cases from published reports compared with an unselected series of 6000 reported by Zülch, 1957.* Statistical significance of differences calculated by χ^2 method.

Type of cerebral tumour	*% of 6000 unselected cases, Zülch, 1957*	*% of 70 psychotic cases*
Glioma (all forms)	37.0	37.1
Meningioma	18.0	14.3
Pituitary adenoma	8.0	17.0 $P < 0.01$
Craniopharyngioma	2.5	5.7
Sarcoma	2.7	2.9
Angioma and aneurysm	2.5	4.3
Granuloma	0.7	2.9
Pinealoma	0.4	2.9
Colloid cyst	—	7.0
Cholesteatoma, epidermoid cyst	—	2.9

Table 9. *Localization of cerebral tumours in 77 psychotic cases from published reports compared with two unselected series.* Statistical significance of differences calculated by χ^2 method. Values of p refer to difference between psychotic group and each of the two unselected series. (Davison & Bagley, 1969).

Site of cerebral tumour	*% of 600 cases (Walther-Büel, 1951)*	*% of 530 cases (Keschner, Bender and Strauss, 1938)*	*% of 77 psychotic cases*	
Frontal	29.0	24.7	19.5	
Temporal	13.0	16.2	35.1	$P < 0.001$
Parietal	10.0	10.6	—	
Occipital	5.3	2.0	1.3	
Cerebellum	10.3	14.0	5.2	$P < 0.01$ (Cerebellum and Cerebello-pontine angle)
Cerebello-pontine angle	8.3	6.8	1.3	
Hypophysis and supra-sellar	9.3	6.8	19.5	$P < 0.01$
3rd ventricle	—	3.0	9.1	
Brain stem	4.7	3.6	3.9	
Mid-brain and basal ganglia	—	2.6	1.3	
Pineal	—	2.0	3.9	
Supra-tentorial	76.7	75.7	89.6	$P < 0.01$ (Supra-tentorial and Infra-tentorial)
Infra-tentorial	23.3	24.3	10.4	

compared with some unselected series of cerebral tumour cases. There is an excess of temporal lobe and hypophyseal lesions in the psychotic group. More recently further evidence has accumulated pointing to the temporolimbic system (Torrey & Peterson, 1974) and sub-cortical brain areas (Cummings, 1985) as the commonest sites for the lesions associated with schizophrenia-like psychoses and this is also demonstrable in Table 3.

Are organically determined schizophrenia-like psychoses clinically distinguishable from spontaneously occurring schizophrenia?

Several studies have found that many of these organic psychoses fulfil operational diagnostic criteria for schizophrenia (Davison, 1983). For example a recent review of 70 epileptic patients with various psychiatric disorders currently in or attending Newcastle

Table 10. *Schneiderian symptoms in epileptic (ES) and 'functional' (FS) schizophrenia.*

Symptoms	*Number with symptoms* ES	FS	*Statistic (χ^2 test)*
Thought insertion	13 (40.6%)	18 (58.1%)	$P = 0.3$
Thought broadcast	13 (40.6%)	16 (51.5%)	$P = 0.5$
Thought echo	9 (28.1%)	11 (35.5%)	$P = 0.72$
Thought block	4 (12.5%)	6 (19.4%)	$P = 0.7$
Thought withdrawal	4 (12.5%)	6 (19.4%)	$P = 0.7$
Delusions of thoughts being read	14 (43.8%)	19 (61.3%)	$P = 0.3$
Third person auditory hallucinations	24 (75%)	24 (75%)	$P = 1.0$
Delusions of passivity	11 (34.4%)	25 (80.6%)	$P = 0.0005$

Table 11. *Clinical features in 50 cases of 'organic schizophrenia' compared with 150 similar cases in published reports and 475 cases of schizophrenia reported by Astrup* et al. *(1962).*

Symptoms	% Displaying symptoms in 50 organic cases	150 organic cases	475 cases of schizophrenia (Astrup et al., 1962)
Primary delusions	26	13	—
Flat/incongruous affect	48*	23*	30
Paranoid delusions	86	85	78
Passivity feelings	44*	36*	62
Catatonic symptoms	28	29*	20
Thought disorder	34	16*	33
Auditory hallucinations	72	69*	87
Visual hallucinations	4*	20	19
Tactile hallucinations	6*	8*	30
Olfactory hallucinations	—	6	13
1 or more Langfeldt's primary symptoms	68	67	71
1 or more Schneider's 1st rank symptoms	64	64	—
Pre-morbid schizoid personality	14*	9*	36
Family history of schizophrenia	14*	9*	33

*statistically significant difference

hospitals revealed 32 who fulfilled RDC criteria for schizophrenia (Oyebode & Davison, unpublished data). A comparison of the frequency of various Schneiderian 1st Rank Symptoms, as defined in the PSE, between these 32 cases and 32 age-matched schizophrenics is shown in Table 10. The only significant difference is an excess of delusions of passivity in the non-organic group. A comparison of the frequency of individual symptoms between 150 reported cases and a series of 475 schizophrenics published by Astrup *et al.* (1962) (Davison & Bagley, 1969) is shown in Table 11.

When comparing the PSE profiles of 11 patients with epileptic psychoses and nine ordinary schizophrenic patients, Perez *et al.* (1985) found them to be remarkably congruent, the only significant differences being an excess of visual hallucinations and grandiose delusions in the non-organic group. Johnstone *et al.* (1988) also found only minor differences between a group of 23 patients with psychosis and organic disorder compared with 92 with non-organic psychoses.

A claim often made is that the 'organic schizophrenias' are distinguishable from ordinary schizophrenia by the retention of a warm affect, and this allows these patients to make relationships and thus be more likely to marry (eg Slater *et al.*, 1963). Table 12 shows some data from my own series of 50 cases and also the 69 epileptic psychoses reported by Slater *et al.*, from which it can be seen that affective flattening is related to age at the onset of the psychosis. Comparisons of the organic psychoses with schizophrenia therefore need to be controlled for age of onset before any conclusion can be drawn about preservation of affect in the organic group. In fact the mean age of onset of the psychosis in my 50 cases was 33 ± 11 years and in 150 literature cases 32 ± 11 years, considerably older than the peak age of onset of schizophrenia. Patients with 'epileptic schizophrenia' (ES) do not necessarily marry as often as patients with 'functional schizophrenia' (FS), for only 40.6% of 32 ES patients were ever-married compared to 64.5% of 32 age-matched FS patients ($p < 0.1$) (Oyebode & Davison, unpublished data).

To recapitulate, I have sought to demonstrate that (a) psychoses resembling schizophrenia occur in association with organic disorders affecting the brain more

Table 12. *Relationship between age and affective flattening.*

'Organic schizophrenia' (Davison, 1966)

		Mean age of onset (years)	
		Brain lesion	*Psychosis*
Flat affect	(n = 11)	12.4	22.7
Preserved affect	(n = 39)	29.4	36.8
		$P < 0.01$	$P < 0.001$

Epileptic psychoses (Slater *et al.*, 1963)

		Mean age of onset (years)	
		Epilepsy	*Psychosis*
Flat affect	(n = 28)	11.9	26.0
Preserved affect	(n = 41)	18.3	32.6
		$P < 0.05$	$P < 0.02$

frequently than chance expectation; (2) they are not readily distinguishable from ordinary schizophrenia on clinical grounds; (3) they occur in patients without genetic loading for schizophrenia; and (4) in patients with brain lesions the location of the lesion may play an important role in the genesis of the psychosis.

Significance for the schizophrenia concept

The occurrence of psychoses resembling schizophrenia, yet apparently organically determined, supports the syndromic, as opposed to the disease entity, concept of schizophrenia. These cases create nosological difficulties which have not yet been resolved. DSM-III (American Psychiatric Association, 1980) puts them in a separate category of 'organic delusional disorder'. It would be more logical to classify the psychiatric syndrome according to its phenomenology, as schizophrenia if relevant criteria are fulfilled, independently of the associated organic condition. The strength of the association between 'schizophrenia' and various organic concomitants could then be empirically assessed. As it is, these psychoses are given a wide variety of diagnostic labels and are thus lost to epidemiological scrutiny.

The concept of 'secondary mania' has been accepted; why not 'secondary schizophrenia'? The hope is, of course, that it will provide some clues to the pathogenesis of 'ordinary schizophrenia'.

References

American Psychiatric Association (1980): *Diagnostic and statistical manual of mental disorders*, 3rd ed. (DSM-III). Washington, DC: American Psychiatric Association.

Astrup, C., Fossum, A. & Holmboe, R. (1962): *Prognosis in functional psychoses*. Springfield, Ill.: Thomas.

Bolt, J.M.W. (1970): Huntington's chorea in the west of Scotland. *Br. J. Psychiatry* **116**, 259–270.

Creak, M. (1963): Childhood psychosis. A review of 100 cases. *Br. J. Psychiatry* **109**, 84–89.

Cummings, J.L. (1985): Organic delusions: phenomenology, anatomical correlations and review. *Br. J. Psychiatry* **146**, 184–197.

Davison, K. (1966): Schizophrenia-like psychoses associated with organic brain disease. Preliminary observations on 50 patients. *Newcastle Med. J.* **29**, 67–73.

Davison, K. (1983): Schizophrenia-like psychoses associated with organic cerebral disorders: a review. *Psychiatric Devel.* **1**, 1–34.
Davison, K. & Bagley, C.R. (1969): Schizophrenia-like psychoses associated with organic disorders of the CNS: a review of the literature. In *Current problems in neuropsychiatry*, ed. R.N. Herrington, pp 113–184. British Journal of Psychiatry Special Publication No 4. Ashford: Headley Bros Ltd.
Heathfield, K.W.G. (1967): Huntington's chorea. Investigation into the prevalence of this disease in the area covered by the North-East Metropolitan Regional Hospital Board. *Brain* **90**, 203–232.
Holden, N.L. (1987): Late paraphrenia or the paraphrenias? A descriptive study with a 10-year follow-up. *Br. J. Psychiatry* **150**, 635–639.
Johnstone, E.C., MacMillan, J.F. & Crow, T.J. (1987): The occurrence of organic disease of possible or probable aetiological significance in a population of 268 cases of first episode schizophrenia. *Psychol. Med.* **17**, 371–379.
Johnstone, E.C., Cooling, N.J., Frith, C.D., Crow, T.J. & Owens, D.G.C. (1988): Phenomenology of organic and functional psychoses and the overlap between them. *Br. J. Psychiatry* **153**, 770–776.
Keschner, M., Bender, M.B. & Strauss, I. (1938): Mental symptoms associated with brain tumor. A study of 530 verified cases. *J.A.M.A.* **110**, 714–718.
Khaime, T. (1967): Organic diseases of the brain in schizophrenia. *Zh. Nevropatol. Psikhiatr.* **67**, 113–118.
McClelland, H.A., Roth, M. & Neubauer, H. (1966): Some observations on a case material based on patients with certain common schizophrenic symptoms. Proceedings of the World Congress of Psychiatry, Madrid, p. 2955. Amsterdam: Excerpta Medica.
McKenna, P.J., Kane, J.M. & Parrish, K. (1985): Psychotic syndromes in epilepsy. *Am. J. Psychiatry* **142**, 895–904.
Nielsen, J. (1969): Klinefelter's syndrome and the XYY syndrome. *Acta Psychiatr. Scand.* **45**, Suppl. 209.
Oliver, J.E. (1970): Huntington's chorea in Northamptonshire. *Br. J. Psychiatry* **116**, 241–253.
Owens, D.G.C., Johnstone, E.C., Bydder, G.M. & Kreel, L. (1980): Unsuspected organic disease in chronic schizophrenia demonstrated by computed tomography. *J. Neurol. Neurosurg. Psychiatry* **43**, 1065–1069.
Perez, M.M., Trimble, M.R., Murray, N.M.F. & Reider, I. (1985): Epileptic psychosis: an evaluation of PSE profiles. *Br. J. Psychiatry* **146**, 155–163.
Propping, P. (1983): Genetic disorders presenting as "schizophrenia". Karl Bonhoeffer's early view of the psychoses in the light of medical genetics. *Hum. Genet.* **65**, 1–10.
Registrar General (1964): Statistical review of England and Wales for the year 1960: Supplement on mental health. London: HMSO.
Rutter, M. & Lockyer, L. (1967): A five to fifteen year follow-up study of infantile psychosis. I. Description of sample. *Br. J. Psychiatry* **113**, 1169–1182.
Saugstad, L. & Ødegard, Ø. (1986): Huntington's chorea in Norway. *Psychol. Med.* **16**, 39–48.
Slater, E., Beard, A.W. & Glithero, E. (1963): The schizophrenia-like psychoses of epilepsy. *Br. J. Psychiatry* **109**, 95–150.
Spitzer, R., Endicott, J. & Robins, E. (1975): *Research diagnostic criteria.* New York: New York State Psychiatric Institute.
Torrey, E.F. (1987): Prevalence studies in schizophrenia. *Br. J. Psychiatry* **150**, 598–608.
Torrey, E.F. & Peterson, M.R. (1974): Schizophrenia and the limbic system. *Lancet* **ii**, 942–946.
Walther-Büel, H. (1951): Die Psychiatrie der Hirngeschwülste. *Acta Neurochir.* Suppl. II.
Weinberg, W. (1925): In *Handbuch der sozialen Hygiene*, eds A. Gottstein, A. Schlossman & L. Teleky, vol. 1, p 71. Berlin.
Wing, J.K., Cooper, J.E. & Sartorius, N. (1974): *The description and classification of psychiatric symptoms: an instruction manual for the PSE and Catego systems.* Cambridge: Cambridge University Press.
Zülch, K.J. (1957): *Brain tumors, their biology and pathology.* New York: Springer.

Chapter 3
Memory in schizophrenia*

Avraham Calev

The Jerusalem Mental Health Centre, Ezrath-Nashim, P.O. Box 140, Givat Shaul, Jerusalem, Israel

Summary

This chapter reviews the research on memory in schizophrenia. It suggests that schizophrenics are characterized by an associative disturbance which adversely affects recall. Both verbal and non-verbal tasks are affected. This deficit can be ameliorated through meaningfully organizing to-be-remembered materials, or affectively characterizing their encoding. The results of these manipulations, however, show that long-stay (negative symptoms) schizophrenics do not improve to a normal level, unlike short-stay (positive symptoms) patients. The former, unlike the latter patients, also show rapid forgetting of well-organized information, and a recognition memory deficit. Their recall and forgetting rates are better for negative emotion than neutral and positive emotion words. Their remote and recent recognition memories are less severely affected than their recent recall memory. The deficits schizophrenics show seem minor in semantic, procedural (implicit) and primary (short-term) memory. The effects of anticholinergic drugs are minor in chronic (long-stay) patients, but are visible in other patients. Memory deficits of minor magnitude may also be observed in high risk subjects. The implications of the findings for understanding the brain pathology of schizophrenia and for memory treatment are discussed.

Introduction

The study of memory in schizophrenia dates back to the days of Kraepelin (1919) and Bleuler (1911). Kraepelin (1919) wrote that 'memory is comparatively little disordered,' and that 'retention is also often quite well preserved' (pp. 12–17) in schizophrenia, but also noticed the 'disturbance of associations' which may lead to memory dysfunction (eg, Tulving & Donaldson, 1972), and to 'pseudomemories' and 'confabulations,' used to describe memory dysfunction. Bleuler (1911), although impressed by the 'clear sensorium' in schizophrenia, also noticed that 'forgetfulness' was the first or one of the first of the important symptoms of the illness; and that the patients themselves often complain about their memory' (p. 60).

*This chapter was supported by the Doll-Steinberg Research Project in The Jerusalem Mental Health Centre, Ezrath-Nashim. I wish to acknowledge Dr M.P.I. Weller's significant contribution to this effort.

C.L. Hull (1917) was probably the first to conduct an experimental study of memory in schizophrenia. He used a paired associated task in which subjects had to learn to associate Chinese characters with nonsense syllables. He found that schizophrenics had more difficulty, needing more trials, to learn these associations. However, in a retest carried out a week later, no subsequent retention deficit was found. This study used only three patients, and no statistical analysis. This finding of a learning deficit has, however, been the one most frequently replicated in schizophrenics by various investigators since Hull (eg Babcock, 1933; Cohen, 1950; Koh, 1978).

The first comprehensive review of memory in schizophrenia was not written until 1978 by Koh, who had conducted a large number of studies in the Micheal Reese Hospital in Chicago. The main conclusion of this review was that it is 'control processes' of memory, such as the use of associative ability, affect in encoding the to-be-remembered information, and attentional resources which caused the schizophrenic memory dysfunction. When using techniques which could overcome these faulty 'control processes,' no deficits in memory were observed. These techniques consisted of (1) induced sematic organization of memory at encoding (eg Larsen & Fromholt, 1976), or affective encoding of the to-be-remembered materials (eg Koh *et al.*, 1981), and (2) use of tasks which require minimal or no mnemonic organization (associative ability), as in some recognition tasks, rather than recall (Koh & Peterson, 1978). Koh's subjects were, however, young and often acutely ill patients.

When considering chronic long-stay patients, the picture of memory functioning in schizophrenia seems different. Such patients, who usually suffer from so-called negative rather than positive symptoms (eg Crow, 1980; Andreasen & Olsen, 1982), also fail to show total recovery of memory function even when techniques that ameliorate or avoid the faulty 'control processes' are used. In addition, they show memory problems of a different nature from short-stay schizophrenics. They suffer from a larger 'generalized deficit' than short-stay patients, manifested in most of the cognitive tasks they perform (Chapman & Chapman, 1973, 1978; Calev & Monk, 1982), and so they do show deficits in some tasks with which mildly disturbed patients have little difficulty. There are several areas of memory research in which differences between these two types of patients have been found.

Areas of memory research showing differences between short-stay and long-stay patients

Induced meaningful mnemonic organization and affective encoding

An example of a successful use of a technique which ameliorates memory performance is reported in Larsen & Fromholt's (1976) study. They used Mandler & Pearlstone's (1966) sorting consistency task before recall. Subjects were given a list of 'unrelated' nouns, and asked to sort them into categories of their own choosing. The original list was then removed and the same words were presented to the subjects again, but in a different random order. The next task was to sort this second list, using the same categories. This list was presented several times, in different random orders, until the subject achieved two consecutive identical sorts. Larsen & Fromholt found that short-stay schizophrenics needed more learning trials than normal individuals to arrive at two consecutive identical sorts. Those schizophrenics who achieved the sorting consistency criterion also achieved equivalent recall levels to the normal controls.

Calev *et al.* (1983*a*) applied this task to long-stay schizophrenics with at least 2 years of cumulative hospital admission. Only five out of 15 such patients reached the criterion of

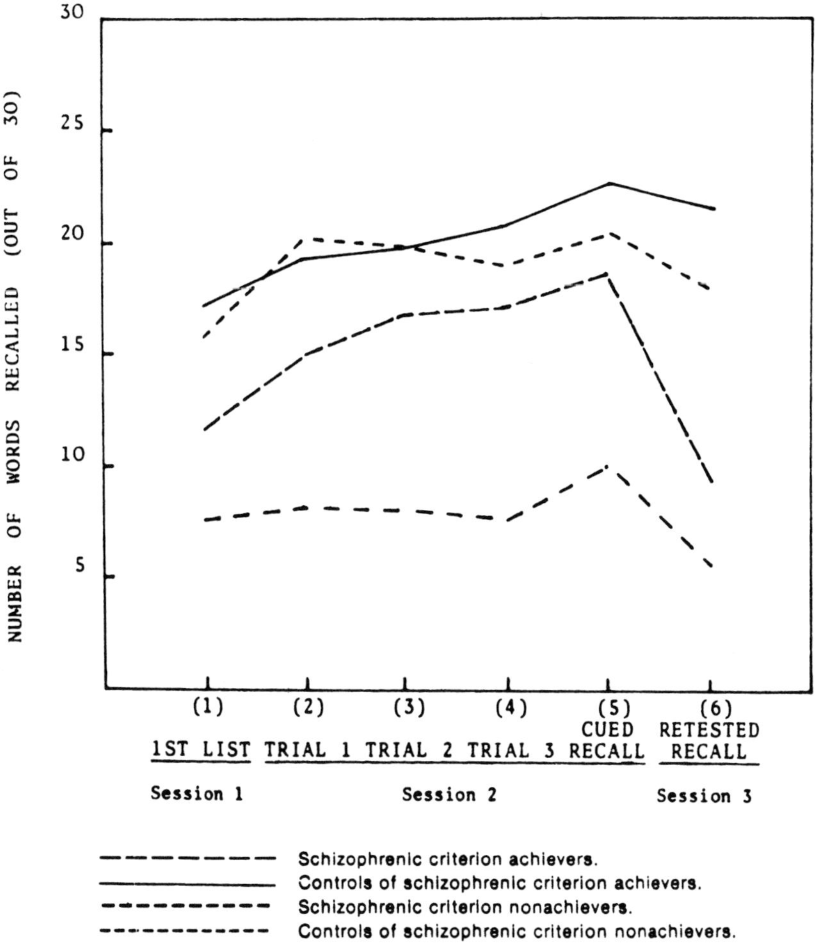

Fig. 1. *(a) The effect of an 'orienting task' performed before having to recall a list of words, and (b) the phenomenon of rapid forgetting in long-stay schizophrenics.* The recall of the 2nd list relative to the 1st is improved in 10 normals and 5 schizophrenics who reached the criterion of 'sorting consistency,' but not in 5 schizophrenics who could not reach this criterion. All groups were helped in their recall by retrieval cues (category names of the words grouped during the 'sorting consistency' tasks). Schizophrenics (n=10) tended to forget the second list in a retest carried out about 24 hours later. (From Calev *et al.*, 1983*a* by permission of *Schizophrenia Bulletin.*)

two consecutive identical sorts, unlike the short-stay patients studied by Larsen & Fromholt who had over 70 per cent success. These patients were less severely disturbed (older when first admitted to hospital), showed less conceptual overinclusion, had longer education in school and higher intelligence (Calev *et al.*, 1980) than the rest of the subjects. Figure 1 presents the results of this study. It shows that the five patients who achieved the sorting consistency criterion had, like the normal subjects, a better recall performance in the sorting task (trial 1, 2nd list) than they did when they performed the same task without achieving the consistency criterion (trial 1, 1st list). Their overall performance was much better than that of the five patients who continued working on the tast without reaching the criterion within 10 trials (another five subjects discontinued the

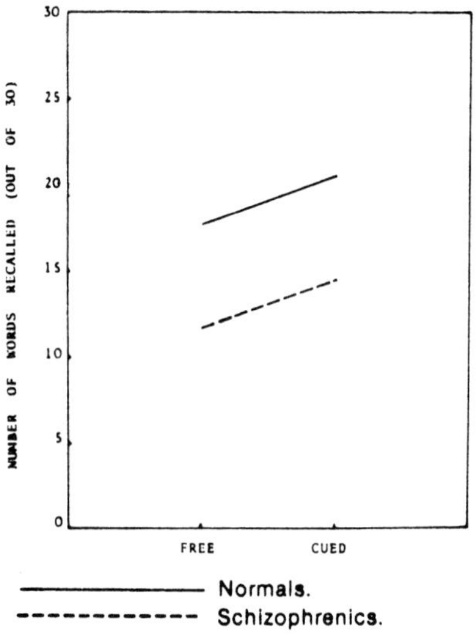

Fig. 2. *The figure, using 10 schizophrenics and 10 normal controls, shows that achieving a 'sorting consistency' criterion does not bring long-stay schizophrenics (unlike short-stay schizophrenics) to the recall level of normal controls, matched for general cognitive functioning, age and sex.* Cued recall (as in Fig. 1) helps both schizophrenics and normals to a similar extent (From Calev *et al.*, 1983*a*, by permission of *Schizophrenia Bulletin*.)

task before 10 trials were completed). However, contrary to the findings in Larsen & Fromholt's (1976) study, criterion achievers' recall performance tended to be poorer than that of the normal controls who were matched for intelligence. The same results were repeated with a further 10 long-stay schizophrenic criterion achievers using another list (Fig. 2). In yet another replication, it seemed that 'midly disturbed' patients with less than 1 year of cumulative hospital admission showed no significant deficit, unlike severely disturbed patients with more than 2 years of cumulative hospital admission (Fig. 3).

In a further replication, in which the immediate and delayed recall tasks were matched for discriminating power using the Chapman & Chapman (1973, 1978) proposed methodology, the difference from normals was again significant (Fig. 4). The results of

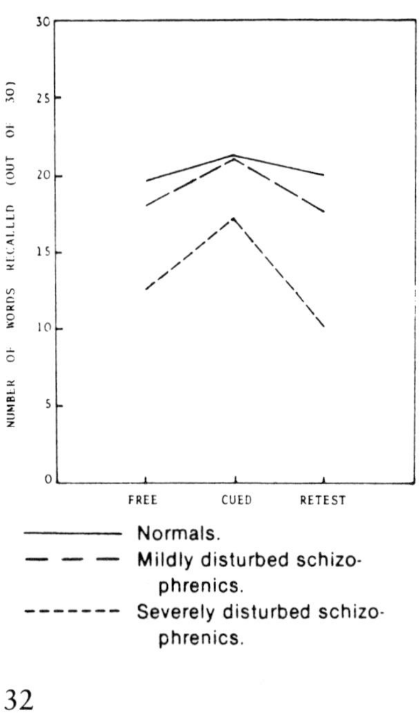

Fig. 3. *This figure shows that short-stay schizophrenics' recall performance, after successfully performing the 'sorting consistency' task, is more similar (non-significantly different) to normals than to long-stay schizophrenics; the latter group also shows significantly more rapid forgetting than short-stay schizophrenics and normal controls.* (The trend for rapid forgetting by short-stay schizophrenics is not statistically significant.) (From Calev *et al.*, 1983*a*, by permission of *Schizophrenia Bulletin*.)

INTERNATIONAL PERSPECTIVES IN SCHIZOPHRENIA

Biological, Social and Epidemiological Findings

Edited by
M.P.I. Weller, MA (Cantab), MB, BS, FRCPsych, CPsychol, FBPsS,

LIST OF CONTRIBUTORS

Dr. T.R.E. Barnes, MB, BS, MRCPsych, Senior Lecturer in Psychiatry, Department of Psycyhiatry, Charing Cross and Westminster Medical School, London, UK

Dr. D.H.R. Blackwood, PhD, BSc, MB, ChB, MRCP, MRCPsych, Senior Lecturer in Psychiatry, Department of Psychiatry, University of Edinburgh, Edinburgh, UK

Dr. J. Brynjolfsson, Cand Med, Research Psychiatrist, Borg Stitalinn, Iceland

Dr. A. Calev, PhD, Lecturer in Psychology, Bar Ilan University and Senior Research Psychologist, Jerusalem Mental Health Centre, Jerusalem, Israel

Dr. P.G. Campbell, MPhil, MA, BM, BCh, MRCP, FRCPsych, Consultant Psychiatrist, Friern Hospital and University College Hospital, London, UK

Dr. J.K. Chivers, Department of Pharmacology, Kings College Hospital, London, UK

Dr. J. Connolly, MPhil, MB, BS, FRCP, MRCS, LRCP, FRCPsych, Consultant Psychiatrist, Maudsley Hospital, London, UK

Professor B. Costall, BPharm, PhD, DSc., Professor of Neuropharmacology, Postgraduate School of Studies in Pharmacology, University of Bradford, Bradford, UK

Dr. T.J. Crow, PhD, MB, BS, FRCP, FRCPsych, DPM, MRCP, Head of Division of Psychiatry and Director Medical Research Council Psychiatric Unit, Northwick Park Hospital, London, UK

Dr. D. Curtis, MA, MB, BS, MRCPsych, Department of Psychiatry, University College and Middlesex School of Medicine, London, UK.

Dr. A. Davis, Department of Pharmacology, Kings College Hospital, London, UK

Dr. K. Davison, MB, BS, DPM, FRCPsych, Consultant Psychiatrist, Newcastle General Hospital and Honorary Lecturer in Psychological Medicine, University of Newcastle, Newcastle, UK

Dr. A.M. Domney, BSc, PhD, Senior Research Fellow in Neuropharmacology, Postgraduate School of Studies in Pharmacology, University of Bradford, Bradford, UK

Dr. G. Dougherty MD, Western Psychiatric Institute and Clinic, Department of Psychiatry, University of Pittsburgh School of Medicine and Highland Drive Veterans Administration Medical Center, Pittsburgh, Pennsylvania, USA

Dr. M.Y. Ekdawi, MB, ChB, DPM, FRCPsych, DPM, Consultant Psychiatrist (Rehabilitation), Netherne Hospital, Coulsdon, Surrey, UK

Dr. I.R.H. Falloon, MB, ChB, MRCPsych, DPM, Consultant Physician (Mental Health), Buckingham Hospital, Buckingham, UK

Dr. H.M.D. Gurling, MD, MB, BS, MPhil, MRCPsych, Senior Lecturer in Psychiatry, Academic Department of Psychiatry, and Honorary Consultant Psychiatrist, University College and Middlesex School of Medicine, London, UK

Dr. C. Harvey, Department of Psychiatry, Charing Cross and Westminster Medical School, London, UK.

Professor A. Jablensky, MB, DM Sc, MRCPsych, Director Institute of Sciences, Medical Academy, Sofia, Bulgaria formerly Assistant Director, WHO Schizophrenia Project

Dr. P. Jenner, PhD, MRC Movement Disorder Research, University Department of Neurology and Parkinson's Disease Society Research Centre, Institute of Psychiatry and Reader in Pharmacology, Kings College Hospital, London, UK

Dr. B.J. Jones, BPharm, PhD, Glaxo Group Research, Neuropharmacology Department, Ware, Hertfordshire, UK

Dr. M.E. Kelley, BSc, PhD, Lecturer in Pharmacology, Postgraduate School of Studies in Pharmacology, University of Bradford, Bradford, UK

Professor S.S. Kety, AB, MD, HonScD, Emeritus Professor of Neuroscience, Harvard University and Senior Scientist, Intramural Research Program, National Institute of Mental Health, Bethesda, Maryland, USA

Dr. G. Kilpatrick, Department of Pharmacology, Kings College Hospital, London, UK

Dr. J. Leff, BSc (Anat), MD, MB, BS, MRCP, FRCPsych, Professor of Social Psychiatry, Institute of Psychiatry, De Crespigny Park, London, UK

Dr. P.F. Liddle, BM, BCh, Senior Lecturer in Psychiatry and Honorary Consultant Psychiatrist, Charing Cross and Westminster Medical School, London, UK

Dr. B.J. Mankoo, PhD, Research Assistant, Molecular Psychiatry Laboratory, University College and Middlesex School of Medicine, London, UK

Dr. I.M. Marks, MB, ChB, MRCPsych, DPM, Professor Experimental Psychopathology, Institute of Psychiatry and Consultant Psychiatrist, Bethlem Royal and Maudsley Hospitals, London, UK

Professor C.D. Marsden, MB, BS, FRS, FRCP, MRCP, MRCPsych, Professor of Neurology, The Institute of Neurology, The National Hospital, London, UK

Dr. R.G. McCreadie, BSc, MD, MB, ChB, FRCPsych, DPM, Director Clinical Services, Director Clinical Research and Consultant Psychiatrist, Crichton Royal Hospital, Dumfries, UK

Dr. M. Muijen, MD, Lecturer in Psychiatry, Institute of Psychiatry, De Crespigny Park, London, UK

Dr. W.J. Muir,, BSc, MB, ChB, MRCPsych, Clinician Scientist Fellow, University of Edinburgh, Edinburgh, UK

Professor R.J. Naylor, BPharm, PhD, BSc, MPs, Professor of Pharmacology, Postgraduate School of Studies in Pharmacology, University of Bradford, Bradford, UK

Dr. T. Neylan, MD, Western Psychiatric Institute and Clinic, Department of Psychiatry, University of Pittsburgh School of Medicine and Highland Drive Veterans Administration Medical Center, Pittsburgh, Pennsylvania, USA

Dr. C. Pantelis, MB, BS, MRCPsych, Lecture in Psychiatry, Charing Cross and Westminster Medical School, London, UK

Dr. J.L. Peters, MD, Western Psychiatric Institute and Clinic, Department of Psychiatry, University of Pittsburgh School of Medicine and Highland Drive Veterans Administration Medical Center, Pittsburgh, Pennsylvania, USA

Dr. H. Petursson, PhD, FRCPsych, Cand Med, Director, Department of Psychiatry, Borg Stitalinn, Iceland

Dr. M. Potter, BMedSci, MB, BS, MRCPsych, Clinical Lecturer, Department of Psychiatry, University College and Middlesex School of Medicine, London, UK

Dr. T. Read, BSc, MB, BS, MRCPsych, Clinical Lecturer, Department of Psychiatry, University College and Middlesex School of Medicine, London, UK

Dr. M.A. Reveley, PhD, BA, MD, MRCPsych, Senior Lecturer and Honorary Consultant in Psychiatry, London Hospital Medical College, London, UK

Dr. G. Roberts, BSc, PhD, Lecturer in Neuroanatomy, St. Mary's Hospital Medical School, London, UK

Professor Sir Martin Roth, MA, MD, ScD (Hon),MB, BS, FRCP, MRCS, LRCP, FRCPsych, Emeritus Professor of Psychiatry, University of Cambridge Clinical School and Fellow of Trinity College, Cambridge, UK

Dr. N.M.J. Rupnaik, Department of Pharmacology, Kings College Hospital, London, UK

Dr. D. Shaw, PhD, Western Psychiatric Institute and Clinic, Department of Psychiatry, University of Pittsburgh School of Medicine and Highland Drive Veterans Administration Medical Center, Pittsburgh, Pennsylvania, USA

Dr. D.M. St. Clair, BM, BCh, FRCS, MRCPsych, BA, MPhil, Wellcome Fellow, Human Genetics Unit, Western General Hospital, Edinburgh, UK

Mr. P. Sherrington, BSc, Research Assistant, Molecular Psychiatry Laboratory, University College and Middlesex School of Medicine, London, UK

Dr. J. Taylor, MB, BS, MRCPsych, Locum Consultant Psychiatrist, Whittington Hospital, London, UK

Dr. M.R. Trimble, MPhil, BSc, MB, ChB, FRCP, FRCPsych, Consultant Physician in Psychological Medicine, National Hospital for Nervous Diseases and Raymond Way Lecturer in Behavioural Neurology, Institute of Neurology, London, UK

Dr. D.P. Van Kammen, MD, PhD, Professor of Psychiatry and Chief of Staff, Veterans Administration Medical Center, Pittsburgh, Pennsylvania, USA

Dr. W.B. Van Kammen, PhD, Western Psychiatric Institute and Clinic, Department of Psychiatry, University of Pittsburgh School of Medicine and Highland Drive Veterans Administration Medical Center, Pittsburgh, Pennsylvania, USA

Dr. P.H. Venables, Honorary Research Professor, Department of Psychology, University of York, York, UK

Mrs. M.T. Walker, BSoc, Dip.Soc.Sc., Senior Social Worker, University Department of Psychiatry, Royal Edinburgh Hospital, Edinburgh, UK

Dr. M.P.I. Weller, MA (Cantab), MB, BS, FRCPsych, CPsychol, FBPsS, Consultant Psychiatrist, Friern, Whittington and Royal Northern Hospitals and Honorary Senior Lecturer, Royal Free School of Medicine, London, UK

Dr. J.K. Yao, PhD, Western Psychiatric Institute and Clinic, Department of Psychiatry, University of Pittsburgh School of Medicine and Highland Drive Veterans Administration Medical Center, Pittsburgh, Pennsylvania, USA

INTERNATIONAL PERSPECTIVES IN SCHIZOPHRENIA
(0 86196 145 5)

Published by

John Libbey and Co. Limited, 13 Smith's Yard,
Summerley Street, London, SW18 4HR

these studies clearly show that long-stay schizophrenic recall performance, unlike that of short-stay patients, cannot be equated with that of IQ-matched normal controls even after effective encoding for organizing the material is induced.*

It is worth noting that another method, namely affective encoding, also used to induce normal recall in short-stay schizophrenics, was attempted by Koh (Koh *et al.*, 1976; Koh *et al.*, 1981). Again, recall levels equivalent to normal emerged after the subjects rated to-be-remembered words for their affective quality (pleasantness-unpleasantness). However, this method has not yet been applied to chronic long-stay schizophrenics. A study of this kind may be of importance since it may produce different results from the sorting consistency studies.

Rapid forgetting

Another finding apparent in these studies (Figs 1–4) which seems to characterize chronic long-stay but not short-stay (Fig. 2) schizophrenics, is their forgetfulness from day to day (see Figs 1–4). Calev *et al.* (1983*a*) suggested that this characterizes patients who are on neuroleptic drugs, either given alone or in combination with anticholinergic drugs. A matched tasks check (Tables 1 and 2) suggested that poor short-term memory was not due to differences in discriminating power between the early and the late recall tasks. More recently Calev *et al.* (1988) replicated the finding of rapid forgetting in drug-free schizophrenics, using the same matched tasks 3–4 weeks after drug withdrawal in patients who showed no appreciable change in symptoms or signs of relapse. As the tasks were matched, it is unlikely that the finding was due to differences in discriminating power. To make sure that rapid forgetting was not due to the specific verbal task requiring sorting consistency before recall, another verbal task — word-associated learning and retention

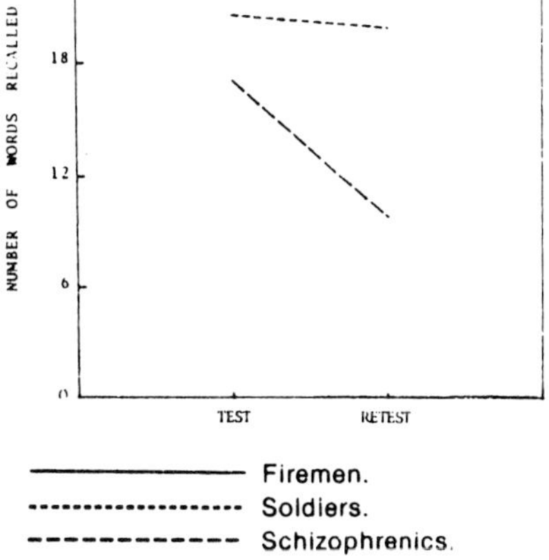

Fig. 4. *Rapid forgetting, using matched immediate and delayed tasks, in long-stay schizophrenics (n=12) who reached the 'sorting consistency' criterion before the first day recall.* At the 3rd day (retest), their recall performance is far worse than their earlier recall performance. This is unlike fireman (n=44) and soldier (*n*=12) controls. (From Calev *et al.*, 1983*a*, by permission of *Schizophrenia Bulletin*.)

*This may have been caused partially but not fully by 'regression to the mean' when matching subjects for IQ. Otherwise one cannot explain the success achieved by the shorter-stay schizophrenics.

Table 1. *Matching of immediate and delayed recall tasks (for the results presented in Fig. 4):* Tests means, variances, reliabilities, true-score variances, and shapes of distribution (skewness, kurtosis) and the means, variances and shapes of distribution of item-difficulty are very similar for normals [validation by Firemen (n=44) and cross validation by Soldiers (n=12)]. (From Calev *et al.*, 1983*a*, by permission of *Schizophrenia Bulletin.*)

	Firemen (n=44)		*Soldiers (n=12)*		*Schizophrenics (n=12)*	
	Test	*Retest*	*Test*	*Retest*	*Test*	*Retest*
Mean	22.227	22.591	20.500	19.917	17.083	10.083
Observed variance	16.831	21.271	43.182	68.447	10.265	18.992
Alpha coefficient (reliability)	0.693	0.690	0.898	0.929	0.443	0.793
Estimated true-score variance	11.665	14.671	38.786	63.710	4.547	15.042
Estimated true-score variance (after z-score transformation)	0.693	0.690	2.304	2.988	0.232	0.708
Mean item difficulty	3.643	3.752	3.403	3.292	2.847	1.680
Variance of item difficulty	0.054	0.099	0.212	0.349	0.101	0.082
Skewness	−0.169	0.228	0.604	0.048	−0.011	0.052
Kurtosis	0.416	0.750	−0.472	0.867	−1.003	−1.006

Table 2. *Close match procedure for the items included in the matched tasks check, for the larger normal sample (n=44).* In this check, categories were used as items. Very similar match to this, shown in Fig. 1, was reached also when alternatively using words as items. (From Calev *et al.*, 1983*a*, by permission of *Schizophrenia Bulletin.*)

Item	*Means*		*Observed variance*[1]		*Skewness*		*Kurtosis*	
no.	*Test*	*Retest*	*Test*	*Retest*	*Test*	*Retest*	*Test*	*Retest*
1.	3.477	3.523	1.372	2.023	−0.398	−0.048	1.148	1.078
2.	3.591	3.432	1.038	1.228	−0.327	0.234	0.221	0.004
3.	3.409	3.568	0.712	1.228	0.056	0.733[2]	−0.496	0.169
4.	4.045	4.273	1.347	1.500	−0.900	−0.394	2.207[2]	−0.112
5.	3.614	3.773	1.033	1.668	−0.254	−0.107	−0.384	−0.451
6.	3.795	3.955	1.608	1.393	−0.743[2]	−1.153[2]	1.024	2.209[2]

[1]All distributions unimodal.
[2]Deviation from normality ($P < 0.05$).

over 24 hours — was used. Again no difference in the rate of forgetting on and off drugs emerged. Sengel & Lavallo (1983) also reported rapid forgetting using another verbal task. It seems therefore that poor short-term memory does characterize long-stay but not short-stay patients, and that is is not caused by drugs.

Emotional and verbal factors affecting the rate of forgetting. Further research on long-stay schizophrenics has revealed that their rate of forgetting is affected by the degree of negative and positive emotion involved in the to-be-remembered material, and by whether these materials are verbal or visuo-spatial. Calev *et al.* (1988) found that a non-verbal task (Rey-Ostereith complex figure) was not forgotten from one day to another when patients were off drugs, and that only marginally significant forgetfulness occurred on both neuroleptic and anticholinergic drugs. The excessive degree of forgetfulness on drugs

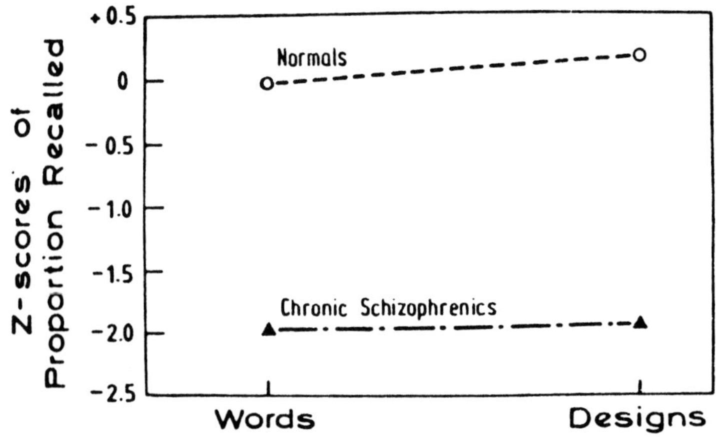

Fig. 5. *After task matching which allows the comparison of 24 words and 24 designs, presented sequentially, in terms of discriminating power, long-stay schizophrenics (n=20) like normals (n=20) show no disparity between the two tasks, although their rate of forgetting of such verbal tasks is larger than their rate of forgetting of non-verbal tasks* (Calev *et al.*, 1988). (From Calev *et al.*, 1987*b*, by permission of *Biological Psychiatry*.)

treatment may have been due to the adverse effect of the anticholinergic drugs (see Drachman & Levitt, 1974). In this study, unlike depressive and normals, long-stay schizophrenics also showed more forgetting of words expressing positive emotion ('kiss', 'love') and neutral emotion ('road', 'moon') than negative emotion ('kill', 'rape'). As in this study, and also in another study using matched tasks consisting of words *versus* designs (Calev *et al.*, 1987*b*) no differences were found in immediate recall performance (Fig. 5), it seems that the rate of forgetting is selectively affected by both the emotional and verbal factors rather than by visuo-spacial factors in long-stay schizophrenics.*

Physiological explanations of the findings of rapid forgetting in long-stay schizophrenics
The main conclusions from these studies are (a) that there is rapid forgetting and (b) that this rapid forgetting is enhanced for verbal positive emotional materials. If this is the case, then two types of organic factors said to characterize long-stay schizophrenics (with negative symptoms) seem to cause this memory disturbance. The first finding is that there may be damage or dysfunction in the limbic system and hippocampus in schizophrenia (eg Brown *et al.*, 1986; Conrad & Scheibel, 1987). If such dysfunction or damage exists, then, like many amnesic patients with the same damage, long-stay schizophrenics may show rapid forgetting. The second finding is that there may be left hemisphere dysfunction or damage in schizophrenia (Gur, 1978; Reveley *et al.*, 1987). If this kind of pathology does exist, one could expect that the rate of forgetting of verbal material and material with a positive emotional content (Tucker, 1981) (both of which are left-hemisphere-mediated) will be affected more than that of non-verbal and negative emotion materials (which are right-hemisphere-mediated).

*This does not exclude the possibility that in immediate recall there is also a deficit in remembering positive emotion material by schizophrenics (anhedonia, Koh *et al.*, 1981). However, in Koh's study, tasks were not matched and therefore the results are somewhat dubious.

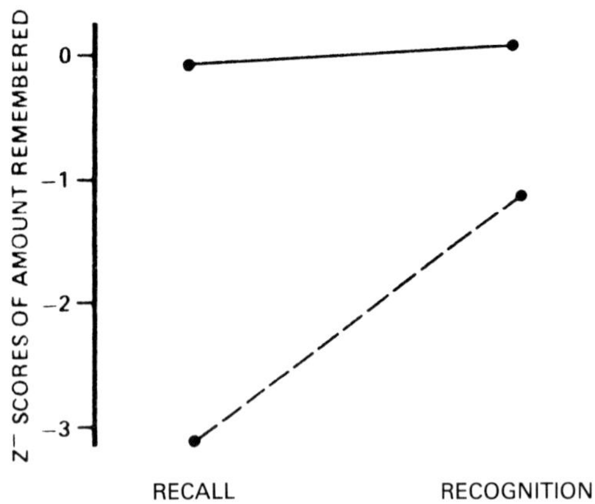

Fig. 6. *Disparity between recall and recognition in long-stay schizophrenics (n=10), after the tasks were compared for discriminating power.* Short stay (n=10) patients (Calev, 1984*b*) did not show a significant disparity between these tasks. Short-stay patients on anticholinergic drugs (n=10) did show a disparity. (From Calev, 1984*a*, by permission of *Journal of Abnormal Psychology*.)

Use of recognition memory tasks

Studies using short-stay and more mildly disturbed schizophrenics have tended to find no recognition memory deficit, although there was a deficit in recall (Bauman & Murray, 1968; Nachmani & Cohen, 1969; Bauman, 1971). Recognition involves selecting familiar items out of a larger number of items. In recall, the subject has first to retrieve, and decide whether to include the item in the output. Recall thus includes both recognition and associative ability (Kintch, 1970; Anderson & Bower, 1972). The findings of deficient recall and intact recognition in schizophrenics were usually interpreted — in line with this contention — as due to their associative disturbance which affects recall but not recognition (Kintch, 1970; Koh & Peterson, 1978). Traupmann (1975, 1980), however, used more severely disturbed long-stay patients and did find a deficit. These tasks, as Koh (1978) pointed out (see also Tulving & Thompson, 1973), were recognition memory tasks which involved little contextual information and therefore the deficit could not be explained by an associative disturbance. Calev *et al.* (1983*a*) also found a recognition memory deficit in long-stay schizophrenics and suggested that there was a very minor deficit in short-stay patients which appears statistically non-significant in single studies. In a subsequent controlled study in which recall and recognition tasks were compared for discriminating power, Calev (1984*a*) found (Fig. 6) a deficit in both recall and recognition, although in long-stay schizophrenics recall performance was worse than recognition. Again, anticholinergic drugs made no appreciable difference. By contrast, when testing short-stay schizophrenics, Calev (1984*b*) found no significant difference between recall and recognition, except in patients who were on anticholinergic drugs. To reconcile these findings, it seems that anticholinergic drugs tend to affect recall and associative memory more than recognition and more automatic tasks (Calev, 1983). In severely disturbed long-stay schizophrenics, there may be habituation and no major effect of these drugs, unlike in less severely disturbed short-stay patients. The latter patients show a disparity between recall and recognition which is at least partially induced by being on the drug.

The main conclusion from these findings is that long-stay schizophrenics, in contrast to short-stay patients, show a recognition 'non-associative' memory deficit. This deficit may be due to a dysfunction in memory in general, not only in the control processes of memory, as suggested by Koh (1978), and may be caused by damage to those brain structures which seem to be affected in schizophrenia (Lesch & Bogerts, 1986; Brown *et al.*, 1986), as well as in amnesia (Butters & Meliotis, 1985), for example the limbic system and the hippocampus.

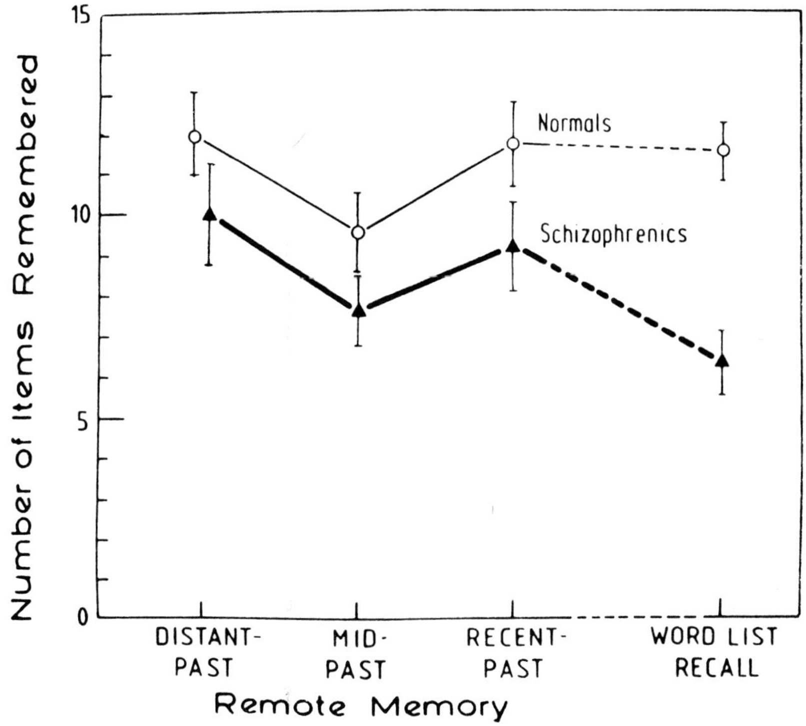

Fig. 7. *(a) No amnesic gradient in remote memory, and (b) larger recent than remote memory deficit, in long-stay schizophrenics (n=16) relative to normals (n=16).* A matched task check suggesting that the results were not due to discriminating power differences. (From Calev *et al.*, 1987*a*, by permission of *Biological Psychiatry*,)

Remote (episodic) memory

Remembering of remote past facts and episodes is of importance in investigating organic memory pathology (Butters & Meliotis, 1985). Only a few studies have addressed the question of remote memory functioning in schizophrenia. Johnson *et al.* (1977) used a recognition memory questionnaire for famous public episodes of the past and found no significant differences between patients who were mainly mildly disturbed (short-stay in terms of cumulative hospital admissions). Liddle & Crow (1984), however, administered a Famous Faces questionnaire to long-stay schizophrenics and found that, unlike Johnson's shorter-stay patients, they were significantly impaired throughout all time periods represented by the faces they recognize, much like subnormal subjects. They suggested, in agreement with Crow, that these patients suffered from dementia manifested by age and time disorientation (Crow & Stevens, 1978). Calev *et al.* (1987*a*) tested the functioning of long-stay schizophrenics and looked at the possibility that patients with medial temporal amnesia who showed schizophrenic symptoms (Butters & Metiotis, 1985; Squire, 1987) will remember famous events from the distant past better than events from the more recent past, in line with Ribot's law of amnesia. Figure 7 shows that no amnesic gradient was found and the results were in agreement with those of Liddle & Crow (1984). However, this figure also shows that remote memory was less impaired than a recent memory task, that is the encoding and subsequent recall of a new list of words. As these remote and recent memory tasks were matched for discriminating power (Chapman & Chapman, 1978; Blaney, 1978; Calev & Monk, 1982), these results are reliable. They suggest that, although long-stay schizophrenics have a more severe remote memory impairment than short-stay patients, this impairment is mild relative to their recent memory loss which involves the use of 'control processes' required for recall. This difference in severity of memory impairment is consistent with the idea of a more definite and more severe brain and biochemical pathology in long-stay (negative symptom) than short-stay (positive symptom) subjects.

Areas of memory research not showing a difference between short- and long-stay schizophrenics — the case of semantic, procedural and short-term memory

'Semantic memory' refers to knowledge (usually verbal) which we know is due to overlearning (Tulving & Donaldson, 1972). In amnesia sematic memory, alongside procedural memory tasks (eg those involving learning of motor skills [Squire, 1987]), seems to remain intact. The studies of short-stay schizophrenics suggested that the organization of semantic memory, both while sorting words and while recalling them, remains intact (Koh *et al.*, 1974; Koh, 1978). Calev (Calev, 1981; Calev *et al.*, 1983*a*) found similar results in chronic long-stay patients (although there were retrieval problems using this structure, thus suggesting that semantic memory structure remains intact in both short- and long-stay schizophrenics.* Several studies have also suggested that this is also the case for memory for skills (Eysenck & Frith, 1977), that is, procedural memory.

The studies of short-term (primary) memory (including also sensory echoic and iconic memory) most of which were reviewed by Koh (1978) and Calev (1981), although important in pointing to other cognitive dysfunction in schizophrenia, were not of major importance in differentiating long-stay (negative symptoms) and short-stay (positive symptoms) schizophrenic patients. I shall not try to define these terms nor review these studies here, but only point out that Koh's (1978) conclusion, after reviewing several paradigms, was that short-term (primary) memory as such is intact in schizophrenia. Koh probably meant that the store itself rather than its function is intact, otherwise it may be difficult to accept this conclusion fully in view of contradictory evidence using measures influenced by 'control processes' (eg Braff *et al.*, 1977; Miller *et al.*, 1979). For this reason further research comparing sub-types of short-term and sensory memory paradigms in schizophrenics may be revealing.

Memory in people with high-risk for schizophrenia

Finally, I shall examine another area in which further research may be of major importance, that is, high-risk subjects (see Chapter 7, Venables). If some of the neurological abnormalities of schizophrenics are present in high risk normal subjects (eg research on hard and soft neurological signs in schizophrenics and relatives), then they may also show memory pathology. Calev *et al.* (1983*b*) conducted such a study and found that non-psychiatric subjects who showed the 2-7-8 MMPI schizophrenic profile, also had poor recall. In particular, they had a minor but significant deficit in recall of verbal

*It is worth noting that general intelligence and vocabulary may suffer in long-stay more than in short-stay schizophrenics (eg Alyward *et al.*, 1984), this deficit remaining constant throughout life. The deficits are, however, probably a consequence of the faulty 'control processes' such as attention and cooperation, and consequently they affect the ability to retrieve the correct response from semantic memory. In the same way, the other abnormalities of schizophrenics, such as catatonia, may interfere with procedural memory.

materials for which there was adequate sorting consistency before recall. This result is most interesting because only long-stay patients showed this deficit. It seems possible therefore that short-stay schizophrenics have a different memory pathology and perhaps a different disease process from long-stay schizophrenics and 2-7-8 normals. This area of research is poor and therefore it would be most interesting to find out whether first and second degree relatives show specific memory profiles, and whether this is correlated with physiological and biochemical measures. Further research along these lines is important.

Conclusion

This review describes several qualitative differences between the memory performance of long-stay and short-stay schizophrenic patients which may be related to different disease processes and brain pathologies. Laterality and hippocampal dysfunctions fit well with the memory pathology of schizophrenic patients. This raises the possibility that the memory pathology in long-stay (usually 'negative symptom') schizophrenics is directly affected by the biological abnormalities of the disease, and is not a secondary phenomenon.

References

Anderson, J.R. & Bower, G.H. (1972): Recognition and retrieval processes in free recall. *Psychol. Rev.* **72**, 97–123.

Andreasen, N.C. & Olsen, S. (1982): Negative and positive schizophrenia: Definition validation. *Arch. Gen. Psychiatry* **39**, 789–794.

Alyward, E., Walker, E. & Bettes, S. (1984): Intelligence in schizophrenia: Meta analysis of the research. *Schizophrenia Bull.* **10**, 430–459.

Babcock, H. (1933): *Dementia praecox: a psychological study.* New York: The Science Press.

Bauman, E. & Murray, D.J. (1968): Recognition versus recall in schizophrenia. *Can. J. Psychol.* **22**, 18–25.

Bauman, E. (1971): Schizophrenic short-term memory: The role of organization at input. *J. Consult. Clin. Psychol.* **36**, 14–19.

Blaney, P.H. (1978): Schizophrenic thought disorder: Why the lack of answers? In *Language and cognition in schizophrenia*, ed. S. Schwartz. Hillside, NJ: Lawrence Erlbaum.

Bleuler, E. (1950 [1911]): *Dementia praecox and the group of schizophrenias.* New York: International University Press.

Braff, D., Callaway, E. & Naylor, H. (1977): Very short-term memory dysfunction in schizophrenia. *Arch. Gen. Psychiatry* **34**, 25–30.

Brown, R., Cotlev, N., Carsellis, N., Crow, T.J., Frith, C.D., Jagoe, R., Johnson, E.C. & Marsh, L. (1986): Postmortem evidence of structural brain changes in schizophrenia. *Arch. Gen. Psychiatry* **43**, 36–42.

Butters, N. & Meliotis, P.V. (1985): Amnesic disorders. In *Clinical neuropsychology*, eds K.M. Heilman & E. Valenstein, pp. 403–452. New York: Oxford University Press.

Calev, A. (1981): *Post-organizational memory deficits in severely disturbed schizophrenics.* York, England: University of York. PhD Thesis.

Calev, A. (1983): Anticholinergic drugs and memory. *Br. J. Psychiatry* **143**, 422–423.

Calev, A. (1984*a*): Recall and recognition in chronic nondemented schizophrenics: Use of matched-tasks. *J. Abnorm. Psychol.* **93**, 172–177.

Calev, A. (1984*b*): Recall and recognition in midly disturbed schizophrenics: Use of matched-tasks. *Psychol. Med.* **14**, 425–429.

Calev, A. & Monk, A.F. (1982): Verbal memory tasks showing no deficit in schizophrenia — fact or artefact? *Br. J. Psychiatry* **141**, 528–530.

Calev, A., Monk, A.F. & Venables, P.H. (1980): Sorting consistency as a diagnostic tool for schizophrenics and normals. *Psychiatr. Res.* **2**, 231–239.

Calev, A., Venables, P.H. & Monk, A.F. (1983*a*): Evidence for distinct verbal memory pathologies in severely and mildly disturbed schizophrenics. *Schizophrenia Bull.* **9**, 247–264.
Calev, A., Venables, P.H. & Monk, A.F. (1983*b*): Schizophrenic tendencies and memory deficits in normals. *Personality and Individual Differences* **4**, 89–94.
Calev, A., Berlin, H. & Lerer, B. (1987*a*): Remote and recent memory in long-hospitalized chronic schizophrenics. *Biol. Psychiatry* **22**, 79–85.
Calev, A., Korin, Y., Kugelmass, S. & Lerer, B. (1987*b*): Performance of chronic schizophrenics on matched word and design recall tasks. *Biol. Psychiatry* **22**, 699–709.
Calev, A., Edelist, S., Kugelmass, S. & Lerer, B. (1988): *Effect of emotion on the rate of forgetting in normals, schizophrenics and major depressives.* First international Conference on Individual Differences. Tel Aviv, Israel.
Chapman, L.J. & Chapman, J.P. (1973): *Disordered thought in schizophrenia.* New York: Appleton-Century-Crofts.
Chapman, L.J. & Chapman, J.P. (1978): The measurement of differential deficits. *J. Psychiatr. Res.* **14**, 303–311.
Cohen, J. (1950): Wechsler memory scale performance of psychoneurotic, organic and schizophrenic groups. *J. Consult. Clin. Psychol.* **14**, 371–375.
Conrad, A.J. & Scheibel, A.B. (1987): Schizophrenia and the hippocampus: The embryological hypothesis extended. *Schizophrenia Bull.* **13**, 577–587.
Crow, T.J. (1980): Positive and negative schizophrenic symptoms and the role of dopamine. *Br. J. Psychiatry* **137**, 383–388.
Crow, T.J. & Stevens, M. (1978): Age disorientation in chronic schizophrenia: The nature of cognitive deficit. *Br. J. Psychiatry* **133**, 137–142.
Drachman, D.A. & Levitt, J. (1974): Human memory and the cholinergic system — a relationship to aging? *Arch. Neurol.* **30**, 1343–1349.
Eysenck, H.J. & Frith, C.D. (1977): *Reminiscence, motivation and personality.* New York: Plenum Press.
Gur, R.E. (1978): Right hemisphere dysfunction and left hemisphere overactivation in schizophrenia. *J. Abnorm. Psychol.* **87**, 226–238.
Hull, C.L. (1917): The formation and retention of associations among the insane. *Am. J. Psychol.* **28**, 419–435.
Johnson, J.H., Klinger, D.E. & Williams, T.A. (1977): Recognition in episodic long-term memory in schizophrenia. *J. Clin. Psychol.* **33**, 643–647.
Kintch, W. (1970): Models for free recall and recognition. In *Models of human memory*, ed. D.A. Norman. New York: Academic Press.
Koh, S.D. (1978): Remembering of verbal materials by schizophrenic young adults. In *Language and cognition in schizophrenia*, ed. S. Schwartz. Hillsdale, NJ: Lawrence Erlbaum.
Koh, S.D. & Peterson, R.A. (1978): Encoding orientation and the remembering of schizophrenic young adults. *J. Abnorm. Psychol.* **87**, 303–313.
Koh, S.D., Kayton, L. & Schwartz, C. (1974): The structure of word storage in the permanent memory of nonpsychotic schizophrenics. *J. Consult. Clin. Psychol.* **42**, 879–887.
Koh, S.D., Kayton, L. & Peterson, R.A. (1976): Affective encoding and subsequent remembering in schizophrenic young adults. *J. Abnorm Psychol.* **85**, 156–166.
Koh, S.D., Grinker, R.R., Marusarz, T.Z. & Forman, P.L. (1981): Affective memory and schizophrenic anhedonia. *Schizophrenia Bull.* **7**, 292–307.
Kraepelin, E. (1919): *Dementia praecox and paraphrenia* (translated R.M. Barclay). Edinburgh: Livingstone.
Larsen, S.F. & Fromholt, P. (1976): Mnemonic organization and free recall in schizophrenia. *J. Abnorm. Psychol.* **85**, 61–65.
Lesch, A. & Bogerts, B. (1986): The diencephalon in schizophrenia. Evidence for reduced thickness of the periventricular grey matter. *Eur. Arch. Psychiatr. Neurol. Sci.* **234**, 212–219.
Liddle, P.F. & Crow, T.J. (1984): Age disorientation in chronic schizophrenia is associated with global intellectual impairment. *Br. J. Psychiatry* **144**, 193–197.
Mandler, G. & Pearlstone, Z. (1966): Free and constrained conceptual learning and subsequent recall. *J. Verb. Learn. Verb. Behav.* **5**, 126–131.

Miller, S., Saccuzzo, D. & Braff, D. (1979): Information process deficits in remitted schizophrenics. *J. Abnorm. Psychol.* **88**, 446–449.
Nachmani, G. & Cohen, B.D. (1969): Recall and recognition free learning in schizophrenics. *J. Abnorm. Psychol.* **74**, 511–516.
Reveley, M.A., Reveley, A.M. & Baldy, R. (1987): Left cerebral hemisphere hypodensity in discordant schizophrenic twins. *Arch. Gen. Psychiatry* **44**, 625–632.
Sengel, R.A. & Lovallo, W.R. (1983): Effects of cueing on immediate and recent memory in schizophrenics. *J. Nerv. Ment. Dis.* **171**, 426–430.
Squire, L.R. (1987): *Memory and brain.* New York: Oxford University Press.
Traupmann, K.L. (1975): Effects of categorization and imagery on recognition and recall by process and reactive schizophrenics. *J. Abnorm. Psychol.* **84**, 307–314.
Traupmann, K.L. (1980): Encoding processes and memory for categorically related words by schizophrenic patients. *J. Abnorm. Psychol.* **89**, 704–716.
Tucker, D.M. (1981): Lateral brain dysfunction, emotion and conceptualization. *Psychol. Bull.* **89**, 19–46.
Tulving, E. & Donaldson, W. (1972): *Organization of memory.* New York: Acedemic Press.
Tulving, E. & Thompson, D.M. (1973): Encoding specificity and retrieval processes in episodic memory. *Psychol. Rev.* 80, 352–373.

Chapter 4

The familial sporadic distinction in schizophrenia: the contribution of CT scan studies

Michael A. Reveley

Academic Department of Psychiatry, Alexandra Wing, The London Hospital Medical College, Turner Street, London E1 2AD, UK

Summary

In attempts to reduce the heterogeneity in schizophrenia, the familial-sporadic distinction has become a topic of interest. Schizophrenia is a polygenic multifactorial disorder with important genetic and environmental sources of causation. Studies of identical twins discordant for schizophrenia using computerized tomography have revealed that the schizophrenic twins had larger ventricular size than both normal controls and their own co-twins, showing that environmental factors were associated both with ventricular enlargement and the development of schizophrenia. Further, ventricular size was under a high degree of genetic control. In other studies an absence of a family history for schizophrenia was associated with ventricular enlargement in a larger sample of twins with schizophrenia, while in controls, ventricular enlargement was associated with a history of birth complications. Environmental factors predisposing to ventricular enlargement in adult life might be perinatal complications, such as birth complications or other intrauterine or postnatal events. There may be a continuum of liability to schizophrenia so that those with a lesser genetic load may require more environmental influences to manifest the illness whilst those with a greater genetic predisposition become schizophrenic on that basis alone with a minimum of environmental contribution. Family studies of singletons have also confirmed the high heritability of ventricular size and have shown that ventricular enlargement is more associated with environmental events such as histories of head injuries or birth complications. In 10 published studies examining CT scan findings in schizophrenia with and without a family history, three studies found no relationship while five studies found an inverse correlation between ventricular size and positive family history. Because of the large sample sizes required to show a family history effect in singletons these studies have been less clear-cut than those using discordant twins, in whom environmental effects are particularly important in the development of schizophrenia. This was shown in a study comparing twins and singletons in which the ventricular size was significantly greater in twins than singletons, and the family history effect was more clearly evident among the twins.

Introduction

One of the consultants at the Maudsley Hospital, whenever there was a case or research conference, was fond of pointing out that the only thing we have really shown about schizophrenia is that there is a great deal of variability within any biological or other measure examined. Scattergrams of various characteristics, such as reaction time, show substantial overlap between patient and control samples. There is further a wide variation within the patient sample. The question of whether schizophrenia is one, or several, disorders is central to the familial sporadic distinction. Kraepelin originally conceived of dementia praecox, later renamed schizophrenia by Bleuler, as one disorder, beginning early in life and the progressing throughout life with a certain amount of deterioration. In contrast, Bleuler conceived of schizophrenia as being several disorders; he called them 'the schizophrenias' in the plural. The broad concept was further extended by Adolph Meyer, almost to the point that every schizophrenic person was unique and completely different. Thus, there were as many 'schizophrenias' as there were schizophrenics. More modern approaches are to group schizophrenics together according to common characteristics.

There are a number of different ways of subdividing schizophrenia. Traditional subtypes include hebephrenia, catatonia, paranoid and simple schizophrenia, among others, as in the ICD-9. But these are symptomatic, not aetiological, subtypes. They are not stable over time and are not familial. Another subdivision is 'good' *vs* 'poor' prognosis. Again, this is symptomatic, although there is some evidence for a family history difference between them. A family history of affective disorder is more common in good prognosis patients, and a family history of schizophrenia, in poor prognosis patients. This familial pattern of inheritance, as well as twin and adoption studies, have established the genetic contribution to schizophrenia (Gottesman & Shields, 1982). However, it is clear that there is a substantial environmental contribution to the development of schizophrenia, and it is more accurate to consider schizophrenia a polygenic, multifactorial disorder. What might be some of the important environmental sources of causation? Davison & Bagley (1969) found that schizophrenia associated with organic brain disease was more likely to occur in patients without a family history of schizophrenia. While their disorder was impossible to distinguish on clinical grounds from 'idiopathic' schizophrenia, the illness was often termed a 'secondary' schizophrenia. Kendler & Hays (1982) found that 72% of non-familial but only 43% of familial schizophrenics had a detectable abnormality on EEG, indicative of organic brain dysfunction. It is possible therefore, that environmental factors are more important aetiologically in non-familial cases, and less important in familial cases, in which the presumed genetic factors are more important.

Twin studies of ventricular size

One of the basic questions in relation to ventricular size in schizophrenia is the relative contribution of genetics *versus* environment to the abnormalities. Studies of identical twins provide a useful model to examine genetic environmental interactions. My colleagues and I (Reveley *et al.*, 1982) studied a group of twins from the Maudsley Hospital twin register, the largest hospital-based register of twins in the world. For controls, we used the Institute of Psychiatry normal twin register. The subjects were examined in order to determine the range of variation in CT scan findings within pairs of healthy monozygotic (MZ) and dizygotic (DZ) twins, and to establish the extent of genetic contribution to normal ventricular size. CT scans of MZ twins discordant for schizophrenia were also examined. We proposed that if some individuals were genetically predisposed to large ventricles, and this were a predisposing, but not a direct cause of schizophrenia, then both the twin and well co-twin should have similarly increased ventricular size. If, on the other hand, the ventricular enlargement were the result of external agents or injury to the affected twin, or a secondary consequence of the illness itself, then only the schizophrenic should show the abnormality. We examined eleven monozygotic and eight dizygotic pairs of volunteer twins, who were in good physical and mental health, and seven pairs of MZ twins discordant for schizophrenia. Diagnosis of the latter was established through (a) personal examination using the SADS-L interview, (b) a review of all hospital admissions, and (c) consultation with relatives. All patients met research diagnostic criteria for schizophrenia and none of the co-twins was currently ill or suffered from psychiatric illness. Zygosity was established by blood grouping and physical comparison. Scans were obtained on a CT 1010 scanner and the records were viewed at random on a computerized video display unit. The slice showing the largest ventricular area was selected for analysis and a light pen was used to draw a ventricular and brain circumference manually from the VDU which calculated the area of brain and ventricle in pixels. A ventricular brain ratio was then determined (VBR = ventricular area divided by brain area × 100). We determined the correlation coefficient (r) based on the variability within and between pairs to establish an intra-class correlation coefficient, which was a rough estimate of 'heritability' (h^2): h^2 = r divided by the coefficient of relationship, where the coefficient of relationship was 1 for MZ and 0.5 DZ twins, as MZ share 100%, and DZ, on average 50%, of their genes.

We found that the largest ventricular area was very highly correlated in the healthy MZ twins ($r = 0.98$, $P < 0.01$), while the DZ correlation was about half the MZ value ($r = 0.45$, ns), which would be expected as DZs share half their genes in common. This suggests that the heritabilities are under a high degree of genetic control in normal subjects.

However, in the MZ twins discordant for schizophrenia the correlation for ventricular area and ventricular brain ratio were both 0.87, not as high as in the healthy MZ pairs. This lowered correlation resulted from increased intra-pair variability. The mean intra-pair difference for ventricular area and ventricular brain ratio was six times greater in the MZs discordant for schizophrenia than in the normal MZs. Four individuals had values falling more than three standard deviations beyond the healthy MZ mean and yet others were below it. The schizophrenics also had significantly greater ventricular area and ventricular brain ratio than both the normal controls and their own co-twins; there was a non-significant trend for the co-twins also to have greater values than the normal twins. With the exception of one pair, the schizophrenics always had larger ventricles than their co-twins.

Therefore this comparison showed that as in singletons, schizophrenic twins tended to have larger ventricles. Furthermore, while ventricular size in normal volunteer twins was under a very high degree of genetic control, it was more variable among the MZs discordant for schizophrenia. This produced a lower heritability value in the latter group and implied an additional environmental influence. One possible cause of this increased variability could be the schizophrenic process itself or its treatment. However, co-twins who had never received neuroleptics and did not have schizophrenia also had larger ventricles, suggesting that factors resulting from the illness are unlikely to be the full explanation. Another possibility is that both twins in the discordant pair may have been the subject of some common environmental factor, such as birth complications, or other intrauterine or postnatal events and the more severely affected twins developed schizophrenia. Some studies have reported that perinatal damage might be a factor in schizophrenia. By choosing twins discordant for schizophrenia, one may have assembled a series in which environmental factors were especially important. Five of the 14 individuals in the discordant pairs had low birth weight or complicated delivery. On the other hand every one of the normal MZ pairs also reported either prematurity or birth complications or both. Thus, it may be that environmental factors interact with genetic factors to produce schizophrenia.

In order to explore these relationships further we expanded our series of twins discordant for schizophrenia to eleven pairs. Within this sample the schizophrenics had a larger ventricular brain ratio than normal twin controls. When the twin pairs were examined for adverse pre-morbid events, more were reported for the schizophrenic members of the 11 twin pairs ($t = 4.18$, $P < 0.01$) (Reveley *et al.*, 1984*b*). This suggests that non-specific debilitating illness or injury may play a part in precipitating a schizophrenic illness in a predisposed individual. Such adverse pre-morbid events included gunshot wounds to the body (1), closed head injury with unconsciousness (2), yaws (1), pyloric stenosis (1), hernia operation as infants (2), and birth anoxia (6). The schizophrenic twins had larger cerebral ventricles than their co-twins, though the difference between the two groups was not significant. We also examined the twins according to family history and those pairs with a negative family history for schizophrenia had significantly and consistently (1605 *versus* 1191, $t = 2.47$, $P < 0.05$) larger ventricles than their well unmedicated co-twins. This study showed that the diathesis stress model for the aetiology of schizophrenia offered the best explanation for the data, with variable proportions of genetic and environmental components of liability taking individuals across the threshold for manifestation of the disorder.

This approach was further followed in a study specifically examining family history for a major psychiatric disorder in a group of 21 schizophrenic twins in comparison with 18 normal control twins (Reveley *et al.*, 1984*a*). This study was devised to assess the relationship of genetic predisposition, organic cerebral insults and chronicity and severity of the schizophrenic illness to cerebral ventricular enlargement. The twins were identified from the Maudsley Hospital and Institute of Psychiatry twin registers as before and were interviewed by the SADS using Research Diagnostic Criteria. Births were classified as 'complicated' if they were reported as featuring a breech or difficult forceps delivery, a blue baby, or birth weight less than 3 lb 4 oz (1.48 kg). Family history was regarded as positive if the twin reported and case notes or relatives confirmed that a first or second degree relative had suffered from a major psychiatric illness. CT scans were examined using an independent viewing console and pixels with a density of 0 to 25 Hounsfield units were assigned a CSF space.

The schizophrenic group as a whole had a greater mean total ventricular volume than the controls, but the difference was not significant after square root transformation of the data. Control twins who reported birth complications had significantly larger total ventricular volume than those controls who did not (1015 *versus* 470, $P < 0.01$). Analysis of variance by sex and reported birth complications using age as a covariant showed that the effect of birth complications was highly significant ($F = 16$, $P = 0.001$). The same analysis for the schizophrenics did not yield a significant result. Thus within controls but not schizophrenics birth complications accounted for a substantial part of the variance of ventricular size.

No significant correlations were found between ventricular volume and length of the illness prior to the scan, total time spent as inpatient, or age. Age of onset was significantly correlated ($P < 0.05$); the schizophrenics with later onset had larger ventricles. However, the effect was no longer significant after controlling for present age, although it was still apparent as a trend. By far the most significant association for total ventricular volume among the schizophrenics was with presumed genetic predisposition: those with a positive family history had small ventricular volume (mean = 558 voxels), while those with a negative family history had three times larger ventricular size on average (1503 voxels).

Analysis of variance of volume by family history, twin concordance, and birth complications, controlling for present age by analysis of co-variance, showed family history to be the only significant effect ($F = 7.48$, $P = 0.016$).

Thus the hypothesis that enlarged cerebral ventricles would be found only among schizophrenics without obvious genetic predisposition was confirmed: all the schizophrenics with a positive family history had ventricular volumes below the mean of the schizophrenic group as a whole. Within the control twins the association of perinatal trauma and ventricular size provided direct evidence of association between birth complications and ventricular size in a normal population. Shulsinger *et al.* (1984) has also noted that among the offspring of schizophrenic mothers, signs of prematurity at birth are associated with increased ventricular size in adult life. However, we did not find an effect of birth complications with a group of schizophrenic twins and can only propose that some other unknown process of cerebral injury must have lead to ventricular enlargement.

A variety of cerebral insults may lead to ventricular enlargement. Schizophrenic illness may not be the result of any particular stress or genetic background, but rather there is a continuum of liability to schizophrenia, and those with less genetic load may require more environmental influences to manifest the illness, and even then show less severity, while those with greater genetic predisposition become schizophrenic on that basis alone, or with a minimum of environmental contribution.

It may thus be that a more rational subtyping of schizophrenia would be on the basis of those with a positive and those with a negative family history. This may provide a more aetiological basis for sub-division than the merely symptomatic sub-division based on symptomatology such as paranoid or non-paranoid, negative symptoms, prevalence or absence of nuclear symptoms, response to drug treatment or prognosis. There are of course problems with such a sub-division, based on family history, particularly with the false negatives, incomplete penetrance of the genetic loading, the artefacts of small family size or incomplete ascertainment of illness by family history. There is also the theoretical and somewhat circular argument of whether schizophrenia in the presence of cerebral injury is actually schizophrenia or whether it should be reclassified as an organic psychosis. However, when looking for an organic aetiology for a functional disorder it is irrational, to say the least, to re-classify the diagnosis once an organic aetiology has been found.

Family studies of schizophrenia and ventricular size

Weinberger *et al.* (1981) examined pairs of siblings discordant for schizophrenia and normal siblings. He found a high correlation for ventricular size among the normal sibling pairs, while in those in whom one sibling was schizophrenic the correlation was less. The schizophrenic sibling in all cases had the greater ventricular size. Non-psychotic siblings of schizophrenics, like the co-twins in studies by Reveley *et al.*, also had significantly larger ventricles than normal subjects.

DeLisi *et al.* (1986) examined families with more than one individual of the same generation with a diagnosis of schizophrenia. Brain lateral ventricular size was quantified in 27 schizophrenic subjects from 12 unrelated families and their available siblings ($n = 10$) and 20 non-psychotic controls. Lateral ventricular size was significantly greater in the schizophrenics than in their well siblings and controls. In addition, an analysis of the data showed a significant familial component to ventricular size. Although histories of head injuries and birth complications were also associated with ventricular size, they were not considered sufficient to explain familial aspects of ventricular size and its association with schizophrenia. DeLisi *et al.* found no correlation of the severity of positive or negative symptoms in schizophrenia (as measured by the Krawiecka scale) with measurement of ventricular brain ratio. Nor did severity of illness or poor pre-morbid social adjustment correlate with ventricular size.

Analysis of variance for the frontal horn measurements found that effects due to birth complications ($P = 0.001$) and head injury ($P = 0.0009$) were both significant. The family effect was significant, though less so ($P = 0.031$), while the diagnosis effect was also barely significant ($P = 0.052$). A similar analysis of variance for the lateral ventrical bodies showed that the history of birth complications was not significant, while head injuries were significant ($P = 0.003$) and family history effect was significant ($P = 0.019$), while diagnosis was not significant. The authors interpret these results as suggesting that while birth complications and head injury might be significant factors, they do not explain the familial, ie the genetic effect. However, the birth complications and head injury, that is the environmental effects, were much more powerful than the genetic effects. Furthermore these authors did not have a model which would directly compare the genetic *versus* sporadic effects, as *all* schizophrenics had a positive family history. These results are compatible with the idea of a complementary contribution of genetic and environmental factors.

The familial-sporadic distinction as a strategy

DeLisi *et al.* (1986) conclude from their study that the familial-sporadic strategy is not supported by their findings. The authors concluded that 'increased ventricular size could represent an inherited vulnerability towards schizophrenia'. However, the most significant effect is the association of ventricular enlargement and previous obstetric and childhood environmental insults. All eight of the schizophrenic patients whose ventricles were larger than one standard deviation of the control mean had a history of either childhood head injury, birth complications or intracranial infection. To suggest that these findings represent an inherited vulnerability is not fully supported by the data. The fact that a family effect was found at a much lower level of significance may simply reflect the sample selection procedures. That is, families in which more than one member had schizophrenia were selected. There are no comparison groups of patients without a family history. Thus the family effect does not really suggest a genetic effect in contrast to a non-genetic effect, but simply reflects the finding that some family-history-positive patients had larger ventricles than other family-history-positive patients. Thus, the family effect should not be confused with family history or genetic effect.

To date, 10 published studies have examined CT scan findings in schizophrenia with and without a family history. Three studies (Campbell *et al.*, 1979; Pearlson *et al.*, 1985; Farmer *et al.*, 1985) with small sample sizes found no relationship, while the study of Nasrallah *et al.* (1983) stands alone in reporting a higher rate of schizophrenia in the relatives of patients with large compared to normal ventricles. Five studies have found an inverse correlation between ventricular size and positive family history (see Lewis *et al.*, 1987). In addition, Owens *et al.* (1985) found a curvilinear relationship between definite family history of schizophrenia and ventricular brain ratio in a sample of 112 patients. Thus the weight of the evidence is in favour of the hypothesis that there is an inverse relationship between the presence of cerebral pathology in schizophrenia, as judged by CT scan findings, and the presence of genetic predisposition. This does not suggest that the genetic-environmental or familial-sporadic distinction is absolutely clear cut, but rather that there is a continuum of liability, with individuals falling more or less along that continuum. Thus far, there have been no convincing studies to disprove this hypothesis.

In the twin studies performed so far the familial-sporadic distinction has been particularly clear cut. On the other hand in studies of singletons, large sample sizes have been required to demonstrate the effect. It may therefore be that there is something special about twins or twinning which makes the effects of cerebral damage more apparent. In order to pursue this further, we have examined a group of adult twins of MZ and DZ birth and compared them with age matched singletons, all normal volunteers under the age of 50 (Reveley & Reveley, submitted for publication). We found that lateral ventricular size was significantly larger for the twins than non-twins ($P = 0.009$). We proposed that, since twins are subjects to increased perinatal morbidity compared to non-twins from factors such as cerebral anoxia or intracerebral haemorrhage, it is likely that the enlarged ventricular brain ratio reflects previous sub-clinical brain damage. Thus the study of twins will make the effects of birth complications and perinatal injury particularly apparent.

In order to investigate the effects of twinning in a sample of schizophrenics, we examined a group of twin and singleton schizophrenics and controls. The singleton schizophrenics were matched for age and severity of illness to the non-twin schizophrenics. We found that ventricular brain ratio was significantly greater among the twins (Revely & Reveley, 1987) and analysis of co-variance, correcting for the effects of age, found that twin birth ($P = 0.038$) and family history ($P = 0.035$) accounted for the main effects. There was a two way interaction of twin and family history ($P = 0.028$), which reflected the fact that the family history effect was more apparent in the twins than in the singletons. Twins with schizophrenia had a larger ventricular brain ratio than singleton schizophrenics ($P < 0.05$), while control twins had larger ventricles than control singletons ($P < 0.01$). Control twins had a ventricular brain ratio only slightly greater than singleton schizophrenics and the difference was not significant. These results show that within these subjects the familiy history effect is more clearly evident among the twins. This is probably because of the high prevalence of perinatal and birth complications within the twins, making more apparent the effect of adverse environmental effects in the development of schizophrenia. However, clearly a genetic predisposition of some sort is required, as the singleton schizophrenics had almost as large a ventricular size as the control twins. Thus birth complications themselves do not lead to schizophrenia, but they must interact with some degree of genetic predisposition. Studies which attempt to replicate the familial-sporadic design using singletons will require particularly careful methodology and large samples in order to demonstrate the effect.

References

Campbell, R., Hays, P., Russell, D.B. & Zacks, T.J. (1979): CT scan variants and genetic heterogeneity in schizophrenia. *Am. J. Psychiatry* **136**, 722–723.

Davison, K. & Bagley, C.R. (1969): Schizophrenia-like psychoses associated with organic disorders of the central nervous system. In *Current problems in neuropsychiatry: schizophrenia, epilepsy and the temporal lobe*, ed. R. Herrington. London: British Journal of Psychiatry Special Publication No. 4.

DeLisi, L..E., Golden, L.R., Hammowit, J.R., Maxwell, E., Kurtz, D. & Gershon, E.S. (1986): A family study of the association of increased ventricular size with schizophrenia. *Arch. Gen. Psychiatry* **43**, 148–153.

Farmer, A., McGuffin, P., Jackson, R. & Storey, E. (1985): Classifying schizophrenia. *Lancet* **i**, 1333.

Gottesman, I.I. & Shields, J. (1982): *Schizophrenia: The epigenetic puzzle.* Cambridge: Cambridge University Press.

Kendler, K.S. & Hays, P. (1982): Familial and sporadic schizophrenia: A symptomatic, prognostic and EEG comparison. *Am. J. Psychiatry* **42**, 770–779.

Lewis, S.W., Reveley, A.M., Reveley, M.A., Chitkara, B. & Murray, R.M. (1987): The familial-sporadic distinction as a strategy in schizophrenia research. *Br. J. Psychiatry* **151**, 306–313.
Nasrallah, H.A., Kuperman, S., Hamra, B.J. & McCalley-Whitters, M. (1983): Clinical differences between schizophrenic patients with and without large cerebral ventricles. *J. Clin. Psychiatry* **44**, 407–409.
Owens, D.G.C., Johnstone, C., Crow, T.J., Frith, C.D., Jagoe, J.R. & Kreel, L. (1985): Lateral ventricular size in schizophrenia: Relationship to the disease process and its clinical manifestations. *Psychol. Med.* **15**, 27–41.
Pearlson, G.D., Garbacz, D.J., Moberg, P.J., Ahn, H.S. & De Paulo, J.R. (1985): Symptomatic, familial, perinatal and social correlates of computerised axial tomography (CAT) changes in schizophrenics and bipolars. *J. Nerv. Ment. Dis.* **173**, 42–50.
Reveley, A.M. & Reveley, M.A. (1987): The relationship of twinning to the familial-sporadic distinction in schizophrenia. *J. Psychiatr. Res.* **21**, 306–313.
Reveley, A.M., Reveley, M.A., Clifford, C.A. & Murray, R.M. (1982): Cerebral ventricular size in twins discordant for schizophrenia. *Lancet* **i**, 540–541.
Reveley, A.M., Reveley, M.A. & Murray, R.M. (1984*a*): Cerebral ventricular enlargement in non-genetic schizophrenia: A controlled twin study. *Br. J. Psychiatry* **144**, 89–93.
Reveley, A.M., Reveley, M.A. & Murray, R.M. (1984*b*): Hypothesis for the aetiology of schizophrenia: A genetic perspective. *Psychopharmacol. Bull.* **20**, 505–508.
Schulsinger, F., Parnas, J., Peterson, E.T., Schulsinger, H., Teasdale, T.W., Mednik, S.A., Moller, L. & Silverton, L. (1984): Cerebral ventricular size in the offspring of schizophrenic mothers. *Arch. Gen. Psychiatry* **41**, 602–606.
Weinberger, D.R., DeLisi, L.E., Neophytides, A.N. & Wyatt, R.J. (1981): Familial aspects of CT scan abnormalities in chronic schizophrenic patients. *Psychiatr. Res.* **4**, 65–71.

Chapter 5

Brain development and CCK systems in schizophrenia: a working hypothesis

Gareth W. Roberts

Department of Anatomy and Cell Biology, St Mary's Hospital Medical School, London W2 1PG, UK

Summary

Non-invasive imaging techniques have shown structural differences in the brains of schizophrenics. Planimetric studies indicate that the structural changes are localized to the medial temporal lobe (parahippocampal cortex, hippocampus and amygdala). Such changes may result from a developmental anomaly in a sub-group of temporal lobe neurons. Temporal lobe abnormalities in schizophrenics have previously been suggested on the basis of clinical and psychological observations.

Alterations in brain dopamine systems have been advanced as the major factors in the development of the clinical symptoms of schizophrenia. However, the dopamine hypothesis does not explain how alterations in sub-cortical dopamine systems relate to the recently described structural changes in the temporal lobe.

Cholecystokinin octapeptide (CCK, a putative neurotransmitter) is one of the most abundant neuropeptides in the human brain. CCK is thought to play a role in brain development. In the adult brain intrinsic CCK-containing circuits are present in the temporal lobe and in limbic system pathways connecting the temporal lobe with other brain regions. Reductions in CCK content of the temporal cortex, hippocampus and amygdala of schizophrenics have been reported and appear to correlate with increasing frequency of negative symptoms. CCK and dopamine interact physiologically and are co-localized in the ventral tegmental area.

Consideration of recent neuropathological and neurochemical data allows the generation of an alternative to the dopamine hypothesis of schizophrenia which may have greater explanatory power and generate further progress in our understanding of the disease state.

Introduction

Implicit in the concept of schizophrenia devised by Kraepelin (1907) and Bleuler (1916) is the belief that the syndrome is an organic disorder of the central nervous system with a definite pathology. Pathologists laboured in vain for over 50 years in an attempt to elucidate the pathological substrate of schizophrenia (Weinberger *et al.*, 1983; Jellinger, 1985; Kovelman & Scheibel, 1986; Roberts & Crow, 1987), a situation which resulted in the rise of psychogenic theories to explain the evolution of 'functional' psychosis. The successful use of neuroleptics (dopamine antagonists) to treat psychotic symptoms led to the proposal that schizophrenia was due to overactivity of the dopamine system — this is in essence the dopamine hypothesis (Randrup & Munkvad, 1972). Numerous studies have used tissue from schizophrenic brains to examine this hypothesis (see Owen & Crow, 1987, for review). Studies have shown that dopamine (D_2) receptor numbers are increased in the striatum and accumbens (Owen *et al.*, 1978), dopamine turnover is largely unaltered and dopamine content is unchanged (except in the amygdala and accumbens, Bird *et al.*, 1979; Reynolds, 1983). The increase in receptor number is taken as evidence of dopamine system overactivity and the dopamine hypothesis is still the major neurochemical hypothesis of schizophrenia (Meltzer & Stahl, 1976; Owen & Crow, 1987).

Preliminary evidence that schizophrenic patients had enlarged cerebral ventricles (a sign of brain atrophy) was confirmed and extended with the introduction of computerized axial tomography (Weinberger *et al.*, 1983; Kovelman & Schiebel, 1986 for review). However, ventricular enlargement is a common finding in neurodegenerative diseases (eg Huntington's chorea, Alzeimer's disease, alcohol addiction) and it might have no special relevance for schizophrenia. In addition, the presence of enlarged ventricles offers few clues as to the location of the presumed atrophic process. Indirect evidence for the association of schizophrenia with a particular brain region arises from clinical, psychological and electroencephalographic studies. In an influential review Davidson & Bagley (1969) concluded that the association between brain pathology and schizophrenia was influenced more by the location of pathology than by the type, and specifically this association was with lesions of the temporal lobe (left side). The relationship between temporal lobe epilepsy and the development of schizophrenia-like psychoses has also been highlighted (Slater, 1969; Perez & Trimble, 1980; Sherwin *et al.*, 1982). EEG abnormalities in the left temporal lobe of schizophrenics had been noted and reviewed at length by Flor-Henry (1974) who postulated a left temporal lobe dysfunction in schizophrenia.

While all these data were suggestive, they were not conclusive or concrete enough for significant progress to be made in the formulation of a more specific hypothesis which could link the site of damage and the dopamine hypothesis with the data derived from observing symptoms. The necessary additional data have come from two further sources — the traditional methods of neuropathology and the new field of neuropeptides. By integrating these data with the known pharmacological data on interactions between CCK and dopamine systems, a hypothesis can be constructed with may be useful in developing future research strategies.

Neuropathology of schizophrenia

Non-invasive visualization of the brain by computerized axial tomography (CT) and nuclear magnetic resonance (NMR) scans has revolutionized neurology and, by allowing large numbers of schizophrenics to be screened safely, has provided new evidence for the presence of structural changes in the brains of schizophrenics. The first controlled CT investigation of schizophrenia was published in 1976 (Johnstone *et al.*, 1976). Confirming earlier pneumoencephalographic work (reviews in Weinberger *et al.*, 1983; Kovelman & Scheibel, 1986), the study reported the presence of significant ventricular enlargement in chronic schizophrenics and showed that this enlargement related to cognitive functioning. Subsequent studies (reviewed in Weinberger *et al.*, 1983; Kovelman & Scheibel, 1986*a*) are in general agreement that many schizophrenics, and perhaps those with chronic forms of illness in particular, have a degree of ventricular enlargement.

The CAT scan studies highlighted the discrepancy between neuroradiological findings of atrophy and the inconclusive results of earlier pathological studies (Roberts & Crow, 1987). Efforts to resolve this discrepancy have been made using improved diagnostic criteria, blindness in experimental design and quantitative techniques.

Jellinger (1985) reported that in an autopsy series (93 schizophrenics) 13% of the brains examined had evidence of cerebral atrophy and/or internal hydrocephalus. Bogerts *et al.* (1985) used planimetric methods to make a detailed study of schizophrenic material obtained from the Vogt collection. Their data show considerable shrinkage of temporal lobe structures — hippocampal formation, amygdala, parahippocampal gyrus and a moderate shrinkage of the inner pallidal segment (−20%) in the schizophrenic group. The outer pallidal segment, caudate, putamen and nucleus accumbens did not show significant volume differences. This was taken to suggest that volume shrinkage was localized rather than general. Further study on the same material showed that the volumes of thalamic and hypothalamic nuclei were not significantly altered (Bogerts, 1986). In this study the volume decrements in schizophrenic striatal and limbic structures were compared with controls and also with cases of Huntington's chorea and postencephalitic Parkinson's disease. Volume losses in amygdala, corpus callosum and internal pallidum in Huntington's chorea and in the substantia nigra in Huntington's chorea and/or Parkinson's disease (both with *no* schizophrenic symptoms) were greater than in schizophrenics. It was concluded that the atrophy of these structures may not necessarily be related to the occurrence of schizophrenic symptoms; by comparison with Huntington's chorea and Parkinson's disease the only change which was specific to schizophrenia was in hippocampus and associated cortex.

In the largest planimetric study of schizophrenics to date Brown *et al.* (1986) used cases of affective disorder as a control group. The cases (41 schizophrenic and 29 affective) were screened for the presence of senile or vascular change and the findings were controlled for age, sex and year of birth. This study further confirmed the presence of structural change reported in CAT scan studies. The schizophrenic brains were 6% lighter (equivalent to the loss of some 50 grams of brain substance reported in some earlier studies, see Brown *et al.*, 1986, for discussion), and had lateral ventricles that were larger in the anterior horn (by 19%) and temporal horn (by 97%) cross-sectional areas. The schizophrenic group also had a significantly thinner parahippocampal cortex (by 11%). No significant differences were noted in the areas of basal ganglia structures, third ventricle, cingulate cortex and insular opercula cortex.

The two planimetric studies are in general agreement. They both found evidence of atrophy in schizophrenic brain although the degree of atrophy is less than that found in Alzeimer's disease or Huntington's chorea. Neither study provides support for the notions of *generalized* cortical atrophy or that the basal ganglia are particularly affected. Both studies conclude that the temporal lobe, and in particular the medial temporal lobe structures (hippocampus and associated cortex), are selectively affected (Fig. 1). Such a relationship between the temporal lobe (limbic system) and the clinical symptoms of schizophrenia has a long pedigree (Davidson & Bagley, 1969; Flor-Henry, 1974). However, these regions are not central to the dopamine hypothesis.

The structures of the temporal lobe — the hippocampus in particular — have been the subject of intensive study. In a qualitative study, Scheibel & Kovelman (1981) reported that the pyramidal cells of the left hippocampal formation showed varying degrees of structural disorganization which could be visualized with Golgi impregnation methods. A second larger study (Kovelman & Scheibel, 1984) using improved controls and quantitive techniques replicated their initial finding of neuronal disorganization. Disruption was

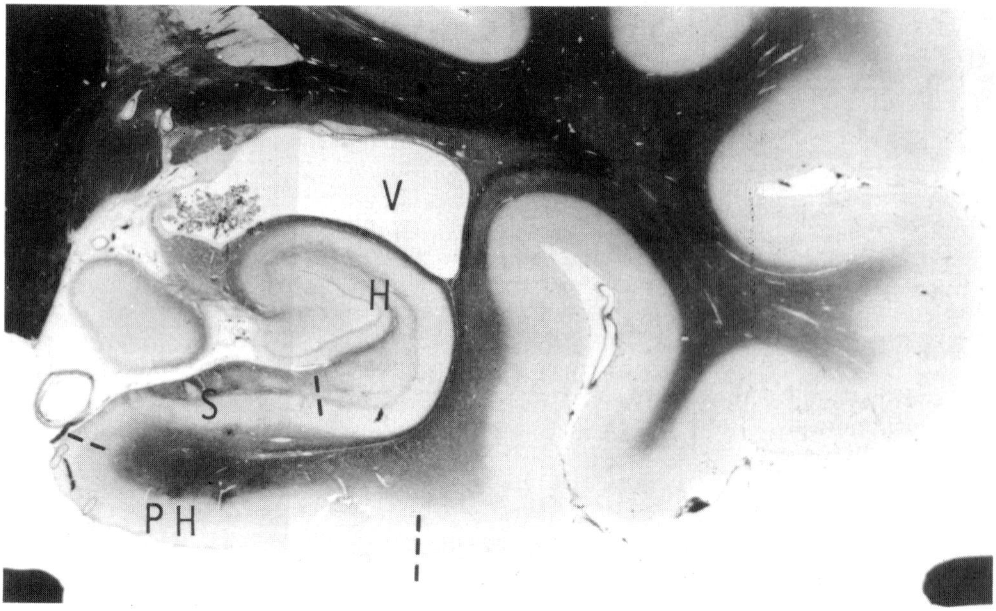

Fig 1. *Coronal section through human temporal lobe showing the temporal horn of the ventricle (V), hippocampus (H), subiculum (S) and parahippocampal gyrus (PH).* (Heidenhains stain × 2).

maximal in the anterior and middle portions of the hippocampus, particularly at the interface zones between the entorhinal cortex and the CA1 region, and between the CA2 and CA3 regions. Minimal change was found posteriorly. These changes were considered suggestive of defective patterns of neuronal migration.

Further data indicating hippocampal damage in schizophrenic brains have been provided by Falkai & Bogerts (1986). Using schizophrenic material from the Vogt collection (previously shown to be atrophic) they reported that volumes of the hippocampal formation, pyramidal cell band and hippocampal segments CA1/CA2, CA3 and CA4 were decreased in the left hemisphere. Pyramidal cell loss was more noticable in paranoid than catatonic patients. A trend towards volume reduction was identified in the pre and para subiculum and the perforant path. No significant reductions in volume of the alveus, fimbria and prosubiculum/subiculum were noted. The absolute number of pyramidal cells diminished in CA1/CA2, CA3 and CA4 zones. Pyramidal cell numbers were unaltered in other regions. The reduction of hippocampal nerve cells was not accompanied by gliosis (as indicated by glial cell counts).

A detailed description of putative morphological changes in the temporal lobe of schizophrenics has recently been presented by Jakob & Beckman (1986). They reported cytoarchitechtonic changes in the allocortical lamination pattern of the ventral insula (claustrocortex) and rostral entorhinal cortex in the parahippocampal gyrus. In the parahippocampal cortex the development of the second layer pre-α cells was abnormal (nomenclature of Braak, 1980) with layer II pre-α nerve cells misplaced in the third layer pre-β. Atypical pre-α neurones were also irregularly arranged as a superficial row, instead of in islands. These disturbances in cytoarchitecture were spread over the whole width of the parahippocampal gyrus, the medial and central portion being most disturbed and the lateral (transitional) region less affected. These changes were localized and did not extend anteriorly to the prepiriform cortex nor posteriorly to the occipital level of the temporal cortex. A defined region at the base of the insular (claustro-) cortex showed cell losses of 20–3% in cortical layers II and III.

The cytoarchitecture of the remaining temporal neocortex was normal. The architectural abnormalities were present in both hemispheres but were more conspicuous in the left hemisphere. It was notable that patients with marked pathological abnormalities tended to have an earlier age of onset of psychotic symptoms. No correlation was found between degree of cytoarchitectonic damage and duration of hospitalization. It was suggested that these findings indicate abnormal ontogenetic development of a small part of the entorhinal cortex probably occurring during gestation.

The above studies favour a developmental defect as the primary cause of the structural change in the brains of schizophrenics. However, previous neuropathological studies have reported pathological degrees of gliosis in schizophrenia (Nieto & Escobar, 1972; Fisman, 1975; Stevens 1982). These findings are important in determining the aetiology of the structural changes in schizophrenia since the presence of gliosis is not compatible with a developmental explanation.

Following brain injury (trauma, toxic injury, viral infections, etc) astrocytes proliferate (gliosis) to form scars marking the sites of neuronal loss or damage. The presence of gliosis is indicative of pathology and marks the site of the pathological process. If gliosis could be documented this would be of considerable importance in confirming the presence of organic change in the brain and clarifying its nature.

Nieto & Escobar (1972) reported gliosis in the diencephalon of schizophrenics but not in controls; evidence of gliosis was also found in the reticular formation, septum, hypothalamus and periaqueductal grey matter. Fisman (1975) also reported changes, included gliosis, in the cranial nerve nuclei of schizophrenics. In a larger qualitative study Stevens (1982) used the Holzer technique for staining glial fibrils and reported widespread gliosis in 70% of schizophrenic brains — particularly in the periaqueductal and periventricular regions. These findings are consistent with one another and recall earlier claims. The results might have been predicted on the basis of CT scan evidence of pathology. Neuronal damage can give rise to atrophy, ie cell loss in Alzeimer's disease and Huntington's Chorea, and the same damage can also be detected by the presence of gliosis. So do schizophrenic brains with atrophy have gliosis? Recent quantitative studies have attempted to answer this question (Roberts *et al.*, 1986*a*, 1986*b*; Roberts *et al.*, 1987).

Immunoreactivity attributable to glial fibrillary acidic protein (GFAP — a structural protein of astrocytes which is increased as a consequence of astrocyte reaction) has been quantified in two groups of schizophrenic brains with demonstrable atrophy (Roberts *et al.*, 1986*b* and Roberts *et al.*, 1987, using the material of Bogerts *et al.*, 1985 and Brown *et al.*, 1986). These studies were conducted blind and showed that levels of gliosis in schizophrenic brains were no different in degree or distribution from those found in the control groups without psychiatric symptoms. The lack of pathologically significant gliosis in schizophrenic brains is supported by other studies. The series of 100 schizophrenic brains investigated qualitatively by Jellinger (1985) showed no evidence of increased levels of gliosis, and studies of glial cell numbers in the hippocampus (Falkai & Bogerts, 1986) and cortical areas (Benes *et al.*, 1986) showed no differences between schizophrenics and controls. A study of MAO–B (an enzyme associated with glial cell function) failed to show an increase (expected if gliosis is present) in MAO-B levels in the temporal cortex of schizophrenics (Owen *et al.*, 1987). Together these findings do not support the concept of a pathological increase in gliosis in the brains of schizophrenics. Although there appears to be cell loss or absence in the schizophrenic brain, there is no evidence of gliosis. The conclusion argues against an ongoing process of neuronal degeneration in the adult brain.

However, it should be noted that gliosis is well established as an accompaniment of neuronal loss-degeneration/destruction only in the *adult or developed brain*. Newborn animals' reactivity to CNS trauma is limited and the immature nervous system shows no reactive gliosis or mesenchymal proliferation of the type seen in adults (Larroche, 1984). It has been shown that lesions to the cortex of the embryonic nervous system provoke degeneration but no reactive gliosis (Oyanagi *et al.*, 1986). When such lesioned animals reach adulthood they are found to have smaller numbers of cortical neurones and an abnormal distribution compared to controls, but no evidence of reactive gliosis. Therefore cell loss without gliosis can take place provided that the cell loss occurs during the development of the brain — probably before the final cell divisions.

The concept of a developmental anomaly in schizophrenic brains finds some support in other work (Kovelman & Scheibel, 1984; Jakob & Beckmann, 1986; Falkai & Bogerts, 1986). The quantitative gliosis studies are consistent with the interpretation developed above — that the structural change in schizophrenic brain may be due to an embryonic insult or developmental anomaly of some kind. This interpretation leads to the hypothesis that the injury (perinatal, toxic, viral, genetic) takes place at the embryonic stage (possibly in the 2nd or 3rd trimester when development of the limbic system is taking place). The injury results in cellular atrophy or aplasia but nor reactive gliosis.

Cholecystokinin (CCK) and CCK receptors in schizophrenia

CCK is of particular interest in schizophrenia because it is found in high concentrations in the limbic lobe and is present in many limbic system pathways. A pilot study of peptides in the limbic system of schizophrenics (five controls *vs* five schizophrenics, Crow *et al.*, 1982) reported that the CCK content of the hippocampus was reduced by 50% in schizophrenics; no change in CCK content was seen in temporal cortex, cingulate cortex or amygdala. A similar small (12 controls *vs* five schizophrenics) investigation of CCK content in the entorhinal cortex (Perry *et al.*, 1981) showed no differences in CCK content. In the largest survey to date of neuropeptides in schizophrenics (Roberts *et al.*, 1983) substance P, vasoactive intestinal polypeptide, neurotensin, somatostatin and CCK, were assessed in 10 brain areas (cortical and subcortical regions). The patients had all been interviewed and rated in life and were divided into two sub-groups on the basis of the presence or absence of negative symptoms (Type 1 and Type 2 patients after Crow, 1980). Analysis of covariance showed that significant reductions (35%) in CCK content were seen in temporal cortex (Brodman areas 21,22) of the whole schizophrenic group. Analysis of the sub-group showed that significant reductions in CCK content were found in the hippocampus and amygdala of the Type 2 patients (patients with negative symptoms). The finding of CCK reductions in limbic structures of Type II patients which correlate with the ratings of negative symptoms is one of very few markers of the defect state (Ferrier *et al.*, 1983; 1985). The finding of significant reductions in the amygdala of schizophrenics was replicated by Carruthers *et al.* (1983) but no clinical subtyping was possible in this study. Kleinman *et al.* (1984) reported normal CCK levels in amygdala, hippocampus and temporal cortex from a group of psychotic patients (although only some of this group appeared to suffer from schizophrenia as defined by the Research Diagnostic Criteria). Reduced CCK in the lumbar CSF of schizophrenics has been reported (Verbanck *et al.*, 1984) but this has not been replicated (Gerner *et al.*, 1985). In addition, significant reductions in hippocampal and frontal cortex CCK receptor number (by 40% and 20% respectively) have been reported, with receptor numbers in temporal cortex, caudate and amygdala remaining unaltered (Farmery *et al.*, 1985). These alterations in CCK content and receptor number in the limbic system may reflect changes in production, storage or secretion of the peptide or atrophy/aplasia of CCK-containing intrinsic cells of afferent fibres.

Other intrinsic peptide systems in the temporal lobe (eg vasoactive intestinal polypeptide, somatostatin and neuropeptide Y) are substantially unaffected and underline the specificity of the change in CCK-containing circuits.

Cholecystokinin in the temporal lobe

CCK is present in high concentrations in many brain regions. In cortical regions the concentration is greater than 4 nmol/g protein (Crawley, 1985), one of the highest of any peptide reported to date and an order of magnitude greater than the concentration of dopamine in the rat cerebral cortex. CCK is present mainly as the sulphated octapeptide in animal and human brain, and the temporal lobe structures — temporal cortex, hippocampus and amygdala — contain some of the largest concentrations in the brain (Beinfeld *et al.*, 1981; Beinfeld, 1983; Roberts *et al.*, 1983*a*; Sakamoto *et al.*, 1984; Crawley, 1985; Rehfeld, 1985).

Immunocytochemical studies have shown that CCK-containing neurones are widely distributed and rival monoamine and amino-acid-containing neuronal systems in complexity (Roberts 1981; Roberts *et al.*, 1981; Greenwood *et al.*, 1981; Handelmann *et al.*, 1983; Peters *et al.*, 1983; Woodhams *et al.*, 1983; Roberts 1984*a*, 1984*b*; Emson & Hunt 1984; Fallon & Seroogy, 1985). In the fore-brain of all species, CCK-containing cell bodies are most prominent in the cerebral cortex, particularly the limbic cortex. Cell bodies are found in most layers of all cortical regions, with higher numbers in the piriform, anterior cingulate, entorhinal and prefrontal cortices. Cell bodies are also abundant in the hippocampal formation and the amygdala (Fig. 2). In the temporal allo-cortex cell bodies are prominent in layer II of the piriform and entorhinal cortices; cells are also present in layers III, V, VI and are predominantly medium sized bipolar and multipolar, with processes coursing perpendicular to the pial surface. Horizontal fusiform-shaped neurones are present in layer 1. Multipolar-shaped cell bodies are found mainly in layers V and VI (Roberts *et al.*, 1982*a*, Peters *et al.*, 1982; Emson & Hunt 1984; Fallon & Seroogy, 1985). Few cortical cells are thought to be pyramidal neurones and accordingly most cortical neurones and the polymorphic neurones found in the hippocampus are thought to be local circuit neurones which have symmetric synaptic connections with pyramidal neurones (Hendry *et al.*, 1983). Long projections are present including one from layer V and VI neurones of prefrontal cortex to the midline thalamus (Fallon & Serrogy, 1985), and from the hippocampus and amygdala to the lateral septum, bed nucleus of the stria terminalis and hypothalamus (Handelman *et al.*, 1983; Roberts *et al.*, 1981, 1982*a*, 1983*b*, 1984*a*). Interhemispheric connections and association projections (Meyer 1982*a*; Roberts *et al.*, 1984; Fallon & Seroogy, 1985) have also been reported.

In the amygdala CCK neurones are prevalent in the medial central, basolateral and cortical nuclei (Roberts *et al.*, 1982*a*). Many of these neurones appear to contribute to local circuits, but CCK-containing fibres are found in the stria terminalis (an amygdaloid efferent pathway) and from the entorhinal cortex and amygdala to the ventral striatum (Roberts *et al.*, 1982*a*; Meyer *et al.*, 1982*b*; Zaborszky *et al.*, 1985; Fallon & Seroogy, 1985) and the ventral amygdalo-fugal bundle (Roberts *et al.*, 1982*a*). Hippocampal CCK-containing neurones are found predominently in the subiculum, stratum molecular and stratum radiatum (Greenwood, 1981; Roberts, 1981; Roberts *et al.*, 1982*b*, 1984*a*). The cells are small and bipolar or multipolar (basket cells) and innervate the pyramidal cell layer (Harris *et al.*, 1985; Nunzi *et al.*, 1985; Hendry & Jones, 1985; Totterdell &

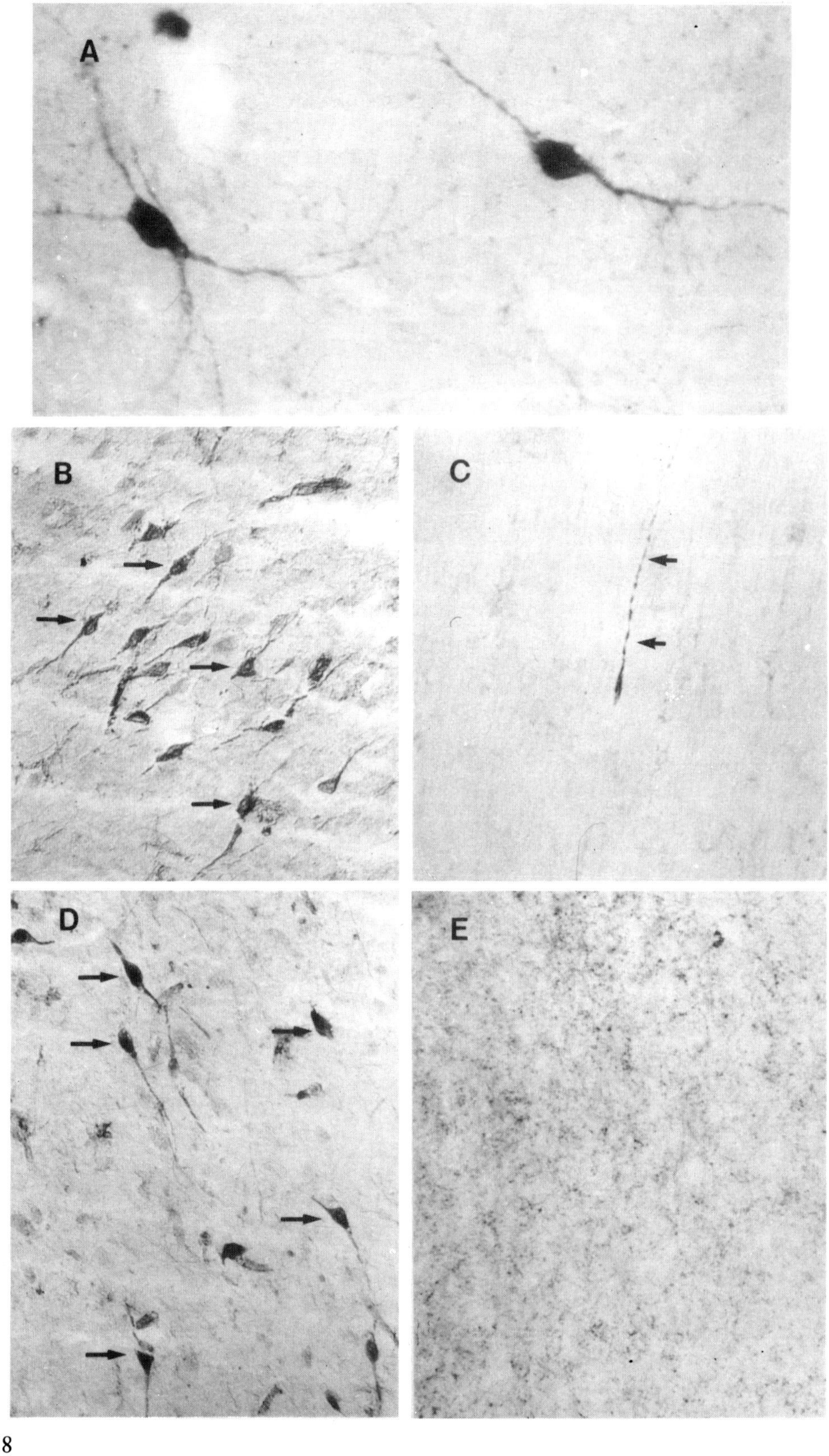
A
B
C
D
E

Smith, 1986). Large numbers of CCK-containing fibres are found within the hippocampal formation, and fibres are found within the perforant path, fornix, and commissural-associational system in animals (Roberts, 1981; Köhler & Chan-Palay, 1982; Handelmann *et al.*, 1983; Roberts *et al.*, 1984*a*; Fredens *et al.*, 1984; Fredens *et al.*, 1986) and humans (Roberts, 1982*b*, 1983*b*, 1983*c*).

The CCK neuronal system is one of the most complex in the central nervous system. Within the temporal lobe, CCK is present within the local circuit neurones of the cortex, hippocampus and amygdala and additionally the peptide is present in a number of pathways which link these limbic system components to each other, such as the perforant path and amygdala-hippocampal path (Fig. 3).

In recent studies virtually all the CCK immunoreactive neurones in rat and monkey neocortex (Hendry *et al.*, 1984) and in the cat hippocampus (Somogyi *et al.*, 1984) were found to be immunoreactive for glutamate decarboxylase, the biosynthesizing enzyme for α-aminobutyrate (GABA). Glutamate decarboxylase terminals form symmetric synaptic contacts which are inhibitory in the neocortex and hippocampus (Curtis *et al.*, 1970). This fact raises questions about the interactions between CCK and GABA at hippocampal and cortical sites, since although both are present in symmetric (inhibitory) synapses (Hendry & Jones 1985; Totterdell & Smith, 1986), CCK has been shown to have an excitatory effect on cortical and hippocampal neurones (Dodd & Kelly, 1981; Kelly, 1982; Rehfield, 1985).

Specific receptors for CCK are widely distributed in the central nervous system (Saito *et al.*, 1980; Zarbin *et al.*, 1983; Van Dijk *et al.*, 1984) with high numbers in the hippocampus, amygdala and temporal cortex. In the cerebral cortex CCK receptors have a distinct laminar organization, the highest densities being found in layer II–VI with a sparsity of receptors in layers I and V. The presence of numerous CCK-containing neurones in cortical layers II and III, hippocampus and amygdala coupled with high receptor density support the idea that CCK plays a role in local circuitry.

Cholecystokinin and dopamine interactions

CCK is co-localized with dopamine in the pars compacta of the substantia nigra A9 and the ventral tegmental area A10 (Hökfelt *et al.*, 1980; Markstein & Hökfelt, 1984). These CCK/dopamine cells project topographically along previously described dopamine pathways (Lindvall & Björklund, 1978) to the nucleus accumbens, amygdala hippocampus and entorhinal cortex as well as to the prefrontal cortex (Hökfelt *et al.*, 1980; Fallon & Seroogy, 1985). CCK has also been shown to affect the functioning of the dopamine system (see Wang *et al.*, 1984, and Nair *et al.*, 1985, for reviews). CCK peptides decrease dopamine turnover, dopamine release and spiroperidol (dopamine receptor ligand) binding (Mashal *et al.*, 1983; Voigt & Wang, 1984). Dopamine neurones in the substantia nigra which have CCK receptors are excited by the application of CCK (Skirboll *et al.*, 1982). In some studies CCK peptides have been shown to have

---

Fig. 2. *CCK-like immunoreactivity in the human temporal lobe.* (a) CCK-containing interneurones in the stratum molecular of the hippocampus (×450). These neurones innervate and synapse symmetrically on pyramidal neurones. (b) CCK-positive neurones in the entorhinal cortex (×320). Projections from these neurones innervate the hippocampus via the medial perforant pathway. (c) CCK-immunoreactive fibre in the fornix (× 450). (d) Numerous CCK-positive neurones are found in the dopamine-poor cortico-medial amygdala (×320). (d) Dense plexus of CCK-containing fibres is present in the medial amygdaloid nucleus (× 350). CCK immunoreactivity was visualized using a specific antibody and the PAP method as described in Roberts *et al.*, 1982*a*, 1983*b*.

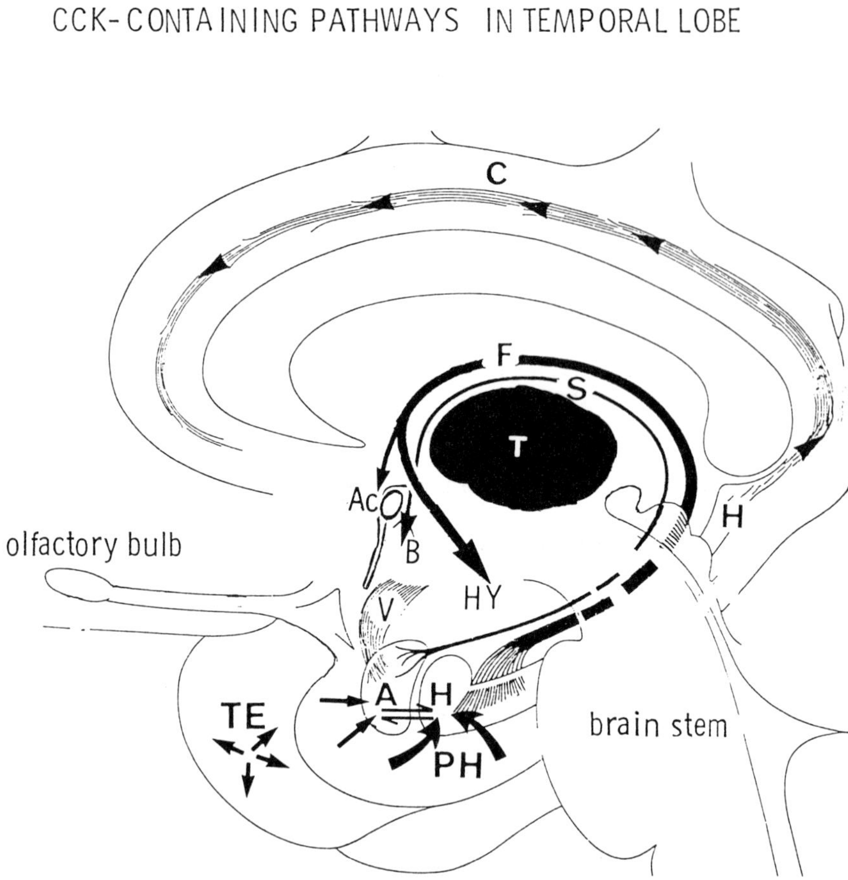

Fig. 3. *Schematic diagram of possible CCK-containing pathways in the temporal lobe.* Note the CCK-containing links between the regions showing structural change in schizophrenics — the parahippocampal gyrus and hippocampus. A, amygdala; Ac, accumbens; B, bed nucleus of the stria terminals; C, cingulate bundle; F, fornix; H, hippocampus; HY, hypothalamus; PH, parahippocampal gyrus; S, stria terminals; T, thalamus; TE, temporal cortex; V, ventral amygdalofugal bundle. (Data derived from Roberts 1981; Roberts *et al.*, 1982*a*, 1983*a*, 1984*a*.)

neuroleptic-like profiles antagonizing stereotyped behaviour induced by methylphenidate, apomorphine, amphetamine and levodopa (see Nair *et al.*, 1985 for reviews). Chronic treatment with neuroleptics increases CCK receptor number in the frontal cortex and meso-limbic regions (Change *et al.*, 1983) and increase CCK concentrations in the striatum and limbic system (Frey, 1983). The clinical effects of CCK and synthetic forms of the peptides on schizophrenic symptoms are still uncertain, as some studies have been unable to replicate earlier positive results (see Nair *et al.*, 1985 for review).

Cholecystokinin and brain development

Changes in the levels of CCK and in the numbers of CCK receptors occur during brain development. These alterations may be of considerable importance in determining adult cortical circuitry. In the developing rat brain, CCK levels rise steadily from birth to adult levels on postnatal day 27. Levels of CCK receptors rise from low levels (postnatal day 2) to a high on postnatal day 12 before declining to adult levels by postnatal day 30 (Hays *et al.*, 1981). A more detailed immunocytochemical investigation of the developing rat brain (Westenbroek *et al.*, 1987) has shown that dramatic increases in the number of CCK-labelled structures in the cortex occurs between postnatal days 6–9 and 13–21. The latter increase in immunoreactivity coincides with the ingrowth and development of associational and corticofugal fibres in the prepiriform cortex. The pattern of increased immunoreactivity is *not* homogeneous for all cortical regions and the patterns in different cortical regions may be related to the development of function in that region. Supporting evidence for the role of CCK in the development of cortical circuitry comes from studies on the developing cat brain (Chun *et al.*, 1987). These show that subplate cells immunoreactive for CCK occupy distinct tangential domains within the cortex. It is thought that these cells may act as temporary targets for ingrowing afferent systems and that they may influence particular sections of cortex during development. The amount of CCK expressed in the cortex could also be crucial for normal development. When newborn animals are treated with CCK peripherally and then subsequently examined, significant reductions in CCK content are found in the cerebral cortex and hippocampus and a trend towards cortical thinning is found (Johnson *et al.*, 1987). Such effects were not seen in adult animals treated with CCK, implying that over-expression of CCK in the developing animal could result in the retardation of brain development.

Summary

(a) The successful use of neuroleptics (dopamine antagonists) led to the proposal that schizophrenic symptoms are due to overactivity of the dopamine system — the dopamine hypothesis. Dopamine is significantly increased in the amygdala and accumbens and dopamine receptor numbers are increased in the striatum and accumbens.
(b) Neuropathological data show that medial temporal lobe structures — primarily the entorhinal cortex/parahippocampal gyrus and hippocampus, and to a lesser extent the amygdala, show evidence of aplasia in the brains of schizophrenics. In particular there is evidence of a developmental anomaly in the pre-α pre-β cell layers of the parahippocampal cortex and the subicular and pyramidal cell zones of the hippocampus. Other cortical and subcortical regions appear relatively unaffected.
(c) Selective deficits of CCK have been found in the temporal cortex, hippocampus and amygdala. These changes correlate with clinical symptoms. Reductions in CCK receptors have been reported in the hippocampus.
(d) Immunocytochemical studies have revealed an extensive and complex CCK-containing network of cells and fibres within the limbic system. Numerous CCK-containing neurones are located in layer II and III (pre-α and pre-β) of the parahippocampal cortex in the hippocampus and throughout the subnuclei of the amygdala. CCK-containing fibres link temporal lobe structures with each other and distant brain regions.
(e) CCK may be essential for the normal development of cortical structure. Over-expression of CCK during development could result in retardation of brain growth.

The dopamine hypothesis revisited

The dopaminergic hypothesis of schizophrenia is the leading neurochemical explanation for the symptoms of schizophrenia, and the nucleus accumbens, located at the striatal limbic crossroads (Mogenson *et al.*, 1980), is central to this hypothesis (Stevens, 1973; Mathyse, 1981). The relationship between the neuropathological findings in schizophrenia (smaller brain structure due to abnormal development) and the neurochemical evidence of dopamine system abnormalities is not addressed by the dopamine hypothesis. Other limitations of the dopamine hypothesis have also been raised (Crow, 1987).

CCK and dopamine are intimately related to one another. The two are co-localized in the A9 and A10 dopamine cell groups and CCK/dopamine projections from this region innervate the accumbens (where D_2 receptors are increased in schizophrenia) and central amygdaloid nucleus (where dopamine levels are increased). The dopamine projection to the striatum (where D_2 receptors are increased in schizophrenia) does not contain CCK. However, pharmacological research has indicated that the therapeutic actions of antipsychotic drugs may be related to the reduction of dopamine activity in the mesolimbic and neocortical regions rather than in the nigrostriatal area (Wang *et al.*, 1984). That is to say the CCK/dopamine system is therapeutically more important than the dopamine system.

Preliminary attempts to understand the relationship between CCK and dopamine in schizophrenia have focused on the meso-limbic dopamine system (where CCK and dopamine are co-localized) and the region of the nucleus accumbens (Hökfelt *et al.*, 1980; Wang *et al.*, 1984; Nair *et al.*, 1985; Totterdell & Smith, 1986). The anatomy of CCK and dopamine systems suggests possible areas of interaction between the two transmitters in: (a) the accumbens due to co-localization of CCK and dopamine in the meso-limbic dopamine system, (b) the temporal lobe — where there is evidence of a functional dopaminergic input to the temporal cortex, hippocampal formation and amygdala (Ishikawa *et al.*, 1982; Verney *et al.*, 1985; Bruinik & Bischoff, 1986) and (c) via an indirect connection between temporal lobe and subcortical dopamine systems, as has been demonstrated for the hippocampus (DeFrance *et al.*, 1981).

No evidence has been found for subcortical alterations in CCK systems in schizophrenia, whilst dopamine levels are increased. Within the amygdala, CCK is reduced and dopamine is increased. A significant proportion of the local CCK system in the amygdala is in the dopamine-poor cortico-medial region, ie a separate system from the CCK/dopamine A10 projection (Roberts *et al.*, 1982*a*). It should be noted that the CCK reduction in the amygdala was found in patients with negative (neuroleptic-resistant [Crow, 1980]) symptoms (Roberts *et al.*, 1983*a*). Dopamine content and receptor numbers in temporal cortex and hippocampus are low (Verney *et al.*, 1985; Bruinick & Bischoff, 1986) and there is no evidence of alterations in the dopamine system of the hippocampus or temporal cortex — the regions showing most structural change in schizophrenics.

On the basis of the above data, damage to either the CCK/dopamine containing projection of the ventral tegmental area or *direct* connections between dopamine and 'local' CCK systems in the parahippocampal gyrus/entorhinal cortex and hippocampus is unlikely. The third possibility, an *indirect* link via neural pathways connecting medial temporal lobe structure and nucleus accumbens, needs further study. Hippocampal pyramidal cells project to the nucleus accumbens via the fornix (Groenwegen *et al.*, 1981; Alonso & Köhler, 1982; Kelley & Domesick, 1982; Phillipson & Griffiths, 1985), and this projection is excitatory (DeFrance *et al.*, 1981; Lopes da Silva *et al.*, 1984; Yang & Mogenson, 1984). Damage to the hippocampus results in increased dopamine content and binding of haloperidol in the accumbens (the changes found in schizophrenic brains) due to decreased release and use of dopamine (Isaacson, 1984). This approach has been expanded by Totterdell & Smith (1986). They suggest that the hippocampal contribution to the excitatory input of the accumbens may be controlled in part by CCK-interneurones. Thus loss of interneurones in schizophrenia results in a decreased flow of impulses from hippocampus to accumbens. This leads to an imbalance in the accumbens with inhibitory dopaminergic input uncompensated for by the excitatory drive from the hippocampal formation. The result is similar to lesioning the hippocampus — increased dopamine content from decreased use leading to increased neuroleptic binding (receptor supersensitivity) in the accumbens. Antipsychotic drugs would correct this imbalance as a result of their ability to block dopaminergic transmission in the accumbens by occupying dopamine receptor sites (Bunney, 1985). Whilst being a useful extension of the dopamine hypothesis this hypothesis is limited. It fails to take account of recent developments in neuropathology (particularly the proposed developmental aetiology) and ignores the reductions of CCK found in the temporal cortex and amygdala and the increases of D_2 receptors reported in the striatum.

Brain development and CCK systems in schizophrenia — a hypothesis

Using all the information available a hypothesis can be formulated which accounts for both the neurochemical and the neuropathological features of schizophrenia. CCK-containing structures in the cortex appear to have an important role in the development of normal cortical structures. CCK-containing neurones act as target cells for afferent projection systems and the appearance of CCK-containing fibres coincides with the development of associational systems. It is proposed that the core event in schizophrenia is a developmental anomaly affecting the CCK-containing cells in the pre-α and pre-β layers of the parahippocampal/entorhinal cortex. The anomaly may be due to genetic factors governing cell surface markers on CCK neurones (so that cells do not recognize their location) or the induction or regulation of CCK production (so that the appropriate levels of CCK are not present at the correct time.). *Alterations in the embryonic environment which effect cell-cell recognition or CCK production could also produce similar results.* The extent of the developmental disruption in CCK systems is probably *variable* (as is common in developmental defects, Larroche, 1984) and in more extreme cases CCK-containing local circuit neurones in the hippocampus and amygdala may also be affected. Extensive involvement of separate 'local' CCK systems (ie the hippocampal system, the amygdala system) may well produce an earlier age of onset of symptoms and increasing degrees of negative symptoms. CCK-containing systems will be disrupted (not necessarily destroyed) and thus the processing of the input and output of these regions by CCK circuits will be reduced. Cortical information converges onto the entorhinal cortex and reaches the hippocampus proper via polysynaptic relays in the parahippocampal gyrus and subiculum (Van Hoesen, 1982; Goldman-Rakic *et al.*, 1984). Hippocampal output is organized in a similar fashion. In this respect the parahippocampal gyrus and subiculum serve to 'gate' all the information leaving and entering the hippocampus (Goldman-Rakic *et al.*, 1984). Connections also exist between the entorhinal region and the striatum and amygdala (Krettek & Price, 1977; Van Hoesen *et al.*, 1981). So alterations in entorhinal CCK could affect hippocampal, amygdala and striatal function. CCK-containing pathways have been shown to link each of these regions (Roberts *et al.*, 1982*a*, 1984*a*, Fallon & Seroogy, 1985). In relation to the hippocampus, CCK-containing neurones in the entorhinal cortex project through the medial perforant path and terminate in the hippocampus (possibly on the apical dendrites of pyramidal cells [Roberts *et al.*, 1984*a*; Fredens *et al.*, 1984]). Even without loss of CCK cells intrinsic to the hippocampus (proposed by Totterdell & Smith, 1986), loss of the CCK-mediated perforant path input may lead to a loss of excitatory pyramidal input.

Loss of such excitatory input during *development* could lead to dystrophy ('windswept look' of Scheibel & Kovelman, 1981) or loss of pyramidal cells bearing CCK receptors during development. Cells bearing CCK receptors project to the accumbens (Totterdell & Smith, 1986). It has been shown that damage to the hippocampus in rats results in an increase in the dopamine content of the accumbens due to decreased release and use of dopamine, ie increases of dopamine but no change in metabolites (Isaacson, 1984) and such lesions also cause an increase in haloperidol binding (increasing in receptor binding). These are the findings which are present in schizophrenic brains and form the basis of the dopamine hypothesis.

Using the above hypothesis it should be possible to make predictions of the findings in schizophrenia. The temporal cortex will be primarily affected, followed by the hippocampal formation and amygdala. Neuropathological and biochemical findings should reflect this order of vulnerability. Increasing involvement of limbic structures should result in earlier age of onset of symptoms and increased degree of negative symptoms. CCK and dopamine systems will show relation to each other at sites of physiological interaction, though these are not necessarily the same as the sites where both are present.

It is hoped that the above argument will be a useful synthesis of data from neuropathological and neurochemical studies and allow the development of experimental strategies to examine the role of development on transmitter systems. The concept of a 'working' hypothesis underlines the tentativeness which should accompany all efforts to account for the symptoms of schizophrenia as the truth is 'rarely pure and never simple'.

Acknowledgements—I thank Dr T.J. Crow for his patience and critical insight which aided crystallization of these thoughts, Drs Bruton and Reynolds and Nigel Colter for long and useful discussions and Asmita Soni for her expert secretarial skills.

References

Alonso, A. & Köhler, C. (1982): Evidence for separate projections of hippocampal pyramidal and non-pyramidal neurones to different parts of the septum in the rat brain. *Neurosci. Lett.* **31**, 209–214.

Beinfeld, M.C. (1983): Cholecystokinin in the central nervous system: a minireview. *Neuropeptides* **3**, 411–427.

Beinfeld, M.C., Meyer, D.K., Eskay, R.L., Jansen, R.T. & Brownstein, M. (1981): The distribution of cholecystokinin immunoreactivity in the central nervous system of the rat as determined by radioimmunoassay. *Brain Res.* **212**, 51–57.

Benes, F.M., Davidson, J. & Bird, E.D. (1986): Quantitative cytoarchitectural studies of the cerebral cortex of schizophrenics. *Arch. Gen. Psychiatry* **43**, 31–35.

Bired, E.D., Spokes, E.G.S. & Iverson, L.L. (1979): Increased dopamine concentration in limbic areas of brain from patients dying with schizophrenia. *Brain* **102**, 347–360.

Bleuler, E. (1916): Psychich und Psychisch in der Pathologie. *Z. Gesamte Neurol. Psychiatr.* **30**, 426–475.

Bogerts, B., Meertz, E. & Schonfeldt-Bausch, R. (1985): Basal ganglia and limbic system pathology in schizophrenia. *Arch. Gen. Psychiatry* **42**, 784–791.

Bogerts, B. (1986): Evidence for structural changes in the limbic system in schizophrenia. Proceedings of the IVth world congress of Biological Psychiatry. Amsterdam: Elsevier/North Holland.

Braak, H. (1980): *Studies of brain function 4: Architectronics of the human telecephalic cortex.* Berlin: Springer Verlag.

Brown, R., Colter, N., Corsellis, J.A.N., Corw, T.J., Frith, C.D., Jagoe, R., Johstone, E.C. & Marsh, L. (1986): Postmortem evidence of structural brain changes in schizophrenia. *Arch. Gen. Psychiatry* **43**, 36–42.

Bruinik, A. & Bischoff, S. (1986): Detection of dopamine receptors in homogenates of rat hippocampus and other brain areas. *Brain Res.* **386**, 78–83.

Bunney, B.S. (1985): Antipsychotic drug effects on the electrical activity of dopaminergic neurons. In *Neurotransmitters in action*, ed. D. Bousfield, pp 289–296. Amsterdam: Elsevier.
Carruthers, B., Dawharn, D., de Quidt, M., Emson, P.C., Hunter, J. & Reynolds, G.P. (1984): Changes in neuropeptide content of amygdala in schizophrenia. *Br. J. Pharmacol.* **81**, 139.
Chang, R.S.L., Lotti, V.J., Martin, G.E. & Chen, T.B. (1983): Increase in brain cholecystokinin (CCK) receptor binding following chronic haloperidol treatment, intracisternal 6-hydroxydopamine or ventral tegmental lesions. *Life Sci.* **32**, 871–878.
Chun, J.J.M., Nakamura, M.J. & Shatz, C.J. (1987): Transient cells of the developing mammalian telencephalon are peptide immunoreactive neurons. *Nature* **325**, 617–620.
Crawley, J.N. (1985): Comparative distribution of cholecystokinin and other neuropeptides. *Ann. N.Y. Acad. Sci.* **448**, 1–8.
Crow, T.J. (1980): Molecular pathology of schizophrenia: more than one disease process? *Br. Med. J.* **280**, 66–68.
Crow, T.J. (1987): The dopamine hypothesis survives, but there must be another way ahead. *Br. J. Psychiatry* **151**, 460–465.
Crow, T.J., Ferrier, I.N., Johnstone, E.C., Owens, D.G.C., Roberts, G.W., Lee, Y.C., Bloom, S.R. & Polak, J.M.: (1982): Neuroendocrine aspects of schizophrenia. In *Neuropeptides: Basic and clinical aspects*, eds G. Fink & L.J. Whaley, pp 22–239. Edinburgh: Churchill-Livingstone.
Curtis, D.R., Felix, D. & McLennan, H. (1970): GABA and hippocampal inhibition. *Br. J. Pharmacol.* **40**, 881–87.
Davidson, K. & Bagley, C.R. (1969): Schizophrenia and the limbic system. In *Current problems in neuropsychiatry*, R.N. Special Publication No 4, ed. R.N. Hertington. Ashford: *Br. J. Psychiatry.*
DeFrance, J.F., Sikes, R.W., Palmer, G.C. & Chronister, R.B. (1981): Frequency specific effects of dopamine in the nucleus accumbens. *Neurosci. Lett.* **22**, 245–301.
Dodd, J. & Kelly, J.S. (1981): The actions of cholecystokinin and related peptides on neurons of the mammalian hippocampus. *Brain Res.* **205**, 337–350.
Emson, P.C. & Hunt, S.P. (1984): Peptide containing neurons of the cerebral cortex. In *The cerebral cortex* eds E.G. Jones & A. Peters, pp 145–169. New York: Plenum Press.
Falkai, P. & Bogerts, B. (1986): Cell loss in the hippocampus of schizophrenics. *Eur. Arch. Psychiatr. Neurol. Sci.* **236**, 154–161.
Fallon, J.H. & Seroogy, K.B. (1985): Distribution and some connections of CCK neurons in the rat brain. *Ann. N.Y. Acad. Sci.* **448**, 121–132.
Farmery, S.M., Owen, F., Poulter, M. & Crow, T.J. (1985): Reduced high infinity cholecystokinin binding in hippocampus and frontal cortex of schizophrenic patients. *Life Sci.* **36**, 473–477.
Ferrier, I.N., Roberts, G.W., Crow, T.J., Johnstone, E.C., Owens, D.G.C., Lee, Y.C., O'Shaughnessy, D., Adrian, T.E., Polack, J.M. & Bloom, S.R. (1983): Reduced cholecystokinin-like and somatostatin-like immunoreactivity in limbic lobe is associated with negative symptoms in schizophrenia. *Life Sci.* **33**, 475–482.
Ferrier, I.N., Crow, T.J., Farmery, S.M., Owens, F., Roberts, G.W., Adrian, T.E. & Bloom, S.R. (1985): Reduced CCK in the limbic lobe in schizophrenia: a marker for pathology underlying the defect state? *Ann. N.Y. Acad. Sci.* **448**, 495–506.
Fisman, M. (1975): The brain-stem in psychosis. *Br. J. Psychiatry.* **126**, 414–422.
Flor-Henry, P. (1974): Psychosis, neurosis and epilepsy. *Br. J. Psychiatry* **124**, 144–150.
Fredens, K., Steingaard-Pedersen, K. & Larsson, L.I. (1984): Localisation of enkephalin and cholecystokinin immunoreactivities in the perforant path terminal field of the rat hippocampal formation. *Brain Res.* **304**, 255–263.
Fredens, K., Stengard-Pedersen, K. & Wallace, M.N. (1986): Localisation of cholecystokinin in the dentate commissural-associational system of the mouse and rat. *Brain Res.* **401**, 68–78.
Frey, P. (1983): Cholecystokinin octapeptide levels in rat brain are changes after subchronic neuroleptic treatment. *Eur. J. Pharmacol* **95**, 87–92.
Gerner, R.H., Vankammem, D.P. & Ninan, P.T. (1985): Cerebrospinal fluid cholecystokinin, bombesin and somatostatin in schizophrenia and normals. *Prog. Neuropsychopharmacol. Biol. Psychiatry* **9**, 73–80.
Goldman-Rakic, A., Selemon, L.D. & Schwartz, M.L. (1984): Dual pathways connecting the dorsolateral prefrontal cortex with the hippocampal formation and the parahippocampal cortex in rhesus monkey. *Neuroscience* **12**, 719–743.

Greenwood, R.S., Godar, E., Reaves, T.A. & Hayward, J.N. (1981): Cholecystokinin in hippocampal pathways. *J. Comp. Neurol.* **203**, 335–350.
Groenwegen, H.G., Arnold, D. & Lopes da Silva, F.H. (1981): Afferent connections of the nucleus accumbens in the cat, with special emphasis on the projections from the hippocampal region: an anatomical and electrophysiological study. In *Neurobiology of the nucleus accumbens* eds R.B. Chronister & J.F. De France, pp 41–74. Brunswick, Main: Haer Institute for Electrophysical Research.
Handelman, G.E., Benfield, M.C., O'Donohue, I.L., Nelson, J.B. & Brenneman, D.E. (1983): Extra-hippocampal projections of CCK neurons of the hippocampus and subiculum. *Peptides* **4**, 331–334.
Harris, K.M., Marshall, P.E. & Landis, D.M.D. (1985): Ultrastructural study of cholecystokinin-immunoreactive cells and processes in area CA1 of the rat hippocampus. *J. Comp. Neurol.* **233**, 147–158.
Hays, S.E., Houston, S.H., Beinfield, M.C. & Paul, S.M. (1981): Post-natal ontogeny of cholecystokinin receptors in rat brain. *Brain Res.* **213**, 237–241.
Hendry, S.H.C. & Jones, E.G. (1985): Morphology of synapses formed by cholecystokinin-immunoreactivity axon terminals in regio superior of rat hippocampus. *Neuroscience* **16**, 57–68.
Hendry, S.H.C., Jones, F.G. & Beinfield, M.C. (1983): Cholecystokinin-immunoreactive neurons in rat and monkey cerebral cortex make symmetric synapses and have intimate associations with blood vessels. *Proc. Natl. Acad. Sci. U.S.A.* **80**, 2400–2404.
Hendry, S.H.C., Jones, F.G., DeFelipe, J., Schmechel, D., Brandon, C. & Emson, P.C. (1984): Neuropeptides containing neurons of the cerebral cortex are also GABAergic. *Proc. Natl. Acad. Sci. U.S.A.* **81**, 6526–6530.
Hökfelt, T., Rehfeld, J.F., Skirboll, L., Ivemark, B., Goldstein, M. & Markey, K. (1980): Evidence for coexistence of dopamine and CCK in mesolimbic neurons. *Nature* **285**, 476–478.
Isaacson, R.L. (1984): Hippocampal damage-effects on dopaminergic systems of the basal ganglia. In *International review of neurobiology* eds J.R. Symthies & R.J. Bradley, pp 339–361. Orlando: Academic Press.
Ishikawa, K., Oh, T. & McGaugh, J.L. (1982): Evidence for dopamine as a transmitter in dorsal hippocampus. *Brain Res.* **232**, 222–226.
Jakob, H. & Beckmann, H. (1986): Prenatal developmental disturbances in the limbic allocortex in schizophrenics. *J. Neurol. Transmission* **65**, 303–326.
Jellinger, K. (1985): Neuromorphological background of pathochemical studies in major psychoses. In *Pathochemical markers in major psychoses*, eds H. Bekman & P. Riederer, pp 1–23. Heidelberg: Springer.
Johnson, F.E., Hudd, C., LaRegina, M.C., Beinfield, M.C., Tolbert, D.L., Spain, J.W., Szucs, M. & Coscia, C.J. (1987): Exogenous cholecystokinin (CCK) reduces neo-natal rat brain opioid receptor density and CCK levels. *Dev. Brain Res.* **21**, 139–146.
Johnstone, E.C., Crow, T.J., Frith, C.D., Husband, J. & Kreel, L. (1976): Cerebral ventricular size and cognitive impairment in chronic schizophrenia. *Lancet* **ii**, 924–926.
Kelley, A.E. & Domesick, V.B. (1982): The distribution of the projection from the hippocampal formation to the nucleus accumbens in the rat: an anterograde-horseradish peroxidase study. *Neuroscience* 7, 2321–2335.
Kelley, A.E., Domesick, V.B. & Nauta, W.J.H. (1982): The amygdalostriatal projection in the rat — an anatomical study by anterograde and retrograde tracing methods. *Neuroscience* 7, 615–630.
Kelly, J.S. (1982): Electrophysiology of peptides in the central nervous system. *Br. Med. Bull.* **38**, 283–290.
Kleinman, J.E., Iadarola, M., Govoni, S., Hong, J., Gillin, J.C. & Wyatt, R.J. (1982): Postmortem measurements of neuropeptides in human brain. *Psychopharmacol. Bull.* **19**, 375–377.
Köhler, C. & Chan-Palay, V. (1982): The distribution of cholecystokinin-like immunoreactive neurons and nerve terminals in the retrohippocampal region in the rat and the guinea pig. *J. Comp. Neurol.* **210**, 136–146.
Kovelman, J.A. & Scheibel, A.B. (1984): A neurohistological correlate of schizophrenia. *Biol. Psychiatry* **191**, 1601–1621.
Kovelman, J.A. & Scheibel, A.B. (1986*a*): Biological substrates of schizophrenia. *Acta. Neurol. Scand.* 73, 1–32.

Kovelman, J.A. & Scheibel, A.B. (1986*b*): A neurohistologic correlate of schizophrenia. *Biol. Psychiatry* **19**, 1601–1621.

Kraepelin, E. (1917): Introduction à la psychiatrie clinique. Translated from the second German edition by A. Devaux & P. Merklen. Paris: Vigot Freres.

Krettek, J.E. & Price, J.L. (1977) Projections from the amygdaloid complex and adjacent olfactory structures to the entorhinal cortex and to the subiculum in the rat and cat. *J. Comp. Neurol.* **172**, 723–752.

Larroche, J.C. (1984): Malformation of the nervous system. In *Greenfield's neuropathology*, 4th edn, eds J.M. Adams, J.A.N. Corsellis & L.W. Duchen, p. 385. London: Edward Arnold.

Lindvall, O. & Björklund, A. (1978): Organisation of catecholamine neurons in rat central nervous system. In *Handbook of psychopharmacology*, Vol. 9, eds L.L. Iversen, S.D. Iversen & S.H. Snyder, pp. 139–231. New York; Plenum Press.

Lopes da Silva, F.H.L., Arnols, D.E.A.T. & Neijt, H.C. (1984): A functional link between the limbic cortex and ventral striatum-physiology of the subiculum accumbens pathway. *Exp. Brain Res.* **55**, 205–214.

Markstein, R. & Hökfelt, T. (1984): Effect of cholecystokinin-octapeptide on dopamine release from slices of cat caudate nucleus. *J. Neurosci.* **4**, 570–575.

Mashal, R.D., Owen, F., Deakin, J.F.W. & Poulter, M. (1983): The effects of cholecystokinin on dopaminergic mechanisms in rat striatum. *Brain. Res.* **277**, 375–376.

Mathyse, S. (1981): Nucleus accumbens and schizophrenia. In *Neurobiology of the nucleus accumbens*, eds R.B. Chronister, J. F. De France, pp. 351–359. Brunswick, Maine, USA: Haer Institute for Electrophysiological Research.

Meltzer, H.Y. & Stahl, S.M. (1976): The dopamine hypothesis of schizophrenia. *Schizophrenia. Bull.* **2**, 19–76.

Meyer, D.K., Beinfeld, M.C. & Brownstein, M.J. (1982*a*): Corpus callosum lesions increase cholecystokinin concentrations in cortical areas with homeotopic connections. *Brain Res* **240**, 151–153.

Meyer, D.K., Beinfeld, M.C., Oertel, W.H. & Brownstein, M.J. (1982*b*): The origin of the cholecystokinin containing fibers in the rat caudatoputamen. *Science* **215**, 187–188.

Mogenson, G.J., Jones, D.L. & Yim, C.Y. (1980): From motivation to action: functional interface between the limbic system and the motor system. *Proc. Neurobiol.* **14**, 69–97.

Nair, N.P., Lal, S. & Bloom, D.M. (1985): Cholecystokinin peptides, dopamine and schizophrenia. *Prog. Neuropsychopharmacol. Biol. Psychiatry* **9**, 515–524.

Nieto, D. & Escobar, A. (1972): Major psychoses. In *Pathology of the nervous system*, vol. 3. ed. J. Minckler, pp 2654–2665. New York: McGraw-Hill.

Nunzi, M.G., Gorio, A., Milan, F. M., Freund, T.F., Somogyi, P. & Smith, A.D. (1985): Cholecystokinin-immunoreactive cells from symmetrical synaptic contacts with pyramidal and nonpyramidal neurons in the hippocampus. *J. Comp. Neurol.* **237**, 485–505.

Owen, F. & Crow, T.J. (1987): Neurotransmitters and psychosis. *Br. Med. Bull.* **43**, 651–671.

Owen, F., Cross, A.J., Crow, T.J., Longden, A., Poulter, M., & Riley, G.J. (1978): Increased dopamine-receptor sensitivity in schizophrenia. *Lancet* **ii**, 223–226.

Owen, F., Crow, T. J., Frith, C.D., Johnson, J.A., Johnstone, E.C., Lofthouse, R., Owens, D.G.C., & Poulter, M. (1987): Selective decreases in MAO-B activity in post-mortem brains from schizophrenic patients with the 'Type II' syndrome. *Br. J. Psychiatry* **151**, 514–519.

Oyanagi, K., Yoshida, Y. & Ikuta, F. (1986): The chronology of lesion repair in the developing rat brain: Biological significances of the pre-existing extracellular space. *Virchows Arch.* [A] **408**, 347–359.

Peters, A., Miller, M. & Kimerer, L.M. (1983): Cholecystokinin-like immunoreactive neurons in rat cerebral cortex. *Neuroscience* **8**, 431–448.

Perez, M.M. & Trimble, M.R. (1980): Epileptic psychoses — diagnostic comparison with process schizophrenia. *Br. J. Psychiatry* **137**, 245–249.

Perry, R.H., Dockra, G.J., Dimaline, R., Perry, E.K., Blessed, G. & Tomlinson, B.E. (1981): Neuropeptides in Alzeimers disease, depression and schizophrenia. *J. Neurol. Sci.* **51**, 465–472.

Phillipson, O. T. & Griffiths, A. C. (1985): The topographical order of inputs to nucleus accumbens in the rat. *Neuroscience* **16**, 275–296.

Randrup, A. & Munkvad, I. (1972): Evidence indicating an association between schizophrenia and dopaminergic hyperactivity in the brain. *Orthomolecular Psychiatry* **1**, 2–7.
Rehfeld, J.F. (1985): Neuronal cholecystokinin: one or multiple transmitters? *J. Neurochem.* **44**, 1–9.
Reynolds, G.P. (1983): Increased concentrations and lateral asymmetry of amygdala dopamine in schizophrenia. *Nature* **305**, 527–529.
Roberts, G.W. (1981): Neuropeptides in the limbic system: Distribution pathways and possible functions. University of London: PhD Thesis.
Roberts, G.W. & Crow, T.J. (1987): Neuropathology of schizophrenia: A progress report. *Br. Med. Bull.* **43**, 599–615.
Roberts, G.W., Polak, J.M. & Crow, T.J. (1981): The peptidergic circuitry of the amygdaloid complex. In *The amygaloid complex*, ed. Y. Ben-Ari, pp 185–196. Amsterdam: Elsevier/North Holland.
Roberts, G.W., Woodhams, P.L., Polak, J.M. & Crow, T.J. (1982*a*): Distribution of neuropeptides in the limbic system: the amygaloid complex. *Neuroscience* 7, 89–131.
Roberts, G.W., Crow, T.J. & Polak, J.M. (1982*b*): Immunocytochemical localization of neuropeptides in the human hippocampus. *J. Histochem. Cytochem.* **30**, 577.
Roberts, G.W., Ferrier, I.N., Lee, Y., Crow, T.J., Johnstone, E.C., Owens, D.G.C., Barcarese-Hamilton, A.J., McGregor, G., O'Shaughnessy, D., Polack, J.M. & Bloom, S.R. (1983*a*): Peptides, the limbic lobe and schizophrenia. *Brain. Res.* **288**, 199–211.
Roberts, G.W., Allen, Y., Crow, T.J. & Polak, J.M. (1983*b*): Immunocytochemical localization on neuropeptides in the fornix of rat, monkey and man. *Brain Res.* **263**, 151–155.
Roberts, G.W., Crow, T.J., Bloom, S.R. & Polak, J.M. (1983*c*): Immunocytochemical localization of peptide in the human temporal lobe. *J. Pathol.* **139**, 482–483.
Roberts, G.W., Woodhams, P.L., Polak, J.M. & Crow, T.J. (1984*a*): Distribution of neuropeptides in the limbic system of the rat: the hippocampus. *Neuroscience* **11**, 37–77.
Roberts, G.W., Polak, J.M. & Crow, T.J. (1984*b*): Peptide circuitry of the limbic system. In *The psychopharmacology of the limbic system*, eds M.R. Trimble & E. Zarifian, pp 226–243. Oxford: Oxford University Press.
Roberts, G.W., Colter, N., Lofthouse, R., Brown, R., Bogerts, B., Zech, M. & Crow, T.J. (1986*a*): Is there gliosis in the brains of schizophrenics? Proceedings of the IVth World Congress in Biological Psychiatry, 1018–1020. New York: Elsevier.
Roberts, G.W., Colter, N., Lofthouse, R., Bogerts, B., Zech, M. & Crow, T.J. (1986*b*): Gliosis in schizophrenia. *Biol. Psychiatry* **21**, 1043–1050.
Roberts, G.W., Colter, N., Lofthouse, R., Johnstone, E.C. & Crow, T.J. (1987): Is there gliosis in schizophrenia? Investigation of the temporal lobe. *Biol. Psychiatry* **22**, 1459–1468.
Saito, A., Sankaran, H., Goldfine, I.D. & Williams, J.A. (1980): Cholecystokinin receptors in the brain: characterization and distribution. *Science* **208**, 1155–1156.
Sakamoto, N., Takatsuji, K., Shioska, S., Tateishi, K., Hashimura. E., Muira, S., Hamaoka, T. & Tohyama, M. (1984): Cholecystokinin-8-like immunoreactivity in the pre- and post-central gyri of the human cerebral vortex. *Brain. Res.* **307**, 77–83.
Scheibel, A.B. & Kovelman, J.A. (1981): Disorientation of the hippocampal pyramidal cell and its processes in the schizophrenic patient. *Biol. Psychiatry* **16**, 101–102.
Sherwin, I., Peron-Magnan, P., Bancaud, J., Bonis, A. & Talairach, J. (1982): Prevalence of psychosis in epilepsy as a function of the laterality of the epileptogenic lesion. *Arch. Neurol.* **39**, 621–625.
Skirboll, L.R., Grace, A.A., Hommer, D.W., Rehfield, J., Goldstein, M., Hökfelt, T. & Bunney, B.S. (1981): Peptide monamine co-existence: studies of the actions of cholecystokinin-like peptide on the electrical activity of midbrain dopamine neurons. *Neuroscience* **6**, 2111–2124.
Slater, E. (1969): The schizophrenia like illness of epilepsy. In *Current problems in psychiatry*, ed. R.N. Herrington. *Br. J. Psychiatry* Special Publ. No 4 Ashford: Headly.
Somogyi, P., Hodgson, A.J., Smith, A.D., Nunzi, M.G., Gorio, A. & Wu, J.Y. (1984): Different populations of GABAergic neurons in the visual cortex and hippocampus of cat contain somatostatin- or cholecystokinin-immunoreactive material. *J. Neurosci.* **4**, 2590–2603.
Stevens, J.R. (1973): An anatomy of schizophrenia. *Arch. Gen. Psychiatry* **29**, 177–189.
Stevens, J.R. (1982): Neuropathology of schizophrenia. *Arch. Gen. Psychiatry* **39**, 1131–1139.

Totterdell, S. & Smith, A.D. (1986): Cholecystokinin immunoreactive boutons in synaptic contact with hippocampal pyramidal neurons that project to the nucleus accumbens. *Neuroscience* **19**, 181–192.

Van Dijk, A., Richards, J.G., Trzeciak, A., Gillessen, D. & Möhler, H. (1984): Cholecystokinin receptors: biochemical demonstration and autoradiographical localization in rat brain and pancreas using ^{3}H cholecystokinin as radioligand. *J. Neurosci.* **4**, 1021–1033.

Van Hoesen, G.W. (1982): The parahippocampal gyrus. New observations regarding its cortical connections in a monkey. *Trends Neurosci.* **5**, 145–350.

Van Hoesen, G.W., Yeterian, E.H. & Lavizzo-Mourey, R. (1981): Widespread corticostriate projections from temporal cortex of the Rhesus monkey. *J. Comp. Neurol.* **199**, 205–219.

Verbanck, P.M.P., Lotstra, F., Gilles, C., Linkowski, P., Mendlewicz, J. & Vanderhaechen, J.J. (1984): Reduced cholecystokinin immunoreactivity in the cerebro-spinal fluid of patients with psychiatric disorders. *Life Sci.* **34**, 67–72.

Verney, C., Baullac, M., Berger, B., Alvarez, C., Vigny, A. & Helle, K.B. (1985): Morphological evidence for a doperminergic terminal field in the hippocampal formation of young and adult rat. *Neuroscience* **14**, 1039–1052.

Voigt, M.M. & Wang, R.Y. (1984): *In vivo* release of dopamine in the nucleus accumbens of the rat: modulation by cholecystokinin. *Brain Res.* **296**, 189–193.

Wang, R.Y., White, F.J. & Voigt, M.M. (1984): Cholecystokinin, dopamine and schizophrenia. *Trends Pharmacol. Sci.* **5**, 436–438.

Weinberger, D.R., Wagner, R.L. & Wyatt, R.L. (1983): Neuropathological studies of schizophrenia: A selective review. *Schizophrenia Bull.* **9**, 193–212.

Westenbroek, R.E., Westrum, L.E., Hendrickson, A.E. & Wu, J.Y. (1987): Immunocytochemical localisation of cholecystokinin and glutamic acid decarboxylase during normal development in the prepyriform cortex of rats. *Dev. Brain Res.* **34**, 191–206.

Woodhams, P.L., Roberts, G.W., Polak, J.M. & Crow, T.J. (1983): Distribution of neuropeptides in the limbic system of the rat: the bed nucleus of the stria terminals, septum and pre-optic area. *Neuroscience* **8**, 677–703.

Yang, C.R. & Mogenson, G.J. (1984): Electrophysiological responses of neurons in the nucleus accumbens to hippocampal stimulation and the attenuation of the excitatory responses by the mesolimbic dopaminergic system. *Brain Res.* **324**, 69–84.

Zaborszky, L., Alheid, G.F., Beinfeld, M.C., Eiden, L.E., Heimer, L. & Palkovits, M. (1985): Cholecystokinin innervation of the ventral striatum: a morphological and radioimmunological study. *Neuroscience* **14**, 427–453.

Zarbin, M.A., Innis, R.B., Wamsley, J.K., Synder, S.H. & Kuhar, M.J. (1983): Autoradiographic localization of cholecystokinin receptors in rodent brain. *J. Neurosci.* **3**, 877–906.

Chapter 6
Epilepsy and chronic psychosis

Michael R. Trimble

Department of Psychiatry, National Hospital for Nervous Diseases, The National Hospital, Queens Square, London WC1, UK

Summary

The relationship between epilepsy and chronic psychoses is briefly reviewed. This is followed by the description of a clinical study in which 24 patients with chronic psychoses of epilepsy were evaluated using the PSE and their phenomenology compared with 11 non-epileptic schizophrenic patients. It was shown that patients classified as nuclear schizophrenia all had epilepsy derived from the temporal lobes, and that in the majority left sided lesions were present. It is suggested that using epilepsy as a model for the development of psychotic symptoms, the dominant hemisphere and the temporal lobes are important neuroanatomical sites underlying some psychotic phenomena.

Introduction

The historical relationship, and the changing but evolving concepts between psychosis and epilepsy, have been reviewed in detail elsewhere and are only mentioned briefly here (Trimble, 1982*a*, *b*, *c*).The link goes back to ancient times, but was most clearly stated by the French and German authors of the 19th century. A suggested association between the temporal lobes and psychiatric disturbances derives from the report of Bouchet & Cazauveilh (1825) of cases in which epilepsy and insanity were associated, the pathology being noted in the 'cornes d'ammon'. An early British author of importance was Hughlings Jackson, who clearly delineated the forerunner of what became referred to as temporal lobe epilepsy, and introduced the term 'epileptic insanity', suggesting that the epilepsy was the actual cause of the psychiatric disorder.

The early part of this century was dominated by the suggestion of an inverse relationship between epilepsy and schizophrenia, and the supposed introduction of electroconvulsive therapy on account of this for the treatment of psychosis. Nevertheless the idea of an association between the two disorders was still discussed, and more clearly revived by such authors as Gibbs (1951), Hill (1953), and Pond (1957), who noted patients with temporal lobe epilepsy and chronic paranoid hallucinatory states in which the epileptic attacks usually began prior to the onset of the psychosis. An extensive series was reported by Slater & Beard (1963) who, on statistical grounds, suggested that patients with epilepsy developed a schizophrenia-like illness with increased frequency, especially noting in this group an absence of abnormal premorbid personality traits or family history of psychiatric disturbance that might suggest a predisposition to schizophrenia, and noted that while catatonic phenomena seemed rare, affective responses were warm and preserved. They also commented that the epilepsy tended to precede the onset of the psychosis, and re-emphasized what had been stated earlier by Glaus (1931), namely that in some cases the psychotic symptoms appeared as the fit frequency declined.

A further important consideration was introduced by Flor-Henry in 1969. He suggested that left sided temporal lobe lesions in particular were associated with a schizophreniform presentation of the psychosis, and a right sided abnormality with a manic-depressive picture.

A criticism of much of the work in this area however is that the term 'psychosis' has been used without definition by some of the authors and little attempt has been made to specify the precise phenomenology of the patients who are examined (Trimble, 1982*b*). It is noteworthy that the Anglo-Saxon authors tend to use Schneiderian concepts for the diagnosis of a schizophreniform illness, in particular relying on the presence of first rank symptomatology. In psychiatry over the past 20 years more definitive methods have been adopted for quantification of psychopathology, which mainly use rating scales to increase reliability of clinical observation. A more recent development in this field has been the use of structured or standardized interviews, in which the manner in which the symptoms are elicited, as well as the way in which they are recorded, is laid down. Questions are asked in a specific order, and ratings of patients' answers are made based on standardized definitions. The Wing Present State Examination (PSE) (Wing *et al.*, 1974) is used more commonly in Great Britain. The interview technique is based on the examination of the patient, and the clinician decides whether a particular symptom is present or not after all the questions laid down, and appropriate probes, have been asked. The questions relate to the patient's experiences during the month prior to the interview, and this of necessity excludes most of the psychiatric history, which becomes the subject of a separate enquiry.

The results from the PSE schedule are analysed by a computer program known as the Catego, in which the original items pass through a progressive series of condensations, and decisions about the actual diagnosis are postponed until the final stage. The item content is thus reduced to a number of 'symptoms', which are then further refined to 38 basic 'syndromes'. Mean syndrome profiles can be derived from the PSEs to compare groups, or to monitor change with time. The final output of the program is an allocation of 1–50 subclasses, which are collapsed into broader classes.

This technique has been used by us to try to clarify in detail the phenomenology of the psychoses associated with epilepsy (Perez & Trimble, 1980).

PSE evaluation of the chronic psychoses of epilepsy

Twenty-four patients, consecutively referred to the National Hospitals and suffering from unequivocal epilepsy and active psychosis which had continued for more than a month and in whom consciousness was clear, were examined using the PSE. The results were compared with a group of 11 schizophrenic patients who were previously assessed by two psychiatrists, both of whom agreed the diagnosis was schizophrenia. In the analysis of the results Fisher's Exact Probability Test was used.

Of the 24 patients, 12 received a class diagnosis of schizophrenic psychosis, and of these, analysis of the subclass revealed 11 who were classified as nuclear schizophrenia, 10 who were classified as having some kind of affective disturbance, and one as having a paranoid psychosis. In contrast to this group, nine of the patients with schizophrenia were classified as nuclear schizophrenia, one as paranoid psychosis, and one as psychotic depression (Table 1).

Table 1. *Catego subclasses and classes — diagnostic comparison between epileptic psychotic and schizophrenic patients.*

Subclass diagnoses	*Epileptics (n = 24)*	*Schizo-phrenics (n = 11)*	*Class diagnoses*	*Epileptics (n = 24)*	*Schizo-phrenics (n = 11)*
Nuclear schizophrenia	11	9	Schizophrenic psychosis	12	9
Schizophrenia without first rank symptoms	1	—	Manic psychosis	3	—
Residual schizophrenia mania	1	—	Depressive psychosis	3	1
Mania	3	—	Paranoid psychosis/ retarded depression	3	—
Psychotic depression	3	1	Paranoid psychosis	2	1
Paranoid psychosis/ retarded depression	3	—	Borderline psychosis	1	—
Paranoid psychosis/ affective psychosis	1	—			
Paranoid psychosis	1	1			
Total	24	11	Total	24	11

In a further analysis, the type of psychosis present in those patients classified clinically as having complex-partial seizures of probable temporal lobe origin was compared with those having generalized epilepsy. As can be seen from Table 2 classification of nuclear schizophrenia was exclusively associated with the temporal lobe group, the other diagnostic categories being present in both groups. One patient who had a diagnosis of schizophrenia without first-rank symptoms came from the generalized group. A more comprehensive account of these data is given in Perez & Trimble (1980).

Figure 1 shows the syndrome profiles of those patients with left sided or predominantly left sided lesions, compared with those who have right sided lesions. In this figure the various syndromes are referred to using the standardized notation of the Catego system. Patients with the left sided lesions show significantly more ideas of reference and nuclear syndrome than the right sided patients. This latter result may be all the more significant in that the patients who did rate as nuclear syndrome who had right sided lesions were left handed, and their dominance cannot therefore be accurately stated. Although not significant, it is important to note the increased occurrence of delusions of persecution,

Table 2. *Catego subclasses and classes — diagnostic comparison between psychotic patients with temporal lobe (TLE) and with generalized (GEN) epilepsy.*

	TLE (n = 17)	*GEN (n = 7)*
Nuclear schizophrenia	11	—
Schizophrenia without first rank symptoms	—	1
Residual schizophrenia — mania	—	1
Manic psychosis	1	2
Psychotic depression	1	2
Paranoid psychosis/retarded depression	3	—
Paranoid psychosis/affective psychosis	1	—
Paranoid psychosis	1	1

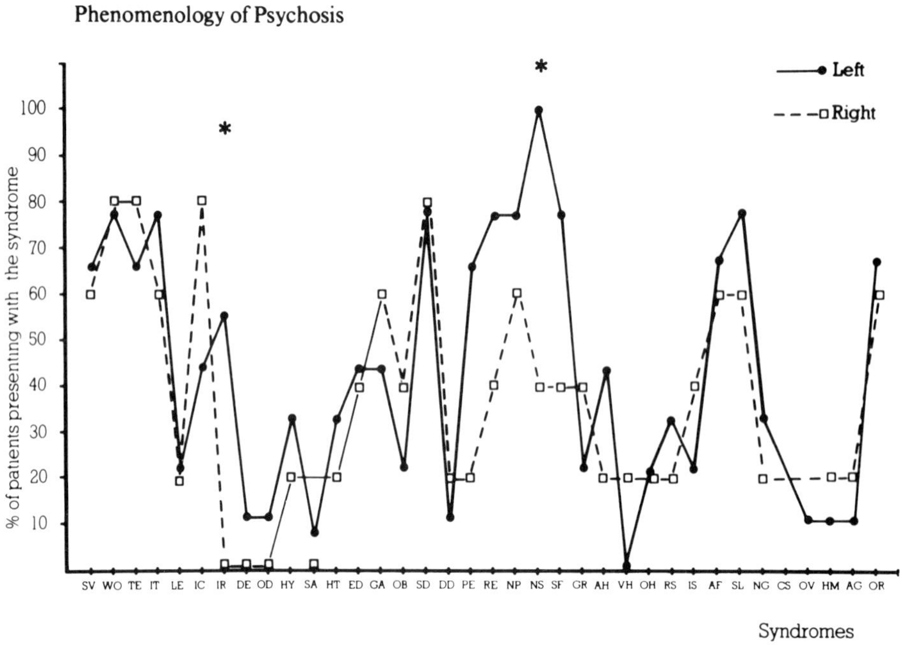

Fig. 1. *PSE profiles of patients with left and right temporal lobe focus.* Significant differences noted for IR (ideas of reference) and NS (nuclear schizophrenia).

delusions of reference, fantastic delusions, and auditory hallucinations in the left temporal lobe patients and their absence of visual hallucinations.

Discussion

These data lend support to the suggestions that the psychotic states associated with complex-partial seizures of temporal lobe origin vary in relationship to the laterality of the focus. It is noteworthy that the authors who have demonstrated a laterality effect have tended to be British, and their diagnostic criteria for the assessment of the schizophreniform psychosis has been based on Schneiderian principles. Several authors have failed to detect such a relationship (eg Kristensen & Sindrup, 1978; Jensen & Larsen, 1979), although they also fail to use precise diagnostic criteria as outlined above.

There is a growing literature on laterality in psychiatric patients which points in a similar direction to our studies, namely to abnormalities of left hemisphere function in association with schizophrenia (eg Gruzelier, 1981). Clearly further work needs to be carried out in this area, in particular in patients with a schizophrenia-like illness in association with temporal lobe epilepsy. Attempts to examine brain function and structure in such patients in detail, with modern techniques, have been carried out, and largely confirm the laterality findings discussed in this paper. However, the well documented cases of psychoses in epilepsy that develop after temporal lobectomy (eg Jensen & Larsen, 1979: Stevens, 1980; Sherwin, 1982) and the similarity of neuropathological abnormalities recently described in patients with schizophrenia and schizophreniform psychosis of epilepsy, which include not only focal pathology in the temporal lobes but also gliosis in periventricular, periaqueductal, mid-brain tegmentum and basal forebrain areas (Stevens, 1982), suggest that we must look beyond the temporal lobe for our fuller understanding of this relationship.

References

Bouchet, M. & Cazauveilh, M. (1825): De l'épilepsie considérée dans ses rapports avec l'aliénation mentale. Recherche sure la nature et le siège de ces deux maladies. *Arch. Gen. Med.* **9**, 510–542.
Flor-Henry, P. (1969): Psychosis and temporal lobe epilepsy. *Epilepsia* **10**, 363–395.
Gibbs, F. A. (1951): Ictal and non-ictal psychiatric disorders in temporal lobe epilepsy. *J. Nerv. Ment. Dis.* **113**, 522–528.
Glaus, A. (1931): Ueber Combinationen von Schizophrenic und Epilepsie. *Z. Diegesante Neurol. Psychiatr.* **135**, 450–500.
Gruzelier, J. H. (1981): Cerebral laterality and psychopathology — fact and fiction. *Psychol. Med.* **11**, 219–227.
Hill, D. (1953): Psychiatric disorders of epilepsy. *The Medical Press* **229**, 473–475.
Jensen, K. & Larsen, J. K. (1979): Mental aspects of temporal lobe epilepsy. *J. Neurol. Neurosurg. Psychiatry* **42**, 256–265.
Kristensen, O. & Sindrup, E. H. (1978): Psychomotor epilepsy and psychosis. *Acta Neurol. Scand.* **57**, 361–370.
Perez, M.M. & Trimble, M.R. (1980): Epileptic psychosis. A psychopathological comparison with process schizophrenia. *Br. J. Psychiatry* **137**, 245–249.
Pond, D. (1957): Psychiatric aspects of epilepsy. *J. Indian Med. Prof.* **3**, 1441–1451.
Sherwin, I. (1982): The effect of the location of an epileptogenic lesion on the occurrence of psychosis in epilepsy. In *Temporal lobe epilepsy, mania and schizophrenia and the limbic system,* eds W. Koella, M.R. Trimble, pp. 81–97. Basel: Karger.
Slater, E. & Beard, A.W. (1963): The schizophrenia-like psychoses of epilepsy. *Br. J. Psychiatry* **109**, 95–150.
Stevens, J.R. (1980): Psychoses in epilepsy and epilepsy in psychiatric patients: A re-examination. *Epilepsia* **21**, 184.
Stevens,. J. R. (1982): Risk factors for psychopathology in individuals with epilepsy. In *Temporal lobe epilepsy, mania and schizophrenia, and the limbic system,* eds W. Koella & M.R. Trimble, pp. 56–80. Basel: Karger.
Trimble, M.R. (1982*a*): The phenomenology of epileptic psychosis: a historical introduction to changing concepts. In *Temporal lobe epilepsy, mania and schizophrenia, and the limbic system,* eds W. Koella & M.R. Trimble, pp. 1–11, Basel: Karger.
Trimble M.R. (1982*b*): The interictal psychoses of epilepsy. In *Psychiatric aspects of neurologic disease,* 2nd edn, ed. F. Benson & D. Blummer, pp. 75–92. New York: Grune and Stratton.
Trimble, M. R. (1982*c*): Psychosis and epilepsy. In *A textbook of epilepsy,* 2nd edn, eds J. Laidlaw, & A. Richens, pp. 393–405. Edinburgh: Churchill Livingstone.
Wing, J.K., Cooper, J.E. & Sartorius, N. (1974): *The description and classification of psychiatric symptoms.* London: Cambridge University Press.

Chapter 7
Developmental precursors of adult disorder

Peter H. Venables

Department of Psychology, University of York, York YO1 5DD, UK

Summary

Research on psychiatric disorders is no longer confined to study of the patient. Important insights are gained by work on the 'patient-to-be', on the recovered patient, and on the normal person possessing some of the characteristics of the patient. The advantages of these approaches lie in the potential decrease in the blurring of investigation of the fundamental mechanisms of the disorder by 'patienthood' and particularly by medication. This chapter describes some of the work that has been undertaken with the 'high-risk' model where those who have an elevated risk for developing disorders are followed up through the developmental years and after.

Introduction

Former emphasis on research on psychiatric disorders concentrated on adult subjects, with little attention being paid to the development of the condition which they manifest. The impetus for change resulted from the publication in 1968 of a paper by Mednick & McNeil which suggested (in the context of schizophrenia) that it was important to examine the fundamental mechanisms underlying a disorder and that it was necessary to recognize that the characteristics of the adult patient were an amalgam of fundamental aetiological factors and a set of reactions to those factors. What eventually brought the patient or disordered person into contact with the psychiatric or other services was often not the fundamental disorder *per se* but the secondary features seen by the subject's contacts to distinguish his behaviour from that of normal persons. The patient as investigated by the researcher in the institution often had characteristics which were the result of additional factors such as institutionalization or medication. Going back further, it was Meehl's seminal article in 1962 on the development of schizophrenia which provided the scientific climate required for the change of emphasis. In this he put forward the concept of schizotaxia as the fundamental disorder developing into schizotypy or schizophrenia, depending on the benign or malign environment to which the subject was exposed.

In consequence, with this background research has broadened so that it now takes place in five areas: on (1) adult patients in the morbid state; (2) adult patients in remission; (3) children at risk for psychiatric breakdown; (4) normal relatives of patients; and (5) normal subjects with characteristics of patients but in an attenuated form.

Thus, in this latter group we have research on schizotype, whereas if instead of patients we read delinquents or criminals, we have research on refractory children or those people in the community who exhibit some form of antisocial behaviour which has not yet brought them into contact with the law. One of the outcomes of this approach and where psychophysiological work in particular is of importance is the development of work which has as its aim the identification of markers. Markers may conveniently be grouped into three categories as suggested by Iacono in 1985:
(1) Episode or state markers which are present only in the first class of subjects above, ie when there is a state of symptom exacerbation;
(2) Vulnerability markers which identify those prone to the disorder; and
(3) Genetic markers, which are vulnerability markers for which there is evidence that they constitute heritable traits. Such markers would, for instance, be expected to be evident in the normal relatives of those who are disordered. It should, perhaps, be noted that this use of the term 'genetic marker' is looser than those of some geneticists where the implication of the usage of the term would be that a gene locus has been identified. An example of a genetic marker would be that of Meehl's indices of schizotaxia in that he describes schizotaxia as 'all that can be properly spoken of as inherited'. In the same way it may be reasonable to view measures of schizotypy as vulnerability markers.

Obviously, behind the idea of the use of childhood markers for adult disorders is the general notion of a stress-diathesis approach. With no diathesis there would be nothing to look for as the characteristic of subjects who may become disordered. However, in emphasizing the use of markers it is important not to forget the 'stress' part of the diathesis equation and to recognize that the term stress is perhaps in this context too limited a concept. For example it is necessary to include conditions from conception onwards which may not be considered as stress factors in particular, in so far as they do not elicit a stress reponse in the Selye (1950) sense but rather are events in the development of the child which may or may not be disadvantageous. An example would be the role of perinatal birth complications in the development of schizophrenia. Parnas *et al.* (1982), analysing data from the 1962 Copenhagen High Risk Study, have shown that subjects from the high risk group diagnosed as borderline schizophrenics have a lower than normal level of perinatal birth complications in comparison with those later diagnosed as schizophrenic, who have a higher than normal level of birth complications. Thus, perinatal birth complications themselves do not lead to schizophrenia in those who are not genetically predisposed to the disorder. However, there is a tendency for those who have what Meehl would call a schizotaxic predisposition to display schizotypic characteristics if not exposed to a malign interuterine environment, while those exposed to a malign environment exhibit schizophrenia.

As suggested earlier the main impetus for change in work on disorder has been that of high risk studies. The foundation for these studies was the recognition in 1957 by Pearson & Kley that it is essential to take into account the base rate of disorders to enable researchers to obtain populations for study which are likely to make research economically feasible. Thus a study on schizophrenia which starts from a childhood sample from the general population and follows that sample for, say, 20 years, will only find that one per cent of the original population develop schizophrenia. It has therefore become essential to obtain populations for study which are likely to have a higher expectation of developing a disorder than the general population. The majority of studies which are known as high risk studies, but which are possibly better designated as elevated risk studies, are those which adopt the use of familial factors to increase risk. The majority of these have used children of schizophrenic parents as the population to study. In these children the lifetime morbid risk may be seen to be elevated from about one per cent in the general population to some 15% in children with one schizophrenic parent or perhaps

45% in children with two schizophrenic parents. There are, however, some anomalies in this procedure in that looking at the statistics the other way round, only 10% of adult schizophrenics have a schizophrenic parent, and thus, by taking only children of schizophrenic parents as a risk population, there is a chance of introducing bias in studying a disorder like schizophrenia with a low fertility rate. Those schizophrenics who do not have children may possess characteristics which are not those of 'negative symptom schizophrenics' (Andreason & Olson, 1982) and may, according to some authors, eg Kety 1980, be likely to form the strictly defined population of Kraepelian schizophrenics. Other principles of selection have been used to obtain high risk populations. For example, bearing in mind the excess of schizophrenics in Social Class V, which contains a high proportion of unskilled workers, Asarnow *et al.* (1983) used as their experimental population unemployed workers drawn from a Labour Exchange. Another technique adopted by Venables (1978) was to select on the basis of psychophysiological responses, and it is this study, carried out in Mauritius, which will form the major content of the remainder of this chapter.

Study of developmental precursors in Mauritius

The study was started in 1972 by Mednick, Schulsinger and Venables with the screening of the total population of three-year-olds in two towns in Mauritius chosen to be representative of the racial distribution of the whole island. Thus some 50% were of Hindi or Tamil origin, 20% of Moslem origin and 26%, known in the island as the 'general' or Creole population, were those whose background was of African origin. The remainder of the population is made up of Chinese and English ancestry. Over a period from August 1972 to July 1973, psychophysiological data comprising skin conductance and heart rate measurements were obtained from 1795 subjects and the electrodermal data were used for the selection of 200 children who were to form a more intensively studied population. Of these, 99 were designated as hyper-responders because they gave skin conductance responses which were of high amplitude, short latency and fast recovery, a pattern of responses which had been shown to be characteristic of those in the Danish High Risk Study who later succumbed to schizophrenia. Thirty-seven were electrodermal non-responders, a characteristic shown by some 40–50% of the adult schizophrenic population in hospital. Fifty-three were drawn from the centre of the electrodermal distribution, being neither hyper- nor hypo-responders, and a small sub-sample of eleven subjects had the characteristic of long recovery times of the electrodermal response, which had been shown to be especially common in those with criminal or delinquent tendencies (eg Loeb & Mednick, 1977).

The 200 children were divided into four groups of 50, two of which were placed in two specially instituted nursery schools and the other two groups, which were matched to them, went through the normal process of four-year-olds in the Mauritian population, some not going to school until the age of six when primary schooling started, and some going to what, in this country, might be called 'Dame' schools.

This study was initiated at the behest of the World Health Organization which, in 1968, published a special report urging the development of more high risk studies which, for the purposes of generalization, might be carried out in non-Western countries. So that more knowledge of the development of disorders might be gained, these studies were to be started at an earlier age than those which had, at that time, been undertaken, and hence it was proposed that they should start at nursery school level. Mauritius was chosen as a community with a reasonable background of health services, which might enable follow-up to be readily effected, and it was also a community which, because of its geographical isolation, might be expected to remain available for the length of the study. Nevertheless, it was criticized by Garmezy (1974) because of the procedures which were used. Garmezy stated, 'the critical question that remains, however, is the appropriateness of using deviant psychophysiological functioning in children as a criterion of risk. Issues related to the legitimacy of using such a criterion on the basis of existant data, the stability of such measures over time when obtained from preschoolers, and the markedly different social and psychophysiological environment of Mauritius are only several of the factors that raise questions about the direction of the projected study.'

The research which has been conducted since has been largely concerned with attempting to show that the original selection procedure at 3 years of age was valid and that the environment in Mauritius was not so exotic that it might invalidate the work being carried out. In relation to this last point, a subsidiary cross-sectional study was carried out on a population of 640 subjects, drawn from all the racial groups at ages of 5, 10, 15, 20 and 25 years, the expected ages to be covered by the duration of the longitudinal study, where data were collected during the cool, dry and hot, wet seasons of the year. The data gathered were heart rate and skin conductance, together with measures of ambient temperature, humidity and pressure collected at the same time. Analyses showed the seasonal or racial effects were minimal and that variance due to sex and age were what might be expected in a study carried out in Western society. The variance due to climatic variables was minimal and, in fact, only evident in the 20- and 25-year-olds. There is, thus, no reason to expect that, from the point of view of the area in which the study is carried out, it cannot be generalized to a wider population.

The other factor which was raised by Garmezy (1974) is the stability of the psychophysiological function. This raises a particular point of issue. It is possible that a measure of psychophysiological function taken at the age of 3 years may be a good predictor of later behaviour while not necessarily being a good predictor of a later measure of the same psychophysiological function. Thus, from the point of view of test-retest reliability, the measure may be poor but from the point of view of its validity as a predictor, it may be satisfactory. The research which will be described has been able to show that the original selection procedure at age 3 years has had some validity, in that the psychophysiological selection predicted different kinds of behaviour in its group members. This has taken place, however, in a background where test-retest reliabilities of the measures used have been of the order of 0.3 or less.

Validation of psychophysiological selection procedures

The first study, which attempted to show that the psychophysiological selection procedures at the age of 3 years have been effective in producing subject samples in which behaviour was different, took place when the children were aged 6 years, just prior to their entry into primary school. A special observation area was created in a house which was different from those used by the two nursery schools. Fresh observers were trained who did not know the children and children were brought in in groups of four, dressed in identical uniform, so that they could not be distinguished on the basis of dress (children in nursery schools had been provided with school uniform). They played for a time in a sandpit before being taken into the observation area in which toys were available for them to play with, none of which had previously been used in the nursery schools. The children's behaviour was timed in three categories while they were in this play situation. The three categories were 'Constructive Play', in which each child took a toy and went off and played with it on his own; 'Watching', in which they stood and watched the other children but did not actively participate themselves; and 'Social Interaction', in which they spent time going round talking to other children or to an adult.

The most interesting data were derived from the measures of 'Constructive Play' and 'Watching'. The control children, ie those whose psychophysiological indices were drawn from the centre of the electrodermal distribution, spent more time in constructive play if they had previously been in a nursery school than if they had not. In the two 'high risk' groups, there was no significant effect of having been or not having been in nursery school. However, in the children rated as hyper-responders, the time spent in constructive play was higher than that of the control children who had not been in nursery school. The biggest differences from normal in watching behaviour occurred in the children classed as electrodermal non-responders at the age of 3 years. They spent a large amount of time watching, whether or not they had been in nursery school, which was not the case with the hyper-responders or those control children who had been in nursery school. However, the control children who had not been in nursery school spent the same amount of time watching as the non-responders. Thus, although it could not be said that the behaviours shown by the children were necessarily related to later development of schizophrenia, nevertheless it did show that the psychophysiological selection 3 years earlier had produced groups whose social behaviour was different. This material is described more fully in Venables *et al.* (1978).

At age 9 the children were rated by their teachers on the Rutter (1967) Children's Behaviour Questionnaire. The factor analysis of the data derived from this questionnaire resulted in two clear factors, which are similar to many shown in the analysis of material of this type. The first factor was labelled 'Hyper-activity/aggression', with weighting on such items as fighting, irritability, restlessness, disobedience, bullying; the second factor was labelled 'Worried/fearfulness', with weighting on items such as being miserable, fearful, worried, solitary. Separate factor analyses were conducted on subjects divided by sex or by racial group and in no instance did the resulting factor structure differ from that which resulted from the analysis of the total data. This material is described in Venables *et al.*. (1983). Measures of performance and verbal IQ were also available on these children. This material enabled a rather direct test to be made on whether a pattern of findings described by Roff & Knight (1980) could be replicated. These workers showed that measures of aggression and IQ gathered at age 11 were able to predict schizophrenic outcome at age 40. Those subjects who as children had both low IQ and low levels of aggressiveness were significantly more likely to show an unfavourable schizophrenic outcome than other groups.

Factor scores on the aggression/hyperactivity factor were first examined for the three 'risk groups', which had been selected psychophysiologically 6 years before at age 3 years. In the case of the control group, aggression factor scores were positive, but in both the electrodermal hyper-responders and the non-responders the aggression factor scores were negative. No significant difference was shown in the groups on performance IQ. However, in the case of verbal IQ, the male non-responders were different from all the other groups in showing a negative verbal factor score. Thus, if we combine the material showing that male electrodermal non-responders have both low aggression and low verbal scores, these data are in line with those of Roff & Knight, which were derived entirely from male subjects. It is also worth noting that Offord (1974) showed that school IQ was related to adult schizophrenic status only in males where the pre-schizophrenics in school showed a significantly lower IQ than control groups which consisted of their own male or female sibling or unrelated controls. It is also worthwhile noticing that the factor labelled in the Mauritius Study as Worried/fearfulness did not relate to psychophysiological status. This again is in line with data from Roff & Knight, who showed no relation of a similar measure taken while in school to later schizophrenic outcome.

At age 11, a considerable amount of psychophysiological data were gathered on the children, including measures of smooth pursuit eye movement. Referring to the discussion on genetic markers earlier in this chapter, smooth pursuit eye movement is, perhaps, one of the few psychophysiological measures which may be considered as having the status of a genetic marker, and thus if the original selection procedure at 3 years did not result in differences in smooth pursuit eye movement at age 10/12, this would cast considerable doubts on the validity of that procedure. An initial analysis showed that there was no difference in three measures of smooth pursuit eye movement between the three psychophysiological risk groups. These measures were (1) a quantitative rating, (2) a measure of velocity arrests derived by counting the number of times that eye movement showed zero velocity in relation to a sinusoidally moving target, and (3) a measure of signal-to-noise ratio derived by the spectral analysis of the eye movement response: if the subject was smoothly tracking the target, his eye movements would match the target movement exactly and he would exhibit a high signal value; if the subject track deviated from the input track this was considered as noise and an increase in noise would therefore lower the signal-to-noise ratio. The finding that there was no difference between the risk groups of any of these three measures was an initial set-back. However, it was thought that the factor of IQ might again be of importance as an intervening variable in the relationship between smooth pursuit eye movement and group membership. The first reason for this has already been discussed in relation to the data derived at age 9 years. The second reason, however, is that Kimmel & Deboskey had in 1978 published a paper in which they showed that electrodermal activity in gifted children had the same sort of pattern shown by the hyper-responsive children in the present study, whereas the electrodermal activity of average IQ children was similar to that of the control group in the present study.

A second analysis of the data taking IQ into account showed that the hyper-responsive risk group, who were of high IQ, showed normal eye tracking. However, those who were of low IQ exhibited abnormal eye tracking scores. In the electrodermally selected control group, eye tracking was normal in both high and low IQ sub-groups. Thus, IQ on its own was not related to eye tracking behaviour. It would, therefore, appear that the original selection of electrodermally hyper-responsive children at age 3 years produced a group which contained two classes of subject: firstly, those who might be likely later to develop schizophrenia, and secondly those who might be considered as particularly gifted.

If we return to the data on children at age 6 years which were previously presented, it was noted that the hyper-responsive group displayed more constructive play than the control group, who had not been to nursery school. This may be due to the presence of the gifted children amongst the hyper-responders, who on average elevated the score of constructive play in this group. The issue of the role of IQ is presented nicely in a hypothesis by Lehmann (1966) who states, 'non-paranoid schizophrenic patients have a primary, possibly constitutional, susceptibility ... to be subject to the impact of a higher number of discrete sensory stimuli per time unit than other individuals. If a person can cope with a super-normal influx of stimuli then he might become creative.' As Dellas & Gaier (1970) say, 'creative individuals deploy their attention more widely and tend not to screen out the irrelevant'. On the other hand, Lehmann says, 'if the patient's central processing apparatus does not match in performance the extraordinary sensitivity of his input apparatus, then his integration breaks down and he may become psychotic'. If then, we translate a 'good central processing apparatus' as a high intellectual capacity, high IQ may be seen as protective against one characteristic of the pre-schizophrenic, ie that he has a 'broadened' range of intelligence and attention.

Conclusion

The value of the data collected in Mauritius is that they may be used for examination of relationships other than those concerned particularly with the development of schizophrenia, and in particular they have been used to look at possible relations between psychophysiological data and the development of antisocial behaviour. Data which suggested that the long recovery of the skin conductance response might be related to later delinquent behaviour were described earlier. One attempt to look at this more closely in the present data was made by Clark (1982). She looked at the relationship between recorded fighting at 9 years of age reported by teachers and skin conductance half-recovery time at 3 years and showed that in male subjects there was a significant difference between those who were reported as fighting and those who were not, with longer recovery in the former group. This was not the case in female subjects. A further study used skin conductance data collected at 10–12 years of age and related this to measures taken from the Revised Behaviour Checklist (Quay & Peterson, 1987). The measure used was that of conduct disorder, which as part of the scale reports behaviour similar to that derived from the aggression hyper-activity factor in the Rutter (1967) scale. In this instance it was shown that those with high levels of conduct disorder, whether male or female, showed lower levels of skin conductance than those rated as having low levels of conduct disorder. This finding is a direct replication of that by Borkovec (1970).

Thus, it would appear that the use of psychophysiological variables as methods of screening populations and selecting those who may be at biological risk for the later development of disorders is at least a possibility. If what is done is screening on the basis of diathesis, then perhaps it is the function of society to make sure that the environment to which these biologically defined 'risk' subjects are exposed is adequately benign.

References

Andreason, N.C. & Olsen, S. (1982): Negative v positive schizophrenia. *Arch. Gen. Psychiatry* **39**, 789–794.

Asarnow, R.F., Nuechterlein, K.H. & Marder, S.R. (1983): Span of apprehension performance, neurophysiological functioning, and indices of psychosis proneness. *J. Nerv. Ment. Dis.* **171**, 667–669.

Borkovec, T.D. (1970): Autonomic reactivity to sensory stimulation in psychopathic, neurotic and normal juvenile delinquents. *J. Consult. Clin. Psychol.* **35**, 217–222.

Clark, F.A. (1982): Relationship of electrodermal activity in 3-year-olds to their level of aggression at age 9: a study of a physiologic substrate of temperament. PhD dissertation: University of Southern California, Los Angeles, California.

Dellas, M. & Gaier, E.L. (1970): Identification of creativity: The individual. *Psychol. Bull.* **73**, 55–73.

Garmezy, N. (1974): Children at risk: The search for the antecedents of schizophrenia. Part 11: Ongoing research programs, issues and intervention. *Schizophrenia Bull.* **9**, 55–125.

Iacono, W.G. (1985): Psychophysiological markers of psychopathology: A review. *Can. Psychol.* **26**, 96–112.

Kety, S.S. (1980): The syndrome of schizophrenia: unresolved questions and opportunities for research. *Br. J. Psychiatry* **136**, 421–436.

Kimmel, H.D. & Deboskey, D. (1978): Habituation and conditioning of the orienting reflex in intellectually gifted and average children. *Physiol. Psychol.* **6**, 377–380.

Lehmann, H. (1966): Pharmacotherapy of schizophrenia. In *Psychopathology of schizophrenia*, eds P. Hoch & J. Zubin, New York: Grune & Stratton.

Loeb, J. & Mednick, S.A. (1977): A prospective study of predictors of criminality: electrodermal response patterns. In *Biological bases of criminal behaviour*, eds S.A. Mednick & K.O. Christiansen, pp. 245–254. New York: Gardner Press.

Mednick, S.A. & McNeil, T.F. (1968): Current methodology in research on the aetiology of schizophrenia. Serious difficulties which suggest the use of the high-risk group method. *Psychol. Bull.* 70, 681–693.
Meehl, P.E. (1962): Schizotaxia, schizotypy and schizophrenia. *Am. Psychol.* **17**, 827–838.
Offord, D.R. (1974): School performance of adult schizophrenics, their siblings and age mates. *Br. J. Psychiatry* **125**, 12–19.
Parnas, J., Schulsinger, F., Teasdale, T.W., Schulsinger, H., Feldman, P.M. & Mednick, S.A. (1982): Perinatal complications and clinical outcome within the schizophrenic spectrum. *Br. J. Psychiatry* **140**, 416–420.
Pearson, J.S. & Kley, I.B. (1957): On the application of genetic expectancies as age-specific base rates in the study of human behaviour disorders. *Psychol. Bull.* **54**, 406–420.
Quay, H.C. & Peterson, D.R. (1987): Manual for the revised behaviour problem checklist.
Roff, J.D. & Knight, R. (1980): Pre-schizophrenics: Low IQ and aggressive symptoms as predictors of adult outcome and marital status. *J. Nerv. Ment. Dis.* **168**, 129–132.
Rutter, M. (1967): A children's behaviour questionnaire for completion by teachers. *J. Child Psychol. Psychiatry* **8**, 1–11.
Selye, H. (1950). *Stress.* Montreal: Acta.
Venables, P.H. (1978): Psychophysiology and psychometrics. *Psychophysiology* **15**, 302–315.
Venables, P.H., Menick, S.A., Schulsinger, F., Raman, A.C. & Bell, B. (1978): Screening for risk of mental illness. In *Cognitive defects in the development of mental illness,* ed. G. Serban. New York: Brunner Mazel.
Venables, P.H., Fletcher, R.P., Dalais, J.C., Mitchell, D.A. & Schulsinger, F. (1983): Factor structure of the Rutter Children's behaviour questionnaire in a primary school population in a developing country. *J. Child Psychol. Psychiatry* **24**, 313–222.
World Health Organisation (1968): Neurophysiological and behavioural research in psychiatry. *WHO Technical Report Series No. 381.* Geneva: WHO.

Chapter 8

Prefrontal and subcortical dysfunction in schizophrenia

Peter F. Liddle

Charing Cross and Westminster Medical School, Charing Cross Hospital, London W6 8RF, UK

Summary

Examination of the relationships between persistent schizophrenic symptoms demonstrates that these symptoms fall into three distinguishable groups: the Psychomotor Poverty syndrome (poverty of speech and flatness of affect); the Disorganization syndrome (disorders of the form of thought and inappropriate affect); and the Reality Distortion syndrome (various delusions and hallucinations). The Psychomotor Poverty syndrome and the Disorganization syndrome resemble two distinguishable syndromes seen in patients with damage to their frontal lobes. Anatomical studies reveal two networks of neurones which connect frontal cortex with subcortical nuclei: one network connects dorsal prefrontal cortex with the dorsal striatum, while the other connects orbital prefrontal cortex with the ventral striatum. We propose that schizophrenic patients tend to have persistent underactivity of the prefrontal cortex. Underactivity of the dorsal prefrontal cortex would result in Psychomotor Poverty symptoms, while underactivity of the orbital cortex would result in Disorganization symptoms. By virtue of the links between frontal cortex and subcortical nuclei, prefrontal hypofunction might predispose to overactivity of dopamine in subcortical nuclei, and consequently to symptoms of the Reality Distortion syndrome.

Introduction

Many studies provide evidence that the function of the brain is disturbed in schizophrenia, but this abundant evidence had not yet revealed a specific brain dysfunction characteristic of the illness. Two clinical observations provide starting points for the attempt to delineate this brain dysfunction. First, there is the observation made by Kraepelin (1919), and by many clinicians subsequently, that the disorganized or impoverished mental life of patients with persistent schizophrenia closely resembles the inappropriate or apathetic behaviour of patients with frontal lesions. Secondly, the hallucinations and delusions characteristic of acute schizophrenic episodes respond to treatment with neuroleptic drugs which block dopamine receptors, suggesting that the overactivity of dopaminergic neurones plays a part in the pathogenesis of at least some of the symptoms of schizophrenia.

These two clinical observations appear to point in different directions: on the one hand the similarities between some manifestations of schizophrenia and the effects of frontal lobe lesions direct our attention to the frontal lobes, while on the other hand the efficacy of neuroleptic medication has focused attention on putative overactivity in the mesolimbic dopaminergic system. In this chapter, I intend to examine a hypothesis which unites the apparently disparate strands of evidence implicating the frontal lobes and the mesolimbic dopamine system. This hypothesis is based on contributions from many researchers, including Ingvar & Franzen (1974), Pycock *et al.* (1980) and Weinberger *et al.* (1986)

Anatomy of the prefrontal cortex and relevant subcortical nuclei

The cortex of the anterior part of the frontal lobes is called the prefrontal cortex (Fig. 1). It can be defined as that part of the frontal cortex which receives afferent fibres from the dorsomedial nucleus of the thalamus, and its anatomy and connections have been described in detail by Fuster (1980). Three features are of special relevance to the hypothesis we shall be considering. First, the prefrontal cortex has reciprocal connections with many parts of the limbic system, including the hippocampus, amygdala and septal area. These connections provide a potential route for prefrontal regulation of limbic activity. Secondly, the prefrontal cortex is not homogeneous, but can be subdivided into regions which differ in their connections and probably differ also in their function. In

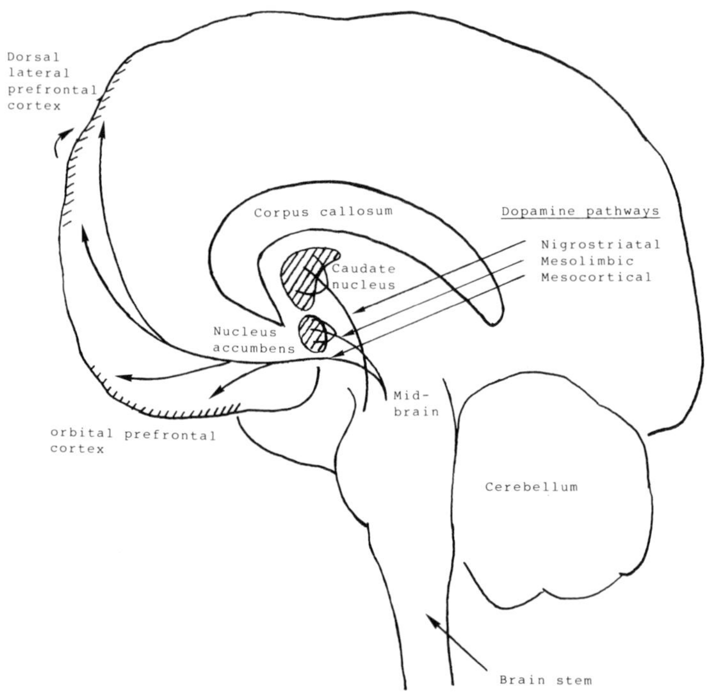

Fig. 1. *Diagrammatic representation of the nigrostriatal, mesolimbic and mesocortical dopamine pathways in the human brain.* It should be noted that the mesolimbic system sends fibres not only to the nucleus accumbens, but also to other parts of the limbic system including the amygdala.

particular, the distinction between the dorsolateral prefrontal cortex and the orbital prefrontal cortex is important for our hypothesis. The dorsolateral prefrontal cortex has its main connections with the lateral thalamus, anterodorsal caudate, hippocampus and neocortex. The orbital prefrontal cortex has its main connections with the medial thalamus, hypothalamus, ventrolateral caudate and amygdala. Thirdly, the pre-frontal cortex receives a dopaminergic input from the mid-brain. This input is via a dopaminergic system designated the mesocortical dopaminergic system. This system consists of neurones with cell bodies in the ventral tegmental area of the mid-brain and with terminals in the cerebral cortex, especially the prefrontal cortex.

Two other dopaminergic systems arise in the mid-brain. These are the mesolimbic dopamine system and the nigrostriatal system. The *mesolimbic system*, like the mesocortical system, arises from the ventral tegmental area of the mid-brain, and terminates in various limbic structures including the amygdala and the nucleus accumbens. The evidence we shall consider relates largely to the nucleus accumbens. This is a nucleus which lies near the head of the caudate nucleus, in the vicinity of the septum that lies between the anterior horns and central portions of the two lateral ventricles. In some species, such as the rat, the nucleus accumbens is clearly defined, but in man it is less clearly demarcated.

The *nigrostriatal system* comprises neurones with cell bodies in the substantia nigra, which lies in the mid-brain, and with terminals in the caudate nucleus and putamen. This system plays an important role in the regulation of movement. It might possibly play some role in cognitive and emotional functions also, but this is a subject of debate. In schizophrenia, cognitive, perceptual and emotional disturbances are usually predominant, but movement disorders also occur. In the light of some of the evidence we shall consider subsequently, we should not ignore the possible importance of the nigrostriatal system in schizophrenia.

Evidence for increase of dopamine receptors in sub-cortical nuclei

In 1978, Owen and his colleagues at Northwick Park Hospital published evidence from a post-mortem study suggesting that schizophrenic patients had an increase in the number of dopamine receptors in limbic and striatal nuclei (Owen *et al.*, 1978). They measured the binding of the ligand ^{3}H-spiperone in the nucleus accumbens, caudate and putamen, and found that the amount of ligand bound in all three of these nuclei was significantly greater in schizophrenic patients than in controls. Since ^{3}H-spiperone is a ligand which binds specifically to the D_2 type of dopamine receptor, this finding implies that the schizophrenic patients have an increased number of D_2 receptors in these subcortical nuclei.

This finding has been received with a degree of scepticism, mainly on account of the fact that the majority of the patients studied had previously been treated with dopaminergic blocking drugs. Such treatment might be expected to produce a compensatory increase in the number of dopamine receptors. However, the possibility that the increased number of receptors was not merely an artifact arising from treatment was supported by the observation that the small number of cases who had never been treated with dopamine blocking agents also had an increased number of dopamine receptors.

The possibility that the abnormality is associated with the illness itself has recently received further support from a study by Wong *et al.* (1986) at the Johns Hopkins Hospital in Baltimore. They used positron emission tomography (PET) to measure the binding of the D_2 ligand, ^{11}C-N-methyl spiperone, in the striatal nuclei of living subjects. They found evidence of an increased number of D_2 receptors in the striatal nuclei of previously untreated schizophrenic patients. However, a more recent PET study by Farde *et al.* (1987) of the striatal binding of a different D_2 ligand, ^{11}C-Raclopride, did not find evidence of an increase in the number of D_2 receptors in schizophrenic patients. Thus the question remains unanswered.

The relevance of the heterogeneity of schizophrenia

In general, the various brain abnormalities that have been described in schizophrenic patients are found in only a proportion of the patients. In the studies of binding to D_2 receptors performed by the Northwick Park group and by the group at Johns Hopkins Hospital, the range of variation in the amount of binding to D_2 receptors observed in the patients overlapped with the range of variation observed in normal subjects. Thus it appears that in some schizophrenic patients the number of D_2 receptors is within the normal range. This suggests that if there is an abnormality of D_2 receptors, it might not be a characteristic of all cases of schizophrenia but might be associated with some particular aspect of the illness.

The clinical observation that some schizophrenic symptoms, especially delusions and hallucinations, are more responsive than others to medication which blocks dopamine receptors, suggests that abnormality of D_2 receptors might be associated with some specific symptoms of schizophrenia. The Northwick Park group examined this possibility and found it to be the case. They classified schizophrenic symptoms into positive symptoms, defined as abnormalities involving the presence of a mental activity not occurring in normal people, and negative symptoms, which consist of a decrease or absence of a normal mental activity. They compiled a composite score for positive symptoms by adding scores for delusions, hallucinations and incoherence of speech, and found that this positive symptom score was strongly correlated with the amount of D_2 ligand binding, suggesting that positive symptoms are associated with an excess of D_2 receptors. They compiled a score for negative symptoms by adding the scores for poverty of speech and flatness of affect and found that the negative symptoms score was not correlated with the amount of D_2 receptor binding, suggesting that negative symptoms are not associated with an excess of D_2 receptors.

There are a number of studies (eg Crow, 1980; Andreasen *et al.*, 1986) which suggest that negative symptoms of schizophrenia are associated with various indices of structural damage to the brain. Thus the evidence suggests that different aspects of schizophrenia are associated with different abnormalities of brain function. One interpretation of this state of affairs is that there are different types of schizophrenia, and in particular, that positive and negative schizophrenia might be different diseases. However, this approach is unsatisfactory because in many cases of schizophrenia positive and negative symptoms occur either concurrently, or at different times in the course of the illness. An alternative interpretation is that the brain abnormalities underlying positive and negative symptoms respectively are related in some way, such as in sharing a common cause. One approach to investigating this question is to explore the relationship between positive and negative symptoms in more detail.

Syndromes of persistent symptoms in schizophrenia

Crow (1980) has pointed out that positive symptoms tend to occur during acute episodes, whereas negative symptoms are more characteristic of chronic illness. This raises the possibility that the differences in the brain dysfunction associated with these two groups of symptoms might reflect differences in the brain dysfunction associated with acute and chronic disorder. In other words, it might be the degree of chronicity of the symptoms rather than the symptom type *per se* which is determined by the pattern of brain dysfunction. It is therefore important to determine whether persistent positive symptoms and persistent negative symptoms differ in their pattern of association with evidence of brain dysfunction.

In order to address this question, I studied symptoms and neuropsychological performance in a group of patients with persistent symptoms (Liddle, 1987*a*, 1987*b*). Because clinicians differ in their opinion as to which symptoms should be regarded as positive symptoms and which should be regarded as negative, I made no *a priori* assumptions about the classification of symptoms. Instead, my first step in analysing the data was to examine the correlations between the various symptoms to determine which symptoms tended to occur together. Contrary to expectation based on the view that symptoms can be classified into two categories, I found that the symptoms segregated into three groups. These three groups of symptoms are shown in Table 1. The correlations between symptoms within each group were high, while all correlations between pairs of symptoms from different groups were virtually zero. Thus this study suggests that persistent schizophrenic symptoms segregate into three syndromes.

One of the syndromes, which I have designated the Psychomotor Poverty syndrome, comprises poverty of speech, decreased spontaneous movement and various aspects of affective flattening, and is similar to the group of symptoms which the Northwick Park group regard as negative symptoms. The second syndrome, which I have designated the Disorganization syndrome, comprises various types of disorder of the form of thought and inappropriate affect. Clinicians have differed in their opinions as to whether these symptoms should be regarded as positive or negative. The third syndrome, which I have designated the Reality Distortion syndrome, comprises various delusions and hallucinations. These would generally be classified as positive symptoms. Thus the segregation of

Table 1. *Syndromes of persistent symptoms in schizophrenia.* The right hand column shows the neuropsychological impairments associated with each syndrome.

Symptoms in each syndrome	*Impaired neuropsychological function*
Psychomotor Poverty Syndrome	
Poverty of speech	Conceptual reasoning
Decreased spontaneous movement	Long-term memory
Unchanging facial expression	Object naming
Paucity of expressive gesture	
Affective non-response	
Lack of vocal inflection	
Disorganization Syndrome	
Inappropriate affect	Concentration
Poverty of content of speech	New learning
Tangentiality	
Derailment	
Pressure of speech	
Distractibility	
Reality Distortion Syndrome	
Voices speak to the patient	Figure-ground perception
Delusions of persecution	
Delusions of reference	

symptoms observed in this population of patients with persistent symptoms bears some similarity to the positive-negative classification, but differs in the identification of a separate group of symptoms which do not fit into a positive-negative dichotomy. The segregation of persistent schizophrenic symptoms into the three syndromes has been confirmed in a separate study of a different population of patients (Liddle & Barnes, to be published).

The second step in analysing the results of my study was an examination of the correlations between the scores for each of the syndromes, and performance in a battery of neuropsychological tests designed to measure various aspects of brain function. I found that each syndrome was associated with a specific pattern of neuropsychological impairment. The pattern of impairment associated with with syndrome is summarized in Table 1. (Results are published in detail elsewhere [Liddle, 1987*b*]).

Although the results of this study cannot easily be compared with other studies of neuropsychological performance in schizophrenia, because no other study has used the same method to classify the schizophrenic symptoms, previously published studies do lend support to my findings. For example, Robertson & Taylor (1985) found that a sub-group of schizophrenic patients, whom they designated simple schizophrenics and who had symptoms similar to the Psychomotor Poverty syndrome, had widespread intellectual impairment, including impairment in conceptual reasoning. This pattern of impairment resembles that which I found to be associated with the Psychomotor Poverty syndrome. Robertson & Taylor also found that a sub-group of patients suffering from delusions were impaired in a figure-ground perception. In my study, the Reality Distortion syndrome, which includes delusions and hallucinations, was associated with poor performance in a very similar figure-ground perception task. Thus the findings of Robertson & Taylor support mine with regard to the neuropsychological impairment associated with the Psychomotor Poverty and Reality Distortion syndromes. Robertson & Taylor did not distinguish a group with symptoms closely resembling the Disorganization syndrome. However, in a study of attentional impairment in schizophrenia, Oltmanns *et al.* (1978) found that the symptom most strongly associated with attentional impairment was incoherence of speech, consistent with my observation of an association between the Disorganization syndrome and attentional impairment.

The segregation of symptoms of persistent schizophrenia into three syndromes suggests that several different pathological processes occur in this condition. Furthermore, the observation that each syndrome is associated with a characteristic pattern of neuropsychological impairment suggests that each syndrome is associated with dysfunction of a different part of the brain.

Just as it would be inappropriate to regard positive and negative syndromes in schizophrenia as distinct illnesses, the three syndromes of persistent symptoms identified in my study should not be regarded as separate illnesses. Although there was no significant correlation between any pair of syndromes, the three syndromes were not mutually exclusive. Some patients had substantial scores for more than one syndrome, and all possible pairings of syndromes were observed. This suggests that the pathological processes underlying the three syndromes are related in some manner.

Localization of the pathological processes underlying the three syndromes

Comparison of these persistent schizophrenic syndromes with the clinical sequelae of focal lesions in specific parts of the brain suggests a tentative localization of the pathological process underlying each of the three syndromes. In particular, two of the schizophrenic syndromes bear a striking resemblance to two syndromes associated with damage to the frontal lobes. These two frontal lobe syndromes were clearly delineated by Kleist (1934). Blumer & Benson (1975) named these syndromes pseudodepression and pseudopsychopathic syndrome. The characteristics of pseudodepression are apathy, loss of initiative, lack of overt emotion and poverty of speech. This syndrome closely resembles the Psychomotor Poverty syndrome. The pseudopsychopathic syndrome includes silly or disinhibited behaviour and abnormal speech which suggests an inability to maintain specific meanings. A transcript of the speech of a patient with the pseudopsychopathic syndrome quoted by Blumer & Benson includes apparent tangentiality and derailment, the two types of disorder of thought occurring most commonly in the Disorganization syndrome. Thus there is a substantial resemblance between the pseudopsychopathic syndrome and the Disorganization syndrome.

Blumer & Benson (1975) propose that pseudodepression and the pseudopsychopathic syndrome arise from lesions in different regions of the prefrontal cortex. They suggest that pseudodepression arises from dorsolateral prefrontal lesions and the pseudopsychopathic syndrome from orbital prefrontal lesions. Other authors suggest that laterality of the lesion also plays a part in determining the clinical features. Kolb & Whishaw (1980) propose that pseudodepression is more likely when the lesion is in the left frontal lobe and the pseudopsychopathic syndrome is more commonly seen with right frontal lesions.

Various studies suggest that delusions and hallucinations might arise from temporo-limbic lesions. In particular, the observation by Slater *et al.* (1963) that schizophreniform psychoses occurring in association with temporal lobe epilepsy are characterized by delusions and hallucinations, but relatively little flattening of affect, supports the proposal that the Reality Distortion syndrome might be associated with temporo-limbic dysfunction.

The observed patterns of neuropsychological impairment support the proposed localization of the pathological processes underlying the three syndromes, although unambiguous localization of dysfunction on the basis of neuropsychological performance is difficult because an impaired performance in a particular test can arise from dysfunction of various brain regions. The proposal that the Psychomotor Poverty syndrome, which was found to be associated with impairment of conceptual reasoning and memory, arises from dysfunction of the dorsolateral prefrontal cortex is supported by Hamlin's (1970) finding that patients who had had surgical removal of the upper frontal cortex had much greater subsequent intellectual and memory impairment than matched patients who had had surgical removal of orbital frontal cortex.

Attentional impairment can occur as a result of a lesion in one of many locations in the brain, but there is evidence that the orbital prefrontal cortex plays an especially important part in the maintenance of attention, eg Fuster (1980) reports that intracellular recording from neurones in the brains of primates demonstrates that there are neurones in the orbital prefrontal cortex that appear to play a role in the maintenance of attention during certain tasks. This supports the proposal that the Disorganization syndrome, which was found to be associated with impairment of attention, arises from dysfunction of the orbital prefrontal cortex.

Impairment of figure-ground perception is one of the abnormalities characteristic of temporal lobe lesions (Kolb & Whishaw, 1980). This supports the proposed temporo-limbic location of the process underlying the Reality Distortion syndrome, since this syndrome was found to be associated with impairment of figure-ground perception.

The relationship between the three syndromes

Any attempt to identify the nature of the pathological processes underlying the three syndromes should take account of the clinical evidence that the processes are related. The three brain regions proposed as possible sites of the pathological processes underlying the syndromes share a potentially relevant characteristic. Each of the three is the site of termination of dopaminergic neurones the cell bodies of which are located in the ventral tegmental area of the mid-brain. Furthermore, there is substantial evidence from studies of rats that the prefrontal cortex can play an important part in the regulation of subcortical dopaminergic systems. In general, damage to the prefrontal cortex leads to enhancement of activity of sub-cortical dopamine systems. For example, Pycock *et al.* (1980) demonstrated that destruction of dopamine terminals in the prefrontal cortex by the administration of 6-hydroxy-dopamine following pretreatment with desmethyl-imipramine produces an increase in the number of dopamine receptors in the striatum and in the nucleus accumbens.

Studies of the effect of prolonged isolation on dopaminergic activity in rats have provided further evidence of a reciprocal relationship between prefrontal cortical and subcortical dopamine systems. Blanc *et al.* (1980) found that isolation produces a decrease in prefrontal dopamine activity and a corresponding increase in subcortical dopamine activity. In addition, isolation produces an increased susceptibility to stress.

In view of the important part which stress can play in the exacerbation of schizophrenia, it is of interest that in rats an increase in prefrontal dopaminergic activity is a characteristic component of the response to the stress of repeated foot shocks (Thierry *et al.*, 1976). In the case of hypofunction of the frontal lobes, it might be predicted that susceptibility to stress would be increased.

These observations lead to the hypothesis that there is a persistent underactivity of the prefrontal cortex in schizophrenia. Depending on the part of the prefrontal cortex most affected, this can lead directly to the symptoms of the Psychomotor Poverty and/or Disorganization syndrome. Furthermore, by virtue of the reciprocal relationship between prefrontal cortical and subcortical domapine activity, the prefrontal hypofunction will tend to be associated with subcortical dopaminergic hyperfunction leading to the symptoms of the Reality Distortion syndrome.

Direct evidence of frontal hypofunction in schizophrenia

Evidence from studies of neuropsychological performance (Flor-Henry & Yeudall, 1979; Taylor & Abrams, 1984), regional cerebral blood flow (Ingvar & Franzen, 1974; Weinberger *et al.*, 1986), regional cerebral metabolism (Buchsbaum *et al.*, 1982; Farkas *et al.*, 1984; Wolkin *et al.*, 1985; De Lisi *et al.*, 1985), and brain electrical activity mapping (Morihisa *et al.*, 1983) provide evidence of frontal lobe dysfunction in schizophrenic patients.

The study of cerebral blood flow by Weinberger *et al.* (1986) is an example of a particularly thorough study which revealed evidence of hypofunction of the prefrontal cortex. They used the ^{133}Xe inhalation technique, in which the rate of accumulation of radioactivity in a specified cerebral region following the inhalation of radioactive xenon provides a measure of the blood flow in that cerebral region. They found that under resting conditions schizophrenic patients had a lower ratio of blood flow in the dorsolateral prefrontal cortex to flow in non-frontal regions than control subjects. In addition, the regional blood flow was measured during the performance of the Wisconsin Card Sorting Test, a task which would be expected to involve activity of the dorsolateral prefrontal cortex, since patients with dorsolateral prefrontal lesions are impaired in the performance of the test. The control subjects showed an increase in the blood flow to the dorsolateral prefrontal cortex during the performance of this task, but the schizophrenic patient group did not. Furthermore, in the schizophrenic group, dorsolateral prefrontal blood flow was correlated with performance in the task, suggesting that the blood flow deficit was specifically related to the deficit in function of the dorsolateral prefrontal cortex.

However, not all studies which have examined frontal lobe function in schizophrenic patients have found evidence of dysfunction. For example, the study by Sheppard *et al.* (1983) of regional cerebral metabolism in acute, predominantly never treated, schizophrenic patients did not find evidence of frontal hypometabolism. There are several possible explanations which must be considered.

First, could frontal hypofunction be a consequence of treatment with neuroleptic medication? The evidence suggests that current medication is not responsible for the reported deficits in frontal blood flow or metabolism. In the case of Weinberger's study of blood flow described above, medication had been withdrawn at least 4 weeks before the study. Furthermore, in a subsequent study comparing medicated patients with normal controls, the results were qualitatively identical to those reported in the study of medication-free patients (Berman *et al.*, 1986). The studies using positron emission tomography which have addressed the question of the influence of current medication on regional cerebral metabolism have found no evidence that neuroleptics produce frontal hypometabolism. Wolkin and colleagues (1985) found lowered metabolic rate in the frontal and temporal lobes of schizophrenic patients before treatment and the hypofrontal pattern persisted after treatment. De Lisi *et al.* (1985) measured glucose metabolism before and during treatment with neuroleptic medication and found that the glucose uptake increased during treatment, but the relative hypofrontality persisted. Thus hypofrontality cannot be attributed to concurrent treatment, though the possibility that it is the consequence of prior treatment with neuroleptic medication has not yet been excluded.

Secondly, could differences between the findings of different studies reflect clinical differences in the schizophrenic patients included in the study? The hypothesis I am considering in this chapter implies that this possibility is likely, since it is only patients with marked Psychomotor Poverty or Disorganization who would be expected to have pronounced hypofrontality. Recruitment of patients during their first episode of acute illness is likely to discriminate against patients with marked Psychomotor Poverty symptoms, and thus the failure of Sheppard *et al.* (1983) to find hypofrontality in a group of acute, predominantly never treated patients is not inconsistent with the hypothesis that we are considering. In those studies which have found evidence of hypofrontality in schizophrenic patients, the range of observed frontal blood flow or metabolism in the schizophrenic patients has overlapped with the range observed in normals, indicating that some schizophrenic patients do not have hypofrontality. There is a need for further studies in which blood flow or metabolism are measured in groups of patients who have been subjected to a comprehensive clinical assessment.

Does prefrontal abnormality precede the onset of illness?

I have considered evidence for abnormality of the prefrontal cortex and of subcortical nuclei in schizophrenia, and have also examined the evidence that a regulatory mechanism acts to achieve a reciprocal relationship between prefrontal and subcortical dopaminergic activity. From the point of view of understanding the aetiology of schizophrenia, it is important to seek to establish the site of the primary abnormality.

There is at present little direct evidence indicating the likely site of the primary abnormality. However, indirect evidence implicates the frontal lobes. The tendency for the onset of schizophrenia to occur in early adult life suggests that the illness arises from an abnormality of brain development. The prefrontal cortex is the last brain region to mature, and the completion of its maturation in adolescence coincides with the beginning of the high risk period for the onset of schizophrenia. This coincidence would be explained if faulty development of the prefrontal cortex played a primary role in the genesis of schizophrenia (Morice, 1986).

There is some direct evidence supporting this hypothesis. In a post-mortem study comparing the brains of schizophrenic patients with those of controls, Benes *et al.* (1986) found a decreased number of neurones in several regions of cerebral cortex. This decrease was most marked in the prefrontal cortex. In addition, they found a decreased number of glial cells, so that the ratio of neurones to glia was normal. Since glial cells proliferate during degeneration of brain tissue, this finding suggests that the decreased number of neurones reflects abnormal development rather than degeneration.

Conclusion

There is substantial evidence for prefrontal cortical hypofunction and for subcortical dopaminergic overactivity in schizophrenia. There is evidence suggesting that at least in some cases the prefrontal deficit is a developmental deficit. These observations support the hypothesis that there is a persistent underactivity of the prefrontal cortex in this condition. Patients in whom the dorsolateral prefrontal cortex is substantially underactive would be expected to exhibit the Psychomotor Poverty syndrome, while cases in which the orbital prefrontal cortex is substantially underactive would be expected to exhibit the Disorganization syndrome. Furthermore, by virtue of the regulatory process which acts to achieve a reciprocal relationship between prefrontal cortical and subcortical dopamine activity, prefrontal hypofunction will produce a predisposition to subcortical dopaminergic hyperfunction and consequently to the symptoms of the Reality Distortion syndrome.

References

Andreasen, N.C., Nasrallah, H.A., Dunn, V., Olson, S.C., Grove, W.M., Ehrhardt, J.C., Coffman, J.A. & Crossett, J.H.W. (1986): Structural abnormalities in the frontal system in schizophrenia. *Arch. Gen. Psychiatry* **43**, 136–144.

Benes, F.M., Davidson, J. & Bird, E.D. (1986): Quantitative cytoarchitectural studies of the cerebral cortex of schizophrenics. *Arch. Gen. Psychiatry* **43**, 31–35.

Berman, K.F., Zec, R.F. & Weinberger, D.R. (1986): Physiologic dysfunction of dorsolateral prefrontal cortex in schizophrenia. II. Role of neuroleptic treatment, attention and mental effort. *Arch. Gen. Psychiatry* **43**, 126–135.

Blanc, G., Herve, D., Simon, H., Lisoprawski, A., Glowinski, J. & Tassin, J.P. (1980): Response to stress of mesocortico-frontal dopaminergic neurones in rats after long term isolation. *Nature* **284**, 265–267.

Blumer, D. & Benson, D.F. (1975): Personality changes with frontal lobe lesions. In *Psychiatric aspects of neurological disease*, eds D.F. Benson & D. Blumer, pp. 151–170. New York: Grune & Stratton.

Buchsbaum, M.S., Ingvar, D.H., Kessler, R., Waters, R.N., Cappelletti, J., van Kammen, D.P., King A.C., Johnson, J.L., Manning, R.G., Flynn, R.W., Mann, L.S., Bunney, W.E. & Sokoloff, L. (1982): Cerebral glucography with positron tomography. *Arch. Gen. Psychiatry* **39**, 251–259.

Crow, T.J. (1980): Molecular pathology of schizophrenia: more than one disease process? *Br. Med J.* **280**, 1–9.

De Lisi, L.E., Holcomb, H.H., Cohen, R.M., Pickar, D., Carpenter, W., Morihisa, J.M., King, A.C.

Kessler, R. & Buchsbaum, M.S. (1985): Positron emission tomography in schizophrenic patients with and without neuroleptic medication. *J. Cerebr. Blood Flow Metab.*5, 201–206.
Farde, L., Weisel, F.-A., Hall, H., Halldin, C., Stone-Elander, S. & Sedvall, J.S. (1984): Regional brain glucose metabolism in chronic schizophrenia. *Arch. Gen. Psychiatry* **41**, 293–300.
Farkas, T., Wolf, A.P., Jaeger, J., Brodie, J., Christman, D.R. & Fowler, J.S. (1984): Regional brain glucose metabolism in chronic schizophrenia. *Arch. Gen. Psychiatry* **41**, 293–300.
Flor-Henry, P. & Yeudall, L.T. (1979): Neuropsychological investigation of schizophrenia and manic depressive psychoses. In *Hemisphere asymmetries of function in psychopathology*, ed J.G. Gruzelier & P. Flor-Henry, pp. 341–362. Amsterdam: Elsevier.
Fuster, J.M. (1980): *The prefrontal cortex*. New York: Raven Press.
Hamlin, R.M. (1970): Intellectual function 14 years after frontal lobe surgery. *Cortex* **6**, 299–307.
Ingvar, D.H. & Franzen, G. (1974): Abnormalities of cerebral blood flow distribution in patients with chronic schizophrenia. *Acta Psychiatr. Scand.* **50**, 425–462.
Kleist, K. (1934): *Gehirnpathologie*. Leipzig: Barth.
Kolb, B. & Whishaw, I.Q. (1980): *Fundamentals of human neuropsychology*. San Francisco: Freeman.
Kraepelin, E. (1919): *Dementia praecox and paraphrenia,* trans. R.M. Barclay, Facsimile edition published 1971. New York: Kreiger.
Liddle, P.F. (1987*a*): The symptoms of chronic schizophrenia: a re-examination of the positive-negative dichotomy. *Br. J. Psychiatry* **151**, 145–151.
Liddle, P.F. (1987*b*): Schizophrenic syndromes, cognitive performance and neurological dysfunction. *Psychol. Med.* **17**, 49–58.
Morice, R. (1986): Beyond language — speculations on the prefrontal cortex and schizophrenia. *Aust. N.Z. J. Psychiatry* **20**, 7–10.
Morihisa, J.M., Duffy, F.H. & Wyatt, R.J. (1983): Brain electrical activity mapping (BEAM) in schizophrenic patients. *Arch. Gen. Psychiatry* **40**, 719–728.
Oltmanns, T.F., Ohayon, J. & Neale, J.M. (1978): The effect of antipsychotic medication and diagnostic criteria on distractibility in schizophrenia. In *The nature of schizophrenia: new approaches to research and treatment*, eds L.C. Wynne, R.L. Cromwell & S. Matthysse, pp. 196–204. New York: John Wiley.
Owen, F., Cross, A.J., Crow, T.J., Longden, A., Poulter, M. & Riley, C.J. (1978): Increased dopamine receptor sensitivity in schizophrenia. *Lancet* **ii**, 223–226.
Pycock, C.J., Kerwin, R.W. & Carter, C.J. (1980): Effects of lesion of cortical dopamine terminals on sub-cortical dopamine receptors in rats. *Nature* **286**, 74–77.
Robertson, C. & Taylor, P.J. (1985): Some cognitive correlates of schizophrenic illnesses. *Psychol. Med.* **15**, 81–98.
Sheppard, G., Gruzelier, J., Manchanda, R., Hirsch, S.R., Wise, R., Frackowiak, R. & Jones, T. (1983): ^{15}O positron emission tomographic scanning in predominantly never-treated acute schizophrenic patients. *Lancet* **ii**, 1448–1452.
Slater, E., Beard, A.W. & Glithero, E. (1963): The schizophrenia-like psychoses of epilepsy. *Br. J. Psychiatry* **109**, 95–150.
Taylor, M.A. & Abrams, R. (1984): Cognitive impairment in schizophrenia. *Am. J. Psychiatry* **141**, 196–201.
Thierry, A.M., Tassin, J.P., Blanc, G. & Glowinski, J. (1976): Selective activation of the mesocortical DA system by stress. *Nature* **263**, 242–244.
Weinberger, D.R., Berman, K.F. & Zec, R.F. (1986): Physiologic dysfunction of dorsolateral prefrontal cortex in schizophrenia. II. Regional cerebral blood flow evidence. *Arch. Gen. Psychiatry* **43**, 114–124.
Wolkin, A., Jaeger, J., Brodie, J.D., Wolf, A.P., Fowler, J., Rotrosen, J., Gomez-Mont, F. & Cancro, R. (1985): Persistence of cerebral metabolic abnormalities in chronic schizophrenia as determined by positron emission tomography. *Am. J. Psychiatry* **142**, 564–571.
Wong, D.F., Wagner, H.N., Tune, L.E., Dannals, R.F., Pearlson, G.D., Links, J.M., Tamminga, C.A., Broussolle, E.P., Ravert, H.T., Wilson, A.A., Toung, J.K.T., Malat, J., Williams, J.A., O'Tuama, L.A., Snyder, S.H., Kuhar, M.J. & Gjedde, A. (1986): Positron emission tomography reveals elevated D_2 dopamine receptors in drug-naive schizophrenics. *Science* **234**, 1558–1563.

Chapter 9

Organic findings and pharmacotherapy in the spectrum of schizophrenia

Malcolm P. I. Weller

Friern Hospital, Friern Barnet Road, London N11 3BP, UK

Summary

The early phases of schizophrenia are difficult to recognize for what they are and the more stringent and exclusive criteria of diagnosis now current in America do not diagnose schizophrenia in the same manner as Bleuler & Kraepelin, and do not recognize schizophrenia simplex, ie a disorder which has the hallmarks of schizophrenia in the deterioration of personality but where there are no hallucinations or delusions. This condition is now described in the American system of classification as a Personality Disorder, but this term carries some opprobrium, and the boundaries of personality disorder traditionally are wide and stretch the concept of illness.

The spectrum of schizophrenic disorders discussed in Chapter 11 by Seymour Kety suggests that there is a strong genetic relationship between these disorders and delusional and hallucinatory schizophrenia. This genetic relationship was perceived by the classic authors and suggests the possibility that anti-psychotic medication may be helpful in such conditions, however they are termed, a possibility supported by some recent evidence.

Introduction

Schizophrenia is diagnosed as a subset of psychosis but includes more besides, and it is this additional domain that excites particular contention. The subtle boundaries of the non-psychotic conditions continue to vary yet are important in many practical ways, including forensic and community psychiatric care issues (Weller, 1989; Weller *et al.* 1987). Most diagnostic schemes concur on the psychotic symptoms that define schizophrenia, universally according Schneider's symptoms of the first rank a central place (Weller, 1984). Disagreements rest, in part, on how long these psychotic symptoms should have been present for the diagnosis to be certain, whether there were overwhelming precipitants and how the illness resolved, with spontaneous and complete recovery from acute, florid symptoms casting doubts on a diagnosis of schizophrenia.

The term schizophrenia thereby comes to denote a chronic disorder. Short-lived, often self-terminating illnesses have been variously termed schizophreniform, cycloid psychosis, boufée delirante (Johnson-Sabine *et al.*, 1983), the emotion psychoses of Rohr and Labhart, or the reactive psychoses of Wimmer (see Roth, 1979 and this volume p.

110), and include a number of syndromes allegedly limited to specific cultures, such as amok (Kraepelin, 1904) and spirit possession or *boufée delirante aigue* (Sanseigne & Desrosiers, 1960). These terms describe transient conditions which by implication are different from schizophrenia. However, those who suffer from these transient psychoses tend to re-present subsequently with indubitable schizophrenia. The genetic evidence is contradictory; for example in reactive schizophrenia, in which the individual has a clear psychotic episode with short-lived, schizophrenic symptoms following a severe stress, succeeded by spontaneous recovery with no residual signs of defects, the typical hereditary pattern is not apparent (Kety *et al.*, 1968; Rosenthal *et al.*, 1971). On the other hand, the transient psychoses tend to be over-represented amongst family members of schizophrenic probands and in addition certain introverted personality characteristics are genetically related to schizophrenia (Kendler *et al.*, 1986) (which is discussed more fully later), and organic findings have been demonstrated in this group which are interesting to review.

The relationship of such non-psychotic symptoms to schizophrenia is complicated by the fact that the prodromal symptoms of schizophrenia are difficult to recognize. Kraepelin (1919) described affective and neurotic symptoms as sometimes being early manifestations, whilst 'the general trend of volition and also the higher emotions might form the first point of attack', with 'dullness and indifference' being early symptoms. Bleuler (1923) described a related situation: 'Where only the basic symptoms are visible, we speak of *schizophrenia simplex* (the primary dementia of earlier authors). It is usually a case of a dementia in the sense of schizophrenia that increases gradually in the course of decades. The anamnesis invariably indicates that the disease has been mistaken for years; it was a latent schizophrenia.' This concept of latent schizophrenia has been ridiculed as nonsensical and the possibility of prospectively recognizing such a condition had been doubted, but there are many who feel they have seen similar situations to those that Bleuler described in characteristic oddities of personality which on follow-up have declared themselves indeed to be early manifestations of schizophrenia. Whilst hesitating to be emphatic, in routine clinical practice one often believes that one is dealing with such a case of evolving schizophrenia in which the symptoms have not yet crystallized sufficiently to justify the term. It is unlikely that these suspicions will be voiced, particularly to young patients, who are inevitably passing through periods of difficult adjustment which might explain the reactions, yet who represent the group in whom the onset of schizophrenia is most likely.

The early manifestations can be completely misleading to experienced clinicians. Hoch & Polatin were treating apparently neurotic patients and were concerned by the unexpected emergence of psychoses in some during their analytic therapy. Their experience led them to emphasize (Hoch & Polatin, 1949) that neurotic symptoms are common in evolving schizophrenia. This possibility of schizophrenia developing in neurotic conditions had been noted earlier by Jung (1907) in his correspondence with Freud. 'I have often had cases that passed with apparent smoothness from hysteria or obsessional neurosis straight into D. pr', (dementia praecox) and the same relationship has been subsequently emphasized in follow-up studies (Carter, 1949; Ljungberg, 1957; Ziegler *et al.*, 1960; Slater, 1965).

Vulnerability to schizophrenia and the premorbid personality

A study of psychosocial indicators (Hartmann *et al.*, 1984), based on the follow-up of an earlier study of delinquent boys aged 10 to 17, conducted in 1940–1942 by Glueck & Glueck (1950) demonstrated a number of vulnerability factors for schizophrenia that encompass psychopathic traits and establish the youthful, behavioural features that predict a psychotic outcome.

Almost 90% of the group of 500 delinquent boys and 500 controls in the Gluecks' original study were traced; 24 were found to have received hospital diagnoses of schizophrenia over the previous 10–20 years, according to DSM-I and DSM-II diagnostic criteria, and three more might have had the disease. Rather surprisingly, the schizophrenic cases were equally divided between the delinquent and non-delinquent groups but the latter had been followed up 15 years longer — to age 47, in contrast to the delinquent group, to age 32 years — allowing considerable additional time for the disease to develop. Taking this into account, it suggests that there was more schizophrenia in the delinquent group.

Disregarding the uncertain cases, the frequency of schizophrenia was about six times the epidemiological expectation. The high prevalence figures overall may well derive from the loose diagnostic criteria incorporated in DSM-II and particularly in DSM-I, and it is a pity that the researchers were unable personally to interview their sample. The 24 schizophrenics were matched with two controls for each patient from the original cohort of 500 controls for age, intelligence (IQ) and ethnic group; the controls were further selected by the exclusion of those with a first degree relative with schizophrenia, or with personality traits which might lie within the spectrum of schizophrenia, thereby sharpening any between group differences.

Features in the original records, assessed after many years by researchers blind to which individuals subsequently developed schizophrenia, distinguished the schizophrenic patients on a number of variables in youth, including difficulties in interpersonal relationships, delays in developmental milestones, disturbance of gait and minor ('soft') neurological signs, together with unusual reactions to marijuana, alcohol and other drugs, all of which were overrepresented to a statistically significant extent. Some of these characteristics are consistent with early brain damage. (IQ was used as a matching factor.) The loner characteristics of the schizophrenic group were emphasized by poor adjustment to schoolmates and cruelty or bullying.

Hartmann *et al.* (1984) emphasize that they consider it quite possible that each of their indicators 'involves information on one or several aspects of a single underlying vulnerability (to schizophrenia) that is simply manifested more clearly in some sorts of behaviour in one case and other sorts in other cases'.

Discriminant analysis assigned 88% of the total sample correctly. If 25% of the sample with the lowest IQ was eliminated, on the grounds that some of the measures might be contaminated by low IQ, 52 of the 54 remaining subjects were correctly assigned to the schizophrenic or non-schizophrenic groups (96%) (it is interesting that the mean IQ of the 24 subjects who became schizophrenic was 89.6, whereas the overall mean IQ of the Gluecks' sample was reported inconsistently to be either 93.3 or 91.4).

These findings are similar to those of earlier, retrospective studies by Roff *et al.* (1976), and Watt (1972, 1978) and associates (1970), who found that half his schizophrenic probands were maladjusted a decade before their illnesses and concluded that pre-schizophrenic boys tended to exhibit 'unsocialized aggression'.

Some researchers claim an overlap between borderline and schizotypal personality disorder, with common features to the characteristic premorbid disposition of schizophrenics, and others argue for separate disorders with differing outcomes (Torgersen, 1983; Plakum *et al.*, 1985). In the most recent third edition of the American Diagnostic and Statistical Manual (DSM-III) the two terms are defined separately, schizotypal personality disorder being characterized by suspicious, paranoid attitudes, sensitivity to criticism, ideas of reference, poor rapport, and odd ways of communication. The DSM-III criteria for borderline personality disorder, in its typical unambiguous but unweighted way, which has uncharitably been referred to as the Chinese menu approach, require at least four of the following: impulsiveness, self-damaging acts, unstable interpersonal relationships, intolerance of being alone, empty and bored, and identity disturbance, the last seeming more akin to schizophrenia and the first to psychopathy.

Genetics

Bleuler (1923, pp. 432–433) remarked on a number of peculiarities in the relatives of his schizophrenic patients, which stopped short of frank schizophrenia but had features in common with the disease. Kraepelin (1919) similarly observed that 'not infrequently one learns further that among the brothers and sisters of the patient there are found striking personalities, criminals, queer individuals, prostitutes, suicides, vagrants, wrecked and ruined human beings, all being forms in which more or less well-developed dementia praecox may appear'. (p. 234). Similar observations have continued to be made, with an excess of borderline conditions in the first degree relatives, while some relatives have 'clearly schizoid or paranoid personalities as well as others characterized by schizoid features and serious emotional disorders ... ' (Alanen, 1978).

Kendler, Gruenberg & Strauss (1981) confirmed the higher incidence of schizotypal personality disorders in the biological relatives of adopted-away schizophrenics found by Kety *et al.* (1971), using a methodology that met criticisms of earlier studies (Liebowitz, 1979). However, they pointed out that there is some circularity in the arguments, because the DSM-III concept of schizotypal personality was derived from an examination of the case summaries of the biological relatives of the adopted-away schizophrenics in the extended family study of Kety *et al.* (1971). (Other criticisms have been made of the methodological issues [eg Weller, 1984, pp. 131–133].)

These same personality deficiencies are found as prodromal features of later schizophrenia, and, as already mentioned, psychopathic features also occur, emphasizing a relationship between the two conditions which have many biological features in common (Weller, 1986), and psychopathy is over-represented in the families of schizophrenic probands (Heston, 1966; Stephens *et al.*, 1975). If these non-schizophrenic individuals with allegedly schizophrenic spectrum traits, a term first used by Inouye (1961), are included in statistical comparisons, the genetic transmission of schizophrenia is more convincing (Kety *et al.*, 1968; Kety *et al.*, 1971; Wender *et al.*, 1974).

The relatives of schizophrenics are at greater risk of developing schizophrenia than a random population, the risk being proportional to the degree of consanguinity. Where a family history is absent, sporadic cases of schizophrenia betray evidence of brain damage (Reveley, this volume p. 47; Reveley *et al.*, 1984). A recent family study, in which the probands were followed up over a long period and in many cases personally interviewed by the researchers, showed that short-lived schizophreniform psychoses, schizo-affective psychoses and psychotic affective illness have a schizophrenic pattern of inheritance (Kendler *et al.*, 1986).

Organic findings

In view of these genetic findings it is of great interest that claims have been made that the relatives betray cognitive dysfunction and formal thought disorder on objective tests (Romney, 1984; Callahan & Saccuzzo, 1986), in addition to certain personality factors which are allegedly detected in the apparently unaffected first degree relatives.

Neurological abnormalities similar to those found in schizophrenics have also been found in their seemingly unaffected first degree relatives, initially as eye tracking dysfunction (Holzman *et al.*, 1973; Latham *et al.*, 1981; Solomon *et al.*, 1987) but more recently on a battery of conventional neurological tests (Kinney *et al.*, 1986). This suggests that the neurological signs in schizophrenia are unlikely to be dependent solely on previous medication. Intriguingly, the extent of the dysfunction is modestly but significantly, associated with the degree of thought disorder (Solomon *et al.*, 1987).

Treatment

Neuroleptic treatment of schizotypal personality disorder produces a perceptible improvement, but is poorly tolerated (Francis, 1985), and also modestly improves borderline disorders (Brinkley *et al.*, 1979; Leone, 1982), as evaluated in double-blind trials (Serban & Siegel, 1984; Soloff *et al.*, 1986). The improvement produced by neuroleptics typically includes improvement in depression and anxiety, and Goldberg *et al.* (1986) also found benefits in obsessive-compulsive problems, suggesting that these are components of the total complex rather than independent features, particularly since the use of the tricyclic antidepressant amitriptyline produced a deterioration in some patients. One study found improvement in those borderline patients who took trifluoperazine for 6 weeks for anxiety symptoms and suicidal ideas, but found that the dysphoric component could be dissected out of the total complex and improved with tranylcypromine, whilst carbamazepine specifically reduced anger and acting-out behaviour (behavioural dyscontrol), which, however, was increased with the benzodiazepine alprazolam (Cowdry & Gardner, 1988).

A particularly vivid example from the author's own experience is worth recounting. Excerpts from a letter, written by a psychopathic man at constant odds with the law, show the growth of empathetic understanding when he was treated with a neuroleptic, with a striking change in his insight and attitude. Following one offence, a colleague had written despairingly: 'He is subject to serious personality disorder and can be described as being unstable, insecure and manipulative, and is prone to various hysterical symptoms, but personality disorders are unfortunately not amenable to conventional psychiatric treatment…'. The patient subsequently wrote: 'Since taking the medication you prescribed for me (pimozide 4 mg daily), I find that I am more relaxed, more calm and am now able to cope with normal daily life and decisions. I can now enter into discussions with other people, being able to hold a normal conversation knowing what we are speaking about. I now take the time to listen to their point of view, realizing it is just as important as mine, and think things over with great consideration before making any rash decisions (sic).… I now feel that I have a purpose in life and that one of the main factors is to stay away from trouble, not just for myself but for others who have stood by me. I think how I would be hurting others if I were to get into trouble. It is the hurt of those near me and also the hurt of those whose property taken or damaged, (sic) I would not wish it to happen to me and they're no different.… I also feel the love, consideration, affection and understanding shown by others, especially my wife.… Looking back at how I used to be, I think how irrational I used to be in both my actions and conversation, my point of view had to be the one which was correct or I would flare up and lose my temper… *it seemed like a dream and yet I was awake, sometimes I could not remember doing certain things* (my italics) … (see Chapter 1). I did at one stage during taking my medication stop taking my tablets and after two or three days I found that once again I was becoming irrational and withdrawn, however I proceeded with the medication again and after a further two to three days I felt calm and responsible again.'

These comments were accompanied by a pleasing change in the man's demeanour, a new warmth and attraction in his personality and a change in his way of life from habitual crime to responsible social behaviour.

Conclusion

It is not always clear where the spectrum of schizophrenia begins and ends but borderline, schizotypal and psychopathic personalities seem to lie within that spectrum. Relationships with schizophrenia have been established for the DSM-III asocial type of personality disorder (Lowing *et al.*, 1983; Kendler *et al.*, 1984) and paranoid personality disorder (Kendler & Gruenberg, 1982), and Barron *et al.* (1983) demonstrated a possible genetic-familial link with schizotypal personality disorder. These personality characteristics may be early manifestations of an evolving schizophrenic illness, or render the sufferer vulnerable to schizophrenia like psychoses, and in many cases they improve with low doses of antipsychotic medication.

Acknowledgement—This chapter is based on a leading article in the Postgraduate Medical Journal, 1987, **63**, 1021–1024.

References

Alanen, Y.O. (1978): In search of the international origin of schizophrenia. *Research in the schizophrenic disorders: The Stanley R. Dean Award Lectures*, ed. R. Cancro & S.R. Dean, vol. 1, p. 253. Jamaica: Spectrum Publications.

Barron, M., Gruen, R., Asnis, L. *et al.* (1983): Familial relatedness of schizophrenia and schizotypal states. *Am. J. Psychiatry* **140**, 1437–1442.

Bleuler, E. (1923): *Textbook of psychiatry*, Trans. A.A. Brill. London: George Allen and Unwin.

Brinkley, J.R., Beitman, B.D. & Friedel, R.O. (1979): Low dose neuroleptic regimes in the treatment of borderline patients. *Arch. Gen. Psychiatry* **36**, 319–326.

Callahan, L.A. & Saccuzzo, D.P. (1986): Associative intrusions in the verbal behaviour of the first-degree relatives of adult schizophrenics. A preliminary study. *J. Nerv. Ment. Dis.* **174**, 240–242.

Carter, A.B. (1949): The prognosis of certain hysterical symptoms. *Br. Med. J.* **1**, 1076–1079.

Cowdry, W. & Gardner, D.L. (1988): Pharmacotherapy of borderline personality disorder: Alprazolam, carbamazepine, trifluoperazine, and tranylcypromine. *Arch. Gen. Psychiatry* **45**, 111–119.

Francis, A. (1985): Validating schizotypal personality disorders: Problems with the schizophrenia connection. *Schizophrenia Bull.* **11**, 595–597.

Glueck, S. & Glueck, E. (1950): *Unraveling juvenile delinquency*. New York: Commonwealth Fund.

Goldberg, S.C., Schulz, S.C., Schulz, P.M., Resnick, R.J., Hamer, R.M. & Friedel, R.O. (1986): Borderline and schizotypal personality disorders treated with low-dose thiothixene *vs* placebo. *Arch. Gen. Psychiatry* **43**, 680–686.

Hartmann, E., Milofsky, E., Vaillant, G., Oldfield, M., Falke, R. & Ducey, C. (1984): Vulnerability to schizophrenia. *Arch. Gen. Psychiatry* **41**, 1050–1056.

Heston, L. (1966): Psychiatric disorder in foster home reared children of schizophrenic mothers. *Br. J. Psychiatry* **112**, 819–825.

Hoch, P.H. & Polatin, P. (1949): Pseudoneurotic forms of schizophrenia. *Psychiatr. Q.* **23**, 248.

Holzman, P.S., Proctor, L.R. & Hughes, D.W. (1973): Eye tracking patterns in schizophrenia. *Science* **181**, 179–181.

Inouye, E. (1961): Similarity and dissimilarity of schizophrenia in twins. In *Proceedings of the third World Congress of Psychiatry*, vol. 1, pp. 524–530. Montreal: University of Toronto Press.

Johnson-Sabine, E.C., Mann, A.H., Jacoby, R.J., Wood, K.H., Peron-Magnan, P., Olie, J.P. & Deniker, P. (1983): Boufée délirante: an examination of its current status. *Psychol. Med.* **13**, 771–778.

Jung, C.C. (1907): *The Freud/Jung Letters*, eds R. Manheim & R.F.C. Hull, pp. 35–38. London and Henley-on-Thames: Hogarth Press and Routledge and Kegan Paul.
Kendler, K.S. & Gruenberg, A.M. (1982): Genetic relationship between paranoid personality disorder and the 'schizophrenic spectrum' disorders. *Am. J. Psychiatry* **139**, 1185–1186.
Kendler, K.S., Gruenberg, A.M. & Strauss, J.S. (1981): An independent analysis of the Copenhagen sample of the Danish adoption study of schizophrenia: II. The relationship between schizotypal personality disorder and schizophrenia. Arch. Gen. Psychiatry **88**, 982–984.
Kendler, K.S., Masterson, C.C., Ungaro, R. *et al.* (1984): A family history study of schizophrenia-related personality disorders. *Am. J. Psychiatry* **141**, 424–427.
Kendler, K.S., Gruenberg, A. & Tsuang, M.T. (1986): A DSM-III family study of nonschizophrenic psychotic disorders. *Am. J. Psychiatry* **143**, 1098–1105.
Kety, S., Rosenthal, D., Wender, P. & Schulsinger, F. (1968): The type and prevalence of mental illness in the biological and adoptive families of adopted schizophrenics. In *The transmission of schizophrenia*, ed D. Rosenthal & S. Kety. Oxford: Pergamon Press.
Kety, S., Rosenthal, D., Wender, P. & Schulsinger, F. (1971): Mental illness in biological and adoptive families of adoptive schizophrenics. *Am. J. Psychiatry* **128**, 302–306.
Kiev, A. (1972): *Transcultural psychiatry*. Harmondsworth, Middlesex: Penguin Books.
Kinney, D.K., Woods, B.T. & Yurgelun-Todd, D. (1986): Neurologic abnormalities in schizophrenic patients and their families: II. Neurologic and psychiatric findings in relatives. *Arch. Gen. Psychiatry* **43**, 665–668.
Kraepelin, E. (1904): Vergleichende Psychiatrie (Translated as Comparative psychiatry). In *Themes and variations in European psychiatry*, eds S.R. Hirsch & M. Shepherd. Bristol: Wright, 1974.
Kraeplin, E. (1919): *Dementia praecox and paraphrenia*, trans. R.M. Barclay. Edinburgh: E. and S. Livingstone.
Latham, C., Holtzman, P.S., Manschreck, T.C. & Tole, J. (1981): Optokinetic nystagmus and pursuit eye movements in schizophrenia. *Arch. Gen. Psychiatry* **38**, 997–1003.
Leone, N.F. (1982): Response of borderline patients to laxapine and chlorpromazine. *J. Clin. Psychiatry* **43**, 148–150.
Liebowitz, M.R. (1979): Is borderline a distinct entity? *Schizophrenia Bull.* **5**, 23–38.
Ljungberg, L. (1957): Hysteria: A clinical, prognostic and genetic study. *Acta Psychiatr. Neurol. Scand.* **32**, Suppl. 112.
Lowing, P.A., Mirsky, A.F. & Pereira, M.A. (1983): The inheritance of schizophrenia spectrum disorders: a reanalysis of the Danish adoptee study. *Am. J. Psychiatry* **140**, 1167–1171.
Plakum, E.M., Burkhardt, P.E. & Muller, J.P. (1985): 14-year follow-up of borderline and schizotypal personality disorders. *Compr. Psychiatry* **26**, 5, 448–455.
Reveley, A.M., Reveley, M.A. & Murray, R.M. (1984): Cerebral ventricular enlargement in non-genetic schizophrenia: A controlled twin study. *Br. J. Psychiatry* **144**, 89–93.
Roff, J.D., Knight, R. & Wertheim, E. (1976): A factor-analytic study of childhood symptoms antecedent to schizophrenia. *J. Abnorm. Psychol.* **85**, 543–549.
Romney, D.M. (1984): Formal thought disorder amongst schizophrenics: a new look at some old data. *J. Clin. Psychol.* **40**, 51–52.
Romney, D.M. (1987): A simplex model of the paranoid process: Implications for diagnosis and prognosis. *Acta Psychiatr. Scand.* **75**, 651–655.
Rosenthal, D., Wender, P.H., Kety, S.S., Welner, J. & Schulsinger, F. (1971): The adopted-away offspring of schizophrenics. *Am. J. Psychiatry* **128**, 307–311.
Roth, M. (1979): Problems of diagnosis and treatment in the borderlands of schizophrenia. In *Proceedings of an International Symposium on Neuroleptics and Schizophrenia, Cambridge 1978*, ed. J.M. Simister, pp. 63–81. Luton: Lundbeck.
Sanseigne, A. & Desrosiers, M. (1960): Evaluation of psychopharmaceuticals in an undeveloped country. In *Psychiatry in the underdeveloped countries: report of a roundtable meeting*, APA Annual Meeting Atlantic City, 12 May, ed. N.S. Kline, pp. 52–8 (cited Kiev, 1972, p. 103, *q.v.*).
Serban, G. & Siegel, S. (1984): Response of borderline and schizotypal patients to small doses of thiothixene and haloperidol. *Am. J. Psychiatry* **141**, 1455–1458.
Slater, E. (1965): Diagnosis of 'hysteria'. *Br. Med. J.* **1**, 1395–1399.
Soloff, P.H., George, A., Nathan, R.S., Schulz, P.M., Ulrich, R.F. & Perel, J.M. (1986): Progress in

pharmacotherapy of borderline disorders. A double-blind study of amitriptyline, haloperidol, and placebo. *Arch. Gen. Psychiatry* **43**, 691–697.

Solomon, C.M., Holzman, P.S., Levin, S. & Gale, H.J. (1987): The association between eye-tracking dysfunctions and thought disorder in psychosis. *Arch. Gen. Psychiatry* **44**, 31–35.

Stephens, D.A., Atkinson, M.W., Kay, D.W.K., Roth, M. & Garside, R.F. (1975): Psychiatric morbidity in parents and sibs of schizophrenics and non schizophrenics. *Br. J. Psychiatry* **127**, 97–108.

Torgersen, S. (1983): Genetics of neurosis: the effects of sampling upon the twin concordance ratio. *Br. J. Psychiatry* **142**, 126–132.

Watt, N.F. (1972): Longitudinal changes in the social behaviour of children hospitalized for schizophrenia as adults. *J. Nerv. Ment. Dis.* **155**, 42–54.

Watt, N.F. (1978): Patterns of childhood social development in adult schizophrenics. *Arch. Gen. Psychiatry* **35**, 160–170.

Watt, N.F., Stolorow, R.D., Ludensky, A.W. & McClelland, D.C. (1970): School adjustment and behaviour of children hospitalized for schizophrenia. *Am. J. Orthopsychiatry* **40**, 637–657.

Weller, M.P.I. (1984): Some problems in the diagnosis of schizophrenia and the concept of clear consciousness. In *Aspects of consciousness*, ed. R. Stevens, vol. 4, pp. 117–166. London, New York, Tokyo: Academic Press.

Weller, M.P.I. (1986): Medical concepts in psychopathy and violence. *Med. Sci. Law* **26**, 131–143.

Weller, M.P.I. (1989): Mental illness – who cares? *Nature* 399, 249–252.

Weller, B.G.A., Weller, M.P.I., Cocker, E. & Mahomed, S. (1987): Crisis at Christmas 1986. *Lancet* i, 553–554.

Wender, P., Rosenthal, D., Kety, S., Schulsinger, F. & Weiner, J. (1974): Crossfostering research strategy for clarifying the role of genetic and experimental factors in the etiology of schizophrenia. *Arch. Gen. Psychiatry* **30**, 121–128.

Ziegler, F.J., Imboden, J.B. & Meyer, E. (1960): Contemporary conversion symptomatology. *Am. J. Psychiatry* **116**, 901–910.

Chapter 10

Theories regarding the causation of paranoid disorders and their relationship to other psychiatric syndromes

Sir Martin Roth

University of Cambridge Clinical School, Addenbrooke's Hospital, Hills Road, Cambridge CB2 2QQ, UK

Summary

The influential view which regarded all forms of paranoid psychosis not due to organic disease as being variants of schizophrenia is not supported in its original form by the findings of the past few decades. The hereditary link with schizophrenia is found in some syndromes but its strength and importance have probably been overstated. The classification and diagnosis of the paranoid disorders cannot be decided on the basis of genetical evidence alone. Follow-up studies undertaken on a large scale, by Scandinavian workers in particular, have shown that paranoid psychotic and other disorders enjoy a more favourable clinical and social outcome. However, in about 50% of cases symptoms become chronic (though encapsulated), but personality deterioration of schizophrenic type is rare. Stress has to be laid on the indeterminancy of outcome in the individual case. There are no reliable means of predicting at first presentation whether recovery, a chronic course with some paranoid symptoms, or a schizophrenic illness (which evolves in a small proportion of cases), will follow. There is a developmental and historical dimension in certain forms of paranoid illness. This comprises a link between pre-morbid personality and stressful circumstances which impinge on it, and the illness which follows. But the term 'psychogenic psychosis' overstates the influence of 'key events' in the premorbid state and their adequacy as explanations of paranoid delusional states. Knowledge and understanding of the aetiology of these conditions remains limited.

Neuroleptic treatment has improved the prognosis of patients with paranoid disorders. The treatment has to be provided along many fronts: biological, psychotherapeutic in appropriate cases, and where possible through improvement of social circumstances to correct physical illness and sensory deficit.

Introduction

The relationship between paranoid disorders and other forms of psychiatric illness and the theories that have been advanced about their causation will be considered in this chapter.

The evidence bearing on these issues needs to be taken into account in making a diagnosis in cases with paranoid symptoms and in making decisions about treatment.

The international pilot study of schizophrenia (1973) showed that many psychiatrists in different parts of the world consider most cases of psychosis dominated by paranoid delusions, whether or not they are associated with hallucinations, to be variants of schizophrenic illness. In consequence many of the cases classed by the 'Catego' program as paranoid psychosis in this enquiry had been diagnosed as schizophrenic. The participants in the enquiry were expressing allegiance to one of the more influential views expressed in the course of the long controversy regarding the affiliations of the paranoid disorders. The failure to resolve this controversy is rooted in the fact that it does not admit of any simple categorical solution in terms of a simple unifying theory.

Three main groups of theories have been advanced since the beginning of this century regarding the character, nosological status and outcome of paranoid states. The first theory has emanated from the school of Kraepelin and implicit in it is the view that mental disorders dominated by paranoid delusions have a close kinship with schizophrenia. In his early writings Kraepelin had described 'paranoia' and 'paraphrenia' as distinct from schizophrenia in their clinical picture and long-term outcome. In particular, observations over a long period showed that the type of deterioration of personality that occurred in schizophrenia did not take place in these conditions. However, Kraepelin later accepted the testimony favouring a close kinship with schizophrenia produced by a number of his pupils.

The second theory is highly influential in the Scandinavian countries where a wide range of paranoid disorders is subsumed under the heading 'psychogenic psychosis'. These disorders are regarded as arising from an interaction between certain types of predisposition and the onerous life events which impinge upon vulnerable facets of the personality (Wimmer, 1916; Strömgren, 1940; Faergeman, 1963; Retterstöl, 1966 & 1970). The benign outcome of patients with psychogenic psychoses such as 'paranoia' is contrasted with the chronic deterioration of personality in a high proportion of schizophrenic patients. Paranoid symptoms are prominent both in Kasanin's 'schizoaffective' syndrome (1933) and the schizophreniform disorder of Langfeldt (1937). Each mentions that traumatic life events precede the onset personality factors and that there is a favourable outcome; they may therefore be classed with the other 'reactive' theories in the second group. Langfeldt's concept has been extensively tested in the studies of Retterstöl which will be described in this chapter. A relatively large body of observations has been published about the treatment and the other aspects of schizo-affective disorder and this will therefore be mainly considered in the section devoted to therapy.

A third theory is implicit in the French concept of *bouffée délirante* which refers to an acute paranoid hallucinatory syndrome that terminates in a matter of days or weeks in a clear remission without lasting deficit. It is considered to be entirely *distinct from schizophrenia* and antecedent life events are not mentioned as an aetiological factor of a consistent feature of the condition. Bouffée délirante is therefore regarded in France as a third psychosis.

The Scandinavian school had been powerfully influenced in its early stages by a number of German psychiatrists who considered that at least some paranoid states arose as an understandable historical development culminating in the delusional syndrome. They included Gaupp who investigated the psychiatric disorder of the mass murderer Wagner (Gaupp, 1914, 1920), and his pupil Kretschmer (1918). The ideas of Jaspers were also widely influential. He divided paranoid states into those in which the delusional ideas were primary and the result of a 'psychic process' beyond the reach of understanding, in contrast to developmental conditions that were 'understandable'. He also formulated criteria for the diagnosis of 'psychogenic' disorders including psychoses (Jaspers, 1910).

These disputes continue to be of importance for contemporary psychiatry. They are relevant for clinical psychiatrists and investigators whether they employ DSM III R in diagnosis and classification or utilize other systems. Since the evidence about the nature, causation and the lines of demarcation of paranoid states is complex, account has to be taken of all the dimensions selected by these different theories for special emphasis. Each has some relevance for one or more of the syndromes to be described later.

Delusional paranoid states as a form of schizophrenia

Kraepelin described paranoia as 'the insidious development of a permanent and unshakeable delusional system arising from internal causes which is accompanied by perfect preservation of clear and orderly thinking, will and acting'. Paranoia was distinct in his view from the paranoid forms of dementia praecox, in that it evolved on the basis of an abnormal constitution which had a hereditary basis. He laid stress on the absence of hallucinations in this condition but later contributors were less inflexible about the weight to be attached to this feature. He judged paraphrenia, a delusional psychosis with florid hallucinations, to occupy an intermediate position between schizophrenia on the one hand and paranoia on the other. However a number of pupils of Kraepelin published evidence which appeared to constitute a rebuttal of his views. Thus Mayer-Gross (1931) found evidence of schizophrenic deterioration of personality in more than half of 78 patients diagnosed as paraphrenic by Kraepelin himself.

The work of Kolle (1931) provided further support for the view that paranoia and kindred delusional states were forms of schizophrenic illness. Kolle investigated 66 patients with this condition. He regarded 62 as showing delusions of a primary and incomprehensible character. He also cited genetic observations which purported to show that paranoia and schizophrenia had a common hereditary basis. Kolle considered that the 'true delusion' was incomprehensible and always the symptom of a psychosis. This was usually schizophrenic but occasionally due to organic disorder.

Although he was influenced by the findings of his pupils, Kraepelin continued to defend the view which gave independent nosological status to paranoia and paraphrenia. Both conditions are separately treated in the eighth edition of this textbook (1909–1915). Paranoia was described as incurable and paraphrenia as pursuing a chronic course as far as the persistence of symptoms was concerned but uncomplicated by the deterioration of personality. At a later stage advances in treatment were to uphold the discriminating nature of Kraepelin's clinical insight in relation to this controversy. But some of his views came to be regarded as inflexible and lacking in the historical and dynamic dimension appropriate for study of the origins of some paranoid states.

As far as paranoia was concerned it was the views of Kraepelin's pupils rather than those of the master himself that were to exert the greater influence in the decades that followed.

A number of German psychiatrists ranged themselves on the side of Kolle on the basis of phenomenological evidence about the character of delusions found in paranoia and paraphrenic psychosis. These were judged by Gruhle (1951), a pupil of Jaspers, as having the character of true delusion which '... does not originate from subliminal wishes or from repressed emotions. It is an organic cerebral symptom which cannot be traced back to any source and with which one cannot empathize.' Another distinguished member of the Heidelberg school, Mayer-Gross (1950), was later to express the opinion that most delusional psychoses were variants of schizophrenic illness. He adopted a view regarding the delusions identical with that of Schneider (1952) who considered that there was a sharp categorical distinction between understandable delusional reactions which had no specific diagnostic significance and true delusions or 'delusional perception'. He was referring to a two stage phenomenon; the first comprised an ordinary perception and the second the attachment of an abnormal significance to this perception for reasons that defied comprehension.

The findings of Kolle that favoured a genetic link with schizophrenia have been confirmed in the case of 'late paraphrenia' by the demonstration of a raised morbid risk for schizophrenic illness in the relatives of patients with this disorder. A substantial proportion of those with paranoid psychoses and other disorders associated with paranoia pursue a chronic course. In more recent years some support for the closeness of these disorders to schizophrenia has come from the response made by 'late paraphrenia' among other paranoid disorders to treatment with neuroleptic drugs.

But there is also evidence which calls in question the view of Kolle and others and argues in favour of a relatively distinct status for the paranoid disorders. As far as genetics are concerned, morbid risks which are thought to be greater than in the relatives of normal subjects, are substantially smaller in first degree relatives of paranoic and paraphrenic patients (Kay, 1959) than in the relatives of schizophrenics. Moreover a genetic kinship does not establish clinical identity. Inheritance of the same gene may result in markedly divergent clinical consequences. Each clinical syndrome has therefore to be judged in its own right. The chronic deteriorating course pursued by a high proportion of Kolle's paranoiac patients and reported also in more recent studies represents an out-of-date picture at the present time. 'Late paraphrenia' was described from the outset as a psychosis in which personality was well preserved and did not undergo deterioration despite the typical schizophrenic features present in a high proportion of cases (Roth & Morrissey, 1952; Roth, 1955; Kay & Roth, 1961). The prognosis of late paraphrenia and related forms of disorder has been transformed by the advent of neuroleptic compounds. The precise extent to which the prospects for other paranoid syndromes have been favourably altered remains to be determined with the aid of clinical trials in different sub-groups. But there is a body of evidence from trials in schizo-affective illness with predominantly paranoid symptomatology that neuroleptic drugs (or their combination with antidepressant compounds) promote remission in a substantial proportion of cases.

Paraphrenic and paranoid psychoses of middle life respond to modern treatments in a manner similar to the corresponding psychoses of the aged. Moreover in a large cohort of Swedish patients first admitted to hospital before neuroleptics came into general use and followed up after many years, the observations of Retterstöl (1966, 1970) and his colleagues (Opjørdsmoen, 1986) have shown that 'paranoid' and 'paranoiac' psychoses (regarded as reactive psychoses by Retterstöl) have a distinctly more favourable outcome than that of DSM III schizophrenia. It is the far higher proportion of social recovery in the former that is particularly noteworthy since it rules out the possibility that schizophrenic deterioration could have been anything like as common as suggested by Kolle's original findings. This general conclusion remains valid despite the less favourable outcome in these cases reported by some other observers.

Towards the end of his life Kolle (1957) was to depart from his earlier views, according to which delusional states were endogeneous, determined by genetical and constitutional factors and closely related to schizophrenia. He acknowledged the existence of a group of 'developmental paranoias'. These were delusional states which could be partly understood in the light of historical development of the individual in contrast to 'process paranoia' in which delusions were beyond such attempts at empathy and comprehension. The former comprised such conditions as conjugal paranoias, morbid states of jealousy and the paranoid states of litigious, fanatical, imprisoned and deaf individuals.

By this time the view that there was a distinct group of 'psychogenic' or 'reactive' paranoid psychoses with a benign prognosis had received influential support from the work of Gaupp, Kretschmer and Scandinavian psychiatrists such as Strömgren (1970) and Faergeman (1945).

Delusional (paranoid) states as psychogenic or 'reactive' disorders

From the second decade of the present century onwards a number of attempts have been made to separate 'paranoia' from dementia praecox by observations purported to establish that: (1) they were to an extent psychologically understandable developments; (2) they emerged from interaction between a predisposed individual with an Achilles heel in his personality and traumatic life events; (3) there followed a paranoid delusional psychosis that divorced the patient from his environment; and (4) despite this rift from reality the personality remained intact in terms of thought, affect and volition. The classical description by Gaupp in 1914 and 1920 of the notorious mass murderer Wagner was a massively documented paradigm of cases of this nature. Ernst Wagner was a highly educated intelligent schoolmaster, poet and novelist who on the night of 3rd September 1913 killed his wife and four children by cutting their throats while they slept. He then travelled by train and bicycle from Stuttgart to Mühlhausen. On the following night he started four fires in the sleeping village and when the inhabitants tried to escape from their houses he fired shots from two pistols at all the male inhabitants, killing eight of them and severely wounding 12 others. He was then brought down by some of the inhabitants and prevented from completing his entire plan, which was to murder his brother's family, to start other fires in the village and to set fire to the neighbouring castle where he was to commit suicide by shooting himself. The mass murders had been meticulously planned and kept secret over a decade.

Wagner was committed to an asylum where he spent the rest of his life and was observed by Gaupp over a period of almost 25 years. He considered that Wagner suffered from a paranoid illness which had begun abruptly after he committed a number of acts of indecency with animals while making his way from an inn to his home in a drunken state. Almost immediately he began to observe others commenting, laughing, making derisory and contemptuous remarks about him. The whole village of Mühlhausen and people wider afield were aware of his perverted behaviour. He developed an intense hatred of his tormentors and planned to murder his enemies in Mühlhausen out of revenge and to kill his family out of compassionate concern for the sufferings they would otherwise endure after his death. Wagner had already experienced ideas of self-reference in relation to the practice of masturbation from the age of 18. He believed everyone knew his guilty secret.

Gaupp considered Wagner's psychotic disorder to be the delusional reaction of a man of paranoid personality to the emotional stress occasioned by indecent acts that caused him guilt and shame. Over a period of 25 years his delusions remained unshakeable except for short-lived intervals when they would recede, only to be replaced by a fresh delusional system in which he felt persecuted by Jews whom he saw all round him, and in particular by the poet Franz Werfel whom he accused of plagiarizing his works. He welcomed the advent of the Nazi regime and its racial policies with a joyous satisfaction. He died in 1938 at the age of 64. There was at no time any sign of intellectual impairment or personality deterioration. He remained quick-witted, powerful in argument, verbally fluent and coherent to the end, when he died of tuberculosis.

Most of Gaupp's psychiatric colleagues including Eugen Bleuler thought Wagner suffered from a mild paranoid schizophrenic illness. Gaupp rejected this view although he admitted that two of Wagner's maternal relatives were clearly schizophrenic. In fact one uncle suffered from delusional ideas of self-reference centering around his masturbation which were strongly reminiscent of earlier stages of his nephew's mental development.

The concept of psychogenic psychosis was carried forward by Gaupp's pupil Kretschmer (1918) in his work on the sensitive delusion of reference (Der sensitive Beziehungswhan). Kretschmer's monograph described patients who were sensitive, endowed with a depressive and pessimistic outlook, high ambition and low frustration tolerance. The psychosis was initiated by a 'key event' which gave rise to a 'mental avalanche' after impinging upon vulnerable facets of the individual's morbid personality. The event was usually some error or indiscretion at variance with the individual's moral code, often a minor misdemeanour of a sexual nature. Kretschmer was partly influenced by his familiarity with the case of Wagner whom he regarded as exemplifying his syndrome. Subsequent investigations were to show that a substantial proportion of Kreschmer's cases developed symptoms of a chronic psychosis. But it is not clear whether the picture in those found to be ill on follow-up was one of schizophrenic personality deterioration with negative symptoms or no more than an encapsulated psychosis which had left the personality essentially intact.

Despite the criticisms levelled against it, Kretschmer's work was widely influential in directing attention to the dynamic aspects of certain paranoid states. The Scandinavian concept of psychogenic psychosis which Kretschmer's work had helped to create (Strömgren, 1940; Retterstöl, 1966, 1970) was considerably wider than Kretschmer's syndrome and embraced paranoia and paraphrenia (a late form of schizophrenia) as well as schizophreniform psychosis, which are all regarded as 'reactive'. The Danish psychiatrist Wimmer (1916) was an early pioneer in this field. He was influenced by French authors such as Magnan and Janet as well as Kraepelin and Jaspers in Germany.

More recently the comprehensive long-term studies conducted by Retterstöl and his colleagues have adduced a large body of evidence regarding the clinical profile, course and prognosis of paranoid psychosis. He followed up and compared the outcome of 78 delusional patients with schizophreniform psychosis, 173 cases of reactive psychosis and 52 patients with schizophrenia (originally diagnosed by Langfeldt). Five to 19 years after discharge, 81% of the reactive psychotics had pursued a favourable course compared with 61% of those with schizophreniform psychosis and only 23% of those with schizophrenia. Fifty-four of per cent the reactive psychotics achieved a complete and lasting remission, 36% suffered further attacks with good remissions, and 10% pursued a chronic course. In contrast only 10% of patients with schizophrenia made a complete recovery.

However a more recent investigation by Opjordsmoen (1986) on a sub-sample of 125 patients with the same material after a follow-up period of 15–18 years, and 35–37 years after the original remission, shows that a further proportion of paieints had undergone deterioration as assessed with the aid of the Global Assessment Scale. Fifty-eight per cent of the patients were unchanged, 30% had deteriorated and 13% improved. The proportion whose status had declined increased with the length of time that had elapsed since discharge from hospital.

Particular interest attaches to the detailed results regarding social outcome and the proportion who remained under psychiatric care. A variety of different criteria were applied in the evaluation of these patients at follow-up.

On the basis of DSM III criteria for 'schizophreniform' disorder, 68.1% were at work at the end of the follow-up period and 87.1% were residing at home; the corresponding figures for schizophrenia were 18.4 and 68.4%. Among those diagnosed as 'reactive psychosis' by ICD 9 criteria, 68% were at work and 92% were living at home. The findings for paranoid states (ICD 9) and schizo-affective disorder (RDC criteria) were closely similar, while among delusional states (Kendler, 1980) 51.6% were at work and 87.1% living at home.

However from the data provided by Opjordsmoen it would seem that a substantial proportion of patients continued to suffer from psychiatric symptoms. Nearly half of those with reactive psychosis were receiving psychiatric treatment. The proportion under care among schizophreniform disorders was 58%, and 'schizo-affective' and 'reactive' psychoses about 48%. The status of schizophrenic patients was far less satisfactory; four fifths were continuing under psychiatric treatment and only 18.3% were in employment.

Some components of the Retterstöl thesis that certain paranoid psychoses are relatively distinct from schizophrenia are therefore supported by his own and others' published data. These disorders pursue on the whole a more benign course than schizophrenic disorders. Schizophrenic deterioration of personality leading to a 'burnt-out' state is uncommon. Chronicity of some symptoms is more common but the illness is encapsulated permitting a satisfactory social adjustment in more than two thirds of the cases. Ninety per cent of each group were living at home. Retterstöl's conclusions were derived from the largest cohort of patients with paranoid psychosis ever studied and therefore have a firm factual basis. But the verdict that emerges from the observations of other workers is more ambiguous. Forty-three out of 160 of Faergeman's patients (Faergeman, 1945, 1963) originally diagnosed by Wimmer as suffering from 'psychogenic' psychosis, proved to be suffering from schizophrenia or a closely similar disorder when followed up many years later. The Norwegian study (Noreik, 1970) showed 56% of patients with 'reactive' psychosis to have pursued a course consistent with a diagnosis of schizophrenic illness. Variations in the criteria used in diagnosis and in sampling are the most likely explanation for some of these seemingly contradictory findings. But the most telling statistics come from Retterstöl's own data and those of Opjordsmoen. Of the patients with 'uncertain' diagnosis (almost a quarter of the total material) 30% were judged to be schizophrenic on follow-up. A third of the sub-sample of 125 patients re-examined decades after the initial admission were found to have deteriorated. And at this time almost 50% of patients with 'reactive' psychoses were under psychiatric care though only a small proportion were in institutions. The outcome of paranoid psychoses, though relatively favourable overall, is indeterminate.

Jaspers' line of demarcation between 'psychogenic' and 'endogenous' psychoses

The differential diagnostic criteria of Jaspers (1963) were the first to be set down in specific terms and continue to be influential among contemporary psychiatrists in Europe in particular. He drew a sharp distinction between psychiatric disorders which could be regarded as the result of 'a process'. This term referred to a qualitative change in psychic life which emerged spontaneously without any adequate and ascertainable psychological cause. In 'development' on the other hand the disorder arises during the unfolding of the individual's life history; it can be understood in terms of this history and the personality that had evolved in the course of it. In the former there was a break in continuity of psychic life followed by subjective experiences and behaviour beyond the range of normal psychological phenomena. In the latter the disorder is merely a variant of normal psychological experience. During a 'process', 'true delusions' are often manifest. These cannot be comprehended when set in the context of the patient's life history and situation. In the 'developmental' type of disorder any delusions are closely and comprehensibly related to the prevailing emotional state and the patient's life predicament.

In Jaspers' view, psychotic delusional (paranoid) disorders may be regarded as psychogenic when they satisfy the following criteria:

(i) The onset of illness bears a clear time relationship with some stressful life event.
(ii) The precipitating stress must be adequate; in other words the disorders that follow stress must not be disapproportionately severe.

(iii) There is a meaningful relationship between the content of the precipitating adverse event and that of the mental illness that follows it. It should be possible to construe it as a form of defence, a wish fulfilment or an escape from onerous circumstances and symptoms.
(iv) When the primary or precipitating cause is removed the illness ('abnormal reaction') comes to an end.

Wimmer, the influential Danish psychiatrist who formulated criteria similar to those of Jaspers, added that reactive psychoses *never end in deterioration.*

A small proportion of paranoid disorders would qualify for diagnosis as 'psychogenic psychosis' according to these criteria. They include the paranoid psychoses of prisoners, some of the paranoid reactions of the deaf and of those placed in a situation of isolation, and induced psychoses such as 'folie à deux'. But the majority of cases of persecutory paranoia, paranoid jealousy or erotomania, and schizo-affective and schizophreniform disorders with predominantly paranoid features seen in clinical practice would fail to qualify for admission to the class of 'psychogenic' disorders. When these paranoid syndromes follow onerous life events they are disproportionate in severity and duration, meaningful connections will usually be few, tenuous or non-existent, and elimination of the 'primary' event will very rarely eliminate the mental illness that has followed it. This should not be taken to mean that the patients' vicissitudes and personalities may be omitted from consideration in the treatment given them.

As far as delusions are concerned, even if one accepts the validity of the broad distinction between 'true delusions' and those more comprehensibly related to prevailing emotional state and the patient's predicament, the sharp and unmistakable dividing line applied by Jaspers is open to question. Hallucinations in clear consciousness and delusions of reference and persecution are at times described in cases of 'psychogenic' paranoid psychosis as 'understandable'. But if this is accepted, the same verdict has to be passed on delusions of indubitably schizophrenic patients by the criteria of Schneider (1959). Connections between the themes of delusion and pre-morbid personality there may be, but the fixed and lasting nature of all such ideas and their impregnability to all evidence that refutes them are beyond 'understanding'.

Theories of paranoid states as a distinct but non-reactive psychosis

The French concept of bouffée délirante (bd)

The special interest of the French concept resides in the fact that a number of the paranoid psychoses and disorders described in ICD 9, DSM III and other classifications appear to be subsumed under a single heading 'bouffée délirante' (bd). Pichot (1986) has recently traced the origins of the concept to the contributions of Magnan and Legrain in the late 19th century and reviewed his earlier work in an attempt to bring it into relationship with the related rubrics in ICD 9 and DSM III in particular.

The psychosis in question is of sudden onset, the delusions overpowering in character and protean in form, incorporating persecutory, grandiose, mystical, erotic and other themes. Hallucinations are a secondary and inessential feature. There may be some clouding of consciousness and emotional disorder manifest in anxiety, agitation, impulsiveness or inertia. Physical signs are absent and there is a rapid return to pre-morbid functioning in a matter of '... a few hours, days or weeks'.

Pichot considers that four of the diagnoses presented in DSM III could be subsumed under the rubric of 'bouffée délirante'. DSM III 205–40, schizophreniform disorder, differs only in that there is no reference either to emotional instability or fragile personality. This would receive a diagnosis of 'bd' in France. DSM III 298–90, 'atypical psychosis', would also qualify except for the limitation to a duration of 2 weeks or less. The same statement applies to DSM III 298–30, acute paranoid disorder. This approximates the reactive form of the 'bd' syndrome except that the symptoms do not display the wide variation which is regarded as characteristic of 'bd' whether or not it is reactive. DSM III 298–80, brief reactive psychosis, which is expected to resolve in 2 weeks or less, is regarded by Pichot as the exact French equivalent of reactive 'bd'.

However Pichot points out that the French concept of 'bd' places emphasis upon inherent constitutional aspects of aetiology (only 15% being judged reactive) whereas DSM III, and also the Scandinavian systems, place more emphasis upon the reactive character of the disorder. Whether the four syndromes mentioned by Pichot could indeed be brought together could only be decided by investigations of natural history outcome and treatment response. If there were parallel characteristics in all these respects, there would be economy in classification and decision making with respect to prognosis and treatment could be simplified.

However, the jealous, erotomanic, somatic, grandiose types of delusional (paranoid) disorder (197.10) and schizo-affective disorders could not be subsumed under the heading of a psychosis such as 'bd', which is acute, florid, of short duration and self-terminating in the great majority of cases. The outcome of 'schizophreniform' disorders is also indeterminate.

Further, although 'bd' is stated to carry a favourable prognosis with a return to pre-morbid functioning in '... a few hours, days or weeks'; it would seem that 40% can be expected to prove non-recurrent, another 40% will suffer relapses and 20% have an outcome closely similar to that of schizophrenia. In fact we appear to be not very remote from the findings of Retterstöl. There is the same indeterminacy; there are no available criteria for predicting in which of the classes of outcome described by Pichot individual patients will be found some years after initial presentation. Yet the aetiological basis of 'bd' is conceived quite differently in France than that of 'psychogenic' or 'reactive' psychoses in Scandinavia. Only 15% of 'bd' cases were considered 'reactive' and no more than 6% of the '*paranoid*' cases. This last term is employed in France exclusively in relation to schizophrenia.

The Viennese concept of paranoid psychoses

The Viennese group of Berner has arrived at a body of theory as distinctive as that of the French and Scandinavian schools. Yet common ground between all can be defined.

The Viennese School (Berner, 1965; Berner *et al.*, 1983) divided the paranoid psychoses on the strength of background features such as apathy, disturbance of mood and affect, disorders of biological rhythms such as sleep disturbance, and neurological or phenomenological evidence suggesting a contribution by an organic lesion. Using such background features they defined three relatively distinct syndromes:

(i) A schizophrenic axial syndrome associated with thought disorder and affective impoverishment.
(ii) A cyclothymic axial syndrome the leading features of which were disturbances of mood and drive, sleep disorder and derangements of biological rhythm.
(iii) The organic axial syndrome derived from biological evidence of organic brain damage or phenomenological changes in thought and language suggesting organic impairment.

Utilizing research criteria derived from these axial syndromes they have classified their patients into four groups: (i) an 'endogenomorphic-schizophrenic syndrome', (ii) an 'endogenomorphic-cyclothymic syndrome', (iii) an 'organomorphic syndrome' and (iv) a fourth group made up of those patients who could not be assigned on the basis of the criteria employed to any one of the first three groups. The terms employed imply phenomenological rather than aetiological affinities.

Only five patients fell into the first group. This was one of the reasons for the conclusion of the Viennese workers that the 'classical' teaching, according to which the majority of paranoid syndromes have a close kinship with schizophrenia, is erroneous. Of the 18 patients classified into the second group more than two thirds pursued an episodic course and a third became chronic, suggesting kinship of cases with affective disorders. Eight of the 12 patients who fell into the organomorphic syndrome pursued a chronic course. The largest was the fourth group made up of 49 of the cases. More than two-thirds became chronic and less than a third pursued an episodic course.

Only a small group of patients with stable paranoid symptoms was therefore classified as a nuclear schizophrenic group. The remainder fell into two main classes; episodic cases on the one hand and those with a chronic pattern of outcome on the other; five-eighths of the patients fell into this latter outcome group.

Although the chronicity rate was high, the findings do not appear markedly discrepant from those of Retterstöl, for the proportion of cases in which a schizophrenic burnt-out state with negative symptoms emerged proved to be very small. In the remainder, one group constituting about a third of cases had clear affinities with episodic affective disorders. The second and main group exhibited chronic paranoid illusions. The quality of social adaption of the patients in the different outcome groups would be of interest. Berner and his colleagues were undecided as to whether there is an adequate case for a third distinct class of psychotic disorders in addition to manic depressive and schizophrenic psychosis.

Summary

The evidence makes a strong case that there is a developmental and historical dimension in the form of personality factors and threatening events and circumstances in *a proportion* of patients with paranoid disorder. Long-term follow-up investigations established that the pattern of outcome of paranoid disorders is more favourable on the whole than that of schizophrenia. But the term 'psychogenic psychosis' overstates the causal importance of key events and the pre-morbid state. These probably contribute to the development of the disease but we do not yet understand how they do so and their aetiology remains largely obscure. Even in so-called 'psychogenic' cases the condition pursues a chronic course in a substantial proportion, though in encapsulated form, and personality deterioration is much more uncommon than in schizophrenia. One inference to be drawn at this stage is that although treatment with neuroleptic drugs has transformed the prospect for some cases, such treatment should be combined with attention to personality and life situation by appropriate methods of psychotherapeutic support and correction of possibly contributory factors such as social isolation and physical disease. These conclusions are largely derived from the large scale prospective studies undertaken by Scandinavian workers such as Strömgren and Retterstöl and studies of late paraphrenia and kindred conditions in Great Britain. Although French and Austrian workers have employed different clinical concepts, their findings are mainly in accord with these conclusions.

Acknowledgement—A substantial part of this chapter has been published in *Treatment of psychiatric disorders*, 'A Task Force Report of the American Psychiatric Association, Vol 2', by Toksoz Byram Karasu; and is reprinted here by permission of the American Psychiatric association.

References

American Psychiatric Association. (1980): Diagnostic and statistical manual of mental disorders, 3rd edn. Washington: American Psychiatric Association.
Berner, P., Gabriel, E., & Katschnig, H. (1983): Diagnostic criteria for schizophrenia and affective disorders. London: World Psychiatric Association.
Berner, P. (1965): *Das Paranoische Syndrom*. Berlin: Springer.
Faergeman, P.M. (1945): *Der Psykogene Psykoser belyst gennem Katamnestiske Undersogelser*. Copenhagen: Munksgaard.
Faergeman, P.M. (1963): *Psychogenic psychoses. A description and follow-up of psychoses following psychological stress*. London: Butterworths.
Gaupp, R. (1914): *Zür Psychologie des Massenmordes*.Berlin: Hauptlehrer Wagner von Degerloch.
Gaupp, R. (1920): Der Fall Wagner. Eine Katamnese, zugleich ein Beitrag zur Lehre von Paranoia. *Z. Gesamte Neurol. Psychiatr.* **60**, 312–327.
Gruhle, H.W. (1951): Uber den Wahn. *Nervenarzt* **22**, 125–126.
Jaspers, K. (1910): Eifersuchtswahn. *Z. Gesamte Neurol. Psychiatr.* **1**, 567–637.
Jaspers, K. (1963): *General psychopathology (1913)*; translated from 7th edition Hoenig and Hamilton. London: Manchester University Press.
Kasinin, J. (1933): The acute schizoaffective psychoses. *Am. J. Psychiatry* **13**, 97–126.
Kay, D.W.K. (1959): Observations on the natural history and genetics of old age psychosis: Stockholm material 1931–1937 (Abridged). *Proc. R. Soc. Med.* **52**,
Kay, D.W.K. & Roth, M. (1961): Environmental and hereditary factors in the schizophrenias of old age ('late paraphrenia') and their bearing on the general problem of causation in schizophrenia. *J. Ment. Sci.* **107**, 649–686.
Kendler, K.S. (1980): The nosological validity of paranoia (simple delusional disorder). *Arch. Gen. Psychiatry* **37**, 699–706.
Kolle, K. (1931): *Die primare Verrucktheit*. Leipzig: Georg Thieme.
Kolle, K. (1957): *Der Wahnkranke im Lichte alter und neuer Psychopathologie*. Stuttgart: George Thieme.
Kraepelin, D. (1909–1915): *Psychiatrie. Ein Lehrbuch fur Studierende and Arzte*. 8. Aufl. Leipzig: J.A. Barth.
Kretschmer, E. (1918): *Der sensitive Beziehungswahn*. Berlin: Julius Springer.
Landfeldt, G. (1937): The prognosis of schizophrenia and the factors influencing the course of the disease. *Acta Psychiatr. Neurol. Scand.* **suppl 13**, 302, 308, 309, 483.
Langfeldt, G. (1951): The hypersensitive mind. *Acta Psychiatr. Scand. Suppl.* 73.
Mayer-Gross, W. (1931): Some symptoms of organic brain disease. *Arch. Psychiatr. Nervenkr.* **92**, 433–613.
Mayer-Gross, W. (1950): Psychopathology of delusions. Congres International de Psychiatrie I. Tome I, 59–87.
Noriek, K. (1970): Follow-up and classification of functional psychoses with special reference to reactive psychoses. Oslo: Universitetsforlaget.
Opjørdsmoen, S. (1986): Long-term follow-up of paranoid psychoses. *Psychopathology* **19**, 44–49.
Pichot, P. (1986): The concept of 'Bouffee Delirante' with special reference to the Sandinavian concept of reactive psychosis. *Psychopathology* **19**, 35–43.
Retterstöl, N. (1966): *Paranoid and paranoiac psychoses*. Oslo: Universitetsforlaget.
Retterstöl, N. (1970): *Prognosis in paranoid psychosis*. Springfield: Thomas.
Roth, M. (1955): The natural history of mental disorders in old age. *J. Ment. Sci.* **101**, 281.
Roth, M. & Morrissey, J.D. (1952): Problems in the diagnosis and classification of mental disorder in old age. *J. Ment. Sci.* **98**, 66.
Schneider, K. (1952): *Uber den Wahn*. Stuttgart.

Schneider, K. (1959): *Klinische Psychopathologie*, 12th ed. 1980. Stuttgart: Thieme. English edition translated by M.W. Hamilton & E.W. Anderson. New York: Grune & Stratton.
Strömgren, E. (1940): *Episodiske Psykoser*. Copenhagen: Munksguard.
Strömgren, E. (1974): Psychogenic psychoses. In *Themes and variations in European psychiatry. An anthology*, ed. S.R. Hirsch & M. Shepherd. Bristol: John Wright.
Wimmer, A. (1916): *Psykogene Sindssygdomsformer* (in Danish). Copenhagen: Lunds.
World Health Organization (1973): The international pilot study of schizophrenia, vol. I. Geneva: World Health Organization.

II

GENETICS

Introduction

The core, or nuclear, symptoms of schizophrenia are auditory hallucinations discussing the patients, external influences on the thought, will, or emotion, and characteristic disturbances of thinking (thought disorder). In an interesting analysis Warner has pointed out that although very different diagnostic systems have been used there has been a strong correlation between chronicity and the economic circumstances of America, the UK, and Scandinavian countries, and the prognosis is very much better in third world countries. Other evidence has convincingly linked schizophrenia to hostility and high emotional tone in the family situation.

Clearly some factor additional to social circumstances is involved since the population at large is exposed to similar problems and only about 3–4000 of the population suffer from schizophrenia in any one year, and only about 1% over a lifetime (see Jablensky, this volume, p. 169).

The concept that disease rests on cellular pathology dates back to Virkow. Psychiatric disturbance has been difficult to fit into the disease concept because no unique cellular pathology has been demonstrated in any of the psychiatric illnesses, although organic findings have been found in several, increasingly so with the new imaging techniques. This has been particularly true in the case of schizophrenia, a disorder with many manifestations. The diagnostic criteria have expanded and shrunk since the original formulations of Kraepelin, who named the condition dementia praecox, and Bleuler who coined the term schizophrenia. Since then there has been an increasing emphasis on psychotic manifestations, with a corresponding de-emphasizing of the chronically disabling symptoms of disintegration of the personality, social withdrawal, and lack of drive and ambition, described as lack of volition. There has been a difficulty in explaining to the clinically naive how to recognize the wider diagnostic criteria. This has bolstered the confidence of the critics of psychiatry, who have gone as far as to protest that schizophrenia is a myth; but as Seymour Kety (Chapter 11) wryly comments, 'If schizophrenia is a myth it is a myth with a strong genetic element'.

The genetic arguments have been based on the increased likelihood of developing the disease with increased closeness to a related family member, and the increased frequency of schizophrenia in the offspring of schizophrenic parents when placed in adopted families.

The genetic pattern has proved very complicated and difficult to fit into a clear Mendelian model. Because the illness typically occurs in the late teens or early twenties, but may occur much later, the figures are difficult to obtain and the first figure in the Table (overleaf) is based on few cases. The lack of symmetry between child and parent is attributed to social withdrawal and lower fertility in affected individuals.

One of the more attractive models has been that of stress and diathesis, so that what is inherited is a vulnerability which can be highlighted by certain environmental factors; these include an adverse obstetric and perinatal history, which seems to explain some of the variance in identical twins who are discordant for schizophrenia, where the lighter of the two twins and the second born of the two twins has a greater likelihood of manifesting the disease (see Reveley, this volume, p. 44).

Gun shot wounds to the left temporal lobe and epilepsy in this same area lead to schizophrenia-like psychosis more often than damage or malfunction in other parts of the

Table *Genetic risk of schizophrenia.*

Relationship	*Risk* (%)
Both parents	46.3
Sibling plus parent	16.7
Child	12.8
Sibling	10.1
Parent	5.6
Uncles/aunts/nephews/nieces	2.8
Grandchild	3.7
Unrelated	0.86

brain, and the left handed twin is more likely to suffer from schizophrenia if there is a handedness discrepancy, suggesting the possibility of left hemisphere damage. A thinning of the left parahippocampal gyrus and an excess of dopamine in the amygdaloid nucleus on the left side of the brain occur in schizophrenics, and the latter finding is consistent with the beneficial effects of neuroleptic drugs. These same drugs seem to be beneficial in a range of disorders (see Weller, Chapter 9), including schizotypal and borderline personality disorders, which has been named the schizophrenic spectrum of disorders (see Kety, p. 124). The genetic concordance is increased if these disorders are included with schizophrenia.

The current fashion to hive off such spectrum disorders and to separate them from the nuclear symptoms has supported the critics of psychiatry and promoted the reduction of psychiatric facilities. It has been argued that this has contributed to the increase in the prison population, and the correspondence between the two is sufficiently great for more than 90% of the variance in the prison population to be explained by variations in the psychiatric bed occupancy figures (Weller *et al*, 1988) and great difficulty in transferring mentally disturbed offenders from prison to psychiatric care (Cheadle *et al.*, 1982; Coid, 1988).

The public attitude and perception has been bolstered by persuasive and influential figures, and the teaching of psychiatry has been influenced by writings of people like Lange and Szasz, not only in prestigious sociology departments, but also in departments of psychology and social work, from which clinical psychologists and approved social workers eventually emanate. Both public policy and clinical practice are shaped by anti-psychiatry concepts which have sought to challenge the medical model and the medical contribution to the treatment of nuclear schizophrenia, let alone the spectrum of schizophrenic disorders. These are interpreted as distress which has been 'medicalized' for little purpose other than the self-advancement of psychiatrists.

Gurling and his colleagues (Chapter 13) provide important support for the genetic transmission of a disease with many manifestations. Other examples abound in medicine, for example the atopic disorders of asthma, urticaria and hay fever can be clustered together on the basis of common pathology, and may be treated with psychotherapy. Asthma particularly was commonly treated in this way until the advent of more successul drugs. An indisputable genetic disorder like phenylketonuria can be modified by diet. The diathesis-stress model does not rule out the beneficial effects of environmental control, and the relapse of schizophrenia can certainly be reduced by careful attention to emotional climate in the household (see Leff, Chapter 24).

The findings of Gurling *et al.* therefore should not be seen as vindication for an organic view so much as a reconciliation between opposing factions for a disease which causes much suffering and social problems and which requires expertise in many areas. It is hoped that the recognition of the medical basis will affect psychiatric planning in a favourable direction.

References

Cheadle, J. & Ditchfield, J. (1982): *Sentencing mentally ill offenders*. London: Home Office Research and Planning Unit.

Coid, J.W. (1988): Mentally abnormal prisoners on remand. I. Rejected or accepted by the NHS? *Br. Med. J.* **296**, 1779–1782.

Weller, M.P.I., Weller, B.G.A. & Badenoch, D. (1988): Mentally abnormal prisoners on remand. *Br. Med. J.* **297**, 559–560.

Chapter 11

The significance of genetic factors in the aetiology of schizophrenia: results from the National Study of Adoptees in Denmark*

Seymour S. Kety

National Institute of Mental Health, National Institutes of Health, Bethesda, MD, USA

Summary

The prevalence of schizophrenic illness in the biological and adoptive relatives of schizophrenic adoptees has been examined in a total sample of adoptees in Denmark. The sample was studied in two stages, beginning with the Copenhagen sample of adoptions granted by the courts in the city and county of Copenhagen, and the results have been reported previously. The adoptions granted by the courts in the remainder of Denmark comprised the Provincial sample, the preliminary results of which appear to confirm those obtained earlier. Schizophrenia was found in both samples to concentrate significantly in the biological relatives of schizophrenic adoptees as compared to their controls, but not in their adoptive relatives, indicating the operation of genetic, but not of family-related environmental factors in this disorder. Milder syndromes, described as latent, borderline, or uncertain schizophrenia, and in current practice in the United States as schizotypal personality disorder, were also concentrated significantly in only the biological relatives of the schizophrenic adoptees. These milder and marginal syndromes resembling schizophrenia occurring in the families of schizophrenic patients confirm the observations of Bleuler and others who succeeded him. Their presence in the biological families of schizophrenic adoptees is compatible with genetic relationship to schizophrenia.

Introduction

The old 'nature *vs* nurture' arguments have worn themselves thin and, with very few exceptions, biological and behavioural scientists now agree that mental qualities and disorders, like those in the somatic area, are the result of genetic and epigenetic, or environmental influences. There is still a need to delineate and evaluate their components in particular disorders and to examine their interaction. Psychiatric nosology is largely phenomenological, diagnosis is imprecise, rarely based on objective and pathognomonic

*A lecture presented in London at the conference "Perspectives in Schizophrenia", under the auspices of the National Schizophrenia Fellowship, 14–17 July, 1988, based on earlier publications and on the most recent study, to be published with Wender, Jacobsen, Jansson, Faber, Ingraham, Kinney, Schulsinger & Rosenthal.

criteria, and the same genetic deviance may have a variety of alternative expressions by virtue of the complexities of the brain.

Demonstration of genetic contributions and their examination has been the object of several different methodological approaches. Occurrence of schizophrenia in families, which has been known to be characteristic and may be the resultant of genetic or environmental factors, does not constitute conclusive proof for any degree of genetic transmission unless shared environment can be shown to have a negligible effect. The high concordance for schizophrenia (40–50%) which is found in monozygotic twins, with a lower concordance (10–15%) in dizygotic twins, comparable to that in siblings, has constituted presumptive evidence for a genetic contribution. This is based on the assumption that identical and fraternal twins differ only in their degree of genetic overlap while the environment is constant. However the former share many more psychosocial influences than the latter and these influences may play an aetiological role.

The study of adopted individuals and their biological and adoptive families offers a means of disentangling genetic and family-associated environmental variables since adoptees share their genetic endowment with one family and their environment with another.

Study of adopted individuals

Beginning in 1962, I have been engaged, in collaboration with David Rosenthal and others at the National Institute of Mental Health, Paul Wender at the University of Utah, Fini Schulsinger and associates in Copenhagen, and colleagues at Harvard, in a programme of studies which uses adoption as a means of separating genetic and environmental influences in the aetiology of schizophrenia and a number of other psychiatric disorders.

We entered this collaboration from different vantage points and with different aims: as a better means of evaluating a diathesis:stress model of schizophrenia, or a valuable means of testing parental schizophrenogenic hypotheses without genetic interference. For me it permitted an examination of the prevalence of schizophrenia in the biological and adoptive families of schizophrenic adoptees in order to learn how much of the well known familial tendency of schizophrenia might be accounted for by genetic or environmental factors. When, with the invaluable collaboration of Fini Schulsinger, we were given access under strict rules of confidentiality to the pertinent records in Denmark and were able to compile the Danish Adoption Registers, first for Greater Copenhagen and more recently for all of Denmark, it was possible to pursue these aims using the diligently maintained records, and exhaustive interviews by Danish psychiatrists. We developed a research design to minimize ascertainment, selective, and subjective bias, and to separate to the maximum degree possible the genetic and family-related environmental influences operating in the adoptees and families who would be studied.

We have now completed four studies examining the incidence of schizophrenia or affective disorder in the biological and adoptive relatives of affected adoptees (Kety *et al.*, 1968, 1975; Wender *et al.*, 1986; Kety *et al.*, to be published), and each has found a significantly higher incidence of the particular type of disorder among the biological siblings, half-siblings or parents of the affected adoptees than in their controls.

Prevalence of schizophrenia in relatives of schizophrenic adoptees

The hypothesis to be tested in the first study (Kety *et al.*, 1968) was stated as follows: ‘If schizophrenia were to some extent genetically transmitted, there should be a higher prevalence of disorders in the schizophrenia spectrum among the biological relatives of the index cases (ie schizophrenic adoptees) than in those of their controls'. Blind consensus diagnoses based on detailed abstracts of hospital records found a prevalence of that spectrum in the biological index relatives of 8.7% compared with 1.9% in the biological relatives of the control adoptees, the prevalence in the adoptive index relatives being no higher than that in their controls. Without the inclusion of the two personality disorders, 'schizoid' and 'inadequate', the prevalence of chronic or latent schizophrenia, definite or uncertain, in the biological index and control relatives was 7.3 *vs* 1.9%. Although there were insufficient cases to permit testing individual components of the spectrum with any reliability, an absence of any schizophrenia disorders was noted in the 30 biological relatives of the seven adoptees diagnosed as acute schizophrenia. On the other hand, 10 of the 13 spectrum disorders in the index biological relatives were diagnosed as 'latent' or 'uncertain' schizophrenia, confirming Bleuler who rejected 'acute' schizophrenia but noted the prevalence of latent or borderline forms of schizophrenia in the relatives of his schizophrenic patients. These results strengthened the surmise that schizoid and inadequate personality as well as acute schizophrenia would more appropriately have been omitted from the schizophrenia spectrum, a hypothesis which would be tested later.

To come closer to defining the boundaries of schizophrenia it was necessary to enlarge the sample or obtain more information regarding the mental and behavioural status of the relatives. It was decided to do both by extending the study to all of Denmark and by conducting exhaustive interviews with the relatives. Bjorn Jacobsen joined the collaboration and spent the next 3 years interviewing the relatives in the Copenhagen sample. Analysis of the interviews amplified the results obtained in the same sample from hospital records alone (Kety *et al.*, 1975). The original spectrum was significantly concentrated as before in the biological relatives of the schizophrenic adoptees, but now in addition to the two cases of schizoid or inadequate personality in the relatives who were in hospital, 26 instances were found among the relatives who were not hospital inpatients, dividing themselves evenly between index and control relatives. When these non-discriminating personality disorders were excluded, the remaining diagnoses were highly concentrated in the biological relatives of the schizophrenic adoptees. There were no diagnoses of chronic schizophrenia in the biological relatives of the controls but five cases of this most severe form in the biological relatives of the schizophrenic adoptees. There was, moreover, a large number of latent and uncertain schizophrenias among the biological relatives, highly concentrated in the index relatives (11.0 *vs* 3.4%). Control adoptees were interviewed blindly along with the relatives and 23 were found to be free of schizophrenia spectrum or serious mental disorder. When their biological relatives were compared with those of the schizophrenic adoptees, the preponderance of latent and uncertain schizophrenia in the biological relatives of the schizophrenic adoptees was even more striking (11.0 *vs* 0.9%) (Kety *et al.*, 1975).

The concept of latent schizophrenia had been vaguely defined by Bleuler, and our criteria for uncertain schizophrenia were equally ill-defined — enough of the features of schizophrenia to make it the most likely diagnosis, but not sufficiently severe or typical to be certain. With all their vagueness, however, which could only increase the opportunity for error and make it more difficult to find a significant difference, these diagnoses, made blindly, were almost exclusively in the biological relatives of the schizophrenic adoptees. Bleuler's recognition of a mild form of the disorder in the relatives of severely ill schizophrenic patients was confirmed, but now in relatives who grew up apart from the patients and unlikely to have been influenced by the patients' family environment or their thought processes and behaviour.

Provincial Sample

The collection of what would be called the Provincial Sample, ie the adoptees throughout

Denmark outside of Copenhagen, began in 1975, accumulating first the records of adoptions granted outside of the City and County of Copenhagen, approximately 9300 in number. Using the same procedures employed in the Copenhagen study, the index adoptees were selected by unanimous agreement on a diagnosis of schizophrenia: chronic, latent, or acute. The matched controls, presumably mentally healthy, or at least with no record of admission to a mental institution, were then selected. The control and index biological and adoptive parents, siblings and half-siblings were identified, and the Psychiatric Register searched for any record of their admission to a mental institution. Blind consensus diagnoses based on these records were made, and the results were quite consistent with those of the 1968 Copenhagen study, also based on institutional records.

In 1980, Dr Jacobsen and two associates began interviewing the relatives with the same high rate of compliance which was achieved in Copenhagen. The 36 page English transcripts were blindly rated independently by two raters and a consensus diagnosis arrived at. This, in conjunction with abstracts and extensive summaries of hospital records of those subjects who had been in hospital 10 or more years earlier were the basis of a final diagnosis made on relatives and probands, both index and control, all made without knowledge of the relationship of a subject to any other (Kety *et al.*, to be published).

A preliminary analysis of the findings in the Provincial Sample indicates, as did the Copenhagen Sample, that the frequency of psychiatric diagnoses outside of the schizophrenia spectrum is almost identical in the biological relatives of the schizophrenic and control adoptees and no particular diagnosis shows a significant difference. There are significantly more diagnoses of chronic, latent, acute and uncertain schizophrenia and schizoid or inadequate personality in the biological relatives of the total sample of schizophrenic adoptees than in the biological relatives of the controls. The difference is markedly enhanced when, as was indicated by the Copenhagen Study, the schizoid and inadequate personality disorders as well as acute schizophrenia are removed from the spectrum and comparison is made with controls who were interviewed within the past 5 years and found to be free of serious mental illness (11.6 *vs* 2.2%). In each analysis the prevalence in the adoptive relatives is low and no significant difference is found between index and control relatives.

There is good agreement as well between the Provincial and Copenhagen Studies in respect of certain constituents of the schizophrenia spectrum. The relationship of these to classical schizophrenia was explored by examining serially the prevalence of the disorders of the schizophrenia spectrum in the biological relatives of adoptees with classical chronic schizophrenia and of control adoptees who, on psychiatric interview, revealed no evidence suggestive of schizophrenia or other serious mental illness (Fig. 7). Chronic schizophrenia, definite or probable, was found at prevalence of 5.2 and 5.8% in the biological relatives of the Provincial and Copenhagen index adoptees respectively, compared with 0 and 0.9% in the control relatives. For latent schizophrenia, definite or probable, the corresponding values were 8.6 and 12.5% with control levels of 2.2 and 0.9%. All of the differences between index and control values were significant. When the analysis is made by families instead of relatives, similar differences are found.

Discussion

It cannot be emphasized too often that findings which substantiate genetic influences do not exclude the operation of environmental factors in aetiology and pathogenesis. Since these have been the focus of most attention and conviction until recently, there is reason to examine current hypotheses relating to the possible role of specific environmental influences.

The risk for schizophrenia in genetically vulnerable children is quite insensitive to fairly drastic extremes of rearing milieu. Heston & Denney (1968) found no significant difference in the prevalence of schizophrenia or other psychopathology between children at high genetic risk for schizophrenia reared by foster families or in foundling institutions. Higgins (1976) studied 50 young adults, all born of schizophrenic mothers, half of whom had been reared by their mothers, the other half separated from their mothers early in life and reared by agents without history of psychiatric illness. Chronic schizophrenia as well as other types of psychopathology were found in each group at equal prevalence. Wender and associates (1974) studied individuals born of normal biological parents but reared by adoptive parents with severe psychopathology or psychosis, comparing them with offspring of a psychotic parent adopted by normal individuals. The risk for schizophrenia in the offspring appeared to be determined by the psychiatric status of the biological rather than the adoptive parents. In additon, a comparison of the amount of psychopathology in the adoptive siblings of ill and well adoptees could shed some light on the possible effects of rearing.

On the other hand, a substantial number of studies have appeared in the past decade which appear to demonstrate an important influence of family interactions not on aetiology but on the severity of symptoms and rate of relapse in schizophrenia.

The two-fold higher prevalence of schizophrenia in the lower socioeconomic classes of large cities has suggested a number of environmental stresses that might exist to a greater extent in economically deprived classes. A large number of social and psychological stressors are associated with poverty, status, role perception, values and child rearing practices. These provide a number of aetiological hypotheses pertinent to schizophrenia which have not been sufficiently evaluated (Kety, 1980).

Certain biological hazards associated with lower social class should also be considered. To the extent that perinatal injuries, malnutrition and infection may play roles in the environmental aetiologies of schizophrenia, their impact would be exaggerated in the lower socioeconomic class in large cities. Several infectious diseases, especially those of viral origin, occur significantly more frequently in lower socioeconomic classes. The evidence is quite good that some perinatal stresses operate in schizophrenia. The findings of an earlier study were confirmed by data collected in our adoption sample (Jacobsen & Kinney, 1980).

Knight (1982) has advanced compelling arguments that autoimmune processes operate in some forms of schizophrenia as they are now known to operate in myasthenia gravis, thyrotoxicosis and diabetes, disorders which share with schizophrenia a monozygotic concordance rate of 30–50%, a variable age of onset in such pairs, and a juvenile grace period. This heuristic hypothesis requires experimental evaluation.

Conclusions

Although there is still much more to be learned about schizophrenia if we are to treat it more effectively and eventually to prevent it, we have made progress in elucidating some aspects of its aetiology. There is compelling evidence that genetic factors play a significant role, and although neither the genes involved nor their mode of transmission have been characterized, there is reason to believe that with modern molecular genetic techniques such knowledge is obtainable. It is also clear that environmental factors are important and although there have been numerous plausible hypotheses regarding specific possibilities, few have been rigorously identified. While parental attitudes and family interactions undoubtedly affect the severity of symptoms and the course of the illness, the notion that these influences play a dominant role in producing schizophrenia has not been substantiated.

References

Heston, L.L. & Denney, D. (1968): Interactions between early life experience and biological factors in schizophrenia. In *The transmission of schizophrenia*, eds D. Rosenthal & S.S. Kety, pp. 363–376. Oxford: Pergamon Press.

Higgins, J. (1976): Effects of child rearing by schizophrenic mothers: A follow up. *J. Psychiatr. Res.* **13**, 1–9.

Jacobsen, B. & Kinney, D.K. (1980): Perinatal complications in adopted and nonadopted schizophrenics and their controls: Preliminary results. *Acta Psychiatr. Scand. (Suppl)*, **285**, 337–346.

Kety, S.S. (1980): The 52nd Maudsley Lecture. The syndrome of schizophrenia: Unresolved questions and opportunities for research. *Br. J. Psychiatry* **136**, 421–436.

Kety, S.S., Rosenthal, D., Wender, P.H. & Schulsinger, F. (1968): The types and prevalence of mental illness in the biological and adoptive families of adopted schizophrenics. In *The transmission of schizophrenia*, eds D. Rosenthal & S.S. Kety, pp. 345–62. Oxford: Pergamon Press.

Kety, S.S., Rosenthal, D., Wender, P.H., Schulsinger, F. & Jacobsen, B. (1975): Mental illness in the biological and adoptive families of adoptive individuals who have become schizophrenic: A preliminary report based on psychiatric interviews. In *Genetic research in psychiatry*, eds R.R. Fieve, D. Rosenthal & H. Brill, pp. 147–65. Baltimore: The Johns Hopkins University Press.

Knight, J.G. (1982): Dopamine-receptor-stimulating autoantibodies: a possible cause of schizophrenia. *Lancet* **ii**, 1073–1076.

Wender, P.H., Rosenthal, D., Kety, S.S., Schulsinger, F. & Welner, J. (1974): Cross-fostering: A research strategy for clarifying the role of genetic and experential factors in the etiology of schizophrenia. *Arch. Gen. Psychiatry* **30**, 121–128.

Wender, P.H., Kety, S.S., Rosenthal, D., Schulsinger, F., Ortmann, J. & Lunde, I. (1986): Psychiatric disorders in the biological and adoptive families of adopted individuals with affective disorders. *Arch. Gen. Psychiatry* **43**, 923–929.

Chapter 12

Genetic trait markers in schizophrenic probands and their unaffected relatives

D. H. R. Blackwood, W. J. Muir, D. M. St. Clair and M. T. Walker

Department of Psychiatry, Royal Edinburgh Hospital, Morningside Park, Edinburgh, UK

Summary

Over the past few years several psychophysiological changes have been observed in schizophrenia and some of these are now emerging as promising candidates for consideration as biological markers. Eye tracking dysfunction is one of the most studied of these physiological dysfunctions and changes in averaged event-related potentials, in particular the auditory P50 response recorded using a conditioning testing paradigm and the P300 response to an 'odd-ball' stimulus, may also give clues about the underlying neuronal dysfunction in schizophrenia and may help clarify the mode of inheritance of the disease.

In this study both P300 latency and eye tracking function were recorded in 93 schizophrenic patients and 166 controls and abnormalities in both physiological measures were more common in the schizophrenic group. The same measures were recorded from 105 members of 10 families in which there was more than one schizophrenic member. Amongst first degree relatives there was an increased incidence of both types of abnormality and this occurred in family members with schizophrenia, a variety of other psychiatric diagnoses and in some relatives who were asymptomatic. The results suggest the autosomal dominant mode of transmission in these families of a trait which may manifest as schizophrenia or as a disorder of P300 and eye tracking, either alone or in combination.

Introduction

A major obstacle to all research into the causes, genetic or otherwise, of schizophrenia is that we can define this condition only by its clinical features. The boundaries of what we term schizophrenia remain an unsolved mystery (Kendell, 1987). The picture is further confused because the same clinical symptoms may arise for a variety of diverse and quite unrelated reasons. In this respect the major psychoses including schizophrenia may follow the pattern we are familiar with in other medical conditions, for example, diabetes mellitus, where both genetic and non-genetic sub-types have been identified and the same pattern of disease may be the end result of a number of different causative factors. (Eisenbarth, 1986).

The problem of diagnostic uncertainty requires a solution if we are to elucidate the mode of inheritance of schizophrenia in some families and to pursue research into the genetics of the condition using linkage studies. It is not surprising that over many years attempts have been made to find a biological variable which, like the measurement of blood glucose concentration in diabetes, will help clarify the diagnosis of schizophrenia.

Before a vulnerability trait can be considered useful in genetic research a number of criteria should be fulfilled. Firstly, we are looking for a biological variable which is abnormal in a large proportion of schizophrenic patients but normal in patients with other diagnoses. Furthermore, the variable should not be unduly influenced by medication and should remain unchanged in a subject whether he is in an acute phase of the illness or in remission. The marker should be known to be under genetic control and within families of patients the abnormality should segregate with the illness. With these criteria in mind interesting candidate diagnostic markers have included the enzymes associated with the metabolism of dopamine and noradrenaline, measured in peripheral blood samples and cerebrospinal fluid. Despite initial promise that low levels of the enzyme monoamine oxidase measured in blood platelets might be a useful marker for schizophrenia, the difference in levels between patients and controls was not sufficiently marked and the effect of medication was not sufficiently excluded for this enzyme to be employed as a useful vulnerability trait (Baron, 1986). More promising candidates are a range of physiological measures, notably eye tracking disorders and evoked potential abnormalities, which are found with increased frequency amongst schizophrenic patients.

Eye tracking dysfunction

The first report of abnormal eye tracking movements amongst patients with schizophrenia was made by Diefendorf & Dodge in 1908 but it is the extensive and more recent research of Holzman and his colleagues which has established eye tracking dysfunction as a possibly useful biological marker for schizophrenia (Holzman *et al.*, 1973, 1974, 1984). During the test, subjects watch a smoothly moving target such as a swinging pendulum or a spot moving to and fro across a screen. The electro-oculogram is recorded or alternatively the direction of gaze is measured by reflecting infra-red light from the pupil. The disorders of eye tracking which are noted most commonly amongst schizophrenic patients include a larger than expected number of jerky or saccadic intrusions during pursuit movements and bursts of 'saccadic smooth pursuit tracking'. Eye tracking dysfunction is present in over 50% of schizophrenic patients in contrast to around 8% of a normal population. The abnormality is independent of neuroleptic drug treatment and cannot be explained by low motivation or inattention in the patient population (Levy *et al.*, 1983). Eye tracking disorder is under a degree of genetic control because twin studies show that monozygotic twins discordant for clinical schizophrenia have remarkably similar rates of eye movement disorder ($r = 0.77$) whereas dizygotics showed much less similarity ($r = 0.39$) (Holzman *et al.*, 1980). The disorder appears not only in schizophrenic patients but in about 45% of their parents and siblings who may not show clinical signs of schizophrenia. In order to explain their finding that some schizophrenics with good eye tracking have relatives showing bad tracking even when those relatives have no psychotic symptoms, Matthysse *et al.* (1986) have proposed that schizophrenics inherit a latent trait that is not directly observable but can cause either schizophrenia or poor eye tracking or both. This latent trait may be regarded as a disease process affecting the brain. Different symptoms are caused by different regions of the brain being more severely involved. More recently a twin study in Norway (Holzman *et al.*, 1988) provides evidence that eye tracking disorder and clinical schizophrenia can be considered expressions of a single underlying trait that appears to be transmitted by an autosomal dominant gene. They suggest the measurement of eye tracking dysfunction in schizophrenia is an important non-invasive and easy-to-perform technique which should improve the chances of success of genetic linkage studies considerably in schizophrenic families.

Changes in event-related potentials

Other promising candidates for vulnerability markers in schizophrenia are abnormalities of the electroencephalogram (EEG), and in particular techniques which average EEG activity over a period of time and examine it for changes in response to stimuli. These waveforms are known as averaged evoked responses or event-related potentials.

Since the pioneering work of Lennox *et al.* (1945) it has been amply confirmed that brain electrical activity is strongly influenced by genetic factors. Several twin studies have shown that monozygotic twins are strikingly similar in a number of EEG measures including event-related potentials following auditory and visual stimuli. For example Buchsbaum (1974) observed that both the wave form and the change in amplitude to increasing intensity of stimulus were similar in monozygotic but not in dizygotic twins. A possible role for auditory event-related potentials as trait markers in schizophrenia has been most fully investigated in the case of the so-called P50 response during a conditioning testing paradigm, and the P300 response using an auditory 'odd-ball' task.

The P50 auditory-event-related potential

An impairment of information processing could account for some of the clinical manifestations of schizophrenia. Freedman and his colleagues have shown that subjects with schizophrenia show a defect in the P50 auditory-event-related potential (Adler *et al.*, 1982; Freedman *et al.*, 1983). In this test an averaged EEG response is recorded from the scalp while the subject listens through headphones to pairs of brief sounds presented at 10 second intervals. Individual clicks in the pair are 0.5 seconds apart. In normal subjects the second of two sounds thus presented generates a much smaller EEG response than does the first of the two stimuli. A large proportion of schizophrenic subjects show no such habituation of response, and this failure to habituate has been measured in the EEG at around 50 ms after stimulus. The failure to suppress the P50 wave is not altered by neuroleptic medication and is found in half of the first degree relatives of schizophrenic subjects (Siegel *et al.*, 1984). Further studies within families are required to determine more precisely the mode of inheritance of this defect.

Auditory P300 response

The P300 response is a scalp potential recorded some 300 ms after a stimulus which is unexpected or surprising. It is most conveniently recorded from a subject listening to a series of tones through headphones. The subject is asked to count infrequent high pitched tones embedded randomly in a series of low pitched tones. The amplitude of the P300 response is thought to reflect the degree of surprise when the individual hears the infrequent tone and the latency of the response, the stimulus evaluation time. As with the P50 response, a defect in P300 may be due to an underlying disorder of information processing. P300 latency is abnormal in over 50% of schizophrenic subjects and once again it has been shown the abnormality is not influenced by either medication or the

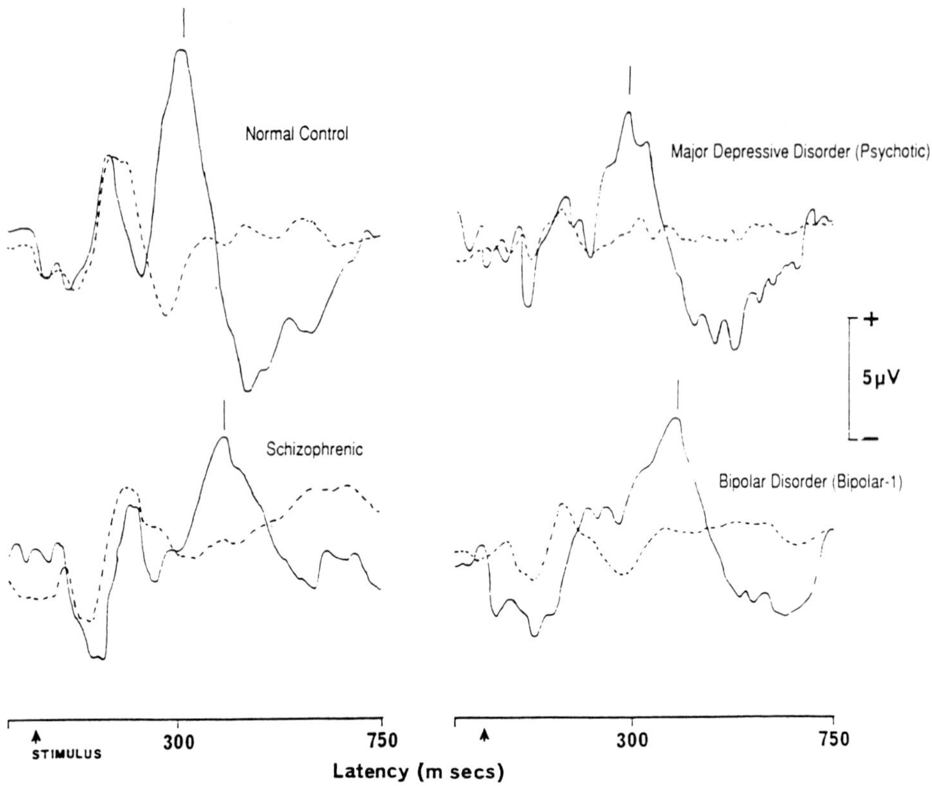

Fig. 1. *Event-related potentials recorded during a two-tone discrimination task.* The discontinuous line is the response to frequent 'unattended' tones. The continuous line, which includes the P300 wave form, is the averaged response to infrequent 'attended' tones. P300 shows changes in amplitude and latency in schizophrenia and bipolar affective disorder in comparison with unipolar depression and controls.

clinical status of the patient (Blackwood *et al.*, 1987). Figure 1 illustrates the reduced amplitude and delayed latency found in many schizophrenics and patients with bipolar but not unipolar affective disorder. Twin studies have confirmed that P300 is under a high degree of genetic control (Polich & Burns, 1987).

Differences in P300 latency and eye tracking function between schizophrenics and controls

Recent progress in the identification of physiological markers of schizophrenia has been encouraging and the question arises as to how these differing measurements relate to each other and the extent to which eye tracking disorder and information processing disorders, as measured by the P50 and P300 responses, reflect the same or differing underlying brain pathologies. We have recently recorded the P300 response in 93 subjects with a schizophrenic illness and in 166 control subjects in the age range 16–60 years. Eye tracking was also recorded in 56 of these schizophrenics and 93 of the control subjects using techniques similar to those employed by Holzman *et al.* (1973) as described by Muir

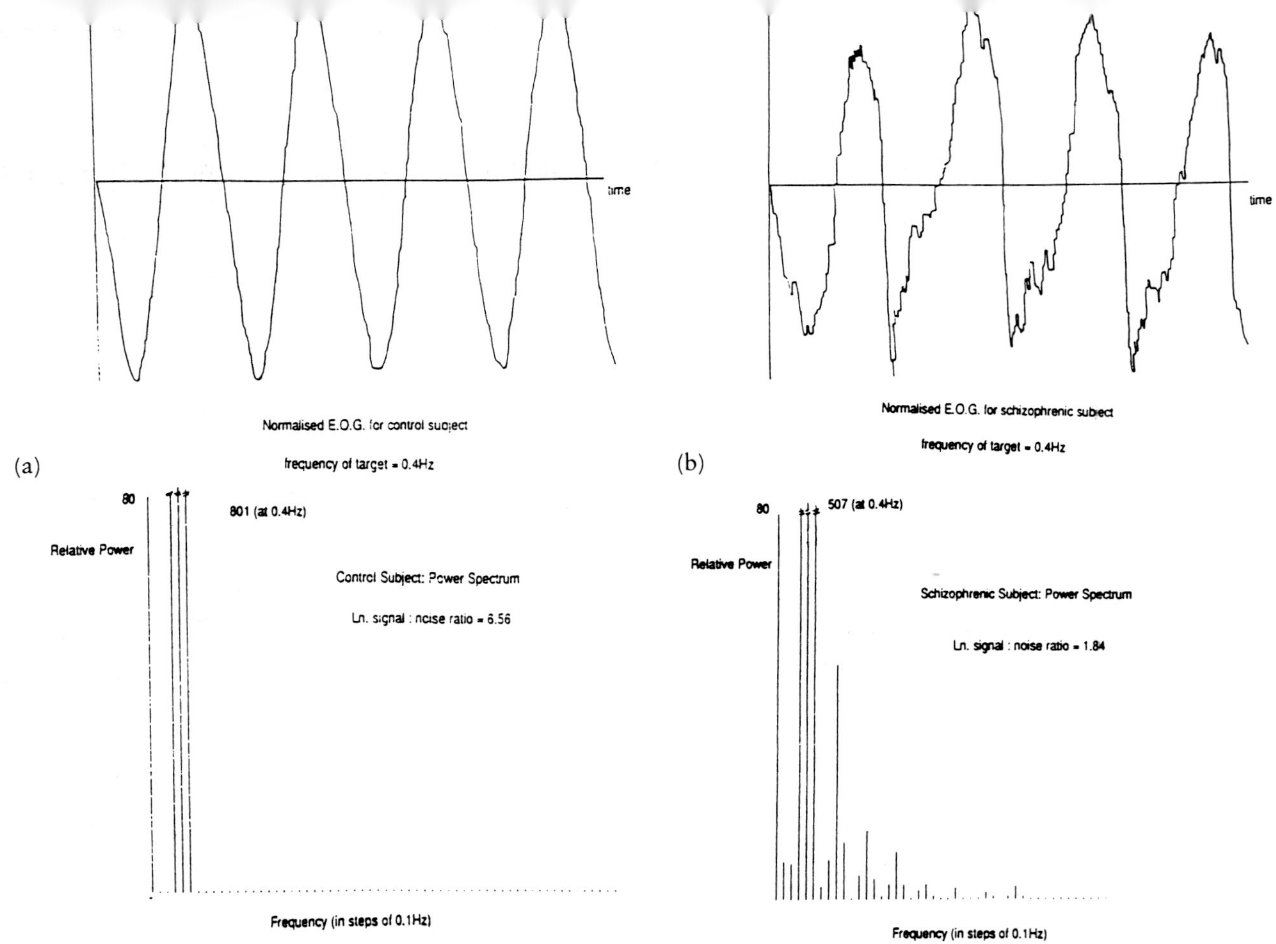

Fig. 2. *Electro-oculograms from normal and schizophrenic subjects.* (a) Normal electro-oculogram from a control subject visually tracking a light target traversing a screen at 4 cycles per second. Frequency analysis shows insignificant high frequency (saccadic) movements. (b) Electro-oculogram from a schizophrenic subject performing the same tracking task. Increased high frequency saccadic movements are quantified by frequency analysis and lead to a reduced signal/noise ratio.

Table 1. *P300 latency and eye tracking in schizophrenic and control subjects.*

	P300 latency (ms) (mean ± SD)	Eye tracking Ln S/N (mean ± SD)
Control	300 ± 22.1 (n = 166)	5.1 ± 0.8 (n = 93)
Schizophrenia	341 ± 37.1 (n = 93)	4.3 ± 1.2 (n = 56)

P300 latency $P < 0.01$ (Wilcoxon).
Eye tracking $P < 0.05$ (Wilcoxon).

Table 2. *Per cent of subjects with P300 and eye tracking abnormalities in a group of schizophrenic patients.*

	Control	Schizophrenia
Prolonged P300 latency (> 340 ms)	2.5	52
Eye tracking disorder (Ln S/N < 3.4)	2.5	26
Both P300 and eye movement disorder occurring in the same subject	0	12

et al. (1988, submitted for publication). Figure 2*a* shows a normal electro-oculogram and Fig. 2*b* the recording from a schizophrenic subject showing increased saccadic movements. The recorded electro-oculogram was analysed by a fast Fourier transform. Spectral power density in the range of the signal (0.3 to 0.5 Hz) was compared to power density in the range 0.8 to 8 Hz ('noise'). The natural logarithm of the signal-to-noise ratio was used as the measure of smooth pursuit eye movement. Lower ratios result from an increased proportion of high frequency saccadic movements indicative of eye tracking dysfunction.

Table 1 shows that in schizophrenic subjects P300 latency is prolonged and eye tracking function is impaired compared with a group of population controls. Both the P300 latency and the eye movement data were normally distributed about the mean in the control population and the 95th percentile was used to define the 'normal' range used in Table 2. Fifty two per cent of schizophrenics showed an abnormal P300 latency (greater than 340 ms) and 26% had eye tracking disorder (Ln S/N < 3.4). Both abnormalities were present together in 12% of schizophrenics and in none of the controls. The results indicate that P300 latency increase and smooth pursuit eye tracking abnormalities can occur separately or in combination in schizophrenia.

P300 latency and eye tracking function in families of schizophrenic probands

We have extended these observations of altered physiology in schizophrenia by recording P300 and eye movement from 105 members of 10 families selected on the basis of there being a large sibship with more than one schizophrenic member. Using the 95th percentile of control data as the cut-off, a high incidence of abnormal physiology was found.

Differences between control and family data shown in Table 3 were significant. Less than 5% of 'normals' would be expected by chance to show either P300 or eye tracking abnormality, and as Table 2 shows it is very rare to find both P300 and eye movement abnormality occurring together in the same person in the general population. P300 latency

Table 3. *Number of family members having abnormal P300 latency (> 340 ms) and eye tracking functions (Ln S/N < 3.4).*

Diagnosis of family member	*Normal P300, normal eye tracking*	*Abnormal P300, normal eye tracking*	*Normal P300, abnormal eye tracking*	*Both P300 and eye tracking abnormal*	*Total*
Schizophrenia	6	10	3	4	23
Other major psychoses	4	4	0	1	9
No current or previous psychotic illness	49	9	9	6	73
Total	59	23	12	11	105

was prolonged in 23 family members ($\chi^2 = 18.5$ $P < 0.001$) and eye tracking alone was impaired in 12 ($\chi^2 = 9.6$ $P < 0.01$). In a further 11 relatives but none of the controls both P300 latency and eye tracking were abnormal ($\chi^2 = 37.5$ $P < 0.001$).

In these families there was a clear segregation of physiological abnormality with schizophrenic illness since 17 out of 23 subjects with schizophrenia showed abnormal P300, eye tracking or both. However, P300 and eye tracking were not specific to schizophrenia but were abnormal in five out of nine subjects with other major psychoses, including bipolar illness and unclassified functional psychosis. Surprisingly of the 73 members who had no history of psychotic illness 24 showed physiological abnormalities, a significant increase over the control population ($\chi^2 = 19.6$ $P = 0.001$). P300 latency was prolonged in nine, eye tracking impaired in nine and both P300 latency and eye tracking were abnormal in seven. In keeping with our earlier studies this group included the four family members diagnosed as schizotypal personality disorder (Blackwood *et al.*, 1986; Kutcher *et al.*, 1987). There are thus indications that as physiological trait markers P300 latency and eye tracking function may help delineate so-called spectrum disorders related to schizophrenia.

Figures 3*a* and 3*b* show the distribution of P300 latency and eye tracking function in these families. The data from a volunteer control sample are superimposed (dotted line) for comparison. The distribution of both P300 latency and eye tracking function in families is bimodal (confirmed by Phi-P graph; Everitt & Hand, 1981). Inspection of the data shows, in both figures, two peaks corresponding to the mean of the control group and the mean of the schizophrenic population. Estimation of the mixing proportions revealed approximately equal numbers in the two distributions.

These results are preliminary and are being extended. The finding of P300 or eye tracking abnormality either alone or in combination in 46 out of 105 family members and the analysis of the distribution of the data in Fig 3*a* and *b* can be interpreted as showing an autosomal dominant transmission in these families of a trait manifested by psychotic symptoms or physiological abnormalities or a mixture of these. This is in keeping with the views of Matthysse *et al.* (1986) and Karlsson (1988). Further analysis of a larger sample of subjects will help resolve whether these two psychophysiological measures are independent variables or reflect the same underlying pathology in schizophrenia. The ability to identify family members with clear psychophysiological abnormalities will help resolve some of the diagnostic uncertainties which still present a formidable obstacle to genetic studies in schizophrenia.

(a)

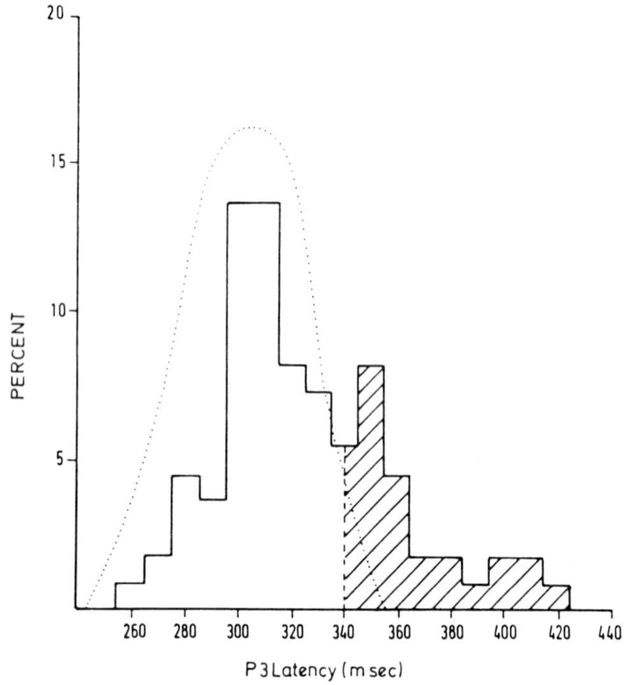

(b)

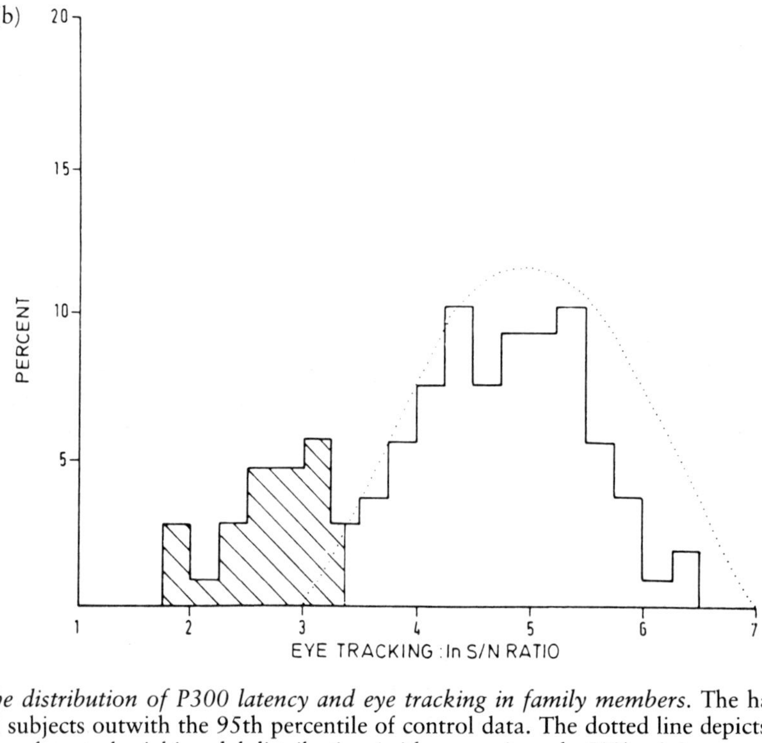

Fig. 3. *The distribution of P300 latency and eye tracking in family members*. The hatched areas include all subjects outwith the 95th percentile of control data. The dotted line depicts the normal distribution of controls. A bimodal distribution (with approximately 50% mixing proportions) was confirmed for both P300 latency (a) and eye tracking data (b) in families.

Conclusion

There is now growing evidence that eye movement disorder and evoked potential abnormality, both of which are simple to record, go some way to fulfilling the criteria for genetic trait markers in schizophrenia. A major unanswered question in all cases is the specificity of these changes to one type of psychosis. With more extensive data these markers may help to define the genetic boundaries between schizophrenic and manic-depressive psychoses and related schizotypal and borderline personality disorders. Since no studies have found physiological abnormalities in all schizophrenic patients it is possible that these markers may also help to resolve the question of heterogeneity by defining sub-groups of the disease.

Finally genetic linkage studies on DNA from multiply affected families should be much easier through the use of markers which can identify within families members who are at risk, in addition to those who have actual clinical signs of schizophrenia.

References

Adler, L.E., Pachtman, E., Franks, R.D., Pecevich, M., Waldo, M.C. & Freedman, R. (1982): Neurophysiological evidence for a defect in neuronal mechanisms involved in sensory gating in schizophrenia. *Biol. Psychiatry* **17**, 639–654.

Baron, M. (1986): Genetics of schizophrenia: II Vulnerability traits and gene markers. *Biol. Psychiatry* **21**, 1189–1211.

Blackwood, D.H.R., St. Clair, D.M. & Kutcher, S.P. (1986): P300 event-related potential abnormalities in borderline personality disorder. *Biol. Psychiatry* **21**, 557–560.

Blackwood, D.H.R., Whalley, L.J., Christie, J.E., Blackburn, I.M., St. Clair, D.M. & McInnes, A. (1987): Changes in auditory P3 event-related potential in schizophrenia and depression. *Br. J. Psychiatry* **150**, 154–160.

Buchsbaum, M.S. (1974): Average evoked response and stimulus intensity in identical and fraternal twins. *Physiol. Psychol.* **2**, 365–370.

Diefendorf, A.R. & Dodge, R. (1908): An experimental study of the ocular reactions of the insane from photographic records. *Brain* **31**, 451–489.

Eisenbarth, G.S. (1986): Type 1 Diabetes Mellitus: A chronic autoimmune disease. *N. Engl. J. Med.* **314**, 1360–1368.

Everitt, B.S. & Hand, D.J. (1981): *Finite mixture distributions*. London: Chapman & Hall.

Freedman, R., Adler, L.E., Waldo, M.C., Pachtman, E. & Franks, R.D. (1983): Neurophysiological evidence for a defect in inhibitory pathways in schizophrenia: comparison of medicated and drug-free patients. *Biol. Psychiatry* **18**, 537–551.

Holzman, P.S., Proctor, L.R. & Hughes, D.W. (1973): Eye tracking patterns in schizophrenia. *Science* **181**, 179–181.

Holzman, P.S., Proctor, L.R., Levy, D.L., Yasillo, N.J., Meltzer, H.Y. & Hurt, S.W. (1974): Eye-tracking dysfunction in schizophrenic patients and their relatives. *Arch. Gen. Psychiatry* **31**, 143–151.

Holzman, P.S., Kringlen, E., Levy, D.L. & Shelby Haberman, J. (1980): Deviant eye tracking in twins discordant for psychosis: A replication. *Arch. Gen. Psychiatry* **37**, 627–631.

Holzman, P.S., Solomon, C.M., Levin, S. & Waternaux, C.S. (1984): Pursuit eye movement dysfunctions in schizophrenia. *Arch. Gen. Psychiatry* **41**, 136–139.

Holzman, P.S., Kringlen, E., Matthysse, S., Flanagan, S.D., Lipton, R.B., Cramer, G., Levin, S., Lange, K. & Levy, D.L. (1988): A single dominant gene can account for eye tracking dysfunctions and schizophrenia in offspring of discordant twins. *Arch. Gen. Psychiatry* **45**, 641–647.

Karlsson, J.L. (1988): Partly dominant transmission of schizophrenia in Iceland. *Br. J. Psychiatry* **152**, 324–329.

Kendell, R.E. (1087): Diagnosis and classification of functional psychoses. *Br. Med. Bull.* **43**, 499–513.

Kutcher, S.P., Blackwood, DH.R., St. Clair, D.M., Gaskell, D.F. & Muir, W.J. (1987): Auditory P300 in borderline personality disorder and schizophrenia. *Arch. Gen. Psychiatry* **44**, 645–650.
Lennox, W.G., Gibbs, E.L. & Gibbs, F.A. (1945): The brain-wave pattern, an hereditary tract. Evidence from 74 "normal" pairs of twins. *J. Hered.* **36**, 233–243.
Levy, D.L., Lipton, R.B., Holzman, P.S. & Davis, J.M. (1983): Eye tracking dysfunction unrelated to clinical state and treatment with haloperidol. *Biol. Psychiatry* **18**, 813–819.
Matthysse, S., Holzman, P.S. & Lange, K. (1986): The genetic transmission of schizophrenia: Application of Mendelian latent structure analysis to eye tracking dysfunctions in schizophrenia and affective disorder. *J. Psychiatr. Res.* **20**, 57–65.
Polich, J. & Burns, T. (1987): P300 from identical twins. *Neuropsychologia* **25**, 299–304.
Siegel, C., Waldo, M., Mizner, G., Adler, L.E. & Freedman, R. (1984): Deficits in sensory gating in schizophrenic patients and their relatives. *Arch. Gen. Psychiatry* **41**, 607–612.

Chapter 13

Molecular genetic research into schizophrenia

H. M. D. Gurling[1], R. Sherrington[1], J. Brynjolfsson[2], T. Read[3], D. Curtis[4], B. J. Mankoo[1], M. Potter[4], and H. Petursson[2]

[1]*Molecular Psychiatry Laboratory, University College and Middlesex School of Medicine, University of London;* [2]*Department of Psychiatry, Borgarspitalinn, Reykjavik, Iceland;* [3]*Department of Psychiatry, University of College and Middlesex School of Medicine, London;* [4]*Department of Psychiatry, Middlesex Hospital, London.*

Summary

The difficulties caused by incomplete penetrance and an uncertain mode of transmission for schizophrenia have not prevented the first successful localization of a susceptibility gene for a subtype of schizophrenia. It is argued that the strategy of employing linkage methods and DNA polymorphisms as markers is the most useful of the possible molecular genetic strategies because it leads on to both enhanced clinical genetic investigation as well as further recombinant DNA research to clone and sequence schizophrenia susceptibility mutations. Future recombinant DNA research can now employ long range mapping and cloning techniques such as the chromosome walking/jumping approach and the strategy of cloning brain specific cDNAs from brain mRNA. The identification of carriers for high risk studies and the genetic validation of diagnosis appear to be the most promising clinical developments. Prenatal counselling will only become widely feasible when much more is known about the extent of heterogeneity of linkage in schizophrenia.

Introduction

Schizophrenia has tended to occupy a special position in the genes *versus* environment debate over human behaviour, and geneticists have often tended to be cautious with their hypotheses and claims concerning the genetics of schizophrenia. Quite recently scientific papers were being written which put schizophrenia beyond the grasp of the genetic linkage methodology that has recently been so successful in detecting single major gene effects in the classical Mendelian disorders. It was claimed that the evidence for single major gene transmission for susceptibility to schizophrenia was untenable (O'Rourke *et al.*, 1983; Sturt & McGuffin, 1985; McGuffin & Sturt, 1986). No such claims were ever made for certain medical disorders such as multiple endocrine neoplasia (MEN2a) which nevertheless shows as much incomplete penetrance and apparent 'polygenic' or uncertain mode of inheritance as schizophrenia (Ponder *et al.*, 1988).

Despite the superficial difficulties of working genetically with a disorder that had never shown a consistent pattern of genetic transmission, it has nevertheless proven possible to identify a locus on chromosome 5 that confers susceptibility to the development of schizophrenia (Sherrington *et al.*, 1988). In this instance the fact of finding genetic linkage in multigenerational families also proved that a specific type of genetic transmission was operating for at least one subtype of schizophrenia. The stage is now set to employ recombinant DNA techniques in order to close the genetic gap between the linkage markers and the schizophrenia mutation itself. It seems likely there will once again be a body of thought which believes that the cloning and sequencing of the first schizophrenia mutation cannot be achieved because of the problems of incomplete penetrance, heterogeneity of linkage, and diagnostic uncertainty. One favourable factor that can be invoked to counter this argument is, paradoxically, the very fact that schizophrenia does seem to have a complex genetic aetiology. This may increase the chance that further cytogenetic abnormalities associated with schizophrenia may be found. Such findings may rapidly lead on to the precise identification of a schizophrenia susceptibility gene. The complexity might also be due to a high rate of mutation and this too might assist rather than hinder specific molecular genetic strategies.

A strategy for studying schizophrenia with genetic linkage analysis

Schizophrenia is associated with reduced fertility, social isolation, and probably a greater than expected familial association with other non-schizophrenic psychiatric disorders. Therefore it should not have been surprising that these factors could have masked or inhibited the recognition by segregation analysis of single gene susceptibility to schizophrenia. The susceptibility identified has been shown to be transmitted as an autosomal dominant gene with incomplete penetrance (Sherrington *et al.*, 1988). Other types of schizophrenia could be recessive, polygenic, or environmental. The factors that contributed to the first localization of a schizophrenia susceptibility allele were not described in great detail at the time of publication. In order to make the design of the study more explicit the various criteria that were employed are listed below:

(1) The UK/Icelandic study chose only to sample medium to large sized pedigrees with schizophrenia in at least three generations. In such families a lod score* suggestive of linkage could be computed within a single family. The lod scores could therefore be analysed using computer programmes written by Ott (1985, 1986) and Risch (1988) to test the hypothesis that the sample of families was genetically homogeneous.

(2) The study chose to select high density pedigrees so that a suggestive lod score could be computed by considering affected schizophrenics alone. This circumvented the problem of incomplete penetrance which can rapidly lower the power of the linkage approach if there are many unaffected individuals who are in fact carriers of the susceptibility allele.

(3) Careful attention was paid to selecting families without manic depression (bipolar disorder) present. Families in which both schizophrenia and bipolar disorder (circular manic depression) was present were in fact encountered. However in each instance it was established that there were two independent genetic sources of the two diseases present. This suggested that coexistence of the two disorders within a family was probably due to

*A lod score is the log to the base 10 of the odds ratio of observing a family at a specified recombination fraction as opposed to 50% recombination.

assortative mating by social homogamy. This was made possible by extensive pedigree tracing work and showed up in the presence of schizophrenia on one side of a family and manic depression on another (ie 'marrying in' of the disorders).

(4) Considerable attention was paid to obtaining families in which there was only one possible source for a schizophrenia allele segregating into the kindred. This necessitated considerable knowledge about the past histories of the families that were sampled. If this criterion is not satisfied then the results of genetic linkage analysis can be confounded. A false negative lod will result even in the presence of linkage. In Iceland the research was aided by the existence of genealogical information which was very extensive and which sometimes recorded the presence of mental illness even though the records were not specifically psychiatric in origin.

(5) The study was carried out mainly on a population which has the characteristics of a genetic isolate and this increased the chance of obtaining a homogeneous sample with a single genetic subtype of schizophrenia.

Diagnostic issues in schizophrenia genetics research

Genetic linkage research is very sensitive to diagnostic error, especially to false positive diagnoses. Failure to identify a true case has less severe consequences because such individuals will join the pool of individuals who are either showing recombination or who are non-penetrant carriers. This group of individuals can receive special attention in the linkage analysis, unlike false positive cases which will continue to have a hidden negative effect on all types of analysis.

An important element in coming to a valid decision over caseness is the need to obtain information about the life time history of the patient and the illness rather than using a single 'snapshot' of the illness at a one episode. Kraepelin, who coined the term dementia praecox to differentiate schizophrenia from manic depressive psychosis (MDP), emphasized a deteriorating course, while Bleuler used diagnostic criteria emphasizing psychiatric phenomenology rather than prognosis. Schneider's attempt (1959) to use first rank symptoms to increase reliability of diagnosis was of limited success (Taylor, 1972; Wing & Nixon, 1975), although influential in British psychiatry.

Thus there appeared to be increasing confusion in the early sixties and seventies as competing diagnostic ideologies led researchers to study and describe very different populations (Cooper *et al.*, 1982). Attempts to standardize diagnosis over the last 15 years have led to the introduction of Feighner (1972), RDC (Spitzer *et al.*, 1978) and DSM criteria (American Psychiatric Association 1980) which are widely used and have narrower definition, greater reliability and better prediction of prognosis (Brockington *et al.*, 1978). Such diagnostic criteria are now routinely used in genetic linkage research with a resultant improvement in the comparability of findings. Fortunately some of the new diagnostic systems have been investigated in identical co-twins of schizophrenics and in the families of schizophrenics in order to give an idea of how sensitive they are for identifying psychopathology genetically related to schizophrenia.

Gottesman & Shields (1972) found that very broad or very narrow definitions of schizophrenia reduced the ratio of MZ to DZ concordance in twins and suggested that the most genetic forms of the illness are found by using definitions of medium specificity. Pope *et al.* (1982) found that using DSM-III criteria gave low heritability in first degree relatives of schizophrenics and this suggests that DSM-III is too restrictive, perhaps because of an overemphasis of positive symptoms and underrecognition of the diagnostic importance of negative symptoms. McGuffin *et al.* (1984) tested six sets of operational criteria in MZ and DZ twins and found that RDC and Feighner definitions gave the highest concordance in schizophrenia which would make these criteria the most useful for linkage research. Schneiderian and PSE criteria gave very low scores, indicating that they would be mainly of academic interest when used in genetic linkage studies. In an extension of this work Farmer *et al.* (1987b) found that the maximum difference in MZ/DZ concordance (ie the diagnostic criteria that detected the most heritable schizophrenic features) were for schizophrenia with mood incongruent delusions, schizotypal personality and atypical psychosis. The effect of including paranoid disorder and all other affective disorders was a reduction in the concordance ratio, suggesting that they were not genetically related to schizophrenia.

The inclusion of bipolar disorder and related schizo-affective illness in family studies of schizophrenia is an important issue. It is already known that schizo-affective disorder is found amongst pedigree samples of bipolar disorder showing linkage either to chromosome 11 or the X chromosome (Gurling *et al.*, 1988). Schizo-affective disorder therefore has already been investigated sufficiently for us to know that it is sometimes part of manic depression. Family studies also show that it occurs in association with schizophrenia (Baron *et al.*, 1982). It is not certain whether the association between schizophrenia and schizo-affective disorder in some families is due to the marrying in of two disorders or the consequence of a separate type of psychosis. A further reason for the apparent coexistence of the two disorders within a family may be simple error in diagnosis because it is well known that young manic depressive patients can receive a schizophrenia diagnosis that is overturned after the passage of time. Because there are overlapping symptoms in schizophrenia this does not mean that such individuals will share the same prognosis and genetic aetiology.

Recent proposals (Kendell & Brockington, 1980; Crow, 1984) for a unitary concept for both the functional psychoses now look increasingly inappropriate given that both chromosome 11 and X chromosome linkages in manic depression have been confirmed in two separate samples with total lod scores of above 9.00 for each of the subtypes (Mendlewicz *et al.*, 1972; Baron *et al.*, 1987; Egeland *et al.*, 1987; Mendlewicz *et al.*, 1988). It seems that the weight of historical opinion, the evidence from monozygotic twin studies (Bertlesen *et al.*, 1972), as well as the recent linkage studies of both schizophrenia and manic depression show that the two disorders 'breed true' and segregate independently. The most recent of these is the dual mating study carried out by Gottesman & Bertlesen (personal communication) which also shows that the two disorders are independent.

Until it is established that there is a true schizo-affective psychosis that is independent of schizophrenia and manic depression (Baron *et al.*, 1982) it seems illogical to include such cases in family studies of schizophrenia because they will introduce an avoidable source of heterogeneity for linkage on chromosome 11 and the X chromosome.

Diagnosis in the UK/Icelandic study of schizophrenia

Prior to the advent of successful linkage studies diagnosis has always been based on recurring clusters of clinical symptoms and such a system may have little or no relation to aetiology. Thus the recent finding of the susceptibility locus for schizophrenia on chromosome 5 represents an opportunity to start an aetiological classification based on genetic markers.

The UK/Icelandic study employed the RDC system to study a sample of seven British and Icelandic families containing 104 individuals amongst whom there were 39 schizophrenics (DOMS model) and five people with schizoid personality with or without schizotypal features. These groups of patients were classified as schizophrenic spectrum disorders (DOMSS model) and their presence in the sample supports the concept (eg Kety, 1983; Kendler & Gruenberg, 1984) of a continuum of schizophrenia ranging from personality disorder to psychosis. There were other non-psychotic or fringe disorders, (DOMSSF model) some of which are rather atypical and required neuroleptic treatment.

The finding that all the traditional subtypes, ie paranoid, hebephrenic, catatonic, undifferentiated and unspecified psychosis, were present in the same families within the sample shows that one genotype can give rise to clinical diversity. This fact, together with the findings that hebephrenic schizophrenia may be more heritable than the paranoid variety (Winokur *et al.*, 1974; McGuffin *et al.*, 1984) lends some support to Tsuang & Winokur's (1974) concept of a hebephrenic-paranoid continuum of illness, with the hebephrenic type being the most advanced and severe form.

The highest concordance for linkage was with the broadest definition of psychiatric disorder or caseness including the fringe phenotypes (DOMSSF). The lod score for this model is now above 7.00. This analysis was planned prior to data collection and therefore the lod was calculated with a prior hypothesis. This suggests that the schizophrenia genotype predisposes to other psychiatric conditions apart from schizophrenia *per se* and that these represent a subtle prepsychotic or 'forme fruste' of schizophrenia. Such fringe cases may masquerade as a state that appears to be a 'depression' or as other neurotic disorders. However there was clear evidence from clinical appraisal that there were additional psychological abnormalities present in the fringe cases which were related to schizophrenia for which the SADS-L/RDC system had no adequate categorization. For example a patient who appeared chronically and atypically depressed may have been suffering from the effect of a schizophrenia genotype which had manifested in blunted affect, anhedonia and poverty of thought/speech found in the negative or type 2 schizophrenic (Crow, 1980). Further evidence that these fringe phenotypes are indeed variant expressions of the same underlying mutation is needed because elevation of the lod that occurred when they were included as cases for linkage was only about 2.00 (from 5.20 to 7.09 approximately) and this could have arisen by chance. The lod score for schizophrenia, schizoid personality and schizotypal disorders was significantly in favour of linkage (lod = 5.20) independently of the fringe cases, so that the evidence for linkage did not depend on the atypical cases.

Comparison of the chromosome 5 linked subtype with the Swedish/USA and other schizophrenia linkage studies

The proportion of schizophrenia cases in most populations that are related to the chromosome 5 mutation is as yet unknown. A similar study in a large Swedish pedigree (Kennedy *et al.*, 1988) with a high density of schizophrenia failed to demonstrate chromosome 5 linkage, suggesting that the genetic factors underlying schizophrenia are heterogeneous. There were quite obvious differences in the way these two samples were ascertained. In the UK/Icelandic study, whenever a sibship was found with affected individuals, all normal individuals and all those with uncertain diagnoses within a sibship were systematically sampled. The Swedish study adopted a different (equally valid) approach by sampling only definite cases of schizophrenia. This therefore gave the impression that there were few schizophrenia spectrum or schizophrenia 'fringe' phenotypes present in the Northern Swedish sample (Kennedy *et al.*, 1988) when in fact the sampling procedure tended to exclude them (Wetterberg, personal communication). The two samples are not therefore comparable for rates and types of the non-psychotic schizophrenia-related disorders but are comparable in terms of the schizophrenia subtypes (paranoid, catatonic, hebephrenic, etc.) amongst the definite cases of schizophrenia. So far the Swedish sample has not been submitted to an investigation of RDC schizophrenia subtypes but when this has been done it will be possible to compare the two samples for any obvious differences in the distribution of subtypes.

Taking the UK/Icelandic and Swedish studies together strongly suggests that genetic heterogeneity must exist for schizophrenia, with some families being chromosome 5 linked and others not. The proportion which are linked can only be estimated within wide limits at present. One possibility is that almost all schizophrenia is chromosome-5-linked and that the Swedish pedigree represents one rare exception to this rule occurring in a genetically isolated population. At the opposite extreme, it is possible that chromosome 5 schizophrenia is in fact rather a rare subtype.

Ott and Risch have proposed formal mathematical tests to detect whether a group of families show linkage heterogeneity. Both tests use as data the lod scores for each family, calculated at different recombination fractions, and proceed to produce a maximum likelihood estimate of the true recombination fraction. Ott's computer program, HOMOG, uses the A-test (admixture test) to compare the hypothesis that all families are linked to the marker against the alternative hypothesis that some families are linked but others are unlinked; whereas Risch's program (BTEST) is designed also to detect other types of heterogeneity, for example some groups being more strongly linked than others, as well as being less sensitive to variations in family size and recombination fraction. Quite a large amount of data may be necessary to detect heterogeneity when it exists. Ott calculates that one would need 10 phase-known double backcross families with five meioses each to obtain a power of 67% to detect heterogeneity at a 5% level of significance.

When these homogeneity tests were carried out on the families from the UK/Icelandic study the maximum likelihood estimate for the proportion of families to be linked to chromosome 5 was 100% so that not only could homogeneity not be rejected, it was actually the favoured hypothesis over heterogeneity in those families. However this does not necessarily mean that all the families were indeed chromosome-5-linked, and some had only weakly positive lod scores. The power of these tests to reject homogeneity is in fact rather low and it will be necessary to be able to incorporate further data from large numbers of other families in the future to detect heterogeneity and accurately assess its extent.

If in fact all seven of the UK/Icelandic families are linked to chromosome 5 then it is possible to use a simple binomial formula to provide a lower limit on the estimated proportion of all such families which are linked. Since 0.65 to the power of 7 is less than 0.05, one would be unlikely (within 95% confidence limits) to find seven families all linked if the actual proportion of linked families were anything less than 65%. It should be stressed however that this figure applies only to families which could have been ascertained with equal probability, ie families in the UK and Iceland with a high density of multiple cases of schizophrenia.

Another recent study of families containing both bipolar disorder and schizophrenia from Edinburgh (Blackwood *et al.*, 1988; St. Claire *et al.*, 1989) has claimed negative results for the chromosome 5 markers found to be linked with schizophrenia in the UK/Icelandic study. This result needs to be interpreted with caution because of the fact that a substantial proportion of the cases for genetic analysis were bipolar or schizoaffective rather than schizophrenic individuals.

Before the chromosome 5 schizophrenia result is accepted as a confirmed linkage, a lod of above 3.85 (Lander, personal communication) needs to be obtained in two laboratories. This is slightly higher than the usual lod of 3.00 because both the recombination fraction and penetrance must be estimated jointly. So far the schizophrenia locus has been implicated in one laboratory with a probability of about 0.00001 against the result having occurred by chance. If there had been no prior hypothesis that the susceptibility locus was indeed on chromosome 5 because of the observation of the trisomy/translocation in association with schizophrenia (Bassett *et al.*, 1988) then the evidence against the linkage having occurred by chance would have been slightly weaker.

An independent confirmation of this result, at an early stage, showing widespread involvement of the chromosome 5q11-q13 susceptibility locus would put a high priority on the chromosome 5 molecular genetic approach to schizophrenia. If the subtype of schizophrenia we have identified is rare then it will serve as a useful model for other types of schizophrenia and may also help to unravel which brain systems are involved, even though different loci may be involved for each subtype.

Future clinical genetic research

Identifying schizophrenia susceptibility loci

There are pitfalls for those trying to replicate the chromosome 5 linkage result unless adequate attention is paid to the problems of incomplete penetrance, diagnostic uncertainty and the presence of multiple disease alleles within a single kindred. To some extent these problems depend on the precise objectives of the research. For example whether the aim is to estimate the degree to which there is heterogeneity of linkage in sibling pairs or an attempt to find linkage within large single kindreds. However once chromosome 5 linkage has been conclusively excluded in a sample of multiplex schizophrenia families then there are three further ways of proceeding to find a linkage. The most productive method is likely to be the systematic investigation of loci that have some *a priori* reason to contain a genetic locus that is involved in schizophrenia. This strategy has already proven successful and there are many more loci at which cytogenetic abnormalities have been reported in association with schizophrenia. A further method of choosing loci that may be involved is by the observation of an association at the clinical level between a genetic disorder and schizophrenia, where it is plausible that a dual pathology has been caused by the same cytogenetic abnormality. Two genetic diseases associated with schizophrenia are albinism (Baron, 1976) and Marfan's syndrome (Romano & Linares, 1987). Linkage markers at or near these loci could be used to find linkage in non-chromosome-5 families. The second is the candidate gene approach in which genes with a plausible role in the aetiology of schizophrenia are used as linkage markers on the assumption that mutant alleles at the same locus cause susceptibility to schizophrenia. A recently cloned neurotransmitter receptor gene, the D_2 dopamine receptor, has yet to be investigated by the use of linkage genetics (Bunzow *et al.*, 1988). The last approach is the random search, which has the advantage of the use of highly polymorphic linkage markers which will provide linkage information in most families.

Heterogeneity of linkage and family size

The difficulties that schizophrenia poses for the geneticist lie principally with the tendency for schizophrenic patients to have few children (especially schizophrenic fathers) thus making sibship size in schizophrenia pedigrees rather small in many cultures. Therefore it is very difficult to prove chromosome 5 linkage in any given family unless there are at least five or six affected individuals in a sample of other like-sized families (Ott, 1985; 1986). The sibling pair approach (the sampling of small nuclear families with or without parents) could in theory estimate the proportion of chromosome-5-linked pairs in a sample of sibling pairs (Suarez *et al.*, 1978) but cannot provide information about which specific sibling pairs are linked as opposed to which sibling pairs are unlinked. An accurate estimate of the recombination fraction (genetic distance) between any marker and schizophrenia would be very difficult to obtain using the sibling pair approach if heterogeneity of linkage is present. If the goal of a research group was to obtain a sample suitable for accurate mapping of a schizophrenia susceptibility locus with the eventual objective of cloning and sequencing alleles at that locus then the sibling pair approach would be of little value. The one exception might be if the sample of sibling pairs came from a genetic isolate where homogeneity was strongly suspected, with prior linkage data in many families, and where the proportion of sibling pairs that were of the linked type was estimated to be maximal (ie complete linkage was present).

Exploring genetic aetiology in relation to known abnormalities in schizophrenia

Unless chromosome 5 linkage can be unequivocally established within a certain family then associated abnormalities in brain morphology and metabolism such as those found at CT scan, EEG and on PET cannot be related to the underlying chromosome 5 disease genotype.

Brain ventricular size is known to be abnormal in some schizophrenics (Johnstone *et al.*, 1976; Turner *et al.*, 1986). Although there is no firm concensus, this may be a marker for a less genetic form of the illness (Reveley *et al.*, 1984) especially when associated with perinatal complications (Turner *et al.*, 1986; Owen *et al.*, 1988). This relationship also seems to hold for some familial cases, suggesting that the two aetiological factors can operate in a cumulative way (Murray *et al.*, 1988) and providing an example of how penetrance might be affected by environmental factors.

The difficulty with much of the previous research dealing with antecedent factors such as birth and perinatal trauma is that it is often uncontrolled for simple demographic variables and is not up to the standard required for good epidemiological research. However, if simple hypotheses are tested with respect to a genetically defined population the power of these studies can increase significantly in the same way that incorporation of specific indices of the environment can enhance path or variance component analysis of the genetic and environmental components of human behaviour (Henderson, 1982).

Other workers (Gruzelier, 1987) feel that the fundamental feature underlying specific schizophrenia syndromes (positive/negative or type 1/type 2, see below) is the functional state of imbalance between the two cerebral hemispheres and that symptoms are an expression of the more activated hemisphere, the left in the activated syndrome and the right in the withdrawn syndrome. Eye tracking movements are known to be abnormal in some schizophrenics (Holzman *et al.*, 1974) and in some of their relatives (Matthysse *et al.*, 1986) and may be a marker for a genetic subtype of schizophrenia as suggested by Holzman *et al.* (1988). The role of EEG and evoked potentials is unclear, although it has been claimed (Blackwood *et al.*, 1987) that the auditory evoked potential P300 is characteristically abnormal in schizophrenia and manic depression. It should be possible to determine whether all of the abnormalities described above are found in the chromosome-5-linked subtype of schizophrenia. This should lead to an enhanced ability for psychiatric researchers to pursue separate subtypes of schizophrenia in their own right. However if these measures turn out to be weakly specific for genetic subtypes of schizophrenia and present in other psychiatric disorders then they may be epiphenomena of whole groups of mental illness without any specificity.

Advancing accurate diagnosis and prognosis in schizophrenia

Eventually molecular genetic methods may show that there are truly non-genetic environmentally-caused subtypes of schizophrenia. Comparison between the genetic and non-genetic types may lead to a new aetiological classification and this avenue of research could lead to management and treatment advances even in the absence of further recombinant DNA research to clone and sequence the underlying genetic mutations. A more immediate advance that follows from successful linkage for schizophrenia is in the area of clinical variation in schizophrenia. Crow (1980) has delineated two separate schizophrenia syndromes. Type 1 consists of positive symptoms and response to neuroleptics and is postulated to be due to abnormal brain dopaminergic function. Type 2 consists of negative features and tends not to respond to treatment. The two syndromes are not mutually exclusive; the mixed type may be quite common and the pure type 2 unusual (Farmer *et al.*, 1987a). Investigation in genotypically defined (ie linked) families should help resolve whether these supposed subtypes have any aetiological validity. Twin studies (Dworkin & Lenzenweger, 1984) have indicated that negative symptoms may be characteristic of the more strongly genetic form of schizophrenia, so this may be the type with the worst prognosis.

High risk studies and incomplete penetrance

In the UK/Icelandic study (Sherrington *et al.*, 1988) the best estimate of penetrance was 71% for schizophrenia, rising to 76% for the DOMSS and 86% for the DOMSSF models. This implies that for all definitions of genetic caseness there were a number of individuals with the disease genotype who were clinically normal and did not develop the full syndrome. The Icelandic families studied were genetically isolated and had a high density of illness so they were selected for high penetrance. The factors influencing penetrance are likely to be a productive research area in the future with implications for preventive psychiatry. The true penetrance for genetic cases of schizophrenia as a whole must be much lower than that observed in the recent linkage studies. Eliot Slater calculated that if all of schizophrenia was genetic then the gene frequency would need to be 3.00% and the penetrance approximately 15% with a dominant pattern of transmission. The corollary of this is that it is unwise to assume that an individual who does not have a family history of schizophrenia has a non-genetic type of the illness. If the penetrance really is as low as 15% then most schizophrenics will have inherited the susceptibility from normal parents and will also have unaffected siblings. The cause of the low or variable penetrance of schizophrenia could be environmental, biological or genetic. There may be evolutionarily determined mechanisms specific to the brain that compensate for mutations affecting behaviour so that most individuals with the susceptibility never develop the illness, Polygenic background effects are just as likely to contribute to the variable penetrance as are specific environmental factors such as stressful psychological experiences. However if clear evidence of environmental precipitants for schizophrenia could be identified acting jointly with the genetic susceptibility this could lead on to dramatic and simple methods of prevention.

Molecular genetic methods to clone and sequence schizophrenia mutations

With good fortune it may be possible to localize a schizophrenia susceptibility allele by genetic linkage in affected families to a map resolution of one million base pairs or less. This will entail the cloning of markers that 'step over' recombinants by virtue of being genetically closer than previously used markers. This will need to be carried out with the use of samples biased heavily towards affected cases and not relying on unaffected individuals for linkage information. This approach as described by Sherrington *et al.* (1988) called the 'penetrance free' model can provide a robust estimate of the recombination fraction and will therefore give an accurate map position of the susceptibility locus. The inclusion of unaffected individuals would bring about uncertainty because apparent recombinants may in fact be unaffected carrier individuals. At this stage it will be necessary to utilize several different molecular and genetic approaches.

It is useful to present the possible avenues of research available in the context of the successful application of molecular biology to isolate the affected genes in other genetic disorders. These examples raise the hope that the 'reverse genetics' approach may be more widely successful in the isolation of genes for which the protein product is unknown.

The genetic diseases chronic granulomatous disease (CGD), Duchenne muscular dystrophy (DMD) and retinoblastoma were all found to be associated with cytogenetically identifiable chromosomal deletions. The use of hybrid cell lines containing these deletions enabled the selection of genomic or cDNA clones of candidate genes. The first clues to the identification of the affected locus in DMD came from the observation that females suffering from DMD have balanced X:autosome translocations with breakpoints within Xp21. These females are affected because the normal X chromosome is preferentially inactivated. Subtractive hybridization experiments using a patient with a large deletion at Xp21 (Kunkel *et al.*, 1985) were used to isolate DNA sequences from normal chromosomes which overlapped this deleted region. Sequences conserved across many mammalian species were selected and used to identify a large messenger RNA in fetal muscle cells (Monaco *et al.*, 1985). The rationale for this was that a gene conserved throughout evolution and expressed in muscle would be an obvious candidate for the DMD gene. This RNA species has subsequently been identified as the mRNA (Koenig *et al.*, 1987) for dystrophin, which is the defective protein in DMD (Hoffman *et al.*, 1987). Clones from the Xp21 region allow the detection of deletions in approximately 50% of DMD patients, ranging in size from six thousand to one million base pairs (den Dunnen *et al.*, 1987).

For CGD a B-cell line was created from a patient who exhibited CGD and a cytogenetic deletion at Xp21 to which the disorder was linked. Subtractive screening using messenger RNA from this cell line with complementary DNA from a normal B-cell line identified a phagocyte-specific messenger mRNA that was absent from some patients and which exhibited deletions in others (Royer-Pokora *et al.*, 1986). These workers showed that the protein was a member of the cytochrome family.

A similar methodology has been successful in identifying the molecular basis of retinoblastoma. Dryja *et al.* (1986) demonstrated homozygous deletions greater than 25 kilobases (kb), at 13q14 in two out of 37 retinoblastoma tumours. cDNA clones of the gene encoding esterase D, which is linked to the retinoblastoma susceptibility locus in band 13q14.11, were used to isolate genomic clones of the esterase D locus. Distal DNA fragments of these clones were in turn used to isolate overlapping genomic clones. This chromosome walking technique allowed the isolation of DNA sequences over 500 kb. These were used to isolated cDNA clones from fetal retinal and placental libraries (Lee *et al.*, 1987). Friend *et al.* (1986) described a cDNA clone with properties attributed to the retinoblastoma gene. This clone detected a transcript absent specifically from retinoblastoma cell lines. Fung *et al.* (1987) have shown that 60% of retinoblastomas tested contained no deletion in the retinoblastoma gene, but have aberrant RNA expression.

To date the only chromosome abnormality detected and shown to be linked to schizophrenia is that of a partial trisomy of chromosome 5 (Bassett *et al.*, 1988; Sherrington *et al.*, 1988). The mother of one of these affected individuals had a balanced translocation of 5q11-13 to chromosome 1q32.2 (Bassett *et al.*, 1988). It has been possible to produce a human/hamster hybrid cell line of this deleted chromosome 5 from the mother (Wasmuth, personal communication). This hybrid cell line, in which chromosome 5 is the only human chromosome present, will permit rapid mapping of clones linked to the schizophrenia susceptibility locus at 5q11-13. However, this region contains at least 30 million base pairs and consequently thousands of possible candidate genes. Therefore, the direct approach used for the isolation of the DMD locus is not applicable. The complexity of brain-specific gene expression coupled with the difficulty of obtaining high quality RNA from postmortem brain tissue precludes the approach used to isolate the affected gene in CGD.

The application of recombinant DNA techniques has been very successful in the pursuit of the cystic fibrosis (CF) gene, although there was no observed cytogenetic abnormality. Genetic linkage studies of CF and DNA markers localized the CF mutation to chromosome 7q22-31 (White *et al.*, 1985). The recombination fraction between the marker MET and CF was found to be 0.004 centimorgans*, and 0.003 centimorgans between J3.11 and CF. Greater than 95% of CF families show linkage to the 7q markers. A degree of non-random association is observed between specific marker alleles (RFLPs) and the cystic fibrosis gene. This non-random association between a marker and a disease is known as linkage disequilibrium or allelic association. Although as a rule the relationship between physical and genetic distance is not linear, linkage disequilibrium becomes stronger as physical distance between two loci decreases. If little or no recombination occurs between a marker and disease locus during evolution, and assuming no new mutations have occurred, then these will reveal a population association among unrelated affected individuals. The above-mentioned markers linked to CF are therefore immediately amenable to fine genetic mapping and molecular cloning techniques. Using chromosome-mediated gene transfer (CMGT), several mouse/human hybrid cell lines were constructed that contain transgenomes including the markers most closely linked to CF. This was possible as a result of using the MET oncogene as a selectable marker for cell lines carrying this region of chromosome 7 (Estivill *et al.*, 1987). From these hybrid cell lines cosmid libraries were obtained that were enriched for HTF (Hpa II tiny fragment) islands. The rationale for this is that HTF islands, containing clustered sites for restriction enzymes that cleave unmethylated CpG dinucleotide sequences, are often found in association with genes (Bird, 1986). Estivill *et al.* (1987) selected cosmid clones that showed strong linkage disequilibrium to CF. Sequences from these clones that were found to be conserved in many vertebrate species were used to isolate, as candidates, clones expressed in the lung.

A similar approach could be utilized for identifying the schizophrenia susceptibility locus from tightly linked clones. However, CMGT can be used only where there is a selectable marker in the region to be cloned; furthermore, molecular rearrangements are known to accompany CMGT, and there is little control over the size of fragments transferred. If the average size transferred is greater than five million bases detailed mapping becomes difficult. Therefore CMGT is unlikely to be of much application. Fortunately the deleted chromosome 5 mentioned above provides a method of rapidly identifying clones mapping to 5q11-13 by Southern blotting. Those cosmid clones containing HTF islands of this region can be orientated and ordered using a combination of linkage analysis and long range restriction mapping by pulse field gel electrophoresis (PFGE) (Schwarz & Cantor, 1984). PFGE allows the analysis of DNA fragments of 50 – 10 000 kb, a range not covered by molecular cloning and classical genetics. This approach was exploited to generate probes close to the CF marker MET (Michiels *et al.*, 1987) and

*One centimorgan is represented approximately by 1 million base pairs.

around the 5' region of the DMD locus (Anand *et al.*, 1987). Although still in its infancy, cloning by yeast artificial chromosomes (YACs) in conjunction with preparative PFGE to enrich for sequences of selected regions of the genome promises to be a powerful cloning technique.

Using classical genetic linkage analysis with affected families as described previously it may be possible to identify a chromosomal region of one to five centimorgans containing the schizophrenia susceptibility gene. This would require a hundred or more informative meioses, preferably from affected individuals only. The observed heterogeneity (Kennedy *et al.*, 1988) may make this difficult. However, the advantage of the deleted chromosome 5 is that it should be possible to produce a long range restriction map including the schizophrenia locus, of ordered but not overlapping clones. These maps will provide information on the spatial arrangement of HTF islands which will indicate the presence of possible candidate genes. The selection of specific clones where physical distances match the genetic distance from a known tightly linked marker may enable us to identify candidate loci by chromosome walking and/or jumping. Confirmation of the fact that the gene is expressed in the brain can be carried out by hybridization with brain specific cDNAs to the genomic locus and to northen blots of brain mRNA. The identification of markers in strong linkage disequilibrium with the schizophrenia susceptibility locus will greatly facilitate the cloning of the affected gene.

The problems of heterogeneity for the establishment of linkage disequilibrium may be overcome in several ways. For example, by collecting a large number of affected individuals each from a chromosome-5-linked family. Alternatively, by obtaining a large sample of affected individuals from many families it may be possible to identify linkage disequilibrium with a particular subtype showing through the 'noise' of unlinked subtypes. The success of this latter approach depends on the degree of heterogeneity in schizophrenia and the proportion caused by the chromosome 5 locus. The proportion affected could be increased by studying a genetically isolated population which has been subject to genetic drift. The search for linkage disequilibrium could be facilitated by the identification of a particular clinical marker associated with the chromosome-5-linked disorder. It is possible that schizophrenia linked to chromosome 5 may be caused by more than one mutation at the same locus. This would make the search for linkage disequilibrium more difficult. However, this does not present an insurmountable obstacle to successful cloning of the gene, as such problems were present in the search for the retinoblastoma gene.

The rapidly moving field of molecular genetics and the ingenuity of molecular biologists will ultimately allow the cloning of the schizophrenia genes. This will provide a precise knowledge of the biochemistry of the disease pathways. Consequently, new and more appropriate therapies will be developed.

Acknowledgements—The research was funded by the Wellcome Trust and the Rothschild Schizophrenia research fund. We would like to thank Icelandair for the generous transportation of blood samples to London and for other assistance.

References

American Psychiatric Association (1980): *Diagnostic and statistical manual of mental disorders*, 3rd ed. Washington DC.

Anand, R., Honeycombe, J., Whittaker, P.A., Elder, S.K. & Southern, E.M. (1987): Clones from an 840 kb fragment containing the 5' region of the DMD locus enriched by PFGE. *Genomics* **3**, 177–186.

Baron, M. (1976): Albinism and schizophreniform psychosis: A pedigree study. *Am. J. Psychiatry* **133**, 1070–1073.

Baron, M., Gruen, R., Asnis, L. & Kane, J. (1982): Schizoaffective illness, schizophrenia and affective disorders: morbidity risks and genetic transmission. *Acta Psychiatr. Scand.* **65**, 253–262.
Baron, M., Risch, N., Hamburger, R., Mandel, B., Kushner, S., Newman, M., Drumer, D., & Belmaker, R.H. (1987): Genetic linkage between X chromosome markers & bipolar affective disorder. *Nature* **326**, 289–292.
Bassett, A.S., McGillivray, B.C., Jones, B., Pantzar, J.T. & Langlois, S. (1988): Partial trisomy chromosome 5 co-segregating with schizophrenia. *Lancet* i, 779–780.
Bertlesen, A., Harvald, B. & Hauge, M. (1972): A Danish twin study of manic depressive psychosis. *Br. J. Psychiatry* **130**, 330–351.
Bird, A.P. (1986): CpG-rich islands and the function of DNA methylation. *Nature* **321**, 209–213.
Blackwood, D.H.R., Whalley, L.J. & Christie, J.E. (1987): Changes in P3 auditory evoked potential in schizophrenia and depression. *Br. J. Psychiatry* **150**, 154–160.
Blackwood, D. *et al.* (1988): Oral communication, Royal College of Psychiatrists winter quarterly meeting, London.
Brockington, I.F., Kendall, R.E. & Leff, J. (1978): Definitions of schizophrenia concordance and prediction of outcome. *Psychol. Med.* **8**, 387–398.
Bunzow, J.R., Van Tol, H.H.M., Grandy, D.K., Albert, P., Salon, J., Christie, M., Machida, C., Neve, K.A. & Civelli, O. (1988): Cloning and expression of a rat D2 dopamine receptor cDNA. *Nature* **336**, 783–785.
Cooper, J.E., Kendell, R.E., Gurland, B.J., Sharpe, L., Copeland, J.R.M. & Simon, R. (1982): *Psychiatric diagnosis in New York and London.* Maudsley Monograph No 20. Oxford: Oxford University Press.
Crow, T.J. (1980): Molecular pathology of schizophrenia; more than one disease process. *Br. Med. J.* **1**, 66–68.
Crow, T.J. (1984): A re-evaluation of the viral hypothesis; is psychosis the result of retroviral integration at a site close to the cerebral dominance gene? *Br. J. Psychiatry* **145**, 243–253.
Den Dunnen, J.T., Bakker, E., Klein Breteler, E.L.G., Pearson, P.L. & Van Ommen, G.J.B. (1987): Direct detection of more than 50% of Duchenne muscular dystrophy mutations by field inversion gels, *Nature* **329**, 640–642.
Dryja, T.P., Rapaport, J.M., Joyce, J.M. & Petersen, R.A. (1986): Molecular detection of deletion involving band q14 of chromosome 13 in retinoblastomas. *Proc. Natl. Acad. Sci. USA* **83**; 7391–7394.
Dworkin, R.H. & Lenzenweger, M.F. (1984): Symptoms and genetics of schizophrenia, implications for diagnosis. *Am. J. Psychiatry* **141**, 1541–1545.
Egeland, J.A., Gerhard, D.S., Pauls, D.L., Sussex, J.N., Kidd, K.K., Allen, C.R., Hostetter, A.M. & Housman, D.E. (1987): Genetic linkage between X chromosome markers & bipolar affective disorder. *Nature* **326**, 289–292.
Estivill, X., Farrall, M., Scambler, P.J., Bell, G.M., Hawley, K.M.F., Lench, N.J., Bates, G.P., Kruyer, H.C., Frederick, P.A., Stanier, P., Watson, E.K., Williamson, R. & Wainright, B.J. (1987): A candidate for the cystic fibrosis locus isolated by selection for methylation-free islands. *Nature* **326**, 840–845.
Farmer, A.E., Jackson, R., McGuffin, P. & Storey, P. (1987a): Cerebral ventricular enlargement in chronic schizophrenia. *Br. J. Psychiatry* **150**, 324–330.
Farmer, A.E., McGuffin, P. & Gottesman, I.I. (1987b): Twin concordance for DSM-III defined schizophrenia. *Arch. Gen. Psychiatry* **44**, 634–641.
Feighner, J., Robins, E., Guze, S., Woodruff, R., Winokur, G. & Munoz, R. (1972): Diagnostic criteria for use in psychiatric research. *Arch. Gen. Psychiatry* **26**, 57–63.
Friend, S.H., Bernards, R., Rogelj, S., Weinberg, R.A., Rapaport, J.M. Albert, D.M. & Dryja, T.P. (1986): A human DNA segment with properties of the gene that predisposes to retinoblastoma and osteosarcoma. *Nature* **323**, 643–646.
Fung, Y-H.T., Murphree, A.L., T'ang, A., Qian, J., Hinrichs S.H. & Benedicts, W.E. (1987): Structural evidence for the authenticity of the human retinoblastoma gene. *Science* 236, 1657–1661.
Gottesmann, I.I. & Shields, J. (1972): *Schizophrenia and genetics.* London: Academic Press.
Gruzelier, J.H. (1987): In *Cerebral dynamics, laterality and psychopathology*, eds R. Takahashi, P. Flor-Henry, J.H. Gruzelier & S.I. Niwa, pp. 23–54. Amsterdam: Elsevier.

Gurling, H.M.D., Sherrington, R.P., Brynjolfsson, J., Potter, M., McInnis, M., Petursson, H. & Hodgkinson, S. (1988): Molecular genetics and heterogeneity in manic depression. *Mol. Neurobiol.* **2**, 1–7.

Henderson, N. (1982): Behaviour genetics. *Annu. Rev. Psychol.* **33**, 403–440.

Hoffman, E.P., Brown, R.H., Jr. & Kunkel, C.M. (1987): Dystrophin: The protein product of the Duchenne muscular dystrophy locus. *Cell* **51**, 919–928.

Holzman, P.S., Proctor, L.R. & Levy, D.L. (1974): Eye tracking dysfunction in schizophrenics and their relatives. *Arch. Gen. Psychiatry* **31**, 143–151.

Holzman, P.S., Kringlen, E., Matthysse, S., Flanagan, S.D., Lipton, R.B., Cramer, G., Levin, S., Lange, D.L. & Levy, D.L. (1988): A single dominant gene can account for eye tracking dysfunctions and schizophrenia in offspring of discordant twins. *Arch. Gen. Psychiatry* **45**, 641–647.

Johnstone, E.C., Crow, T.J., Frith, C.D., Husband, J. & Kreel, L. (1976): Cerebral ventricle size and cognitive impairment in chronic schizophrenia. *Lancet* **ii**, 924–926.

Kendell, R.E. & Brockington, I.F. (1980): The identification of disease entities and the relationship between schizophrenia and affective psychoses. *Br. J. Psychiatry* **137**, 324–331.

Kendler, K.S. & Gruenberg, A.M. (1984): An independent analysis of the Danish adoption study of schizophrenia. *Arch. Gen. Psychiatry* **41**, 982–984.

Kennedy, J.L., Giuffra, L.A., Moises, H.W., Cavalli-Sforza, L.L., Pakstis, A.J., Kidd, J.R., Castiglione, C.M., Sjogren, B. & Kidd, K. (1988): Evidence against linkage of schizophrenia to markers on chromosome 5 in a northern Swedish pedigree. *Nature* **336**, 167–170.

Kety, S.S. (1983): Mental illness in the biological and adoptive relatives of schizophrenic adoptees. *Am. J. Psychiatry* **140**, 720–727.

Koenig, M., Hoffman, E.P., Bertelson, C.J., Monaco, A.P. Feener, C. & Kunkel, L.M. (1987): Complete cloning of the Duchenne muscular dystrophy (DMD) DNA and preliminary genomic organization of the DMD gene in normal and affected individuals. *Cell* **50**, 509–517.

Kunkel, L.M., Monaco, A.P. Middlesworth, W., Ochs, H.D & Latt, S.A. (1985): Specific cloning of DNA fragments absent from the DNA of a male patient with an X chromosome deletion. *Proc. Natl. Acad. Sci. USA* **82**, 4778–4782.

Lee, W.-H., Bookstein, R., Hong, F., Young, L-H., Shew, J-Y. & Lee E. (1987): Human retinoblastoma susceptibility gene: cloning, identification and sequence. *Science* **235**, 1394–1399.

McGue, M., Gottesman, I.I. & Rao, D.C. (1985): Resolving genetic models for the transmission of schizophrenia. *Genet. Epidemiol.* **46**, 44–55.

McGuffin, P., Farmer, A.E., Gottesman, I.I., Murray, R.M. & Reveley, A.M. (1984): Twin concordance in operationally defined schizophrenia. *Arch. Gen. Psychiatry* **41**, 541–545.

McGuffin, P. & Sturt, E. (1986): Genetic markers in schizophrenia. *Hum. Hered.* **36**, 65–88.

Matthysse, S., Holsman, P.S. & Lange, K. (1986): The genetic transmission of schizophrenia. *J. Psychiatr. Res.* **20**, 52–76.

Mendlewicz, J., Fleiss, J.L. & Gieve, R.R. (1972): Evidence for X linkage in the transmission of manic depressive illness. *JAMA* **222**, 1624–1627.

Mendlewicz, J., Simon, P., Sevy, S., Charon, F., Brocas, H., Legros, S. & Vassart, G. (1987): Polymorphic marker on X chromosome and manic depression. *Lancet* ii, 1230–1231.

Mendlewicz, J., *et al.* (1988): Molecular genetic studies of manic depression. Oral presentation, 16th. Collegium Internationale Neuro-Psychopharmacologium Meeting, Munich.

Michiels, F., Burneister, M. & Lehrach, H. (1987): Derivation of clones close to MET by preparative pulse field gel electrophoresis. *Science* **236**, 1305–1308.

Monaco., A.P., Bertelson, W., Middlesworth, W., Collett, C.A., Aldridge, J., Fishbeck, R., Bartlett, R., Pericak-Vance, M.A., Roses, A.D. & Kunkel, L.M. (1985): Detection of deletions spanning Duchenne muscular dystrophy locus using a tightly linked DNA segment. *Nature* **316**, 842–845.

Murray, R.M., Lewis, S.W., Owen, M.J. Foerster, A. (1988): The neurodevelopmental origins of dementia praecox. In *Schizophrenia: the major issues*, eds P. Bebbington & P. McGuffin. London: Heinemann.

O'Rourke, D.H., Gottesman, I.I., Suarez, B.K., Rice, J. & Reich, T. (1983): Refutation of the single major locus model in the aetiology of schizophrenia. *Am. J. Hum. Genet.* **34**, 630–649.

Ott, J. (1985): *Analysis of human genetic linkage*. Baltimore, USA: Johns Hopkins University Press.

Ott, J. (1986): The number of families required to detect of exclude linkage heterogeneity. *Am. J. Hum. Genet.* **39**, 159–165.
Owen, M.J., Lewis, S.W. & Murray, R.M. (1988): Obstetric complications of schizophrenia: A CT study. *Psychol. Med.* **18**, 331–340.
Ponder, B.A.J., Coeffey, R., Gagel, R.F., Semple, P., Ponder, M.E., Pembrey, M.E., Telenius-Berg, M. & Easton, D.F. (1988): Risk estimation and screening in families of patients with medullary thyroid carcinoma. *Lancet* i, 397–400.
Pope, H.G., Jonas, J.M. & Cohen, B.H. (1982): Failure to find evidence of schizophrenia in first degree relatives of schizophrenic probands. *Am. J. Psychiatry* **139** 826–828.
Reveley, A.M., Reveley, M.A. & Murray, R.M. (1984): Cerebral ventricular enlargement in non genetic schizophrenia: A controlled twin study. *Br. J. Psychiatry* **144**, 89–93.
Risch, N. (1988): A new statistical test for linkage heterogeneity. *Am. J. Hum. Genet.* **42**, 353–364.
Romano, J. & Linares, R.L. (1987): Marfan's syndrome and schizophrenia: a case report. *Arch. Gen. Psychiatry* 32, 466–476.
Royer-Pokora, B., Kunkel, L.M., Monaco, A.P., Goff, S.C., Newburger, P.E., Baehner, R.L., Sessions Cole, F.S., Curnutte, J.T. & Orkin, S.H. (1986): Cloning the gene for an inherited human disorder-chronic granulomatous disease on the basis of its chromosomal location. *Nature* **322**, 32–38.
St. Claire, D., Blackwood, D., Muir, W., Ballie, D., Hubbard, A., Wright, A. & Evans, J.J. (1989): No linkage to chromosome 5q11-q13 markers in schizophrenia in Scottish families. *Nature* **339**, 305–309.
Schneider, K. (1959): *Clinical Psychopathology*, translated by M.W. Hamilton. New York: Grune & Stratton.
Schwartz, D.L. & Cantor, C.R. (1984): Separation of yeast chromosome sized DNA's by pulsed fluid gradient gel electrophoresis. *Cell.* **37**, 67–75.
Sherrington, R., Brynjolfsson, J., Petursson, H., Potter, M., Dudleston, K., Barraclough, B., Wasmuth, J., Dobbs, M. & Gurling, H.M.D. (1988): Localisation of a susceptibility locus for schizophrenia on chromosome 5. *Nature* **336**, 164–167.
Spitzer, R.L., Endicott, J. & Robins, E. (1978): Research diagnostic criteria; rationale & reliability. *Arch. Gen. Psychiatry* **35**, 773–82.
Sturt, E. & McGuffin, P. (1985): Can linkage and marker association resolve the genetic aetiology of psychiatric disorders? Review and argument. *Psychol. Med.* **15**, 455–462.
Suarez, B.K., Rice, J. & Reich, T. (1978): The generalized sib pair IBD distribution: its use in the detection of linkage. *Ann. Hum. Genet.* **42**, 87–94.
Taylor, M.A. (1972): Schneiderian first rank symptoms and clinical prognostic features in schizophrenia. *Arch. Gen. Psychiatry* **26**, 64–67.
Tsuang, M.T. & Winokur, G. (1974): Criteria for subtyping schizophrenia. Clinical differentiation of hebephrenic and paranoid schizophrenia. *Arch. Gen. Psychiatry* **31**, 43–47.
Turner, S.W., Toone, B.K. & Brett-Jones, J.R. (1986): Computerised tomography scan changes in early schizophrenia preliminary findings. *Psychol. Med.* **16**, 219–225.
White, R.S., Woodward, S., Leppert, M., O'Connel, P., Hoff, M., Herbst, J., Lalouel, J.M., Dean, M. & Vande Woude, A. (1985): A closely linked genetic marker for cystic fibrosis. *Nature* **318**, 382–384.
Wing, J. & Nixon, J. (1975): Discriminating features in schizophrenia. *Arch. Gen. Psychiatry* **32**, 853–859.
Winokur, G., Morrison, J., Clancy, J. & Crowe, R. (1974): The Iowa 500. The clinical and genetic distinction of hebephrenic and paranoid schizophrenia. *J. Nerv. Men. Dis.* **159**, 12–19.

Chapter 14

Integrated viral genes as potential pathogens in the functional psychoses*

T. J. Crow

Division of Psychiatry, Clinical Research Centre, Watford Road, Harrow, Middlesex, HA1 3UJ, UK

Summary

According to the retrovirus-transposon hypothesis, psychosis is due to the expression of a pathogenic sequence (a 'virogene') integrated in the genome and either inherited from an affected or predisposed parent or acquired in the course of reproduction by a genetic rearrangement (eg a transposition or the generation of a tandem repeat). The psychoses are viewed as a continuum extending from unipolar through bipolar and schizo-affective disorder to schizophrenia with increasing severity of defect, movement along this continuum occurring by such genetic rearrangements. The locus at which these changes take place is envisaged as related to the genetic determinants of cerebral lateralization (the 'cerebral dominance gene'), the interaction between potential pathogen and growth factor gene having possible growth enhancing effects. Such beneficial effects may have ensured the survival of this 'hot-spot' in the genome.

Introduction

It is often argued that discordance for psychosis in monozygotic twins is a measure of the role of non-genetic factors in aetiology. While there is reasonable concensus from twin and adoption studies on a contribution from genes, the nature of the non-genetic component remains obscure. Whether it is supposed that genes predispose to an environmental agent or that there are separate genetic and non-genetic types of illness, few specific hypotheses of the non-genetic element have been formulated.

Prominent amongst these is the viral hypothesis. This seems first to have been clearly expressed by Menninger (1928) and Goodall (1932). These authors observed the psychotic sequelae of the epidemic of influenza in 1918 and that of encephalitis lethargica which succeeded it. Some of these psychoses presented with schizophrenia-like symptoms. On this basis arose the proposal that schizophrenia itself might be caused by a viral agent.

In recent years the concept has derived support from the challenge to the established dogma that the incidence of schizophrenia is relatively constant with respect to time and place. For example, Hare (1983) marshalled evidence that there was a real increase in incidence in the course of the nineteenth century and Torrey (1980) argued that there are significant variations in different countries. Such conclusions encourage the view that schizophrenia spreads in the manner of an epidemic.

If the disease spreads within populations it must be assumed that it is passed from one individual to another. The notion of schizophrenia as an infectious disease is perhaps unfamiliar although it has historical precedents (Hofbauer, 1846; Baillarger, 1857). Some data from family studies are consistent with it (Crow, 1983). According to this concept the environmental contribution arises from exposure to an individual who already has the disease.

A test of contagion

The contagion hypothesis has been tested in pairs of siblings. If the disease is passed from an affected individual to a genetically-susceptible sibling, an earlier age of onset will be expected in the younger sibling. Examination of five series of siblings in the literature revealed a highly significant trend in this direction (Crow & Done, 1986). This appears consistent with *contagion*. However, other explanations must be considered, for example that the effect is due to *earlier detection* in a younger sibling as a result of the disease being already known in the family, and *ascertainment bias* which arises from systematic under-inclusion of late onsets in younger siblings if the data are collected at the time of onset of illness in a proband. The three explanations generate different predictions about age-shift (toward younger onset in younger sibling) in elder-sibling ill first pairs. Both the contagion and early detection hypotheses predict the shift will occur; the ascertainment bias hypothesis does not. The findings support this latter explanation. When possible ascertainment bias is taken into account (ie by excluding the younger-sibling ill first pairs), it appears there is no significant shift toward younger age of onset in the younger sibling.

The result is damaging to the contagion hypothesis and also to the more general concept that age of onset is determined by an environmental pathogen. Any explanation that invokes an agent which occurs at a defined point in time (eg psychological trauma) and which might be shared by two siblings would predict earlier age of onset in the younger sibling. Yet when ascertainment bias is allowed for, this is not seen. It appears that age of onset is intrinsic to predisposition to the disease. Some individuals are predisposed not only to get the disease but to get it at a predetermined age. It is as though a clock is ticking away to ensure that the individual will develop psychosis at a particular point in his life span.

The findings set limits for the role of an environmental factor. If such a factor exists, it appears that (at least for the generality of cases of psychosis) it does not exert its effects in postnatal life. However, prenatal influences are not excluded as siblings do not share an environment at this time.

Is a virus integrated in the genome?

Another finding which suggests a role for early events is the tendency for individuals who later develop psychosis to have been born in the winter months (Dalen, 1975). Such seasonality is compatible with a role for infection, but only if a latent period of 20 years or more is invoked. A somewhat complicated theory is that the individual with psychosis i genetically predisposed to *in utero* infection with a virus which remains latent for decades before replicating to cause disease. A simpler hypothesis is that predisposing gene and pathogen are one and the same, ie that the virus is integrated in the genome, but can be expressed as viral particles (Crow, 1984). This concept can explain episodicity of illness as well as its long latency. According to this hypothesis, the disease is genetic because the pathogen can be inherited from an unaffected or prediposed parent. The non-genetic component arises from acquisition of the pathogen at an early (perhaps very early) stage of development. Such acquisition might represent *de novo* exposure to an exogenous virus (ie prenatal contagion) although this seems improbable. More likely, perhaps, is that the agent is already within the genome and becomes pathogenic by transposition to a critical site or by some modification of structure. Temperature-dependence of such early genetic rearrangements could account for seasonality of birth.

A prediction generated by this explanation is an inverse relationship between family history and the excess of births in the winter months. Such a relationship was reported by Kinney & Jacobsen (1978) although on a small sample. Similar trends were detected by Shur (1982) and McNeil (1987).

Disease caused by integrated viruses in animals is well known — mammary tumours and leukaemia in mice are both caused by retroviruses inherited as genes (Teich, 1982). In these cases the individual mouse is affected at a particular age. A motor neurone disease in mice is also described (Murphy *et al.*, 1983) in which an integrated retrovirus plays a role. In these retrovirally-caused diseases, the disturbance arises from expression of the integrated sequence as autonomous viral particles in the target tissue.

Because they code for the enzyme reverse transcriptase and can integrate in the host genome as a DNA provirus, retroviruses are of particular interest as potential pathogens. They can be considered as a member of the wider class of transposable genetic elements. This includes long- and short-interspersed nuclear elements (LINES and SINES, Singer & Skowronski, 1985) and the THE-1 element (Paulson *et al.*, 1985) all of which, along with retrovirus sequences (Mager & Henthorn, 1984), are present in the human genome. Also in this category are the highly variable sequences described by Jeffreys *et al.* (1985). Each of these types of element is a possible candidate for the role of virogene in the sense that they are more labile within the genome than conventional genes; some may have an autonomous existence outside the genome. Whether or not the other transposons are sometimes pathogenic in the way that retroviral sequences can be remains to be shown.

Does season influence early genetic rearrangements?

The tendency for persons with psychosis to have been born in the winter months of the year gives no clue as to the stage of development at which the influence of season occurs, ie whether in the perinatal period or much earlier.

According to the retrovirus — transposon hypothesis early genetic rearrangements (eg transpositions) have the same consequence (the development of psychosis after an interval of 20 years or more) as inheritance of the psychosis 'virogene' from an affected or predisposed parent. Such genetic rearrangements are equivalent to new mutations. That psychosis might be associated with a high mutation rate has often been considered (eg Böök, 1953; Lewis, 1958; Penrose, 1968; Moran, 1972) as a possible explanation of the persistence of a genetically determined condition which reduces fertility.

In the case of ecotropic murine leukaemia viruses, the rate of acquisition of new retroviral sequences in the genome may be high. For example, in AKR strains it is estimated that one new copy appears every four generations of inbreeding and in SWR/J strains congenic for two closely linked proviral loci 18.6% of progeny acquire new proviruses (Jenkins & Copeland, 1985). Such mutation rates are more than enough to accommodate the estimates of Böök and Penrose, although whether the phenomenon described by Jenkins & Copeland is of general significance remains to be established.

In the case of experimental retroviral insertion into the germ cell line (Jaenisch, 1976), the time of exposure of the embryo (ie pre-implantation) is critical. If, as suggested, the mutational event represents rearrangement by transposition within the germ cell line this may occur at an early stage of development, eg early embryogenesis, fertilization or even gamete formation. Transposition is sometimes temperature-dependent, for example, in Ty elements in yeast (Paquin & Williams, 1984) and Tn3 elements in bacteria. How temperature might have a significant influence on mutation rate in a homeothermic organism appears obscure. However, it should be noted that gametogenesis in the male by its location in the scrotal sac is exposed to external temperature in a way that female gametogenesis is not. It seems worth considering, therefore, that the season of birth effect (and the role of new mutations) relates particularly to the paternal contribution of the zygote.

There is also evidence that transposition events are more frequent or confined to the germ cell line, eg in the case of LINE elements in the mammalian genome and P elements in Drosophila (eg Laski *et al.*, 1986). Therefore, there are grounds for suggesting that mutational events do occur in the manner that is being suggested for psychosis, ie at a specific site within the genome, in the germ cell line and in a temperature-dependent manner.

The continuum of psychosis

According to the concept outlined above, the psychosis locus is a 'hot-spot' of genetic variation. What has to be explained is why this hot-spot persists within the genome, ie why, if it is associated with decreased fertility (Lewis, 1958) it is not selected out by evolutionary pressure. One answer is that schizophrenia is but part of a broader spectrum of genetic variation, and that advantages lie elsewhere in the spectrum. For example, it is suggested (Crow, 1986a) that schizophrenia represents one end of the 'continuum of psychosis' that stretches from unipolar through bipolar and schizo-affective disorder to schizophrenia with increasing degrees of defect. The evidence for this view includes the fact that no clear demarcation can be drawn between affective and schizophrenic psychoses on phenomenological grounds (but see Cloninger *et al.*, 1985, for the argument regarding outcome) and in family studies that schizo-affective illness cannot be separated from either affective disorder or schizophrenia. Of relevance to the retrovirus-transposon concept are observations that the descendants of individuals with a disorder at one point on the continuum are at increased risk of disease of greater severity. Thus, bipolar affective illness is increased in the children of unipolar probands, schizo-affective illness in the children of affective parents, and schizophrenia in the offspring of schizo-affective parents. There is a degree of stability in the continuum — on the whole relatives of patients with schizophrenia suffer from schizophrenic psychoses — but there is also the possibility of change, and such change between generations is sometimes in the direction of increased severity.

The continuum concept suggests that the gene is subject to quantitative variations and that these occur in the course of reproduction. One possibility is that tandem repeats of the element or a component of the element are generated. Such changes might occur at gamete formation or fertilization.

The continuum concept is a refinement of the virogene (integrated virus) hypothesis. High rates of mutation are required to explain the persistence of psychosis and it variability. It appears that the element both has potential autonomy and is subject to variation in form. Such considerations provide clues to its structure. A recently described model of interest is the L1 Md repetitive sequence in the mouse (Loeb *et al.*, 1986). This element includes protein coding sequences and a variable number of tandem repeats at the 5′ end. It is suggested (Loeb *et al.*, 1986) that transcriptional activity is a function of the number of tandem repeats present.

Where is the virogene located?

Some clues are avilable to the location of the psychosis gene. Evidence from CT scan studies, brain electrical activity mapping (BEAM) and two recent post-mortem studies supports the view that schizophrenia is a disease of the left or dominant hemisphere (Crow, 1986*b*). In a recent CT scan study (Crow *et al.*, in press), the width asymmetries in the posterior part of the brain were reduced in early (before age 25 years) onset patients by comparison with late onset schizophrenic and other psychiatric patients. It appeared as though the onset of schizophrenia was associated with an arrest of the development of brain lateralization.

Selectivity of the schizophrenic disease process for the left hemisphere could be explained if the agent were directly associated with the mechanisms of lateralization. Gross morphological asymmetries (for example, the greater extent of the planum temporale on the left side) are now well documented (Geschwind & Levitsky, 1968), and presumably depend upon asymmetrical brain growth. Such asymmetries are probably a relatively recent evolutionary development and are associated with the human capacity for speech. It may be supposed that they depend upon the presence within the genome of a growth factor (the 'cerebral dominance gene'), equivalent to the right shift factor postulated by Annett (1985), which is differentially expressed in the left hemisphere. If the psychosis 'virogene' were located close to the cerebral dominance gene it might be similarly expressed.

The ability of retroviruses to incorporate genes coding for growth factors and to enhance their expression is established in the field of neoplasia. Similar associations between growth factors and other retroposons (eg LINE elements, Katzir *et al.*, 1985) and other types of mobile element (eg IS elements, Rechavi *et al.*, 1982) are described. Such associations may be relevant to the survival of the gene. If the element interacts with the cerebral dominance gene to promote the development of those brain areas involved in lateralization and speech, this could be advantageous. One can envisage that this might be associated with particular creativity. Such abilities are seen in some patients with manic-depressive illness (Jamison, 1987) and perhaps also in some relatives of patients with schizophrenia (Karlsson, 1984).

Conclusion

Although the findings of family and twin studies of schizophrenia leave room for significant environmental contributions to aetiology, no such pathogenic factors have been identified. Moreover as indicated by a study in siblings, age of onset rather than being dependent upon the postnatal environment is intrinsic to the individual. These conclusions suggest the disease is determined by genes to a greater extent than is generally assumed, but a naive genetic theory has difficulty in explaining the persistence of the disease, as well as its periodicity and age of onset. According to the retrovirus–transposon hypothesis, these features are accounted for as follows:

(i) Psychosis is due to the expression of a pathogen (a 'virogene') integrated in the genome.
(ii) The virogene is either inherited from an affected or predisposed parent or acquired as a result of a genetic rearrangement (eg transposition or the generation of a tandem repeat) which occurs early in development (perhaps even at meiosis). Seasonality of birth of psychotic individuals may indicate that such new mutations (particularly in the male gonads) are temperature-dependent. The rate at which these genetic rearrangements occur indicates that the locus is a 'hot-spot' of genetic variation.
(iii) The element is integrated at a site close to the 'cerebral dominance gene', the growth factor determining the asymmetric development of brain areas concerned with the human capacity for speech and communication.
(iv) The gene is expressed in the course of development to enhance brain growth. This may account for the survival of the gene and the persistence of this hot-spot of variation within the genome. In episodes of illness in predisposed individuals the gene is expressed in an aberrant manner as viral particles which interfere with local brain function.
(v) Psychosis is seen as a continuum extending from unipolar through bipolar to schizo-affective disorder and schizophrenia with increasing degrees of defect. Movement along this continuum occurs in the course of reproduction and represents quantal changes in the virogene.

References

Annett, H. (1985): *Left, right, hand and brain: the right shift theory*, London: Erlbaum.

Baillarger, L. (1857): Example de contagion d'un delire monomanique. *La Moniteur des Hospitaux* **45**, 353–354.

Böök, J.A. (1953): Schizophrenia as a gene mutation. *Acta Genet.* **4**, 133–139.

Cloninger, C.R., Martin, R.L., Guze, S.B. & Clayton, P.J. (1985): Diagnosis and prognosis in schizophrenia. *Arch. Gen. Psychiat* **45**, 15–25.

Crow, T.J. (1983): Is schizophrenia an infectious disease? *Lancet* **i**, 173–175.

Crow, T.J. (1984): A re-evaluation of the viral hypothesis: is psychosis the result of retroviral integration at a site close to the cerebral dominance gene? *Br. J. Psychiatry* **145**, 243–253.

Crow, T.J. (1986*a*): The continuum of psychosis and its implication for the structure of the gene. *Br. J. Psychiatry* **149**, 419–429.

Crow, T.J. (1986*b*): Left brain, retrotransposons and schizophrenia. *Br. Med. J.* **292**, 3–4.

Crow, T.J. & Done, D.J. (1986): Age of onset of schizophrenia in siblings: a test of the contagion hypothesis. *Psychiatr. Res.* **18**, 107–117.

Crow, T.J., Colter, N., Firth, C.D., Johnstone, E.C. & Owens, D.G.C. (1989): Developmental arrest of cerebral asymmetries in early onset schizophrenia. *Psychiatr. Res.* (in press).

Dalen, P. (1975): *Season of births: A study of schizophrenia and other mental disorders.* Amsterdam: North Holland.

Geschwind, N. & Levitsky, W. (1968): Left-right asymmetry in temporal speech region. *Science* **161**, 186–187.

Goddall, E. (1932): The exciting cause of certain states, at present classified under 'schizophrenia' by psychiatrists, may be infection. *J. Ment. Sci.* **78**, 746–755.

Hare, E.H. (1983): Was insanity on the increase? *Br. J. Psychiatry* **142**, 439–455.

Hofbauer, B. (1846): Infectio psychica. *Oest. Med. Woch.* **39**, 1184–1188.

Jaenisch, R. (1976): Germ line integration and Mendelian transmission of the exogenous Moloney leukemia virus. *Proc. Natl. Acad. Sci. USA* **73**, 1260–1264.

Jamison, K.R. (1989): Manic-depressive illness and accomplishment: creativity, leadership and social class, In *Manic-depressive illness*, ed. F.K. Goodwin & K.R. Jamison, Oxford: Oxford University Press. (in press).

Jeffreys, A.J., Wilson, V. & Thein, S.L. (1985): Hypervariable 'minisatellite' regions in human DNA. *Nature* **314**, 67–73.

Jenkins, N.A. & Copeland, N.G. (1985): High frequency germ-line acquisition of ecotropic MuLV proviruses in SWR/J-RF/J hybrid mice. *Cell* **43**, 811–819.

Karlsson, J. (1984): Creative intelligence in relatives of mental patients. *Hereditas* **100**, 83–86.

Katzir, N., Rechavi, G., Cohen, J.B., Unger, T., Simoni, F., Segul, S., Cohen, D. & Givol, D. (1985): 'Retroposon' insertion into the cellular oncogene c-myc in canine transmissible venereal tumor. *Proc. Natl. Acad. Sci. USA* **82**, 1054–1058.

Kinney, D.K. & Jacobsen, B. (1978): Environmental factors in schizophrenia: new adoption study evidence. In *The Nature of schizophrenia,* ed. L.C. Wynne, R.L. Cromwell & S. Matthysse, pp. 38–51. New York: John Wiley.

Laski, F.A., Rio, D.C. & Rubin, G.M. (1986): Tissue specificity of *Drosophila* Pelement transposition is regulated at the level of mRNA splicing. *Cell* **44**, 7–19.

Lewis, A.J. (1958): Fertility and mental illness. *Eugenics Rev.* **50**, 91–106.

Loeb, D.D., Padgett, R.W., Hardies, S.C., Shehee, W.R., Comer, M.B., Edgell, M.H. & Hutchinson, C.A. (1986): The sequence of a large L1 Md element reveals a tandemly repeated 5′ end and several features found in retrotransposons. *Mol. Cell. Biol.* **6**, 168–182.

Mager, D.L. & Henthorn, P.S. (1984): Identification of a retrovirus-like repetitive element in human DNA. *Proc. Natl. Acad. Sci. USA* **81**, 7510–7514.

McNeil, T.F. (1987): Perinatal factors in the development of schizophrenia. In *Biological perspectives in schizophrenia*, ed. F.A. Henn, & H. Helmchen. Chichester: John Wiley.

Menninger, K.A. (1928): The schizophrenic syndrome as a product of acute infectious disease. *Arch. Neurol. Psychiatry* **20**, 464–481.

Moran, P.A.P. (1972): Theoretical considerations on schizophrenia genetics. In *Genetic factors in schizophrenia* ed. A.R. Kaplan, pp. 294–309. Springfield: C. C. Thomas.

Murphy, W.H., Nawrocki, J.F. & Pease, L.R. (1983): Age-dependent paralytic viral infection in C58 mice: possible implications in human neurologic disease. *Prog. Brain Res.* **59**, 291–303.

Paquin, C.E. & Williams, V.M. (1984): Temperature effects on the rate of Ty transposition. *Science* **226**, 53–55.

Paulson, K.E., Doka, N., Schmid, G.W., Misra, R., Schindler, C.W., Rush, M.G., Kadyk, L. & Leinwand, L. (1985): A transposon like element in human DNA. *Nature* **316**, 359–361.

Penrose, L.S. (1968): Critical survey of schizophrenia genetics. In *Modern perspectives in world psychiatry* ed. J.G. Howells, pp. 3–19. Edinburgh: Oliver & Boyd.

Rechavi, G., Givol, D. & Canaani, E. (1982): Activation of a cellular oncogene by DNA rearrangement: Possible involvement of an IS-like element. *Nature* **300**, 607–611.

Shur, E. (1982): Season of birth in high and low genetic risk schizophrenics. *Br. J. Psychiatry* **140**, 410–415.

Singer, M.F. & Skowronski, J. (1985): Making sense out of LINES: long interspersed repeat sequences. *Trends Biochem. Sci.* **10**, 119–122.

Teich, N. (1982): Endogenous viruses. In *RNA tumour viruses*, 2nd edn, ed. R. Weiss, N. Teich, H. Varmus & J. Coffin. pp. 1109–1203. New York: Cold Spring Harbor Laboratory.

Torrey, E.F. (1980): *Schizophrenia and civilisation.* New York: Jason Aronson.

III

EPIDEMIOLOGY

Introduction

Epidemiological studies fall into two categories, macro studies, such as the comparative incidence in various parts of the world, and micro studies, examining regional variations, such as differences in urban and rural settings, and in the centre and periphery of cities. The following chapters discuss these issues from various perspectives.

Chapter 15

Interaction of environmental and endogenous factors in schizophrenia

A. Jablensky

Medical Academy, Sofia, Bulgaria

Summary

The study of the multiple interactions which determine the course of schizophrenia seems to support the belief that the outcome of this potentially disabling disorder should not be regarded as pre-determined or pre-programmed, but rather as resulting from numerous but essentially modifiable daily transactions between the patient, his family, the therapeutic team, and the wider social environment. The process contains sufficient degrees of freedom to warrant the investment of time, effort, and reasonable optimism in the management of every schizophrenic person.

Introduction

Nearly one hundred years after the original formulation of the concept of dementia praecox by Emil Kraepelin, schizophrenia, as the disorder was renamed by Eugen Bleuler in 1909, continues to be an unresolved puzzle to psychiatry and the neurosciences, and a major public health problem on a global scale. Compared to other domains of mental morbidity, in which effective treatment, management, and, in some instances, preventive measures have been developed over the past decades, schizophrenia appears to be refractory to understanding and control. This state of affairs, originating in the lack of a critical breakthrough in our understanding of the biological basis and neurobehavioural mechanisms implicated in the clinical manifestations of schizophrenia, results in a variety of disparate, and often incompatible, notions about its nature.

Concepts of schizophrenia

Schizophrenia is conceptualized today in a number of different ways: as a single disease (Kraepelin, 1899); as a group of aetiologically different diseases sharing a 'common final pathway' (Bleuler, 1972); as an aberrant personality development (Bleuler, 1972); as a diathesis conferring on the person a special kind of vulnerability (Zubin *et al.*, 1983); or as a 'myth' contrived by a social conspiracy for the control of deviance (Szasz, 1976).

What are the characteristics that make schizophrenia unique, as if it were a disorder in a class of its own? The principal features may be summarized as follows:

(1) Schizophrenia is a very complex disorder, with multiple and variable psychopathological manifestations, which at present cannot be reduced to a few basic, underlying disturbances, as is the case with some of the organic brain syndromes or the mood disorders.

(2) In spite of promising new leads in neurobiology and molecular genetics, no validated disease marker and no laboratory test is yet available for its reliable identification. As in the times of Kraepelin, the diagnosis of schizophrenia depends almost entirely on clinical observation and examination, judgement, and diagnostic convention.

(3) The disease model which is at the root of the currently dominant diagnostic concepts and classifications of schizophrenia is inferential and draws support from circumstantial rather than direct evidence.

(4) As yet, no single biological factor has definitively been demonstrated as necessary for the causation of schizophrenia, and no combination of different factors has been shown to be sufficiant to explain its manifestations.

(5) The symptoms of schizophrenia are the expression of disturbances at the highest (and least understood) levels of integration of specifically human cognitive functions, such as the delimitation of the self from the external world, the encoding and decoding of information critical for social interaction, and other high-order information processing for which no animal model is available to assist experimental research.

If we accept, on the basis of knowledge generated by the neurosciences, that the environment plays a critical role in the ontogenesis of such functions, it would be logical to look for environmental determinants of some of the major dysfunctions in schizophrenia. The environment, in this context, should be defined broadly, as the sum total of factors and influences which are external to the genome and interact with it to produce the phenotypical expression that gives the disorder its clinical and behavioural reality. Such factors and influences may be located anywhere on a continuum ranging from molecular and cellular events to social interactions.

The view of the environment as a broad range of non-social and social variables would allow an integrated approach to be adopted to the interpretation of the large volume of research data which at present tend to receive less attention than the exciting new perspectives opened up by molecular genetics. Bringing the data concerning the environmental determinants of schizophrenia into a clear focus would provide a heuristic counterpart to molecular research. Without such a counterpoint our attempts at understanding the nature of the disorder may miss potentially important clues.

Pointers to a role of the environment

Evidence pointing to a significant environmental contribution to the development and manifestations of schizophrenia is presented below in the form of several propositions about the features that characterize this group of disorders, with a view to localizing them on the general map of human pathology. Empirical support for part of what is stated below derives from a multi-centre research programme on schizophrenia, coordinated by the World Health Organization, and including, over a period of 20 years, the work of research centres and investigators in 24 countries, representing among themselves a broad spectrum of cultural variation (WHO, 1973, 1979; Sartorius *et al.*, 1986).

Schizophrenic disorders occur in all populations and cultures

To date, no sizeable human group (ethnic, social, or occupational) has been shown to be free of schizophrenic illness. Moreover, there is now evidence that schizophrenia tends to occur at comparable incidence rates (ie the number of new cases per 100 000 population at risk, per unit of time) in populations that are geographically and culturally wide apart. Support for this conclusion was provided by the most recent WHO investigation (Sartorius *et al.*, 1986) in which a total of 1352 persons meeting screening criteria for possible schizophrenic illness were identified at the point of their first-in-lifetime contact with various helping agencies in 12 geographical areas in 10 countries. Following a detailed and standardized clinical assessment and a diagnostic evaluation, which was repeated at one-year and two-year follow-up examinations, it was possible to calculate age- and sex-specific annual incidence rates (Fig. 1). These rates were in the range 0.18–0.37 per 1000 for males in age groups 15–54, and 0.12–0.48 for females in the same age groups. An important finding was the reduction in the variation in incidence estimates

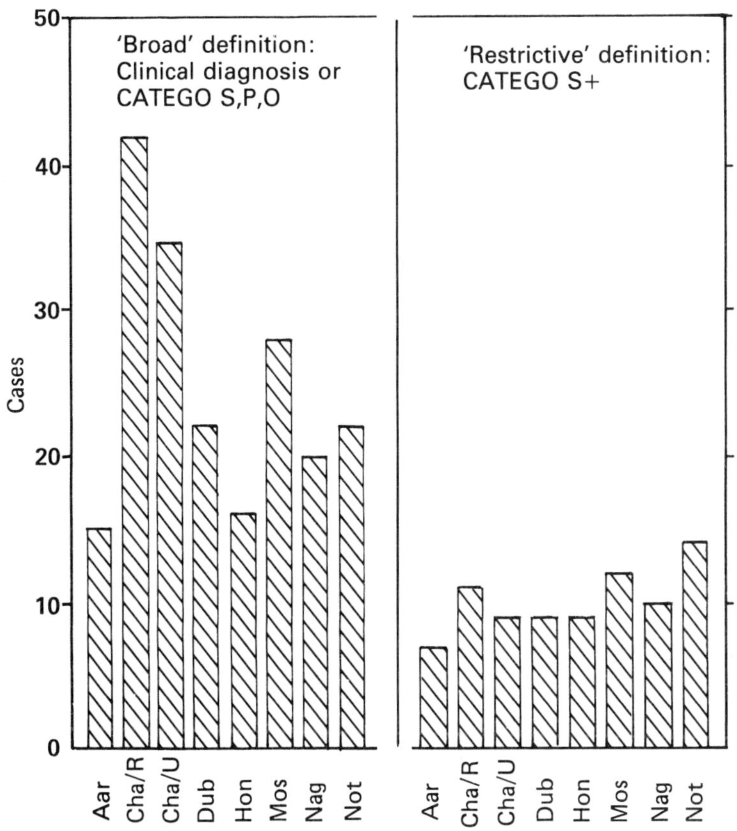

Fig. 1. *Incidence rates per 100 000 population aged 15–54 (both sexes) for the 'broad' and for the 'restrictive' definition of schizophrenia in Aarhus, Chandigarh (rural and urban), Dublin, Honolulu, Moscow, Nagasaki, and Nottingham.*

among the study sites when, instead of a 'broad' clinical definition of the disorder, a more restrictive set of diagnostic criteria (class S+ of the CATEGO computer program, Wing *et al.*, 1974) was applied to select only cases of the 'nuclear' schizophrenic syndrome. In other words, the 'core' of schizophrenic psychopathology, defined by subjectively experienced thought disorder, delusions of control and passivity, and a particular type of auditory hallucinations (the so-called first-rank symptoms of schizophrenia), was found to occur in comparable proportions of the adult populations in areas as different from one another as rural India, the fishing villages of Denmark, and the inner city of Nottingham. The conclusion that the similarity in incidence rates was not an artefact of a diagnostic evaluation based predominantly on the symptomatic presentation (in the sense that fundamentally different disorders might have a similar phenotypical expression in the populations concerned) was strengthened by another finding of the WHO study — that of very similar patterns of age and sex distribution of the onsets of the disorder. The nearly identical shapes of the distributions in contrasting populations (Fig. 2) suggest strongly that the study identified the same disease in the different cultures.

The basic symptomatology of schizophrenia is similar across the different cultures

This proposition can only be examined if standardized methods of investigation are uniformly applied by skilled clinical researchers in the different cultures. In the WHO programme, the common tool used to assess the clinical manifestations of schizophrenia

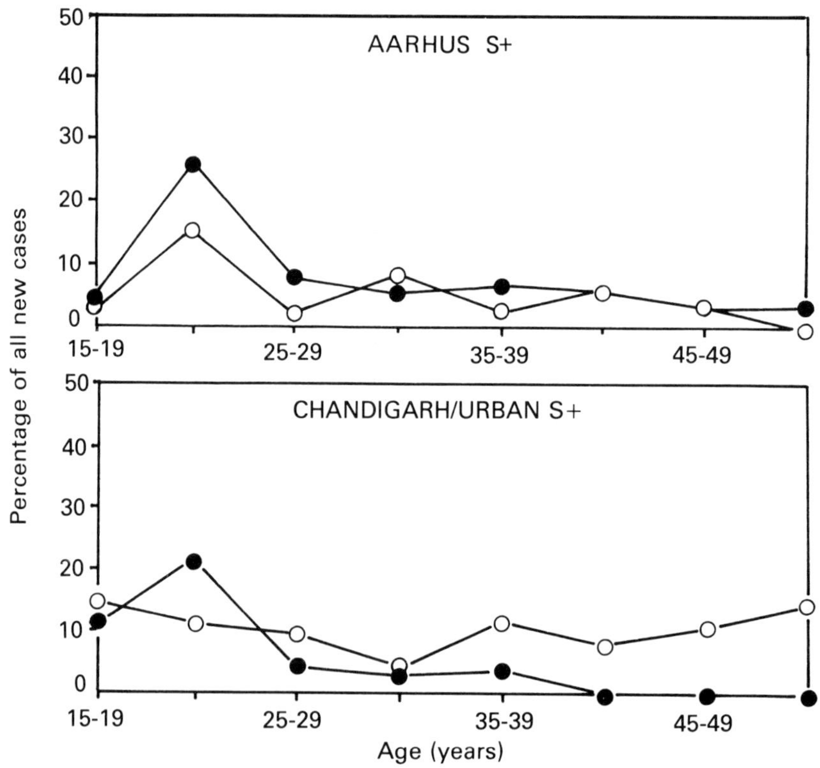

Fig. 2. *Age – and sex specific distribution of onsets of 'nuclear' schizophrenia (CATEGO class S+) in Aarhus (Denmark) and Chandigarh (India)* ● *males* ○ *females.*

was the Present State Examination (PSE), a structured clinical interview designed to elicit and score a total of 140 symptoms and signs (Wing *et al.*, 1974). The PSE data can be presented either as individual symptom profiles or as averaged profiles describing groups of patients. The profiles computed for patients in the developing countries and for patients in the developed countries were very similar, although certain differences did appear, eg in the relative frequency of affective symptoms (more common in patients in developed countries) and visual hallucinations (more common in patients in developing countries). However, the most marked difference in symptoms found in this study was not between patients in different cultures but between cases of 'nuclear' schizophrenia (exhibiting first-rank symptoms) on one hand, and disorders broadly classified as schizophrenic but not manifesting the first-rank symptoms on the other. Such differences between 'nuclear' and 'non-nuclear' schizophrenia were about equally pronounced in the developing and the developed countries (Fig. 3).

The course and outcome of schizophrenia are highly variable both within and across cultures

In contrast to the overall similarity in incidence and symptomatology, the longitudinal aspects of schizophrenia disorders exhibited a highly significant variation. Such variation could not be predicted from either the manifest symptomatology at the point of onset of the disorder, or the observed correlation between the pattern of course and the diagnostic classification of the clinical subtype (which generally was of a low order). It seems that in any population there are, on the one hand, schizophrenic illnesses in which a clinically severe initial episode is followed by a complete recovery and a remission which may last for years, if not for a lifetime. On the other hand, there are also conditions which tend to run a continuous course, in which chronicity and social disability set in at a very early stage. Between these two extremes are the intermediate patterns which include a recurrent type with acute episodes and good remissions (resembling the course of a recurrent affective illness), and a type characterized by an irregular sequence of psychotic relapses and incomplete remissions occurring against a background of a progressive impoverishment of the personality and loss of social skills. These different patterns are represented in varying proportions in the different populations studied. A general trend, however, could be discerned, and it was extensively documented in the WHO studies.

First, significant and consistent differences were found in the distribution of the various patterns of the course of the illness between the developing and the developed countries (Table 1). In the developing countries, a high proportion of the schizophrenic patients exhibited a pattern characterized by a single acute or subacute psychotic episode followed by a complete recovery without further attacks. For example, 58% of the Nigerian patients and 51% of the Indian patients had a single psychotic episode followed by a complete remission (while, in contrast, only 6% of the Danish patients had this type of course). The other extreme, ie the pattern of a continuous, deteriorating psychotic illness, occurred more frequently in the developed countries than in the developing countries. A chronic unremitting psychotic illness was established in as many as 50% of the patients in Denmark, 47% in the USA, and 30% in the UK and Czechoslovakia, compared to only 7% in Nigeria and 20% in India.

Secondly, some of the variables which were used as indices of the pattern of course (eg the cumulative percentage of the length of the follow-up period during which the patients were in psychotic episodes) showed a clear trend towards a bimodal distribution. The majority of the cases clustered at the two extremes of a mild remitting course and of a severe continuous or relapsing psychotic illness. The bimodality of the patterns of course

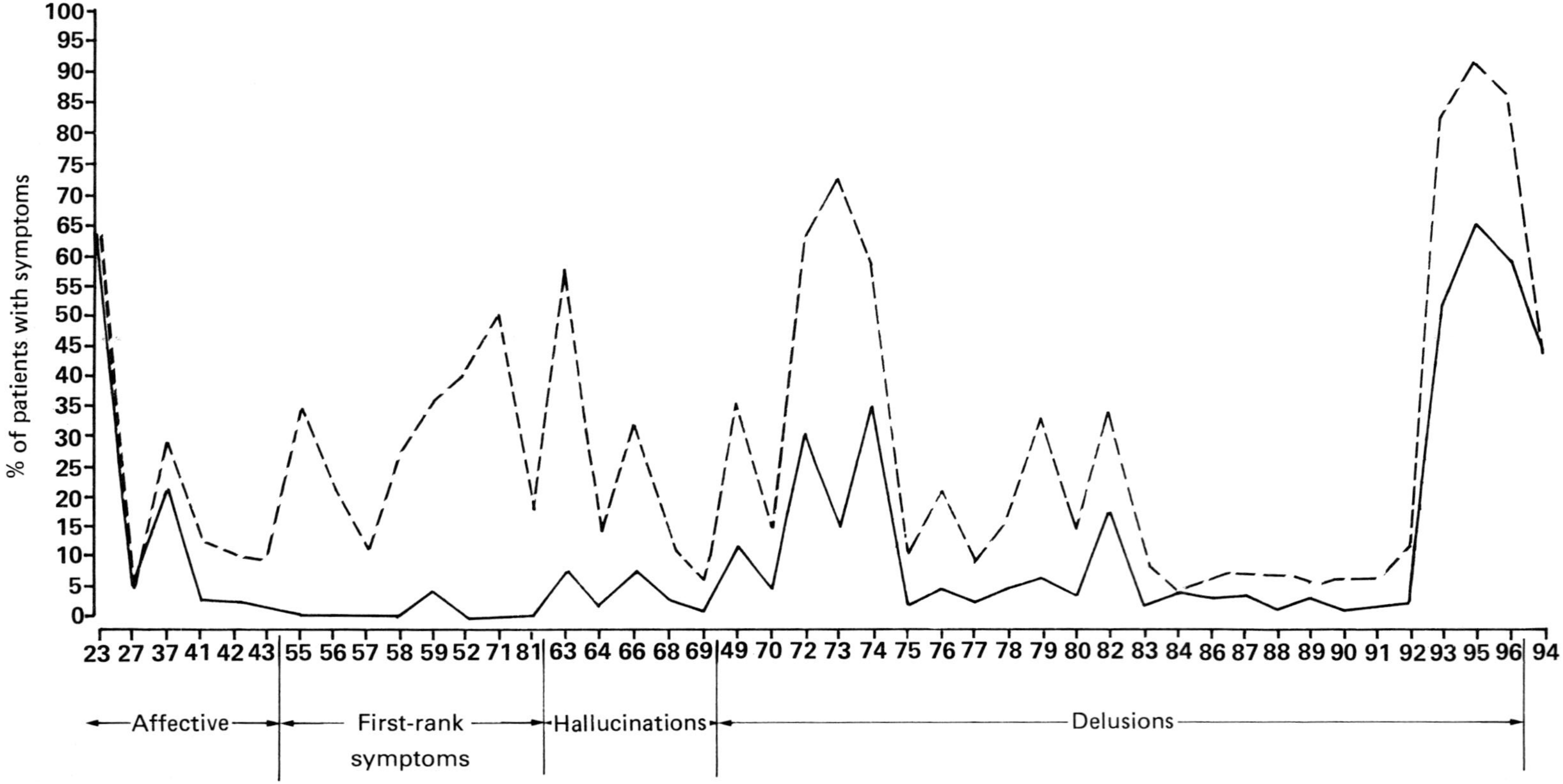

Fig. 3. *Symptom profiles of 727 CATEGO S+ patients and of 389 CATEGO S? P,O patients on 44 selected PSE items (all centres, numbers on the abscissa are the PSE symptom numbers).* ___ *CATEGO S? P,O;* ------ *CATEGO S+.*

Table 1. *Pattern of course (2-year follow-up) by type of onset and setting (percentages).*

Setting	*Type of onset*	*Pattern of course*		
		Mild	*Intermediate*	*Severe*
Developed countries	Acute	52.1	25.1	22.6
$\chi^2 = 40.3$	Subacute	41.3	23.9	34.7
$P < 0.001$	Gradual	29.8	17.5	52.6
	All types	38.9	21.1	39.8
Developing countries*	Acute	62.0	21.0	16.9
$\chi^2 = 26.4$	Subacute	58.7	23.8	17.4
$P < 0.001$	Gradual	40.2	16.3	43.4
	All types	55.7	20.2	24.0

*Ibadan excluded

was present in both the developed and the developing countries. Its existence raises the possibility of a prognostic subtyping of the schizophrenic disorders on the basis of patterns of course observed in the first 2 years after its onset.

There is strong evidence for a significant genetic component in the causation of schizophrenia

The genetic transmission of a predisposition to schizophrenia, or of a physiological dysfunction directly responsible for its symptoms, has been studied extensively since the formulation of the concept of schizophrenia. The major pieces of evidence to date (Gottesman & Shields, 1982) come from four sources: (1) pedigree studies; (2) twin studies; (3) adoption studies; and (4) longitudinal observation on children at high risk (offspring of schizophrenic parents; see Chapter 11). The evidence is consistent in the sense that genetic proximity to a person with a manifest schizophrenic illness significantly increases the risk of developing the disorder. This, however, can only be expressed in terms of a statistical probability, and, in spite of recent inroads made by molecular genetics, we do not yet know *what* is being inherited, or *how* the individual predisposition is determined. The attempts to fit the observational data into alternative models of genetic transmission — single major locus, polygenic, threshold effects, etc — have produced inconclusive results. As in many heritable diseases, the possibility exists that schizophrenia is a genetically heterogeneous group of disorders which includes several different genetic subtypes. The new research strategies based on molecular genetics and making use of recombinant DNA techniques open an entirely new perspective on the issue (see Chapter 13; Matthysse, 1987; Sherrington *et al.*, 1988), but it is unlikely that a quick solution is in sight in this immensely complex field. Another point concerning genetic research is that, whatever the molecular basis of the inherited liability to schizophrenia, it is implausible as a single and sufficient condition for developing the disease. A reminder of this is the fact that the concordance rate in monozygotic twins in the more recent studies ranges from about 10 to 50%. This suggests that, in addition to inherited liability, a non-genetic factor is required to trigger the process resulting in manifest schizophrenic dysfunction and symptomatology.

A variety of environmental factors have been implicated in the causation and course of schizophrenia but the knowledge about their mode of action is inconclusive

It is customary to divide the putative environmental influences on the pathogenesis of schizophrenia into social and non-social ones (the latter including agents or events such as viruses, birth complications or injuries). Although this distribution is not as clear as it might appear (because the action of biological or physicochemical agents is also mediated by social factors), it presents a convenient way of summarizing the research evidence. There is an extensive body of research data, stretching over several decades, which indicates that the occurrence and course of schizophrenia are significantly associated with a variety of macrosocial and microsocial influences. In this brief overview only the main findings can be enumerated (Jablensky, 1988):

(1) There is an over-representation of persons of a low socioeconomic status among schizophrenic patients.

(2) In circumstances of social, educational and economic disadvantage, ethnic minorities have higher rates of admission to hospital for schizophrenia than comparable non-minority groups.

(3) Under certain conditions migrants and uprooted persons have an excess of schizophrenic morbidity.

(4) There is a significant excess of new cases of schizophrenia in urban areas characterized by low status, poverty, and social disorganization.

(5) Exacerbations of schizophrenic symptoms, leading to increases in the hospital admission rates, have been shown to occur in periods of economic recession and mass unemployment.

(6) There is significant cultural variation in the course and outcome of schizophrenia. One of the several hypotheses which have been proposed to explain this suggests that cultures differ from one another by the degree of complexity of the cognitive and social role demands they impose of their members: such differences may be relevant to the precipitation, manifestations and course of schizophrenia.

(7) Stressful life events, critically straining the individual's coping resources, have been shown to be significantly associated with the onset of acute psychotic episodes in schizophrenic patients. This finding has been replicated in several different cultures.

(8) The intensity and special quality of emotional interaction within the family are related to the risk of a psychotic relapse in schizophrenic patients. A high index of 'expressed emotion' (a combination of emotional overinvolvement with the patient and hidden rejection or hostility) in a close relative spending much time in face-to-face contact with the patient increases the probability of an acute exacerbation of the so-called 'positive' schizophrenic symptoms. Conversely, social and emotional isolation, monotony and lack of stimulation tend to aggravate the so-called 'negative' symptoms of schizophrenia, expressed as apathy, withdrawal, poverty of thinking, stereotypy, and affective flattening. These findings also have received a socio-cultural validation and appear to be a universal pattern of response of schizophrenic individuals to environmental stimulation.

The main problem with the plethora of data generated by social and behavioural research lies in the difficulty in distinguishing a causal relationship from mere statistical association. There are serious methodological obstacles with which this type of research has to cope, and high quality behavioural science databases are costly to develop. This may partially explain the low tide of social research in schizophrenia at the present time, without implying that the field would not become fertile once again if more rigorous methods were applied.

As regards the non-social environmental influence on the risk of developing the disease, and on its course and outcome, research in the last decade has been focused on two groups of factors: (1) the possible role of a viral infection and (2) the significance of obstetric events, in particular anoxia at birth. The search for a 'schizophrenic' virus has been prompted both by advances in virology (which have demonstrated the capacity of certain classes of viruses to become integrated in the genome — a property which theoretically could be consistent with some of the genetic findings in schizophrenia; see Chapter 14) and by the observation that there is an excess of winter births among schizophrenic patients. However, to date, the results of virological studies in schizophrenia have been negative (Kaufmann *et al.*, 1988). In contrast, the search for obstetric risk factors has resulted in the finding that evidence of prolonged labour and anoxia at birth can be found more often in the birth records of subjects who later develop schizophrenia than in control subjects (McNeil, 1987). Other early environmental influences may affect the maturation of the brain during critical periods of development; see Chapter 4). Events interfering with the normal plasticity of the maturing CNS, whether due to genetic, intrauterine or perinatal causes, may interact with environmental stimulation and result in patterns of neuronal connectivity that are prone to unusual responses in complex situations in adult life.

There has been considerable progress in the standardization of the diagnosis of schizophrenia and in the development of refined tools for the assessment of psychopathology

Diagnosis and classification play a key role in research into the causes, course and outcome of schizophrenia. Some 80 years ago Kraepelin (1904) proposed the method of 'comparative psychiatry' as a new approach in the understanding of the causes and mechanisms of mental disorders. However, he warned that 'reliable comparison is of course, only possible if we are able to draw clear distinctions between identifiable illness, as well as between clinical states; moreover, our clinical concepts vary so widely that for the foreseeable future such comparison is possible only if observations are made by one and the same observer.' It took indeed a long time to develop an alternative to Kraepelin's single-handed observer as a means of ensuring sufficient reliability of diagnosis and psychopathological assessment for the purposes of epidemiological and cross-cultural research. Instruments for standardizing the clinical diagnostic interview, such as the Present State Examination (PSE), have been developed and many psychiatrists and psychologists in different parts of the world trained in their use. Data elicited with such methods can be processed by computer programs (eg CATEGO) which incorporate explicit diagnostic rules and eliminate some of the sources of bias in the diagnostic process. A related development has been the formulation of operational criteria for the diagnosis of schizophrenia which began with the so-called Feighner criteria in the United States and resulted in the widely used Research Diagnostic Criteria (RDC) and DSM-III. A similar approach was adopted by the World Health Organization in the development of the 10th revision of the International Classification of Diseases (ICD-10) which will be introduced for official use world-wide in 1990 (Cooper, 1988). The mental disorders chapter of ICD-10 contains detailed definitions and diagnostic criteria for schizophrenia and related disorders which are based on a broad international consensus. Nevertheless, even the most rigorous standardization of the diagnosis of schizophrenia will remain a sterile exercise in the absence of progress in the development of external validating criteria for the diagnosis. For some purposes it may be important to have diagnostic criteria which predict the course and outcome of the disorder; for other research purposes it may be essential to predict the heritability of schizophrenic illness; and in yet another situation the main concern might be the correspondence between the diagnosis and the symptoms profile.

As no set of diagnostic rules is capable of performing equally well in all of these areas, a research strategy which has emerged in recent years emphasizes the so-called polydiagnostic approach (Berner *et al.*, 1983), whereby each case is simultaneously diagnosed according to several alternative diagnostic systems. An illustration of this approach is the use of the clinician's diagnosis (according to ICD-9) and the computer CATEGO diagnostic classification in the WHO studies on schizophrenia. The polydiagnostic method can be used to create a data base for the testing of alternative hypotheses about the correlations between diagnostic description and various genetic, pathophysiological ot environmental characteristics.

The study of interactions as a research strategy

The overview of selected areas of schizophrenia research where significant progress has been achieved in the past decade suggests that the study of interactions among variables belonging to different areas or levels of functioning is a productive strategy. By interaction we mean that the joint effect of two or more variables is quantitatively or qualitatively different from a simple additive effect. Improved statistical techniques, such as multivariate analysis of variance, stepwise multiple regression, and log-linear models, are now available to tease out individual from joint effects.

Two further examples from the WHO cross-sectional studies illustrate the importance of the study of interactions, especially with a view to drawing practical conclusions about the management of schizophrenic patients.

Once the finding was established that the course of schizophrenia was highly variable and that the overall prognosis was better in the developing countries than in the developed countries, it was important to determine predictors of the pattern of course in the two types of setting. As no single factor was suspected to account for this variation but rather an interaction of multiple factors, log-linear analysis was employed to examine the contribution of each one among a large number of potential predictors, as well as the joint effects of various combinations of predictors. The results of the analysis indicated that the principal contributors or the variation of course and outcome were, on the one hand, the mode of onset (which may be under genetic control) and, on the other hand, several environmental and life history variables. It is important to note that neither the symptom profile, nor the diagnostic classification of the initial episode of illness were among the best predictors. By this analysis it was possible to explain part of the overall effect of culture in terms of other specific variables; however, some residual effect of 'centre' (ie study area) remained that could not be reduced to other factors.

In an attempt to make a step beyond earlier cross-cultural research, the design of the latest WHO investigation has incorporated an exploratory study of stressful life events (Day *et al.*, 1987) and the index of expressed emotion (Leff *et al.*, 1987) in different cultures. The results indicated that both life events and expressed emotion predicted a risk of psychotic relapse in Danish and Indian patients in much the same way as these variables had performed in the original British sample. More importantly, however, life events and expressed emotion (EE) interacted in such a way that the occurrence of a stressful life event to a patient with a high EE risk significantly increased the probability of relapse, while a low index of EE seemed to have a protective effect against the triggering action of stressful events. The interaction was even more complex when a third factor — that of

Table 2. *Distribution of expressed emotion (EE) components among relatives from London, Aarhus and Chandigarh.*

	London	*Aarhus*	*Chandigarh*
Mean number of *critical comments*	8.4[1]	4.5	1.9
Proportion of relatives showing *hostility*	18%[1]	21%	16%
Proportion of parents showing *over-involvement*	36%[1]	n.a.[3]	4%
Mean score on *warmth*	2.3[1]	2.5	2.0
Mean number of *positive remarks*	2.6[2]	3.1	0.8
Proportion of relatives classed as *high-EE*	54%[1]	54%	23%
Proportion of hostile relatives with low criticism	0%	0%	29%
Correlation between warmth and critical comments	−0.44	−0.57	0.10
Number of patients assessed	37	28	78
Number of relatives assessed	46	28	104

[1]Data from Vaughn & Leff (1976)
[2]Data from Leff *et al* (1982)
[3]Danish data not comparable with Indian and English

neuroleptic maintenance treatment — was added. It has been shown that higher doses of phenothiazines (or any other maintenance neuroleptic) are needed to prevent relapse in patients who live in high EE homes than to control symptoms and prevent relapse in patients who live with low-EE relatives. A goal of the rational management of schizophrenia, therefore, must be the careful assessment and adjustment ('titration') of at least three groups of interacting factors: (1) the level of stimulation and arousal associated with adjustment to rapid environmental change; (2) the level of stimulation and arousal associated with the day-to-day emotional interaction with significant others (reduction of EE); and (3) the dosage of antipsychotic medication. To these three factors in the management equation a fourth one might be added, based on the WHO data on the prediction of course and outcome. Considering the non-negligible baseline probability that a schizophrenic illness may take a relatively benign, or remittent, pattern of course, a careful evaluation of the patient on a checklist of predictors may enable the clinician to dispense with long-term neuroleptic medication altogether in those cases where the odds favour a good prognosis. Such an approach would require considerable skills but the pay-off in terms of prevented late sequelae of neuroleptic overload and improved quality of life would be significant.

As to the better outcome of schizophrenic patients in the traditional cultures of the developing countries, a potentially significant factor may be the generally lower incidence of high EE families, as shown in Table 2 comparing data from UK, Denmark and India. Why Western cultures and families produce more emotional overinvolvement and, at the same time, more hidden hostility towards their mentally ill members as compared to their counterparts in the developing countries is an issue to be addressed by anthropologists and sociologists.

Acknowledgement—The chief collaborating investigators in the WHO study are: Aarhus: E. Strömgren; Agra: K.C. Dube; Cali: C. Leon; Chandigarh: N.N. Wig (1976–80) and V. Varma (1980–); Dublin: D. Walsh; Honolulu: A. Marsella and M. Katz; Ibadan: M. Olatawura; Moscow: R.A. Nadzharov and N.N. Zharikov; Nagasaki: R. Takahashi (1976–84) and Y. Nakane (1984–); Nottingham: J.E. Cooper; Prague: L. Hanzlicek (1976–81) and J. Gebhart (1981–); Rochester: L.C. Wynne and T. Gift. At WHO Headquarters, Geneva, the study was coordinated by N. Sartorius (principal investigator) and A. Jablensky (co-principal investigator).

References

Berner, P., Gabriel, E., Katschnig, H., Kieffer, W., Koehler, K., Lenz, G. & Simhandl, Ch. (eds) (1983): *Diagnostic criteria for schizophrenic and affective psychoses.* Vienna: World Psychiatric Association.

Bleuler, E. (1911): *Dementia praecox oder die Gruppe der Schozophrenien.* (English translation by J. Zinkin. New York: International Universities Press. 1950).

Bleuler, M. (1972): *Die schizophrenen Geistesstorungen im Lichte langjahriger Kranken — und Familiengeschichten.* Stuttgart: Thieme.

Cooper, J.E. (1988): The structure and presentation of contemporary psychiatric classifications with special reference to ICD-9 and 10. Br. J. Psychiatry **152**, suppl. 1, 21–28.

Day, R., Nielsen, J.A., Korten, A., Ernberg, G., Dube, K.C., Gebhart, J., Jablensky, A., Leon, C., Marsella, A., Olatawura, M., Sartorius, N., Strömgren, E., Takahashi, R., Wig, N., Wynne, L.C. (1987): Stressful life events preceding the acute onset of schizophrenia: a cross-national study from the World Health Organization. *Culture Med. Psychiatry* **11**, 123–205.

Gottesman, I.I. & Shields, J. (1982): *Schizophrenia. The epigenetic puzzle.* Cambridge: Cambridge University Press.

Jablensky, A. (1988): Schizophrenia and the environment. In: *Handbook of social psychiatry*, eds S. Henderson & W. Burrows, pp. 103–116. Amsterdam: Elsevier.

Kaufmann, C.A., Weinberger, D.R., Stevens, J.R., Asher, D.M., Kleinman, J.E., Sulmia, M.P., Gibbs, C.J. & Gajdusek, D.C. (1988): Intracerebral innoculation of experimental animals with brain tissue from patients with schizophrenia. *Arch. Gen. Psychiatry* **45**, 648–652.

Kraepelin, E. (1899): *Psychiatrie: Ein Lehrbuch fur Studierende und Aerzte.* Leipzig: Abel.

Kraepelin, E. (1904): Comparative psychiatry. In: *Themes and variations in European psychiatry*, eds S.R. Hirsch & M. Shepherd, pp. 3–6. Bristol: John Wright.

Leff, J., Wig, N.N., Ghosh, A., Bedi, H., Menon, D.K., Kuipers, L., Korten, A., Ernberg, G., Day, R., Sartorius, N., Jablensky, A. (1987): Influence of relatives expressed emotion on the course of schizophrenia in Chandigarh. *Br. J. Psychiatry* **151**, 166–173.

Matthysse, S., (1987): 'The middle game' in the genetics of schizophrenia. In *Biological perspectives of schizophrenia*, eds H. Helmchen & F.A. Henn, pp 7–17. Chichester: Wiley.

McNeil, T.F. (1987): Perinatal influences in the development of schizophrenia In: *Biological perspectives of schizophrenia*, eds H. Helmchen & F.A. Henn. Chichester: Wiley.

Sartorius, N., Jablensky, A., Korten, A., Ernberg, G., Anker, M., Cooper, J.E. & Day, R. (1986): Early manifestations and first-contact incidence of schizophrenia in different cultures. *Psychol. Med.* **16**, 909–928.

Sherrington, R., Brynjolfson, J., Petursson, H., Potter, M., Dudleston, K., Barraclough, B., Wasmuth, J., Dobbs, M. & Gurling, H. (1988): Localization of a susceptibility locus for schizophrenia on chromosome 5. *Nature* **336**, 164–167.

Szasz, T.S. (1976): Schizophrenia: the sacred symbol of psychiatry. *Br. J. Psychiatry* **129**, 308–316.

WHO (1973): *Report of the International Pilot Study of Schizophrenia*, vol. 1. Geneva: World Health Organization.

WHO (1979): *Schizophrenia. An international follow-up study.* Chichester: Wiley.

Wing, J.K., Cooper, J.E. & Sartorius, N. (1974): *The measurement and classification of psychiatric symptoms.* Cambridge: Cambridge University Press.

Zubin, J., Magaziner, J. & Steinhauer, S.R. (1983): The metamorphosis of schizophrenia: from chronicity to vulnerability. *Psychol. Med.* **13**, 551–571.

Chapter 16

The Nithsdale schizophrenia surveys 1981–1988: An overview

R. G. McCreadie

Crichton Royal Hospital, Dumfries, Scotland

Summary

A review of all known schizophrenics from a discrete geographical area, Nithsdale in South West Scotland, found a point prevalence of 2.38 per 1000 of the total population. Negative schizophrenic symptoms were prominent, positive symptoms uncommon. The prevalence of both tardive dyskinesia (TD) and parkinsonism was 31%. The TD group was older and more often showed negative schizophrenic symptoms. Patients' and relatives' assessment of the patients' overall adjustment, using the Social Adjustment Scale by Self-Report (SAS-SR), correlated very closely, thus suggesting that a schizophrenic person can satisfactorily describe his own adjustment. The patients were less well adjusted than a normal community population. The Morningside Rehabilitation Status Scale, the Krawiecka Scale for chronic psychotics and the SAS-SR together provide a quick and comprehensive assessment of a patient's rehabilitation status.

Introduction

Nithsdale, a historically ancient and geographically discrete part of Dumfries and Galloway Region, has an area of 550 square miles and a population of 56 000. It is largely rural, but contains the market town of Dumfries (population 31 000) and three other small towns along the banks of the River Nith. Psychiatric services are provided by Crichton Royal Hospital. It is probable that very few patients from Nithsdale receive treatment elsewhere, especially as the Crichton has had amenity beds for many years and the two nearest psychiatric hospitals are 35 and 60 miles from Dumfries.

The principal Nithsdale surveys carried out over the past 7 years have been published elsewhere (McCreadie, 1982; McCreadie *et al.*, 1982 a and b; McCreadie & Baron, 1984; Robinson & McCreadie, 1986; McCreadie & Robinson, 1987; McCreadie *et al.*, 1987; McCreadie & Phillips, 1988). The present paper focuses on four main areas, namely the identification of patients and a description of their psychopathology; the prevalence of movement disorders; patients' social handicaps; and a comparison of scales which assess rehabilitation status.

Patient identification and psychopathology

Patients included in the survey were all the inpatients, day patients and outpatients of Crichton Royal Hospital who, on 1 March 1981, had a firm case record diagnosis of schizophrenia and whose home address was in Nithsdale. All general practitioners (n = 32) in Nithsdale were sent a list of schizophrenics in their practice currently in contact with the Crichton. They were asked if there were any other schizophrenics known to the practice and receiving treatment. The Feighner criteria for schizophrenia (Feighner *et al.*, 1972) were then applied to each patient, using information obtained from the case record and the clinical assessment. In this way 133 schizophrenics were identified of whom 28% were inpatients, 17% were day patients, and 32% were outpatients or supervised by community psychiatric nurses; 23% were known only to the family doctor. Therefore 73% of patients were living in the community.

In a catchment population of 56 000 this number of schizophrenics gives a point prevalence of 2.38 per 1000 of the general population. When the Feighner criteria were applied the prevalence fell to 1.73 per 1000. The point prevalence in Nithsdale lies between the point prevalence in Camberwell in South East London and Salford in Manchester (Wing & Fryers, 1976).

Over the 4 weeks following the census the mental state of 89% of patients was assessed using the Krawiecka Scale for chronic psychosis (Krawiecka *et al.*, 1977). This scale assesses three main areas: positive schizophrenic symptoms (delusions, incoherence, hallucinations and incongruous affect); negative symptoms (flatness of affect and poverty of speech); and non-schizophrenic symptoms (retardation, anxiety and depression). Eighteen per cent had no abnormality in their mental state. Twenty-six per cent had delusions, 14% incoherence, 10% hallucinations and 8% an incongruous affect. However, more patients showed negative symptoms: 45% showed flatness of affect and 29% poverty of speech. Twenty-three per cent showed retardation, 28% anxiety and 23% depressive symptoms.

Seventy-two per cent of patients were also assessed using the Wing Ward Behaviour Scale (Wing, 1961) which with minor modifications was used to rate patients living outside hospital. Sixty-one per cent of patients showed social withdrawal, 50% a lack of leisure interests, 48% poverty of conversation and 33% slowness of movement. More disturbed behaviour such as laughing and talking to oneself or the exhibition of threatening or violent behaviour was found in a small percentage of patients, 12% and 8% respectively.

Thus, although almost three-quarters of Nithsdale schizophrenics were living out of hospital, social and psychiatric disability was still considerable. Psychiatric disability, however, was 'quiet'. Flattening of affect and social withdrawal were most prominent; florid positive symptoms and embarrassing behaviour were uncommon.

Movement disorders

A community review of movement disorders was also carried out at the same time as assessment of mental state and behaviour. Eighty-eight per cent were examined for evidence of parkinsonism using the T.A.K.E. Scale (Wojcik *et al.*, 1980) and tardive dyskinesia using the AIMS Scale (US Dept. of Health, 1976). It was found that 31% of patients showed at least mild parkinsonism on the global scale. With regard to individual signs, 29% showed slowness of movement, 21% rigidity, 23% tremor, but only 2% akathisia. Thirty-one per cent of patients had at least mild tardive dyskinesia on the AIMS global scale; 4% showed movements of the face, 17% of the lips, 14% of the jaw and

19% of the tongue. Abnormal movements in other parts of the body were less common; 9% had abnormal movements of the upper limbs, 6% of the lower limbs and 4% of the trunk. Patients with TD were older, had been ill longer, and more showed flattening of affect. Twelve patients (33% of both the TD and parkinsonism group) had symptoms of at least mild TD *and* parkinsonism.

This community survey, the first of its kind, has thus identified a high prevalence of both TD and parkinsonism. This illustrates well the cost to schizophrenics of taking neuroleptics. Such drugs are effective in controlling the positive symptoms of the disorder, but the price to be paid is considerable (see Barnes, p. 217, Jones, p. 235, and Costal *et al.*, p. 247).

Social adjustment

Since approximately three quarters of all known Nithsdale schizophrenics are probably living outside hospital, and since many continue to have psychiatric and social handicaps, further rehabilitation is usually necessary after discharge from inpatient care. The efficacy of such rehabilitation needs to be evaluated and any assessment should include a measure of social adjustment. Patients were therefore assessed using the Social Adjustment Scale by Self Report (Weissman & Bothwell, 1976). The review aimed firstly to determine the acceptability to patients of the self-report, secondly to compare patients' and relatives' assessment of the patient, and thirdly to compare patients' social adjustment with that of a normal population.

The social adjustment of 82 Nithsdale schizophrenics was examined; 48% were daypatients, 33% were outpatients, and 19% were known only to their family doctor at the time of the survey. Forty-one relatives of the 82 patients also completed the questionnaire; 37% were spouses, 50% parents and 13% other relatives living with the patient.

The SAS-SR, which takes 10–15 minutes to complete, is a 54 item questionnaire examining adjustment during the previous 2 weeks. It yields an overall adjustment score and a rating of six role areas: work as a worker, housewife or student; social and leisure activities; relationships with extended family; and marital roles as a spouse, parent and member of the family unit. A final question asks about economic circumstances. A higher score indicates greater impairment. In 24 pairs, both patients and relatives answered more than 90% of relevant questions. Correlation between patients' and relatives' scores for overall adjustment were measured by the product moment correlation coefficient. Correlations were positive and high (the correlation coefficient ranged from + 0.77 to + 0.89) in overall adjustment and in role areas except relationships with the extended and immediate family.

Patients' assessment of themselves was compared with self-assessment of a normal population (Weissman *et al.*, 1978). The patients were significantly more handicapped in overall adjustment and in all role areas except the parental role.

Replies to individual questions help to describe the patients' adjustment. Only 25% worked in open employment and 24% were married. Thirty-nine per cent said that they had no friends, 34% had not gone out socially in the past two weeks, and 33% of the unmarried said they were completely uninterested in going out with a member of the opposite sex. Fifty-two per cent had spent no time on interests or hobbies in the previous 2 weeks except watching television, and although the vast majority depended on social security benefits, 79% said that they had enough money for their needs.

The review suggests that the SAS-SR can be used reasonably successfully with chronic schizophrenics. The nature of the questionnaire was readily understood by most patients and relatives. The assessment of overall adjustment by a patient corresponded very closely with that by his relative. An accurate assessment of overall adjustment can probably be made by the patient himself. This is an advantage as many schizophrenics in the community live alone. As with the review of patients' mental state (see above) the psychiatric and social handicaps suggest that patients are withdrawn. In short they lead a quiet life and probably the majority cause little disturbance to most people in the community.

Comparison of scales for assessing rehabilitation status

In a busy community psychiatric service a short simple inexpensive assessment of rehabilitation status is required. The last Nithsdale review reported in the present paper examined three scales: the Morningside Rehabilitation Status Scale (MRSS) (Affleck & McGuire, 1984), the Krawiecka Scale (see above) and the Social Adjustment Scale by Self-Report (SAS-SR) (see above). The MRSS is a short scale which takes 10–15 minutes to complete. It gives an overall assessment of rehabilitation status and also examines separately dependency, inactivity, isolation and symptoms. In brief, the dependency scale assesses the amount of support given by staff and relatives, the inactivity scale assesses how the patient occupies himself during the day, the isolation scale assesses relationships and participation in activities, and the symptom scale assesses current symptoms and anomalous behaviour. A higher score indicates greater disability. As little work had been carried out using this scale, inter-rater reliability of the MRSS was first examined. Secondly, the three scales were used with the same patients to see whether or not they assessed the same behaviours.

Twenty-four Nithsdale schizophrenic daypatients were examined, 10 females and 14 males, 88% of whom satisfied the Feighner criteria. Two psychiatrists rated the patients independently using the MRSS after interviewing the patient and discussing him or her with nursing staff. One psychiatrist knew the patients well, the other had had little previous contact with them. The mental state of the same patients was assessed by a third psychiatrist using the Krawiecka Scale, and during the same week the patients also rated their own social functioning using the SAS-SR.

The inter-rater correlations using the MRSS were high for both the overall score and the four sub-scales (the correlation coefficient ranged from +0.62 to +0.83). The correlation between the overall score on the MRSS and the Krawiecka total score was quite high ($r = +0.67$). However, the contribution to the positive correlation of the overall score on the MRSS came largely from the symptom sub-scale. The correlation between the MRSS and the SAS-SR was low ($r = +0.46$) and the correlation between the Krawiecka and the SAS-SR negligible (+0.16).

Thus the inter-rater reliability of the MRSS was high; this suggests that it can be used by an investigator with little previous knowledge of the patient. This makes it very useful, especially from the research point of view. The correlations among the MRSS, SAS-SR, and the Krawiecka were not great, except between the symptom sub-scale of the MRSS and the Krawiecka, which was to be expected. It is thus probable that the three scales are examining different aspects of the patients' functioning. All three scales therefore might profitably be used in an everyday NHS setting, especially as they are quick and easy to use.

References

Affleck, J.W. & McGuire, R.J. (1984): The measurement of psychiatric rehabilitation status: a review of the needs and a new scale. *Br. J. Psychiatry* **145**, 517–525.

Feighner, J.P., Rubins, E., Guze, S., Woodruff, R.A., Winokur, G. & Monoz, R. (1972): Diagnostic criteria for use in psychiatric research. *Arch. Gen. Psychiatry* **26**, 57–62.
Krawiecka, M., Goldberg, D., & Vaughan, M. (1977): A standard psychiatric assessment scale for rating chronic psychotic patients. *Acta Psychiat. Scand.* **55**, 299–308.
McCreadie, R.G. (1982): The Nithsdale Schizophrenia Survey I: Psychiatric and social handicaps. *Br. J. Psychiatry* **140**, 582–586.
McCreadie, R.G. & Barron, E.T. (1984): The Nithsdale Schizophrenia Survey IV: Social Adjustment by Self-report. *Br. J. Psychiatry* **144**, 547–550.
McCreadie, R.G. & Robinson, A.D.T. (1987): The Nithsdale Schizophrenia Survey VI: Relatives' expressed emotion: prevalence, patterns, and clinical assessment. *Br. J. Psychiatry* **150**, 640–644.
McCreadie, R.G. & Phillips, K. (1988) The Nithsdale Schizophrenia Survey VII: Does relatives' high expressed emotion predict relapse? *Br. J. Psychiatry* **152**, 477–481.
McCreadie, R.G., Barron, E.T. & Winslow, G.S. (1982): The Nithsdale Schizophrenia Survey II: Abnormal Movements. *Br. J. Psychiatry* **140**, 587–590.
McCreadie, R.G., Crorie, J., Barron, E.T. & Winslow, G.S. (1982): The Nithsdale Schizophrenia Survey III: Handedness and tardive dyskinesia. *Br. J. Psychiatry* **140**, 591–594.
McCreadie, R.G., Affleck, J.W., McKenzie, Y. & Robinson, A.D.T. (1987): A comparison of scales for assessing rehabilitation of patients. *Br. J. Psychiatry* **151**, 520–522.
Robinson, A.D.T. & McCreadie, R.G. (1986): The Nithsdale Schizophrenia Survey V: Follow-up of tardive dyskinesia at three and a half years. *Br. J. Psychiatry* **149**, 621–623.
US Department of Health, Education and Welfare (1976): Abnormal Involuntary Movements Scale (AIMS). In *ECDEU assessment manual*, ed. W. Guy pp. 534–7. Rockliffe, Maryland: US Department of Health, Education and Welfare.
Weissman, M.M. & Bothwell, S. (1976): Assessment of social adjustment by patients self-report. *Arch. Gen. Psychiatry* **33**, 1111–1115.
Weissman, M.M., Prusoff, B.A., Thompson, W.D., Harding, P.S. & Myers, J.K. (1978): Social adjustment by self-report in a community sample and in psychiatric outpatients. *J. Nerv. Men. Dis.* **166**, 317–326.
Wing, J.K. & Fryers, A. (1976): *Psychiatric services in Camberwell and Salford.* London: MRC Social Psychiatry Unit, Institute of Psychiatry.
Wing, J.K. (1961): A simple and reliable sub-classification of schizophrenia. *J. Mental Sci.* **107**, 862–875.
Wojcik, J.D., Gelenberg, A.J., LaBrie, R.A. & Mieske, M. (1980): Prevalence of tardive dyskinesia in an outpatient population. *Compr. Psychiatry* **21**, 370–379.

Chapter 17

Studies of schizophrenia in a large mental hospital proposed for closure, and in two halves of an inner London borough served by the hospital

P. G. Campbell[1], J. Taylor[2], C. Pantelis[3] and C. Harvey[4]

[1]Friern Hospital and University College Hospital, London; [2]Whittington Hospital, London; [3]Charing Cross and Westminster Medical Schools, London, and Academic Unit, Horton Hospital, Surrey; [4]St. Mary Abbots and Charing Cross Hospitals, London, UK

Summary

In 1982 the North East Thames Regional Health Authority proposed the closure by 1992 of two of the Region's six large mental hospitals. With a view to learning more about the disparate needs of individuals who were likely to be affected by these changes and to establishing a data base for a safety net computerized information system targeted at providing clinical monitoring and support for at-risk individuals, three studies were undertaken.

The authors describe a survey undertaken in 1983 at Friern Hospital (one of those destined for closure) and detail the responses to findings. Two community point prevalence studies were also undertaken within the London borough of Camden, to examine the current pattern of resource allocation and the needs of individuals with schizophrenia (and their families) in two districts currently served by Friern Hospital. The findings of very high point prevalence figures in both halves of the borough (and particularly so in South Camden) and of large numbers of individuals with active psychotic symptoms and behavioural problems have important implications for the way service planning should be basied if a serious commitment to community care is envisaged.

Background history

The studies we are going to present were prompted by urgent practical necessity. In 1982, the North East Thames Regional Health Authority proposed the closure by 1992 of two of the Region's six large mental hospitals and a move to reliance on District General Hospital Units and Community Care (N. E. Thames Regional Health Authority, 1982). One of these two hospitals destined for closure is Friern Hospital, which now serves a total population of over half a million people in four contiguous health Districts in North London.

In our studies we have aimed to learn more about the disparate needs of individuals with schizophrenia who may be affected by these changes. We have focussed on two of the Health Districts currently using Friern, in the area which makes up the London borough of Camden. An important aim has been to prepare the basis for information systems which could assist the allocation of resources to people who are at special risk of falling through the incomplete and fragmented network of services for severe mental disorder. At a time when the major focus of change is centred on the population of the mental hospital, we wanted to know how the hosiptal service stands in relation to the larger (but how much larger?) number of people with schizophrenia who live outside it.

Friern Hospital was opened in 1851 by Prince Albert as the Colney Hatch Pauper Lunatic Asylum, in its time the largest mental hospital in Europe, with 1250 beds. That number grew to over 2700 by the 1930s, a peak from which it has steadily declined, most rapidly since the 1960s as active discharge policies came to be adopted. The Regional Authority proposed, in 1982, that Friern's nominal 900 remaining beds could be replaced by 300, and the savings thereby achieved could build an improved service in the community.

The failure of medical advice

When the bare outline of the closure plan was first announced in 1982, an initial period of consultation was allowed, in which it became clear that medical and nursing advice based on clinical experience of the service was no match for the powerful combination of ideology, financial expediency and wishful thinking which had inspired the plan, in the formulation of which the Authority's officers at that time had already acted against the advice of its expert Policy Group on Mental Illness (Policy Group Report, 1980). A very detailed account by Friern Hospital staff of the hospital's services and role was condensed into half a sentence in the report on its consultation exercise the Authority's officers put before its members. The closure plan was endorsed by the Authority, but a further period of about 3 months was available before the Districts using Friern were expected to complete their outline proposals for alternative services

Factual evidence

During this interval, the Medical Committee of Friern attempted to illuminate the debate by some factual evidence: it undertook a comprehensive survey of all the patients resident in the hospital at a census point on midnight of the 6th/7th January 1983. The intention was to provide as objective and detailed an enumeration as possible of the patients' needs and disabilities. With the help of 30 doctors and over 100 nurses, and the generous help of the Department of Clinical Epidemiology of the Royal Free Hospital (and particularly of its statistician, Mr Derek Cooke) the survey was completed in 7 weeks from the moment of conception through to publication of an analysis of results. An important deadline was imposed by a planned meeting of the hospital management team with Mrs Thatcher, in whose constituency Friern lies. She was the first person outside Friern to see the analysis of the data collected.

Some findings of the 1983 survey

The survey covered a very wide range of personal details about the patients' histories, their social circumstances, daily behaviour and activities, their treatment, reasons for being in

Table 1. *Friern Hospital inpatient survey, January 1983.*

	Number of patients	*(%)*
Males	392	(46.7)
Females	447	(53.3)
Informal status	794	(94.6)
Married/cohabiting	109	(13.0)
Job to return to	15	(1.8)
Address still available	256	(30.5)
Total	839	

hospital and assessments of future need. But some of the most compelling facts about them are evident from simple total numbers.

There were 839 people resident in hospital (see Table 1: male 392; female 447) on the night of the census. The majority (87%) of the 827 patients for whom marital status could be ascertained were single or separated. Hardly any of the patients had any prospect of employment on leaving hospital: 7/246 (2.8%) acute patients had a job to return to and eight longer-term residents were working in open employment from the hospital. Nearly all of the patients (94.6%) were in hospital voluntarily. Only 256 patients (30.5% of the total) had an address even theoretically available to return to: this number included those patients among 195 demented people in the hospital (23% of the total) who still nominally had an address, even if they could never return to it.

The closure plans published in 1982 painted a picture of an outmoded institution with custodially-minded staff caring for long-stay patients in old-fashioned restrictive ways. Even today the plans envisage that longer-term residents will be rehoused in permanent residential accommodation without replacement of the hospital beds they vacate: in this way, it is claimed, the Friern service will be 'reprovided'. No amount of evidence has been able to shift this extraordinary assumption, which cannot be supported by figures showing the activity and discharge rates of the hospital — rates which cannot be assumed to be sustainable when patients are replaced in hostel accommodation outside the hospital. At least for recent new longer-stay patients the hospital provides an escalator leading back to life outside in community settings; the escalator may move slowly, but it is by no means altogether stationary nor as sluggish as is found in most hostels for discharged longer-stay patients.

As shown in Table 2, at the time of the survey 246 (29%) of the patients were classed as acute, having been in the hospital for not more than a year. Most of them would be staying in hospital for only a few weeks. There were 228 (27%) who had stayed between 1 and 5 years, and 365 (44%) who had stayed more than 5 years. The hospital has some 1400 admissions a year. (Acute admissions to Friern from Bloomsbury district have more than doubled since the time of the study, as beds within the District have fallen in numbers.)

Table 2. *Duration of stay in Friern Hospital (approximately 1400 admissions per year).*

	Duration of stay	*(%)*
Short stay (≤ 1 year)	246	(29)
New long stay (1–5 years)	228	(27)
Old long stay (> 5 years)	365	(44)

Table 3. *Year of current admission to Friern Hospital.* (52% of patients had stayed less than 4 years; 50 patients had stayed longer than 50 years.)

Year of admission	*Number of patients*
Before 1920	5
1920–1924	12
1925–1929	18
1930–1934	26
1935–1939	28
1940–1944	16
1945–1949	25
1950–1954	30
1955–1959	33
1960–1964	37
1965–1969	43
1970–1974	37
1975–1979	138
1980–1983	391

When one looks at the duration of stay in the hospital as a whole (Table 3), it is striking that over half the patients (52%) had been resident less than 4 years. Fifty had been resident for over 50 years. As one goes back in time to 1920, there appears to have been about 30 patients from each 5 year period (with a slight dip during the war years) who have remained in hospital, often after community placement had failed, sometimes repeatedly.

Four hundred and seventy five patients had schizophrenia as a primary (444 patients) or subsidiary (31) diagnosis. Inspection of the age structure of the hospital and its

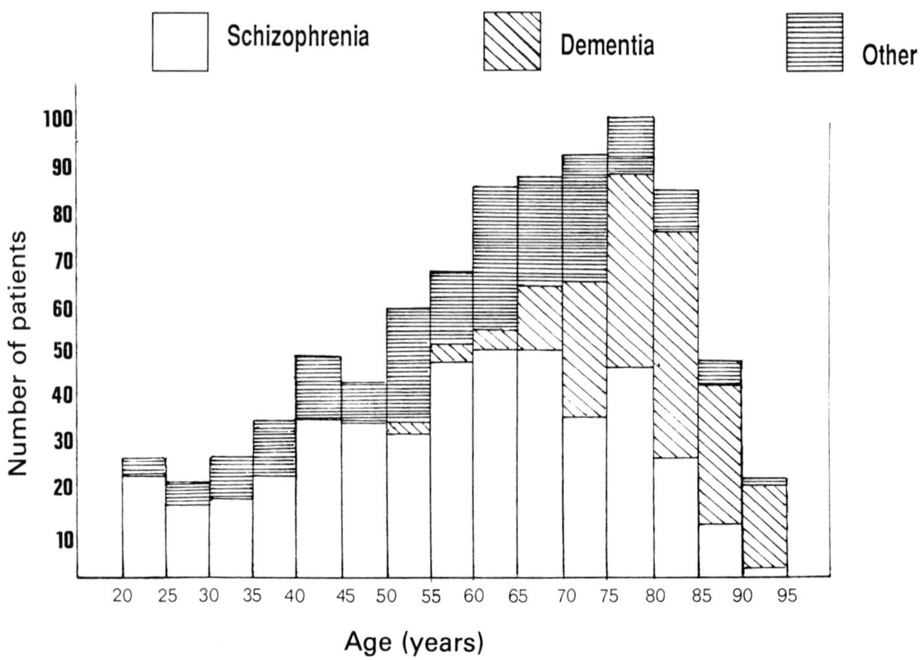

Fig. 1. *Age structure and diagnosis.*

Table 4. *Schizophrenia population* (percentages in parentheses).

	Length of stay (years)				
	≤ 1	*1–5*	*5–10*	*> 10*	*All*
Total	100 (21)	87 (18)	38 (8)	250 (53)	475
Married	7 (7)	3 (3)	1 (3)	5 (2)	16 (3)
Job to return to	5 (5)	0	0	0	5 (1)
Address available	58 (58)	18 (21)	11 (29)	23 (9)	110 (23)
Section order on admission	23 (23)	18 (21)	9 (24)	161 (64)	211 (44)
Relapse	66 (66)	43 (49)	20 (53)	88 (35)	217 (46)
Non-compliance	36 (36)	21 (24)	7 (18)	9 (2)	73 (15)
Previous Fiern admission	77 (77)	71 (89)	32 (84)	78 (31)	258 (54)
Previous other hospital admission	55 (55)	61 (70)	21 (55)	130 (52)	267 (56)
No contacts outside Friern	20 (20)	32 (37)	9 (24)	136 (54)	197 (41)
No family	11 (11)	22 (25)	2 (5)	113 (41)	148 (31)

Table 5. *Schizophrenia: disabilities and problems* (percentages in parentheses). N/A = not applicable.

	Length of stay (years)				
	≤ 1	*1–5*	*5–10*	*> 10*	*All*
Total	100 (21)	87 (18)	38 (8)	250 (53)	475
Hallucinations	34 (34)	35 (40)	15 (39)	89 (36)	173 (36)
Delusions	55 (55)	48 (55)	19 (50)	89 (36)	211 (44)
Exacerbations	N/A	55 (63)	22 (58)	119 (48)	196 (52)
Physical illness	11 (11)	17 (20)	10 (26)	63 (25)	101 (21)
Physical handicap	8 (8)	12 (14)	8 (21)	43 (17)	71 (15)
Upsets others	25 (25)	27 (31)	14 (37)	87 (35)	153 (32)
Incontinence of urine	10 (10)	19 (22)	10 (26)	79 (32)	118 (25)
Incontinence of faeces	4 (4)	9 (10)	6 (16)	62 (25)	81 (17)
Medication problem	48 (48)	37 (43)	10 (26)	72 (29)	167 (35)

relationship to diagnosis (Fig. 1) show that schizophrenia (which increases in preponderance with increasing duration of stay) is distributed through all age groups, with a median age of 59 years. Dementia, by contrast, becomes predominant only in the very elderly, the median age being over 80 years. A very brief snapshot view of the population in the hospital whose disorder had been disgnosed as schizophrenia (a total of 475 people) is provided by Tables 4 & 5. Striking features include indices of social disadvantage and isolation, the frequency of active psychopathology and behavioural problems in all stay groups, and of physical illness and disabilities, including urinary and faecal incontinence, particularly in the longer-stay. An illustration of the degree of active mental illness among patients staying over 1 year, besides the continuing evidence of overt hallucinations and delusions, is the high prevalence of 'exacerbations', which were defined as the occurrence of 'marked fluctuation in mood, other symptoms or behaviour, amounting to more than one period per year of overt mental illness'. In the 100 acute patients with schizophrenia who had been resident for less than 1 year, especially striking are the extent of social isolation and unemployment, the frequency of relapse of illness as the main reason for admission (in 66%), the high proportion (23%) of compulsory orders at admission, and the large number of patients (36%) in whom non-compliance with medicine-taking appeared to be a major contributory factor is necessitating admission

Table 6. *District populations* (percentages in parentheses).

	Total	*Hampstead*	*Bloomsbury*	*Haringey*	*Islington*	*Other*
Total	839	109	123	177	258	172
Male	392	48 (44)	60 (49)	67 (38)	111 (43)	106 (62)
Female	447	61 (56)	63 (51)	110 (62)	147 (57)	66 (38)
Single	460	51 (47)	61 (50)	92 (52)	124 (48)	132 (77)
Address	256	46 (42)	34 (28)	87 (49)	76 (29)	13 (8)
No fixed abode	65	8 (7)	10 (8)	6 (3)	14 (5)	27 (16)
Stay >5 years	365	33 (30)	39 (32)	63 (36)	85 (33)	145 (84)
Schizophrenic	444	45 (41)	48 (39)	82 (46)	131 (51)	138 (80)

despite quite well-developed community nursing and other services outside hospital. Problems with medicine-taking continue to be common in hospital, even in many of the long-stay residents, and are a further pointer to the need for expert care and supervision if patients are to be discharged to the community.

The two Districts we went on to look at in subsequent community surveys were Hampstead and the South Camden sector of Bloomsbury, which together make up the London Borough of Camden. In Table 6, some details are given of the patients in Friern who originated from these two parts of the borough. The severe social deprivation which is a feature of the Bloomsbury sector is evident, for example, in the fact that only 34 out of 123 patients (28%) had an address even theoretically available to return to. (Among new acute admissions to Friern from Bloomsbury, the frequency of homelessness continues to rise, and in 1987 was over 22%.) The table also shows that Friern houses many people, predominantly male, who originated from outside the four Districts now using the hospital. They make up 49% of the 250 patients with schizophrenia resident for over 10 years.

Implications for Revenue Transfer Plans

The planning proposals award a standard 'dowry' payment of revenue equal to the current revenue of the hospital divided equally between all residents, whatever their disability or age. Gross disparities exist between the Districts in the average duration of stay and age of their patients in Friern, particularly between Haringey (which has many elderly long-stay residents who have moved to its wards over the years from other District wards) and Islington.

Response to the 1983 survey: Friern tries again

Our findings were attentively studied by Mrs Thatcher in February 1983, but subsequently they were not welcomed by the Regional Health Authority or any of the District Authorities. Critics said that the study was motivated by medical pessimism and the vested interest of psychiatrists in preserving hospital empires. In 1985, therefore, we carried out another survey of all patients who had been resident in the hospital for more than 1 year in order to try to overcome the reluctance to attend to or act on the findings of our first survey. We used standardized research measures of 'dependency' which were accepted by the Districts as an acceptably non-medical survey instrument and we sought active participation from them in planning and executing the survey. No very new findings emerged and the results were no more welcome. Since then many people have carried out further assessments on smaller groups of patients. The findings obstinately seem to stay much the same. They indicate that Friern is more than a resource for local Districts: it is also part of the larger national resource serving a particularly disadvantaged, dislocated, overtly disordered and disabled clientele of rejected people for whom the community has not yet been able to provide.

Description of the community surveys

The broad aims of the Camden surveys were to identify those individuals suffering from schizophrenia and to describe their psychopathology and social difficulties. This is of particular relevance in view of the planned closure of Friern Hospital.

South Camden schizophrenia survey

South Camden is an inner-city area of London which lies within Bloomsbury Health District and is served by Camden Social Services. It has a population of around 54 000. Into it drain three major railway termini which connect with the north of the country (King's Cross, St Pancras and Euston stations). It is the first port of call for many individuals arriving in London from across the country.

Indices (Jarman, 1983) for North and South Camden, which highlight the degree of social deprivation in these areas, are of interest. South Camden ranks 9th (Jarman Index 35.59) and has a higher level of deprivation than North Camden which ranks 18th (Jarman Index 22.13) in comparison with other health districts in England and Wales.

Aspects of the service

Of particular interest within South Camden are the hostels for homeless people which provide an essential service. Those included in the present study are Arlington House, providing refuge for some 600 men, St Mungo's Hostel catering for 106 men, Camden Womens' Resettlement Unit providing 40 places for women, Cecil House which also caters for women, and the Simon Community Night Shelter, providing temporary accommodation for up to 3 nights. Day centres are mostly located in North Camden, except for the Cromer day centre for elderly people. Part III homes for the elderly are exclusively outside South Camden. A recent initiative is the Compass Project which will be a shopfront providing a service to the longer-term mentally ill in South Camden. It aims to identify those individuals who have little or no contact with services.

Methods

Entry criteria and patient identification

Criteria for inclusion in the surveys were as follows: affected individuals were aged 18 or over and were effectively treated as suffering from schizophrenia on the census day (10 October 1985). They were (1) listed as receiving supervision from community psychiatric nurses based in the South Camden sector of Bloomsbury Health District, and/or (2) by psychiatrists in the South Camden area, and/or (3) South Camden general practitioners, and/or (4) were residing in a mental aftercare amenity supported by Camden, having been admitted there from a South Camden address or psychiatric service, and/or (5) were attending a Camden daycare amenity from a South Camden address, or (6) were identified by other agencies, eg hostels within South Camden.

A broad definition of schizophrenia was employed and this will be refined by the application of the Feighner Criteria (Feighner *et al.*, 1972). All patients receiving long-acting depot neuroleptic medication were included even if the diagnosis of schizophrenia was not established.

Patients were identified from visits to these various agencies. Letters were also written to GPs and social and probation services in order to identify those individuals who might not be in contact with the psychiatric service. This was followed up by a further letter, telephone calls and visits to the various people concerned. In this way a list of 530 individuals was built up.

Questionnaire and interview schedules

A detailed questionnaire consisting of 160 items of information was developed for use in the survey. Good questionnaire design was felt to have facilitated the co-operation of the various agencies who helped in completing it. It was piloted with the assistance of the community psychiatric nurses prior to the census data and this highlighted problem areas which were subsequently revised. The questionnaire was divided into six sections which could be completed separately if necessary. The six sections were laid out as follows:-

Section A indicated how the patient was identified for the study.
Section B provided basic demographic details as well as some information about social networks, daily activities and problem areas.
Section C related to community psychiatric nursing contact.
Section D contained relevant data about length of illness, number of admissions (including day hospital) and the circumstances of the patient's last admission, including follow up. Information about diagnosis and medication was also included.
Section E was an interview of the patient using the Manchester scale developed by Krawiecka *et al.* (1977), which is an interview schedule used for the assessment of psychotic patients. It consists of nine items rated on a 5-point scale. This scale has also been found to be sensitive to changes in symptoms of patients with chronic psychosis (Vaughan & Krawiecka, 1979).
Section F is an interview with the best informant (eg relative, CPN, social worker, psychiatrist) using the Social Behaviour schedule developed by Wykes & Sturt (1986) which is used for rating the behaviour of psychotic patients.

During the course of the study, about 10% of patients were co-rated to check inter-rater reliability.

Problems of researching in the community

We should like to highlight some of the challenges we faced in trying to carry out our research. The first difficulty we encountered was that the number of patients identified was far in excess of the estimate in the research protocol. The identification of patients presents particular difficulties in a community survey. Problems encountered included the need to identify individuals from a wide spectrum of sources from within and outside the borough. The fragmented nature of this exercise necessitated enormous care in preventing the error of duplicating counts. This was achieved by the allocation of a specific code number to each patient and by the establishment of a temporary administrative database which detailed names, addresses and contacts and which was maintained on a microcomputer. Diagnosis of individuals with no psychiatric contact at the time of census and identified by a range of sources often required a detailed search for previous psychiatric contact and an exploratory diagnostic interview.

In general terms a wide variety of services expressed interest and enthusiasm in assisting us with the project. Occasionally however we met resistance and this took a number of forms. At some contact points for instance the residents were asked as a group by a key worker whether they were prepared to participate in the survey. This initially led to a global refusal. Where applicable, patients were approached through their key workers and sometimes were excluded on the grounds that the key worker concerned felt such an interview would be damaging to a relationship that had taken time to establish. We respected these views and some refusals relate to these issues. Larger organizations such as social services took 10 months to respond to our request for cooperation, despite numerous and detailed letters. Individual social workers were, however, enthusiastic from the start of the project.

Finally, interviewing this particular population proved both interesting and on occasions frustrating. In general terms we were struck by the large numbers of individuals living in the community who were preoccupied with psychotic experiences and by those individuals who lived in squalid circumstances with little occupation and often heavily dependent on relatives. A substantial minority of patients seen for interview were still in bed at 3 o'clock in the afternoon, some interviews being conducted in semi-darkness. At Arlington House where some 600 men live, only 4% were identified for the survey. This contrasts with the 25% identified in the other, smaller homeless-person hostels. The probable reason for this was that residents at Arlington House tended to live anonymous existences and were often not forthcoming about their lives and experiences to staff members.

Overall, some patients proved elusive and we received no response despite repeated letters and at least three visits to see them. One resident at Arlington House was particularly elusive. During episodes of psychosis he would climb up the drainpipe and through a window to his room thus evading any contact with staff or researchers. A proportion of individuals were no longer resident at the most recent address detailed in their notes, and the bed-and-breakfast landlord would tell us that they had moved on some time ago. Some of the people we visited were overtly paranoid and hostile and refused to open the door or slammed it in our faces.

We identified 530 individuals. Wherever possible the mental state rating and the social behaviour schedule were carried out within a period of 1 month of each other. Often they were completed on the same day. Almost 400 individuals were interviewed and almost 500 informants were seen.

Results of the South Camden Survey

The preliminary results of this survey have been reported (Pantelis *et al.*, 1988). We summarize the main findings below.

Service distribution

In the South Camden Survey 19.8% of the total sample of 530 were resident as inpatients, and 80.2% of the sample were resident in the community of whom 24.3% were under the care of the community psychiatric nursing service, 22.4% attended outpatients, 15.2%

were resident in homeless person hostels, 2.5% were day hospital patients and 24.9% were under the sole care of GPs. These figures give a prevalence of 9.81 per 1000 on a population of 54 000.

Social and demographic features

The mean age of the inpatient group was very similar to that of the community population and was approximately 47 years. Of the analysed sample 43% were male and 57% female; 63% were single and only 13% were married or cohabiting; 63% were born in the United Kindom and 10% in Ireland. South Camden has a large immigrant Greek Cypriot community and 4% of the sample originated from Cyprus.

Accommodation arrangemens were as follows: 48% of the sample lived in council accommodation, 10% were resident in bed-and-breakfast hotels or were lodging with friends, and 2% were identified as living rough; 28% were resident with relatives. Thirty per cent of those with family members outside the home had no contact with their relatives and 37% of the total analysed sample had no contact with friends or acquaintances. Fifty-six per cent had no daytime occupation, 14% attended a day centre and only 10% were in full or part-time employment.

Twenty-one per cent of the South Camden population had strong links with the borough: 45% of the sample had developed links in adult life whilst 16% had formed links only through mental aftercare services. Six per cent had no strong links with Camden and were liable to move on shortly.

Diagnosis

Seventy-six per cent of the sample analysed had a primary diagnosis of schizophrenia. A further 8% were diagnosed as suffering from a paranoid state and 5% as having a schizo-affective disorder. The commonest secondary diagnosis was of personality disorder (12%), whilst 60% had no secondary diagnosis.

Admission and compulsory order

Ninety-one per cent of the sample had had at least one admission to a psychiatric hospital, and 45% had been detained on one or more occasions under a compulsory order. Of the most recent admissions recorded in the notes, 32% were at least partially related to poor drug compliance.

Mental state (inpatients versus *community)*

The groups (Fig. 2) would appear comparable in terms of identified depression, anxiety, and positive symptoms of schizophrenia. Fifty-seven per cent of inpatients and 59% of the community sample were deluded; 50% of inpatients and 40% of the community sample suffered from hallucinations.

The inpatients scored highly with regard to incoherence of speech, poverty of speech, and flattened affect. These findings may be explicible in terms of the effect of the longstay population on the inpatient group. Information on mental state was unavailable for a variety of reasons on almost 40% of the community sample. We shall be examining this group of patients in more detail with information gleaned from notes and from an analysis of the Social Behaviour Schedule.

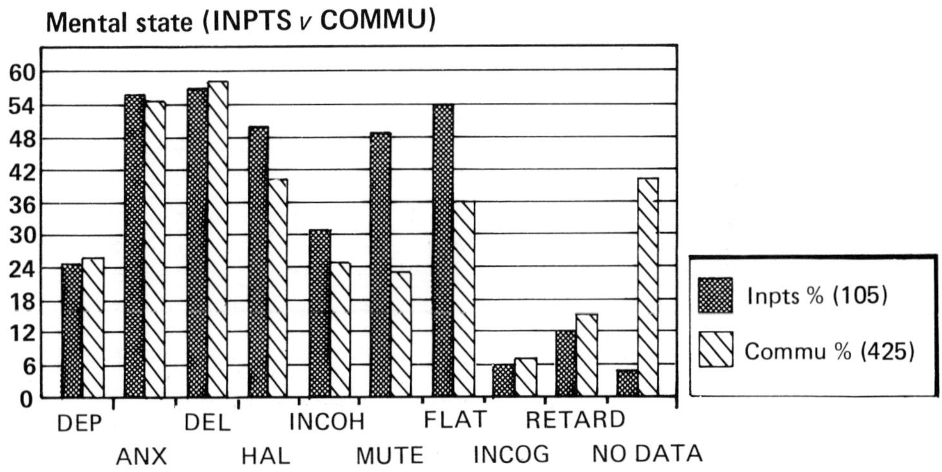

Fig. 2. *Percentage of patients with mental ratings scores of 2 or more on the Manchester scale among inpatients (Inpts) and community care population (Commu) in South Camden.* DEP = depression; ANX = anxiety; DEL = delusions; HAL = hallucinations; INCOH = incoherent speech; MUTE = mutism; FLAT = flat affect; INCOG = incongruity; RETARD = psychomotor retardation.

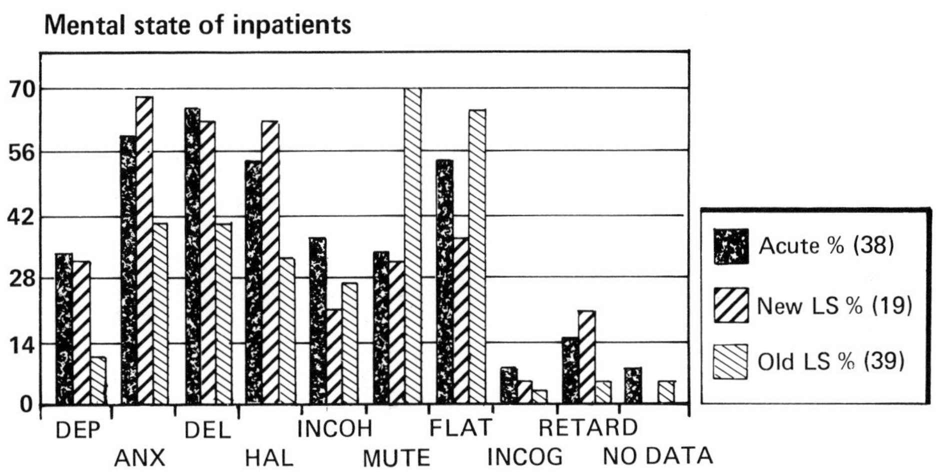

Fig. 3. *Percentage of inpatients in different categories in South Camden with mental ratings scores of 2 or more on the Manchester scale.* LS = long stay. For other abbreviations, see Fig. 2.

Mental state of the inpatients

The inpatients were subdivided (Fig. 3) into acute (in hospital for less than 1 year), new long stay (in hospital for 1–5 years) and old long stay (in hospital more than 5 years). The degree to which the old long stay population are handicapped by negative symptoms contrasts markedly with the acute and new long stay populations.

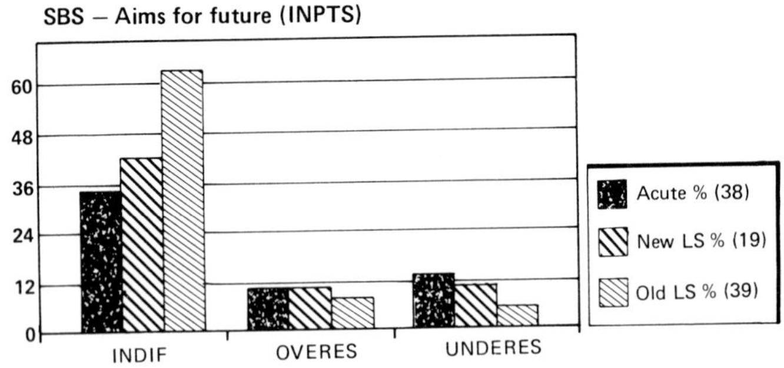

Fig. 4. *Percentage of inpatients in different categories in South Camden with behavioural ratings scores of 2 or more on the Social Behaviour Scale.* LS = long stay; INDIF = appears indifferent to future; OVERES = overestimates abilities; UNDERES = underestimates abilities.

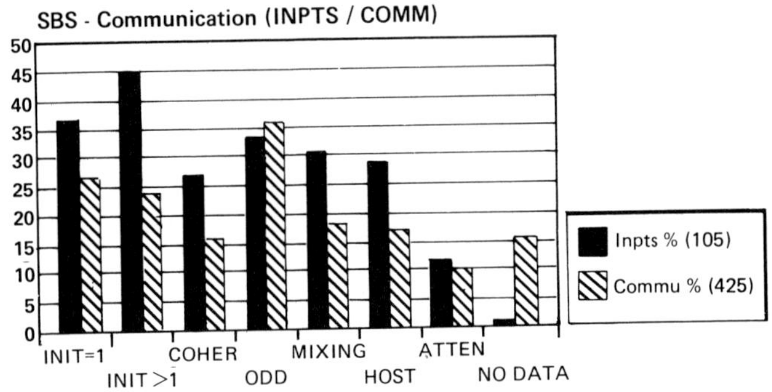

Fig. 5. *Percentage of patients with behavioural ratings scores of 2 or more on the Social Behaviour Scale among inpatients (Inpts) and community care population (Commu).* INIT = 1 > 1 = difficulty in initiating conversation with one or more others; COHER = problems with coherent speech; ODD = preoccupied with odd topics; MIXING = problems with normal social mixing; HOST = hostile behaviour; ATTEN = attention-seeking.

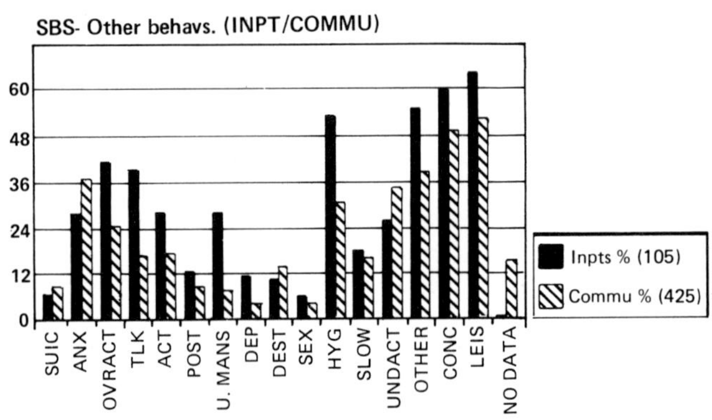

Fig. 6. *See legend to Fig. 5.* SUIC = suicidal; OVRACT = overactive; TLK = laughing and talking to self; ACT = acts out delusional ideas; POST = abnormal postures; U.MANS = unacceptable mannerisms; DEST = destructive behaviour; SEX = inappropriate sexual behaviour; HYG = problems with hygiene; SLOW = slowed up thoughts/actions; UNDACT = underactivity; OTHER = other behaviours, eg suspicion, stealing; CONC = impaired concentration; LEIS = lack of leisure activities. See Fig. 2 for other abbreviations.

Social behaviour schedule ratings

Of the inpatients the long stay population were rated on the social behaviour schedule as displaying the greatest indifference to the future (Fig. 4). The inpatient population scored more highly on problems relating to initiating conversation, coherence of speech, difficulties with social mixing, and hostility (Fig. 5). Other behaviours (Fig. 6) on which the inpatients rated highly were: overactivty, poor hygiene, undesirable manners, poor concentration and lack of leisure activities. The community sample scored more highly on the presence of recent anxiety and on suicidal thoughts and behaviour.

The North Camden Schizophrenia Survey

North Camden is co-terminus with Hampstead health district and has a population of 105 700 (1981 census data). It is a predominantly residential area with light industry, business and services.

The social characteristics present a mixed picture of the area. North Camden has a higher percentage of residents in professional, managerial and non-manual occupations than the national average, with correspondingly a below average percentage in unskilled and manual occupations. In contrast the area has a smaller percentage of owner-occupier households (29% compared with 56%) and a higher percentage of other rented accommodation (not local authority) than the national average (38% compared with 13%).

Other population indices associated with relatively greater deprivation include the high proportion of Hampstead residents born outside the UK (30% compared with 24% for inner London as a whole). There is also a relatively high level of mobility within the populations compared with the national figure.

Outline of service

The service provision in North Camden is broadly similar to that for the southern half of the borough except that there is only one facility for homeless persons (a house which is run as a night shelter by the Simon Community). Nearly all the Part III accommodation is situated in North Camden.

Methods

The census date for the North Camden Schizophrenia Survey was 28 July 1986. In response to the identification of such an unexpectedly large number of individuals for the study, the methodology was modifed in order to incorporate some sample stratification. The 590 individuals were randomly divided into five subgroups which contained equivalent numbers of patients primarily managed by their GPs. In addition, there were equal numbers of patients across the five subgroups who lived in two 'special needs areas' within the district. These are areas identified from census data by the Community Health Unit as having the greatest socioeconomic deprivation.

This procedure offered a logical strategy for interviewing the 590 patients, since assessments were carried out group by group. In addition, if it became impossible to assess all patients due to lack of time, it could be assumed that those already interviewed constituted a representative sample of the whole. Finally, sample stratification offered the opportunity to analyse some of the data in relation to two identified subpopulations from the special needs areas and thus to examine the previously reported association of higher rates of schizophrenia with geographical areas of lower social status.

Results of the North Camden Survey

Of the 590 individuals identified, 14% were hospital-based and 86% were resident in the community, of whom 31% attended psychiatric outpatients, 5% attended day hospitals and 16% were under the care of the community psychiatric nursing service; 23% were in contact with their general practitioner only. These figures give a point-prevalence of 5.62 per 1000 on a population of 105 000.

The following data represent an analysis of group 1 (a representative subsample of 119 individuals).

Social and demographic findings

Fifty-seven per cent of the population were female, and 43% male; the mean age was 47 years. The distribution of age was bimodal, with the older age group being accounted for both by the elderly long stay schizophrenic population in Friern and by the fact that the Part III homes for Camden are almost exclusively in North Camden. Fifty-nine per cent of the sample were single, a finding consistent with other surveys. The largest group after UK born originated from other European countries (19%) and this reflects the nature of the Hampstead population. Patients of West Indian (6%) and African (5%) origin also form a sizeable minority.

By and large, the North Camden population of schizophrenics have strong links with the area, 27% having been born and raised in Camden and a further 60% developing their links in adult life through residence, job or family contact. Relatively few of the patients acquired their association with Camden via mental aftercare services or were part of a transitory population. These figures contrast markedly with those from the South Camden study where individuals' links with the borough are generally less well established.

The schizophrenic patients identified were over represented in council accommodation where 46% were resident at census, and under represented in rented accommodation and in owner-occupier households (11% and 9% respectively). Forty per cent of the sample were living with relatives and at least 70% maintained some face-to-face contact with family members outside their home. However, in contrast, 15% of individuals were completely isolated from their family, neither living with relatives nor having any contact with family outside the home. Contacts with friends seemed to fall into two groups: 38% had no contacts whilst 31% had fairly frequent contacts on the basis of at least weekly meetings.

The substantial majority of subjects (58%) were not engaged in any daily occupation. However, 21% were attending a day hospital or other day facility at the time of census and 14% were engaged in full or part-time employment.

Diagnosis

Examination of the primary diagnosis at the time of census shows that 71% had a diagnosis of schizophrenia, 5% had a diagnosis of schizo-affective disorder, 10% had a diagnosis of paranoid state and 1% a diagnosis of schizophreniform psychosis. Seventy-five per cent of the sample had no secondary diagnosis.

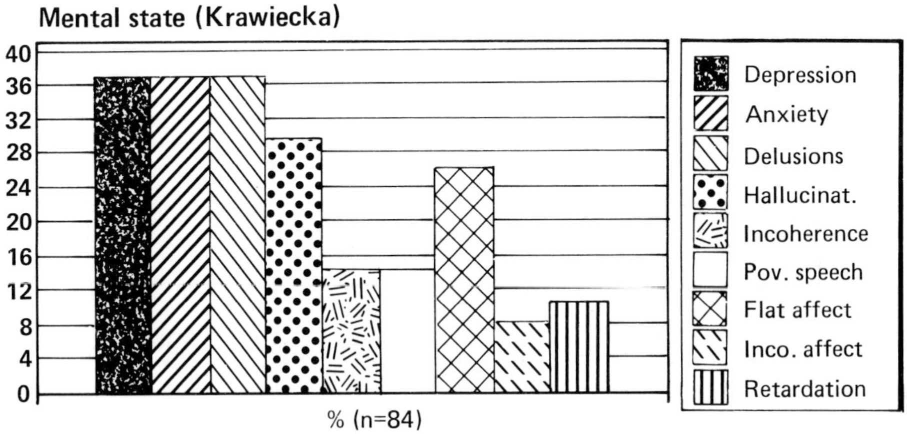

Fig. 7. *Percentage of patients with mental ratings scores of 2 or more on the Manchester scale in the North Camden survey.*

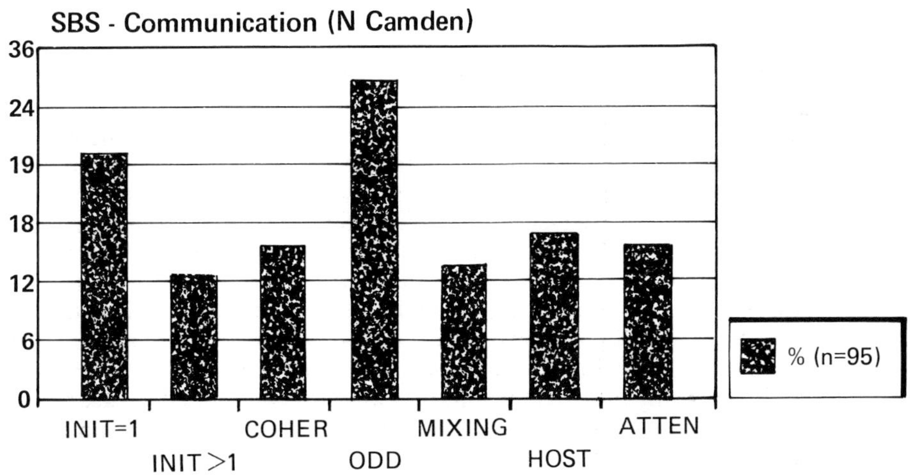

Fig. 8. *Percentage of patients with behavioural ratings scores of 2 or more on the Social Behaviour Scale in the North Camden survey, subdivided by behavioural category.* See Fig. 5 for abbreviations.

Clinical findings

The mental state findings were in stark contrast to those of McCreadie in Nithsdale (McCreadie, 1982, and this volume, page 179). In the North Camden population the positive symptoms were most prominent and the negative symptoms least. Thus more than one third of the patients were deluded and almost as many exhibited hallucinations (Fig. 7). Nevertheless, over a quarter of the patients were rated for flatness of affect. It is also striking that depression and anxiety were as prominent as delusions, a finding in keeping with several other studies which have highlighted the significance of these symptoms in schizophrenia.

The data from the social behaviour schedules echo some of these findings (Fig. 8). For instance, anxiety and depression were rated as significant problems by informants in approximately one quarter of cases. Thirty-three per cent of subjects exhibited odd or

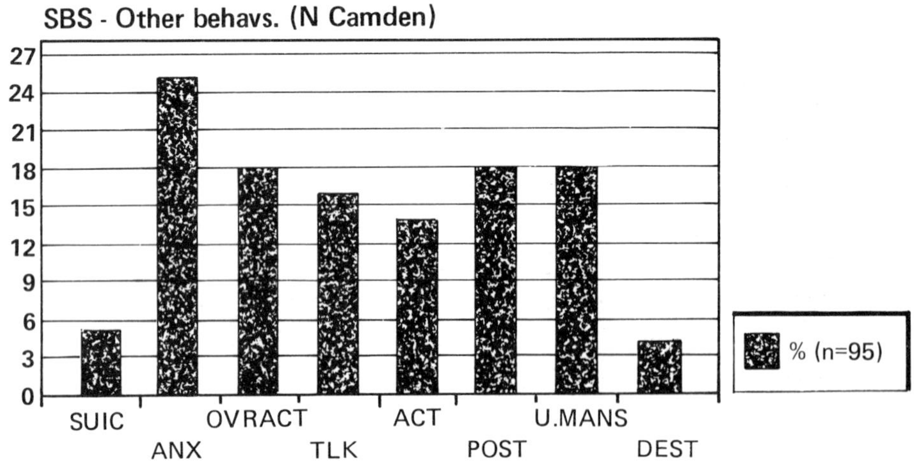

Fig. 9. *Percentage of patients with behavioural ratings scores of 2 or more on the Social Behaviour Scale in the North Camden survey, subdivided by behavioural category.* See fig. 6 for abbreviations.

inappropriate conversation (mostly of delusional content). Fourteen per cent had acted out bizarre ideas, whilst 16% were noted to laugh or talk to themselves in the preceeding month. Patients frequently showed problems in communication skills. For instance, 25% had a limited ability to initiate and maintain conversation and a further 13% had little or no spontaneous conversation. Other areas of difficulty (Fig. 9) included personal hygiene, where one fifth were rated as deficient. Some limitation of concentration was reported in one half of the patients. One fifth were underactive on occasions and two fifths had some impairment of the ability to occupy their leisure time.

Eight per cent of this first group of patients had no psychiatric admissions, whilst a further 5% had not been in hospital over the preceding 10 years. The maximum length of stay over the 10 years preceding the census was less than 1 year for 73% of individuals; similarly the duration of the last admission was less than 1 year in 79% of cases. A link between problems with compliance with medication and the most recent admission was identified from notes in almost a quarter of patients.

Conclusions

The point prevalence figures in both halves of the borough are strikingly high. We have yet to apply the Feighner criteria to these figures. The contrast in point prevalence between the two surveys is likely to reflect the different socio-demographic features of North and South Camden.

Amongst the more important differences are the presence of the homeless person hostels in South Camden and its railway links with the rest of the country, which probably attract a more transient population. The data which support this view include the greater number of individuals in South Camden with weaker links with the borough, the higher percentage in temporary accommodation and the fact that fewer people were identified as living with relatives. Important findings in both surveys were that over 55% of individuals had no daytime occupation, approximately 37% had no contact with friends or acquaintances and that over 90% had been admitted to a psychiatric hospital on at least one occasion (Fig. 10). In comparison with a similar study in a rural setting (Nithsdale —

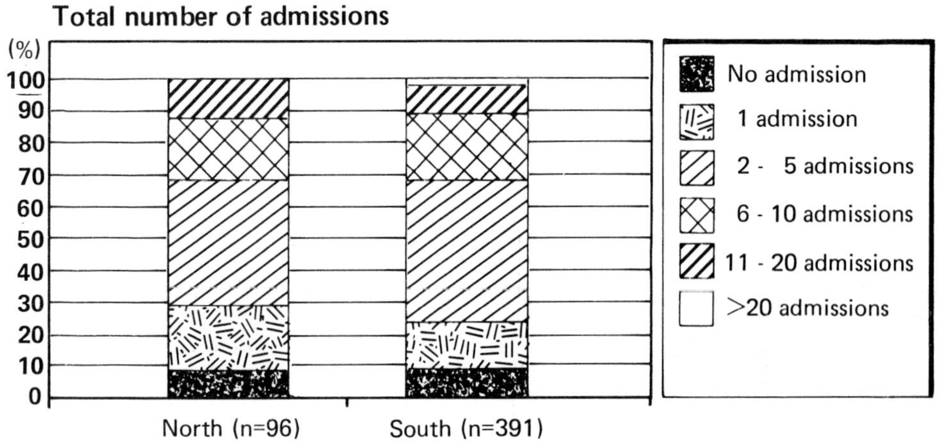

Fig. 10. *Stacked bar chart comparing percentages of patients with previous admissions in the two community surveys.*

McCreadie, this volume, p. 179) a greater percentage of individuals were found to suffer from positive symptoms such as delusions and hallucinations.

These findings will have important implications for service planning and provision in the two districts.

Implications for community care

If we may try to draw a conclusion from the mass of detail which has been briefly sketched out here, we would suggest that our studies support the view that a serious commitment to Community Care must demand that planning should be based on knowledge of the current pattern of resource allocation and of the needs of the identifiable community of suffering individuals and their families as a whole. Focussing just on the hospital population at one point in time and relying on normative figures for community service needs and simplistic ideological formulae cannot be good enough. By concentrating its planning on the closure of Friern and the reprovision of accommodation for that cross-section of patients resident now in the hospital, there is a very real danger that the Regional Health Authority will achieve the very opposite of the more equitable and cost-effective distribution of resources it promised, thereby confirming the accuracy of medical advice it received 6 years ago. Instead of funds being released for the people outside hospital who desperately need them, there is a very great danger that a still larger proportion of the scant resources will go to reproviding very expensive accommodation and care for those whose stay in hospital already attracts the major expenditure.

We know we have identified only a proportion of the people with schizophrenia outside hospital. We want to extend the survey to include a longitudinal view of the people newly identified each year.

Our main efforts at present are directed towards trying to obtain funding to use the data assembled in the surveys for the purpose of establishing a practical computerized system of individual patient-monitoring and supervision, which we have called ‘safety net’. We believe every District, and particularly those fragmented inner-city areas like Camden to which dislocated people with mental illness tend to drift, should have one. There is much to be done.

References

Feighner, J.P., Rubins, E., Guze, S., Woodruff, R.A., Winokur, G. & Munoz, R. (1972): Diagnostic criteria for use in psychiatric research. *Arch. Gen. Psychiatry* **26**, 57–62.

Jarman B. (1983): Identification of underprivileged areas. *Br. Med. J.* **286**, 1705–1708.

Krawiecka, M., Goldberg, D. & Vaughn, M. (1977): A standardised psychiatric assessment scale for rating chronic psychotic patients. *Acta Psychiatr. Scand.* **55**, 299–308.

McCreadie, R.M. (1982): The Nithsdale Schizophrenia Survey: I. Psychiatric and social handicaps. *Br. J. Psychiatry* **140**, 582–586.

North East Thames Regional Health Authority (1982): *The future provision of services for the mentally ill: A consultative document.* London: NETRHA.

Pantelis, C. Taylor, J. & Campbell, P. (1988): The South Camden Schizophrenia Survey — an experience of community based research. *Bull. R. Coll. Psychiatrists* **12**, 98–101.

Policy Group Report (1980): The Mental Illness Service in NETRHA. London: North East Thames Regional Health Authority.

Vaughan, M. & Krawiecka, M. (1979): Sensitivity to change in symptoms of new scales for rating chronic psychotic patients. *Int. Pharmacopsychiatr.* **14**, 121–126.

Wykes, T. & Sturt, E. (1986): The measurement of social behaviour in psychiatric patients: An assessment of the reliability and validity of the Social Behaviour Schedule. *Br. J. Psychiatry* **148**, 1–12.

Chapter 18
Mental illness and social policy

Malcolm P. I. Weller

Friern Hospital, Friern Barnet Road, London N11 3BP, UK

Summary

The prevalence of schizophrenia depends on precisely which population is being surveyed. The destitute are likely to be excluded from census-based population surveys, whilst the probability of schizophrenia is high in this group. London is a magnet to which such people are drawn and this population was repeatedly surveyed in London over several years at the Christmas period, when people generally make an effort to be reunited with their families. The results indicate that many are grossly deluded and hallucinated and are failing to obtain their benefit entitlements. They are generally in poor physical health and the failure of outreaching and low levels of provision for psychosis in Central London is probably contributing to the high level of prison records in this group, generally for petty crime but occasionally for violent crime.

Introduction

Together with colleagues, I have been involved in three surveys which found a relationship between mental illness and imprisonment, but which also illustrate the appalling misery and degradation that befalls the mentally ill in 'the community'.

First survey

Seventy-two men were interviewed over Christmas 1985 (Weller & Weller, 1986) in three settings, in and outside *Crisis at Christmas,* a charity providing shelter, meals and entertainment for the destitute over the Christmas period, at Bruce House, a long stay hostel under the auspices of Westminster local authority, and Great Peter Street Salvation Army hostel. Seventeen of those interviewed had been to prison and of those 15 had previously had psychiatric treatment or were actively hallucinating at the time of the interview. One of the remaining two men was unsure whether or not he had heard voices and the other had severe memory impairment following a head injury and could not remember very much! Forty per cent of the 72 men had psychiatric disorders at some time which had been treated in psychiatric hospitals, as against 14% in the general population treated for any psychiatric condition in any setting, in 95% of cases in a general practitioner's surgery (Shepherd, 1974). Three, who had never received treatment, were actively hallucinating at the time of the interviews.

The plight of some of these men was extreme, most having no friend, no contact with their families, no general practitioner and many not receiving benefits of any kind, particularly if they had received psychiatric treatment in the past.

Second Survey

In a subsequent survey (Weller *et al.*, 1987), 100 men and women were interviewed on Christmas Eve 1986, at *Crisis at Christmas.* Having excluded those who appeared intoxicated with alcohol or drugs and, of necessity, those who declined to be interviewed, 34 were actively psychotic at the time of interview (42% of those replying to questions), of whom 12 had been in contact with psychiatric services, 10 were not receiving any of their benefit entitlements, and 25 (81%) had been to prison, including one who had been to Broadmoor for attempted murder.

These results show a deterioration since the previous survey, with over one in five having florid schizophrenic symptoms in one night of public, superficial interviews (18 out of 81 examined, 22%), and nearly one in three with definite or probable schizophrenia (24 out of 81, 30%), approaching one in two with active psychotic symptoms (34 out of 81, 42%).

Thirty-two admitted to having been to prison, out of the combined group of 46 who had either been admitted to psychiatric hospital before or who were actively psychotic at the time (including a murderer, on Home Office licence from his life sentence, who declined to answer). This number was significantly in excess of the residual group who had no previous psychiatric history. The likelihood of such an excess having occurred by chance was less than five chances in a thousand ($P < 0.005$). If these findings are aggregated with our previous survey, the likelihood of this being a spurious association decreases further, to less than one chance in a thousand ($P < 0.001$). The most conservative form of statistics were used in making these assertions and the probabilities could not be expressed more precisely because they come off the scale of standard statistical tables.

Fifty-seven out of 90 respondents had slept in the open immediately prior to coming to *Crisis at Christmas*, and of these only eight were applicants for housing. Sixty-six per cent had no contact with a medical General Practitioner, although during cursory examination 26% were considered to have some physical problem requiring treatment. Thirty-six per cent were not receiving any benefits of any kind, an enormous increase from the previous year's proportion of 9%. A long separation from family was common, averaging 11.1 years.

In both surveys 90% or more, with or without a psychiatric history, were born outside London and gravitated to the metropolis in line with our own and others' earlier studies of migration and wandering in schizophrenia (Jauhar & Weller 1982; Weller & Jauhar 1987). The extent of this migration is shown in the Table. Considerable migration to London is indicated. Only eight out of the 119 destitute people interviewed were born in London (6.8%).

In this sample there was a significant increase in the concentration of the mentally ill amongst these who had migrated to London. This concentration rose significantly over the two surveys, probably reflecting the preponderance of seriously ill in the second sample, which avoided the more settled population in Bruce House and the Salvation Army hostel.

These findings, which accord with those of the Royal College of General Practitioners

Table 1. *Place of birth, where known.*

	Total			Psychotic at time of interview		
	1985	*1986*	*1985 + 1986*	*1985*	*1986*	*1985 + 1986*
Greater London	0	8	8	0	5	5
Elsewhere England	15	38	53	6	20	26
Scotland	5	11	16	0	5	5
Ireland	9	21	30	2	13	15
Wales	0	1	1	0	1	1
Abroad	6	5	11	2	5	7
Total	35	84	119	10(28.6%)	49(58.3%)	59(49.6%)
% Outside London	100	90.5	93.2	100	89.8	91.5

(1981) in their survey, question the wisdom of the policy of decreasing expenditure on medical services in London, by the application of the Resource Allocation Working Party (1976) (RAWP) formula. The situation has subsequently deteriorated; the Camberwell Resettlement Centre, the largest in Europe, closed in September 1986, the number of beds available at Bruce House has dropped precipitously, whilst access has been made more restrictive, and about 1000 lodging houses are closing each year in London.

Over a 2 year period, 25 000 people were estimated to have used the Camberwell Reception Centre, in which tuberculosis was rife, as it now is at Bruce House, a long standing problem in such inadequate arrangements (Scott *et al.*, 1966; British Thoracic and Tuberculosis Association, 1971). The authorities audaciously redesignated the centre a Resettlement Centre shortly before closure, having found alternative accommodation for 14 individuals over a 2 year period — 10 in Part Three accommodation, two in local authority housing and two with housing associations. Although it ostensibly provides for the vulnerable homeless (see R. *v.* Waveney D. C. ex Bowers [1983] 1 QB 238) the Housing (Homeless Persons) Act 1985 does not provide for the single drifters and wanderers (Brahams & Weller, 1985).

Third Survey

On Christmas Eve 1988 we interviewed 58 people living at Arlington House, a long stay hostel for people in housing need, in Camden, North London, and the St. Mungo Community Hostel in Endell Street in the West End. In addition, early on New Year's Day, in conjunction with the Simon Community tea run, we interviewed 43 men who had slept the previous night on the street (Weller *et al.*, 1989).

In the Christmas data, 17 men were actively psychotic at the time of interview, and a further 11 had a previous history of psychosis, having received in-patient psychiatric care. Despite the fact that these were men who were in stable accommodation and paying rental, seven (13%) were not receiving benefits of any kind.

On the New Year's Day Survey, 19 of the men we interviewed (44%) were actively psychotic when we interviewed them and a further seven had had previous hospital care for psychosis (16%). Thirty-one per cent of the entire sample were not receiving any benefits of any kind. Seventy-two per cent of the total sample were not registered with a GP, although 52% had conditions requiring medical treatment (67% of the actively psychotic men).

There was a significant association ($P < 0.005$) between present and previous psychosis and imprisonment, as we had been found in the earlier surveys.

Comment

All three surveys revealed a similar pattern of cold, hunger, sickness, and self neglect, interwoven with serious mental illness. There is a spectrum of severity of psychopathology. Some manage fairly orderly, if bleak lives, atuned to the anonymity of cheap shelter. A step below this the better organized live in loose combinations at well established places, often chosen because of shelter and relative warmth from the ventilation systems of buildings. From time to time the police break up well known haunts, such as the one at Waterloo Station. Others, less sociable and less well, shelter in doorways wherever they can.

With limited resources and no special funding we have conducted surveys over a number of years. These surveys suffer from a number of sources of bias and cannot be considered to be appropriate epidemiological surveys. Nevertheless, they are the best data that are available and they paint a picture of a persistent drift of people from all parts of the world and particularly of the British Isles to London. This group, at best, has tenuous adequacy and contains many who suffer from persisting psychoses that disable them from securing their minimal entitlements.

An indifference to the rigours of the life was paralleled by a failure to attend to physical ill health, dental decay and failing eyesight. It is romantic but inaccurate to represent this extraordinary behaviour as a rational choice and the promotion of this lonely, cold and uncomfortable life has been inappropriately promoted by men like Robert Louis Stevenson, who ironically died of consumption: 'Give the jolly heaven above and the byway nigh me'.

Although psychosis was not identified in about half the people we interviewed others were of a quirky, suspicious nature and were vague and slightly disorganized in their responses to questions. A striking feature of the surveys was that many of the people who were approached were too suspicious and paranoid to enable assessment using orthodox methods. Some of these seemed to be very unwell, keeping themselves entirely to themselves and shunning all contact with the voluntary services and with those who congregate around them. When approached further they may voice paranoid ideas or betray formal thought disorder, but in general their hostility prevents appropriate assessment. However, one feels that it is this group who are perhaps the most ill, despite our hesitancy in pressing to determine this because of mounting hostility, unwillingness to be over-intrusive, and desire to avoid any unpleasantness.

An interesting feature of our surveys is that those who drink heavily often have persisting alcoholic hallucinations with first rank Schneiderian symptoms of schizophrenia. However, they have better preserved personalities and a warmth of rapport that is not common amongst schizophrenia sufferers. This presentation is unusual in hospital clinical practice.

Even when schizophrenic sufferers remain in contact with psychiatric services, clinical depression is common (Johnson, 1981; Shanfield *et al.*, 1970; Knights & Hirsch, 1981; Singh & Kay, 1979), and destitution and untreated disease are inevitable accompaniments to neglect. There are those who argue that anything is better than the imagined horror of psychiatric hospitals and believe that 'we' should take the risk of inadequately funded and misconceived community care. Mr Hebditch, a national director of Mind, is reported in *The Times* to accept that life outside psychiatric hospitals implies a necessary risk — 'Perhaps that is a price we have to pay', but it is the patients who must endure the consequences.

The willingness to admit patients with predominantly social problems to psychiatric hospitals has progressively diminished, partly in response to the vehement criticism of psychiatry that it 'medicalizes' distress and partly because of the reduction in psychiatric beds. The difficulty in transferring from prison to hospital may take some impetus from the other criticism of psychiatry that is intemperately voiced, that it has become an instrument of social control.

There is much evidence of adverse consequences of this tragic muddle. In December 1985 I interviewed a man sleeping in a cardboard box under the arches beside Embankment station in central London, who had active tuberculosis and no medication, and another who was attending a psychiatric day hospital. There seemed to be far more people at this site at the end of 1986, with 26 bedded down at 9.15pm on Christmas Eve. It is noteworthy that community care of psychiatric patients has been pressed energetically in America, where two out of every five suffering from psychosis never receive treatment (Dohrenwend *et al.*, 1980). Psychiatric patients are unsettled by discharge, being most likely at such times to commit crimes and to take their own lives (Stein, 1978; Roy, 1982). With only the most capable patients discharged and cared for in the community, this group, compared to those patients in hospital, has increased rates for accidents, cancer and suicide (Haugland *et al.*, 1983; Sturt; Amdur & Souchek, 1981). Amongst mentally disordered offenders with various diagnoses, the rate of suicide and violent death in 1982 was five times the general population for those aged 25–29 and two to three times greater for men in most age groups (Robertson, 1987). There are difficulties in making reliable estimates of suicide, because of an unwillingness to bring in such a verdict, combined with the uncertainty of intention amongst psychotics. In any particular psychiatric group there may be an added problem of diagnosis, which is particularly difficult in schizophrenia. Bearing these caveats in mind, the suicide rate for male schizophrenics has been estimated at 17 times greater than expected based on the general population (Pokorny & Kaplan, 1976) and this as long ago as 1976, before the enthusiasm for hospital closures.

The term 'released' is commonly applied to the ejection of such patients, the overwhelming majority of whom are voluntary patients. At Friern hospital for example, destined soon to close, only 11 of the 495 long-stay patients are there by compulsion, most of whom are constrained by Court orders. There are those who will see what they wish to see and who zealously argue for an elimination of psychiatric hospitals with the utmost speed, citing Italy as an example. Programmes such as 'Italy's Mad Laws?' on ITV turned a Nelsonian eye to all contrary arguments. As a participant one could observe how steadfastly any adverse comments were restricted and how the few that crept in were edited out. However, we should heed the lessons of Italy, where the destitute and homeless roam the streets (MacKenzie, 1984; Jones & Poletti, 1984–5) and where the meaning of the term *abbandonati* has shifted from 'psychiatric hospital patients' to 'the outcasts from psychiatric hospitals'. The inevitable pressure that is placed on acute admission beds in Italy is not satifsied by the meagre provision in district general hospitals, which is the only provision allowed and amounts to 15 beds for a population of 150 000. Private hospitals, with less regulation than that public ones, now provide 4000 beds in Rome, against only 30 public ones (Jones & Poletti, 1984–5). A recent supplement to *Acta Psychiatrica Scandinavica* (1985, **316**) describes a similar disaster in the Naples area. The words of Paparo & Bacigalupi (1982) have a familiar ring here in Britain (Cold, 1988). 'The very high pressure on admission beds ... forces the psychiatric team on duty to dedicate most of its time to screening admissions (trying to avoid them at all costs!).'

We ought to be providing comprehensive and continuous care within a network of local facilities, providing this care, moreover, with staff who are as well trained as they are enthusiastic. At present we are obviously far from this goal with a particular weakness in the inexperience of local authority staff (Barclay, 1982).

Follow-up study

Two groups of in-patients at two different psychiatric hospitals, St. Mary's, Stannington, Northumberland (n=40) and Friern, in North London (n=23), were surveyed, together with out-patients from both hospitals (n=40, St. Mary's; n=16 Friern), all of whom were actively supported by community nurses (Weller *et al.*, 1987). The Friern in-patients were significantly older than the out-patients ($P < 0.001$) (ie there is less than one chance in a thousand that this result would have occurred as a chance finding): in-patients mean age 56.5 years, range 37.73, s.d. 11.2: out-patients mean age 40.9 years, range 20–64, s.d. 13.8. However they were carefully matched for age and sex in the St. Mary's groups: in-patients mean age 51.3 years, range 23–77, s.d. 15.1; out-patients mean age 50.4 years, range 24–73, s.d. 13.9. Patients in hospital were significantly advantaged (Mann-Whitney, two tailed probabilities) in terms of: attending social gatherings ($P < 0.05$ both groups); going to places of entertainment ($P < 0.001$, St Mary's); number of meals per week ($P < 0.001$, Friern); number of hot meals ($P < 0.001$, St Mary's; $P < 0.001$, Friern); and the number of baths per week ($P < 0.005$, St. Mary's). However the Friern in-patients were disadvantaged in terms of company, if the contacts with nursing, medical and paramedical staff were excluded ($P < 0.01$), although there is no reason to exclude these contacts. Perhaps because of frequent staff contact they attentively listened less to the radio ($P < 0.005$).

Conclusion

Lionel Penrose's (1938) findings of an inverse correlation between psychiatric bed provisions and the prison population of European countries still holds in this country. He also found an inverse correlation with the homicide rate, suicide rate and general death rate, and there is some disquieting evidence on these associations even now (Robertson, 1987). With only the most capable patients discharged from long-term psychiatric care, they still have increased rates for suicide, accidents and cancer, compared to those in hospital (Haugland *et al.*, 1983; Sturt, 1983; Amdur & Souchek, 1981), with a surge in suicide (Roy, 1982) and violent crime (Stein, 1982) around the time of discharge.

In the words of the Richmond Fellowship report (1983) 'We deplore the use of the term 'community care' as a slogan that diverts attention from the real issues of quality of life for the mentally disordered, distressed or disabled people, whether or not they are living in 'institutions'. ... the age-long neglect of the mentally ill, although ameliorated ... is still a marked feature of present-day society in Britain.' Sir Douglas Black (1984) maintained that the overriding test of the value of a health service lies in what it does for patients. In a good service the patient may spend time in hospital or be cared for in the community, according to his needs, rather than according to value judgments on the importance of the two sectors.

Demographic changes generate an increase of 1% annually on the demand for NHS resources, whilst there has been no growth in resource volume over the past four years (O'Higgins, 1987). Local authorities are squeezed by reduced funding and perhaps rate capping, and the provision for the elderly is decreasing. Local authority provisions overall have barely increased at all, and indeed there was an effective fall in local authority residential places in the 6 years up to 1982, which has been exacerbated by a decrease in the provision of home helps and meals-on-wheels (Andrews, 1985). Some authorities honestly stress their inability to provide for mental illness in no uncertain terms; 'It cannot be emphasized enough that the district is not funded to provide a comprehensive local service (ie meeting all mental health needs in the District) and is not statutorily required to provide such a service.' (Islington Health Authority, 1986).

There should be disquiet because it is clear that current planning is inadequately funded. The charity MIND estimates that it seems to require £500 million a year more, plus an additional £500 million a year for 5 years as a central bridging fund, and one may readily agree with Donovan (1982) that as things stand 'The initial promise of a constructive life in the community for every mentally ill person is the psychiatric equivalent of a cure for cancer. Such promises need to be brought into line with reality.'

This situation was recognized and frankly acknowledged as long ago as 1975 in the Government White Paper *Better Services for the Mentally Ill:*

> 'Those who work in the health and social services fields have to recognize that families and relatives, and indeed the public at large, cannot be expected to tolerate under the name of community care the discharge of chronic patients without adequate arrangements being made for after-care and who perhaps spend their days wandering the streets or become an unbearable burden on the lives of their relatives; hostels which are so selective that they are only half full while people needing residential care are told they are unsuitable; appeals which go unanswered for help in crises while authorities or professional officers debate boundaries of responsibility.' (para 2.27).

The problem cannot be left solely to the local authorities and the recommendations of the current Griffiths report to place the primary responsibility on local authorities causes disquiet. Even the most caring neglect their current statutory responsibilities to the most vulnerable, such as the 12 homeless families for whom Camden could not find temporary accommodation, including a mother with three children, aged $2\frac{1}{2}$, 18 months, and *four days* left to sleep on the railway station (Amery, 1985). It is cumbersome to redress the issue, which was not tested before the Courts until October 1988 when Lord Justice May, sitting with Mr Justice Ian Kennedy in the High Court, condemned the treatment given to the homeless in Camden by restricting the opening of its Homeless Persons Unit at Bidborough House, St. Pancras to between 9.30 am and 12.30 pm on weekdays; 'having read all the material more than once I am quite satisfied that the borough's cavalier treatment of the applicants, who are *prima facie* homeless and have a priority need for some sort of roof over their heads, would be considered to be inadequate by any reasonable council properly directing themselves in the circumstances of this case'. (Hampstead and Highgate Express, 14 October 1988, p. 123, cols. 1 and 2).

Psychiatric hospitals have been known to take up some of the slack, working in harmony with social services to admit predominantly social problems in an emergency. Their capacity to do so has been eroded by a decrease in the number of beds, and problems of nurse recruitment, which applies to London hospitals generally, 16 in the North-West Thames region put on 'red alert' by London's emergency bed service in March 1986, closing them to all but emergency cases, and 13 large hospitals in the South East Thames region being put on 'yellow alert', cancelling all non-emergency admissions. The cause of this catastrophic situation, apart from the run-down of resources – a cold spell! 'All around the London area closure of emergency admission facilities is now a regular occurrence in many parts, especially during winter' (Dr Robert Brown, cited in *The Times*, 7th March 1986, p. 1). A previous female patient of mine died of hypothermia in Haringey, weeks after this was recognized as a likely outcome, because of a lack of social facilties.

The existing community care priorities are clearly inadequate and housing legislation seems defective for mental illness in the UK, as previously discussed by Brahams & Weller (1985). The cost of keeping people in prison is comparable to looking after them in a psychiatric hospital, and is substantially more expensive in some cases; the cost of maintaining a prisoner in Brixton gaol is £12 000 pa, £15 300 at a youth open prison, and

£25 000 in a dispersal prison. As emphasized by Titmuss (1961), to this must be added the additional costs of probation officers, unemployment benefits and, ironically, on research to find out why crime is increasing.

One way to close hospitals is to move patients to other hospitals. The first hospital to close in the UK was St. Wulstan's in Malvern and one of the ones most deserving and needful of remaining open, with its specialist expertise in psychiatric rehabilitation. The closure was achieved by moving the patients, not to some stable situation but to Powick hospital near Worcester, the closure of which is being celebrated. One patient, who was moved in this fashion, has already been removed four times and is due to be moved again. The patients at Banstead Hospital, Epsom, now a site for a prison, were moved to Horton, seven miles away, which is due to close in 1993, as are three other London hospitals in Kensington, Paddington and SW1, and a home for demented patients in Chiswick; so much for the argument of moving the base of health care closer to the patients' relatives, which is advanced as a persuasive reason for closure in the first place.

The policy of community care of psychiatric patients currently living in psychiatric hospitals must succeed in settling such patients in alternative provision and in reaching out to those who do not actively seek help (see Ekdawi, this volume, p. 317). I recognized one of the psychotic men I interviewed at Christmas 1986 as a person I had previously interviewed when he was sleeping rough. That interview happened to take place on a winter day, in which the night temperature was the lowest recorded in that year, and I had wondered if he had survived. Every patient who wanders away represents a serious failure, and every patient who is lost to psychiatric follow-up in this manner must be considered to be at considerable hazard of finishing up as destitute, imprisoned, or dead. The overcrowded prisons seem to be fulfilling a role that they are ill equipped and inappropriate to serve, for a vulnerable population who deserve better, but who often suffer worse. It is economically sensible to revise our present policies, but we should hope for other considerations to prevail, with adequate provision for the most vulnerable members of our society, in a response that combines compassion with generosity.

References

Amdur, M.A. & Souchek, J. (1981): Death in aftercare. *Comp. Psychiatry* **22**, 619–626.

Andrews, K. (1985): Demographic changes and resources for the elderly. *Br. Med. J.* **290**, 1023–1024.

Barclay, P.M. (1982): Social workers: their role and task. London: Bedford Square Press.

Brahams, D. & Weller, M.P.I. (1985): Crime and homelessness among the mentally ill. *New Law J. 135* (1), 761–763; *135* (2), 626–629; reprinted with appendices, *Medico-legal J.* **54** (1), 42–53.

British Thoracic and Tuberculosis Association (1971): Report of the Research Committee. *Tubercle* **52**, 1–8.

Coid, J.W. (1988): Mentally abnormal prisoners on remand. 1. Rejected or accepted by the NHS? *Br. Med. J.* **296**, 1779–1782.

Dohrenwend, B.P., Dohrenewend, B.S., Gould, M.S., Link, B., Neugebauer, R. & Wunsch-Hitzig, R. (1980): *Mental illness in the United States: Epidemiological estimates.* New York: Praeger Publishers.

Donovan, C.M. (1982): Problems of psychiatric practice in community mental health centres. *Am. J. Psychiatry* **139**, 456–460.

Haughland, G., Craig, T.J., Goodman, A.B., & Siegel, C. (1983): Mortality in the era of deinstitutionalization. *Am. J. Psychiatry* **23**, 377–385.

Jauhar, R. & Weller, M.P.I. (1982): Psychiatric morbidity and time zone changes. A study of patients from Heathrow Airport. *Br. J. Psychiatry* **140**, 231–235.

Johnson, D.A.W. (1981): Studies of depression in schizophrenia. *Br. J. Psychiatry* **139**, 89–101.

Jones, D.K. & Poletti, A. (1984): Transformation of the asylum: The Italian experience. V. Commentary and review. *Int. J. Men. Health Services.* Winter/Spring 1984–5.

Knights, A. & Hirsch, S.R. (1981): Revealed depression and drug treatment for schizophrenia. *Arch. Gen. Psychiatry* **38**, 806–811.
MacKenzie, D. (1984): Italian madhouses. *New Scientist*, 30th Aug. p. 9.
O'Higgins, M. (1987): Health spending — a way to sustainable growth. Available from the Institute of Health Service Management, 75 Portland Place, London W1 4AN; cited *Lancet* 1987, **ii**, 54.
Paparo, F. & Bacigalupi, A. (1982): Community health and psychiatry: The Italian experience. In *The individual and the group*, eds M. Pines & L. Rafaelson. London: Plenum.
Penrose, L.S. (1938): Mental disease and crime: Outline of a comparative study of European statistics. *Br. J. Psychol. Med.* **18**, 1–15.
Pokorny, A. & Kaplan, H. (1976):Suicide following psychiatric disorders. *J. Nerv. Ment. Dis.* 162, 499–506 (1976).
Robertson, G. (1987): Mentally abnormal offenders: manner of death. *Br. Med. J.* **295**, 632–634.
Roy, A. (1982): Suicide in chronic schizophrenia. *Br. J. Psychiatry* **141**, 171–177.
Royal College of General Pratitioners (1981): *Survey of primary care in London.* Occasional Paper 16. London: RCGP.
Scott, R., Gaskell, D.G. & Morrell, D.C. (1966): Patients who reside in common lodging houses. *Br. Med. J.* **ii**, 1561–1564.
Shanfield, S., Tucker, G., Harrow, M. & Detre, T. (1970): The schizophrenic patient and depressive symptomatology. *J. Nerv. Ment. Dis.* **151**, 203–210.
Shepherd, M. (1974): General Practice. Mental illness and the British National Health Service. *Am. J. Public Health* **64**, 320–332.
Singh, M.M. & Kay, S.R. (1979): Dysphoric response to neuroleptic treatment in schizophrenia: its relationship to autonomic arousal and prognosis. *Biol. Psychiatry* **14**, 277–294.
Stein, G.S. (1982): Dangerous episodes occurring around the time of discharge of four chronic schizophrenics. *Br. J. Psychiatry* **141**, 586–589.
Sturt, E. (1983): Mortality in a cohort of long-term users of community psychiatric services. *Psychol. Med.* **13**, 441–446.
Titmuss, R.M. (1961): Community care — fact or fiction? (Annual Conference Report, National Association for Mental Health). Reprinted (1963) In: *Trends in mental health services*, eds H. Freeman & J. Farndale. London: Pergamon.
Weller, M.P.I. & Jauhar, P. (1987): Wandering at Heathrow airport. *Med. Sci. Law* **27**, 37–39.
Weller, B.G.A. & Weller, M.P.I. (1986): Health care in a destitute population: Christmas 1985. *Bull. R. Coll. Psychiatr.* **10**, 233–235.
Weller, B.G.A., Weller, M.P.I. & Cheyne, A. (1986): Long-term psychiatric patients in the community. *Br. J. Psychiatry* **151**, 862 (letter).
Weller, B.G.A., Weller, M.P.I., Cocker, E. & Mohamed, S. (1987): Crisis at Christmas 1987. *Lancet* **i**, 553–554.
Weller, M.P.I., Tobiansky, R. & Hollander, D. (1989): Destitution in the festive season. *Lancet* **i**, 220 (letter).

IV

NEW DIRECTIONS IN PHARMACOLOGY

Neurotransmitters — Introduction

The dopamine hypothesis fails to provide a complete understanding of the biochemical nature of schizophrenia (Meltzer, 1979; Crow, 1985), and conventional dopamine blocking neuroleptics are only successful in a proportion of patients, which furthermore often entail immediate and long-lasting side effects. Alternative hypotheses and therapeutic strategies are to be welcomed and the following chapters exemplify current research in noradrenaline and serotonin neurotransmitters in schizophrenia.

References

Meltzer, H.Y. (1979): Studies in schizophrenia, in *Disorders of the schizophrenic syndrome,* ed. L. Bellak. New York: Basic Books.

Crow, T.J., Baker, H.F., Cross, A.J. *et al.* (1985): Monoamine mechanisms in chronic schizophrenia: Post-mortem neurochemical findings. *Br. J. Psychiatry* **134**, 249–256.

Chapter 19

Drug-induced akathisia and tardive dyskinesia

Thomas R. E. Barnes

Academic Unit, Horton Hospital, Epsom, Surrey KT19 8PZ, UK

Summary

Akathisia and tardive dyskinesia are movement disorders associated with antipsychotic drugs. Acute akathisia as a dose-related phenomenon has an incidence around 20%, but akathisia also occurs as a chronic condition. It can be a source of considerable distress, is often unrecognized or misinterpreted and can interfere with treatment and rehabilitation. Diagnosis is based upon the report of a typical subjective experience of restlessness and the presence of characteristic patterns of restless movement. The condition may prove difficult to treat but anticholinergic agents and low-dose beta-blockers can be effective. Tardive dyskinesia is usually a late-onset condition. The movements are principally a social handicap, but they can interfere with functions such as eating and speech and the condition may also carry an excess burden of mortality. There is evidence that oro-facial dyskinesia and trunk and limb dyskinesia constitute discrete subsyndromes of tardive dyskinesia. Risk factors for the condition include advancing age, brain damage and a diagnosis of affective disorder. Prevention and treatment probably rest upon the judicious use of antipsychotic drugs although specific antidyskinetic agents may sometimes be indicated.

Introduction

The administration of antipsychotic drugs may be associated with a variety of movement disorders which can be divided conveniently into early and late onset conditions. The early-onset motor syndromes such as parkinsonism, acute dystonic reactions and acute akathisia, generally arise soon after starting antipsychotic medication or following an increase in drug dose, and tend to be considered as relatively transient problems. The late-onset disorders, such as tardive dystonia and tardive dyskinesia, tend to occur in older patients on maintenance antipsychotic medication and are generally chronic, persistent conditions.

This paper focuses on akathisia and tardive dyskinesia. Perhaps more than the other conditions, these two movement disorders constitute a major constraint upon the use of antipsychotic drugs. Akathisia is probably the commonest of these motor problems, and is often a serious cause of distress to patients (Anonymous, 1986*a*), while tardive dyskinesia has come to symbolize the potential, long-term, harmful complications of these drugs (Barnes, 1987*a*). Both conditions can prove resistant to treatment.

Acute akathisia

The term 'akathisia' was coined by Haskovec in 1903 to describe two psychoneurotic patients who were unable to remain seated. The name derives from the Greek and literally means 'not to sit'. He considered this akathisia to be of compulsive origin, while later authors attributed it to a phobia of sitting down (Oppenheim, 1911; Bing, 1939).

Subsequently, the term was employed to describe an apparently similar phenomenon occurring in patients with Parkinson's disease and post-encephalitic parkinsonism (Sicard, 1923; Bing, 1939). Following the introduction of antipsychotic drugs, Sigwald (1947) and later Steck (1954) noticed restless or rhythmic movements, often in the feet, of patients on these drugs. These manifestations of motor restlessness were referred to as 'neuroleptic-induced akathisia'.

Clinical features

Unlike the other motor syndromes induced by antipsychotic drugs, the movements of akathisia are not dyskinetic in that they are not qualitatively different from normal movements and may be easily mimicked. However, particular patterns of restless movement have been recognized as characteristic of drug-induced akathisia (Braude *et al*., 1983; Gibb & Lees, 1986). These include rocking from foot to foot or treading on the spot when standing, and shuffling or tramping of the legs, repeated leg crossing and swinging of one leg when sitting. In addition, a low frequency, jerky tremor of the feet may be observed (Braude *et al*., 1984). Patients with the severe form of the condition are unable to tolerate any position, such as sitting, lying or standing, for more than a few minutes. They may pace rapidly up and down, a presentation referred to as tasikinesia or the marching syndrome. These signs of motor restlessness may be infrequent or absent in mild cases of acute akathisia (Braude *et al*., 1983), referred to by Van Putten & Marder (1986) as 'subjective akathisia'. In practice, it may be difficult to differentiate between this condition and subtle manifestations of anxiety.

The subjective component of akathisia is the experience of inner tension and emotional unease. More specifically, patients with the condition are commonly aware of tension and discomfort in their limbs, an inability to remain still, or a compulsion to move which may be particularly referable to the legs. Many patients complain that the condition is least tolerable when they are required to stand still, for example, when queuing.

It is paradoxical that the so-called 'major tranquillisers' should produce such a state of agitation, insomnia and restlessness. The overwhelming and intense nature of the subjective experience in severe cases is illustrated by reports where akathisia, often unrecognized, has been thought to have contributed to violent, aggressive behaviour (Kekich, 1978; Kumar, 1979; Schulte, 1985), or impulsive suicidal behaviour (Shear *et al*., 1983; Schulte, 1985; Drake & Erlich, 1985).

Despite the considerable distress that can be associated with akathisia, the condition often goes unrecognized by clinicians (Van Putten, 1975). For example, Weiden & coworkers (1987) diagnosed 27 cases of akathisia out of a sample of 58 acutely psychotic patients admitted to hospital. However, the patients' clinicians, who were blind to the purpose of the study, identified the condition in only seven patients. Of the other 20 patients considered to have akathisia by the researchers, the condition went unnoticed by the clinicians in nine cases. In seven patients the symptoms were attributed to restlessness, agitation or 'acting out', and in the remaining four cases, diagnosis was delayed for more than a week.

As the findings of this study (Weiden *et al.* 1987) illustrate, it is not common for the motor phenomena of akathisia to be misinterpreted as the signs and symptoms of psychiatric illness (Braude *et al.*, 1983; Van Putten & Marder, 1987). If akathisia is misdiagnosed as an exacerbation of agitation or psychotic excitment, this error may prompt an increase in antipsychotic drug dose. Such a response will almost certainly aggravate, rather than relieve the problem.

Akathisia, as an acute, dose-related side-effect, is clinically important for five main reasons. First, it is probably the commonest drug-induced movement disorder. The reported incidence of acute akathisia is commonly around 20% (Ayd, 1961) and in our study of 104 consecutive acute psychiatric admissions requiring antipsychotic drug treatment, the figure was 25%, including mild cases (Braude *et al.*, 1983). Secondly, it is a disabling and distressing condition. Thirdly, as Van Putten (1974) has emphasized, it is an important cause of refusal to take medication. Fourthly, its development in a particular patient may limit the dose that can be administered, and therefore prevent adequate and effective drug treatment. Lastly, the motor phenomena may be misdiagnosed as an exacerbation of psychotic agitation or excitement.

Treatment

The only reliable treatment for akathisia is withdrawal of the antipsychotic medication (Braude *et al.*, 1983), a manoeuvre which may be unrealistic in many acute psychiatric patients. Various pharmacological agents have been tested as potential remedies.

Anticholinergics have an uncertain reputation; some investigators claim that successful treatment with these drugs is virtually diagnostic of akathisia (Van Putten, 1975). For example, in a double-blind, placebo-controlled, crossover study, Friis *et al.*, (1983) found a significant reduction in akathisia score with the anticholinergic biperiden, but not with sodium valproate. However, others suggest that the response is unsatisfactory (Kruse 1960; Marsden *et al.*, 1975; Sovner & DiMascio, 1978), and Adler *et al* (1987a) recently reported a relative lack of effect on akathisia with benztropine.

The variable response of anticholinergic agents as a treatment for akathisia may be partly explained by a finding in our study (Braude *et al.*, 1983). We found that akathisia was an invariable accompaniment of severe parkinsonism, and in such cases both conditions tended to respond to anticholinergic treatment. However, in the majority of patients, akathisia was not associated with severe parkinsonism and in these cases anticholinergics provided little or no benefit. These findings prompted the suggestion that there may be two types of acute akathisia, one related to severe parkinsonism and one not, possibly reflecting different pathophysiological mechanisms.

There are isolated reports of catecholamine agonists such as methylphenidate and amantadine producing an improvement in akathisia (Carman, 1972; Zubenko *et al.*, 1984), and claims have also been made for the efficacy of the alpha$_2$-agonist, clonidine (Zubenko *et al.*, 1984) in the condition.

The therapeutic potential of benzodiazepines, like diazepam (Donlon, 1973; Gagrat *et al.*, Director & Muniz, 1982), lorazepam (Adler *et al.*, 1985; Bartels *et al.*, 1987) and clonazepam (Kutcher *et al.*, 1987) has also been tested and some success has been claimed. Recently, claims have been made for the efficacy of the alpha$_2$-agonist, clonidine (Zubenko *et al.*, 1984) in akathisia, but Adler *et al.*, (1987*b*) found it difficult to differentiate between a specific therapeutic effect and sedation.

The most encouraging and consistent treatment response has been to a modest dose of a beta-adrenoceptor blocker, such as propranolol (Wilbur & Kulik, 1983; Lipinski *et al.*,

1983). A dose of 30–80 mg a day can produce a marked improvement in drug-induced akathisia, often within a few hours of the first dose (Adler *et al.*, 1986). Maximal clinical response seems to occur within 24–48 hours (Lipinski *et al.*, 1983).

Several studies have attempted to elucidate the mechanism of action of beta-blockers in akathisia in terms of whether the effects are central or peripheral, and whether they are mediated via β_1 or β_2-adrenoceptors. With regard to a central or peripheral action, beta-blockers that are hydrophilic and enter the brain poorly generally have been found to be less effective than lipophilic drugs, so supporting the idea of a central action.

With regard to the relevant receptor population, studies have tended to find non-selective β_1 and β_2 blockers, like propranolol, to be more effective than selective β_1 blockers like metoprolol (Zubenko *et al.*, 1984) or atenolol (Reiter, 1987). Such findings suggest that a β_2-adrenoceptor blockade is the relevant pharmacological action. However, this notion is challenged by recent studies by Dupuis *et al.* (1987) and Adler *et al.* (1989) who found improvement with selective β_1 blockers like betaxolol and metoprolol.

Currently the balance of evidence favours a central action but both β_1 and β_2-adrenoceptor blockers appear to be therapeutic. However, further investigation is required as it remains unexplained how drugs such as clonidine and beta-blockers which affect central noradrenergic mechanisms can produce improvement in a condition considered to be related to dopamine receptor antagonism (Marsden & Jenner, 1980; De Keyser *et al.*, 1987).

Chronic akathisia

As mentioned above, akathisia is usually thought of as an early onset phenomenon. However, it can be a persistent problem, and recent studies suggest that symptoms of akathisia can be detected in a third or more of psychiatric patients on chronic antipsychotic treatment (Ayd, 1961; Barnes & Braude, 1985; Gibb & Lees, 1986). Further, the signs and symptoms of akathisia and tardive dyskinesia have been found to co-exist relatively commonly in psychiatric patients receiving maintenance treatment with antipsychotic drugs (Barnes & Braude, 1985). In such cases there may be difficulty in discriminating between the restless movements of akathisia, the abnormal movements of tardive dystonia and tardive dyskinesia, and motor disturbances such as tics, sterotypies and mannerisms which are related to the schizophrenia illness.

To add to the diagnostic confusion, in patients on long-term antipsychotic medication several variants of the acute akathisia picture have been identified. A few patients manifest obvious, complex, repetitive movements resembling those seen in acute akathisia, but do not report a sense of inner restlessness or a compulsion to move. This condition has been called pseudo-akathisia (Munetz & Cornes, 1982; Barnes & Braude, 1985).

A tardive akathisia variant has also been identified which emerges during chronic drug treatment and is unresponsive to anticholinergic agents. Both the subjective and objective components are present. The condition is associated with oro-facial dyskinesia and shares the pharmacological characteristics of tardive dyskinesia in that it is exacerbated or provoked by drug dose reduction or withdrawal, and improves, at least temporarily, when the dose is increased (Fahn, 1983; Braude & Barnes, 1983; Barnes & Braude, 1985). Whether these akathisia subtypes represent stages in the progression of the condition is unclear. Whilst the natural history of akathisia remains obscure, there is some evidence that the feelings of restlessness and associated distress may become less intense with time.

Pathophysiology

There is no satisfactory explanation of the pathophysiological mechanism underlying the development of akathisia. For acute akathisia, Marsden & Jenner (1980) have suggested that the condition may result from dopamine receptor blockade in the mesocortical dopamine system. This notion is based upon influential animal work that suggests that the prefrontal dopamine system may exert an inhibitory influence on spontaneous locomotor behaviour (Carter & Pycock, 1980; Pycock *et al.*, 1980). Lesions of the prefrontal cortex can lead to increased activity in the subcortical dopamine systems with a concomitant increase in locomotor activity. In man, dopamine blockade in the mesocortical system by drugs may lead to a similar increase in locomotor activity, manifested as the restlessness of akathisia.

Recently, it was suggested that the capacity for antipsychotic drugs to ligate with iron was relevant to their ability to induce akathisia (Blake *et al.*, 1986; Pall *et al.*, 1986). These authors noted the association between iron deficiency and Ekbom's syndrome, or restless legs syndrome, a condition which has some similarity to akathisia (Ekbom, 1960). They speculated that there might be a similar association with akathisia and this proved to be the case in a study by Brown *et al.* (1987) in which patients with akathisia were found to have significantly lower serum iron levels compared with non-akathisic controls. The proposed mechanism was that low serum iron produces dopamine D_2 receptor hypofunction which in turn renders patients on antipsychotic drugs particularly susceptible to the development of akathisia. Further investigation of this intriguing relationship between akathisia and iron status is warranted.

Tardive dyskinesia

Clinical features

The core sign of this condition is oro-facial dyskinesia, being the most familiar and prevalent feature of the condition. The syndrome was first described by Schonecker (1957) within 5 years of the introduction of antipsychotic drugs. It comprises involuntary movements of the tongue, jaw and face, such as protrusion or twisting of the tongue, lip smacking, puffing of the cheeks, pursing and sucking actions of the lips, chewing or lateral jaw movements and movements of the peri-orbital muscles. The particular combinations of movements seen vary considerably between patients, but tend to be relatively consistent for an individual. In addition to oro-facial movements, abnormal involuntary movements of the trunk and limbs, usually described as choreiform or choreo-athetoid, are commonly included within the syndrome.

Patients rarely complain of tardive dyskinesia, being unaware of the movements in most cases. The patient's friends and relatives are often not conscious of the movements as a discrete condition, accepting them as part of the person's behaviour. This may reflect the fact that such movements are familiar as a natural consequence of aging in that a syndrome of oro-facial dyskinesia, indistinguishable from tardive dyskinesia, is seen in 5–15% of elderly people of who have never received antipsychotic drugs (Blowers, 1982; Kane *et al.*, 1982; Varga *et al.*, 1982).

Subsyndromes of tardive dyskinesia

The results of a series of studies (Kidger *et al.*, 1980; Barnes *et al.*, 1983*a*; 1983*b*) suggested that oro-facial and trunk and limb dyskinesia should be considered as separate clinical subsyndromes that are pathophysiologically distinct. This conclusion is supported by other epidemiological studies in which the two subsyndromes have emerged as discrete phenomenological clusters following the application of multivariate statistical methods

(Crane *et al.*, 1971; Kennedy *et al.*, 1971; Glazer *et al.*, 1988). From their findings, Glazer *et al.* (1988) concluded that the subsyndromes may have different prognostic and aetiological determinants. In addition, several pharmacological investigations have discovered a discrepant response between oro-facial and trunk and limb dyskinesia (see Barnes & Weller, 1986), reinforcing the notion that different pathophysiological mechanisms underlie the two subsyndromes.

Further support for these subsyndromes is provided by a report by Waddington and colleagues (1987) who found a strong association between both cognitive dysfunction and negative symptoms and the presence and severity of oro-facial dyskinesia in chronic schizophrenic patients. However, there was no such association with trunk and limb movements, additional evidence that these two regional distributions of dyskinesia do not constitute a unitary syndrome.

Prevalence

Comprehensive reviews of the relevant literature have concluded that there has been a true increase in the prevalence of tardive dyskinesia in the last 20 years. However, the reported prevalence figures vary widely, from 0.5 to 56%, with a mean 20% (Kane & Smith, 1982). In more elderly samples, figures of around 50% are relatively common. However, once the condition has developed it does not tend to show a steady increase in severity, and follow-up studies reveal a fluctuating course with spontaneous remissions (Barnes *et al.*, 1983*a*; Casey, 1983; Bergen *et al.*, 1989).

In a prospective study of tardive dyskinesia, Kane (1987) found an incidence of 4% a year over the first 6 years of treatment with antipsychotic drugs. Although patients may be at a relatively high risk of developing the condition in the first few years of drug therapy (Casey & Toenniessen, 1985), nevertheless, it seems that the majority of patients receiving antipsychotic medication will not develop tardive dyskinesia. The identification of factors contributing to individual vulnerability to the condition should be of help in its prediction and in the development of strategies to minimize the risk of development. Furthermore determining the clinical correlates of dyskinesia may give some clue to the possible clinical implications of developing this movement disorder.

Risk factors

Examining treatment variables, the evidence that antipsychotic drugs have a causal role is circumstantial but nonetheless convincing. First, although tardive dyskinesia is frequently described in schizophrenia, bipolar affective disorder and dementia, it cannot be explained simply as a manifestation of psychotic illness. It has been regularly reported in non-psychotic patients with a variety of diagnoses, the common factor being treatment with antipsychotic drugs (Gerlach, 1979).

Secondly, the prevalence of oro-facial and trunk and limb dyskinesia in patients treated with antipsychotics has been found to be consistently higher than in samples of untreated patients, although such groups have tended not to be matched on a number of important variables (Jeste & Wyatt, 1981). Kane & Smith (1982) used data pooled from a large number of surveys and found a mean prevalence of 20% for patients receiving drugs, compared with a figure of 5% for untreated cases. In a study by Owens *et al.* (1982) the prevalence of abnormal involuntary movements in a population of schizophrenic patients with a history of antipsychotic drug treatment was compared with a similar population who had received such medication. Owens (1985) grouped the movement items on the rating scale into syndromes and concluded that oro-facial dyskinesia was significantly associated with past drug treatment. However, he points out that such movements were seen in 30% of those cases never treated with drugs.

Thirdly, there has been a steady increase in reported prevalence since antipsychotics were introduced, which is compatible with an increasing number of patients being exposed to these agents. This evidence supports the notion that receiving antipsychotic medication makes a strong contribution to the development of tardive dyskinesia.

However, no clear association has been shown between developing tardive dyskinesia and drug variables such as the length of time a patient has been receiving medication, the total amount of drug administered, the type or class of drug, or current dosage (Kane & Smith, 1982; Barnes *et al.*, 1983*a*; Morgenstern *et al.*, 1987). One explanation for this absence of a convincing dose-risk relationship in tardive dyskinesia is that most patients studied have been receiving doses of antipsychotic drugs so excessive that they would overwhelm and obscure any relationship which existed (Baldessarini *et al.*, 1988). These authors consider that the risk of tardive dyskinesia may well turn out to be dependent on dose when 'low-effective doses are evaluated and excessive doses are avoided'.

'Drug holidays' for patients on long-term antipsychotic treatment was first advocated as a beneficial strategy by Ayd in 1966. He suggested that intermittent therapy might reduce the risk of developing dyskinesia. The American College of Neuropsychopharmacology — Food and Drug Administration Task Force (1973) supported this notion. However, the findings of clinical studies that have investigated this treatment variable have suggested that rather than reduce the likelihood of tardive dyskinesia, interruptions of drug therapy may increase the risk of persistent dyskinesia as well as the risk of relapse (Jeste *et al.*, 1979; Goldman & Luchins, 1984).

The prescription of anticholinergic drugs has also been considered a possible risk factor. It is a commonplace clinical observation that anticholinergic medication exacerbates existing tardive dyskinesia and that stopping anticholinergics usually improves the condition. A number of studies have found a positive relationship between the severity of tardive dyskinesia and the administration of anticholinergic drugs (Kane & Smith, 1982). However, Gardos & Cole (1983) recently reviewed the evidence for long-term anticholinergic drug administration acting as a risk factor for tardive dyskinesia and found no convincing evidence to support this widely-held notion.

The most important patient variable is undoubtedly age. Advancing age is the factor most consistently predicting an increased risk of tardive dyskinesia. Examining pooled epidemiological data, Smith & Baldessarini (1980) found a strong linear correlation between age and both the prevalence and severity of tardive dyskinesia. In most studies advancing age has been found to be associated with an increased occurrence of tardive dyskinesia, greater severity and a reduced likelihood of spontaneous remission. Smith & Baldessarini (1980) found that tardive dyskinesia in those less than 60 years of age was over three times more likely to remit spontaneously.

It seems likely that the relationship between quantity of antipsychotic treatment and vulnerability to tardive dyskinesia varies with age. However, such a relationship has not been systematically tested. In the minority of studies where a relationship between specific drug variables and tardive dyskinesia has been found, it has been within the first few years of treatment. Csernansky and co-authors (1983) have suggested that in younger, less chronic patients, specific drug exposure may be more important. They consider that tardive dyskinesia developing in such cases may be more directly drug-related than in cases where tardive dyskinesia develops after prolonged drug administration in patients who are likely therefore to be older, and in whom other non-drug variables are likely to be relevant, and obscure any positive relationship with drug variables. The distinction between early and late dyskinesia may be worthy of further study (Barnes, 1987*a*, *b*).

Looking at the influence of gender, a relatively consistent finding has been that women show a greater prevalence of severe dyskinesia, although the available evidence suggests that this is limited to the geriatric age range. Rather than a direct reflection of gender, it has been variously speculated that female sex is a proxy variable for longer duration of hospitalization, higher drug dose and longer duration of treatment.

Early reports on tardive dyskinesia raised the question of an association with brain damage. Several studies have employed a variety of very indirect and tentative measures of brain damage such as evidence of epilepsy or alcoholism, or a history of various physical treatments including leucotomy. Only a few of these studies have revealed an association between brain damage and tardive dyskinesia (see Barnes & Liddle, 1985). However, in several surveys of large samples of psychiatric inpatients tardive dyskinesia has been found to be more prevalent in patients with organic mental syndromes such as epilepsy or mental retardation than in those with schizophrenia (Hunter *et al* 1964; Crane & Paulson, 1967; Yassa *et al.*, 1984).

Computerized tomographic brain scan data from a number of studies have revealed differences between patients with and without tardive dyskinesia, suggesting more structural damage in those cases with the abnormal movements (Famuyiwa *et al.*, 1979; Golden *et al.*, 1980; Bartels & Themelis, 1983). For example, Owens *et al.* (1980) reported a 'linear relationship ... between increasing VBR and increasing prevalence of movement disorders'.

Soft neurological signs including such deficiencies as poor coordination, suggest neurological impairment but lack precise cerebral localization. Wagner *et al.* (1985) selected a battery of tests for soft signs which they considered would not be confounded by the presence of dyskinesia. They compared schizophrenic patients with and without tardive dyskinesia and found a positive relationship between the number of soft signs and tardive dyskinesia. Similarly, Waddington *et al.* (1987) reported a strong association between the presence of developmental, or primitive, reflexes and tardive dyskinesia.

In the same study by Wegner *et al.* (1985), schizophrenic patients with dyskinesia performed significantly more poorly on tests of intellectual function, and the balance of evidence from more recent work confirms this association (Barnes & Liddle, 1985; Waddington *et al.*, 1987). Overall, the findings suggest that signs of organic brain damage may be commoner in patients with tardive dyskinesia.

Susceptibility to drug-induced extrapyramidal side effects as a predictor of tardive dyskinesia was first suggested by Crane in 1972. He considered that tardive dyskinesia was more likely to emerge in patients with drug-induced parkinsonism than in patients not developing this early side effect. A variety of study findings and case report material suggest that patients presenting with symptoms of parkinsonism, acute akathisia and acute dystonic reactions are more likely to manifest tardive dyskinesia (Chouinard *et al.*, 1979; Munetz & Cornes, 1982; Barnes & Braude, 1984; Yassa *et al* 1985).

Kane and co-workers (1984), analysing the data from their 5 year follow-up study, claim that a history of early clinically significant parkinsonism may indicate susceptibility to the subsequent development of tardive dyskinesia, particularly for those patients developing tardive dyskinesia within the first 2 years of exposure to antipsychotic drugs.

Turning to psychiatric diagnosis as a relevant variable, recent work has highlighted affective disturbances as possibly relevant. Both a positive family history of affective disorder, and the presence of depressive features, have been mooted as markers of an increased likelihood of developing both parkinsonism side-effects and tardive dyskinesia, but the evidence is tentative at present (see Barnes, 1987*a*).

Considering next a primary diagnosis of affective disorder, Davis and coworkers in 1976 were struck by a relatively high prevalence of tardive dyskinesia among patients with primary affective disorder, especially depressed patients treated with antipsychotic drugs.

From the preliminary data of the prospective study by Kane *et al.* (1985) psychiatric diagnosis does appear to be a relevant variable. A life-table analysis based on the length of drug administration, and comparing the cumulative incidence of tardive dyskinesia in patients with affective or schizo-affective disorder with that of inpatients with a diagnosis of schizophrenia, revealed that the former have a significantly greater incidence after 6 years of exposure to antipsychotic drugs. The incidence figures were 26% for affective and schizo-affective patients compared with 18% for those with schizophrenia.

Mukherjee *et al.* (1986) found persistent tardive dyskinesia in 35% of a sample of bipolar patients who had received maintenance antipsychotic drugs, while no patients without such a drug history had persistent dyskinesia. This work raises the possibility that bipolar patients treated with maintenance antipsychotic drugs 'may well be at a high risk for developing tardive dyskinesia and this may tend to be the persistent type.'

Finally, the schizophrenic illness itself may be a risk factor (Barnes & Liddle, 1985). Descriptions of abnormal movements similar to tardive dyskinesia appeared in the literature long before the advent of antipsychotic drugs (Kraepelin, 1919; Farran-Ridge, 1926; Jones & Hunter, 1969). Thus, schizophrenia is associated with a tendency to develop abnormal involuntary movements, and Owens (1985) has propounded the notion that antipsychotic drugs act, promote or exacerbate a tendency to develop spontaneous movement disorders inherent in at least some forms of the illness. He has suggested that tardive dyskinesia is part of the Type II syndrome of schizophrenia. If this were true, one would expect tardive dyskinesia to be commoner in patients with negative features of schizophrenia. Reviews of studies that have examined this issue seems to support this view (Barnes & Liddle, 1985; Waddington, 1987). A consistent finding has been a significant association between tardive dyskinesia and blunting of affect. Tardive dyskinesia has also been found to be variously associated with other negative schizophrenic features including social and emotional withdrawal, psychomotor retardation, self-neglect and muteness (Itil *et al.*, 1981; McCreadie *et al.*, 1982; Glazer *et al.*, 1984; Waddington & Youssef, 1986). Our own study has yielded similar findings, with a strong positive association between dyskinesia score and scores for poverty of speech and blunted affect (Barnes, 1987*a*).

The main clinical implication of an association between tardive dyskinesia and negative symptoms is that schizophrenic patients developing dyskinesia may have a poorer prognosis than their non-dyskinetic fellows. The predictive value of abnormal movements in this regard may be true for schizophrenic patients whether or not antipsychotic drugs have been administered. Yarden & DiScipio (1971) reported on a sample of young, drug-free schizophrenic patients presenting with a variety of abnormal movements, labelled as choreiform and athetoid, and including tics, stereotypies and mannerisms. Their follow-up data, after $2\frac{1}{2}$ to $3\frac{1}{2}$ years, led them to conclude that schizophrenic patients distinguished by abnormal movements constituted a group with an early onset, a steadily progressive course, severe deterioration with marked thought disorder and a resistance to pharmacological treatment. They considered choreiform movements to be a 'grave prognostic sign'

Treatment

Despite the apparently endless list of putative treatments for tardive dyskinesia that have been tested, no very satisfactory drug therapy has emerged. Drug and Therapeutics Bulletin (Anonymous, 1986*b*) recommends tetrabenazine for severe cases, but the drug can have serious side-effects and the therapeutic effect may decline over time. More recent remedies for which some success is claimed include calcium channel blockers such as verapamil and diltiazem (Barrow & Childs, 1986; Ross *et al.*, 1987) and alpha-tocopherol (vitamin E) (Lohr *et al.*, 1987) but double-blind, controlled trials are needed to substantiate the initial optimistic reports.

The initial response to the development of tardive dyskinesia should be to prescribe antipsychotic drugs only where the indication is clear. Drug treatment should be continued only where there is evidence of clinical benefit, and then at the minimum effective dose. Interruptions of drug treatment should be avoided. Concurrent anticholinergic agents worsen tardive dyskinesia and should be stopped, if this is possible without precipitating parkinsonism of a moderate to severe degree. The decision to prescribe these drugs for patients with affective disorder should take account of the particular risk of early dyskinesia in such patients. All these considerations apply particularly to patients over 50 years of age.

There is no strong evidence that any antipsychotic drug has a lower liability to cause tardive dyskinesia. Claims have been made for sulpiride (Anonymous, 1984) and clozapine (Marder & Van Putten, 1988) in this regard, but these remain to be substantiated.

References

Adler, L., Angrist, B., Peselow, B. *et al.* (1986): A controlled assessment of propranolol in the treatment of neuroleptic-induced akathisia. *Br. J. Psychiatry* **149**, 42–45.

Adler, L.A., Reiter, S., Corwin, J. *et al.* (1987*a*): Differential effects of benztropine and propanolol in akathisia. *Psychopharm. Bull.* **23**, 519–521.

Adler, L.A., Angrist, B., Peselow, B. *et al.*, (1987*b*): Clondine in neuroleptic-induced akathisia. *Am. J. Psychiatry* **144**, 235–136.

Adler, L., Angrist, B., Duncan, E. *et al.* (1989): Beta blockers in akathisia updated: toward understanding the effect (abstract). *Schizophrenia Res.* **2**, 241.

American College of Neuropsychopharmacology — Food and Drug Administration Task Force (1973): Neurologic syndromes associated with antipsychotic drug use. *N Eng. J. Med.* **289**, 20–23.

Anonymous (1984): Sulpiride: an advance in neuroleptics? *Drug. Ther. Bull.* **22**, 31–32.

Anonymous (1986*a*): Akathisia and antipsychotic drugs. *Lancet* **ii**, 1131–1132.

Anonymous (1986*b*): The management of tardive dyskinesia. *Drug. Ther. Bull.* **24**, 27–28.

Ayd, F.J. (1961): A summary of drug-induced extrapyramidal reactions. *Am. Med. Assoc.* **175**: 1054–1060.

Ayd, F.J. (1966): Drug holidays: intermittent pharmacotherapy for psychiatric patients. *Int. Drug Ther. Newsletter* **8**, 1–3.

Baldessarini, R.J., Cohen, B.M. & Teicher, M.H. (1988): Significance of neuroleptic dose and plasma level in the pharmacological treatment of psychosis. *Arch. Gen. Psychiatry* **45**, 79–91.

Barnes, T.R.E. (1987*a*): The present status of tardive dyskinesia and akathisia in the treatment of schizophrenia. *Psychiatr. Devel.* **4**, 301–319.

Barnes, T.R.E. (1987*b*): Dopamine, schizophrenia and two types of tardive dyskinesia. Proceedings of the Summer Meeting of the British Association of Psychopharmacology 1987. *J. Psychopharmacol.* **1**, (Abstract).

Barnes, T.R.E. (1988): Tardive dyskinesia *Br. Med. J.* **296**, 150–151.

Barnes, T.R.E. & Braude, W.M. (1984): Persistent akathisia associated with early tardive dyskinesia. *Postgrad. Med. J.* **60**, 51–53.

Barnes, T.R.E. & Braude, W.M. (1985): Akathisia variants and tardive dyskinesia. *Arch. Gen. Psychiatry* **42**, 874–878.

Barnes, T.R.E. & Liddle, P.F. (1985): Tardive dyskinesia: implications for schizophrenia? In *Schizophrenia: New pharmacological and clinical developments* eds A.A. Schiff, M. Roth & H.L. Freeman. pp. 81–87. London: Royal Society of Medicine Services.

Barnes, T.R.E. & Weller, M.P.I. (1986): Movement disorders and neuroleptic medication. In *Movement disorders*, eds N.S. Shah & A.G. Donald, pp. 323–341. New York: Plenum Medical.

Barnes, T.R.E., Kidger, T. & Gore, S.M. (1983*a*): Tardive dyskinesia: a 3-year follow-up study. *Psychol. Med.* **13**, 71–81.

Barnes, T.R.E., Rossoe, M. & Trauer, T. (1983*b*): A comparison of purposeless movements in psychiatric patients treated with antipsychotic drugs and normal individuals. *J. Neurol. Neurosurg. Psychiatry* **46**, 540–546.

Barrow, N. & Childs, A. (1986): An anti-tardive dyskinesia effect of verapamil. *Am. J. Psychiatry* **343**, 1485.

Bartels, M. & Themelis, J. (1983): Computerised tomography in tardive dyskinesia. *Arch. Psychiatry. Neurolog. Science* **233**, 371–379.

Bergen, J.A., Eyland E.A., Campbell, J.A. *et al.* (1989): The course of tardive dyskinesia in patients on long-term neuroleptics. *Br J. Psychiatry* **154**, 523–528.

Bing, R. (1939): *Textbook of nervous diseases*, 5th ed. London: Henry Kimpton.

Blake, D.R., Williams, A.C. & Pall, H. (1986): Iron and akathisia. *Br. Med. J.* **292**: 1393.

Blowers, A.J., Borison, R.L., Blowers, C.M. *et al.* (1982): Abnormal involuntary movements in the elderly. *Br. J. Psychiatry* **139**, 363–364.

Braude, W.M. & Barnes, T.R.E. (1983): Late-onset akathisia: an indicant of covert dyskinesia — two case reports. *Am. J. Psychiatry* **140**, 611–612.

Braude, W.M., Barnes, T.R.E. & Gore, S.M. (1983): Clinical characteristics of akathisia: a systematic investigation of acute psychiatric inpatient admissions. *Br. J. Psychiatry* **143**, 139–150.

Braude, W.M., Charles, I.P. & Barnes, T.R.E. (1984): Course, jerky, foot tremor: tremographic investigation of an objective sign of acute akathisia. *Psychopharmacol.* **82**, 95–101.

Brown, K.W. Glen, S.E. & White, T. (1987): Low serum iron status and akathisia. *Lancet* **i**, 1234–1236.

Carter, C.J. & Pycock, C.J. (1980): Behavioural and biochemical effects of dopamine and noradrenaline depletion within the medical prefrontal cortex of the rat. *Brain Res.* **192**, 163–176.

Casey, D.E. (1983): Tardive dyskinesia: what is the natural history. *Int. Drug Ther. Newsletter* **18**, 13–16.

Casey, D.E. & Toenniessen, L.M. (1983): Neuroleptic treatment in tardive dyskinesia: Can it be divided into a clinical strategy for long-term treatment? *Mod. Prob. Pharmacopsychiatry* **21**, 65–79.

Chouinard, G., Annable, L. & Ross-Chouinard, A. (1979): Factors related to tardive dyskinesia. *Am J. Psychiatry* **136**, 79–83.

Crane, G.E. (1972): Pseudoparkinson and tardive dyskinesia. *Arch. Neurol.* **27**, 426–430.

Crane, G.E. & Paulson, G. (1967): Involuntary movements in a sample of chronic mental patients and their relation to the treatment with neuroleptics. *Int. J. Neurol.* **3**, 286–291.

Crane, G.E., Naranjo, E.K. & Chase, C. (1971): Motor disorders induced by neuroleptics — A proposed new classification. *Arch. Gen. Psychiatry* **24**, 179–184.

Csernansky, J.G., Kaplan, J., Holman, C.A. *et al.* (1983): Serum neuroleptic activity, prolactin, and tardive dyskinesia in schizophrenic outpatients. *Psychopharmacology* **81**, 115–118.

Davis, K., Berger, P. & Hollister, L. (1976): Tardive dyskinesia and depressive illness. *Psychopharmacol. Communic.* **2**, 125.

Drake, R.E. & Erlich, J. (1985): Suicide attempts associated with akathisia. *Am. J. Psychiatry* **142**, 499–501.

Ekbom, K.A. (1960): Restless legs syndrome. *Neurology* **10**, 868–873.

Fahn, S. (1983): Long-term treatment of tardive dyskinesia with presynaptically acting dopamine-depleting agents. In *Advances of neurology, Volume 37: Experimental therapeutics of movement disorders*, eds S. Fahn, D.B. Calne, & I. Shoulson. pp. 267–276. New York: Raven Press.

Famuyiwa, O.O., Eccleston, D., Donaldson, A.A. *et al.*, (1979): Tardive dyskinesia and dementia. *Br. J. Psychiatry* **135**, 500–504.

Farran-Ridge, C. (1926): Some symptoms referable to the basal ganglia occurring in dementia praecox and epidemic encephalitis. *J. Ment. Sci.* **72**, 513–523.

Friis, T., Rosted Christensen, T. & Gerlach, J. (1983): Sodium valproate and biperiden in neuroleptic-induced akathisia, parkinsonism and hyperkinesia. *Acta Psychiatr. Scandinavica* **67**, 178–187.

Gardos, G. & Cole, J.O. (1983): Tardive dyskinesia and anticholinergic drugs. *Am. J. Psychiatry*

140, 200–202.

Gerlach, J. (1979): Tardive dyskinesia. *Danish Med. Bull.* **26**, 209–245.

Gibb, W.R.G. & Lees, A.J. (1986): The clinical phenomenon of akathisia. *J. Neurol. Neurosurg. Psychiatry* **49**, 861–866.

Glazer, W.M., Moore, D.L., Schooler, N.R. *et al.* (1984): Tardive dyskinesia, a discontinuation study. *Arch. Gen. Psychiatry* **41**, 623–627.

Glazer, W.M., Morgenstern, H., Niedwiecki, D. *et al.* (1988): Heterogeneity of tardive dyskinesia: a multivariate analysis. *Br. J. Psychiatry* **152**, 253–259.

Golden, C.J., Moses, J.A., Zelazowski, R. *et al.* (1980): Cerebral ventricular size and neuropsychological impairment in chronic schizophrenics. *Arch. Gen. Psychiatry* **37**, 619–623.

Goldman, M.B. & Luchins, D.J. (1984): Intermittent neuroleptic therapy and tardive dyskinesia: a literature review. *Hosp. Community Psychiatry* **35**, 1215–1219.

Haskovec, L. (1903): Nouvelles remarques sur l'akathisia. *Nouvelles iconographie de la Salpetriere* **16**, 287–293.

Hunter, R., Earl. C.J. & Thornicroft, S. (1964): An apparently irreversible syndrome of abnormal movements following phenothiazine medication. *Proc. R. Soc. Med.* **57**, 758.

Itil, T.M., Reisberg, B., Huque, M. *et al.* (1981): Clinical profiles of tardive dyskinesia. *Compr. Psychiatry.* **22**, 282–290.

Iversen, S.D. (1971): The effect of surgical lesions to frontal cortex and substantia nigra on amphetamine responses in rats. *Brain Res.* **31**, 295–311.

Jeste, D.V. & Wyatt, R.J. (1981): Changing epidemiology of tardive dyskinesia: an overview. *Am. J. Psychiatry* **138**, 297–309.

Jeste, D.V., Potkin, S.G., Sinha, S. *et al.* (1979): Tardive dyskinesia — reversible and persistent. *Arch. Gen. Psychiatry* **36**, 585–590.

Jones, M. & Hunter, R. (1969): Abnormal movements in patients with chronic psychiatric illness. In *Psychotropic drugs and dysfunctions of the basal ganglia*, ed. G.E. Crane & R. Gardner, pp. 53–65. Washington: US Public Health Service.

Kane, J.M. (1988): Most encountered problems in chronic treatment for patients. In *Depot neuroleptics: A consensus.* ed. T.R.E. Barnes. pp. 33–39. Mediscript, London.

Kane, J.M. & Smith, J.M. (1982): Tardive dyskinesia: prevalence and risk factors 1959–1979. *Arch. Gen. Psychiatry* **39**, 473–481.

Kane, J.M., Weinhold, P. & Kinon, B. (1982): Prevalence of abnormal involuntary movements ('spontaneous dyskinesias') in the normal elderly. *Psychopharmacology* **77**, 105–108.

Kane, J.M., Woerner, M., Weinhold, P. *et al.* (1984): Incidence of tardive dyskinesia: five-year data from a prospective study. *Psychopharmacol. Bull.* **20**, 39–40.

Kane, J.M., Woerner, M. & Leiberman, J. (1985): Tardive dyskinesia: prevalence, incidence and risk factors. In *Dyskinesia — research and treatment*, eds D.E. Casey, T.N. Chase, A.V. Christensen *et al.*, pp. 72–78. Berlin: Springer-Verlag.

Kekich, W.A. (1985) Violence as a manifestation of akathisia. *J. Am. Med. Assoc.* **240**, 2185.

Kennedy, P.F. Hershon, H.I. & McGuire, R.J. (1971): Extrapyramidal disorders after prolonged phenothiazine therapy. *Br. J. Psychiatry* **118**, 509–518.

Kidger, T., Barnes, T.R.E., Trauer, T. *et al.* (1980): Sub-syndromes of tardive dyskinesia. *Psychol. Med.* **10**, 513–520.

Koob, G.F., Stinus, L. & Le Moal, M. (1981): Hyperactivity and hypoactivity produced by lesions to the mesolimbic dopamine system. *Behav. Brain. Res.* **3**, 341–359.

Kraepelin, E.P. (1919): *Dementia praecox and paraphrenia*, ed. G.M. Robertson. Edinburgh: Livingstone.

Kruse, W. (1960): Persistent muscular restlessness after phenothiazine treatment, report of three cases. *Am. J. Psychiatry.* **117**, 152–153.

Kumar, B.B. (1979): An unusual case of akathisia. *Am. J. Psychiatry.* **136**, 1088.

Lipinski, J.F., Zubenko, G.S., Cohen, B.M. *et al.* (1983): Propranolol in the treatment of neuroleptic-induced akathisia. *Am. J. Psychiatry* **141**, 412–415.

Lohr, J.B., Cadet, J.L., Lohr, M.A. *et al.* (1987): Alpha-tocopherol in tardive dyskinesia. *Lancet* **i**, 913–914.

Marsden, C.D., Tarsy, D. & Baldessarini, R.J. (1975): Spontaneous and drug-induced movement disorders in psychotic patients. In *Psychiatric aspects of neurological disease,* eds D.F. Benson &

D. Blumer, pp. 219–266. New York: Grune and Stratton.
Marsden, C.D. & Jenner, P. (1980): The pathophysiology of extrapyramidal side-effects of neuroleptic drugs. *Psychol. Med.* **10**, 55–72.
McCreadie, R.G., Barron, E.T. & Winslow, G.S. (1982): The Nithsdale schizophrenia survey: II. Abnormal movements. *Br. J. Psychiatry* **140**, 587–590.
Morgenstern, H., Glazer, W.M., Gibowski, L.D. *et al.* (1987): Predictors of tardive dyskinesia: results of a cross-sectional study in an outpatient population. *J. Chronic Dis.* **40**, 319–317.
Mukherjee, S., Rosen, A.M., Caracci, G. *et al.* (1986): Persistent tardive dyskinesia in bipolar patients *Arch. Gen. Psychiatry* **43**, 342–346.
Munetz, M.R. & Cornes, C.L. (1982): Akathisia, pseudoakathisia and tardive dyskinesia: clinical examples. *Compr. Psychiatry* **23**, 345–352.
Oppenheim, H. (1911): *Textbook of nervous diseases for physicians and students.* Edinburgh: Otto Schulze and Co.
Owens, D.G.C. (1985): Involuntary disorders of movement in chronic schizophrenia — the role of the illness and its treatment. In *Dyskinesia — research and treatment*, eds D.E. Casey, T.N. Chase, A.V. Christensen *et al.*, pp. 79–87. Berlin: Springer-Verlag.
Owens, D.G.C. Johnstone, E.C., Crow, T.J. *et al.* (1985): Lateral ventricular size in schizophrenia: relationship to the disease process and its clinical manifestations. *Psycholog. Med.* **15**, 27–41.
Pall, H.S., Williams, A.C. & Blake, D.R. (1986): Iron, akathisia and antipsychotic drugs. *Lancet* **ii**, 1469.
Pycock, C.J., Kerwin, R.W. & Carter, C.J. (1980): Effect of lesions of cortical dopamine terminals on subcortical dopamine receptors in rats. *Nature* **186**, 74–76.
Ross, J.L., Mackenzie, T.B., Hanson, D.R. *et al.*, (1987): Diltiazem for tardive dyskinesia. *Lancet* **i**, 268.
Schonecker M. (1957): Ein eigentumliches Syndrom im oralen Bereich bei Megaphenapplikation. *Nervenarzt* **28**, 35–42.
Schulte, J.R. (1989): Homicide and suicide associated with akathisia and haloperidol. *Am. J. Forensic Psychiatry* **6**, 3–7.
Shear, K., Frances, A. & Weiden, P. (1983): Suicide associated with akathisia and depot fluphenazine treatment. *J. Clinical Psychopharmacol.* 3, 235–236.
Sicard, J.A. (1923): Akathisia and tasikinesia. *La Presse Medicale* **31**, 265–266.
Sigwald, J., Grossiord, A., Duriel, P. *et al.* (1947): Le traitement de la maladie de Parkinson et des manifestations extrapyramidales par le diethylaminoethyl *n*-thiodiphenylamine (2987 RP): resultats d'une année d'application. *Rev. Neurol.* (Paris) **79**, 683–687.
Smith, J.M. & Baldessarini, R.J. (1980): Changes in prevalence, severity and recovery in tardive dyskinesia with age. *Arch. Gen. Psychiatry* **37**, 1368–1373.
Souvner, R. & DiMascio, A. (1978): Extrapyramidal syndromes and other neurological side-effects of psychotropic drugs. In *Psychopharmacology: A generation of progress,* eds M.A. Lipton, A. DiMascio & K.F. Killam, pp. 1021–1032. New York: Raven Press.
Steck, H. (1954): Le syndrome extrapyramidal et diencephalique au cours des traitments au largactil et au Serpasil. *Annales Medico-psychologique* **112**, 734–743.
Tassin, J.P., Stinus, L., Simon, M. *et al.*, (1978): Relationship between the locomotor hyperactivity induced by A10 lesions and the destruction of the frontocortical dopaminergic innervation in the rat. *Brain Res.* **141**, 267–281.
Van Putten, T. (1974): Why do schizophrenic patients refuse to take their drugs? *Arch. Gen. Psychiatry* **31**, 67–72.
Van Putten, T. (1975): The many faces of akathisia. *Compr. Psychiatry* **16**, 43–47.
Van Putten, T. & Marder, S.R. (1986): Toward a more reliable diagnosis of akathisia *Arch. Gen. Psychiatry* **43**, 1015–1016.
Van Putten, T. & Marder, S.R. (1987): Behavioural toxicity of antipsychotic drugs. *J. Clin. Psychiatry* **48**, (Supplement 9): 13–19.
Varga, E., Sugerman, A.A., Varga, V. *et al.* (1982): Prevalence of spontaneous oral dyskinesia in the elderly. *Am. J. Psychiatry* **139**, 329–331.
Waddington, J. & Youssef, H.A. (1986): Late onset involuntary movements in chronic schizophrenia: Relationship of 'tardive' dyskinesia to intellectual impairment and negative symptoms. *Br. J. Psychiatry* **149**, 616–620.

Waddington, J.L., Youssef, H.A., Dolphin, C. *et al.* (1987): Cognitive dysfunction, negative symptoms and tardive dyskinesia in schizophrenia. *Arch. Gen. Psychiatry* **44**, 907–912.
Wegner, J.T., Catalano, F. Gibralter, J. *et al.* (1988): Schizophrenics with tardive dyskinesia: Neuropsychological deficit and family psychopathology. *Arch. Gen. Psychiatry* **42**, 860–865.
Weiden, P., Mann, J.J., Haas, G. *et al.* (1987): Clinical non-recognition of neuroleptic-induced movement disorders: a cautionary study. *Am. J. Psychiatry* **144**, 1148–1153.
Wilbur, R. & Kulik, A.V. (1983): Propranolol for akathisia *Lancet* **ii**, 917.
Yarden, P.E. & DiScipio, W.J. (1971): Abnormal movements and progress in schizophrenia. *Am. J. Psychiatry* **128**, 317–323.
Yassa, R., Ghadirian, A.M. & Schwartz, G. (1988): Tardive dyskinesia: developmental factors. *Can J. Psychiatry* **30**, 344–347.
Yassa, R., Nair, V. & Schwartz, G. (1984): Tardive dyskinesia and the primary psychiatric diagnosis. *Psychosomatics* **25**, 135–138.
Zubenko, G.S., Lipinski, J.F., Cohen, B.M. *et al.* (1984): Comparison of metroprolol and propranolol in the treatment of akathisia. *Psychiatr. Res.* **11**, 143–149.
Zubenko, G.S., Cohen, B.M., Lipinski, J.F. *et al.* (1984): Use of clonidine in treating neuroleptic-induced akathisia. *Psychiatr. Res.* **13**, 253–259.

Chapter 20

New possibilities for the drug treatment of schizophrenia

B. J. Jones*

Department of Neuropharmacology, Glaxo Group Research Ltd, Ware, Hertforshire, SG12 ODP, UK

Summary

The drug treatment of schizophrenia is hopefully entering a new era. There is a growing belief that we have little more to gain by developing additional dopamine receptor blocking drugs; a fresh approach is required. Considerable interest has been generated by antagonists of sigma, 5-HT_2 and 5-HT_3 receptors as potential antipsychotic drugs. Of these, the 5-HT_3 receptor antagonists are the most appealing. From the available evidence, we can deduce that 5-HT_3 receptors in the brain are activated only during periods of high neuronal activity. Consequently, 5-HT_3 receptor antagonists do not affect normal neuronal function, but they do inhibit overactive dopaminergic neurones. This presents the exciting possibility that the 5-HT_3 receptor antagonists may be the first antipsychotic drugs to be devoid of side effects.

Introduction

Our understanding of the neurochemical basis of schizophrenia has been dominated by the 'dopamine hypothesis' for many years. Thus, schizophrenia is believed to be caused by an overactive dopaminergic system. Many of the symptoms of schizophrenia can be understood in terms of dopaminergic malfunctions (McKenna, 1987) and the drugs currently available to treat schizophrenia, the neuroleptics, block dopamine receptors.

A widespread belief in the dopamine hypothesis has led to a proliferation of neuroleptics, yet the archetype, chlorpromazine, is still used extensively. It is salutary to consider that chlorpromazine was introduced more than 30 years ago; the new drugs clearly do not reflect major progress. They are still associated with a very high incidence of side effects. Better drugs are needed and it is apparent that a fresh approach to this problem is long overdue.

Drugs acting at sigma receptors

Thankfully, new ideas have been forthcoming recently and several promising approaches are under investigation. For instance, there is now considerable interest in sigma receptors

*Present address: Beecham Pharmaceuticals Research Division, Harlow, Essex CM19 5AD, UK.

(previously sigma opiate receptors), which are believed to mediate the psychotomimetic effects of certain opiates such as N-allylnormetazocine (SKF 10 047) and cyclazocine (see Deutsch *et al.*, 1988). The psychotomimetic effects of phencyclidine may be attributable to actions at sigma receptors, but phencyclidine has a higher affinity for the N-methyl d-aspartate excitatory amino acid receptor, which is also a source of interest for the development of anti-psychotic drugs. Interestingly, haloperidol has a high affinity for sigma receptors, but this is not a common property among neuroleptics. Other compounds with antagonist actions at sigma receptors but not dopamine receptors have been discovered. For example, rimcazole (Ferris *et al.*, 1986) showed some promise in clinical trials in schizophrenia but was withdrawn because it caused seizures in some patients. BMY 14802 (Taylor & Dekleva, 1987) is also being developed as an anti-psychotic drug. There is now an intensive effort to find more compounds of this type.

Drugs acting at 5-hydroxytryptamine receptors

The growth of research into sigma receptors and schizophrenia shows an interesting parallel with that of 5-hydroxytryptamine (5-HT) and schizophrenia: in both cases, interest arose through the discovery that a psychotomimetic compound interacted with the receptors. In the case of 5-HT receptors, the compound was, of course, LSD. Since the time that this effect of LSD was discovered, interest in 5-HT and schizophrenia has fluctuated. Recently, however, it received a new impetus from the advances that have been made in the classification of 5-HT receptors and the development of new drugs with selective actions at 5-HT receptor subtypes. This research has opened up new possibilities for the treatment of a variety of disorders, but the greatest impact is likely to be in mental health.

There is now a bewildering array of 5-HT receptor subtypes and it is no comfort to know that additional putative subtypes have been proposed. At present, the classification compiled by Bradley *et al.* (1986) is widely accepted. 5-HT receptors are divided into three classes, referred to as 5-HT_1-like, 5-HT_2 and 5-HT_3. The 5-HT_1-like group is made up of several subtypes and includes presynaptic receptors that inhibit the release of neurotransmitter. 5-HT has a high affinity for 5-HT_1-like receptors. In the central nervous system, 5-HT_{1A}, 5-HT_{1B}, 5-HT_{1C} and 5-HT_{1D} have been identified, primarily by radioligand binding. Of these, so far only the 5-HT_{1A} receptor has been linked to mental disorders; compounds with partial agonist activity at this receptor, such as buspirone, have anxiolytic activity (Traber & Glaser, 1987).

On the other hand, both 5-HT_2 and 5-HT_3 receptor antagonists are being explored as potential treatments for schizophrenia. The 5-HT_2 receptor is the classical postsynaptic receptor that responds to high concentrations of 5-HT released into the synaptic cleft. Most of the older 5-HT receptor antagonists, such as methysergide and cyproheptadine, are predominantly 5-HT_2 antagonists. In recent years, compounds with much greater selectivity for 5-HT_2 receptors (eg ritanserin) have been discovered. Although there is some support for the belief that selective 5-HT_2 antagonists will have some anti-psychotic activity by themselves, the greatest interest lies in the use of these compounds as adjuncts to neuroleptic therapy. Alternatively, compounds with combined 5-HT_2 and dopamine D_2 antagonist activity are already showing considerable promise. Risperidone (Janssen *et al.*, 1988) and tiospirone (Jain *et al.*, 1987) are two such compounds. The important features of these compounds appear to be that they have reduced extrapyramidal side-effects and they inhibit negative symptoms. It is of interest to note that some other neuroleptics, including chlorpromazine and clozapine, are also quite potent 5-HT_2 antagonists.

Potentially the most exciting area for the future of the drug treatment of schizophrenia is in the discovery that 5-HT_3 receptor antagonists are very effective in certain animal models of schizophrenia (Costall *et al.*, this volume p. 238). These observations arose from a systematic analysis of the effects of the 5-HT_3 antagonist, GR38032F, in animal models of mental disorders. It was also predicted from these studies that 5-HT_3 antagonists have potential value in the treatment of anxiety (Jones *et al.*, 1988).

5-HT_3 receptor antagonists were discovered by studying peripheral 5-HT_3 receptors in isolated tissue preparations such as the rat vagus nerve (Ireland & Tyers, 1987). 5-HT and the more selective 5-HT_3 agonist 2-methyl 5-HT depolarize neuronal membranes and this can be measured directly in neuronal preparations. In other preparations, such as the isolated rabbit heart or guinea-pig ileum, the neuronal excitation is expressed as a release of another neurotransmitter (eg acetylcholine), which in turn mediates a response such as a contraction. 5-HT_3 anatagonists inhibit these responses. Several 5-HT_3 antagonists have been described and some examples are shown in Fig. 1. They all appear to be highly selective for 5-HT_3 receptors.

For some time, 5-HT_3 receptors were regarded simply as peripheral receptors. The fact that they were located exclusively on neuronal tissue, however, suggested that they might also occur in the central nervous system. Indirect evidence for their existence in the CNS arose from behavioural studies and direct evidence was finally obtained using radioligand binding. A high affinity 5-HT_3 antagonist, ^{3}H-GR65630 (Fig. 1), was shown to bind to rat

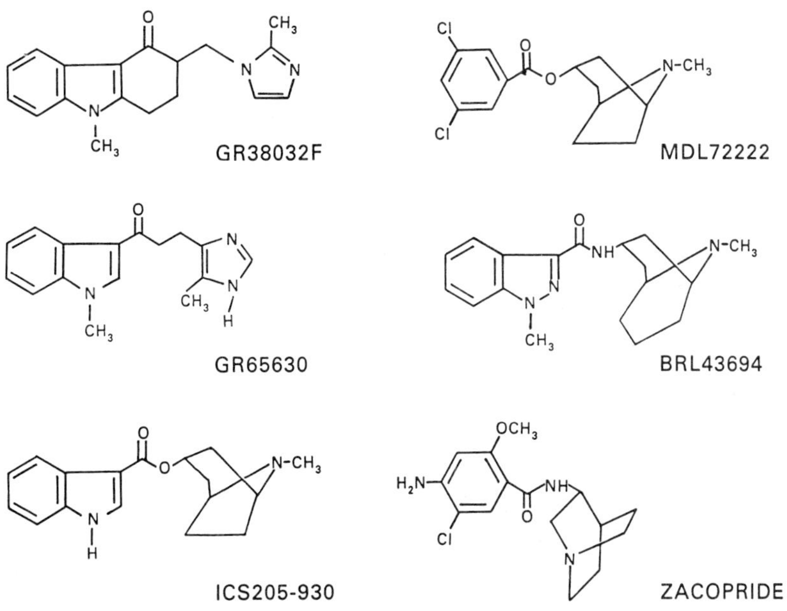

Fig. 1.

brain tissue. The binding sites were distributed unevenly, the highest densities occurring in cortical and limbic areas (Fig. 2) (Kilpatrick *et al.*, 1987). Recently, however, a higher density was observed in the area postrema (Kilpatrick *et al.*, 1988). The specific binding sites in rat entorhinal cortex showed a remarkably good correspondence to the 5-HT_3 receptors in rat vagus nerve: a range of 5-HT_3 antagonists were approximately equipotent on both tissues.

5-HT3 receptors have now been shown to be present in mouse, rabbit, ferret and human brain (Kilpatrick *et al.*, 1989). As in the rat brain, the highest densities in all of

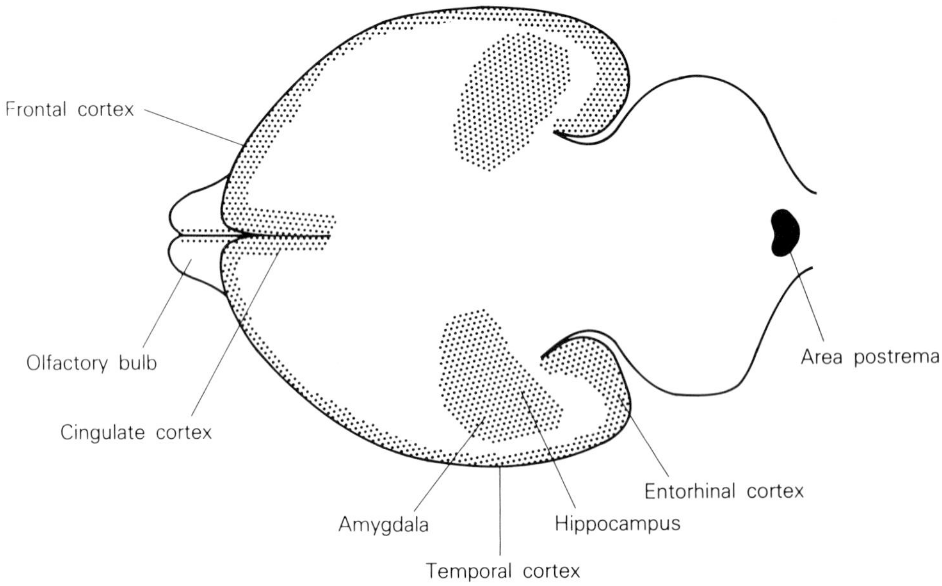

Fig. 2. *Diagrammatic representation of the distribution of* ^{3}*H-GR65630 binding sites in rat brain (adapted from Kilpatrick* et al., *1988).* The density in the area postrema is at least three times higher than that in the stippled areas.

these species were found in the area postrema. This observation has important implications because the area postrema is the site of the chemoreceptor trigger zone in the vomiting reflex and 5-HT_3 antagonists are very effective inhibitors of emesis induced by cytotoxic agents. In ferrets, it was shown that 5-HT_3 antagonists injected directly into the area inhibited the emetic effect of cisplatin (Higgins *et al.*, 1989). Thus a direct link between 5-HT_3 receptor function in the brain and a biological response was demonstrated. This is difficult to achieve because at present there is a void between the radioligand binding and the behavioural tests; there is a need for *in vitro* measures of 5-HT_3 receptor function in the CNS. Blandina *et al.* (1988) made an important contribution recently when they described a 5-HT_3-receptor-mediated release of dopamine from rat striatal slices. Their discovery may provoke others to investigate ways of analysing 5-HT_3 receptor function in the brain.

The roles of 5-HT_3 receptors in the CNS are not understood, but from behavioural evidence it would appear that, under normal circumstances, 5-HT_3 receptors are probably dormant. This can be inferred from the observations that 5-HT_3 antagonists do not modify the behaviour of normal animals. Only when behaviour is perturbed by environmental or pharmacological manipulations do their effects become manifest. Thus in rats or marmosets made hyperactive by stimulating the mesolimbic system, 5-HT_3 antagonists inhibit the hyperactivity (Costall *et al.*, this volume, p. 239). Similarly, experimental animals placed in anxiety-provoking situations show reduced anxiety when treated with 5-HT_3 antagonists (Jones *et al.*, 1988).

At a neuronal level, 5-HT released on to 5-HT_3 receptors would excite neurones or facilitate neurotransmission. This is in keeping with what might be occurring in schizophrenia: dopaminergic overactivity could be caused by activation of 5-HT_3 receptors. Blockade of these receptors would remove the problem and return dopaminergic function to normal. This is an extremely important point; neuroleptics simply inhibit dopaminergic function regardless of its level of activity. This results in extrapyramidal side effects. Such problems could not occur with 5-HT_3 antagonists because there is not normally any 5-HT_3 receptor tone. One can envisage that 5-HT_3 receptors could modulate the functions of several neuronal systems. 5-HT_3 antagonists may therefore have therapeutic value in other mental disorders characterized by a functional overactivity of a neuronal system.

Conclusion

To conclude, we are hopefully entering a new era in the treatment of schizophrenia; some exciting novel approaches are being investigated. The 5-HT_3 receptor antagonists are potentially the first drugs that could re-establish normal behaviour in psychotic individuals without inducing any side effects.

References

Blandina, P., Goldfarb, J. & Green, J.P. (1988): Activation of 5-HT_3 receptor releases dopamine from rat striatal slice. *Eur. J. Pharmacol.* **155**, 349–350.

Bradley, P.B., Engel, G., Feniuk, W., Fozard. J.R., Humphrey, P.P.A., Middlemiss, D.N., Mylecharane, E.J., Richardson, B.P. & Saxena, P.R. (1986): Proposals for the classification of functional receptors for 5-hydroxytryptamine. *Neuropharmacology* **25**, 563–576.

Deutsch, S.I., Weizman, A., Goldman, M.E. & Morihisa, J.M. (1988): The sigma receptor: a novel site implicated in psychosis and antipsychotic drug efficacy. *Clin. Neuropharmacol.* **11**, 105–119.

Ferris, R.M., White, H.L., Tang, F.L.M., Russell, A. & Harfenist, M. (1986): Rimcazole (BW 243U), a novel antipsychotic agent whose mechanism of action cannot be explained by a direct blockade of postsynaptic dopaminergic receptors in brain. *Drug Devel. Res.* **9**, 171–188.

Higgins, G.A., Kilpatrick, G.J., Bunce, K.T., Jones, B.J. & Tyers, M.B. (1989): 5-HT_3 receptor antagonists injected into the area postrema inhibit cisplatin-induced emesis in the ferret. *Br. J. Pharmacol.* **97**, 247–255.

Ireland, S.J. & Tyers, M.B. (1987): Pharmacological characterisation of 5-hydroxytryptamine-induced depolarization of the rat isolated vagus nerve. *Br. J. Pharmacol.* **90**, 229–238.

Jain, A.K., Kelwala, S., Moore, N. & Gershon, S. (1987): A controlled clinical trial of tiaspirone in schizophrenia. *Int. Clin. Psychopharmacol* **2**, 129–133.

Janssen, P.A., Niemegeers, C.J., Awouters, F., Schellekens, K.H., Megens, A.A. and Meert, T.F. (1988): Pharmacology of risperidone (R 64766), a new antipsychotic with serotonin — S2 and dopamine — D2 antagonist properties. *J. Pharmacol. Therap.* **244**, 685–693.

Jones, B.J., Costall, B., Domeney, A.M., Kelly, M.E., Naylor, R.J., Oakley, N.R. & Tyers, M.B. (1988): The potential anxiolytic activity of GR38032F, a 5-HT_3 receptor antagonist. *Br. J. Pharmacol.* **93**, 985–993.

Kilpatrick, G.J., Jones, B.J. & Tyers, M.B. (1987): Identification and distribution of 5-HT_3 receptors in rat brain using radioligand binding. *Nature* **330**, 746–748.

Kilpatrick, G.J., Jones, B.J. & Tyers, M.B. (1988): The distribution of specific ^{3}H-GR65630 binding sites in rat brain assessed by quantitative autoradiography. *Neurosci. Lett.* **94**, 156–160.

Kilpatrick, G.J., Jones, B.J. and Tyers, M.B. (1989): Binding of the 5-HT_3 ligand, ^{3}H-GR65630, to rat area postrema, vagus nerve and the brains of several species. *Eur. J. Pharmacol.* **159**, 157–164.

McKenna, P.J. (1987): Pathology, phenomenology and the dopamine hypothesis of schizophrenia. *Br. J. Psychiatry* **151**, 288–301.

Taylor, D.P. & Dekleva, J. (1987): Potential antipsychotic BMY 14802 selectively binds to sigma sites. *Drug. Devel. Res.* **11**, 65–70.

Traber, J. & Glaser, T. (1987): 5-HT_{1A} receptor-related anxiolytics. *Trends Pharmacol. Sci.* **8**, 432–437.

Chapter 21

Schizophrenia and its treatment

B. Costall, A. M. Domeney, M. E. Kelly and R. J. Naylor

Studies in Pharmacology, The University of Bradford, Bradford, BD7 1DP, UK

Summary

Test procedures have been developed to mimic as closely as possible the persistent and discrete disturbance in mesolimbic dopamine function thought to occur in schizophrenia. Basically, the techniques involve stereotaxic brain surgery for discrete injections or infusions to disrupt mesolimbic dopamine function at the levels of the nucleus accumbens or amygdala.

The behavioural consequences of a mesolimbic dopamine excess, in particular increased psychomotor drive, are inhibited by neuroleptic agents such as fluphenazine, haloperidol and sulpiride. Such agents act by direct blockade of the mesolimbic dopamine receptors. In contrast, the mesolimbic dopamine excess could be shown to be inhibited by blockade of 5-HT_3 receptors using GR38032F (ondansetron). GR389032F was shown to be potent and as effective as the neuroleptic agents. However, it lacked activity on the extrapyramidal system and failed to raise serum prolactin. Thus it is proposed that GR38032F may represent the first of a new class of drug having potential to treat the symptoms of schizophrenia without producing the side-effects associated with present anti-schizophrenia therapy.

The action of GR38032F can be extended to other 5-HT_3 receptor antagonists, and it is suggested that these compounds may provide a major therapeutic advance in the treatment of schizophrenia.

Introduction

The aetiology of schizophrenia has been associated, at least in part, with a raised mesolimbic dopamine function (see review by Costall & Naylor, 1986). The approach to treating the symptoms of this disease has therefore been to use agents which are dopamine antagonists. These are the neuroleptic agents and encompass a breadth of chemicals including the phenothiazines, butyrophenones, thiaxanthines and substituted benzamides. The neuroleptics which are possibly the most widely used as experimental tools are haloperidol and fluphenazine, and these have been used extensively in our laboratories to define neuroleptic action in animal models.

The problem with the neuroleptic agents is that they antagonize indiscriminately at all cerebral dopamine receptors. They will inhibit at the mesolimbic dopamine receptors where there is a link with the disturbance of schizophrenia, but they will also inhibit at normal dopamine receptors, for example in the extrapyramidal system and in the tuberoinfundibular system. This leads to extrapyramidal side effects, including acute dystonias, parkinsonian side effects, tardive dyskinesias, and endocrine disturbances, most notably the elevation of serum prolactin.

The question can be raised as to why, over a period of some two decades, there have been no significant developments in the search for new treatments for schizophrenia. A major limitation has been in the design of the animal test procedures. These have essentially been developed to detect dopamine antagonist compounds. For example, all neuroleptic agents will induce catalepsy, antagonize dopamine agonist-induced stereotyped behaviours, and antagonize dopamine agonist-induced climbing behaviour and increases in locomotor activity. All of these tests depend on the abilities of neuroleptic agents to inhibit dopamine function in both mesolimbic and extrapyramidal dopamine systems, and are therefore to a large degree searching for side-effect potential of the neuroleptics. At best, such experimental approaches can detect compounds similar to those presently available (see review by Costall & Naylor, 1980).

The development of new test procedures for antischizophrenic potential

New approaches to animal models have concentrated on the possibility that the select disturbances of schizophrenia may be more closely mimicked in animals. Firstly, it was decided that the experimentally-induced disturbance should ideally be discrete within the limbic system, and should be persistent.

In order to gain a discrete disturbance, stereotaxic brain surgery was used to localize injections or infusions of substances aimed to increase dopamine function in mesolimbic nuclei. The nucleus accumbens was selected as an area which provides psychomotor drive and the amygdala as an area which is classically involved with the control of emotion and motivational behaviour. Acute disturbances could be effected by injecting an agent such as amphetamine into the nucleus accumbens: the behavioural consequence was increased psychomotor drive which could be inhibited superficially by known neuroleptic agents. More persistent disturbances in mesolimbic dopamine function may be effected by infusing dopamine itself, slowly and persistently over several days, into the mesolimbic nucleus accumbens or central area of the amygdala. Again, the behavioural measure is enhanced psychomotor drive, although it should not be ignored that these test procedures are also linked with changes in anxiety and cognitive function to provide a complex of behavioural disturbances which can be related to those of psychosis. However, the present text will concentrate on the disturbance in psychomotor drive which can be effected in both rodent and primate species.

It is also possible to raise, selectively, endogenous dopamine function in the mesolimbic terminal nuclei by injecting a neurokinin agonist (substance P or a more stable analogue) into the cell body origin of the mesolimbic system, the ventral tegmental area (see Hagan *et al.*, 1987). The approach has the advantage that the excess release of dopamine is endogenous and that biochemical correlates can be determined. It provides answers which are supportive of the developments which will be described here for the use of the intra-accumbens amphetamine model, and the model where dopamine is infused slowly and persistently into the mesolimbic nuclei via chronically indwelling stereotaxically located cannulae and injection units coupled to Alzet osmotic minipumps implanted in the scapular region to provide a constant supply of dopamine, 0.48 μl/h for 24 h each day.

Coupled with the new test procedures we have taken an active approach to eliminating drug action on the extrapyramidal system. Thus, we would require any new compound to show minimal efficacy to induce catalepsy, antagonize stereotypies or other dopamine agonist-induced behaviours. An even more stringent test has been to place the potential antipsychotic agent directly in the striatal area of the extrapyramidal system. Dopamine blockade is seen, after unilateral injection, as a twisting of the body towards the side of injection. In mild form this is seen as a turning of the head and trunk, but this can be exaggerated by peripheral administration of a domapnie agonist such as apomorphine into marked pivoting or rotation, with the body bent nose-to-tail (Costall *et al.*, 1983).

The development of new approaches to inhibit a mesolimbic dopamine excess

With the development of the new test procedures it has become possible to show that a mesolimbic dopamine excess can be inhibited not only by direct influence on the dopamine system, but also by modulation of a system which can control the dopamine function. A major neuromodulating system is that using 5-hydroxytryptamine (5-HT) as neurotransmitter.

It is now known that of the multitude of receptor mechanisms linked to the 5-HT system, it is the 5-HT_3 receptor subtype which is important for the control of mesolimbic dopamine excess. Only with the development of selective tools for the different 5-HT receptor subtypes have we been able to show the importance of 5-HT function in the control of neurotransmitter disturbances in schizophrenia. Yet we have long known of the possible link between 5-HT and schizophrenia. In animal studies we have been able to use the natural ligand 5-HT to reduce or enhance a dopamine response, while some experiments have shown an inactivity (Pijnenburg *et al.*, 1975; Costall *et al.*, 1976, 1979; Makanjuola *et al.*, 1980; Jones *et al.*, 1981). The inconsistencies are now readily explained in terms of an activity of 5-HT on receptor subtypes which can either facilitate or inhibit dopamine activity.

Examples of the importance of 5-HT in schizophrenia have also emerged from the clinic. For example, elevated blood concentrations of 5-HT have been detected in chronic schizophrenics (Delisi *et al.*, 1981); schizophrenic patients with a family history of the disorder have been shown to have elevated 5-HIAA levels in their cerebrospinal fluid (Sedvall & Wode-Helgodt, 1981); blood or platelet levels of 5-HT have been shown to be higher in schizophrenia (Todrick *et al.*, 1960; Freedman *et al.*, 1981; Stahl *et al.*, 1983). There have been reports (King *et al.*, 1985) of an association between elevated 5-HIAA and 5-HT levels in the cerebrospinal fluid and platelets of schizophrenic patients showing symptoms of mannerisms and posturing.

The new test procedures and their value in detecting novel agents influencing mesolimbic 5-HT

When amphetamine is placed bilaterally into rat nucleus accumbens a marked hyperactivity develops within 10 minutes and persists for up to 80 minutes. This can be measured by placing rats individually into activity cages fitted with photocell units; hyperactivity is measured as the number of times the beams have been broken by active movement during a 10 minute observation period. A typical hyperactivity curve can be seen in Fig. 1. The hyperactivity is dose-dependently antagonized by a typical neuroleptic, fluphenazine, injected into the nucleus accumbens (0.5–10 ng) prior to the amphetamine. It is also inhibited by the injection of a selective 5-HT_3 receptor agonists GR38032F (ondansetron) (see Fig. 2, right hand panel). It can be seen that the 5-HT_3 receptor antagonist inhibited the amphetamine hyperactivity at doses of 0.01–1 ng, again given intra-accumbens prior to amphetamine.

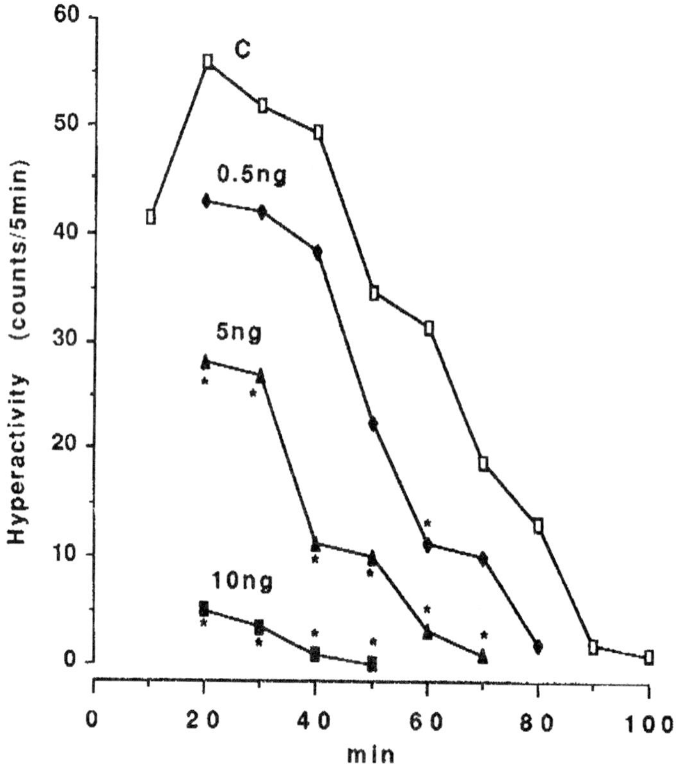

Fig. 1. *Ability of fluphenazine to antagonize the hyperactivity caused by amphetamine injected bilaterally into rat nucleus accumbens.* □———□ (C) = control amphetamine response. ◆ ▲ ■ = amphetamine + fluphenazine given intra-accumbens (doses of fluphenazine given). n = 8. SEMs <13.8%. *$P < 0.01 - P < 0.001$ (two-way ANOVA plus Dunnett's test).

The data in Fig. 2 also show how manipulation of 5-HT_3 function can both enhance and inhibit the amphetamine response. The selective 5-HT_3 receptor agonist 2-methyl-5HT was shown to enhance the hyperactivity caused by amphetamine, and this effect of 2-methyl-5-HT was inhibited by GR38032F (Fig. 2).

While the disturbance in mesolimbic dopamine function caused by intra-accumbens amphetamine is acute, the test procedure has been shown to be valuable in selectively detecting the actions of typical neuroleptics (eg fluphenazine), atypical neuroleptics (eg (−)sulpiride) and novel agents which act via the 5-HT_3 control system (eg GR38032F) (Fig. 3).

The test which has been developed for the persistent disturbance of mesolimbic dopamine function also detects the actions of the 5-HT_3 receptor antagonists. Dopamine is infused persistently into the nucleus accumbens at a rate of 0.48 µl/h, 25 µg dopamine/24 h, for 13 days. This gives rise to characteristic biphasic peaks of hyperactivity over a 13 day infusion period, with peaks generally occurring between days 3 and 5 and again between days 9 and 12 of infusion (Fig. 4). These hyperactivity peaks can be antagonized by a typical neuroleptic (fluphenazine) or by the atypical agent, sulpiride. Figure 4 shows one of the problems of neuroleptic use: the excess motor depression seen at the higher dose of fluphenazine is characteristic and unwanted.

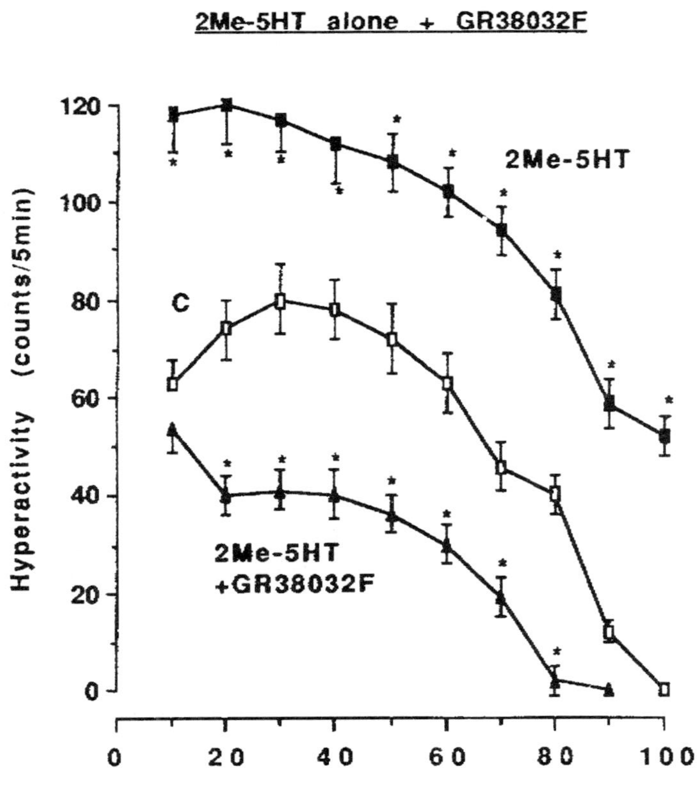

Fig. 2. *Ability of 2-methyl-5HT (2Me-5HT) to enhance the hyperactivity caused by intra-accumbens amphetamine, and the inhibition of this response by GR38032F.* GR38032F is also shown to inhibit the amphetamine hyperactivity dose-dependently. □———□ (C) = Control amphetamine response (10 µg), ■———■ = Amphetamine + 2ME-5HT (10 ng), ▲———▲ = Amphetamine + 2ME-5HT + GR38032F (1 µg), ◆ ■ ▲ = Amphetamine + GR38032F (doses indicated). n = 5. *$P < 0.01$ (two-way ANOVA plus Dunnett's test). Bars = SEM.

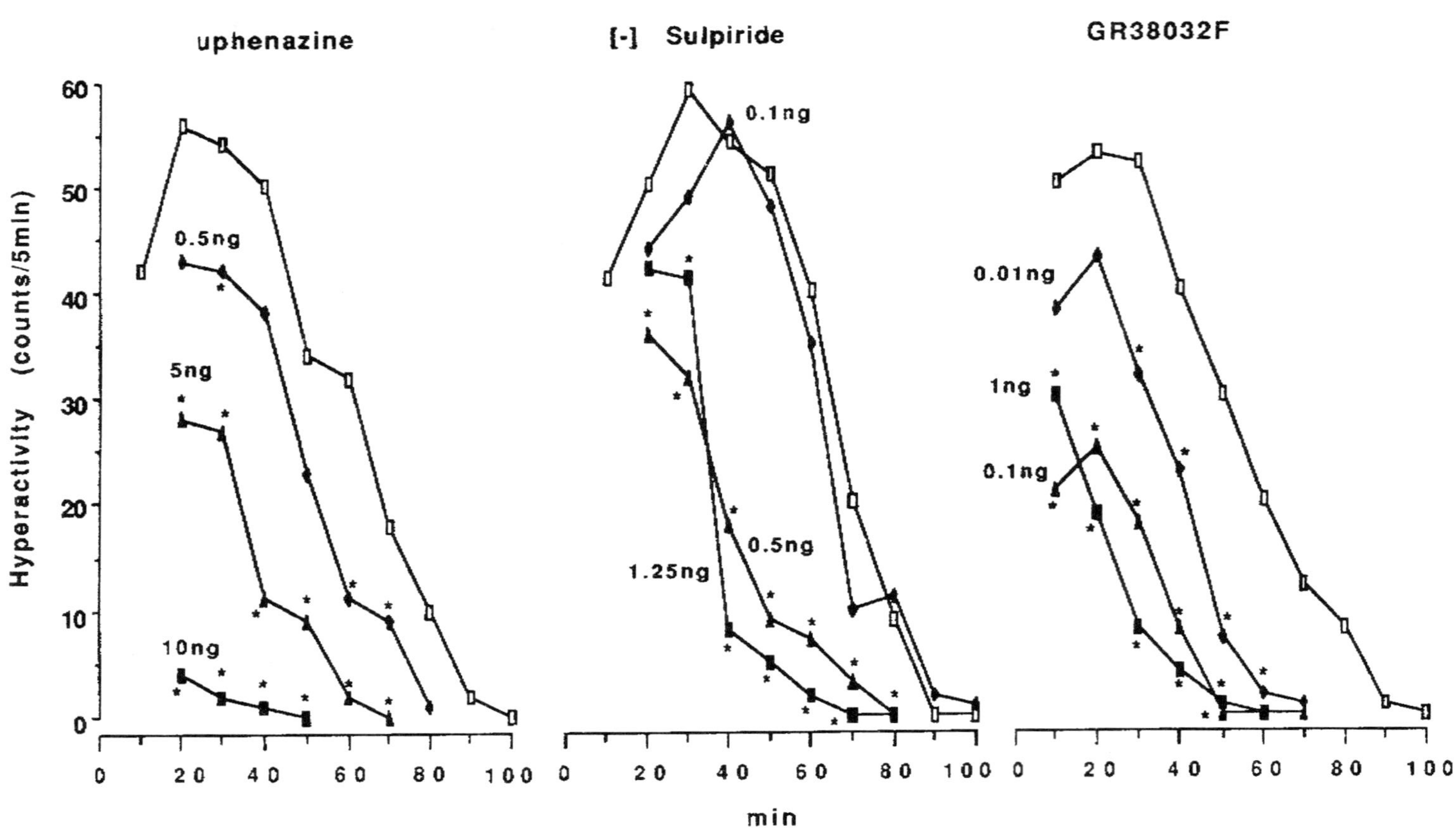

Fig. 3. *Abilities of fluphenazine, (−)sulpiride and GR38032F to antagonize the hyperactivity induced by amphetamine injected bilaterally into rat nucleus accumbens.* □——□ Control amphetamine response (10 µg). ◆ ■ ▲ = Amphetamine + potential antagonists given intra-accumbens. n = 5–10. $^{*}P < 0.01 - P < 0.001$ (two-way ANOVA plus Dunnett's test).

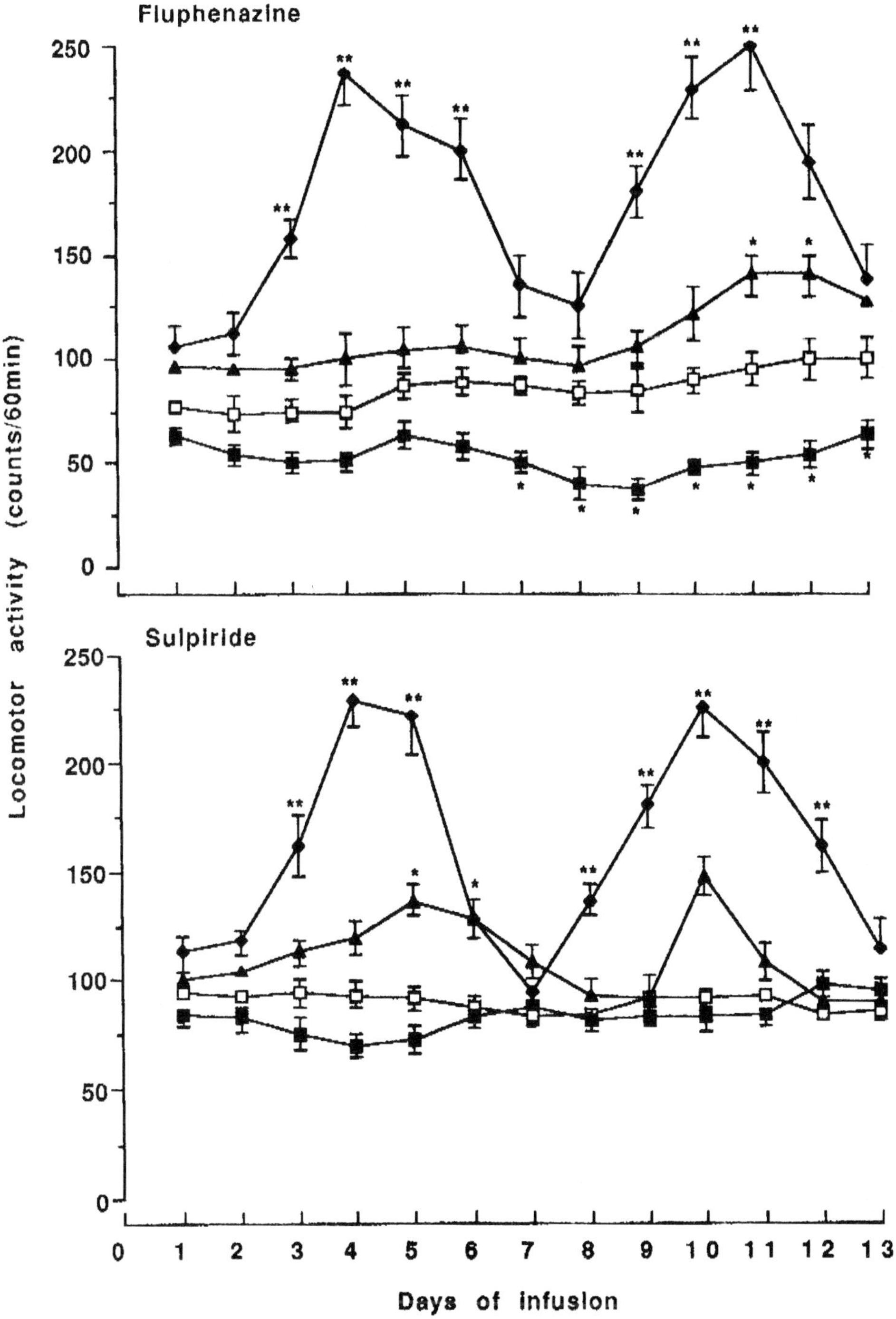

Fig. 4. *Abilities of fluphenazine and sulpiride to antagonize the hyperactivity caused by dopamine infused into rat nucleus accumbens.* □———□ Vehicle (0.48 μl/h). ◆———◆ Dopamine (DA) 25 μg/24 h. For upper block ▲———▲ = DA + Fluphenazine 0.05 mg/kg i.p. b.d., ■———■ = DA + Fluphenazine 0.2 mg/kg i.p. b.d. For lower block ▲———▲ = DA + sulpiride 2.5 mg/kg i.p. b.d., ■———■ = DA + sulpiride 5.0 mg/kg i.p. b.d. n = 6–12. *$P < 0.05$, **$P < 0.01 - P < 0.001$ (two-way ANOVA plus Dunnett's test). Bars = SEM.

Against this background it is important to show that the 5-HT_3 receptor antagonist, GR38032F, is also able to inhibit the phasic hyperactivity caused by dopamine infused bilaterally into the rat nucleus accumbens. This compound is able to effect significant antagonism at low doses and without undue motor depression (Fig. 5).

It is interesting to compare the effective dose ranges for inibition of the dopamine hyperactivity and sedation potential. Fluphenazine, sulpiride and GR38032F will inhibit the dopamine hyperactivity at 0.05–0.5, 2.5–15.0 and at 0.0001–0.5 mg/kg given intraperitoneally twice daily, respectively, with sedation potential which is marked (fluphenazine), apparent only at high doses (sulpiride) or absent (GR38032F). As will be discussed later, this may relate to the selectivity and specificity of action of a compound like GR38032F within the limbic system.

An important finding is that the data obtained from the infusions of dopamine into the mesolimbic nucleus accumbens of rat can be extended to the marmoset. In this primate species the experimental approach is the same as described for the rat. Again, the infusion of dopamine causes phasic hyperactivity, although there is generally a single phase of response during the 13 day infusion period in primate. This hyperactivity is highly sensitive to blockade by fluphenazine and sulpiride. Even at the low doses used (0.01 mg/kg fluphenazine and 0.06 mg/kg sulpiride both given twice daily intraperitoneally) hyperactivity of the primate is suppressed to values below control (Fig. 6). This undue

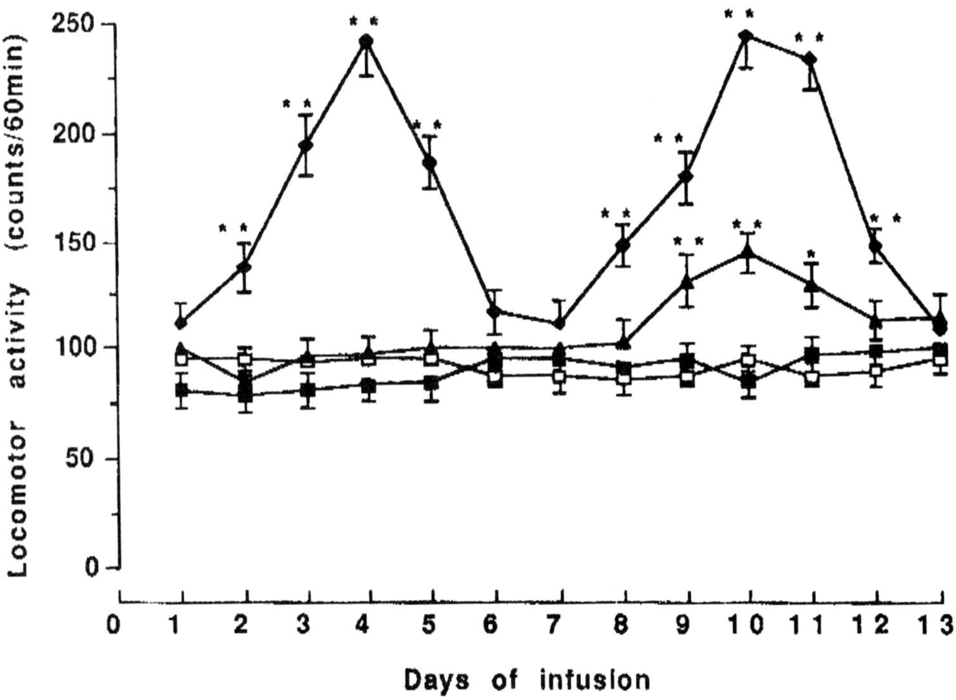

Fig. 5. *Ability of GR38032F to antagonize the hyperactivity caused by dopamine infused into rat nucleus accumbens.* □——□ Vehicle 0.48 µl/h, ◆——◆ = Dopamine (DA) 25 µg/24 h, ▲——▲ = DA + GR38032F 0.0001 mg/kg i.p. b.d., ■——■ = DA + GR38032F 0.001 mg/kg i.p. b.d. n = 6–12. $^*P < 0.05$, $^{**}P < 0.01 - P < 0.001$ (two-way ANOVA plus Dunnett's test). Bars = SEM.

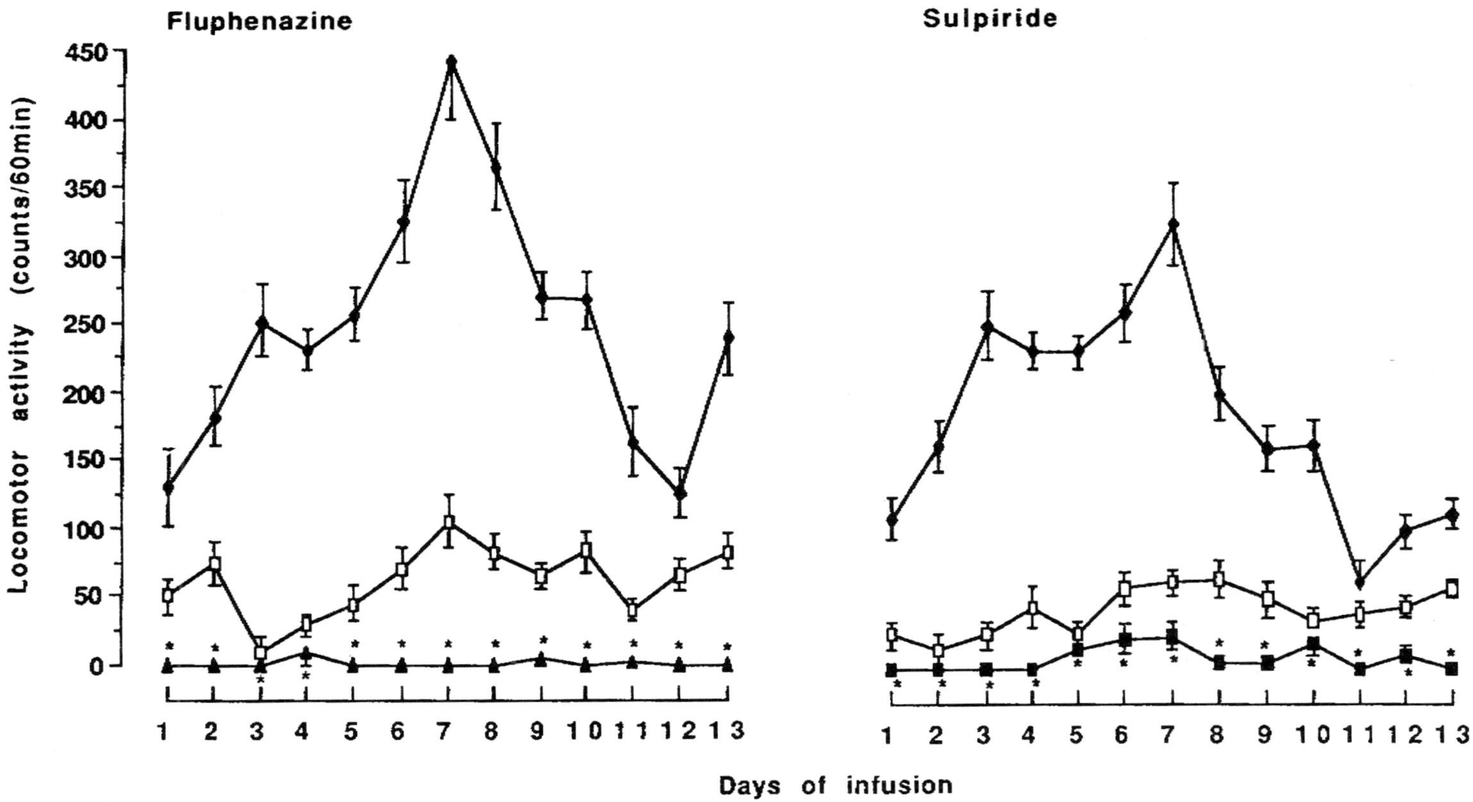

Fig. 6. *Abilities of fluphenazine and sulpiride to antagonize the hyperactivity caused by dopamine infused into the nucleus accumbens (ventral striatum) of common marmosets.* □——□ Vehicle (0.48 μl/h), ◆——◆ Dopamine (25 μg/24 h), ▲——▲ Dopamine + fluphenazine (0.01 mg/kg i.p. b.d.), ■——■ Dopamine + Sulpiride (0.06 mg/kg i.p. b.d.). n = 5. $^*P < 0.001$ (antagonism of dopamine, two-way ANOVA plus Dunnett's test). Bars = SEM.

motor suppression is not seen when the inhibition is effected using the 5-HT_3 receptor antagonist GR38032F (Fig. 7).

The important observation of these studies is that in three test procedures of mesolimbic dopamine excess, where the disturbance is discrete and in some tests chronic, a 5-HT_3 receptor antagonist is potent and effective in inhibiting the behavioural consequences of the dopamine excess. These data were the first indications that the 5-HT_3 receptor antagonists may represent a new therapeutic approach to schizophrenia.

The next stage of the studies was to extend the findings from the nucleus accumbens, an area which provides psychomotor drive, to a mesolimbic area more traditionally associated with emotion and motivational behaviour. For this we selected the amygdala and the dopamine infusion approach. These studies were made difficult by the fact that the amygdala is lateralized in structure, a finding which is not inconsistent with observations in man. For example, left temporal lobe epilepsy is associated with schizophrenic-like disturbances, and Reynolds (1983) showed dopamine levels to be highest in the left amygdala of schizophrenic brain (a finding which cannot be explained away on the basis that patients had been drug treated). We found that dopamine only initiated changed behaviour when infused into the left subdominant amygdala (Bradbury *et al.*, 1985). Cerebral dominance was determined in a simple turn-preference test in

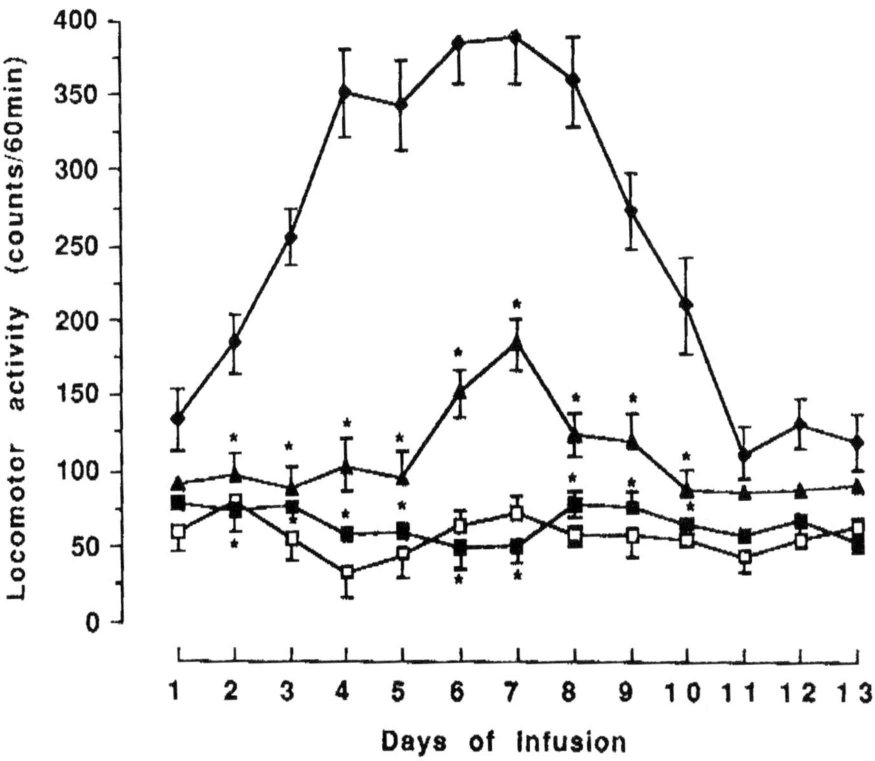

Fig. 7. *Ability of GR38032F to antagonize the hyperactivity caused by dopamine infused into the nucleus accumbens of common marmosets.* □——□ Vehicle (0.48 µl/h), ◆——◆ Dopamine (25 µg/24 h), ■——■ Dopamine + GR38032F 0.001 mg/kg i.p. b.d., ▲——▲ Dopamine + GR38032F 0.0001 mg/kg i.p. b.d. n = 5. *$P < 0.001$ (antagonism of dopamine, two-way ANOVA plus Dunnett's test). Bars = SEM.

which animals were held in two hands and released into an open field. Animals which consistently made an initial move towards the right were categorized as having left cerebral dominancy and *vice versa.*

When dopamine was infused into the central area of the left subdominant amygdala a hyperactivity was observed which tended to be phasic in nature and was neuroleptic-sensitive (Fig. 8). As with infusions of dopamine into the nucleus accumbens the behavioural consequences of infusing dopamine into the amygdala are more complex than simple changes in psychomotor drive, but the latter serves to show the actions of established neuroleptics and 5-HT_3 receptor antagonists.

Like fluphenazine, a 5-HT_3 receptor antagonist can be shown to inhibit the hyperactivity which results from dopamine infusion into rat amygdala. However, an additional fascinating finding is that GR38032F, like a typical neuroleptic, is able to inhibit the dopamine response from the amygdala when injected into the side of the dopamine infusion or into the non-infused side (Fig. 9). Clearly, whilst experimentally one is disturbing directly the function of one amygdala, the consequences are bilateral. This concept is extremely important both for the design of experiments where a unilateral manipulation is envisaged, and for the interpretation of the bilateral consequences of a unilateral intervention. However, the important message of the present work is that a 5-HT_3 receptor antagonist is as effective as a classical neuroleptic in reducing the behavioural consequences of an experimentally induced dopamine excess in the amygdala.

Is the efficacy of a 5-HT_3 receptor antagonist maintained when animals have received prior neuroleptic treatment?

While the 5-HT_3 receptor antagonist GR38032F has been shown to inhibit the behavioural consequences of a mesolimbic dopamine excess, it must be noted that the animals were subject only to the single therapy. In practice in the clinic, patients may present for a new therapy while receiving a traditional neuroleptic. Behaviourally, in animals, there are marked consequences of withdrawing abruptly from traditional neuroleptic treatment, and this raised the question as to whether prior exposure to a neuroleptic may compromise the potential antischizophrenic action of a 5-HT_3 receptor antagonist.

In an attempt to mimic this situation experimentally, rats were subject to an intra-accumbens dopamine infusion with suppression of hyperactivity using a high dose of haloperidol. Treatment was then abruptly withdrawn and a rebound hyperactivity occurred. Although this rebound response was marked, with persistent hyperactivity at levels even higher than achieved by the dopamine infusion alone, it was inhibited by GR38032F (Fig. 10). It should be noted that single acute challenges of 0.001–0.1 mg/kg GR38032F effected inhibition of the rebound hyperactivity which persisted for many days (Fig. 10). It appears that the more marked the mesolimbic disturbance, the more effective is a compound such as GR38032F, and the experimental work does not indicate that prior neuroleptic exposure would compromise the antischizophrenic potential of a 5-HT_3 receptor antagonist such as GR38032F.

Lack of side-effect potential of the 5-HT_3 receptor antagonists

Typical neuroleptic agents such as fluphenazine, by inhibiting mesolimbic and extrapyramidal dopamine function, are able to cause a state of immobility termed catalepsy, and can inhibit the stereotyped licking and biting behaviours caused by

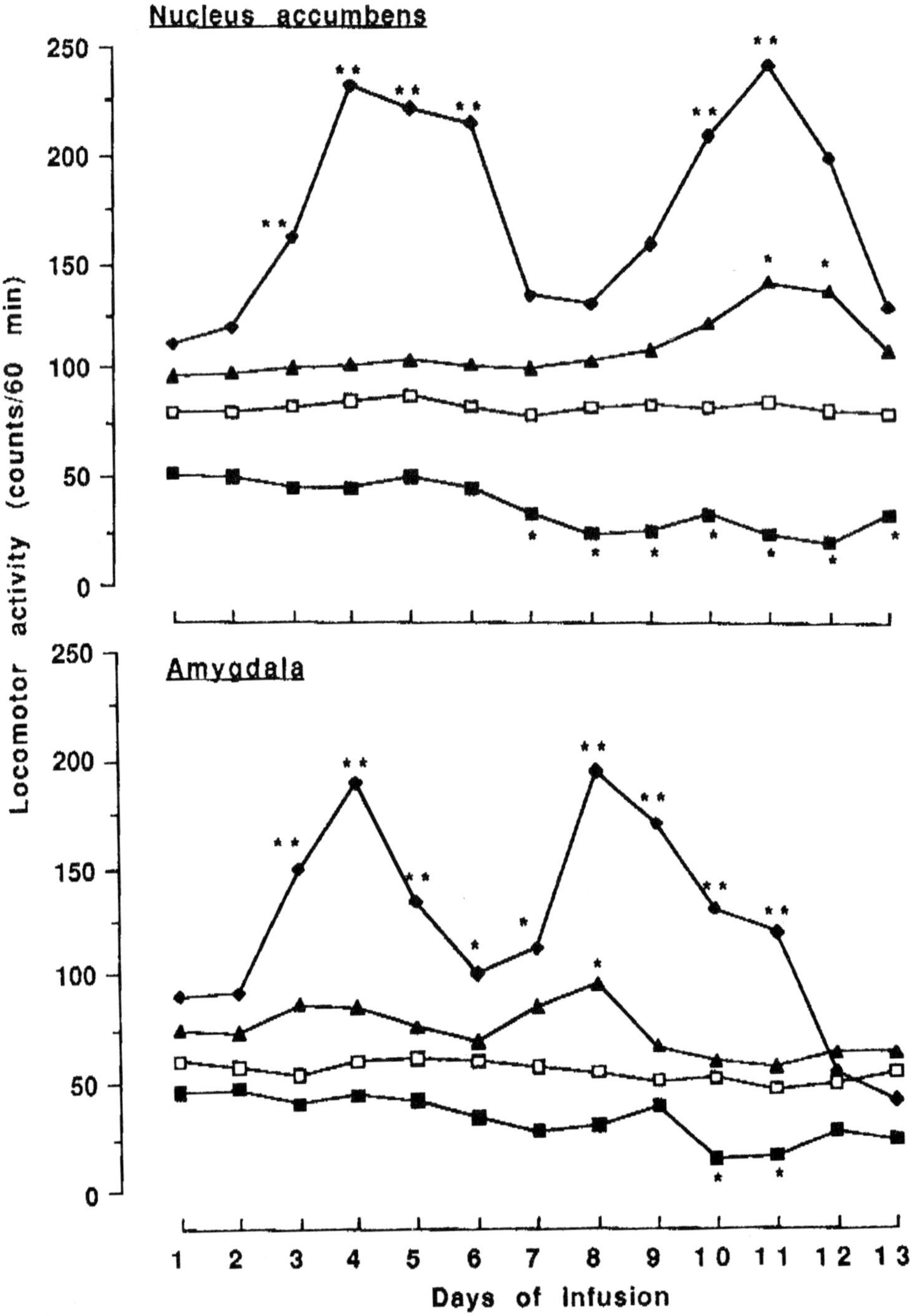

Fig. 8. *Hyperactivity caused by dopamine infused into rat nucleus accumbens or amygdala, and antagonism by fluphenazine.* □———□ Vehicle (0.48 μl), ◆———◆ Dopamine (DA) (25 μg/24 h), ▲———▲ DA + fluphenazine 0.05 mg/kg i.p. b.d., ■———■ DA + fluphenazine 0.2 mg/kg i.p. b.d. Note that infusions into the nucleus accumbens were bilateral, whilst dopamine was infused unilaterally into the left subdominant amygdala. n = 6–12. SEMs <12.6%. $^*P < 0.05$, $^{**}P < 0.01$ – $P < 0.001$ (two-way ANOVA plus Dunnett's test).

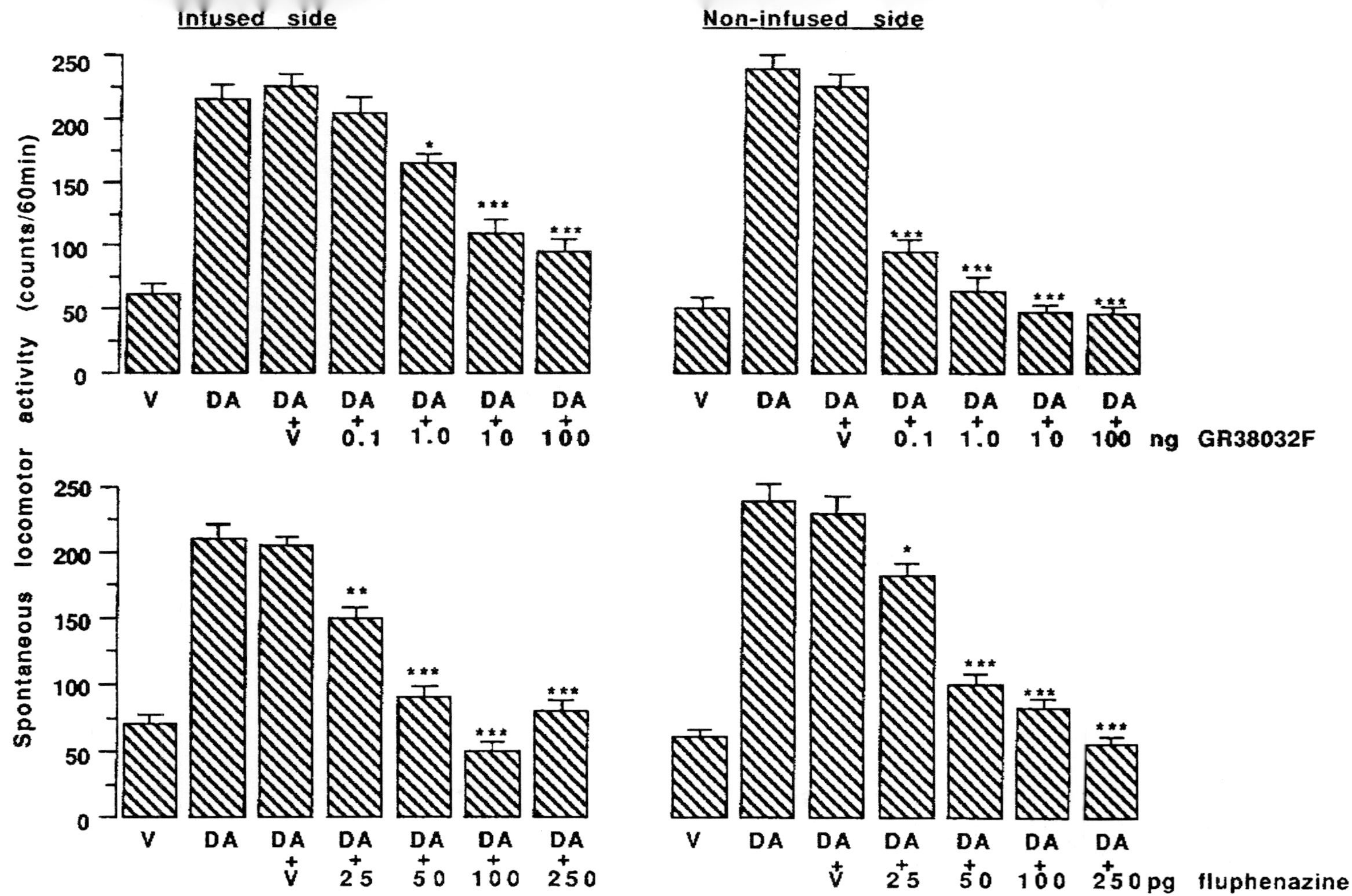

Fig. 9. *Ability of GR38032F or fluphenazine to antagonize the hyperactivity caused by dopamine infused into the left subdominant amygdala of rat.* GR38032F or fluphenazine were injected during a peak of dopamine hyperactivity into the same side as the dopamine infusion (infused side) or into the amygdala of the opposite hemisphere (non-infused side). n = 6. *$P < 0.05$, **$P < 0.01$, ***$P < 0.001$ (one-way ANOVA plus Dunnett's test). Bars = SEM

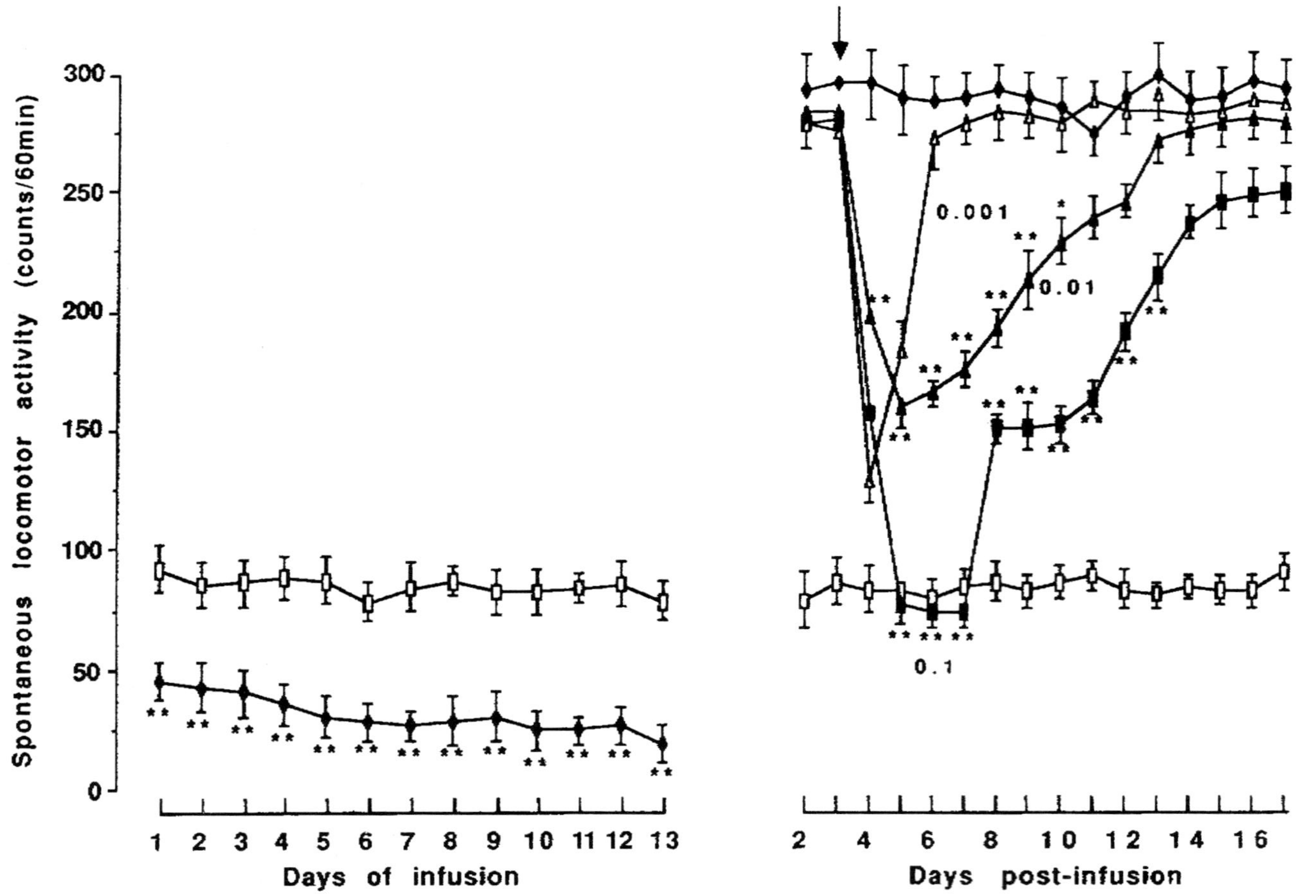

Fig. 10. *Ability of GR38032F to antagonize the rebound hyperactivity after dopamine infusion/neuroleptic treatment in rat.* □——□ Control, ◆——◆ Dopamine (25 µg/24 h) + haloperidol 0.1 mg/kg i.p. t.d.s. After 13 days the dopamine infusion and haloperidol treatment was stopped. The arrow indicates the day of treatment with single doses of GR38032F (mg/kg i.p.). n = 5. $*P < 0.01$, $**P < 0.001$ (two-way ANOVA plus Dunnett's test). Bars = SEM.

amphetamine (5 mg/kg intraperitoneally) in the rat. These effects cannot be mimicked by the 5-HT_3 receptor antagonist GR38032F at doses up to 1.0 mg/kg. Also, when GR38032F was injected into the rat striatum, at doses up to 10 μg, circling behaviour or body asymmetrics did not develop, either spontaneously or when apomorphine was given as a peripheral challenge. This contrasts with the potent ability of neuroleptics to initiate marked body asymmetries and circling when injected unilaterally into the striatum, responses which are exacerbated by apomorphine treatment.

The failure of GR38032F to influence dopamine function directly was further evidenced by its failure to displace (at 10 μM) ^{3}H-spiperone in radioligand binding assays. GR38032F, therefore, appears only to influence mesolimbic dopamine function in order to inhibit the consequences of a dopamine excess. The failure of the 5-HT_3 receptor antagonist to influence the extrapyramidal system was extended to another dopamine system where an influence can give rise to side-effects. Thus, while neuroleptic agents have a marked influence on the dopaminergic tuberoinfundibular system in the hypothalamus to raise hormone levels, and in particular to raise serum concentrations of prolactin, GR38032F was completely without effect in this respect.

Extension of the actions of GR38032F to other 5-HT_3 receptor antagonists

The potential of GR38032F to inhibit the behavioural consequences of a raised mesolimbic dopamine function can be extended to other selective 5-HT_3 receptor antagonists, zacopride, ICS 205–930, BRL43694 (Costall *et al.*, 1988). For all 5-HT_3 receptor antagonists there is loss of efficacy at high dosage, and at present there is no satisfactory explanation for this observation. The emphasis is placed on the therapeutic window which for GR38032F (ondansetron) and zacopride is wide (approximately a 1000-fold dose range).

References

Bradbury, A.J., Costall, B., Domeney, A.M. & Naylor, R.J. (1985): Laterality of dopamine function and neuroleptic action in the amygdala of the rat. *Neuropharmacology* **24**, 1163–1170.

Costall, B. & Naylor, R.J. (1980): Assessment of the test procedures used to analyse neuroleptic action. *Rev. Pure Appl. Pharmacol. Sci.* **1**, 3–83.

Costall, B. & Naylor, R.J. (1986): The neurotransmitter hypothesis of schizophrenia. In *Psychopharmacology and drug treatment of schizophrenia*, eds P.B. Bradley & S.R. Hirsch, pp. 132–165. Oxford: Oxford University Press.

Costall, B., Naylor, R.J., Marsden, C.D. & Pycock, C.J. (1976): Serotonergic modulation of the dopamine response from the nucleus accumbens. *J. Pharmacol. Pharm.* **28**, 523–526.

Costall, B. Hui, S-C.G. & Naylor, R.J. (1979): The importance of serotonergic mechanisms for the induction of hyperactivity by amphetamine and its antagonism by intra-accumbens (3,4-dihydroxy-phenlamino)-2-imidazoline (DPI). *Neuropharmacology* **18**, 605–609.

Costall, B., Kelly, M.E. & Naylor, R.J. (1983): The production of asymmetry and circling behaviour following unilateral intrastriatal administrations of neuroleptic agents: a comparison of abilities to antagonise striatal dopamine function. *Eur. J. Pharmacol.* **96**, 79–86.

Costall, B., Domeney, A.M., Naylor, R.J. & Tyers, M.B. (1988): Inhibition by 5-HT_3 antagonists of hyperactivity caused by dopamine infusion into rat nucleus accumbens. *Br. J. Pharmacol.* **93**, 194P.

Delisi, L.E., Neckers, L.M., Weinberger, D.R. & Wyatt, R.J. (1981): Increased whole blood concentrations in chronic schizophrenic patients. *Arch. Gen. Psychiatry* **38**, 647–650.

Freedman, D.X., Belendiuk, K.C. & Belendiuk, G.W. (1981): Blood tryptophan metabolism in chronic schizophrenics. *Arch. Gen. Psychiatry* **38**, 665–669.

Hagan, R.M., Butler, A., Hill, J.M., Jordan, C.C., Ireland, S.J. & Tyers, M.B. (1987): Effect of the 5-HT_3 receptor antagonist, GR38032F, on responses to injection of a neurokinin agonist into the central tegmental area of the rat brain. *Eur. J. Pharmacol.* **138**, 303–305.

Jones, D.L., Mogenson, G.J. & Wu, M. (1981): Injections of dopaminergic, cholinergic, serotonergic and GABA-ergic drugs into the nucleus accumbens: effects on locomotor activity in the rat. *Neuropharmacology* **20**, 29–37.

King, R., Faull, K.F., Stahl, S.M., Mefford, I.N., Thiemann, S., Barchas, J.D. & Berger, P.A. (1985): Serotonin and schizophrenia: correlations between serotonergic activity and schizophrenic motor behaviour. *Psychiatr. Res.* **14**, 235–240.

Makanjuola, R.O.A., Dow, R.C. & Ashcroft, G.W. (1980): Behavioural responses to steretactically controlled injections of monoamine neurotransmitters into the accumbens and caudate putamen nuclei. *Psychopharmacology* **71**, 227–235.

Pijnenburg, A.J.J., Honig, W.M.M. & Van Rossum, J.M. (1975): Effects of antagonists upon locomotor stimulation induced by injection of dopamine and noradrenaline into the nucleus accumbens of nialamide-pretreated rats. *Psychopharmacologia (Berlin)* **41**, 175–180.

Reynolds, G.P. (1983): Increased concentrations and lateral asymmetry of amygdala dopamine in schizophrenia. *Nature* **305**, 527–528.

Sedvall, G. & Wode-Helgodt, B. (1981): Aberrant monoamine metabolite levels in CSF and family history of schizophrenia. *Arch. Gen. Psychiatry* **37**, 1113–1117.

Stahl, S.M., Wood, D.J., Mefford, I.N., Berger, P.S. & Ciaron-Ello, R.D. (1983): Hyperserotonemia and platelet serotonin uptake and release in schizophrenia and affective disorders. *Am. J. Psychiatry* **140**, 23–26.

Todrick, A., Tait, A.C. & Marshall, E.F. (1960): Blood platelet 5HT levels in psychiatric patients. *Br. J. Psychiatry* **106**, 884–888.

Chapter 22

Noradrenaline, state dependency and relapse prediction in schizophrenia: a hypothesis

Daniel P. van Kammen, Jeffrey L. Peters, Welmoet B. van Kammen, Thomas Neylan, Jeffrey K. Yao, David Shaw and George Dougherty

Western Psychiatric Institute and Clinic, Department of Psychiatry, University of Pittsburgh School of Medicine; and Veterans Administration Medical Centre, Highland Drive, Pittsburgh, PA 15206, USA

Summary

Evidence of elevated noradrenaline levels in the brain and cerebrospinal fluid of drug-free schizophrenic patients is one of the most frequently replicated findings in the literature. However, it is unclear whether this increase is the result of psychosis or neuroleptic drug treatment. By dividing patients into clinically stable and unstable subgroups, some of the reported inconsistencies may be explained. The authors show that noradrenaline release is increased prior to relapse. Similarly, with successful neuroleptic treatment, noradrenaline turnover decreases in stable patients. Increased noradrenaline activity during chronic neuroleptic treatment is associated with relapse following drug withdrawal and also with an increase in both positive and negative symptoms. The authors propose that a dysregulation of the noradrenaline system, ie locus coeruleus, may trigger behaviour in the presence of a dopamine disturbance.

Introduction

Despite the evidence implicating overactive dopamine neuronal systems in schizophrenia, the dopamine hypothesis does not explain in full the clinical symptomatology, drug response or course of this complex disorder (Meltzer, 1979; Crow, 1982). Recent biochemical, behavioural and physical studies suggest a disturbance in the noradrenergic system in schizophrenia as well (Hornykiewicz, 1982; van Kammen & Antelman, 1984). The first major noradrenaline related hypothesis (Stein & Wise, 1971) proposed decreased dopamine beta-hydroxylase (DBH) activity leading to *decreased* noradrenaline levels and more negative symptoms, eg anhedonia. Others have associated decreased DBH with increased dopamine activity, which leads to psychosis (Hartmann, 1976). Subsequent hypotheses have linked the paranoid subtype of schizophrenia with *increased* noradrenaline activity (Farley *et al.*, 1978; Meltzer, 1979; Lake *et al.*, 1980; van Kammen *et al.*, 1981; Sternberg *et al.*, 1983*a*). It now appears that in relapsed patients both positive and negative symptoms are elevated with increased noradrenaline activity (van Kammen *et al.*, 1989*a*, *b*; Rosen *et al.*, 1984), in all likelihood irrespective of DBH activity.

A noradrenergic hypothesis of schizophrenia is not intuitively obvious, since dopamine receptor blackade is believed to mediate the therapeutic effect of antipsychotic drugs (Snyder, 1981). Furthermore, there are many conflicting and paradoxical reports of adrenergic activity in the literature. Elevated noradrenaline levels in the CSF (Lake *et al.*, 1980; Gomes *et al.*, 1980; Kemali, *et al.*, 1982; Gattaz *et al.*, 1983) and in autopsy brains of schizophrenics (Farley *et al.*, 1978; Crow *et al.*, 1979; Carlsson, 1979; Bridge *et al.*, 1985; Kleinman *et al.*, 1985) are some of the most prominent biological findings in schizophrenia. Other evidence of a noradrenaline disturbance is indicated in both abnormally increased (Matussek *et al.*, 1980; Sternberg *et al.*, 1983*a*; Kafka *et al.*, 1985) and decreased alpha$_2$ receptor activity (Mueller-Spahn *et al.*, 1986; Sternberg *et al.*, 1982). Alpha$_2$ receptor function may also be diminished as indicated by decreased cAMP synthesis stimulated by prostaglandin (PG) E_1, eg subsensitive PGE_1 receptors in platelets (Rotrosen *et al.*, 1980; Kafka & van Kammen, 1983; Kafka *et al.*, 1985; Kanof *et al.*, 1986) or impaired adenylcyclase activity (Kafka & van Kammen, 1983). CSF and plasma noradrenaline levels were elevated during a drug-free evaluation in some cases (Gomes *et al.*, 1980; Kemali *et al.*, 1982; Gattaz *et al.*, 1983; Ackenheil *et al.*, 1985), but decreased following neuroleptic withdrawal (Ackenheil *et al.*, 1985; Zander *et al.*, 1985; Bagdy *et al.*, 1985). These confusing results caused some investigators to dismiss a noradrenaline disturbance in schizophrenia as coincidental or drug induced (Post *et al.*, 1975; Lerner *et al.*, 1978; Crow *et al.*, 1979; Berger *et al.*, 1980; Gattaz *et al.*, 1983; Lal *et al.*, 1983; Ackenheil *et al.*, 1985; Bagdy *et al.*, 1985).

What lies behind these conflicting noradrenaline related findings in schizophrenia? If not coincidental, changes in noradrenaline activity may be important to schizophrenia in a number of ways.

(1) They may be serve as *trait markers*. Traditionally, schizophrenic patients have been studied in cross-sectional designs in the hope of identifying diagnostic differences. Typically, noradrenaline related findings obtained in cross-sectional designs have been explained as subtype differences (ie increased noradrenergic activity in paranoid schizophrenia) (Farley *et al.*, 1978; Meltzer, 1979; Lake *et al.*, 1980; van Kammen *et al.*, 1981; Sternberg *et al.*, 1982; Sternberg *et al.*, 1983*a*).

(2) Noradrenergic variables may also be viewed as *state-dependent markers*. In this paradigm clinical changes are associated with, or a consequence of, biochemical dysregulation. This dysregulation in turn signals the onset and end of a psychotic episode or modulates response to pharmacological agents (Sternberg *et al.*, 1981; Hornykiewicz, 1982; van Kammen & Antelman, 1984; Bowers *et al.*, 1984; Bowers *et al.*, 1986). Significant variance in biochemical measures is accounted for by differences in the underlying biochemical conditions leading to changes in clinical state. We propose that inconsistent biochemical findings in schizophrenia may in part be explained by state-dependency, which can only be explained in a longitudinal design. A variable is state-dependent (unstable) if any of the following criteria are met (van Kammen *et al.*, 1985): (a) it is present during the prepsychotic state and early psychotic exacerbations, but absent during stable residual psychotic or non-psychotic states; (b) the marker will disappear or decrease with response to drug treatment; or (c) it will be predictive of short-term behavioural change which occurs either spontaneously or is drug-induced. The increased CSF noradrenaline levels appear to meet such criteria as we discussed elsewhere (van Kammen *et al.*, 1985).

(3) Finally, the noradrenergic system may serve as an *illness modifier*. This concept is illustrated by the role of the locus coeruleus in the brain (Foote *et al.*, 1983; Svensson, 1987). The locus coeruleus receives input from external environmental as well as internal stimuli, including peripheral vegetative stimuli (Svensson, 1987). It modulates and

integrates the input-output characteristics of its target neurones in a functional way (Foote *et al.*, 1983), changing the signal-to-noise ratio. The ability to discriminate significant stimuli seems to be lost in schizophrenia. Patients become frightened by certain autonomic changes and stimuli that may take on an overriding importance over the external reality. Increased activity of the locus coeruleus could intensify thoughts that otherwise would be dismissed as irrational, to the point that they may become delusions or be experienced as hallucinations. Increased noradrenaline activity could give significance to minor events and occurrences, leading to paranoia and ambivalence (Svensson, 1987), and attention deficits (van Kammen & Antelman, 1984). Because of inadequate feedback regulation and poor integration of brain systems, environmental stresses or random changes in autonomic vegetative activity could trigger shifts in locus coeruleus activity, leading to psychotic decompensation or remission (Zahn *et al.*, 1981; van Kammen & Antelman, 1984). We suggest that LC activity influences the course and expression of schizophrenia without necessarily causing the illness (van Kammen *et al.*, 1981). Thus, increased noradrenaline release may intensify schizophrenic symptoms, while subsensitive $alpha_2$ receptor function may lead to behavioural stability. Illness modifers, trait and state markers exemplify three different ways of looking at the data. Illness modifers can also be stable trait markers in the presence of other disturbances, without being diagnostic in themselves. Low CSF DBH is such a marker (Sternberg *et al.*, 1983*b*; van Kammen *et al.*, 1983).

We shall apply the above mentioned concepts of stability and instability to noradrenergic data from schizophrenic patients, in an attempt to bring some clarity to apparent paradoxical and inconsistent observations in the schizophrenia literature. We shall integrate these reports with some of our recent CSF noradrenaline, 3-methoxy-4-hydroxyphenolglycol (MHPG) data from patients on and off haloperidol, both relapsed and non-relapsed. We shall provide evidence that increased noradrenaline release during neuroleptic treatment is followed by relapse after drug withdrawal. This indicates that CSF noradrenaline is increased prior to behavioural decompensation and not because of it; if indeed this is the case, noradrenaline activity may be linked to short-term prognosis,, predicting relapse and drug response. Finally, we shall formulate the role of noradrenaline in schizophrenia as an amplifier of symptoms, indicating that it may play a similar role in other psychiatric illnesses as well.

Stage of psychotic decompensation

Psychotic decompensation is a dynamic process which unfolds in characteristic stages of increasing behavioural disintegration. Docherty *et al.* (1978) have described these stages as overextension, restrictive consciousness, disinhibition, psychotic disintegration, and psychotic resolution. From a stable clinical condition the patient moves through an overextension phase in which he appears dysphoric and distressed, followed by a restricted consciousness or withdrawal phase in which negative and depressive symptoms appear. Any of these stages could reflect changes in noradrenaline activity.

The hyperarousal and increased noradrenaline activity (Zahn *et al.*, 1981; Hornykiewicz, 1982; van Kammen & Antelman, 1984), which has traditionally been explained as secondary to psychotic symptoms (hypothesis A, Fig. 1), may indicate a failure of homeostatic forces. The anxiety and fear of the primary delusional state may reflect outpouring of noradrenaline; the secondary delusional state, as discussed by Jaspers, may indicate a newly found stable homeostasis of relatively decreased noradrenaline activity. In addition, increased arousal and decreased sleep typically *precede* psychotic

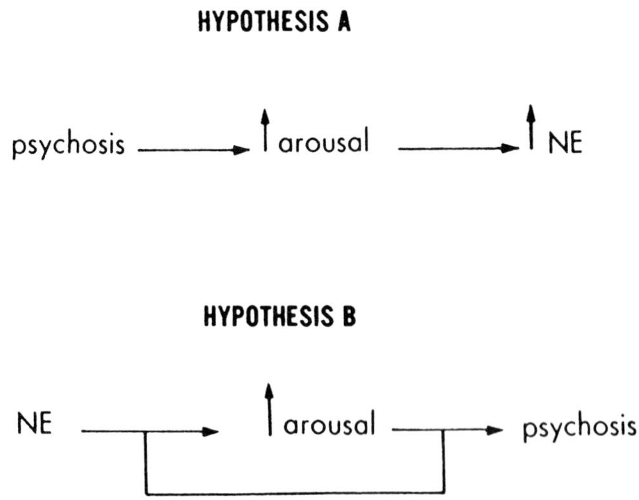

Fig. 1. *We suggest that noradrenaline release is increased prior to relapse, eg that increased noradrenaline release leads to relapse.*

decompensation (Docherty *et al.*, 1978; Szymanski *et al.*, 1980; Herz & Melville, 1984) (hypothesis B). Hyperarousal and loss of sleep are the hallmarks of the disinhibition or prepsychotic phase. Figure 2 shows, as an example, the daily psychosis ratings with the hours of sleep (at night) obtained in a patient who relapsed. During the prodromal phase prior to reaching relapse criteria, sleep decreases while psychosis begins to increase. After relapse is established, duration of sleep bottoms out, and psychosis continues to increase and peaks later.

If we accept the concept of the behavioural prodromes of relapse, it is easy to propose biochemical prodromes. Such biochemical prodromes are hard to study because of the uncertainty about when patients will relapse. One way to approach this methodological problem is to study patients before and after neuroleptic withdrawal when the risk of relapse is high. Most of the previous neuroleptic withdrawal studies drew conclusions from stable drug-free patients rather than from patients who relapsed (Zander *et al.*, 1985; Bagdy *et al.*, 1985; Mueller-Spahn *et al.*, 1986; Glazer *et al.*, 1987). The data from relapsed patients suggest that the increase in noradrenaline activity drives the psychotic relapse rather than the reverse. (See below.)

CSF noradrenaline and sleep

Kemali *et al.* (1985) reported that CSF noradrenaline levels correlated positively with daytime electroencephalographic (EEG) indices of arousal in schizophrenic patients. The exact role of noradrenaline in wakefulness and sleep is uncertain, but it may act as a modulator (Monti, 1985). In a group of drug-free schizophrenic patients we found that elevated CSF noradrenaline levels were associated with fewer hours of sleep the night before the lumbar puncture ($r = -0.44$, $n = 53$, $P < 0.008$) (van Kammen & Antelman, 1984). We also noted that CSF noradrenaline levels declined with pimozide treatment, which paralled a similar decrease in psychosis (Sternberg *et al.*, 1981). This decline in CSF noradrenaline may indicate a neuroleptic-induced inactivation of the locus coeruleus

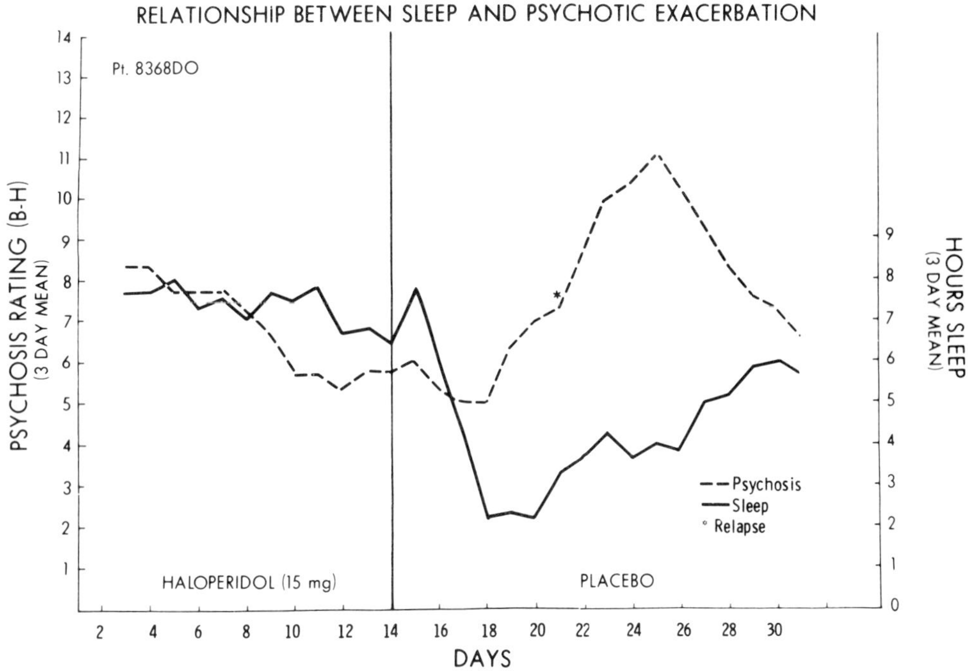

Fig. 2. *Daily psychosis and the hours of nightly sleep (—) are plotted against time.* The values are 3 day running means. Sleep decreased prior to relapse. *Indicates the time point at which relapse criteria are met. Note that sleep returned to normal while psychosis continued to increase, peaked and decreased again. This is one example out of many.

(Dinan & Aston-Jones, 1985). Briefly, chronic neuroleptic exposure leads to a diminished firing rate of spontaneously firing neurones secondary to chronic hyperpolarization. Since disturbed sleep is frequently one of the first prodromal symptoms to improve with neuroleptic treatment (Docherty *et al.*, 1978; Szymanski *et al.*, 1980), this finding points indirectly towards a relationship between changes in CSF noradrenaline levels and changing clinical states, drug-induced or otherwise. The variability of CSF noradrenaline levels taken at different times in an individual patient may also be explained by changes in clinical state from one lumbar puncture to the next (Linnoila *et al.*, 1983). The relationships between CSF noradrenaline and sleep are mainly observed during the prepsychotic stage or early in the decompensation. Our data indicate that sleep EEG studies in drug-free schizophrenic patients will produce variable results (Zarcone *et al.*, 1987; Ganguli *et al.*, 1987), unless differences in clinical and biochemical states are taken into consideration (van Kammen *et al.*, 1989*a*).

CSF noradrenaline, CSF MHPG and psychosis

In addition to finding correlations between CSF noradrenaline and psychosis, we have found a relationship in drug-free schizophrenic patients between CSF MHPG and psychosis ($r = 0.59$, $n = 14$, $P < 0.025$; and $r = 0.66$, $n = 15$, $P = 0.01$, van Kammen, D. P., Karoum, F., Marder, S. R., Wyatt, R., unpublished data, 1979). Recently, we followed up on this potential relationship by measuring CSF noradrenaline and MHPG before and after haloperidol withdrawal (van Kammen *et al.*, 1989*a*). Patients were placed on placebo following haloperidol withdrawal, and monitored for 6 weeks, or until relapse, at which time a lumbar puncture was performed (Fig. 2). CSF noradrenaline was elevated in the relapsed patients, both before and after haloperidol withdrawal. Also, in relapsed drug-free patients, CSF noradrenaline and CSF MHPG correlated significantly with the psychosis ratings of the day before the LP ($r=0.57$, $n = 13$, $P < 0.02$; $r = 0.74$, $n = 13$, $P = 0.002$). During haloperidol treatment similar relationships were not observed. This indicates that the timing of the lumbar puncture in relation to clinical or biochemical stability and medication status determines whether significant correlations between CSF noradrenaline or MHPG and clinical state will be observed.

We dissected further the relationships of CSF MHPG and noradrenaline, psychosis and sleep in the patients who *did* and *did not* relapse in the 6 weeks following haloperidol withdrawal (van Kammen *et al.*, 1989*a*). There were no significant differences in age, duration of illness, age of onset, or family history between these two patient groups. The two groups showed no significant differences during haloperidol treatment in psychosis ratings, hours of sleep, or dose of haloperidol. Following withdrawal, relapsers slept less (5.0± [s.d.] 2.25 *vs* 7.1 ± 0.96 h per night, $P = 0.005$) and had higher CSF noradrenaline (0.91 ± 0.510 *vs* 0.48 ± 0.284 pmol/ml CSF, $P = 0.011$) and MHPG (46.2 ± 16.78 *vs* 35.4 ± 8.89 pmol/ml CSF, $P = 0.056$) levels than non-relapsers. Additionally, a strong negative relationship between sleep and psychosis was found only in the relapsers. However, all drug-free patients showed a similar negative correlation between sleep and CSF MHPG. Interestingly, during haloperidol treatment, sleep and CSF MHPG correlated *positively*. This positive correlation was significant for the patients who would later relapse. The latter finding awaits further study. Figure 3 shows the CSF noradrenaline and MHPG levels in the two groups with and without haloperidol (see table).

Table. *Relationship between CSF noradrenaline and MHPG with sleep and psychosis.*

		Total group		*Relapsers*		*Non-relapsers*	
		Psychosis	*Sleep*	*Psychosis*	*Sleep*	*Psychosis*	*Sleep*
CSF noradrenaline on haloperidol	r	−0.02	0.04	−0.10	−0.12	−0.02	0.17
	n	30	31	12	12	18	18
	P	NS	NS	NS	NS	NS	NS
CSF MHPG on haloperidol	r	0.06	0.39	−0.01	0.60	0.09	0.23
	n	29	29	12	12	17	17
	P	NS	0.019	NS	0.020	NS	NS
CSF noradrenaline drug-free	r	0.55	−0.63	0.57	−0.55	0.06	−0.37
	n	29	28	13	13	16	15
	P	0.001	0.0001	0.020	0.027	NS	NS
CSF MHPG drug-free	r	0.50	−0.41	0.73	−0.34	0.01	−0.03
	n	30	29	12	12	18	17
	P	0.002	0.014	0.004	NS	NS	NS

r = Pearson R; n = number of subjects; *P* = probability that relationship can be explained by chance; NS = non-significant ($p > 0.1$); Sleep: the hours of sleep the night before the lumbar puncture (LP); Psychosis: the psychosis rating the day of the LP; CSF = cerebrospinal fluid; MHPG = 3-methoxy-4-hydroxyphenolglycol. Lumbar punctures were obtained during the last week of haloperidol treatment and after 6 weeks of drug-free treatment after haloperidol withdrawal or before that time when patients met relapse criteria.

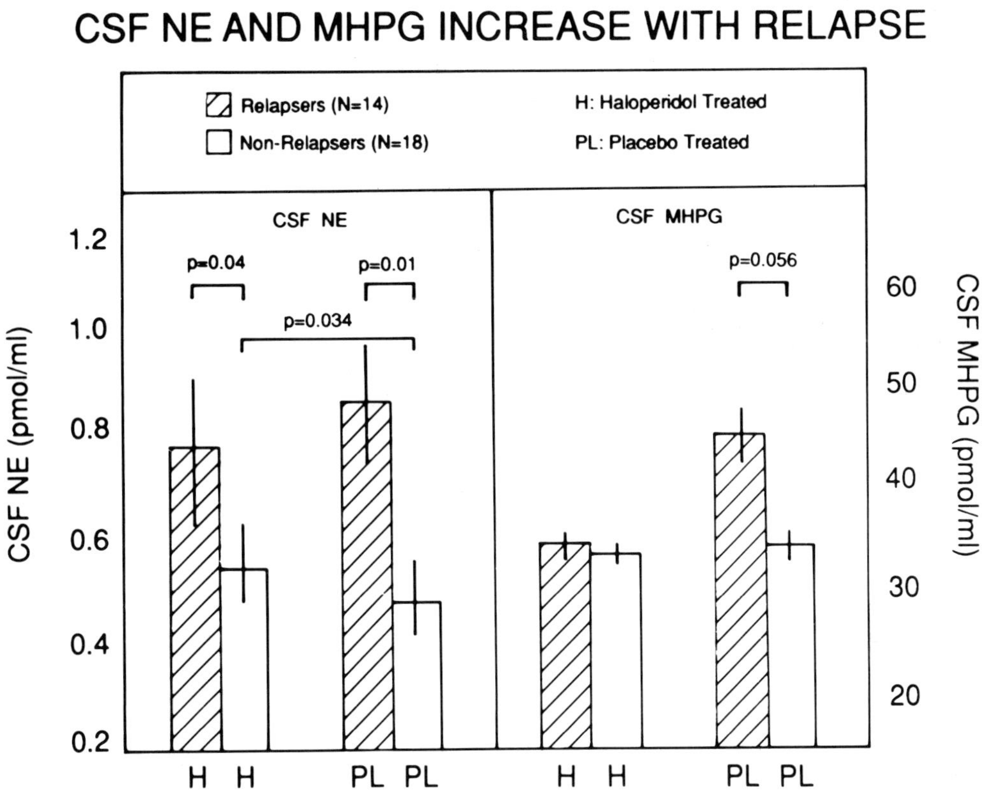

Fig. 3. *During haloperidol treatment, CSF noradrenaline was already elevated in the patients who relapsed after haloperidol withdrawal; following haloperidol withdrawal, CSF 3-methoxy-4-hydroxyphenolglycol and noradrenaline were elevated in the relapsed patients.* This suggests that the increase in CSF noradrenaline is a biochemical prodrome of relapse.

CSF homovanillic and 5-hydroxyindoleactic acid

In contrast to CSF noradrenaline and MHPG, CSF homovanillic acid (HVA) and 5-hydroxyindoleacetic acid (5 HIAA) levels were not significantly different between relapsers and non-relapsers in the haloperidol-treated or in the drug-free condition. In the combined group, psychosis did not correlate positively with CSF HVA in either condition.

In the drug-free *relapsers*, CSF HVA correlated non-significantly with psychosis ($r = 0.36$, $n = 13$, NS), suggesting a potential relationship between psychosis and increased dopamine release. Post *et al.* (1975) reported that acutely ill patients showed higher CSF HVA than remitted patients. In six drug-free patients who received a lumbar puncture when they were acutely ill and again when remitted 2–3 months later, a significant decrease in CSF HVA was observed ($P < 0.05$) (van Kammen, D.P., Marder, S., Gordon, B., Kopin, I., unpublished data, 1978). A similar decrease was observed with CSF MHPG ($P < 0.05$). More recently, we did not observe an increase in CSF HVA during relapse following haloperidol withdrawal (van Kammen *et al.*, 1989*a*). Theoretically, increased dopamine synthesis is present in more acutely ill patients, and may be decreased in the presence of supersensitive dopamine receptors (Bowers & Rozitis, 1974). In the non-relapsers CSF HVA did not correlate significantly with psychosis under either condition. This could be the result of a depolarization block induced by neuroleptics (Skirboll & Bunney, 1979; Grace & Bunney, 1986). For example, residual psychosis levels, not responsive to dopamine blockade, remain unchanged in the presence of decreased dopamine release. Brain atrophy also affects these relationships (van Kammen *et al.*, 1986), and this will be studied when we increase our patient sample.

CSF noradrenaline and MHPG, plasma MHPG and drug response

Neuroleptics are considered to block both noradrenaline and dopamine neurotransmission (Anden *et al.*, 1970; Hyttel, 1974; Robinson *et al.*, 1978), and to be equipotent as alpha$_2$ and dopamine D_2 receptor antagonists (Creese, 1983). In spite of the lack of a relationship between clinical potency and alpha$_2$ receptor blockade *in vitro* (Peroutka & Snyder, 1980), *in vivo* studies have suggested that there is a strong correlation between the ability of a neuroleptic to block the effects of noradrenaline on single neurones and its clinical efficacy (Marwaha *et al.*, 1981). These seemingly paradoxical reports may indicate a neuroleptic effect on noradrenaline mechanisms beyond the receptor itself. It also suggests that a relatively increased noradrenaline release prior to treatment may be necessary for an optimal drug response. This relationship is further supported by the observation that CSF noradrenaline decreased during pimozide treatment parallel with a decrease in psychosis (Sternberg *et al.*, 1981), and that elevated pretreatment plasma MHPG is associated with rapid neuroleptic response (Bowers *et al.*, 1984; Bowers *et al.*, 1986).

In the past van Kammen *et al.* (van Kammen *et al.*, 1982*a*; Angrist & van Kammen, 1984) reported that the acute behavioural change induced by d-amphetamine indicated that the patient was clinically unstable. In addition, they reported that baseline drug-free CSF MHPG levels correlated significantly with the change in psychosis following an infusion of 20 mg d-amphetamine in drug-free schizophrenic patients ($r = 0.58$, $n = 28$, $P = 0.002$) (van Kammen *et al.*, 1982*a*). Furthermore, the response to amphetamine predicted response to pimozide treatment (van Kammen *et al.*, 1982*b*). This indicates that baseline noradrenaline activity may play an important modulatory role in the responses both to antipsychotic drugs and d-amphetamine. A similar relationship between CSF HVA, DOPAC or 5HIAA and the subsequent psychotogenic response to d-amphetamine was not observed (van Kammen *et al.*, 1982*a*).

An alpha$_2$ receptor disturbance?

Chronic schizophrenic patients seem to have lower alpha$_2$ receptor function (Sternberg *et al.*, 1982; Kafka & van Kammen, 1983; Ackenheil *et al.*, 1985; Ko *et al.*, 1985; Mueller-Spahn *et al.*, 1986), whereas acute patients are more likely to have normal (Lal *et al.*, 1983), or increased (Matussek *et al.*, 1980; Sternberg *et al.*, 1983*a*) activity. Kanof *et al.* (1986) found the cAMP response in platelets to correlate with psychosis ratings. We do not know whether the reduced responsiveness of cAMP synthesis to PGE_1 stimulation (alpha$_2$ receptor function) in platelets is also present in the CNS or whether it is associated with either the noradrenaline or dopamine systems or both (Kafka & van Kammen, 1983; Kafka *et al.*, 1985; Kanof *et al.*, 1986). Clonidine treatment was effective in relapsed schizophrenic patients who had relatively elevated growth hormone response to a clonidine challenge (van Kammen *et al.*, 1989*b*).

Relapse Prediction

Attempts to identify patients on neuroleptic maintenance treatment who would relapse following drug withdrawal have included behavioural and endocrine (growth hormone [GH]) responses to d-amphetamine (Angrist *et al.*, 1981; van Kammen *et al.*, 1982*c*) or methylphenidate (Lieberman *et al.*, 1987). Van Kammen *et al.* (1982*c*; 1987) suggested that the worsening observed with d-amphetamine in the presence of dopamine receptor blockade indicated that a role for noradrenaline in the behavioural response to d-amphetamine could not be excluded. When these prediction studies were done with methylphenidate (Lieberman *et al.*, 1987) or levodopa (Davidson *et al.*, 1987) before or after neuroleptic withdrawal, similar results were obtained. Therefore a case could be made for a role for noradrenaline in relapse as well. To test this hypothesis of noradrenergic involvement in relapse, we used the clonidine challenge test (CCT). The growth hormone response to the CCT during haloperidol maintenance treatment was significantly higher in relapsers, but significantly lower in the non-relapsers and lower than in the normal controls (Peters, J., van Kammen, D. P., Gietz, K., *et al.*, unpublished data, 1987). Furthermore, as indicated above, CSF noradrenaline was elevated in these haloperidol-treated patients as well (van Kammen *et al.*, 1989*a*). This suggests that in stable schizophrenic patients noradrenaline release and $alpha_2$ receptor function may be uncoupled, ie both are decreased.

Noradrenaline and dopamine in psychotic decompensation

Both noradrenaline and dopamine are involved in the homeostasis of behaviour. Antelman & Caggiula (1977) reviewed evidence that during minimal stress or activation noradrenaline decreases dopamine dependent behaviours; whereas noradrenaline facilitates dopamine dependent behaviours under steady state conditions. Conceivably, impaired sensory filtering (Freedman *et al.*, 1988) secondary to increased noradrenaline may lead to increased risk of relapse (Geyer & Braff, 1988).

Both noradrenaline and dopamine are present in the limbic system and cerebral cortex, two structures believed to be involved in the pathophysiology and treatment response in schizophrenia (Hornykiewicz, 1982; van Kammen & Antelman, 1984). Because the noradrenaline and dopamine systems do interact (Anden *et al.*, 1970; Costall & Naylor, 1972; Hyttel, 1974; Garattini *et al.*, 1974; Antelman & Caggiula, 1977; Robinson *et al.*, 1978; Hornykiewicz, 1982; van Kammen & Antelman, 1984; Ornstein *et al.*, 1987), particularly in areas that are implicated in schizophrenia (eg the neocortex, amygdala and nucleus accumbens), sustained release of noradrenaline may increase the relapse risk or trigger the psychotic episode. Several groups found CSF noradrenaline to correlate with CSF dopamine (van Kammen & Antelman, 1984; Gattaz *et al.*, 1983) or dopamine sulphate (van Kammen & Antelman, 1984) in drug-free patients, which suggests that dopamine release is simultaneously increased in this condition. CSF MHPG correlated significantly with CSF HVA only in the drug-free relapsed patients. HVA may increase later in the episode than MHPG, because of the reported increase in plasma or CSF HVA with relapse, which we did not observe. Both dopamine and noradrenaline neuronal systems are found to be inactivated following chronic haloperidol treatment (Skirboll & Bunney, 1979; Dinan & Aston-Jones, 1985; Grace & Bunney, 1986). Chronic haloperidol treatment inactivates locus coeruleus neurones (Dinan & Aston-Jones, 1985), but the mechanisms may be different from the depolarization inactivation of the dopamine system induced by haloperidol (Grace & Bunney, 1986; Skirboll & Bunney, 1979). The observed increase in CSF noradrenaline during haloperidol maintenance treatment in the patients who relapsed after haloperidol withdrawal could be due to a reversal of this inactivation, ie a hyperresponsiveness of noradrenaline cells in spite of the inactivating effects of maximum adrenergic blockade, or a failure of inhibitory inputs. Whether this increase in CSF noradrenaline would increase the risk of relapse *during* neuroleptic treatment is unknown.

Recently, van der Heyden *et al.* (1986) reported that noradrenaline activated dopamine-sensitive adenylcyclase, but isoprenaline did not, suggesting a relationship between the D_1 and the $alpha_2$ receptor. There is preliminary evidence that the coupling of dopamine-sensitive adenylcyclase activity is increased in schizophrenic autopsy brains (Memo *et al.*, 1983). Tittler *et al.* (1977) found noradrenaline to interact with D_2 receptors also. Increased D_2 receptor sensitivity has been reported in autopsy brains of some schizophrenic patients (Seeman *et al.*, 1987). These intriguing findings raise interesting issues about the relationship between noradrenaline levels and $alpha_2$ receptor activity on the one hand, and D_1 and D_2 receptor function on the other.

The noradrenaline-dopamine hypothesis of psychotic decompensation and antipsychotic drug response

The thesis of this paper is that elevated noradrenaline releases the risk of psychotic exacerbation or relapse in schizophrenia. We postulate that during the prodromal states, eg during biochemical and clinical instability, excess noradrenaline activity causes, through arousal, decreased sleep and increased psychosis in drug-free patients. Increased noradrenaline activity facilitates improvement with antipsychotic drugs (Sternberg *et al.*, 1981; Bowers *et al.*, 1984; Bowers *et al.*, 1986). Successful neuroleptic treatment is associated with down regulation of dopamine (Grace & Bunney, 1986; Skirboll & Bunney, 1979) and noradrenaline release (Sternberg *et al.*, 1981; Dinan & Aston-Jones, 1985). When the noradrenaline release normalizes, sleep duration returns to normal. Underarousal is present during the stable chronic psychotic state, when noradrenaline activity is decreased. During these chronic conditions CSF noradrenaline can increase again. Patients can become 'stuck' in any stage for some time, which may well explain the large literature reporting over- and underarousal in schizophrenic patients (McGhie & Chapman, 1961; Zahn *et al.*, 1981; Zahn *et al.*, 1987). Increased noradrenaline activity may cause prodromal symptoms and aid environmental stressors in exerting their noxious influence, thus increasing the risk of a psychotic exacerbation. During neuroleptic maintenance treatment, D_2 receptor (and $alpha_1$) blockade may prevent increased noradrenaline release from exerting its major psychotogenic effect. If we accept the dopamine-related abnormalities in schizophrenic autopsy brains (Tittler *et al.*, 1977; Hess *et al.*, 1987; Seeman *et al.*, 1987), the dopaminergic input in the locus coeruleus (Ornstein *et al.*, 1987) and that noradrenaline has a regulatory input of noradrenaline and dopamine neurones (van der Heyden *et al.*, 1986; Grenhoff & Svensson, 1988), it is conceivable that a compensated but dysregulated dopamine receptor function can lead to an increase in psychosis by an increase in noradrenaline activity. We propose that increased release of noradrenaline may be necessary but not solely responsible for the behavioural change in schizophrenia. The locus coeruleus may have a permissive effect on the behaviours mediated by dopamine in schizophrenia. Despite intrinsic differences between the dopamine and noradrenaline systems, both appear to be disturbed in schizophrenia.

Conclusion

We believe that the division of schizophrenic patients into stable and unstable categories is one way to solve the quagmire of increased and decreased noradrenaline activity in schizophrenia. The course of schizophrenia can be described as periods of behavioural and biochemical instability interspersed with periods of stability (Strauss *et al.*, 1985; Zubin *et al.*, 1985). *Chronic* schizophrenic patients are typically in a stable clinical and biochemical state but can become unstable, ie acute. Our data indicate that noradrenaline release is increased preceding psychotic decompensation and increased in patients who respond to neuroleptics (unstable patients). During stabilization noradrenaline levels decrease or return to normal (van Kammen *et al.*, 1981; Sternberg *et al.*, 1981; van Kammen & Antelman, 1984). In stable remitted patients following haloperidol withdrawal, CSF noradrenaline declines further with a small but statistically significant decrease in psychosis (van Kammen *et al.*, 1989*a*). This decrease may explain why some patients improve when antipsychotic drugs are withdrawn (van Kammen *et al.*, 1978; Marder *et al.*, 1979; Zander *et al.*, 1985).

This model of a varying biochemical stability in schizophrenia may help to clarify the large within patient variability, not only of CSF noradrenaline levels (Linnoila *et al.*, 1983) but also of excretion of urinary free cortisol (Sachar *et al.*, 1970), responses to stress (Gruen & Baron, 1984; van Kammen & van Kammen, 1984; Geyer & Braff, 1988), and amphetamine (Kokkinides & Anisman, 1980; van Kammen *et al.*, 1982*a*; Angrist & van Kammen, 1984; van Kammen & van Kammen, 1984). Similarly, this model may explain why patients do not always respond the same way to the same neuroleptics during different episodes (van der Velde, 1976). Furthermore, this may suggest reasons why only a few *chronic* patients have been reported to be responsive to clonidine (Freedman *et al.*, 1982; van Kammen *et al.*, 1989*a*) or propranolol (Yorkston *et al.*, 1974; Manchanda & Hirsch, 1986).

If noradrenaline activity is under state-dependent control, elevated CSF or brain noradrenaline in the presence of paranoid symptoms does not necessarily imply that only patients with a diagnosis of paranoid schizophrenia show these elevated levels. Increased psychotic symptoms may include paranoid symptoms in all subtypes of schizophrenia as well. This suggests that noradrenaline elevation may be a generalized phenomenon in schizophrenic patients; paranoid symptoms may be more evident in psychotic patients when noradrenaline turnover is increased (van Kammen *et al.*, 1989*a*).

Svensson (1987) proposed that internal vegetative autonomic stimuli can activate the locus coeruleus. There may be faulty feedback regulation of the locus coeruleus, which includes dopamine input (Ornstein *et al.*, 1987) and may make the central noradrenergic systems more responsive to internal (central and peripheral) and external stimuli (Zubin *et al.*, 1985). There is also a disturbance in the interpretation of perceptual changes in the prefrontal sensory integration cortex (Zahn *et al.*, 1987). Albus *et al.* (1982) reported evidence that schizophrenia is associated with autonomic dysregulation. If our interpretation of the data is correct, we shall better understand what causes psychotic decompensation when we know what leads to this increase in CSF noradrenaline levels and autonomic dysregulation.

Several questions remain: why are decreased CSF noradrenaline levels and central $alpha_2$ receptor subsensitivity associated with clinical stability? Is this secondary to dopamine input into the locus coeruleus (Ornstein *et al.*, 1987) or *vice versa*? Are noradrenaline release and receptor sensitivity dissociated in stable patients? How do the relative decreases in noradrenaline release associated with chronic neuroleptic treatment lead to decreases in psychosis? Several conditions, including damage to the locus coeruleus (Lohr & Jeste, 1988)and a membrane disorder (Rotrosen *et al.*, 1980; Henn & Henn, 1982; van Kammen & Antelman, 1984; Garver *et al.*, 1988) could lead to this dysregulation of noradrenaline activity. We conclude that noradrenaline activity modulates the pathophysiology of schizophrenia, most likely in the presence of a dopamine disturbance.

Acknowledgements—We thank Ms Doris McAdam, RN, Head Nurse, her nursing staff and the patients of the Schizophrenia Research Unit of the Highland Drive Veterans Administration Medical Centre, Pittsburgh, PA, for their cooperation and participation in the studies described. We are similarly grateful to Ms Sylvia Beal, RN, Head Nurse, her nursing staff and the patients of the NIMH Clinical Research Unit 3-East at the National Institutes of Health, Bethesda, MD. The comments by Dr G. Aston-Jones are very much appreciated. We also thank Mary Kelley, BS, and William Gromley for manuscript preparation. This research was supported in part by the Veterans Administration Research Advisory Group and Merit Reviewing funding.

References

Ackenheil, M., Albus, M., Bondy, B., Muller-Spahn, F., Munch, U. & Naber, D. (1985): Biochemical and neuroendocrine studies in schizophrenics: Attempts to characterize the illness biochemically. In *Pathochemical markers in major psychoses* eds H. Beckmann & P. Riederer pp. 78–87. Berlin: Springer-Verlag.

Albus, M., Engel, R.R., Mueller, F., Zander, K.J. & Ackenheil, M. (1982): Experimental stress situations and the state of autonomic arousal in schizophrenia and depressive patients. *Int. Pharmacopsychiatr.* **17**, 129–135.

Anden, N.E., Butcher, S.G., Corrodi, H. Fuxe, K. & Ungerstedt, U: (1970) Receptor activity and turnover of dopamine and noradrenaline after neuroleptics. *Eur. J. Pharmacol.* **11**, 303–314.

Angrist, B. & van Kammen, D.P. (1984): C. N. S. stimulants as tools in the study of schizophrenia. *Trends in Neurosci.* 7, 388–390.

Angrist, B., Burrows, G.D., Lader, M., Linjaerde, O., Sedvall, G. & Wheatley, D. (1981): Relationships between responses to dopamine agonists, psychopathology, neuroleptic treatment response, and need for neuroleptic maintenance in schizophrenic subjects. In *Recent advances in Neuropsychopharmacology*, eds B. Angrist *et al.* (*Advances in biosciences* vol. 31), pp. 49–54. Oxford: Pergamon Press.

Antelman, S.M. & Caggiula, A.R. (1977): Norepinephrine-dopamine interactions and behavior. *Science* **15**, 646–653.

Bagdy, G., Perenyi, A., Arato, M. & Rotstein, E. (1985): Decrease in CSF dopamine, its metabolites, and noradrenaline after withdrawal of chronic neuroleptic treatment in schizophrenic patients. *Psychiatr. Res.* **12**, 177–178.

Berger, P.A., Faull, K.F., Kildowski, J. Anderson, P.J., Kraemer, H., Davis, K.L. & Barches, J.D. (1980): CSF monoamine metabolites in depression and schizophrenia. *Am. J. Psychiatry* **137**, 174–180.

Bowers, M.B. & Rozitis, A. (1974): Regional differences in homovanillic acid concentrations after acute and chronic administration of antipsychotic drugs. *J. Pharm. Pharmacol.* **26**, 743–745.

Bowers, M.B., Swigar, M.E., Jatlow, P.I. *et al.* (1984): Plasma catecholamine metabolites and early response to haloperidol. *J. Clin. Psychiatry* 1984; 45:248–251.

Bowers, M.B., Swigar, M.E., Jatlow, P.I. & Goicoechea, N. (1986): Early neuroleptic response in psychotic men and women: Correlation with plasma HVA and MPHG. *Comp. Psychiatry* **27**, 181–185.

Bridge, T.P., Kleinman, J.E., Karoum, F. *et al.* (1985): Postmortem central catecholamines and antemortem cognitive impairment in elderly schizophrenics and controls. *Neuropsychology* **14**, 47–61.

Carlsson, A. (1979): The impact of catecholamine research on medical science and practice. In *Catecholamines: Basic and clinical frontiers*, vol. 1, eds E. Usdin, I.J. Kopin & J. Barchas. New York: Pergamon Press.

Costall, B. & Naylor, R.J. (1972): Possible involvement of a noradrenergic area of the amygdala and stereotyped behavior. *Life Sci.* **2**, 1135–1146.

Creese, I. (1983): Receptor interactions of neuroleptics. In *Neuroleptics: Neurochemical, behavioral, and clinical perespectives*, ed. J.T. Coyle. New York: Raven Press.

Crow, T.J. (1982): The two-syndrome concept: origins and current status. *Schizophrenia Bull.* **11**, 471–486.

Crow, T.J., Baker, H.F., Cross, A.J. Joseph, M.H., Lofthouse, R., Longden, A., Owen, F., Riley, G. J., Glover, V. & Killpack, W.S. (1979): Monoamine mechanisms in chronic schizophrenia: Post-mortem neurochemical findings. *Br. J. Psychiatry* **134**, 249–256.

Davidson, M., Keefe, R.S.E., Mohs, R.C. Siever, L.J., Losonczy, M.F., Horvath, T.B. & Davis, K.L. (1987): L-DOPA challenge and relapse in schizophrenia. *Am. J. Psychiatry* **144**, 934–938.

Dinan, T.G. & Aston-Jones, G. (1985): Chronic haloperidol inactivates brain noradrenergic neurones. *Brain Res.* **325**, 385–388.

Docherty, J.P., van Kammen, D.P., Siris, S.G. *et al.* (1978): Stages of onset of schizophrenia psychosis. *Am. J. Psychiatry* **135**, 420–426.

Farley, I.J., Price, K.S., McCullough, E., Deck, J.H., Hordynski, W. & Hornykiewicz, O. (1978): Norepinephrine in chronic paranoid schizophrenia. Above-normal levels in limbic forebrain. *Science* **200**, 456–458.

Foote, S.L., Bloom, F.E., Aston-Jones, G. (1983): Nucleus locus ceruleus: New evidence of anatomical and physiological specificity. *Physiol. Rev.* **63**, 844–914.

Freedman, R., Kirch, D., Bell, J. *et al.* (1982): Clonidine treatment of schizophrenia: double-blind comparison to placebo and neuroleptic drugs. *Acta Psychiatr. Scand.* **65**, 35–40.

Freedman, R., Kirch, D., Bell, J., Adler, L.E., Pecevich, M., Pachtman, E. & Denver, P. (1982): Clonidine treatment of schizophrenia: double-blind comparison to placebo and neuroleptic drugs. *Acta Psychiatr. Scand.* **65**, 35–40.

Freedman, R., Adler, L.E., Gerhardt, G., Waldo, M., Baker, N., Rose, G.M., Drebing, C., Nagamoto, H., Bickford-Wimer, P. & Franks, R. (1987): Neurobiological studies of sensory gating in schizophrenia. *Schizophrenia Bull.* **13**, 669–678.

Ganguli, R., Reynolds, C.F. & Kupfer, D.J. (1987): Electroencephalographic sleep in young, never medicated schizophrenics. A comparison with delusional and nondelusional depressives and with healthy controls. *Arch. Gen. Psychiatry* **44**, 36–44.

Garattini, S., Bareggi, S.R., Marc, V. *et al.* (1974): Effects of piribedil on noradrenaline and MOPEG-SO_4 levels in the rat brain. *Eur. J. Pharmacol.* **28**, 214–216.

Garver, D.L., Kelly, K., Fried, K.A. *et al.* (1988): Drug response patterns as a basis of nosology for the mood-incongruent psychoses (the schizophrenias). *Psychol. Med.* **18**, 1–13.

Gattaz, W.F., Riederer, P., Reynolds, G.P., Gattaz, D. & Beckmann, H. (1983): Dopamine and noradrenaline in cerebrospinal fluid of schizophrenic patients. *Psychiatr. Res.* **8**, 243–250.

Geyer, M. & Braff, D.J. (1988): Startle, sensory motor gating and habitation in schizophrenia and related animal models. *Schizophrenia Bull.* **13**, 643–668.

Glazer, W.M., Charney, D.S. & Heninger, G.R. (1987): Noradrenergic function in schizophrenia. *Arch. Gen. Psychiatry* **44**, 895–904.

Gomes, U.C.R., Shanley, B.C., Potgeiter, L. & Roux, J.T. (1980): Noradrenergic overeactivity in chronic schizophrenia: Evidence based on cerebrospinal fluid noradrenaline and cyclic nucleotide concentrations. *Br. J. Psychiatry* **137**, 346–351.

Grace, A.A. & Bunney, B.S. (1986): Induction of depolarization block in midbrain dopamine neurosis by repeated administration of haloperidol: An analysis using *in vivo* intracellular recordings. *J. Pharmacol. Exp. Ther.* **238**, 1092–1100.

Grenhoff, J. & Svensson, T.H. (1988): Clonidine regularizes substantia nigra dopamine cell firing. *Life Sci.* **42**, 2003–2009.

Gruen, R. & Baron, M. (1984): Stressful life events and schizophrenia. *Neuropsychobiology* **12**, 206–208.

Hartmann, E. (1976): Schizophrenia: A theory. *Psychopharmacology* **49**, 1–15.

Henn, F.A. & Henn, S.W. (1982): Phospholipids as markers for schizophrenia. In *Biological markers in psychiatry and neurology*, eds E. Usdin & I. Hanin, pp. 183–185. New York: Pergamon Press.

Herz, M.I. & Melville, C. (1984): Relapse in schizophrenia. *Am. J. Psychiatry* **137**, 801–805.

Hess, E.J., Bracher, H.S., Kleinman, J.E. & Greese, I. (1987): Dopamine receptor subtype in balance in schizophrenia. *Life Sci.* **40**, 1487–1497.

Hornykiewicz, O. (1982): Brain catecholamines in schizophrenia — a good case for noradrenaline. *Nature* **299**, 484–486.

Hyttel, J. (1974): Effect of neuroleptics on the disappearance rate of (^{14}C)labelled catecholamines formed from (^{14}C)tyrosine in mouse brain. *J. Pharm. Pharmacol.* **26**, 588–596.

Kafka, M.S. & van Kammen, D.P. (1983): Alpha-adrenergic receptor function in schizophrenia: Receptor number, cyclic adenosine monophosphate production, adenylate cyclase activity, and effect of drugs. *Arch. Gen. Psychiatry* **40**, 264–270.

Kafka, M.S., Siever, L.J., Nurnberger, J.I., Uhde, T.W., Targum, S., Cooper, D.M.J., van Kammen, D.P. & Tokola, N.S. (1985): Platelet alpha-adrenergic receptor function in affective disorders and schizophrenia. *Psychopharmacol. Bull.* **21**, 599–602.

Kanof, P.D., Johns, C., Davidson, N., Siever, L.J., Coccaro, E.F. & Davis, K.L. (1986): Prostaglandin receptor sensitivity in psychiatric disorders. *Arch. Gen. Psychiatry* **43**, 987–993.

Kemali, D., DelVecchio, M. & Maj, M. (1982): Increased noradrenaline levels in CSF and plasma of schizophrenic patients. *Biol. Psychiatry* **17**, 711–717.

Kemali, D., Maj, M., Iorio, G., Marciano, F., Nolfe, G., Galderisi, S. & Salvati, A. (1985): Relationship between CSF noradrenaline levels, C-EEG indicators of activation, and psychosis ratings in drug-free schizophrenic patients. *Acta Psychiatr. Scand.* **71**, 19–24.

Kleinman, J.E., Hong, J., Iasarola, M., Govoni, S. & Gillin, C.J. (1985): Neuropeptide in human brain — postmortem studies. *Prog. Neuropsychopharmacol. Biol. Psychiatry* **9**, 91–95.

Ko, G.N., Unnerstall, J.R., Kuhar, M.J., Wyatt, R.J., Raskin, A. & Kleinman, J.E. (1985): Lower $alpha_2$ agonist binding in schizophrenic brains. In *Abstracts of Panels and Posters*. ACNP, 1985, p. 150.

Kokkinides, L. & Anisman, H. (1980): Amphetamine models of paranoid schizophrenia. An overview and elaboration of animal experimentation. *Psychol. Bull.* **88**, 551–579.

Lake, C.R., Sternberg, D.E., van Kammen, D.P., Ballenger, J.C., Ziegler, M.G., Post, R.M., Kopin, I.J. & Bunney, W.E. (1980): Schizophrenia: Elevated cerebrospinal fluid norepinephrine. *Science* **207**, 331–333.

Lal, S., Nair, N.P.V., Thavundayil, J.X., Monks, R.C. & Guyda, H. (1983): Clonidine-induced growth hormone secretion in chronic schizophrenia. *Acta Psychiatr. Scand.* **68**, 82–88.

Lerner, P., Goodwin, F.K., van Kammen, D.P., Post, R.M., Major, L.F., Ballenger, J.C. & Lovenberg, W. (1978): Dopamine-beta-hydroxylase in cerebrospinal fluid of psychiatric patients. *Biol. Psychiatry* **13**, 685–694.

Lieberman, J.A., Kane, M.H., Sarantakos, S., Gadaleta, D., Woerner, M., Alvir, J. & Ramos-Lorenzi, J. (1987): Prediction of relapse in schizophrenia. *Arch. Gen. Psychiatry* **44**, 597–603.

Linnoila, M., Ninan, P.T., Scheinin, M., Waters, R.N., Chang, W.-H., Bartko, J. & van Kammen, D.P. (1983): Reliability of norepinephrine and major monoamine metabolite measurements in CSF schizophrenic patients. *Arch. Gen. Psychiatry* **40**, 1290–1294.

Lohr, J.B. & Jeste, D.V. (1988): Locus coeruleus morphometry in aging and schizophrenia. *Acta. Psychiatr. Scand.* **77**, 689–697.

Manchanda, R. & Hirsch, S.R. (1986): Does propranolol have an antipsychotic effect: A placebo controlled study in acute schizophrenia. *Br. J. Psychiatry* **148**, 701–707.

Marder, S.R., van Kammen, D.P., Docherty, J.P., Rayner, J. & Bunney, W.E. (1979): Predicting drug-free improvement in schizophrenic psychosis. *Arch. Gen. Psychiatry* **36**, 1080–1085.

Marwaha, J., Hoffer, B.J., Geller, H.M. & Freedman, R. (1981): Electrophysiologic interactions of antipsychotic drugs with central noradrenergic pathways. *Psychopharmacology* **73**, 126–133.

Matussek, N., Ackenheil, M., Hippius, H., Mueller, F., Schroder, H.T., Schulteb, H. & Wasilewski, B. (1980): Effect of clonidine on growth hormone release in psychiatric patients and controls. *Psychiatr. Res.* **2**, 25–36.

McGhie, A. & Chapman, J.S. (1961): Disorders of attention and perception in early schizophrenia. *Br. J. Med. Psychol.* **34**, 103.

Meltzer, H.Y. (1979): Biochemical studies in schizophrenia. In *Disorders of the schizophrenia syndrome*, ed. L. Bellak. New York: Basic Books.

Memo, M., Lovenberg, W. & Hanbauer, I. (1983): Coupling of dopamine D_1 recognition sites with adenylate cyclase in nuclei accumbens and caudatus of schizophrenics. *Science* **221**, 1304–1307.

Monti, J.M. (1985): Norepinephrine: Its role in sleep and waking. In *Sleep '84*, eds W.P. Koella, E. Ruether, & H. Schulz. Stuttgart: Fischer Verlag.

Mueller-Spahn, F., Ackenheil, M., Albus, M., Botscher, C., Naber, D. & Welter, D. (1986): Neuroendocrine effects of clonidine in chronic schizophrenic patients under long-term neuroleptic therapy and after drug withdrawal: Relations to psychopathology. *Psychopharmacology* **33**, 190–195.

Ornstein, K., Milon, H., McRae-Degueurce, A., Alvarez, C., Berger, B. & Wurzner, H.P. (1987): Biochemical and radioautographic evidence for dopaminergic afferents of the locus coeruleus originating in the ventral tegmental area. *J. Neurol. Transm.* 70, 183–191.
Peroutka, S.J. & Snyder, S.H. (1980): Relationship of neuroleptic drug effects at brain dopamine, serotonin, alpha-adrenergic, and histamine receptors to clinical potency. *Am. J. Psychiatry* **137**, 1518–1522.
Post, R.M., Fink, E., Carpenter, W.T. & Goodwin, F.K. (1975): Cerebrospinal fluid amine metabolites in acute schizophrenia. *Arch. Gen. Psychiatry* **32**, 1063–1069.
Robinson, S.E., Berney, S., Mishra, R. & Sulzer, F. (1978): The relative role of dopamine and norepinephrine receptor blockade in the action of antipsychotic drugs: Metoclopramide, thiethylperazine and molindone as pharmacological tools. *Psychopharmacology* **64**, 141–147.
Rosen, W.G., Mohs, R.C., Johns, C.A., Small, N.S., Kendler, K.S., Horvath, T.B. & Davis, K.L. (1984): Positive and negative symptoms in schizophrenia. *Psychiatr. Res.* **13**, 277–284.
Rotrosen, J., Miller, A.D., Mandio, D., Tranicante, L.J. & Gershon, S. (1980): Prostaglandins, platelets, and schizophrenia. *Arch. Gen. Psychiatry* **37**, 1047–1054.
Sachar, E.J., Kanter, S.S., Buie, D., Engle, R. & Mehlman, R. (1970): Psychoendocrinology of ego disintegration. *Am. J. Psychiatry* **126**, 1067–1078.
Seeman, P., Bzowej, N.H., Guan, H.C., Beregon, C., Reynolds, G.P., Bird, E.D., Riederer, P., Jellinger, K. & Tourtellotte, W.W. (1987): Human brain D1 and D2 dopamine receptors in schizophrenia, Alzheimer's, Parkinson's, and Huntington's diseases. *Neuropsychopharmacology* **1**, 5–15.
Skirboll, L.R. & Bunney, B.S. (1979): The effects of acute and chronic haloperidol treatment on spontaneously firing neurons in the caudate nucleus of the rat. *Life Sci.* **25**, 1419–1434.
Snyder, S.H. (1981): Dopamine receptors, neuroleptics, and schizophrenia. *Am. J. Psychiatry* **138**, 460–464.
Stein, L. & Wise, C.D. (1971): Possible etiology of schizophrenia: Progressive damage to the noradrenergic reward system by 6-hydroxydopamine. *Science* **171**, 1032–1036.
Sternberg, D.E., van Kammen, D.P., Lake, C.R., Ballenger, J.C., Marder, S.R. & Bunney, W.E. (1981): The effect of pimozide on CSF norepinephrine in schizophrenia. *Am. J. Psychiatry* **138**, 1045–1051.
Sternberg, D.E., Charney, D.S., Heninger, G.R., Lackman, J.F., Hafstad, K.M. & Landis, D.H. (1982): Impaired presynaptic regulation in schizophrenia: Effects of clonidine in schizophrenia patients and normal controls. *Arch. Gen. Psychiatry* **39**, 285–289.
Sternberg, D.E., Charney, D.S. & Heninger, G.R. (1983*a*): Increased sensitivity of post-synaptic $alpha_2$ adrenergic receptors in paranoid schizophrenic patients: Growth hormone response to clonidine. *Sci. Proc. Soc. Biol. Psychiatry*, abstract VR No 27.
Sternberger, W.E., van Kammen, D.P., Lerner, P., Ballenger, J.C., Marder, S.R., Post, R.M. & Bunney, W.E. (1983*b*): CSF dopamine-beta-hydroxylase in schizophrenia. *Arch. Gen. Psychiatry* **40**, 743–747.
Strauss, J.S., Hafex, H., Liberman, P. & Harding, C.M. (1985): The course of psychiatric disorder. III. Longitudinal principles. Am. J. Psychiatry **142**, 289–296.
Svensson, T.H. (1987): Peripheral, autonomic regulation of locus coeruleus noradrenergic neurons in brain: putative implications for psychiatry and psychopharmacology. *Psychopharmacology* **92**, 1–7.
Szymanski, H.V., Simon, J.C. & Gutterman, N. (1980): Recovery from schizophrenic psychosis. *Am. J. Psychiatry* **15**, 381–388.
Tittler, M., Weinreich, P. & Seeman, P. (1977): New detection of brain dopamine receptors with (^{3}H)dihydroergocryptine. *Proc. Natl. Acad. Sci. USA* **74**, 3750–3753.
van der Heyden, P., Ebinger, G. & Kanarek, L. (1986): Vauquelin, epinephrine and norepinephrine stimulation of adenylate cyclase in bovine retina homogenate: Evidence for interaction with the dopamine D_1 receptor. *Life Sci.* **38**, 1221–1228.
van der Velde, C.N. (1976): Variability in schizophrenia. *Arch. Gen. Psychiatry* **33**, 489–496.
van Kammen, D.P. & Antelman, S. (1984): Impaired noradrenergic transmission in schizophrenia? A minireview. *Life Sci.* **34**, 1403–1413.
van Kammen, D.P. & van Kammen, W.B. (1984): The amphetamine challenge test in schizophrenia: A stress response? An episode marker. In *Stress. The role of catecholamines and other neurotransmitters*, vol. 2 eds E. Usdin, R. Kvetnansky & J. Azelrod, pp. 957–966. New York:

Gordon & Breach Science Publishers.
van Kammen, D.P., Marder, S.R., Murphy, D.L. & Bunney, W.E. (1978): MAO activity, CSF amine metabolites, and drug-free improvement in schizophrenia. *Am. J. Psychiatry* **135**, 567–569.
van Kammen, D.P., Malas, K.L., Sternberg, D.E., Murphy, D.L., Lerner, P., Lake, C.R., Dalton, L.A. & Bunney, W.E. (1981): Platelet monoamine oxidase (MAO) and clinical variables in schizophrenia: Interrelationships with spinal fluid norepinephrine (NE) and dopamine-beta-hydroxylase (DBH). *Psychopharmacol. Bull.* **17**, 207–209.
van Kammen, D.P., Bunney, W.E., Docherty, J.P., Marder, S.R., Ebert, M.H., Goodwin, F.K., Rosenblatt, J.E. & Rayner, J.N. (1982*a*): d-Amphetamine induces heterogeneous changes in psychotic behaviour in schizophrenia. *Am. J. Psychiatry* **139**, 991–997.
van Kammen, D.P., Docherty, J.P., Marder, S.R., Schulz, S.C., Dalton, L. & Bunney, W.E. (1982*b*): Antipsychotic effects of pimozide in schizophrenia: Treatment response prediction with acute d-amphetamine response. *Arch. Gen. Psychiatry* **39**, 261–266.
van Kammen, D.P., Docherty, J.P. & Bunney, W.E. (1982*c*): Prediction of early relapse after pimozide discontinuation by response to d-amphetamine during pimozide treatment. *Biol. Psychiatry* **17**, 233–242.
van Kammen, D.P., Mann, L.S., Sternberg, D.E., Scheinin, M., van Kammen, W.B., Ninan, P.T., Marder, S.R., Rieder, R.D. & Linnoila, M. (1983): Dopamine-beta-hydroxylase activity and homovanillic acid in spinal fluid of schizophrenia patients with brain atrophy. *Science* **220**, 974–977.
van Kammen, D.P., Rosen, J., Peters, J., Fields, R. & van Kammen, W.B. (1985): Are there state dependent markers in schizophrenia? *Psychopharmacol. Bull.* **21**, 497–502.
van Kammen, D.P., van Kammen, W.B., Mann, L.S., Seppala, T. & Linnoila, M. (1986): Dopamine metabolism in the cerebrospinal fluid of drug-free schizophrenic patients with and without cortical atrophy. *Arch. Gen. Psychiatry* **43**, 978–983.
van Kammen, D.P., Hommer, D.W. & Malas, K.L. (1987): Effect of pimozide on positive and negative symptoms in schizophrenic patients: are negative symptoms state dependent? *Neuropsychobiology* **18**, 113–117.
van Kammen, D.P., Peters, J., van Kammen, W.B., Nugent, A., Goetz, K.L., Yao, J. & Linnoila, M. (1989*a*): CSF norepinephrine in schizophrenia is elevated prior to relapse after haloperidol withdrawal. *Biological Psychiatry* **26**, 176–188.
van Kammen, D.P., Peters, J.L., van Kammen, W.B., Rosen, J., Yao, J.K., McAdam, D. & Linnoila, M. (1989*b*): Clonidine treatment of schizophrenia: Can we predict treatment response? *Psychiatr. Res.* **27**, 297–311.
Yorkstone, N.J., Zaki, S.A., Malik, M.K.U., Morrison, R.C. & Harvard, C.W.H. (1974): Propranolol in the control of schizophrenic symptoms. *Br. Med. J.* **iv**, 633–635.
Zahn, T.P., Carpenter, W.T. & McGlashan, T.H. (1981): Autonomic nervous system activity in acute schizophrenia. II. Relationships to short-term prognosis and clinical state. *Arch. Gen. Psychiatry* **38**, 260–266.
Zahn, T.P., Rumsey, J.M. & van Kammen, D.P. (1987): Autonomic nervous system activity in autistic, schizophrenic, and normal men: Effects of stimulus significance. *J. Abnorm. Psychol.* **96**, 135–144.
Zander, K.J., Fisher, B., Zimmer, R. & Ackenheil, M. (1985): Long-term neuroleptic treatment of chronic schizophrenic patients: clinical and biochemical effects of withdrawal. *Psychopharmacology* **73**, 43–47.
Zarcone, V.P., Benson, K.L. & Berger, P.A. (1987): Abnormal rapid eye movement latencies in schizophrenia. *Arch. Gen. Psychiatry* **44**, 45–48.
Zubin, J., Steinhauer, S.R., Day, R. & van Kammen, D.P. (1985): Schizophrenia at the crossroads: A blueprint for the 80's. *Compr. Psychiatry* **26**, 217–240.

Chapter 23

Selective interactions of sulpiride with brain dopamine receptors

P. Jenner, A. Davis, G. Kilpatrick, N. M. J. Rupniak, J. K. Chivers and C. D. Marsden

MRC Movement Disorder Research Group, University Department of Neurology and Parkinson's Disease Society Research Centre, Institute of Psychiatry & King's College Hospital Medical School, Denmark Hill, London SE5, UK

Summary

The antipsychotic actions of sulpiride are associated with a low incidence of extra-pyramidal side-effects and improvement of the negative symptoms of schizophrenia.

Sulpiride is a slightly lipophilic dopamine antagonist which exhibits a high degree of specificity for brain dopamine receptors with little or no action on other neuronal systems in brain. Sulpiride is selective for the D_2 dopamine receptor population and perhaps only for one affinity state of those receptors, for its actions show an absolute dependence on the presence of sodium ions.

Sulpiride causes selective inhibition of some dopamine-mediated motor behaviours. In the presence of sulpiride, apomorphine-mediated motor behaviours are modulated such that those due to D_2 receptor activation are suppressed whereas those of D_1 are potentiated.

The molecular interaction of sulpiride with dopamine receptors also may differ from that of typical neuroleptic drugs. Thermodynamic studies of the effects of sulpiride on D_2 receptors suggest that it interacts in a manner expected for a dopamine agonist rather than for a neuroleptic drug.

Sulpiride and related substituted benzamide drugs may form a distinct pharmacological group characterized by moderate lipophilicity, selective D_2 receptor actions, sodium dependence and an agonist-type interaction with dopamine receptors which, in animals, results in the selective modulation of motor behaviours and, in man, produces alerting effects and a low incidence of motor side effects.

Introduction

Since the introduction of chlorpromazine in the early 1950s the development of novel neuroleptic drugs has relied heavily on animal screening techniques. These detect the ability of drugs to inhibit a variety of motor behaviours associated with altered brain dopamine function, looking for agents which mimic the properties of typical neuroleptic compounds, such as chlorpromazine or haloperidol. However, the use of screening techniques based on motor behaviour inevitably has led to the selection of drugs with not only antipsychotic activity but also the ability to induce extrapyramidal disturbances. The consequence of this approach to drug design has been the successful development of a whole variety of different groups of neuroleptic agents, including phenothiazines, thioxanthenes and butyrophenones, but whose properties closely resemble one another.

Against this background, two novel antipsychotic compounds were introduced which are atypical when compared to more classical compounds and whose use is associated with a lower incidence of extrapyramidal side effects. One of these compounds was clozapine which was subsequently withdrawn from many countries due to the production of bone marrow toxicity in a small group of patients in Finland. The other compound is sulpiride which has now been in use in Europe for some 15 years or more. Sulpiride is of interest because, in many, it is claimed to have a number of distinct advantages over typical neuroleptic drugs. Not only is sulpiride a proven antipsychotic agent (Toru *et al.*, 1972, Cassano *et al.*, 1975; Edwards *et al.*, 1980; Harnryd *et al.*, 1984) but it has been suggested that it is useful in treating the negative symptoms of schizophrenia (Borenstein *et al.*, 1969; Alfredsson *et al.*, 1985) and to cause little sedation and few autonomic side effects. In addition, the incidence of extrapyramidal disorders occurring during the use of sulpiride is said to be lower than that observed with more typical neuroleptic drugs. In a recent survey it was found that sulpiride produces akathisia, parkinsonism and acute dystonia in approximately 4% of patients receiving therapy (Alberts, 1985). Perhaps more importantly there have only been four cases of tardive dyskinesia associated with the use of sulpiride and all of those occurred in patients who had long histories of previous treatment with other neuroleptic agents. In addition, sulpiride is itself of use in the treatment of tardive dyskinesia and may suppress such movements without subsequent breakthrough (Gerlach & Casey, 1984; Quinn & Marsden, 1984). As a consequence of these apparent beneficial effects of sulpiride it has been claimed that the drug may be of advantage in treating young schizophrenics at risk from tardive dyskinesia, patients with established tardive dyskinesia, and patients who are either withdrawn or show negative symptoms of schizophrenia.

These unusual properties of sulpiride in man might suggest that the manner in which the compound alters brain function differs from that associated with typical neuroleptic drugs. In the present work we have set out to summarize the evidence which has accumulated to suggest that sulpiride does indeed show differences from typical neuroleptic drugs. We suggest that perhaps sulpiride and some other substituted benzamide drugs should be classed as a distinct pharmacological group in themselves.

Dopamine receptors in brain

A possibility which has fascinated pharmacologists for many years is the existence of different types of dopamine receptors within the brain. Certainly dopamine receptors occur in a number of different brain regions and within any given area such receptors lie at a number of different anatomical locations (see Seeman, 1980). However, it has been debated as to whether these are identical forms of the same receptor or whether different dopamine receptors may exist within any given brain area. In the context of the present work, the existence of multiple dopamine receptors provides a pharmacological challenge, for one type of dopamine receptor might be associated with antipsychotic activity while another might be responsible for extrapyramidal movement disorders. One pharmacological aim has been to design drugs which act on one dopamine receptor population but not on another.

The most influential hypothesis has been that devised by Kebabian & Calne (1979) who suggest that dopamine receptors could be divided into two types, the D_1 receptor linked to the enzyme adenylate cyclase and the D_2 receptor which is not directly linked to this system. Since that time the use of radioactive ligand binding techniques suggested further subdivisions of brain dopamine receptors (see Seeman, 1980). The various schemes devised will not be described here but at one stage it was proposed that up to four different dopamine receptors existed in brain, one linked to adenylate cyclase, the other three being subdivisions of adenylate-cyclase-independent receptors. More recently, however, there has been some rationalization of the concept of multiple dopamine receptors in brain. Presently it is considered that the basic division of dopamine receptors into D_1 and D_2 is correct, but that these two forms of dopamine receptor both exist in high and low affinity states (Grigoriadis & Seeman, 1984; Hamblin *et al.*, 1984; Wreggett & Seeman, 1984). In terms of the action of sulpiride, it is necessary to point out that the interconversion of the high and low affinity forms of the D_2 receptor can be achieved using a number of techniques. Most importantly, the incorporation of high concentrations of guanine nucleotides or of sodium ions will switch the D_2 receptor from its high to its low affinity state. It is in the framework of this concept of dopamine receptors that we shall discuss the actions of sulpiride.

Receptor selectivity of sulpiride

Neuroleptic drugs in general are considered to produce their antipsychotic activity through blockade of brain dopamine receptors. However, most such compounds are not specific for cerebral dopamine systems and will interact with a variety of other neuronal receptors within brain. In contrast, sulpiride is highly selective for brain dopamine receptors. Incorporation of sulpiride into ligand binding assays used to identify a variety of brain neurotransmitter receptors shows that sulpiride has little or no ability to displace ligands from 5HT, alpha-1 and alpha-2 adrenergic, histamine, acetylcholine or GABA receptors (Hyttel, 1979; Leysen, 1982). Other substituted benzamide drugs related to sulpiride show similar selectivity for brain dopamine receptors (Jenner & Marsden, 1983). Recently, more potent substituted benzamide drugs have been introduced, but these do not show the same selectivity as sulpiride (Jenner & Marsden, 1984). This may be related to the increase in lipophilicity inherent in these more potent derivatives.

Sulpiride and other substituted benzamide drugs will displace ligands such as ^{3}H-haloperidol or ^{3}H-spiperone which identify D_2 receptors in brain tissue (Jenner *et al.*, 1978). Other typical neuroleptic compounds are also active in displacing ligands from D_2 receptors. However, sulpiride and other substituted benzamide drugs do not displace ligands such as ^{3}H-*cis*-flupenthixol or ^{3}H-piflutixol which identify D_1 sites (Hyttel, 1980; Fleminger *et al.*, 1983). Nor do these compounds inhibit dopamine's ability to stimulate the enzyme adenylate cyclase (Elliott *et al.*, 1977). This contrasts with neuroleptic drugs of the thioxanthene class such as flupenthixol which are potent in both displacing ligands from D_1 sites and in inhibiting adenylate cyclase activity. Indeed, overall, typical neuroleptic drugs have actions on both D_1 and D_2 receptors although their relative ability may vary (Hyttel, 1978). For example, butyrophenones such as haloperidol are much more potent in blocking D_2 activity than D_1 activity, but can exert a maximal inhibitory effect on both systems.

Recently, the absolute distinction between D_1 and D_2 receptors has been shown to be incorrect. Satoof & Kebabian (1981) have reported that selective inhibition of D_2 receptors by sulpiride enhances the ability of dopamine and synthetic dopamine agonists to stimulate cyclic AMP formation. This implies that D_2 receptor activation is inhibitory on formation of cyclic AMP. So selective D_2 actions of neuroleptics might be expected to produce alterations in cyclic AMP formation. The mechanism by which this occurs is at present not understood but it has obvious bearing on the actions of a drug such as sulpiride which selectively interacts with the D_2 receptor population.

The reason for the selective action of sulpiride on D_2 receptors has been debated. One idea was that the low lipophilicity of substituted benzamide drugs such as sulpiride prevents the drugs reaching the receptor coupled to adenylate cyclase (Woodruff *et al.*, 1980). However, when a series of substituted benzamide drugs are examined in relation to their lipophilicity it is clear that there is no correlation between lipophilicity and D_1 activity (Fleminger *et al.*, 1983). This finding suggests that the structure of substituted benzamide drugs contains configurational or conformational aspects which allow interaction with D_2 receptors, but which are not associated with an action of these drugs at D_1 sites.

Another facet of the interaction of sulpiride with brain dopamine receptors provides evidence that this occurs in a manner distinct from that of typical neuroleptic compounds. By chance we showed that the interaction of ^{3}H-sulpiride with its binding site in brain tissue shows an absolute dependence on the presence of sodium ions in the incubation media (Theodorou *et al.*, 1980, 1983; Jenner *et al.*, 1982). The effect of sodium is specific for it cannot be replaced by any other monovalent or divalent cation. Only lithium shows any ability to restore specific binding of ^{3}H-sulpiride in cation free media, and this is only to some 20 or 30% of that possible in the presence of sodium ions. The reason for the sodium dependency of ^{3}H-sulpiride binding is not understood but may relate to the presence of sulphydryl groups close to the binding site for the ligand (Freedman *et al.*, 1982). The effect of sodium is to cause an alteration in the number of available ^{3}H-sulpiride binding sites rather than to change receptor affinity (Theodorou *et al.*, 1983). One interpretation of these data is that ^{3}H-sulpiride labels a different portion of the dopamine receptor complex from that identified by ^{3}H-spiperone. Sodium effects can also be observed when looking at the ability of substituted benzamide drugs to displace the specific binding of ^{3}H-spiperone. Omission of sodium ions from the incubation buffer decreases the ability of substituted benzamide drugs to displace specific binding of ^{3}H-spiperone but does not affect the actions of neuroleptics of other classes (Stefanini *et al.*, 1980). These findings suggest that ^{3}H-spiperone labels both the sodium-dependent and sodium-independent portion of the dopamine receptor. It may be that the sodium-dependence of the interaction of sulpiride with the D_2 receptor population relates to the affinity state of that receptor. Thus sodium ions are able to convert the D_2 receptor from its high to its low affinity state (Hamblin *et al.*, 1984). Both forms of the receptors are identified by ligands such as ^{3}H-spiperone, but sulpiride may preferentially interact with the low affinity state. In support of this hypothesis is the fact that the number of binding sites identified by ^{3}H-spiperone and ^{3}H-sulpiride are identical.

In conclusion, sulpiride is not only selective for the D_2 receptor population but it may also selectively interact with one affinity form of that receptor population. Clearly we are dealing with a highly selective pharmacological agent.

Behavioural selectivity of sulpiride

A comparison of the acute effects of sulpiride on motor behaviour with those produced by typical neuroleptic compounds reveals a functional selectivity of action of the drug (Jenner & Marsden, 1983). Sulpiride induces little catalepsy, and only weakly antagonizes apomorphine-induced stereotyped behaviour (Elliott *et al.*, 1977). The lack of potency of sulpiride in such motor tests may merely reflect the low lipophilicity of the drug and its poor penetration into brain. However, sulpiride does inhibit one apomorphine-induced motor behaviour at relatively low doses. Sulpiride is approximately four times more potent in inhibiting climbing behaviour than stereotypy. Indeed, this behavioural discrimination is even more marked with some newly described substituted benzamide drugs (Martres *et al.*, 1984).

Lipophilicity, however, may play an important role in the discriminant behavioural actions of substituted benzamide drugs. Newer potent and highly lipophilic substituted benzamide drugs such as YM 09151–2 are indistinguishable from classical neuroleptic agents in terms of their ability to induce catalepsy and to block all motor behaviours (Usuda *et al.*, 1981).

Relevance of the selectivity of sulpiride to its action

The main evidence for the selectivity of sulpiride can be summarized as follows:

(1) Sulpiride selectively inhibits motor behaviour in rodents. This appears to be a true pharmacological effect of the drug unrelated to its ability to penetrate into the brain.

(2) Sulpiride selectively interacts with brain dopamine receptors having little or no ability to displace radioactive ligands labelling other neurotransmitter receptor systems in the brain.

(3) Sulpiride selectively interacts with those dopamine receptors which are not directly linked to adenylate cyclase.

(4) Interaction of sulpiride with brain dopamine receptors is critically dependent on the presence of sodium ions, a feature distinguishing it from other classes of neuroleptic compounds.

(5) Sulpiride may selectively interact with a sub-population of the D_2 adenylate-cyclase-independent receptors, perhaps representing the low affinity state of this receptor population

How do these actions of sulpiride relate to the clinical actions of the compound? Sulpiride possesses at least some of the characteristics of a compound acting as a dopamine receptor antagonist and presumably this is responsible for the antipsychotic action of the drug. Its lack of autonomic side effects may be attributed to its selectivity for brain dopamine receptors, in particular the absence of effects on cholinergic, histaminergic and adrenergic systems. But will its selectivity of action for one dopamine receptor sub-population explain the alerting properties of the compound or the low incidence of motor side-effects?

D_2 receptor selectivity alone would not appear sufficient to explain the clinical profile observed with sulpiride. Thus all functional effects of dopamine receptor antagonism produced by neuroleptic drugs appear correlated with their D_2 actions irrespective of D_1 effects (Seeman, 1980; Schachter *et al.*, 1980; Leysen, 1982). Indeed, members of the butyrophenone series, such as haloperidol and pimozide, are selective for D_2 receptors although in higher doses they can also act on D_1 systems. A compound such as haloperidol produces the usual incidence of motor side effects.

Sodium-dependency alone would not seem sufficient to provide an explanation since YM 09151–2 also shows sodium-dependence of interaction with brain dopamine systems yet acts like a typical neuroleptic (unpublished data). Even if sodium-dependency can be equated with the interaction of substituted benzamide drugs with a low affinity form of the D_2 receptor, the functional significance of such an effect is unknown since no information is available to determine the affinity state of dopamine receptors *in vivo*, nor is the functional significance of changes in affinity state understood.

What other possibilities exist? Potentially a highly selective action of sulpiride on a discrete portion of the dopamine receptor population could act to inhibit some motor behaviours while not affecting or enhancing other motor events. Alternatively, perhaps we are incorrect in classifying sulpiride and other substituted benzamide drugs as atypical dopamine receptor antagonist compounds. Such a definition presumes that the basic mechanism of interaction of such compounds with the dopamine receptor is identical to that observed with classical neuroleptic compounds.

At present there is no definitive evidence to support either of these hypotheses which can be directly related to clinical actions of sulpiride. However, there are some experimental studies which would add substance to this line of investigation.

Differential effects of sulpiride on apomorphine-induced behaviour in the rat

Administration of apomorphine to rats produces a variety of changes in behaviour which are grouped together as a stereotyped response. Certain components of behaviour can readily be distinguished, such as an increase in sniffing and compulsive chewing or biting, and are accepted as being due to D_2 receptor activation (Leysen, 1982). However, pretreatment of rats with sulpiride prior to the administration of apomorphine was found to cause a dose-related inhibition of stereotyped sniffing but potentiated the normal grooming behaviour of the animals (unpublished observation, Fig. 1). In contrast, treatment of animals with haloperidol, fluphenazine or thioridazine produced a dose-related inhibition of all behaviours. So sulpiride appeared able to inhibit some motor events while potentiating other components of the rats' normal behavioural repertoire.

Administration of the selective D_1 antagonist SCH 23390 also caused inhibition of stereotyped sniffing response to apomorphine and decreased grooming behaviour. One explanation for this finding would be that the enhancement of grooming observed after administration of sulpiride is due to its selective blockade of D_2 sites allowing the expression of an action of apomorphine on D_1 receptors. Indeed, administration of the selective D_1 agonist SKF 38393 produced a dose-dependent induction of grooming behaviour with some effect on sniffing, as previously shown (Molloy & Waddington, 1984). In contrast, the selective D_2 agonist LY 141865 induced dose-dependent sniffing with little effect on grooming. The hypothesis must be, therefore, that the ability of sulpiride to enhance the grooming in animals treated with apomorphine is due to a selective inhibition of those behaviours mediated via D_2 receptors, allowing the expression of grooming due to activation of D_1 systems coupled with the ability of sulpiride to enhance D_1 function through the inhibitory link (Stoof & Kebabian, 1981). Indeed, the administration of a range of doses of SKF 38393 or of apomorphine to animals pretreated with a high dose of sulpiride resulted in a marked degree of grooming in the presence of only a small degree of stereotyped sniffing.

Whether or not such a mechanism is responsible for the alerting properties of sulpiride observed in man, it illustrates the principle that sulpiride can cause an elevation of components of normal behaviour while suppressing other dopamine mediated events.

Is the molecular interaction of sulpiride with brain dopamine receptors identical to that occurring with classical neuroleptic agents?

Although ligand binding studies have yielded much information on the pharmacology of dopamine receptor binding sites, the molecular mechanisms underlying the interaction of agonist and antagonist ligands with brain dopamine receptors are not well understood. Thermodynamic changes in drug affinity for neuronal receptors can provide information

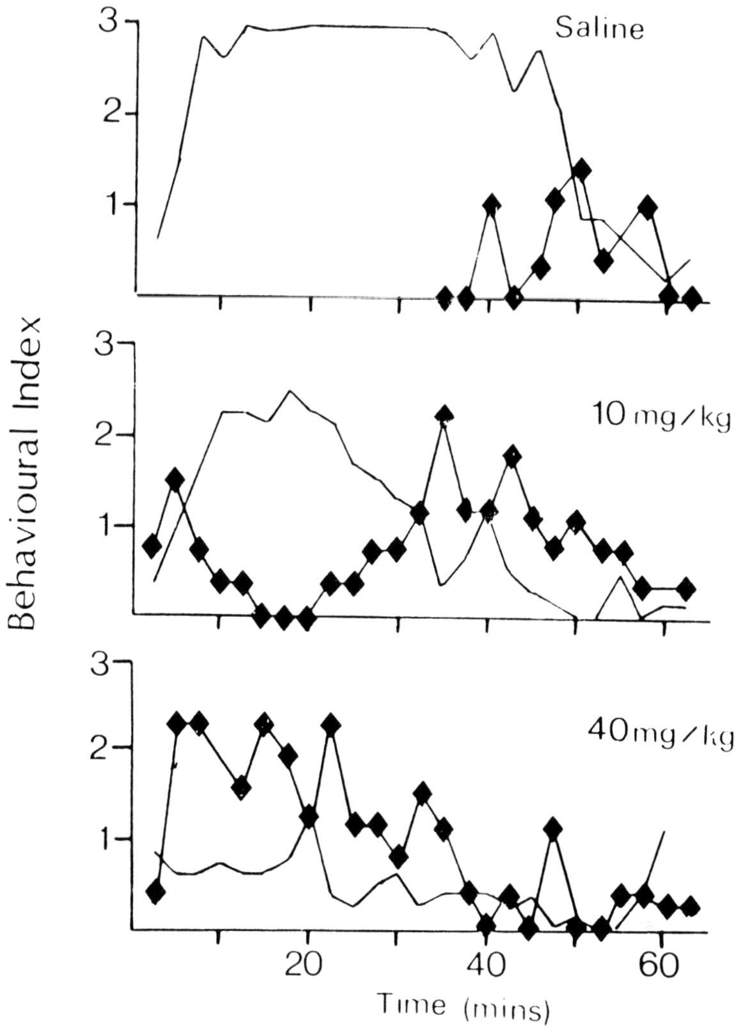

Fig. 1. *Induction of stereotyped sniffing (solid line) and grooming behaviour (—♦—) by administration of apomorphine hydrochloride (0.5 mg/kg subcutaneously) alone or following pretreatment of animals with sulpiride (10 or 40 mg/kg intraperitoneally; 3 h previously).*

on the type of interaction involved (see Weiland *et al.*, 1979; Minneman *et al.*, 1980). For this reason we have measured changes in enthalpy and entropy induced by the interaction of dopamine agonists and groups of typical and atypical neuroleptic drugs with the rat striatal D_2 receptor identified by ^{3}H-spiperone over a range of temperatures.

An initial observation was that the potency of sulpiride and some other substituted drugs to displace ^{3}H-spiperone was greater at 4 °C than at 373°C (Table 1). In general the ability of typical neuroleptic drugs to displace ^{3}H-spiperone was greater at the higher temperature. This is an interesting observation because there has been a worrying discrepancy between the very potent actions of substituted benzamide drugs when injected focally into brain (Costall *et al.*, 1978) compared to their much lower potency in

Table 1. *Ki values of dopamine agonist and antagonist drugs to inhibit binding of ^{3}H-spiperone to membrane preparations of rat striatum at 4° and 37°C.*

	Ki (nM) 4°C	37°C	*Ratio* 4°/37°C
Agonists			
6,7-ADTN	23	657	0.03
Dopamine	379	1999	0.19
Typical antagonists			
Haloperidol	0.79	1.95	0.42
cis-Flupenthixol	20.3	9.8	2.07
(+)-Butaclamol	19.7	1.29	15.3
Substituted benzamide drugs			
Sulpiride	1.28	88	0.014
Tiapride	5700	86830	0.066
Metoclopramide	8 28	104	0.080
Alizapride	7.0	73	0.096
YM 09151–2	0.21	0.12	1.75

IC_{50} values were calculated as the concentration of drug causing displacment of 50% of specified binding (defined using 10^{-5} M (± sulpiride). Ki values are calculated as K = IC_{50}/I + F/KD. Results are mean of three separate experiments. IC_{50} were calculated graphically from each separate experiment.

displacing ^{3}H-spiperone at 37°C. Perhaps the state of the binding site identified by ^{3}H-spiperone at 4°C more closely reflects the *in vivo* situation than occurs at 37°C.

In thermodynamic terms the interaction of dopamine and the dopamine agonist 2-amino,6,7,dihydroxy-tetrahydronaphthalene (ADTN) with the dopamine receptor identified by ^{3}H-spiperone was driven by a decrease in enthalpy allowing an energetically

Table 2. *Enthalpy (ΔH°) and entropy (ΔS°) produced as a result of drugs displacing ^{3}H-spiperone binding from rat striatal membrane preparations.*

	ΔH° *(Kcal mole^{-1})*	*ΔS°* *(cal/mole-deg)*
Agonists		
6,7-ADTN	−16.2	−24.1
Dopamine	−8.7	−1.8
Typical antagonists		
Haloperidol	−4.2	24.6
cis-Flupenthixol	3.5	48.0
(+)-Butaclamol	13.3	83.5
Substituted benzamide drugs		
Sulpiride	−21.0	−35.3
Tiapride	−12.3	−20.4
Metoclopramide	−13.1	−10.2
Alizapride	−11.5	−4.2
YM 09151–2	3.0	54.9

The following thermodynamic relationships were employed: ΔG° = RT 1n Ka where ΔG° is the Gibbs free energy change in Kcal mole^{-1}, R is the gas constant (1.99 cal/mol-deg), T is the temperature in °Kelvin, and Ka is the equilibrium association constant (1/Kd). ΔH° (enthalpy change in Kcal/mole) was calculated from the slope of the Van't Hoff plot (1n Ka vs 1/T). ΔG° = ΔH° − TΔS°. ΔS° is the standard entropy change in calories per mole-degree.

unfavourable decrease in entropy (Table 2). Such a change is associated with an agonist-induced conformational alteration in the nature of the receptor. In contrast, the interaction of the typical antagonists haloperidol, *cis*-flupenthixol and (+)-butaclamol was associated with increases in entropy with a small endothermic component. Such changes are consistent with an interaction with the receptor when no information is transferred. It has been postulated that such reactions are driven by an increase in entropy resulting from the displacement of water molecules ordered around the receptor site. Surprisingly, the interaction of some substituted benzamide drugs including sulpiride appeared to be driven by a decrease in enthalpy. One exception to this was YM 09161–2 where the interaction was entropy-driven, and this drug shows more typical antagonist properties.

It does appear that the interaction of substituted benzamides with the receptor differs in nature from that of classical antagonists and is similar, if not identical, to that of dopamine agonist compounds. For this reason alone it may be improper to classify substitued benzamide drugs of this class as dopamine receptor antagonists. The nature of the thermodynamic change induced might suggest that these compounds belong to a distinct pharmacological class where the interaction is that of an agonist but the effect, at least in part, that of an antagonist. Some precedent exists for such an effect. Compounds classified as 'inverse agonists' have already been identified at benzodiazepine receptors (Mohler, 1984). However, such results are only preliminary and a more detailed investigation of this phenomenon is required before drawing a firm conclusion.

The effects of repeated and long-term chronic administration of sulpiride to rats

Differences in the acute pharmacological profile of sulpiride and its mechanism of interaction with brain dopamine receptors are only of importance if they have bearing on the properties of the drug in man. In this respect it is of interest that sulpiride is believed to produce a lower incidence than typical neuroleptic drugs of tardive dyskinesia, a motor disorder which has been related to the development of dopamine receptor supersensitivity (Klawans, 1973). If the mechanism by which sulpiride alters brain dopamine function differs from that of typical neuroleptic compounds it might be expected that on repeated administration sulpiride would not induce dopamine receptor supersensitivity.

When we administered sulpiride (2 × 100 mg/kg intraperitoneally daily) in rats for 21 days and then withdrew the drug for 3 days animals exhibited an enhanced stereotyped response to apomorphine and showed an increased number of ^{3}H-spiperone, ^{3}H-sulpiride and ^{3}H-NPA binding sites (Table 3). This would suggest that in this paradigm sulpiride, like other neuroleptic drugs, also induces dopamine receptor supersensitivity. However, the conditions under which this experiment was carried out do not mimic those under

Table 3. *The effect of repeated administration of haloperidol (5 mg/kg ip) or sulpiride (2 × 100 mg/kg ip daily) on cerebral dopamine receptor function.*

Treatment	*Sterotypy score*	*Bmax (pmole/g tissue)* ^{3}*H-spiperone*	^{3}*H-sulpiride*	^{3}*H-NPA*
Saline	2.1 ± 0.1	24.0 ± 1.8	33.9 ± 2.6	6.8 ± 0.5
Haloperidol	2.9 ± 0.2[a]	32.3 ± 2.3[a]	51.5 ± 2.2[a]	12.7 − 2.8[a]
Sulpiride	3.0 ± 0.2[a]	29.5 ± 2.4[a]	47.3 ± 2.7[a]	9.7 ± 1.2[a]

Drugs were administered for 21 days followed by a 3–4 days withdrawal period. Sterotypy was assessed 15 min following administration of apomorphine (0.5 mg/kg s.c.). [a]$P < 0.05$ compared to control animals.

Table 4. *The effect of continuous chronic administration for 12 months of haloperidol or sulpiride on striatal dopamine function.*

Drug treatment (dose mg/kg/day)	*Apomorphine-induced sterotypy score*	*^{3}H-spiperone Bmax (pmoles/g)*	*K_D(nM)*	*Cyclic AMP formation stimulated by 50 μM (pmoles/2.5 min/2 min/2 mg tissue)*
Controls (distilled water alone)	3.1 ± 0.2	13.8 ± 1.0	0.13 ± 0.03	32.3 ± 1.9
Haloperidol (1.4–1.6)	3.9 ± 0.1[a]	26.4 ± 2.2[a]	0.20 ± 0.04	25.2 ± 4.2
Sulpride (102–109)	3.5 ± 0.2	17.2 ± 1.4	0.13 ± 0.02	54.1 ± 3.1[a]

[a]$P < 0.05$ compared to age-matched control animals; two-tailed Students *t*-test for parametric data, Mann-Whitney U-test for non-parametric stereotypy scores.

which tardive dyskinesia occurs in man. Thus, we used an intraperitoneal route of administration rather than the oral route, the drug doses used were high and bore no relationship to clinical dose or even to ratio of clinical dose, drugs were administered for only 21 days whereas tardive dyskinesia characteristically appears only after months or years of drug intake, and we only examined dopamine receptor function after a withdrawal period while tardive dyskinesia characteristically first appears while drug administration continues.

Accordingly we have compared the chronic administration of sulpiride or haloperidol by oral administration to rats for a period of up to 1 year (Rupniak *et al.*, 1984). We have used a dosage of each compound in ratio to the clinically used dosage but increased by a 5-fold arbitrary factor to allow for the generally lesser sensitivity of rodents to such compounds. Dopamine receptor function was examined 12 months after starting drug treatment and without withdrawing the neuroleptic drugs (Table 4). After administration of haloperidol (1.4–1.6 mg/kg day) for 12 months, animals exhibited an enhanced stereotyped response to the administration of apomorphine (0.5 mg/kg subcutaneously). In contrast, the administration of sulpiride (102–109 mg/kg day) for a year did not cause any increase in the stereotyped response to apomorphine. At intervals (1, 3, 6, 9 and 12 months) over the period of the study we measured the binding of ^{3}H-spiperone to striatal preparations. The number of dopamine receptors (Bmax) identified by ^{3}H-spiperone was increased throughout the period of administration of haloperidol, but administration of sulpiride had no effect on the Bmax of ^{3}H-spiperone binding. Surprisingly, perhaps, while haloperidol had no effect on the ability of dopamine to stimulate cyclic AMP formation in striatal preparations after 1 year's drug intake, sulpiride produced an approximate doubling of cyclic AMP formed in response to dopamine. Why this selective D_2 drug should produce this effect is unclear but it may relate to the proposed inhibitory influence of D_2 receptors on cyclic AMP formation.

The conclusion from this study is that the administration of sulpiride to rats for long periods may not result in the development of striatal dopamine receptor supersensitivity while drug administration continues. This differs from the results obtained with similar administration of haloperidol and of other neuroleptics such as trifluoperazine, thioridazine and cis-flupenthixol, all of which produced an apparent functional supersensitivity of striatal dopamine receptors (see Rupniak *et al.*, 1983). It may be that this lack of development of striatal supersensitivity is of relevance to the lower propensity of sulpiride to induce tardive dyskinesia in man.

Conclusions

The pharmacological profile of sulpiride gives support to the clinical evidence suggesting this drug may have different actions from classical neuroleptic compounds. Its selective motor actions may explain why the compound does not apparently cause the same degree of motor retardation in schizophrenic patients as is seen with typical neuroleptic drugs and why it may be of benefit in treatment of those patients suffering mainly from negative symptoms of schizophrenia. Its highly selective actions on dopamine receptors may explain the lack of autonomic side effects encountered with this compound. Why sulpiride does not cause the same incidence of extrapyramidal side effects and why the drug may have alerting properties is not understood from a mechanistic point of view. However, there are good reasons from animal experiments for accepting that this may represent a property of the drug due to its different mechanism of action. One difficulty in interpreting the actions of sulpiride is the continued comparison of the drug with typical dopamine receptor antagonists or classical neuroleptic agents. It may be that the mechanism of action of sulpiride is so different from typical neuroleptic drugs that comparison is not justified and that substituted benzamide drugs would be better classified in a pharmacological group of their own. Indeed the term 'neuroleptic drug' implies the possession of a defined spectrum of pharmacological properties (see Janssen *et al.*, 1965). If a compound does not fulfil the criteria as a neuroleptic drug then its classification as 'atypical' is merely an admission that we do not understand its mechanism of action. Certainly many substituted benzamide drugs are classifed at present as atypical neuroleptic agents. From the data currently available it would seem appropriate to attempt a tentative definition of a new pharmacological drug class. The criteria to be fulfilled would be as follows:

(1) Low to moderate lipophilicity.
(2) Selectivity for brain D_2 dopamine receptors.
(3) Sodium-dependence of interaction with D_2 sites.
(4) Enthalpy-driven interaction with dopamine receptors.
(5) Discriminant behaviour actions.

Obviously, at the present time such a classification is only tentative and based on relatively few compounds. Encouragingly, the interaction of ^{3}H-piquindone with striatal dopamine receptors was recently described (Nakajima & Iwata, 1984). This non-benzamide ligand shows sodium-dependent binding to D_2 sites. Substituted benzamide drugs were more potent in displacing ^{3}H-piquindone than ^{3}H-spiperone while the reverse was true for a range of standard neuroleptic drugs; dopamine agonists were also more potent against ^{3}H-piquindone than ^{3}H-spiperone. Interestingly, in a series of pyrroloisoquinoline derivatives examined for the ability to displace the two ligands, the less lipophilic compounds were selective in displacing ^{3}H-piquindone but more lipophilic derivatives did not discriminate between the ligands.

The unusual pharmacological and clinical profile of sulpiride may not be specific for the chemical class of substituted benzamides. But there appears to be a new grouping of 'sulpiride-like' drugs which are becoming more distinct from the 'classical neuroleptics' as time passes.

Acknowledgements—This study was supported by the Medical Research Council, the Wellcome Trust and the Research Funds of the Bethlem Royal and Maudsley Hospitals and King's College Hospital.

References

Alberts, J.L. (1985): *Semaine des Hôpitaux Paris* **61**, 19, 1351–1357.
Alfredsson, G., Harnryd, C. & Wiesel, F-A. (1985): *Psychopharmacology* **85**, 8–13.
Borenstein, P., Champion, C., Cujo, P., Gekiers, P., Olivenstein, C. & Kramarz, P. (1969): *Semaine des Hôpitaux Paris* **45**, 1301–1314.
Cassano, G. B., Castrogiovani, P. & Conti, L. (1975): *Curr. Therap. Res.* **17**, 189–201.
Costall, B., Fortune, D.H. & Naylor, R.J. (1978): *J. Pharm. Pharmacol.* **30**, 796–798.
Edwards, J.G., Alexander, J.R., Alexander, M.S., Gordon, A. & Zuchti, T. (1980): *Br. J. Psychiatr.* **137**, 522–529.
Elliott, P.N.C., Jenner, P., Huizing, G., Marsden, C.D. & Miller, R. (1977): *Neuropharmacology* **16**, 333–342.
Fleminger, S., Van de Waterbeemd, H., Rupniak, N.M.J., Reavill, C., Testa, B., Jenner, P. & Marsden, C.D. (1983): *J. Pharm. Pharmacol.* **35**, 363–368.
Freedman, S.B., Poat, J.A. & Woodruff, G.W. (1982): *J. Neurochem.* **38**, 1459–1465.
Gerlach, J. & Casey, D.E. (1984): *Acta Psychiatr. Scand.* **69**, Suppl. 311, 93–102.
Grigoriadis, D. & Seeman, P. (1984): *Can. J. Neurol. Sci.* **11**, Suppl. 1, 108–113.
Hamblin, M.W., Leff, S.E. & Creese, I. (1984): *Biochem. Pharmacol.* **33**, 877–887.
Harnryd, C., Bjerkenstedt, L., Bjork, K., Gullberg, B., Oxenstierna, G., Sedvall, G., Wiesel, F-A., Wik, G. & Aberg-Wistedt, A. (1984): *Acta Psychiatr. Scand.* **69**, Suppl. 311, 7–30.
Hytell, J. (1978): *Prog. Neuropsychopharmacology* **2**, 329–335.
Hytell, J. (1979): *Psychopharmacology* **65**, 211–214.
Hytell, J. (1980): *Psychopharmacology* **67**, 107–109.
Janssen, P.A.J., Niemegeers, C.J.E. & Schellekens, K.H.L. (1965): *Arzneimittel-Forsch.* **15**, 104–117.
Jenner, P. & Marsden, C.D. (1983): In *Psychopharmacology* ed. D.G. Graham-Smith, pp. 180–247. Amsterdam: Excerpta Medica.
Jenner, P. & Marsden, C.D. (1984): *Acta Psychiatr. Scand.* **69**, Suppl. 311, 109–123.
Jenner, P., Elliot, P.N.C., Clow, A., Reavill, C. & Marsden, C.D. (1978): *J. Pharm. Pharmacol.* **30**, 46–48.
Jenner, P., Theodorou, A. & Marsden, C.D. (1982): In *The benzamides,* eds J. Rotrosen & M. Stanley, pp. 109–141. New York: Raven Press.
Kebabian, J.W. & Calne, D.B. (1979): *Nature (Lond.)* **277**, 93–96.
Klawans, H.L. (1973): *The pharmacology of extrapyramidal movement disorders,* Monographs in Neural Sciences. Basel: Karger.
Leysen, J.E. (1982): In *Clinical pharmacology in psychiatry: neuroleptic and antidepressant research*, eds E. Usdin, S.G. Dahl, L.F. Gram & O. Linghaerde, pp. 35–62. London: Macmillan Press Ltd.
Martres, M.P., Sokoloff, P., Delandre, M., Schwartz, J-C., Protais, P. & Costentin, J. (1984): *Naunyn-Schmiedeberg's Archives of Pharmacology* **325**, 102–115.
Minneman, K.P., Weiland, G.A. & Molinoff, P.B. (1980): *Molecular Pharmacol.* **17**, 1–5.
Mohler, H. (1984): In *Actions and interactions of GABA and benzodiazepines*, ed. N.G. Bowery, pp. 155–166. New York: Raven Press.
Molloy, A.G. & Waddington, J.L. (1984): *Psychopharmacology* **82**, 409–410.
Nakajima, T. & Iwata, K. (1984): *Mol. Pharmacol.* **26**, 430–438.
Quinn, N. & Marsden, C.D. (1984): *J. Neurol. Neurosurg. Psychiatr.* **47**, 844–847.
Rupniak, N.M.J., Jenner, P. & Marsden, C.D. (1983): *Life Sci.* **32**, 2289–2311.
Rupniak, N.M.J., Mann, S., Hall, M.D., Fleminger, S., Kilpatrick, G., Jenner, P. & Marsden, C.D. (1984): *Psychopharmacology* **84**, 503–511.
Schachter, M., Bedard, P., Debono, A.G., Jenner, P., Marsden, C.D., Price, P., Parkes, J.D., Keenan, J., Smith, B., Rosenthaler, J., Horowski, R. & Dorrow, R. (1980): *Nature (Lond.)* **286**, 157–159.
Seeman, P. (1980): *Pharmacol. Revue* **32**, 229–313.
Stefanini, E., Marchisio, A.M., Devoto, P., Vernaleone, F., Collu, R. & Spano, P.F. (1980): *Brain Res.* **198**, 229–233.
Stoof, J.C. & Kebabian, J.W. (1981): *Nature (Lond).* **294**, 366–368.

Theodorou, A., Hall, M.D., Jenner, P. & Marsden, C.D. (1980): *J. Pharm. Pharmacol.* **32**, 441–444.
Theodorou, A.E., Jenner, P. & Marsden, C.D. (1983). *Life Sci.* **32**, 1243–1254.
Toru, M., Moriya, H., Yamamato, K. & Shimzono, Y. (1972): *J. Clin. Pharmacol.* **12**, 221–229.
Usuda, S., Nishikori, K., Noshiro, O. & Maeno, H. (1981): *Psychopharmacology* **73**, 103–109.
Weiland, G.A., Minneman, P & Molinoff, P.B. (1979): *Nature (Lond.)* **281**, 114–117.
Woodruff, G.N., Freedman, S.B. & Poat, J.A. (1980): *J. Pharm. Pharmacol.* **32**, 802–803.
Wreggett, K.A. & Seeman, P. (1984): *Mol. Pharmacol.* **25**, 10–17.

V

SOCIAL ASPECTS

Chapter 24

Autonomic changes and expressed emotion

Julian Leff

MRC Social and Community Psychiatry Unit, Institute of Psychiatry, De Crespigny Park, London SE5 8AF

Summary

This chapter describes the research which has been carried out at the Maudsley Hospital and Friern Hospital on the measurement of stress using psychophysiological indices, and particularly the changes in skin conductance which occur during sweating. It has been found that persons vulnerable to schizophrenia develop a high degree of excitement which is aggravated by relatives with high levels of expressed emotion, particularly when they are overcritical or overinvolved. Conversely recovery is facilitated by relatives with low levels of expressed emotion. Patients exposed to long-standing problems in the family show a greater response to life events than those in more stable family situations, and they are more vulnerable to schizophrenia relapse.

Introduction

For many years our research has concerned the effect of the social environment on the schizophrenic patient, and in particular the attitudes of relatives towards the patient, termed 'expressed emotion' (EE). We have also looked at other aspects of the environment which seemed to lead to episodes of schizophrenia, so-called life events. 'Life events' happen to all of us, sudden and often unexpected occurrences such as births, marriages and deaths — the usual triad — but also events such as changing jobs, moving house and car accidents. All of these happenings, and ones like them, which occur even in the best regulated households, seem able to produce exacerbations of illness. Sometimes they may even appear to precipitate the first episode.

Everyone at some time experiences tension within the family, and everyone encounters one or other of these life events, but most do not respond by developing schizophrenia. Therefore these environmental stresses cannot be considered as causes of schizophrenia, though they may interact with some inherent vulnerability, perhaps genetically determined, to cause the illness. The question as to how these stresses operate on the sufferer to produce a schizophrenic illness is obviously crucial to our understanding of the condition. In this chapter I shall explore the ways in which we may detect the effects of these environmental stresses on the sufferer.

Stress and schizophrenia

When an enquiry is made about the kinds of events mentioned above, it shows that they tend to concentrate in the 3 weeks before the illness appears, whether it is the first or a subsequent episode, so there is obviously only a short time lag between the stressful experience and the development of schizophrenia. This finding, originally reported from the Maudsley Hospital in south east London, has now been replicated in a large scale World Health Organization study in nine different countries in places as diverse as Honolulu, Nagasaki and Nigeria.

The work I shall describe concerns the acute stress of a life event, but there are also more long term stresses involved in the family attitudes to the patients. These are the expressed emotion components, and they can be assessed in the clinical setting. For example, critical attitudes, hostility, 'overinvolvement' and warmth can be measured very reliably. When patients are followed up for 9 months after discharge while they are living at home with relatives, it is found that relapse is likely to occur if a relative is highly critical, hostile or overinvolved. Where relatives are warm and lacking in these other attitudes there is a beneficial effect on the patient. It is thus possible for relatives to influence the outcome of the illness, at least over a short period of time after discharge. This observation is of particular relevance to current studies on psychophysiology.

This finding is not confined to the Maudsley Hospital and south east London and it has now been confirmed in studies involving various different cultures. We characterize the family as being high or low on expressed emotion, depending on the degree of criticism and overinvolvement — excessive criticism or a great degree of overinvolvement scores high; absence of these features scores low. In the original British study in south east London, relapse rates in the first 9 months after discharge were 16% when expressed emotion was low and over 50% when it was high, a very big difference. When the study was repeated 10 years later there were very similar findings. Further studies have been carried out in California on both white Americans and Spanish speaking Mexican Americans, with astonishingly similar results over a 9 month follow up period. We also have some results from Chandigarh in north India, part urban and part rural, and a very different cultural background. Relapse rates here were generally much lower, but this is partly explained by the fact that only first episodes of schizophrenic illness were examined, whereas in the other studies there was a mixture of first episodes and relapses. In spite of this difference in relapse rates, the differential effect of high and low expressed emotion was the same, with three times the rate of relapse in patients from high EE homes. Thus this finding appears to have a solid basis across a variety of cultures.

Measurement of stress

When we were thinking about these relationships between stress and illness we wondered what we could do to try to measure the effect of stress upon the patient. One of the more obvious approaches was through psychophysiology, the study of the responses of the body to the threat of danger. When action is demanded in response to a threat, the body gets ready; blood sugar is mobilized, sweating begins, the heart beats faster, the breathing changes. These changes can readily be measured, either in a laboratory setting or, with modern technology, in the home or elsewhere. Although we have measured all these variables in our studies, the one that proved the most helpful was skin conductance. This is the electrical potential difference measured between two skin electrodes, in this case on the fingers of the hand. The potential difference varies according to the amount of sweating, since the salt in sweat is a conductor of electricity. Skin conductance thus gives a sensitive measure of sweating and is even responsive to insensible sweating. Recordings of skin conductance show fluctuations above a basal value. These fluctuations may occur in response to 'alarming' stimuli such as sudden noise, but also occur spontaneously — 'spontaneous fluctuations' or SF. It is these spontaneous fluctuations that are the main subject of this chapter.

We have evidence that these physiological changes can be related to the patient's symptoms. This has been obtained from studies which have examined changes in auditory hallucinations, which characteristically vary from minute to minute. It is not always possible to rely on the patient telling the interviewer about auditory hallucinations, because he may not want to. However there are various visual clues to the presence of such hallucinations (eye movements, listening posture, and other alerting clues) and we assessed these from video recordings while measuring fluctuations in skin conductance. Figure 1 shows results in one patient. During the cross-hatched periods the patient was apparently hearing voices. At the start of each period of hearing voices the spontaneous fluctuation rate of skin conductance was rising. These results do not tell us whether the patient was excited because he heard voices or whether he heard voices because he was excited; as yet we have not been able to resolve this particular dilemma.

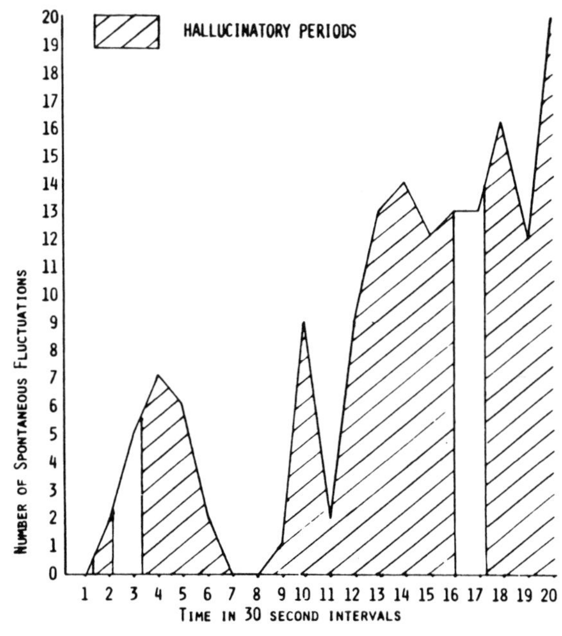

Fig. 1. *Graph of spontaneous fluctuations of skin conductance for patient No 5, with periods of auditory hallucinations superimposed.*

When recordings of skin conductance are made in the resting condition, the frequency of SFs increases with the degree of excitation of the nervous system. An important question in these studies was where they should be conducted. Previous work in this area had been done entirely in the laboratory, but this seemed to us to be irrelevant, since we really needed to know what the patient's responses would be in his normal environment, not in the sheltered setting of the laboratory. We therefore decided to take the risk of performing the measurements at home — 'risk' because there are many variables which cannot be controlled in such an environment.

Results of skin conductance measurements

Patients in remission

Figure 2 shows a record of spontaneous fluctuations in skin conductance over a 30 min recording period. In the first 15 min the subject was sitting at home alone with the experimenter, chatting about neutral subjects. After this the subject's relative was brought in (dashed line in figure) and there was a further period of conversation with both subject and relative, to explore the effect the presence of the relative might have on the subject.

The bottom line on the figure (white diamonds) was the averaged response of 21 control subjects. At the start of the record the control subjects showed about the same number of SFs per minute as the patient groups (black and white triangles). However during the first 15 min of the record the number of SFs in controls declined as they became used to the situation, and though there was a slight increase when the relative came into the room, which is the expected response to any new situation, the overall trend was for the number of SFs to decline throughout the recording.

The black triangles represent the averaged results of SF measurements in 11 schizophrenic patients who had relatives high in expressed emotion (either highly critical or highly overinvolved or both). The white triangles represent the results in 10 schizophrenic patients with relatives low in expressed emotion. Neither group of patients settled down during the first 15 min with the interviewer, the number of SFs remaining high throughout the period. This is characteristic of anyone with a high level of anxiety. When the relative entered the room there was a large response in the number of SFs in patients in the high expressed emotion group and a much lesser response in the low expressed emotion group. The high EE group continued to show high activation throughout the remainder of the recording, while the low EE group showed a striking reduction in activation, their SF rate falling nearly to that of the controls. This seems to

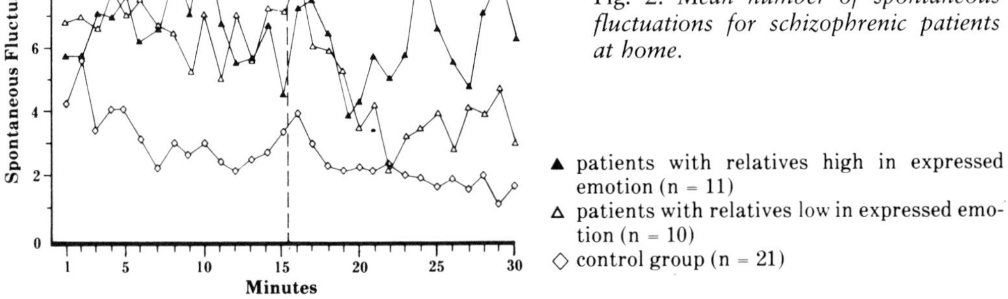

From: "Bodily Reactions to People and Events in Schizophrenia" by N. Tarrier, C. Vaughn, M.H. Lader, and J.P. Leff, 1979, *Archives of General Psychiatry*, 36, 311-315. Copyright 1979, American Medical Association. Reprinted by permission.

Fig. 2. *Mean number of spontaneous fluctuations for schizophrenic patients at home.*

imply that the supportive relative with low expressed emotion is able to help the schizophrenic patient to become accustomed to novel situations. However when this experiment was repeated in 3 months the effects seen in Fig. 2 disappeared and we found no difference between patients and controls. A plausible explanation for this was that the subjects had become accustomed to the interviewer and no longer found the occasion threatening.

We then investigated further the importance of sudden changes in a person's life — life events. We took a history of life events in the 3 weeks before recording sessions and identified seven schizophrenic patients who had experienced such events during this period. Figure 3 shows the results of the skin conductance measurements in these seven patients (a) within 3 weeks of a life event and (b) in the same patients when there was no life event preceding the recording. It can be seen that up to the point when the relative entered there was no difference in the records, but as soon as the relative entered the SF frequency increased greatly when there had been a recent life event and remained at a high level for the remainder of the interview. If there had been no recent life event the activation remained at a low level after the relative entered. This seemed to confirm the view that there is a combination of different stressors which act to increase anxiety and activation — the acute stress of a life event and the chronic stress of a tense home atmosphere. On the first occasion of testing, the novelty of the situation acted like a life event.

A criticism of these studies is that they do not necessarily show an effect of the relatives. The results could have been entirely due to inherent differences in the patients, some of whom were for some reason more activated than others, and this increased level of activation could stimulate critical and overinvolved attitudes in the relatives. One reason to doubt this was that there was no difference between the two groups of patients in the first 15 min alone with the experimenter. However, a further study made it extremely unlikely that the effects seen were inherent in the patients. In this study several patients were examined who lived in families where there was one relative who was low and

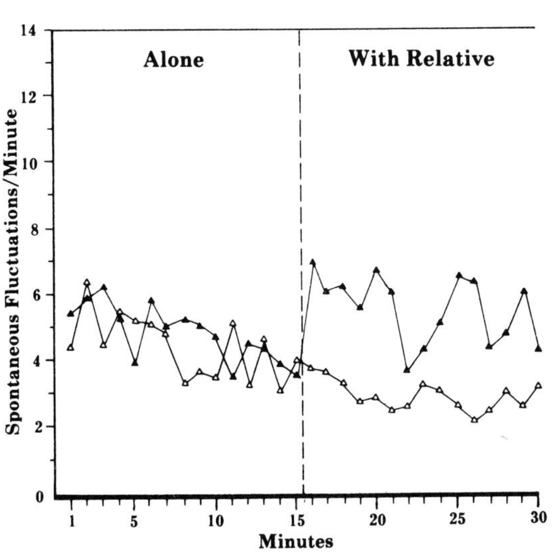

Fig. 3. *Mean number of spontaneous fluctuations for schizophrenic patients after a life event (▲) and when no life event had occurred (△) (n = 7).*

another who was high in expressed emotion. In this situation, when the relatives were brought into the patient's presence in sequence the responses of the patients were entirely appropriate to what one might expect if their activation levels were influenced by the EE of the relative — there was a decline in activation with the low EE relative and an increase in activation with the high EE relative.

Studies on acutely ill patients

The studies described above were performed when the patients were in remission, 2 years after discharge from hospital. The next study was undertaken to investigate the effect of such stresses in patients who were actuely ill. In this study the responses of the patients to the presence of relatives who were assessed as having high or low expressed emotion were studied as before, but on this occasion it was necessary to do the interviews in hospital. The average time interval between admission and study was about 6 weeks. Figure 4 shows the results of this study. Patients with relatives high in expressed emotion had much higher activation levels throughout the interview than those with relatives low in expressed emotion. The responses of the latter were not much different from the responses found during remission in the low EE group. We cannot at present provide a satisfactory explanation as to why there was such a marked difference in activation levels in the two groups *before* the entry of the relative. It is possible however that we did these studies too long after the patients had been admitted to hospital, allowing subjects from low EE homes to calm down and achieve activation levels comparable to those found during remission. If the studies had been done earlier (and there were practical problems which made this difficult) we might have found a very different picture.

We followed up these acutely studied patients and interviewed them again a year later at home. We found that patients from low EE homes showed very little difference in activation between the acute stage (6 weeks after admission) and one year later, and the values were similar to those found in the group of patients who were in remission (at least

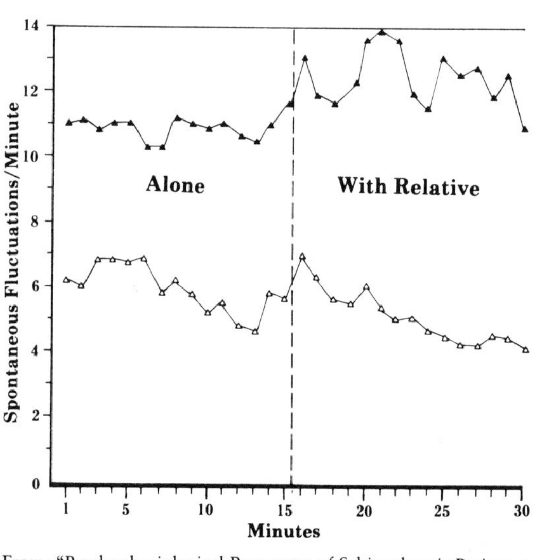

Fig. 4 *Mean number of spontaneous fluctuations for schizophrenic patients during an acute episode.*

▲ Patients with relatives high in expressed emotion (n = 19)
△ Patients with relatives low in expressed emotion (n = 11)

From: "Psychophysiological Responses of Schizophrenic Patients to High and Low Expressed Emotion Relatives: A Follow-up Study" by D. Sturgeon, G. Turpin, L. Kuipers, R. Berkowitz, and J. Leff, *British Journal of Psychiatry* 1984, **145**, 62–69. Reprinted by permission.

2 years out of hospital). The patients from high EE homes showed very high activation in the acute stage, and lower activation at one year, though still raised in comparison with the high EE group in remission. Thus the patients from high EE homes remained in a state of relatively high activation for at least a year after admission. It seems to us that we are dealing with a difference in the rate of recovery which is not related to the acute florid symptoms of schizophrenia, but has more to do with the time it takes to recover from the negative symptoms of the disease. We know it takes up to 2 years for patients to recover from apathy, inertia and absence of emotional responses. We therefore feel we may be charting the progress of these symptoms rather than that of the positive ones.

We then undertook a study in north London at Friern Hospital where we tested acutely ill patients who were not on medication. Unfortunately in this study we had great difficulty in finding any patients from low expressed emotion families. This seems to be a difference between south and north London. In north London many more of the patients were living on their own and the catchment area seemed to be socially much more disrupted. Thus we were not able to compare patients from high and low EE homes, but we could compare patients from high EE homes with those living on their own who had had a recent life event, where we could anticipate that there would be a high level of activation. The results confirmed this. The mean number of spontaneous fluctuations per minute was 16.3 in the high EE homes, very similar to the value found in the acute south London sample, and it was a very high 26/min in patients living alone who had suffered a recent life event.

We then studied a few patients on admission to hospital and again later to see whether our earlier studies at the Maudsley Hospital had been carried out too late in the patients' admission. It was difficult to get more than a few patients for this study because most had left hospital for various reasons when the time came for their retest. However we were able to study a few patients from high EE homes on admission and 4 weeks later, and similarly another small group of patients living on their own who had had a recent life event. We found that activation in the patients from high EE homes was even higher 4 weeks after admission than it was on admission, while patients living on their own with recent life events had a dramatic fall in activation in their first 4 weeks in hospital.

Conclusions

Tentative conclusions from these studies are as follows. A person who is vulnerable to schizophrenia and who has had a recent stress in the form of a life event develops a high level of excitement. As a result of this increased excitability a recurrence (or even the first episode) of the illness develops. Within a few weeks or months the level of excitability diminishes and the schizophrenic symptoms improve (indeed, the rapid improvement which may occur when schizophrenia is precipitated by a recent acute stress is well documented in published reports). If, however, the patient has been exposed to long-standing problems in the family the response to life events is much greater and it also takes much longer to recover to the 'resting' level of activation. Thus such patients remain vulnerable to further episodes for very much longer than those who do not live with difficult relatives.

Much of this is speculative and based on data from small numbers of patients. We need more longitudinal data in much larger groups of patients, to document accurately what happens when life events and family problems occur. In this way we may be able to anticipate a change in clinical state by measuring changes in activation. We have a long way to go but we feel that these results are interesting enough to encourage us to continue this work.

Chapter 25
Family management of schizophrenia

Ian R. H. Falloon

Buckingham Mental Health Service, Buckingham, UK

Summary

Increasing evidence that environmental stress plays an important part in the long-term outcome of schizophrenia suggests that treatment of this disorder should include measures to counter the detrimental effects of major stress factors. Over the past decade a series of approaches has been devised and tested under controlled research conditions. Some have endeavoured to create low stress environments for patients living in the community, others have attempted to train patients and their caregivers in more efficient methods of coping with stresses in their everyday lives. These latter approaches appear to have the advantage of enabling patients to cope with all forms of life stress, including that associated with major life events. Furthermore, the benefits remain after active treatment is tapered. Added benefits include enhanced social and family functioning and lower dosages of medication. A cost-effectiveness analysis suggests that a carer-based approach to stress management is more than twice as efficient as the more usual patient-orientated approaches.

Introduction

Over the past decade there has been a resurgence of interest in family interventions for schizophrenia. However, the value of the family in the management of schizophrenia has been recognized for many years. In the 1913 edition of his textbook of psychiatry Kraepelin advocated early discharge of patients to their families once the most disturbing features of schizophrenia had diminished. He noted, with surprise, that many difficult patients behaved themselves remarkably well on return to the home environment. A decade later Sullivan developed a family-orientated approach to inpatient care of schizophrenia at the Shepherd-Pratt Clinic (Sullivan, 1927). More recently the much criticized work of Laing & Mosher has provided further demonstration of the value of family-style management of the acute phase of schizophrenia (Laing, 1967; Mosher & Menn, 1978).

The value of psychosocial treatments in the management of the acute or florid phase of schizophrenia has been obscured by the advent of highly effective tranquillizing medication. Drug therapy has undoubtedly enhanced the quality of the milieu in the acute hospital ward dramatically. As a result any additional benefits from psychosocial interventions have been comparatively small in such settings (Falloon & Liberman, 1983).

Once the florid episodes of schizophrenia have been controlled the value of neuroleptic drugs has been somewhat less dramatic in preventing recurrences of the disorder. Even when compliance is carefully controlled by giving depot injections, studies have shown that between 30 and 40% of cases suffer recurrent florid episodes in the first year after recovery (Schooler & Severe, 1984). This rate of exacerbation increases to at least 50% by the end of the second year of follow up, and 5-year follow up studies show even less value from continuous neuroleptic administration (Shepherd *et al.*, 1989). Thus the major benefits from drugs appear to be in controlling florid episodes and in preventing recurrent episodes during the first 6 months of aftercare. The emergence of serious side effects, some possibly irreversible, has led to further concern about the benefits of continuous long-term neuroleptic therapy (Schooler & Carpenter, 1983).

Of course the control of florid episodes is only one aspect of the comprehensive management of schizophrenia. Perhaps a more important criterion of successful management is the quality of life of the patient as well as the patient's community caregivers. Drug therapy may reduce clinical morbidity but it cannot win friends for the lonely patient, or provide rewarding employment or interesting leisure pursuits. Psychosocial interventions are needed to facilitate these goals. To date, however, the psychosocial methods that have been employed have not appeared notably cost-effective. Moreover, most studies have contrasted psychotherapy with drug therapy in terms of reducing acute clinical morbidity — a totally unequal contest. Few have attempted to examine combinations of drug and psychological treatment which may prove additive or even synergistic, in conditions that resemble optimal clinical practice (Falloon & Liberman, 1983). I would like to highlight some of the recent developments in the psychosocial management of schizophrenia that attempt to do this, and are all based upon the premise that the family unit (ie, those persons in intimate daily contact with the index patient) may be the greatest natural resource for the comprehensive management of schizophrenia.

The vulnerability-stress model for schizophrenia

Renewed interest in psychosocial interventions in schizophrenia has developed as a direct result of research on the impact of environmental stress on the course of schizophrenia. The first series of studies concerned stress in the everyday home environment. Beginning in the 1950s a series of studies found that the best single prediction of recurrence of florid episodes of schizophrenia has been the level of stress in the home environment, especially stress directed towards the index patient (see Leff, this volume, p. 286). The emotional response and attitudes expressed by household members during the 3 months before the index patient's admission to hospital has been a better predictor of the course of schizophrenia after recovery than any other single variable, such as premorbid adjustment, age at onset, sex, severity of symptoms, etc. The attributes of the household members that make up the index of high expressed emotion are a high level of criticism or rejection, or intrusive overinvolvement. The remarkable feature of this high expressed emotion is that it tends to be the expected reaction to disturbed, upsetting behaviour. Yet surprisingly even during the pre-admission crisis only about half the British relatives show this high response, the other half responding in a calm, supportive manner in the face of often extreme behavioural disturbance and household disruption. Slightly fewer families of patients admitted to Camarillo State Hospital in California showed these calm, coping responses (Vaughn & Leff, 1976; Vaughn *et al.*, 1982).

The expressed emotion index is derived from a series of interviews with every household member except the index patient. We may ask ourselves whether these interview responses show any correspondence with real-life family interactions, and whether the same criticism and intrusiveness is seen in the presence of the index patient, especially during the post-discharge phase once the patient has regained clinical stability.

Figure 1 demonstrates that Expressed Emotion attitudes correspond to similar behaviour when the family are asked to discuss a 'hot' issue in a laboratory setting. This study conducted in collaboration with David Miklowitz & Michael Goldstein at UCLA shows that those family members with high criticism in the Expressed Emotion interviews tended to make the most criticisms in the family discussion of a problem issue (Miklowitz *et al.*, 1984). Those showing high overinvolvement tended to be most intrusive. Thus, Expressed Emotion probably does reflect family behaviour as well as family attitudes, even at times when overt behavioural disturbance is minimal.

Much clinical significance has been attached to a series of *post hoc* analyses made concerning the beneficial effects of reduced contact and regular medication for persons living in high Expressed Emotion households (Vaughn & Leff, 1976). Where contact between the patient and the high Expressed Emotion family member was very low or the patient took neuroleptic medication with almost perfect regularity the relapse rate was substantially reduced. Where both low contact and regular medication were combined the relapse rate approached that of the low Expressed Emotion households. This suggests a simple approach to the treatment of schizophrenia — merely get the patient out of the home as much as possible and make sure he or she takes medication without fail, preferably via intramuscular injections. Unfortunately, this analysis did not account for the fact that those patients in low contact with relatives tended to have better premorbid skills and consequently a lower relapse rate, and those who take drugs perfectly regularly also tend to have a low relapse rate, even when the drugs they take are placebos! (Falloon *et al.*, 1978). In other words time spent out of the home and regular tablet taking are themselves good predictors of clinical outcome.

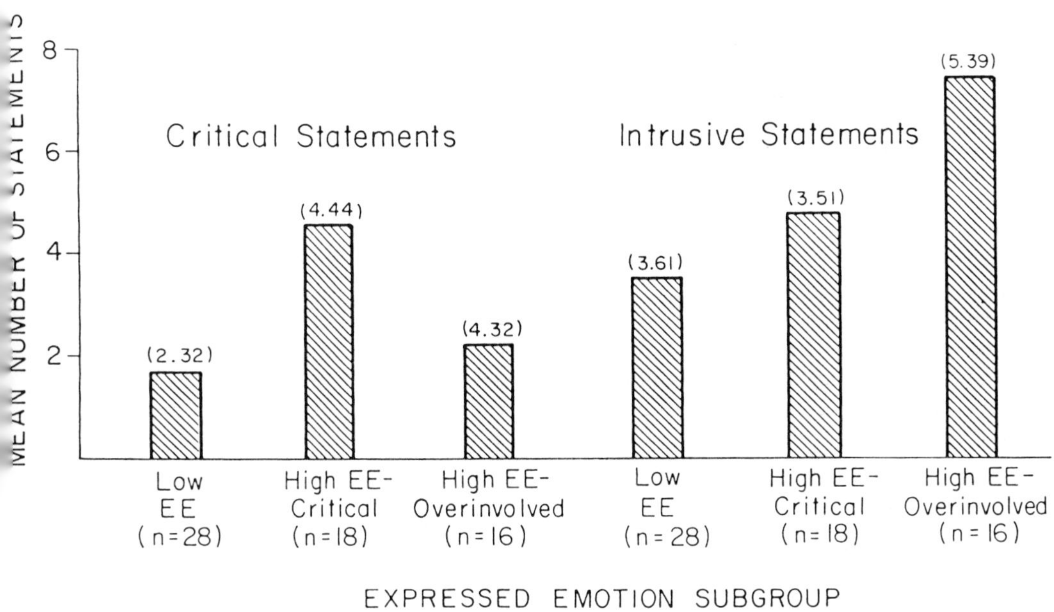

Fig. 1. *Expressed Emotion (EE) attitudes in families of index patients.*

An alternative way of reducing the impact of family stress would involve direct attempts to teach more effective coping behaviour to family members so that they deal with stresses in the calm manner of low Expressed Emotion families. However, it may be important to note that in these low Expressed Emotion families the benefits associated with the low/high contact variable are reversed! In these families low contact increases the risk of recurrent episodes, whereas the best outcome is associated with high contact with a low Expressed Emotion household. Thus it is evident that the low stress environment carries specific health-promoting factors, and these families may enhance the course of schizophrenia (Falloon *et al.*, 1985). In other words, if we are attempting to enhance family coping behaviour we should also ensure that the index patient maintains regular intimate contact with the family unit to derive maximum therapeutic benefits from this endeavour.

Stress in families is not the only variable associated with recurrences of schizophrenia. Environmental stress in the form of life events has been shown to trigger episodes. Where high levels of stress exist on a day-to-day basis only minor events may precipitate episodes (Fig. 2). Where the ambient tension from stress with families, friends, work, etc. is low then major events such as loss of a job or breakup of a close relationship are needed to increase the risk of relapse (Fig. 3). One can assume that stress is cumulative and that there is a stress threshold that when exceeded places any person in the family at a high risk of becoming ill in some way. In other words, everyone has a breaking point.

Neuroleptic medication may reduce the risk of recurrence of schizophrenia when the stress threshold is exceeded, but is not a complete protection and may even enhance stress

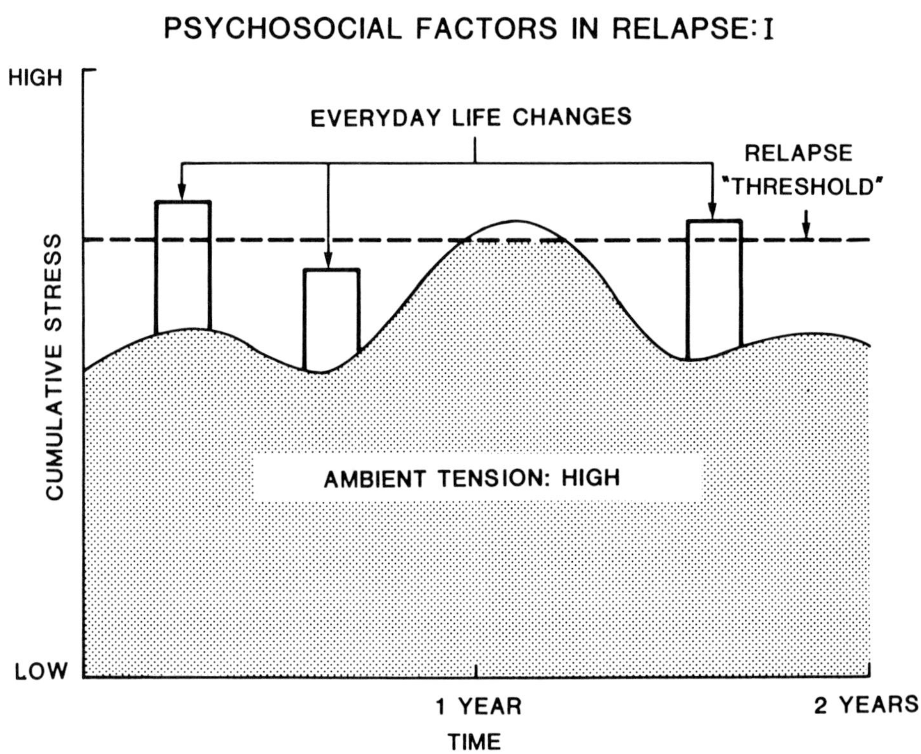

Fig. 2. *Triggering of relapse by minor events when level of ambient tension is high.*

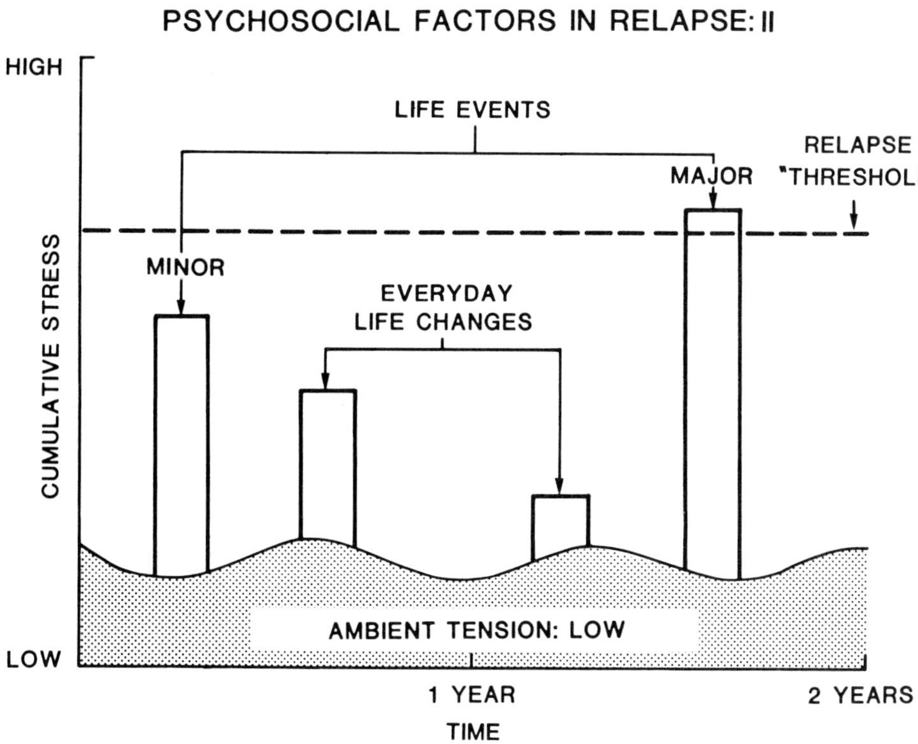

Fig. 3. *Failure to trigger relapse by minor events when ambient tension is low.* Only major events trigger relapse.

if it causes unpleasant side effects. Anything that enables the patient to cope more effectively and resolve the effects of the stress may reduce this risk. This can be achieved by enhancing the efficiency of problem solving behaviour, either through individual psychosocial therapy or through group or family stress management procedures (Fig. 4).

Family-based interventions

The newer family-based therapies have attempted to assist the patient and family to reduce environmental stress and thereby reduce the risk of further clinical episodes of florid symptoms. Perhaps the most straightforward family-based approach is that of Anderson, Hogarty & Reiss (1980). Patients' families are educated about schizophrenia and taught how to tackle the task of rehabilitation in a very gradual manner. They are taught that the effects of an acute episode of schizophrenia last at least 6 months after the effective resolution of the florid symptoms, and that any stress during this period may lead to an exacerbation. After that time families are counselled to assist the handicapped patients to take very small steps towards regaining their former functioning. Overinvolved family members are encouraged to develop their own activities outside the home.

The Maudsley group, led by Leff, Kuipers & Berkowitz (Leff *et al.*, 1982) has developed a rather similar approach. In this approach the patient himself is involved in the education about schizophrenia and in several sessions that focus on ways of reducing contact with relatives with high Expressed Emotion. An additional strategy involves a group for family

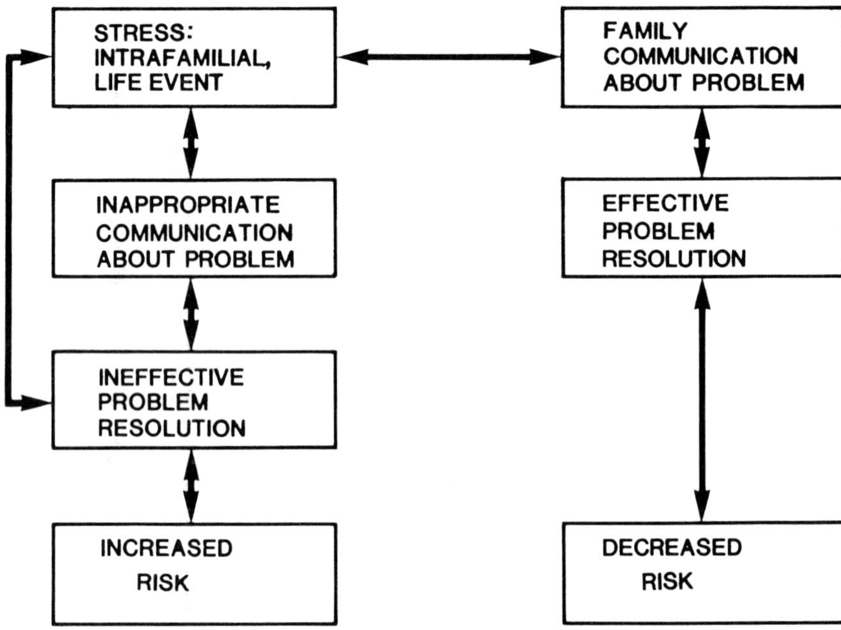

Fig. 4. *The roles of family communication and problem resolution.*

members that includes relatives with low and high Expressed Emotion, and aims to have low Expressed Emotion relatives teach high Expressed Emotion relatives more effective ways of coping with disturbed behaviour and symptoms.

The methods of Goldstein, Liberman & Falloon tackle the stress issue from a somewhat different perspective: that of stress management rather than stress reduction. The aim is to teach patients and families to cope more efficiently with a broad range of idiosyncratic environmental stresses, not merely to attempt to avoid them. Goldstein taught families in six sessions to identify both current and anticipated environmental stresses and to discuss how they would resolve these stresses (Goldstein *et al.*, 1978). These included stress within the family, but in addition, stress from life changes and extrafamilial sources. Less emphasis was placed on teaching families to deal with the symptoms of schizophrenia than in Anderson & Leff's programmes.

The behavioural method developed first at the Maudsley and refined in collaboration with Goldstein & Liberman in Los Angeles is more extensive and focuses less on the content of stresses and more on the basic processes of family stress management. The most parsimonious approach to stress management and community rehabilitation for the entire family unit appears to be that of problem solving (Table).

Table. *Problem solving approach.*

Problem Solving

1. Pinpoint problem
2. Generate potential solutions
3. Evaluate potential consequences
4. Agree on 'best' strategy
5. Plan and implement
6. Review results

In our method, which is derived from behavioural family therapy, patients and their families are taught to sit down together at home and discuss an issue that is a current or anticipated stress for any member of the family (Falloon *et al.*, 1984). It is assumed that problem solving already occurs in the family but that this is not usually carried out in an optimally efficient fashion. In most circumstances 'muddling through' with problems promotes no major disability, but when one or more family member has a predisposition to a stress-related illness then much better than average problem solving may be necessary to minimize the risk of further illness episodes, while at the same time enabling each and every member of the family to maximize his or her functional potential. Thus problem solving is an important aid to enhancing social functioning as well as to resolving stress. It is also assumed that stress that impinges on any member of the household may lead to increased stress for every other household member. So the problem and goals of every family member are considered important, not merely those issues related to schizophrenia and the index patient. Often the person who is recovering from schizophrenia does have many problems and goals deemed to be of high priority within the family. That situation is not always the case and not infrequently the person with schizophrenia is a tower of strength to the family unit, while other family members are experiencing very stressful problems. These concepts need little elaboration for family therapists, but are poorly understood by many mental health professionals.

In stark contrast to the epistemologists among family therapists all these new family approaches accept schizophrenia (as defined by DSM III) as a clearly defined syndrome, in all likelihood a biological disorder associated with specific abnormalities in brain metabolism and genetic predisposition. However, although at least two sessions are devoted solely to discussing the nature and management of schizophrenia, the behavioural approach places less emphasis on teaching families how to deal with the symptoms of schizophrenia and more on generic problem solving within the family, which on occasions includes dealing with disturbed behaviour associated with schizophrenia. The aim is to enable families to deal efficiently with any stress that arises and thereby eventually to become less dependent on professional resources. The other methods described also hope to achieve this goal. Anderson & Leff employ multi-family groups that aim to assist families to support one another after professional support has been withdrawn.

Before learning problem solving it has probably occurred to the reader that providing a structure to family problem solving discussions will only prove effective if family members already sit down and discuss their problems in some fashion. In our experience this seldom occurs on a regular basis. For this reason most families require a number of sessions that focus on enhancing their basic communication skills so that they can meet together at least weekly, pinpoint their problems or goals, listen attentively and work together planning and implementing specific programmes in a cohesive and constructive manner. I should emphasize that we do not aim to avoid the expression of negative feelings and criticism to the index patient. Rather the aim is to express criticism in a constructive manner that is conducive to problem resolution. Families may shout and scream at each other during their meetings but that is of no real concern provided that a constructive plan of how they will deal with the issue at hand is produced at the end of the discussion.

One final comment about differences between the main family management approaches concerns the issue of face-to-face contact. Both the stress reduction approaches of Anderson & Leff attempt to reduce contact between the index patient and his or her family. Patients are expressly excluded from relatives' groups and efforts are made to find ways of either increasing the independence of the index patient or increasing the time spent out of home by caregiving relatives. In contrast, the behavioural approach has no such explicit aims. Consistent with evidence that high contact with supportive family members reduces the risk of exacerbation of schizophrenia we attempt to enhance the quality of family support and encourage family members to spend more time together providing mutual assistance in resolving their everyday problems and achieving their creative potentials. However, families often use their meetings to assist members to achieve a greater range of activities and relationships outside the family. Indeed, they are often encouraged to use the communication skills methods to enhance the social skills of family members who lack competence in interpersonal situations such as joining clubs, job interviews, or dating behaviour. It is recognized that many persons who have suffered serious handicaps as a result of severe schizophrenia will never be able to achieve full independence from family and professional support. The goals for such people are the same as for any other handicapped persons — to maximize the quality of their lives and those of their caregivers. Problem solving enables them to plan their lives with their families and to begin the very small steps towards their long-term aspirations.

The results of family-based management

The results of family management of schizophrenia have been very dramatic. At least they seem this way if one confines one's concern to reducing the risk of major exacerbations of schizophrenia. The reduction in relapse rates, in addition to that achieved by drug treatment, is striking. Even more striking are the consistently low rates of exacerbation found in each of the four major studies (see Fig. 5).

The supreme optimists among us might be tempted to conclude that the scourge of schizophrenia had been conquered by combining stress management with optimal drug therapy. But I suspect that these bald relapse rates tell only half the tale. Worse, they may lead people to conclude that as few as five or six sessions simply teaching relatives how to

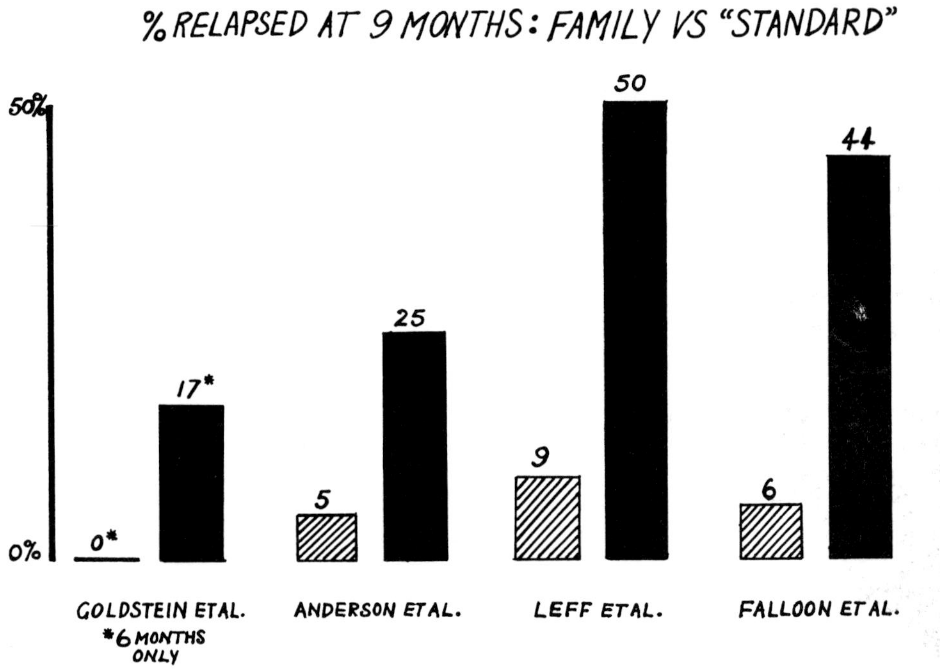

Fig. 5. *Low rates of exacerbation in four major studies of family management of schizophrenia.*

cope with the symptoms of schizophrenia are as beneficial as 20 to 30 hours of more extensive family approaches.

Before we fly off on the wings of promise let us stop to consider a couple of points. First, perhaps we should remind ourselves that the back wards of the old mental asylums were highly effective in controlling florid episodes of schizophrenia and, as Lamb & Goertzel (1971) have pointed out, the same low stress, low expectancy environment can all too readily be developed in the community, even in family homes. Second, we should recall that only about one-third of persons with schizophrenia show a typical relapsing course. The remainder show many different courses, not all readily assessed according to a relapse paradigm. Thus it is crucial also to examine the quality of life of the non-relapsing patient, as well as to examine the psychopathology from perspectives other than from the dichotomous relapse/no relapse angle.

Let us address the psychopathology issue first. At this point a lack of published data prevents comparisons between the four controlled studies I have discussed earlier. For this reason I must confine my comments to the USC study (Falloon, 1985). In this study the clinical benefits included a reduction in severity of persistent psychotic symptoms, an

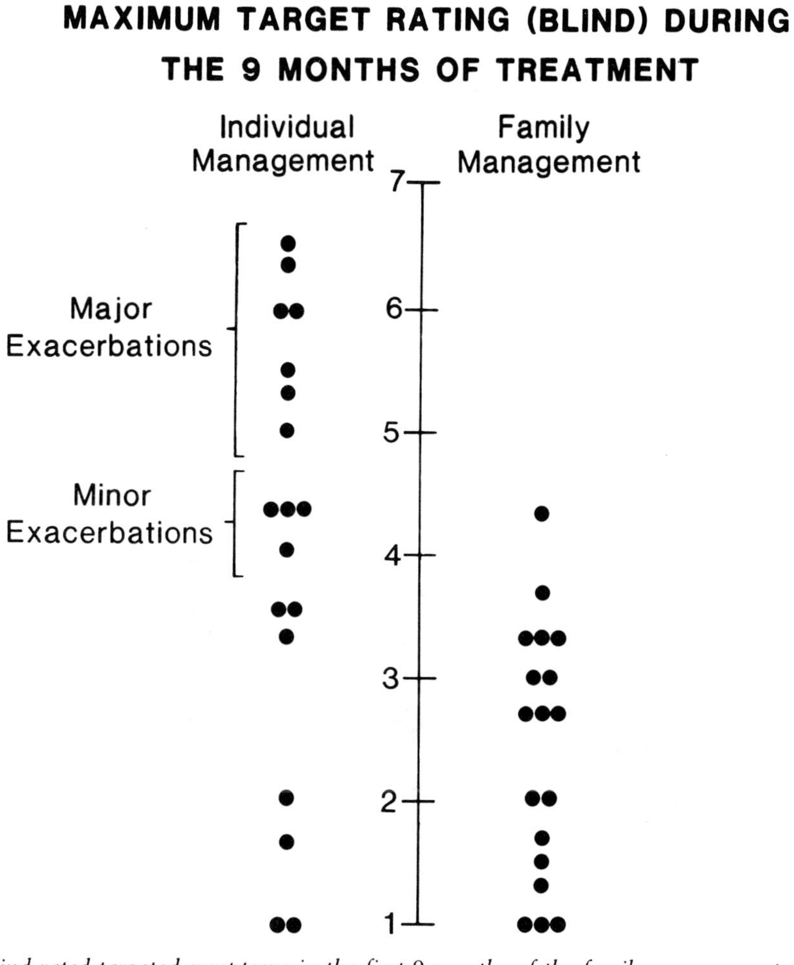

Fig. 6. *Blind-rated targeted symptoms in the first 9 months of the family management study.*

increased rate of full remission of all symptoms, and a trend towards remission of deficit (or 'negative') symptoms (Falloon, 1985).

All patients began this study after maximum clinical stability had been attained with drug and supportive management after a florid episode. During the first 9 months of the study the peaks of blind-rated targeted symptoms were much higher for those cases receiving individual management (Fig. 6). However, it also shows that relatively few family management cases were free of any signs of schizophrenia throughout the first 9 months of the study. Most experienced some minor exacerbations of the disorder, often no more than prodromal features, but at other times amounting to hearing the occasional verbal hallucination or experiencing the occasional episode of delusional perception. The point where one draws the line will largely determine the differential rates of relapse. For example, if we include minor episodes of schizophrenia, say those rated above 2 on our 7-point scale, we would have no difference between the two conditions.

The other limitation of relapse data is that they assume that the typical course of schizophrenia is one of complete remissions and florid relapses. As I have mentioned, perhaps only a third of cases show the typical relapsing pattern. Indeed, the value of family therapies may lie as much in their ability to facilitate remissions or to maintain greater stability of persisting symptoms. For this reason I would advocate the use of serial measurements of specific targeted symptoms of schizophrenia as shown in Fig. 7.

Here we see that family management succeeded in promoting improvement in residual florid symptoms, beyond that achieved by medication and support alone. At the end of 2 years two-thirds of family management patients were free of schizophrenic psychopathology and half showed no symptoms of any mental disorder. Moreover, the overall stability of the family-managed cases was significantly greater than that of individual cases, who continued to show an unstable course with less tendency to achieve full, stable remissions.

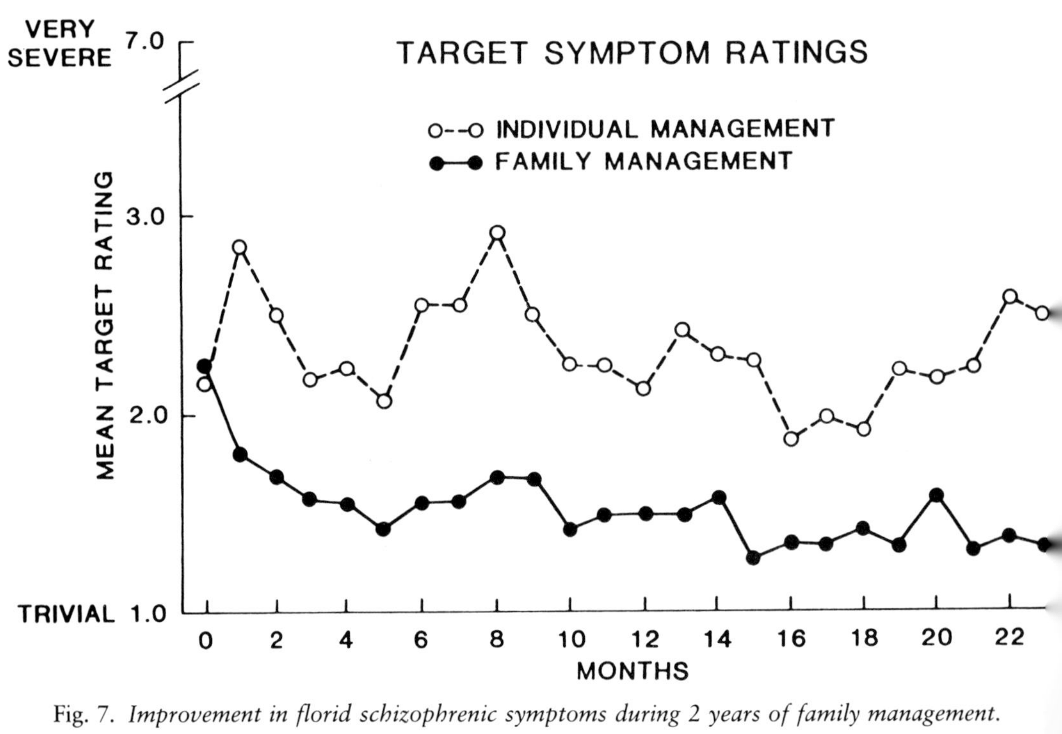

Fig. 7. *Improvement in florid schizophrenic symptoms during 2 years of family management.*

It might be argued that florid symptoms of schizophrenia are less disabling to patients and their caregivers than deficit symptoms or affective symptoms. As I mentioned earlier, family management that attempts only to minimize stress may succeed in eliminating florid symptoms merely by enhancing the social withdrawal characteristic of the deficit syndrome — popularly known as 'negative' symptoms. The data from the USC study suggest that the benefits of family management extended to a reduction in deficit symptoms as well as a reduction in episodes of depression (Falloon *et al.*, 1985).

It is, therefore, evident that the benefits of family-based management may go beyond the early claims for fewer relapses of florid symptoms of schizophrenia, but may facilitate a trend towards full remission of all clinical morbidity in the sufferers of this formerly incurable disorder.

Two-year follow-up results

Before making general claims for all the new family approaches let us examine the 2-year follow-up data to see how well the short-term improvements in stability are maintained once the active phase of treatment is withdrawn. Alas, the results are not nearly so impressive, even when only the crude assessment of relapse is employed. Some researchers have attributed the increased relapse rate in the second year of aftercare to poor compliance with medication (Leff *et al.*, 1985). However, it is clear that failure to continue taking medication represents a failure of education about the importance of medication and of family problem solving that would hopefully have assisted in the rapid resolution of this compliance problem. An increased rate of major episodes of schizophrenia did not occur in the behavioural family therapy study where the aim had been to teach family members to initiate their own problem solving discussions independent of therapist involvement (Falloon *et al.*, 1985). The other methods all depend on family problem solving discussions that are convened by the therapist.

Quality of life of sufferers and carers

So much for the benefits of family management approaches in reducing clinical morbidity. What evidence do we have to indicate that these approaches enhance the quality of the lives of the patients or their caregivers? Once again, the only published data come from our USC study. This study showed that index patients tended to improve in their social functioning at a significantly quicker rate when they received behavioural family therapy (see Fig. 8). In addition the burden that patient care imposed upon the carers was also substantially reduced. For many families this represented a return to a normal life-style with few of the major constraints that they had previously suffered.

The costs of schizophrenia, both emotional and economic, are extremely high. The combined use of optimal neuroleptic drug treatment and family-based stress management would appear to offer considerable benefits. A benefit-cost evaluation of the USC study showed that the application of the new approach was almost 20% cheaper than an excellent patient-orientated case management approach, and two-and-a-half times better value for money in achieving clinical, social and family benefits (Falloon, 1985).

Conclusions

We must await the results of further studies before drawing any definitive conclusions about the value of these family management approaches. It is unlikely that these

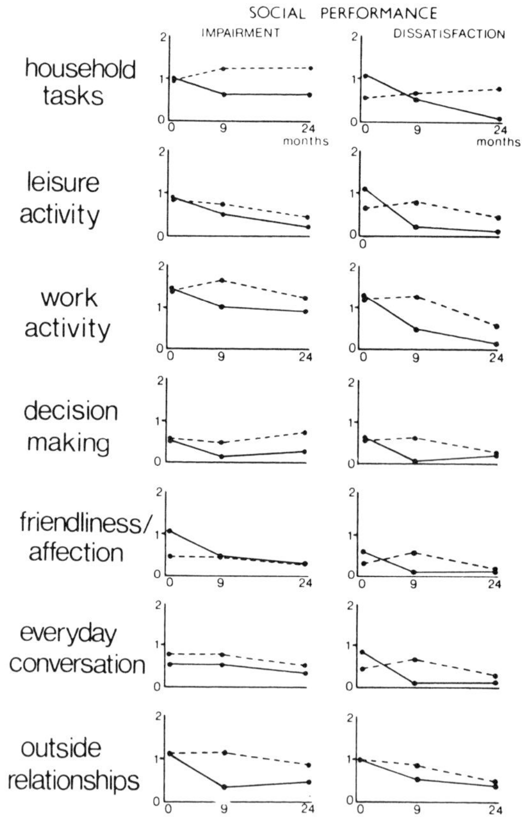

Fig. 8. *Improvement in social functioning by index patients during behavioural family therapy (●——●) compared with control patients (●– – –●). From Falloon et al.*, 1985.

combinations of optimal drug therapy and stress management will provide us with a lasting cure for schizophrenia, no more than insulin and diet provide a cure for diabetes — the vulnerability for schizophrenia is probably a lifelong risk, and even in the best circumstances the stress threshold is likely to be exceeded many times in an active patient's lifetime. However, no longer should any person be filled with dread by the diagnosis of schizophrenia. Furthermore, no family should feel filled with guilt that they have contributed to an incurable disorder in one of their members. Rather families may now take pride in the active role they can play in securing the long-term health and happiness of those among us who succumb to this mysterious yet fascinating disorder.

Acknowledgements—Several figures have been adapted from earlier publications: Fig. 1 from British Journal of Psychiatry, **144**, 482–487; Figs 2, 3, 4, 6 from *Family care of schizophrenia*, London: Guildford Press, 1984; and Fig. 7 from *Family management of schizophrenia*, Johns Hopkins University Press, 1985.

References

Anderson, C.M., Hogarty, G.E. & Reiss, D.J. (1980): Family treatment of adult schizophrenic patients: A psycho-educational approach. *Schizophrenia Bull.* 6, 490–505.

Falloon, I.R.H. (1985): *Family management of schizophrenia: A controlled study of clinical, social, family and economic benefits.* Baltimore: Johns Hopkins University Press.

Falloon, I.R.H., Boyd, J.L. & McGill, C.W. (1984): *Family care of schizophrenia.* New York: Guilford Press.

Falloon, I.R.H. & Liberman, R.P. (1983): Interactions between drug and psychosocial therapy in schizophrenia. *Schizophrenia Bull.* 9, 543–554.

Falloon, I., Watt, D.C. & Shepherd, M. (1978): A comparative controlled trial of pimozide and fluphenazine decanoate in the continuation therapy of schizophrenia. *Psychol. Med.* 8, 59–70.

Goldstein, M.J., Rodnick, E.H., Jones, J.E., McPherson, S.R. & West, K.L. (1978): Familial precursors of schizophrenia spectrum disorders. In *The nature of schizophrenia*, eds L.C. Wynne, R.L. Cromwell & S. Matthysse. New York: John Wiley.

Kraepelin, E. (1913): *Clinical psychiatry.* New York: William & Wood.

Laing, R.D. (1967): *The politics of experience.* New York: Pantheon.

Lamb, H.R. & Goertzel, V. (1971): Discharged mental patients — are they really in the community? *Arch. Gen. LEIN-Vries, R. & Sturgeon, D. (1982): A controlled trial of social intervention in the families of schizophrenic patients. Br. J. Psychiatry* **141**, 121–134.

Leff, J., Kuipers, L., Berkowitz, R. & Sturgeon, D. (1985): A controlled trial of social intervention in the families of schizophrenic patients: two year follow-up. *Br. J. Psychiatry* **146**, 594.

Miklowitz, D., Goldstein, M.J., Falloon, I.R.H. & Doane, J.A. (1984): Interactional correlates of expressed emotion in the families of schizophrenics. *Br. J. Psychiatry* **144**, 482–487.

Mosher, L.K., Menn, A. & Matthews, S. (1975): Soteria: Evaluation of a home-based treatment for schizophrenia. *Am. J. Orthopsychiatry* **45**, 455–469.

Schooler, N.R. & Carpenter, W.T. (1983): New drug treatment strategies in schizophrenia. *Schizophrenia Bull.* 9, 1–4.

Schooler, N.R. & Severe, J.B. (1984): Efficacy of drug treatment for chronic schizophrenic patients. In *The chronically mentally ill: Research and services*, ed. M. Morabi, pp. 125–142. New York: Spectrum.

Shepherd, M., Watt, D., Falloon, I. & Smeeton, N. (1989): Outcome and prediction from a five year follow-up of an epidemiologically representative sample of schizophrenics. *Psychol. Med. Monograph.*

Sullivan, H.S. (1927): The onset of schizophrenia. *Am. J. Psychiatry* 7, 105–134.

Vaughn, C.E. & Leff, J.P. (1976): The influence of family and social factors on the course of psychiatric illness: A comparison of schizophrenic and depressed neurotic patients. *Br. J. Psychiatry* **129**, 125–137.

Vaughn, C.E., Snyder, K.S., Jones, S., Freeman, W.B. & Falloon, I.R.H. (1984): Family factors in schizophrenic relapse: A California replication of the British research on expressed emotion. *Arch. Gen. Psychiatry* **41**, 1169–1177.

Chapter 26

The Daily Living Program: a community programme for the seriously mentally ill

M. Muijen, I. Marks and J. Connolly

Institute of Psychiatry and Mandsley Hospital, Denmark Hill, London SE5

Abstract

The Daily Living Program (DLP) is a controlled study, comparing home care with standard hospital care. Included are patients suffering from a serious mental illness who on presentation are assessed by a psychiatrist as needing hospital admission. If randomized to the control group, patients receive standard hospital and follow-up care at the Maudsley Hospital.

If randomized to the experimental group, patients enter the DLP, which offers intensive home care. Home visits are made as frequently as required. The team consists of 10 staff, and eventually 100 patients will be cared for.

The study will continue for a duration of 3 years. The experimental and control group are evaluated by a team of independent research psychologists at entry and after 3, 9 and 18 months. Outcome criteria are clinical symptomatology, social functioning, family burdens and cost-effectiveness. Patient and family satisfaction with treatment is also measured.

Preliminary data show that home care has reduced the number and duration of hospital admissions. The percentage of admissions in the DLP group of 60% compares well with that of 100% in the control group, as does the duration of stay, 15 and 48 days respectively. The main reasons for admission in the home care group are disturbed behaviour and danger to self and others. Patients and relatives appreciated the service, and very good working relationships have developed with the hospital and local authority departments. In particular the continuity of care provided by the DLP was regarded as a strength.

Present limitations are the absence of a 24 hour service and lack of comprehensive community facilities. Staff find the many aspects of intensive community care demanding, and special skills, including rehabilitative ones, are needed. For these reasons training programs are essential for the dissemination of this model.

Introduction

The Daily Living Program is a 3 year controlled study, funded by the DHSS, which started at the Maudsley Hospital in October 1987. It evaluates whether seriously mentally ill patients can be maintained out of hospital. The experimental community group will be compared with a control group receiving standard hospital treatment on clinical outcome, social functioning, burden on relatives and cost of treatment.

Background

A large amount of published work suggests that many alternatives to hospital benefit the patient clinically and socially. Home, foster, hostel and day hospital care have all been evaluated and have all shown improved outcomes over hospital care on a variety of measures, such as readmission and social functioning (Braun *et al.*, 1981; Kiesler *et al.*, 1982).

Five controlled studies have compared non-residential care with hospital care (Pasamanick *et al.*, 1967; Langsley *et al.*, 1969; Stein & Test, 1980; Fenton *et al.*, 1982; Hoult *et al.*, 1983). There are some important differences between these studies in entry criteria, methodology, duration and treatment models. For example, the Denver study (Langsley *et al.*, 1969) only accepted patients living with relatives, but patients with severe violence or suicidal ideation were excluded. In contrast in Sydney (Hoult *et al.*, 1983) all patients were included, with the exception of those suffering from primary addiction or organic brain damage. None of the studies used the same instruments; many of the rating scales were self-designed and have not been shown to be reliable or valid. However, all studies measured clinical outcome and social functioning and some added family burden and cost-benefit.

The essential element of studies evaluating community care is their treatment model, and the differences between studies are striking (Table 1). In Denver, family therapy was the main ingredient, Sydney offered crisis intervention, and Madison (Stein & Test, 1980) concentrated on a rehabilitative approach. Intensity of care also varied from one weekly visit (Pasamanick *et al.*, 1967) to interventions and support as often as required (Stein & Test, 1980; Hoult *et al.*, 1983). Related to this is the level of staffing. For similar numbers of patients, the staff numbers varied from two (Fenton *et al.*, 1982) to 7.5 (Hoult *et al.*, 1983) (Table 1), strongly suggesting differences in care.

All these studies compare outcomes of their experimental community groups with a standard hospital group, which is used as a control (Table 2). In order to make comparisons between different study results, an assumption has to be made that these control groups are similar. Differences between an American hospital in 1960 (Pasamanick *et al.*, 1967) and an Australian hospital in 1980 (Hoult *et al.*, 1983) make this highly unlikely.

These methodological problems would seriously challenge interpretations of these studies were it not for the remarkable consistency in findings, regardless of measures used. The experimental community groups often showed greater improvements than the hospital groups on clinical symptomatology and social functioning at the end of study

Table 1. *Variables in studies evaluating community care.*

	Treatment variables			
	Staff	*Patients*	*Visits yearly*	*Approach*
Pasamanick *et al.* (1967)	7	57	30	Supportive
Langsley *et al.* (1969)	?	150	5.5	Crisis family
Stein & Test (1980)	10	65	as req.	Rehabilitation
Fenton *et al.* (1982)	2	76	16.5	Crisis
Hoult *et al.* (1983)	7.5	60	as req.	Rehabilitation

Table 2. *Outcome in studies comparing home care with hospital care.*

	Symptoms	*Social*	*Employment*	*Family burden*
Pasamanick *et al.* (1967)	=			
Langsley *et al.* (1969)	+	=	=	
Stein & Test (1900)	+	=	+	+
Fenton *et al.* (1982)	=	=	+	=
Hoult *et al.* (1983)	+	=	=	+

Table 3. *Hospital use by experimental group compared in studies evaluating community care.*

	Admissions yearly (%)	*Days in hospital (Comm/Hosp%)*[1]	*Cost reduction (%)*
Pasamanick *et al.* (1967)	23	110–220	
Langsley *et al.* (1969)	24	32	16
Stein & Test (1980)	18	60	95
Fenton *et al.* (1982)	40	35	60
Hoult *et al.* (1983)	40	41	75

[1]Days spent in hospital by community group as percentage of days in hospital by control group.

periods. Also, patients and relatives were more satisfied with the community services. No programme found a superiority of hospital care on any of the outcome variables. All studies had some failures and significant proportions of patients in the community group needed hospital admission because of the severity of their conditions: 18% in Madison (Stein & Test, 1980) and 40% in Sydney (Hoult *et al.*, 1983). Duration of admission was much briefer for the experimental group in both studies (Table 3). The reason for the long admission duration in the community group of the Pasamanick study is that no continuity of care was offered following hospital entry, in contrast to the other studies, which continued to accept responsibility for their clients during the hospital stay.

No approach claimed to 'cure mental illness'. All experimental samples still showed considerable symptomatology and disability in spite of their comparative improvements. An important finding which supports the effectiveness of the experimental interventions is that after the withdrawal of the community services and the reintroduction of the standard in-patient services the patients gradually lost their acquired gains and the differences between experimental and control groups disappeared (Langsley *et al.*, 1971; Davis *et al.*, 1972; Stein & Test, 1980).

This agreement on the superiority of community care is impressive, although caution is necessary. Findings always confirmed the belief of often charismatic leaders that less restrictive care is superior to traditional hospital care. Staff were highly motivated, aware of their responsibility for a new project and apparently willing to work very hard. The experiences of some community mental health centres in the USA, albeit with a different approach to community care, are not all so positive, often suffering from low staff morale, fast turnover of staff and inefficiency (Sharfstein, 1978; Langsley, 1980).

For this reason, the Madison service is of particular importance. Starting as an experimental project (Stein & Test, 1980), it has continued for over 10 years as a regular service offering a comprehensive community based service for the seriously mentally ill. At present it consists of four units: a crisis intervention service; a mobile community team for a population which needs long term care; the outpatient services for the less needy

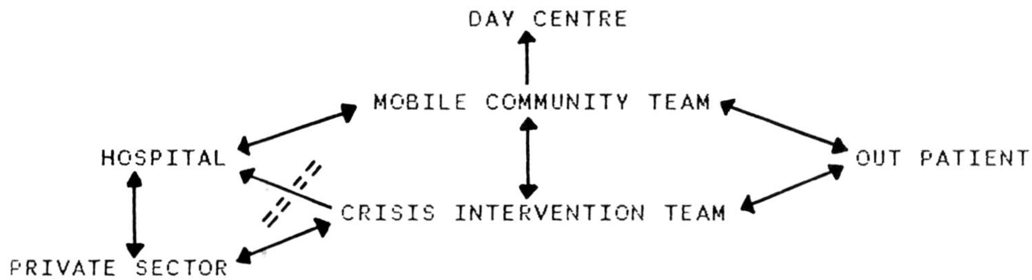

Figure 1. Madison: *psychiatric services*

patients; and a day centre (Fig. 1). Patients enter the system at the crisis intervention service, where they are assessed. If only a short-term intervention seems necessary, patients will be dealt with by the crisis team, but otherwise they will be referred on to appropriate segments of the service. In turn all services can request the crisis team to manage a well-known patient temporarily, using their specific expertise. Flexibility is an essential part of this system. Because it is recognized that a community approach can only function if admissions are monitored and limited, the crisis team is given the task of assessing all patients who may need admission. If admission is avoided the crisis service has a responsibility to provide alternative care. Good use is made of imaginative projects such as foster beds and crisis hostels. In the American system where the private sector provides a substantial proportion of the health care private patients may be admitted directly and offered follow up care based on psychotherapy. Since community care has been demonstrated to be superior to hospital care in most studies, it is somewhat ironic that patients who can afford private treatment receive hospital admission followed by psychodynamic therapies, while those who cannot are provided with community care.

The cost-efficiency of a new service is of great importance in the political climate of the late 1980s. The studies which included a cost-benefit analysis showed small (5%, Stein & Test, 1980) to considerable (25%, Hoult *et al.*, 1983) cost reductions (Table 3). However, capital costs were not included and initially good quality community care may not necessarily save money.

The positive findings of studies in such diverse settings as Australia and North America are encouraging but major differences exist in the UK, such as cultural treatment expectations, legal rights and quality of living. Because of the considerable socioeconomic deprivation, Camberwell is a challenging area for a replication and guidelines on community care may emerge for other UK inner cities.

The study

The Daily Living Program (DLP) accepts a proportion of admissions to the Maudsley Hospital. Patients are included if they: (1) suffer from a serious mental illness (schizophrenia or severe affective disorder) which is deemed to require hospital admission as judged by an independent psychiatrist; (2) are aged 17–64; (3) have no primary addiction (dual diagnosis accepted); (4) have no organic brain damage as primary diagnosis; (5) are connected to South Southwark. Patients with no fixed abode will be included, provided they have links with the area, such as close family ties or attendance of local statutory services.

Patients who are violent, suicidal or presented with a hospital order are all included. Of course many of these will initially need hospital admission, which will be kept as brief as possible. Occasionally it is appropriate to admit patients who are too much of a burden on their relatives, as even an intensive community programme cannot provide 24 hours a day support.

At the time of admission patients are randomly allocated to Daily Living Program or hospital care. A total of 100 patients will be included in each of the DLP and the control hospital groups. The sample consists of two subgroups:

(1) First admissions, because it is hoped that this group will benefit from the prevention of hospital admissions which could lead to the revolving door syndrome.

(2) A proportion of readmissions, to determine the efficacy of community care for the long-term mentally ill.

After randomization, about 20% of all admissions from Camberwell to the Maudsley Hospital are cared for by the Daily Living Program. The proportion of readmissions and first admissions is about equal and it is hoped that the inclusion of a representative patient sample will permit a service evaluation.

Ratings instruments

The DLP and hospital group are compared on clinical outcome, social adjustment, family burden, and economic cost. The following questionnaires are used:

Psychiatric State Examination (PSE)
Brief Psychiatric Rating Scale (BPRS) (20 item version).
Global Assessment Scale (GAS)
Social Adjustment Scale (SAS).
Social Behaviour Assessment Schedule (SBAS), sections c and d.
General Health Questionnaire (GHQ)
Economic Questionnaire (EQ).
Patient & staff satisfaction with care.

The raters, two experimental psychologists, are kept blind regarding patient allocation as much as possible.

The evaluator completes the PSE, BPRS and SAS during an interview with the patient and the SBAS during an interview with the 'significant other'. All adult family members living with the patient are asked to complete a GHQ. The EQ is completed from the information obtained from the patient, the relative or both.

All questionnaires will be administered on admission, and repeated after 3 months, 9 months and 18 months. A satisfaction questionnaire will be given to patients and relatives at follow up (3, 9 & 19 months). Patients who have been discharged from care, moved out of the area or refused to continue in the DLP will continue to be evaluated.

Model of care

The essence of community care is offering patients flexible care which maximizes their functioning in their own environments while minimizing dependency on services. This requires a careful balance between the risks of neglect and over-dependence. The form and intensity of care has to be decided individually for each patient, with a long-term perspective.

The DLP team consists of seven nurses, an occupational therapist, a social worker, a psychiatrist and a coordinator, with a staff:patient ratio of approximately 1:10. It closely collaborates with other services, both in and outside the hospital, such as the Maudsley Emergency Clinic, for crisis cover during the night, the occupational therapy department for basic skills assessments and Day Centres for day-time occupation.

Using a problem-solving approach, key workers present and discuss their patients with the multidisciplinary team, which gives advice or changes plans, based on their background or experience.

It has become clear that care for an individual can only be complete if relatives, neighbours, employers, health professionals or volunteers are involved wherever appropriate. Individual, marital and family therapy all have a role. Often interventions are based on a behavioural model, as this seems relevant for many dependent and chronic patients. Most people are on medication, which is regularly monitored.

Daily Living Program care principles

The principles of care offered by the Daily Living Program are similar to those adopted in the USA by the NIMH (Turner & Ten Hoor, 1978) as guidelines for community support programmes:

(1) Continuity of care is provided. Patients entering the DLP will remain in it for the duration of the study (3 years), unless care is no longer required.

(2) The care is coordinated by a key worker who offers appropriate help to patients and coordinates local resources.

(3) Crisis intervention is provided at the patient's residence, with hospital beds available if brief admission cannot be avoided.

(4) Psychological rehabilitation is given, including evaluation of needs and skills training at the place where these skills will have to be applied, ie at home, with family and friends, or at work.

(5) Support is given to relatives, employers, and statutory and voluntary organizations.

(6) There is flexible support which varies with need.

(7) Twenty four hour care, 7 days a week, is provided (with telephone cover during the night).

(8) The DLP has an advocacy role, both for patients individually and as a group.

Initial observations

The DLP has run for 12 months so far, and only preliminary data are available as yet. About 40 patients have been entered in both the experimental community group and the control group. A considerable proportion of the DLP patients have needed admission (60%), with a mean duration of 15 days. This compares well with an admission rate of 100% and a mean reduction of 60 days in the standard hospital care group. About 20% of both groups were readmitted within 12 months. This suggests that some reduction of hospital beds may be expected from an active community service, with no evidence of the development of a 'revolving door syndrome' for patients in the community group.

The reason for admission in the community group was mainly for disturbed behaviour, which would have put the patient at risk at home. Single people were especially at risk of hospital admission. An indicator of severity is that about 50% of patients in the community group had to be admitted under a Section of the Mental Health Act 1983.

Hospital staff recognized that many of the control hospital admissions could have been avoided if community outreach and close follow-up, as provided by the DLP, had been available. Regrets have often been expressed that patients had been randomized to the hospital group, as 'they would have benefitted so much from community care'.

Comments from patients and relatives confirmed this. Before entry into the study they are asked whether they will agree to receive either hospital care of home care, whichever is available. Without exception the patients and their relatives were delighted to be allocated to the DLP, and expressed surprise that such a service had not been started before. Those relatives who had doubts about the appropriateness of home care were reassured when told that hospital admission could be considered. The agreement between DLP staff and relatives on the need for hospital admission has been very high, perhaps indicating the importance of good and frequent communication. Consistent with this is the experience that much time is spent on advising and supporting relatives.

A large number of patients live on council estates, almost all in deprived circumstances, many of them are young and about half suffer from schizophrenia. Several would fall in the 'young chronic' category and it appears that the DLP has succeeded in developing a good relationship with this group. Much of the staff effort is aimed at achieving medication compliance, budgeting of finances and arranging day-time activities.

Short-comings of the DLP which are regularly commented upon by the staff are the absence of a 24 hour availability, which has necessitated several admissions, and the paucity of local community resources.

The Daily Living Program, the Maudsley and Camberwell

Hard realities often dictate the form of care as much as aims and objectives. Camberwell is among the 10 most deprived areas in England (Jarman, 1984). It is known that these areas have a high prevalence of psychiatric morbidity, with a high need for services (Hirsch, 1988). The high percentage of single parents, unemployment, overcrowding and mixed ethnicity means that many patients will present with severe social problems, in addition to their psychiatric conditions. In a hospital these people are temporarily offered a time-out period by receiving shelter, food, company and some form of occupation. Unfortunately skills acquired in hospital, if taught, are not generalized to their own environment after discharge and the patient is likely to relapse soon (Anthony *et al.*, 1978). A community service which is truly comprehensive can offer most of the functions of a hospital. Essential components of such a community service are walk-in centres, day centres and day hospitals, home-care, crisis beds and long-term housing provisions for people with varying degrees of dependency.

These services will need to cater for the varying needs of client groups of different ages, ethnic backgrounds and sex. Unfortunately many essential provisions in Camberwell are very limited, or non-existent. This has serious implications for a service like the Daily Living Program. Enthusiasm of staff cannot replace basic services and this results in greater use of the Maudsley Hospital facilities than had been planned. Absence of community crisis beds means hospital admission, absence of housing means longer duration of hospital stay, absence of day centres means attending the hospital occupational therapy department, and absence of walk-in centres means social isolation. People suffering most are the young mentally ill, precisely the group most at risk of a future career as chronic patients, without comprehensive and well integrated services (Bachrach, 1982).

Southwark social services are in a difficult position. Overspent and with increasing demands being made as a result of the growth of community care, they are at the receiving end of the 'perverse incentives', as reported by the Audit Commission (1986). These incentives mean that money spent on community care by local authorities is not supported by central government, but that patients in residential settings, frequently not needing that degree of institutionalization, are fully financed by social security payments. Nevertheless the Daily Living Program receives much enthusiasm and support from local organizations, including social services, the housing department and voluntary organizations.

This has resulted in discussions on local developments, such as the availability of community crisis beds, a change in policy at day centres towards care for the young mentally ill and invitations for a DLP representative on the board of some services. It is hoped that a close collaboration between local authorities and the health service, as suggested in the Griffith's Report (1988), will emerge.

Staff training

The objective of a programme can only be achieved if staff expectations and attitudes are realistic and clear. The experience in the USA of Community Mental Health Centres is an important warning. Aiming to offer support for the chronically mentally ill, they gradually drifted towards a concept of prevention of mental illness by offering crisis intervention to the 'unhappy but healthy'. This resulted in the deprofessionalization of staff and low staff morale when the hope of effecting social change was not fulfilled (Stern & Minkoff, 1979; Langsley, 1980). A return to the initial objectives seems to be taking place at present.

Staff working in community care tend to be young, enthusiastic, idealistic and dissatisfied with traditional services. Instant success is expected and they are rarely prepared for the slow progress of chronic patients and the bureaucracy involved in any change. Some have no prior training in the rehabilitation of chronic patients or any experience with problem-solving approaches to treatment.

DLP staff have experienced high levels of anxiety, resulting from the demands of work in the community with the severely mentally ill. Initiative and flexibility are essential, since decisions often need to be made on the spot. In addition expertise in many areas is needed from the team, demanding a genuine multi-disciplinary collaboration.

The special skills required for working in the community with patients and their relatives, after receiving training in a hospital setting, makes the formulation of a training module a priority, as recognized by both the Social Services Committee on community care (1985) and the Griffiths Report (1988).

Future developments of the Daily Living Program

Whatever the results, conclusions will have to be made with caution, due to the inherent limitations of a service evaluation.

Firstly, it could be argued that a research programme like the DLP is in a relatively protected position. Suitable patients are selected and entered into the study in planned numbers. Alternative services, such as hospital, are available for crisis situations. Morale is likely to be high due to selected staff and their perceptions of working on a special project. However, one could also argue that the programme is under a very severe test since suitable back-up services are limited and the DLP is dependent on staff who are not trained and experienced in this field. Acceptance by the traditional services and the community cannot be taken for granted. The initial wave of enthusiasm experienced so far may not continue.

Secondly, the DLP serves South Southwark, which is not representative of the UK as a whole, since it has a high proportion of ethnic minorities, poor people and single people, and few community resources. Therefore any findings, in this district, while applicable to many inner city areas in the UK, may not necessarily be applicable to the whole country. Thus, while a failure of the DLP may prove inconclusive, it is tempting to suggest that a superiority of community care in such a deprived setting indicates a likelihood of successful implementation in better endowed areas. But either way, the confounding effects of being an evaluative study, as described above, should not be overlooked.

A major local concern is the continuing role of the DLP as an integrated part of the clinical services of South Southwark, at the end of the 3 year study. A choice has to be made between a development towards a specialist community service of modest size, serving a subgroup of patients such as chronic schizophrenics, or a more ambitious aim of redeveloping the model of hospital care based on the DLP experience. This decision is likely to be as much political as practical. Observations to date, supported by previous research, are that community care for the seriously mentally ill is possible and successful, provided that services are comprehensive. Eventually the efficacy of the DLP will have to be critically and objectively assessed and hopefully lessons learnt will be incorporated in future programmes.

References

Anthony, W.A., Cohen, M.R., & Vitalo, R. (1978): The measurement of rehabilitation outcome. *Schizophrenia Bull.* **4**, 365–383.

Audit Commission (1986): *Making a reality of community care.* London:HMSO.

Bachrach, L.L. (1982): Young adult chronic patients: an analytical review of the literature. *Hosp. Community Psychiatry* **33**, 189–197.

Braun, P., Kochansky, G., Shapiro, R., Greenberg, S., Gudeman, J.E., Johnson, S. & Shore, M.F. (1981): Overview: Deinstitutionalisation of psychiatric patients, a critical review of outcome studies. *Am. J. Psychiatry* **136**, 736–749.

Davis, A.E., Dinitz, S. & Pasamanick, B. (1972): The prevention of hospitalisation in schizophrenia: Five years after an experimental program. *Am. J. Orthopsychiatry* **42**, 375–388

Fenton, F.R., Tessier, L., Struening, E.L., Smith, F.A., & Benoit, C. (1982): *Home and hospital psychiatric treatment.* London: Croom Helm.

Griffiths, R. (1988): *Community Care, agenda for action.* London: HMSO.

Hirsch, S.R. (1988): Psychiatric beds and resources: Factors influencing bed use and service planning. Royal College of Psychiatrists, Gaskell.

Hoult, J., Reynolds, I., Charbonneau-Powis, M., Weekes, P. & Briggs, J. (1983): Psychiatric hospital *vs* community treatment: the results of a randomised trial. *Aust. N.Z. J. Psychiatry* **17**, 160–167.

Jarman, B. (1984): Validation and distribution of scores. *Br. Med. J.* **289**, 1587–1592.

Kiesler, C.A. (1982): Mental Hospitals and alternative care. *Am. Psychologist* **37**, 349–360.

Langsley, D.G. (1980): The community mental health centre: Does it treat patients? *Hosp. Community Psychiatry* **31**, 815–819.

Langsley, D.G., Flomenhaft, K. & Machotka, P. (1969): Follow-up evaluation of family crisis therapy. *Am. J. Orthopsychiatry* **39**, 753–759.

Langsley, D.G., Machotka, P. & Flomenhaft, K. (1971): Avoiding mental hospital admission, a follow-up study. *Am. J. Psychiatry* **127**, 1391–1394.

Pasamanick, B., Scarpitti, F.R. & Dinitz, S. (1967): *Schizophrenics in the community.* New York: Appleton-Century-Crofts.

Sharfstein, S.S. (1978): Will community health survive in the 1980's? *Am. J. Psychiatry* **135**, 1363–1365.

Social Services Committee, Second Report (1985): *Community care with special reference to adult mentally ill and mentally handicapped people.* London: HMSO.
Stein, L.J. & Test, M.A. (1980): Alternative to mental hospital treatment: 1. Conceptual model, treatment program & clinical evaluation. *Arch. Gen. Psychiatry* 37, 392–397.
Stern, R. & Minkoff, K. (1979): Paradoxes in programming for chronic patients in a community clinic. *Hosp. Community Psychiatry* 30, 613–617.
Turner, J.C. & Ten Hoor, W.J. (1978): The NIMH Community Support Program: Pilot approach to a needed social reform. *Schizophrenia Bull.* 4, 319–348.
Weisbrod, B.A., Test, M.A. & Stein, L.J. (1980): Alternative to mental hospital treatment (2): Economic benefit-cost analysis. *Arch. Gen. Psychiatry.* 37, 400–405.

Chapter 27
The components of psychiatric rehabilitation services

M. Y. Ekdawi

Netherne Rehabilitation Service, Coulsdon, Surrey

Summary

Information gathered from 18 selected British and Continental psychiatric rehabilitation services revealed a good measure of agreement on the services' aims, which were generally based on clinical and social approaches. Seven main components were shared by the services. These consisted of multi-faceted assessments, combined medical and social treatments, multi-disciplinary work, involvement of the recipients and their relatives in the programmes, residential and day care provisions, long-term support and continued evaluation of the facilities and the programmes. Despite varying degrees of emphasis, these are considered to be essential elements in each of the services.

Introduction

Rehabilitation services have, in common, the broad aim of enabling disabled people to achieve and maintain optimal levels of social adjustment in appropriate environments. An enquiry was carried out to elicit those components which characterize services recognized for their work in the field of psychiatric rehabilitation. This paper summarizes findings gleaned from information from 10 British rehabilitation services (including designated National Demonstration Services for Rehabilitation) and from eight Continental contributors to the IV International Congress on Rehabilitation in Psychiatry in Orebro, Sweden (1988).

Target populations

In general, services are concerned with people who have a combination of chronic mental disorder and social difficulties. Chronic disorder is defined by its diagnosis, mainly of functional psychosis, its severity and its duration (usually more than 6 months in hospital or more than 3 admissions to hospital in one year). Rehabilitees tend to share features of increased vulnerability to stress, poor coping abilities, a degree of dependency and difficulties in personal relationships. The 'typical' patients referred for rehabilitation are young or middle-aged, with a chronic or recurrent psychotic illness and with a history of prolonged or repeated hospital admissions. They are mostly referred for training in personal care, domestic and occupational skills, money, management, leisure skills and management of medication. Some 'unwanted' patients are referred as a last resort. The reasons for referral are compatible with the services' aims, which include stabilization, improving social functioning, promoting independence and placement in suitable environments.

Few services seem to exercise strict exclusion criteria when accepting referrals, but certain, mainly behavioural, problems are considered to be contraindications to accepting or persevering with some referred patients. These include dementias and other organic disorders with behaviour difficulties, severe, unstable or uncontrollable symptoms, disturbed, markedly aggressive behaviour and severe substance abuse problems. Poor motivation to cooperate with rehabilitation programmes is viewed by most services as a definite obstacle.

Conceptual framework

Services implicitly or explicitly recognize a disability model, with its constituents of clinical impairment, social disadvantage and maladaptive personal reactions (Wing & Morris, 1981), and their actual operation is therefore based on combined clinical and social approaches. They have an expectation that the patient would have achieved a measure of clinical stability at the point of referral, but most services view the maintenance of medical treatment as one of their essential tasks.

There are three overlapping social paradigms which underpin services' programmes, but with differing emphases in their application. The first is exemplified by the work of Anthony *et al.* (1986) which stresses the development of skills and vocational abilities. The second is mainly concerned with creating suitable environmental supports, including permanent sheltered settings (eg Pepper, 1987) and the third gives precedence to the strengthening of coping abilities, as advocated by Strauss (1986).

Service components

The composite profile of the rehabilitation services' provisions comprise seven main elements: assessment, treatment, multidisciplinary work, patient and family involvement, facilities, follow-up and support, and evaluation.

Assessment

Repeated assessments of the rehabilitees' areas of dysfunction, as well as their strengths, are carried out by means of interviews together with ratings on reliable, valid scales, for example Krawiecka *et al.* (1977) and Affleck & McGuire (1984). Assessments also establish a base-line, record progress and determine the effects of interventions.

Treatment

Medical and social management programmes are designed within each service, but there are, again, variations in emphasis. English services, in particular, attach great importance to medication. Prescription monitoring to assess the type and dosage of medication according to fluctuation in mental state is seen as being essential. Some services provide verbal or written information on the drugs to the rehabilitees and one service includes counselling by the pharmacist, as an additional tool, to encourage a more responsible attitude towards self-medication.

Monitoring also includes attention to side-effects, which may adversely effect compliance and which may further disable the rehabilitees.

Methods of social management mainly consist of skills training, vocational rehabilitation and counselling. The most consistent element is that of skills training, using reinforcers valued by the rehabilitee. In view of the common problems of motivation, generalization of learnt skills and their durability over time, training is more effective if the rehabilitee is involved in goal-setting, if learning takes place in environments where the rehabilitee lives and works and if learnt skills are regularly practised (Shepherd, 1979; Liberman & Evans, 1985).

The use of work and work-related activities is enshrined in rehabilitation practice. Apart from being an indispensable setp towards economic independence for some rehabilitatees, work is a powerful medium for social stimulation (Wing & Brown, 1970) and for social integration (Morgan & Cheadle, 1981). Work activities seem to be, at present, more highly valued by Continental services than by most of their English counterparts.

Although dynamic psychotherapy forms part of the rehabilitation programmes in some Continental services, the majority of services favour counselling on an individual or group basis. Counselling, including problem-solving, education and support, is based on the assumption that social adjustment is dependent on improved behaviour rather than on the acquisition of insights (Ekdawi, 1981: Stewart, 1985).

Multidisciplinary work

The wide spectrum of clinical and social problems presented by each rehabilitee demands a coordinated input from members of the multidisciplinary rehabilitation team. The core membership of teams comprises medical and nursing staff, psychologist, occupational therapist and social worker. Some teams include physiotherapists, speech thereapists and teachers. Difficulties in coordinating team work have led services to adopt the concept of key workers and case managers. However, such workers tend to have insufficient training and seniority, they lack negotiating authority and they are often transient.

Many English services, while supporting the key worker principle, backed by the team, work on the assumption that the consultant remains the point of reference, the coordinator and the provider of continuity.

Patient and family involvement

Rehabilitation programmes may well founder if the rehabilitee's cooperation is not enlisted; moreover, the collaboration of the relatives and other carers is necessary for programme implementation. It has been noted that even those relatives whose contact is only sporadic could exert significant influence on the rehabilitation plans (Collis & Ekdawi, 1984). Involving relatives is occasionally a formidable task; concerned, supportive relatives may feel that their views are being ignored if they differ from those of the rehabilitation team, and problems are magnified in the case of relatives who present as being hostile, and who are labelled as being uncooperative or unrewarding by the professionals.

Facilities

The provision of chains of residential and day care facilities for treatment, training and continuing support to meet the varying needs of the rehabilitees is considered to be a major component of the service. The ideal comprehensive provision does not exist, and there are many identified gaps in each service. The impression gained is that facilities tend to be better developed in areas where mental hospitals exist.

Behaviour can be perceived as a function of the individual's interaction with his environment. For the psychiatrically disabled, supportive environments can compensate for handicaps and help in maintaining stability and adjustment. On the other hand, toxic environments, which increase disability, include those which are cognitively confusing, threatening or demoralizing, those which have poor levels of social stimulation or, alternatively, those which are demanding, critical and intrusive. These features can be present in some so-called sheltered facilities, just as they do in some high expressed emotion families. Although there is agreement amongst the services that they should monitor the facilities with these factors in mind, this does not seem to be done very systematically.

Follow up and support

Many services acknowledge the importance of long-term, systematic follow up and support networks for rehabilitees and their families, although, in practice, this seems to be variable. One of the purposes of careful, detailed follow up assessments is to determine the existence of symptoms and their severity and to plan further treatment accordingly. Apart from psychotic symptoms, high levels of morbidity due to depression and anxiety are frequently found in long-term community patients (Freeman *et al.*, 1979). There is also a wealth of published work which shows that social support for long-term patients and their families, as well as behavioural interventions, can reduce relapse in schizophrenia (Tarrier *et al.*, 1988).

Long-term management and support, in the services' view, is best carried out by staff dedicated to rehabilitation and long-term care, and not by 'generic' staff. Community psychiatric nurses, for instance, whose resources were being absorbed by referrals from general practitioners, were only able to provide an inadequate, reduced service to patients 'in the schizophrenic clinical category, the majority of whom need life-long care' (Woof & Goldberg, 1988).

Evaluation

The performance of rehabilitation services needs to be regularly evaluated so as to justify their existence and to endorse their development plans and consequent expenditure of resources and valuable professional time. Various evaluative measures continue to be explored, but many services still prefer the hard data of hospital readmission (recidivism) rates and employment status on follow-up as indices of performance (Ekdawi, 1972; Acharya *et al.*, 1982; Goering *et al.*, 1984). The advantages of such measures are that they are readily objectified and understood, allowing comparisons among studies. Their disadvantage is that they are dependent on prevailing social, employment and political factors and they could therefore give a distorted picture.

Conclusions

There is remarkable consistency amongst the selected sample of rehabilitation services in their definition of their main components, despite variations in emphasis. Demonstration services include staff training as an additional task, but this training falls within the parameters of the seven components outlined.

References

Acharya, S., Ekdawi, M.Y., Gallagher, L. & Glaister, B. (1982): Day rehabilitation: a six years study. *Soc. Psychiatry* **17**, 1.

Affleck, J.W. & McGuire, R.J. (1984): The assessment of psychiatric rehabilitation status. *Br. J. Psychiatry* **145**, 517–525.

Anthony, W.A., Kennard, W.A., O'Brien, W.F. & Forbess, R. (1986): Psychiatric rehabilitation. *Community Ment. Health J.* **22**, 249–264.

Collis, M. & Ekdawi, M.Y. (1984): *The relatives' story* (A Netherne monograph). Coulsdon: Netherne Hospital.

Ekdawi, M.Y. (1972): The Netherne Resettlement Unit: results of ten years. *Br. J. Psychiatry* **121**, 417–424.

Ekdawi, M.Y. (1981): Counselling in rehabilitation. In *Handbook of psychiatric rehabilitation practice*, eds J.K. Wing & B. Morris. Oxford: Oxford University Press.

Freeman, H.L., Cheadle, A.J. & Korer, J. (1979): A method of monitoring the treatment of schizophrenia in the community. *Br. J. Psychiatry* **134**, 412–416.

Goering, P., Wasylenski, D., Lancee, W. & Freeman, S.J.J. (1984): From hospital to community: six month and two year outcomes of 505 patients. *J. Nerv. Ment. Disease* **172**, 667–673.

Krawiecka, M., Goldberg, D. & Vaughan, M. (1977): A standardised assessment scale for rating chronic psychiatric patients. *Acta Psychiatr. Scand.* **55**, 299–308.

Liberman, R.P. & Evans, C.C. (1985): Behavioural rehabilitation for chronic mental patients. *J. Clin. Psychopharmacol.* **5**, supplement 3.

Morgan, R. & Cheadle, J. (1981): *Psychiatric rehabilitation.* Surbiton: National Schizophrenia Fellowship.

Pepper, B. (1987): A public policy for the long-term mentally ill. *Am. J. Orthopsychiatry* **57**, 452–457.

Shepherd, G. (1979): Social skills training and beyond — environments for the care of chronic patients. *Behav. Psychotherapy* **7**, 31–38.

Stewart, W. (1985): *Counselling in rehabilitation.* London: Croom Helm.

Strauss, J.S. (1986): What does rehabilitation accomplish. *Schizophrenia Bull.* **12**, 720–723.

Tarrier, N., Barrowclough, C., Vaughan, C., Bamah, J.S., Proceddu, K., Watts, S. & Freeman, H. (1988): The community management of schizophrenia. A controlled trial of a behavioural intervention with families to reduce relapse. *Br. J. Psychiatry* **153**, 532–542.

Wing, J.K. & Brown, G.W. (1970): *Institutionalism and schizophrenia.* London: Cambridge University Press.

Wing, J.K. & Morris, B. (1981): *Handbook of psychiatric rehabilitation practice.* Oxford: Oxford University Press.

Woof, K. Goldberg, D.P. (1988): Further observations in the practice of community care in Salford. Differences between community psychiatric nurses and mental health social workers. *Br. J. Psychiatry* **153**, 30–37.

Author index

Subject index